DIARY OF
GIDEON WELLES

IN THREE VOLUMES

VOLUME III

DIARY OF
GIDEON WELLES

IN THREE VOLUMES

VOLUME III

DIARY OF
GIDEON WELLES

SECRETARY OF THE NAVY UNDER
LINCOLN AND JOHNSON

WITH AN INTRODUCTION BY JOHN T. MORSE, JR.

AND

WITH ILLUSTRATIONS

VOLUME III

JANUARY 1, 1867 — JUNE 6, 1869

TOVT
BIEN OV
BIEN

BOSTON AND NEW YORK
HOUGHTON MIFFLIN COMPANY
The Riverside Press Cambridge
1911

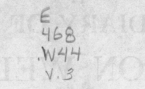

CONTENTS

XLV

JANUARY, 1867

Cabinet Discussion of the Message vetoing the District of Columbia Reorganization Bill — The Bay of Samaná Purchase Scheme meets with Difficulties — Congress overrides the Veto — Representative Ashley of Ohio introduces a Resolution to impeach the President — Seward submits to the Cabinet the Articles of a Proposed Treaty with Prussia — An Amnesty Proclamation agreed upon — The President asks the Opinions of the Cabinet Members in regard to Territorializing the States — Senator Grimes as Chairman of the Naval Committee — General Grant's Position on the District of Columbia Suffrage Bill — His Lack of Political Principles — The Senatorial Fight in Pennsylvania results in the Nomination of Cameron — Roscoe Conkling nominated in New York — Cabinet Discussion of the Right of a Territory to organize itself as a State — The Senatorial Elections — Conkling, Cameron, and Trumbull — The Italian and Chilian Missions — Motley resigns as Minister to Austria — Seward's Calls at the Capitol — The Cabinet decides not to sell out the Dunderberg to the Contractor — The Swatara returning from Nice with Surratt — Action of the House in regard to the Ship Idaho — The President vetoes the Colorado and Nebraska Bills — The Army moving to get Possession of the Indian Bureau — A Committee from North Carolina submits a Reconstruction Proposal to the President   3

XLVI

FEBRUARY, 1867

The Circumstances attending Motley's Resignation discussed in Cabinet — The North Carolina Plan published in the Richmond Papers — The Matter of the R. R. Cuyler, bought by the Colombian Government and seized by the United States — Failure of the Samaná Negotiations — Thaddeus Stevens's Proposal to establish Military Governments in the Southern States opposed in the House — Banks leads the Opposition — Stanton's Sensational Report on the Enforcement of the Civil Rights Act — Plain Talk with the President about Stanton — Stevens's Bill passes the House — Sherman's Substitute adopted in the Senate — The House makes Further Amendments — Impeachment discussed in the Cabinet — The Tenure-of-Office Bill condemned in the Cabinet 34

XLVII

MARCH, 1867

Seward and Stanton prepare the Veto Message on the Tenure-of-Office
Bill — Vetoes of this and the Military Government Bill sent in —
Reverdy Johnson's Extraordinary Course — Butler's Animosity
towards Grant — The Chances of Impeachment — The Close of
One Congress and the Beginning of Another — The Powers of the
Military Governors — The President's Exclamation in regard to
Impeachment — Ex-Congressman Law of Indiana on Andrew
Johnson — The President's Reticence — Randall's Conciliatory At-
titude towards the Radicals — Stanton apparently to select the
Military Governors — Sickles among the Generals chosen as Gov-
ernors — Wall Street's Influence in Congress — The Alaska Pur-
chase Treaty — Death of Charles Eames — His Career — Senator
Foster and the Austrian Mission — No Opposition to the Russian
Treaty in the Cabinet — The ex-Confederate Admiral of the Peru-
vian Navy to be saluted by American Officers — Indian Affairs —
The President wishes to offer the Austrian Mission to General
Blair — Judge Blair's Story of the Action of General Grant and
General Dick Taylor against Seward and Stanton — Private Secre-
tary Moore's Relations with Stanton — Congress refuses to adjourn
— The Alaskan Treaty signed — Seward tells ex-Minister Bigelow
how he shaped Lincoln's Cabinet 54

XLVIII

APRIL AND MAY, 1867

Union Success in the Connecticut Election — Seward seeks to reward a
Political Trimmer with the Cuban Consul-Generalship — The Pre-
sident receives Word that an Injunction against him is to be asked
from the Supreme Court — Conversation with General Butler on
Public Affairs — The Senate confirms the Alaska Purchase Treaty
— Attempts to fill the Cuban Consul-Generalship — Admiral
Goldsborough seeks through his Wife to be retained on the Active
List — Senator Wilson electioneering in the South — Thaddeus
Stevens denies Wilson's Authority to make Promises — Governor
English of Connecticut — Most of his Message to the Legislature
written by Secretary Welles — A Delegation of Japanese visits the
President — The House Judiciary Committee seeking Evidence on
which to impeach — McCulloch talks plainly to the President about
Stanton — The French buying War Vessels in the United States
— Seward considers acquiring Snake Island in the West Indies —
Wilkes Booth's Diary — The Price of the Danish West Indies —
Attorney-General Stanbery examining the Military Government
Act — The Indian Troubles — The Japanese conclude to buy the
Ship Stonewall — The President to visit North Carolina 77

CONTENTS

XLIX

JUNE, 1867

The President goes to North Carolina, accompanied by Seward and Randall — Chief Justice Chase to hold Court in North Carolina — The Judiciary Committee decides against Impeachment but reports a Resolution of Censure against the President — A Visit to the Naval Academy with Admiral Farragut — Parting with Farragut — Farragut the Great Hero of the War — Sheridan's Removal of Governor Wells of Louisiana — Stanbery's Liberal Interpretation of the Military Government Act — Talk with Governor Pease of Texas — A Faction in Colombia proposes to tax Foreign Residents — Seward's Presidential Ambitions and Craze for the Acquisition of Territory — The Attorney-General's Opinion on the Reconstruction Bills an Able Document — Mrs. Goldsborough presses the Admiral's Claims to Retention on the Active List — The President invites Secretary Welles to accompany him on a Journey to Boston — Cabinet Discussion of the Attorney-General's Opinion on the Military Government Law — Commander Roe's Action in seizing Santa Anna — The President starts for Boston — The Publication of Cabinet Proceedings — Sheridan's Insubordination — The President's Faltering Conduct — His Administration a Failure — General Sickles's Letter against the Secretary of the Navy — The President courteously received in New England — Grant's Probable Candidacy — Montgomery Blair's Opinion of Grant as a General — Admiral Farragut sails for Europe with two of the Secretary's Sons accompanying him — Conversation with the President on his Return from the South 101

L

JULY, 1867

Seward proposes to purchase Two Islands from Denmark for $7,400,000 — Cabinet Discussion of Sheridan's Letter to Grant — Maximilian shot in Mexico — Congress meets in Extra Session — General Halleck proposed as Commissioner to go to Alaska — Seward justifies Commander Roe in the Capture of Santa Anna — Stanton ignores the President in addressing a Communication directly to the Speaker of the House — Reconstruction Bill passed — The Influence of Seward and Stanton on the Administration — Conversation with a Member of the British Parliament on Constitutions and Reconstruction — The President vetoes the Reconstruction Bill without consulting the Cabinet — Congress passes a Resolution of Sympathy with Cretan Insurrectionists — General Banks calls to urge a Removal and an Appointment — The President's Leniency in Matters of Pardon — Troops sent to Tennessee — Grant's Change of Views — General Rousseau proposed for Sheridan's Place — Pro-

CONTENTS

posal to appoint Frederick Douglass to the Head of the Freedmen's
Bureau — The President receives Papers revealing a Conspiracy
to manufacture Evidence against him — Sheridan removes Governor Throckmorton of Texas and appoints E. M. Pease in his Place
— McCulloch discouraged at the Political Outlook 124

LI

AUGUST, 1867

The President consults with his Cabinet as to the Advisability of
removing Sheridan — The Conover Allegations — McCulloch's
Compromises — His Great Ability as a Financier — Grant deprecates the Removal of Sheridan — Grant going over to the Radicals
— Conversation with the President as to the Possibility of Stanton's
Retirement — Postmaster-General Randall asks for Leave of Absence — The President requests Stanton to resign — Stanton refuses — The Tenure-of-Office Act in Relation to the Question of
Stanton's Removal — Randall's Shakiness — Thurlow Weed's Attack on Chase — Secretary Welles advises the President to remove
Judge-Advocate-General Holt with Stanton and to appoint one of
the Blairs Secretary of War — The President discusses the Matter
with Montgomery Blair — The Jury in the John H. Surratt Case
disagrees — The President suspends Stanton and appoints General
Grant *ad interim* — General Sickles prohibits Civil Process in his
Military Department — Alleged Conspiracy against Judge-Advocate-General Holt — Stanton's Dismissal makes Little Commotion
— Correspondence between the President and General Grant relative to the Removal of Sheridan — Conversation with Grant on
the Subject of Reconstruction — A Political Ignoramus — General
Sickles announces his Intention of obstructing the United States
Court — Passage between Grant and Assistant Attorney-General
Binckley in Cabinet — Suspicions in regard to Randall — A Reorganization of the Cabinet talked of in the Papers — Conversation
with Montgomery Blair about Grant — Grant, insubordinate in
Cabinet, is rebuked by the President — The President's Strength
and Weaknesses 149

LII

SEPTEMBER, 1867

Grant's Insubordination — Form of a Proclamation of General Pardon
— Newspaper Rumors of Differences between the President and
Grant — Amnesty proclaimed — Newspaper Reports of an In-
tended Prorogation of Congress in case of an Attempt at Impeach-
ment — Exercises at the Antietam Battle-Field — Governor Geary's
Followers try to turn the Affair into a Radical Demonstration —
Death of Sir Frederick Bruce — The President consults with Lewis

CONTENTS

V. Bogy of St. Louis — Jeremiah S. Black as an Adviser of the
President — The Case of Paymaster Belknap — The Sale of Iron-
clads discussed in Cabinet — General Sickles asks for a Court of
Inquiry — The Question of the Power of State and Municipal
Courts to discharge Men enlisted in the United States Service —
The Attorney-General consulted on the Subject — The Matter dis-
cussed in Cabinet — Stanbery's Views as to the Habeas Corpus
Writ — Admiral Godon on the Naval Battle at Port Royal . . . 193

LIII

OCTOBER, 1867

Attorney-General Stanbery reads his Opinion on the Habeas Corpus
Case — The President calls General Sherman to Washington —
Colonel Cooper on the Political Situation in New York State — A
Sketch of Party Politics in New York — James A. Seddon's Application for Pardon — Governor Cox of Ohio mentioned for the War
Portfolio — General Blair's Qualifications for the Position — Sherman's Relations with Grant — Election Returns from Pennsylvania
and Ohio indicate an Overthrow of the Radicals — The President
has a Frank Talk with Grant, who assures him that he should expect to obey Orders — Boutwell disavows any Intention of attempting to arrest the President 218

LIV

NOVEMBER AND DECEMBER, 1867

Cabinet Discussion of the Question of Arrest — The President's Message — The Judiciary Committee of the House reports in favor of
Impeachment — The President's Message to the Senate giving Reasons for suspending Stanton — The Alabama Claims discussed in
Cabinet — A Complaint from Alabama against General Pope's Oppression — Grant's Presidential Aspirations — Senator Nye introduces a Bill to establish a Board of Survey to supervise the Naval
Bureaus — Admiral Porter thought to be behind it — Porter's
Services and Ambition — Thurlow Weed moving for Grant — The
Retirement of Captain R. W. Meade, U.S.N., called up for Revision — Raymond and the Philadelphia Convention 237

LV

JANUARY, 1868

Senator Grimes wishes to reorganize the Engineer Corps of the Navy —
Jealousy between the Line Officers and the Engineers — The Indian
"War" — Stanton's Case in Congress — Charles Francis Adams
resigns the Ministry to England — The President considers appoint-

ing General McClellan to the Place — John Sherman's Instability
— Grant leaves the War Department — His Explanation of his
Course, made in Cabinet — Will Stanton resign? — The Naval
Estimates and the House Committee on Appropriations — Grant
keeps away from the White House — Mrs. Welles's Reception —
Grant's Interview with Stanton — The Political Situation in Con-
necticut — Grant writes the President denying the Reports of his
Action in abandoning his Position as Secretary of War *ad interim* . 252

LVI

FEBRUARY, 1868

Grant's Treachery — Conversation with the President on the Subject
of Preparation for an Emergency — Proposal to make Washington
a Military Department and order Sherman to it — Excitement over
the Correspondence between the President and Grant — Grant's
Account of his Interview with Stanton — Grant's Dislike for and
Subjection to Stanton — His Indifference to Human Life — Stanton goading the Radicals to Impeachment — He dreads being out
of Place — The President sends to the House the Account of his Interview with Grant, with the Statements of the Cabinet Members
— Hancock remonstrates against an Order of Grant's — General
Lorenzo Thomas ordered to resume his Duties as Adjutant-General
at Washington — A New Military Department created at Washington and Sherman placed in Command — Sherman asks to be excused from coming to Washington — The President removes Stanton — McClellan nominated as Minister to England — Excitement
in Congress over Stanton's Removal — Adjutant-General Thomas
arrested — The President nominates Thomas Ewing Secretary of
War — Stanbery an Honest Lawyer and Faithful to the President,
but too Dependent on Precedents in an Emergency — Jeffries, Register of the Treasury, advises the President to use Strong Measures
— Officers summoned from an Evening Party — General Thomas's
Unfitness for the Place of Secretary of War *ad interim* — The Question of the Tenure of the Four Hold-over Members of the Cabinet
— The House votes to impeach the President — Conversation
with John Bigelow on the Situation — Repugnance of the Conservative Senators to the Possibility of Wade's becoming President —
General Lorenzo Thomas arrested and then discharged — Suggestions as to the Democratic Candidate for the Presidency — A Nitro-
Glycerine Scare in Congress — Stanbery considers resigning to devote himself to the President's Cause 269

LVII

MARCH, 1868

Preparations for the Impeachment Trial — The Notice of Impeachment served on the President — Selecting the President's Counsel

— Stanbery determines to resign his Cabinet Position before undertaking the President's Case — Stanton fortified in the War Department — Radical Victory in the New Hampshire Election — A Sketch of New Hampshire Politics — Stanbery hands in his Resignation — The President's Ill-considered Talks with Newspaper Men — Senator Sherman wishes a Naval Lieutenant court-martialed for using Disrespectful Language of Congress — The President's Uncommunicativeness — Judge Black on Seward's Handling of the Alta Vela Affair — The Impeachment Proceedings open with Little Excitement — Judge Black withdraws from the President's Case — Probable Reasons for his Course — A Spirit of Mischief in the Hawaiian Islands — Black's Letter to the President withdrawing from the Case and denouncing Seward's Conduct in the Alta Vela Matter — Wilson and Sumner and the Naval Appropriation Bill — General Butler's Opening in the Impeachment Trial 300

LVIII

APRIL, 1868

Gloomy Political Outlook in Connecticut — English reëlected, however, by an Increased Majority — Curtis opens for the President in the Impeachment Trial — Consultation as to the Introduction of General Sherman's Testimony — The Need of a Lawyer who can meet Butler and Bingham on their own Ground — Sherman's Testimony admitted — Secretary Welles on the Stand — Manager Wilson's Elaborate Speech interjected into the Proceedings — The President nominates General Schofield as Secretary of War — Senator Grimes on the Impeachment Trial — Surmises as to the President's Reasons for nominating Schofield — Vice-Admiral Porter said to be fishing for the Secretaryship of the Navy — The Speeches of Thaddeus Stevens and Thomas Williams — Stanbery, though ill, is confident of Success — Evarts's Speech 328

LIX

MAY, 1868

A Visit to Mount Vernon — The President's Disappointment at Black's Desertion — The Outcome of the Impeachment hanging in the Balance — The Doubtful Senators — The Carpet-Bag Constitutions of Arkansas and South Carolina transmitted to Congress — Bingham's Closing Speech for the Prosecution — Congressional Inquiry into the Sale of the Ironclads Oneota and Catawba — The Case of the Hannah Grant — An Exciting Afternoon and Evening in the Senate — Speeches of Sherman, Grimes, Trumbull, and Fessenden — Hopeful Outlook — The Vote on Impeachment postponed — Illness of Senator Grimes — Public Opinion manufactured in Washington by the Radicals — The Vote on the Eleventh Article fails to

convict the President — A Call on Senator Grimes — Attack on
Ross of Kansas for his Vote in favor of the President — The Candi-
dates before the Republican Convention at Chicago — Grant and
the Radicals — Rumors of Cabinet Changes — Japanese Affairs —
Grant and Colfax nominated at Chicago — The Acquittal of the
President — The News comes to the Cabinet in Session — Charges
of Corruption — Stanton leaves the War Department — His Char-
acter and Abilities and his Administration of the Department —
Schofield's Appointment as Secretary of War sticks in the Senate —
A Seminole Chief on the Written Constitution 343

LX

JUNE, 1868

Whites and Blacks in the Washington Election — Death of ex-President Buchanan — His Character — Oregon goes Democratic —
Stanbery, renominated as Attorney-General, is rejected by the Senate — The Senate compliments Stanton — The Powers of the
Comptrollers and Auditors in the Treasury Department — Chase
talked of for the Presidency — Burlingame and the Chinese Ambassadors — City Election in Washington — Chase's Candidacy
for the Democratic Nomination to the Presidency — Hopelessness of
President Johnson's Desire for the Nomination — Admiral Porter
and the Controversy between the Line and Staff Officers of the
Navy — The *Intelligencer* attacks McCulloch — Congressional Inquiry into the Sale of the Ironclads Oneota and Catawba — The
House accepts the Arkansas Constitution over the President's Veto
— The Attack on McCulloch instigated by Seward — Evarts nom-
inated Attorney-General — Intimations of Another Impeachment
Movement 374

LXI

JULY, 1868

A Proclamation of General Amnesty read in Cabinet — Jefferson Davis the only Person excepted — The President draws up another
making no Exception — The New York Convention nominates
Horatio Seymour and Francis P. Blair — An Unfortunate Nomination — The Result brought about by the Tammany Managers
— Disappointment of the President — Seward Close-mouthed on
the Nominations — Conversation with the President in regard to
Seward, Stanton, and McCulloch — Doolittle invited to become
an Independent Candidate — The President prepares a Message
recommending Certain Changes in the Constitution — Cabinet Discussion of it — A Talk with Montgomery Blair — The Blairs and
the President — Evarts takes his Seat in the Cabinet — The Two
New Cabinet Members, Schofield and Evarts — John A. Griswold

claiming Credit for the Monitor to the Exclusion of the Navy Department — Congress, instead of adjourning, takes a Recess till September 21 — Seward reads in Cabinet a Proclamation relating to the Fourteenth Amendment — General Banks and the Navy Yard Appointments — Conditions in Georgia 393

LXII

AUGUST AND SEPTEMBER, 1868

A Tour of Inspection of the Navy Yards — Talk of an Extra Session of Congress — The Railroads and Congress — Sanford E. Church and Dean Richmond (the younger) on a Political Mission from New York — The Power of State Sheriffs to call on Army Officers for Assistance — Death of Thomas H. Seymour — His Career and the Part played in it by Mr. Welles — Radical Gains in the Maine Election — The "Alexandrine Chain" — Senator Morgan and Representative Schenck issue a Call for Congress to reassemble — Congress meets and adjourns — General John A. Dix's anti-Seymour Letter — His Character and Political Views — Marriage of Robert T. Lincoln — The Pacific Railroad 422

LXIII

OCTOBER AND NOVEMBER, 1868

Dahlgren's Management of the Ordnance Bureau — The Political Outlook — Getting the Election Returns — Proposal to withdraw Seymour and substitute another Democratic Candidate for the Presidency — The Democratic Mistake and how it came about — The Governor of Arkansas asks for Arms — Troops to be sent to Memphis — Seward's Table of Treaties — Dinner of the New York Bar to Attorney-General Evarts — Grant's Spite against Members of the Cabinet — Minister Washburn in Paraguay — Minister Reverdy Johnson submits a Protocol on the Alabama Claims — Discussion of the Subject 445

LXIV

DECEMBER, 1868

Report on the Pacific Railroad — The *New York Evening Post* on Vanderbilt and the Merrimac — The Alabama Claims — Congress assembles — Senator Trumbull makes an Unreasonable Request — The President's Annual Message and its Reception in Congress — Proposal to annex San Domingo — Attorney-General Evarts and the Law relating to Courts Martial — Grant's Probable Course as President — Discussion of the Finances of the Country — Fox's Conversation with Admiral Porter — Formal Acquisition of League

Island for the New Navy Yard — Bowles of the *Springfield Republican* arrested at the Suit of Fisk — Relations of Grant with President Johnson and Members of the Cabinet — Cabinet Discussion of the Currency Question — The End of an Eventful Year . . . 472

LXV

JANUARY, 1869

The President's New Year's Reception — Grant's Failure to call on the President — The President decides not to attend Grant's Inauguration — The Naval Surgeons seeking to be made Commodores — Death of General Rousseau — The Tenure-of-Office Repeal Bill passes the House — Seward concludes his Fifty-sixth Treaty — Evarts favors abandoning Confiscation Proceedings — Senatorial Elections — The Alabama Claims Treaty discussed in Cabinet — Fenton defeats Morgan for the Republican Senatorial Nomination — Seward's Subserviency to Grant — Senator Grimes introduces a Bill to reorganize the Navy 496

LXVI

FEBRUARY, 1869

Students of Georgetown College visit the President — John P. Hale as Minister to Spain — General Schofield advocates consolidating the War and Navy Departments — President Lincoln's Clemency towards the Defeated South — Did Grant and Sherman act under Instructions from him in making the Terms of the Surrender? — Senator Morrill of Vermont compliments the Administration of the Navy Department — Insurrection in Cuba — The Butler and Bingham Factions among the Radicals — General Dix resigns as Minister to France — Hawley urged for Grant's Cabinet — The Panama Canal Treaty — Grant's Nepotism — Simeon Johnson and Coombs's Claim — Johnson's Ignorance of the Duties of the Departments — Grant's Cabinet still in Doubt — The Question of governing Alaska — The Course to be followed by President Johnson and his Cabinet on Inauguration Day 518

LXVII

MARCH, 1869

Discussion of the Inauguration Ceremonies — The President's Last Reception — Good-byes at the Department — How President Johnson and his Cabinet spent the Last Moments of the Administration — The Inaugural Ceremonies and Procession — Grant's Cabinet — A.T. Stewart illegally nominated Secretary of the Treasury — Sumner's Wrath at Grant's Course in regard to his Cabinet

— Stewart, after offering to trustee his Business, finally declines the Secretaryship — Pressure for Boutwell as Secretary of the Treasury — Mr. Faxon and Mr. E. T. Welles leave the Navy Department — Hamilton Fish succeeds Washburne as Secretary of State and the Latter is appointed Minister to France — General Rawlins made Secretary of War — Admiral Porter, in charge of the Navy Department, appoints Chief Engineer King in Isherwood's Place — Porter's Management of the Department — Debate on the Repeal of the Tenure-of-Office Act — Grant's Scheme of reorganizing the Navy — Moses H. Grinnell made Collector at New York — Porter's Intrusion in the Navy Department — The Story of his Appointment as Vice-Admiral — Butler expresses Contempt for Grant — Ex-President Johnson in Tennessee — Montgomery Blair on Colonel Moore and other Associates of Johnson in Washington — Butler outgeneraled and the Tenure-of-Office Repeal Bill compromised 536

LXVIII

APRIL, MAY, AND JUNE, 1869

The Compromise on the Tenure-of-Office Bill passes Both Houses — Porter as "Lord of the Admiralty" — Connecticut goes Radical in the State Election — Possibility of War with Spain — Congress adjourns after placing the Matter of Reconstruction in the President's Hands — Morton's Amendment requiring the Adoption of the Fifteenth Amendment to the Constitution before a State is given Representation — Corruption not confined to one Party — A General Sweep of Official Incumbents — Diplomatic Appointments — Motley goes to England, Washburne to France — The Senate rejects the Alabama Treaty after a Speech against it by Sumner — Regrets at leaving Washington — A Courtesy from Vice-Admiral Porter — Reflections on relinquishing Office — The Return to Hartford — Call on Admiral Farragut in New York — The Admiral suffering from Official Neglect — Changes in Hartford in Eight Years — Getting settled — Grant's Unfitness for the Presidency — Secretary Borie a Nonentity — Admiral Porter's Order to change the Names of Men-of-War — The Alabama Question and the British Public 568

INDEX 591

ILLUSTRATIONS

ANDREW JOHNSON . . . . *Photogravure frontispiece*

JAMES W. GRIMES 14

GIDEON WELLES 86

EDWIN M. STANTON 158

ULYSSES S. GRANT 260

WILLIAM M. EVARTS 308

WILLIAM PITT FESSENDEN 350

WILLIAM FAXON 386

JAMES R. DOOLITTLE 402

DAVID D. PORTER 550

DIARY OF GIDEON WELLES

VOLUME III

JANUARY 1, 1867 — JUNE 6, 1869

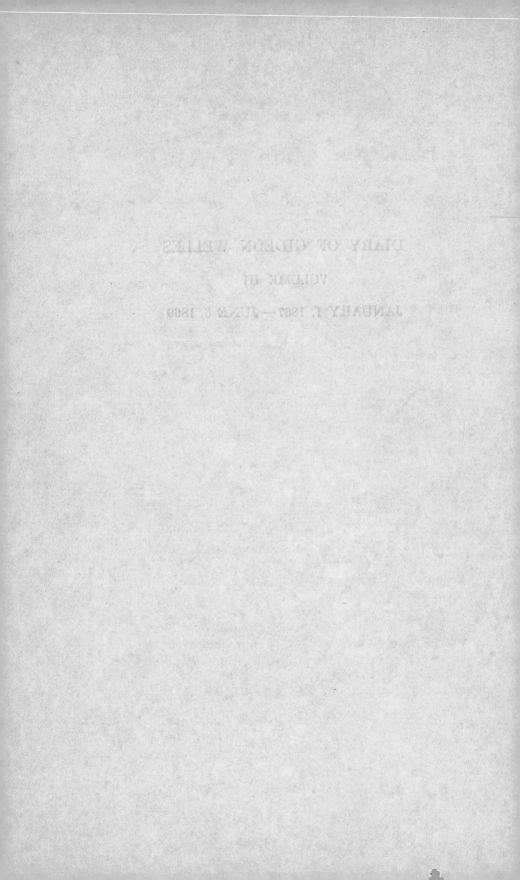

DIARY OF GIDEON WELLES

JANUARY 1, 1867 — JUNE 6, 1869

XLV

Cabinet Discussion of the Message vetoing the District of Columbia Reorganization Bill — The Bay of Samaná Purchase Scheme meets with Difficulties — Congress overrides the Veto — Representative Ashley of Ohio introduces a Resolution to impeach the President — Seward submits to the Cabinet the Articles of a Proposed Treaty with Prussia — An Amnesty Proclamation agreed upon — The President asks the Opinions of the Cabinet Members in regard to Territorializing the States — Senator Grimes as Chairman of the Naval Committee — General Grant's Position on the District of Columbia Suffrage Bill — His Lack of Political Principles — The Senatorial Fight in Pennsylvania results in the Nomination of Cameron — Roscoe Conkling nominated in New York — Cabinet Discussion of the Right of a Territory to organize itself as a State — The Senatorial Elections — Conkling, Cameron, and Trumbull — The Italian and Chilian Missions — Motley resigns as Minister to Austria — Seward's Calls at the Capitol — The Cabinet decides not to sell out the Dunderberg to the Contractor — The Swatara returning from Nice with Surratt — Action of the House in regard to the Ship Idaho — The President vetoes the Colorado and Nebraska Bills — The Army moving to get Possession of the Indian Bureau — A Committee from North Carolina submits a Reconstruction Proposal to the President.

January 1, 1867, *Tuesday.* I neither called on the President nor did I receive this New Year's Day. My nephew, Robert G. Welles, was buried this P.M. Funeral at his father's in Glastonbury.

January 4, *Friday.* At the Cabinet to-day the President read his veto message on the bill reorganizing the District of Columbia, which excluded those who had given comfort to the Rebels but allowed negroes to vote. I was not aware until to-day that the bill had been sent him. When I last conversed with him, about a week since, he said he had not received it. He had, moreover, requested the Cabinet to consider the subject, for he should wish their written opinions. I was therefore surprised, when, without official Cabinet consultation or opinion, he to-day brought forward his proposed message. The document is one of length, too much on the defensive of himself and the Supreme Court, and does not, I think, take hold of some of the strongest points for a veto.

Seward gave it his approval and made quite a random general speech without much point. Said he had always advocated negro suffrage and voted for it in New York. Here and in the States where there was a large preponderating negro population it was different, — if they were not in a majority they were a large minority. That eventually universal suffrage was to prevail, he had no doubt. All governments were coming to it. There are to-day representatives in service in Egypt elected, etc., — but he approved the message.

McCulloch approved the message because he was opposed to giving this privilege to the negro. That was the sentiment of his State, as well as of himself, and he had always voted in conformity to it.

Stanbery occupied much the same position. Had as a member of the Ohio Legislature voted against negro suffrage. Should do the same to-day if there, and believed that on the naked question there were at least one hundred thousand majority against it in that State.

Stanton took from his portfolio a brief and carefully prepared written statement, to the effect that he had examined the bill and could perceive no constitutional objections to any of its provisions; he therefore hoped the President would give it his approval.

I read from some rough notes that the bill proposed to do something more for the blacks than to raise them to an equality with the whites, — it proposed to elevate them above a certain class of whites of admitted intelligence and character who, heretofore, were entitled to and had exercised suffrage. If suffrage is claimed for the blacks on the ground that they are rightfully entitled to it as citizens of the United States, then to deprive the white citizens of that right which they now enjoyed is to inflict a punishment upon them and subject them to a forfeiture, and it is proposed to do this without due form of law, — that is, without trial and conviction, they, by an *ex post facto* law, are to be condemned. The Constitution would thus be violated in two of its most important provisions, deemed essential to the preservation of liberty, and the act, if sanctioned, will stand as a precedent for any similar violation hereafter, etc. On the other points I agreed with the gentlemen that Congress ought to pass no such law until the States had at least gone as far, — that the people of the District (the white people) ought to be heard. I expected that Stanton would have met me defiantly, but he said not a word.

Browning was opposed to the bill for the reasons stated in the veto, and so was Randall.

After all had expressed themselves, Attorney-General Stanbery inquired how long the veto could be delayed. The President said until Monday. Stanbery remarked that would not be sufficient for his purpose. He had reason to believe the Supreme Court would give its opinion on the test oath question on Monday, which he thought would embrace the point which I had raised. He had not turned his mind to the constitutional question, but believed the objection well taken. Stanton still said nothing. I thought, however, that he was of Stanbery's opinion.

General Grant, who was present by invitation, was very emphatic against the bill, not because it disfranchised Rebels, for he said he rather liked that, but he thought it very contemptible business for Members of Congress whose States excluded the negroes, to give them suffrage in this District.

I agreed with him, but remarked there were other and

stronger reasons also, which, in a difference between the President and Congress, should not be overlooked.

McCulloch said he doubted if it would be politic to bring forward the constitutional objection at this time, for the Radicals would seize hold of it and insist that we were in sympathy with the Rebels.

Randall was also decisive against it. The message was just right; he would add nothing nor take anything away.

I stated I had no controversy in regard to the message, but that if there was a constitutional point against a bill which was to be vetoed, that point ought, in my opinion, never to be omitted.

Ten members of the Arkansas Legislature were in waiting when the Cabinet met, and the President proposed to introduce them. They had been appointed a committee to visit Washington and ascertain the views of the Government. The interview was brief. Seward requested them to dine with him to-morrow evening and invited the Cabinet to come also. I promised to call in the course of the evening, but asked to be excused from the dinner. McCulloch and Stanbery concurred.

Not being satisfied that the President should omit the constitutional point in his veto message, I called on him this evening for further conversation. Stanbery was with him. The President produced a file of letters of Forney, Clerk of the Senate, written while he was paying court to the President, strongly urging him to take the position he has pursued, praising and complimenting him. Yet this fellow is now attacking, abusing, and misrepresenting the President summarily in his "two papers, both daily."

The President heard my suggestions in regard to the constitutional objection; agreed with me; admitted, as I urged, the importance of it and of his concurrence with the Court; but did not say, nor did I ask or expect him to say, whether he would make that point in his message. I am inclined to think he will not. The question of expediency raised by McCulloch and Randall, and the point not hav-

ing been original with himself, as all are aware, have their
influence. Yet he hesitates. This is his great infirmity.
The President has firmness, but is greatly wanting in
prompt decision. He is unwilling to take a step, but when
it is once taken he does not recede.

We discussed the whole subject of suffrage and civil
rights after Stanbery left, — the views of Jefferson and
others. I quoted from Jefferson and he wished to know
where he could find the passage. I could not tell him and
promised I would give it to him in the morning.

January 5, Saturday. Seward's scheme to purchase the
Bay of Samaná, St. Domingo, meets with untoward difficulties. His son, who is to be the negotiator, started in
the Gettysburg, which got hard aground before she had
proceeded three miles from Annapolis. The Don was then
ordered round from New York, which took on board pass-
engers, etc., from the G. and proceeded to sea. The Gettysburg got off directly after and was ordered to Hampton
Roads, Norfolk. To-day Admiral Porter telegraphed me
that the Don encountered a gale, lost her mainmast, and
had returned to Norfolk for repairs. He now wants the
Gettysburg. Directed him to take her. I am not in favor
of this purchase. It is a scheme, personal and political, on
the part of Seward. A tub thrown to assure Thad Stevens
and Fessenden.

Gave the President the passage quoted from Jefferson.
It is in the first volume of Jefferson's works, — his Autobi-
ography, page 29. It is quoted by De Tocqueville. I again
advised that the constitutional objection should be presented in his message.

Went with McCulloch to Seward's and spent an hour or
two with the Arkansas gentlemen. Told them I knew of
nothing they had to reconstruct. If Congress admitted
them to their rightful representation, in accordance with
the Constitution, all was well with them. In regard to the
Constitutional Amendment, assured them I was opposed

to it as a Northern man as well as Southern. As an American citizen I wanted no such interpolation in the Constitution.

McCulloch tells me that General Grant urged upon them to adopt the Amendment; said the North was in favor; that they had decided for it in the late election; that if not adopted the Government would impose harder terms. What nonsense! What business has Congress to impose terms upon States? General Grant, not very enlightened, has been led astray, I trust unwittingly on his part, by Stanton and Washburne.

January 7, Monday. The veto went in to-day. But a party vote overrode it, as was expected. The message was courteous in terms, and the argument and reason very well, though not as strong and exhaustive as could have been wished; sufficiently so, however, to have satisfied all who are not partisans or fanatics. No calm, considerate, and true statesman or legislator can believe it correct to impose this bill upon the District against the unanimous voice of the people. The ignorant, vicious, stupid negroes who have flocked hither cannot vote intelligently; are unfit to be jurymen. The States and constituencies from which these came would oppose it within their own jurisdictions.

In the House of Representatives fanaticism, prompted by partisanship, ran wild. The reckless leaders were jubilant; the timid followers were abject and obedient. Ashley [1] introduced a resolution to impeach the President, or to authorize inquiry, and by an almost strict party vote it was adopted and referred to the Judiciary Committee under the previous question. It will never result, even under party drill, in an impeachment and conviction, but it is disreputable and demoralizing that a packed party majority should so belittle the government and free institutions as to entertain such a resolution from such a source. But he has not done it without consulting others.

[1] James M. Ashley of Ohio.

January 8, Tuesday. Seward submitted the articles of a proposed treaty between the United States and Prussia, proposing an arbitrament of claims of citizens of the two governments, which had been prepared and agreed upon by himself and Baron Gerolt, the Prussian Minister. It was asked, first I believe by Stanton, whether it embraced or excluded those Prussians who were domiciled in the Rebel region and who had sustained losses by the War. Seward made a long talk, claiming it did not, because such persons could not come under the law of nations. Browning undertook also to say the commissioners who would be appointed would be sensible men, and would not give such cases consideration. I asked why not, then, insert an article excluding such. Stanton said that if a man were to claim his house and was willing to submit to arbitration to decide if the title was in him, it did not follow that he (S.) would consent to arbitrate. After a long, full, and free discussion the opinion was unanimous against the treaty as presented. Browning, perhaps, finally expressed no opinion either way. Randall was absent. It was one of the frequent mistaken schemes of our Secretary of State, who is not a diplomatist, not a wise statesman, and is always unsafe, notwithstanding he has plausible talent.

The President brought forward the question of issuing a proclamation for more extended amnesty; referred to Mr. Lincoln's successive proclamations, beginning with that of September, 1862, and showing consistency and uniformity of proceedings and views.

Stanton stated that he had this morning received a copy of the act which had just passed the legislature of North Carolina, granting amnesty and oblivion; said that all our officers and soldiers were liable to be harassed and arrested through the Southern States for trespass and injury; thought it would be well there should be reciprocal amnesty. The suggestions struck all favorably and will, I think, receive consideration and action.

Another matter the President remarked he wished to

bring forward, and that was, in view of what was taking
place around us, especially on the subject of dismantling
States, throwing them into a Territorial condition and annulling their present organization and government, he considered it important he should know the opinions and views
of each member of the Cabinet. If we are united, that fact
would carry weight with it, here and before the country; if
we were not united there was weakness.

I had observed through the whole sitting that the President was absorbed and prepared for an energetic movement, and from what he had said to me on Saturday, I anticipated what his purpose was. But he had been slow, and
procrastinated, and until he broached the subject I had not,
after previous experience, much faith that we should reach
it to-day. When he commenced, however, his countenance
indicated firm and fixed resolution. He was pale and calm,
but no one could mistake that he was determined in his
purpose.

I doubt if any one but myself was aware of what was
passing in his mind. Perhaps McCulloch may have thought
of it, for I told him on Saturday evening of my interview.
He said he had repeatedly spoken to the President, and had
similar intimations, but he had little confidence.

Seward was evidently taken by surprise. Said he had
avoided expressing himself on these questions; did not
think it judicious to anticipate them; that storms were
never so furious as they threatened; but as the subject had
been brought up he would say that never, under any circumstances, could he be brought to admit that a sovereign
State had been destroyed, or could be reduced to a Territorial condition.

McCulloch was equally decided that the States could not
be converted into Territories.

Browning, who sat next to him, began to express his
views, — a discourtesy which he not unfrequently commits
but I think will not again, — when Stanton interrupted him
and requested him to wait his turn.

Stanton said he had communicated his views to no man. Here, in the Cabinet, he had assented to and cordially approved of every step which had been taken to reorganize the governments of the States which had rebelled, and saw no cause to change or depart [from it. Stevens' proposition he had not seen, and did not care to, for it was one of those schemes which would end in noise and smoke. He had conversed with but one Member, Mr. Sumner, and that was one year ago, when Sumner said he disapproved of the policy of the Administration and intended to upset it. He had never since conversed with Sumner nor any one else. He did not concur in Mr. Sumner's views, nor did he think a State would or could be remanded to a Territorial condition.

I stated my concurrence in the opinions which had been expressed by the Secretary of War and that I held Congress had no power to take from a State its reserved rights and sovereignty, or to impose terms on one State which were not imposed on all States.

The President interrupted. He said the *power* to prescribe terms was one thing; the *expediency* was another. I said I was opposed to the whole subject or theory of prescribing or imposing terms external to the Constitution on sovereign States on the score of expediency as well as of want of power. If there was no power it certainly could not be expedient. I confessed I had not been as reserved as the Secretary of State and Secretary of War in expressing my opinions. When friends had approached me and conversed on these or indisputable fundamental questions, I had not refrained from stating my views, especially to those who had consulted me. It seemed to me proper that we should do so. I had conversed with Mr. Sumner in the early part of last session, about the period that the Secretary of War had his interview, and then Sumner had taken exception to the omission to give negro suffrage, and for that reason, and that only, he had opposed the President's policy of Reconstruction.

Stanbery said he was clearly and unqualifiedly against

the whole talk and theory of territorializing the States. Congress could not dismantle them. It had not the power, and on that point he would say that it was never expedient to do or attempt to do that which we had not the power to do.

Browning declared that no State could be cut down or extinguished. Congress could make and admit States, but could not destroy or extinguish them after they were made.

The resolution to impeach the President, Seward and others treat lightly. My impressions are that it will not result in a conviction, although infamous charges, infamous testimony, and infamous proceedings will be produced as easily, honestly, and legally as Butler could get spoons in New Orleans; but, the preliminary step having been taken, backed by strong party vote, the Radicals are committed. Ashley, who introduced the resolution, is a calculating fanatic, weak, designing, fond of notoriety, not of very high-toned moral calibre. I do not think, however, that he is, as some suppose, a tool of others entirely, — certainly not an unwilling tool. He seeks the notoriety and notice, and hounds like Boutwell and Williams of Pittsburg edge him on. Colfax, though feeble-minded, is Speaker, seeks to be foremost, and has been an adviser with Ashley and pioneered the way for him to introduce the resolution. Stevens, much shrewder and abler than either, keeps in the background, though the chief conspirator.

It is a necessity for the Radicals to get rid of the President. Unless they do, they cannot carry out their plans of dwarfing the States under the torture of Reconstruction with the judiciary opposed to their revolutionary schemes. At present the Senate is not prepared to convict, even if the conspiracy to impeach should pass the House. But there is not much reliance on the present Senate. The honest instincts of a majority are against the whole scheme, but a considerable portion of them are without moral courage or high integrity. Perhaps they may herd together and hold out; but, individually, very few of them can stand up against the dictates of party.

January 9, Wednesday. Mr. Eames was yesterday touched with a slight fit of apoplexy when arguing the case of the Grey Jacket in the Supreme Court. Called upon him this evening and found him better than I apprehended.

Sent in replies, one to the Senate and one to the House, through the President. The first called for detailed orders issued to officers, mechanics, laborers, etc., in all the navy yards and all correspondence at the Norfolk Yard. The response to this call embraced probably two thousand pages. Most of it mere routine orders, and the whole call is an abuse and valueless. The object was to get at a certain communication from the Radicals at Norfolk, who, while employed at the navy yard, had been active partisans,— had attended, whilst receiving pay from the Government, the sectional Southern delegation at Philadelphia, been displaced or suspended by Admiral Rowan, and his action had been confirmed by the Department. Clements, one of the dismissed men, had been employed here on the Capitol for two or three years, had formed partisan acquaintance with Radical Members of Congress, and believed he could compel the Department to reinstate him. Senator Grimes, to whom he appealed and from whom I have reason to believe he had assurances of support, did not like to appear in the matter, and he therefore induced Senator Henderson of Missouri to offer the resolution. Admiral Smith, who was a good deal disgusted with the unnecessary partisan call, knowing some of the facts, charged Grimes with having instigated the movement. Grimes, who is jealous, suspicious, and intensely sectional in party matters, but proud and ambitious, was enraged to learn that his intrigue was known to and understood by the Department. Under high impulse, immediately on getting to the Senate, he introduced a resolution for discontinuing the Norfolk Yard and putting it in charge of the Commandant of Marines.

This was to get rid of Rowan, whose course I approved. It was a pitiful exhibition of spite, malice, and evil passion, of which I have no doubt he will in due time be ashamed; but it shows the course of action, personal and party motives, and narrow and vindictive malevolence of one of the ablest of the Radical leaders. Strange that a man and Senator of his good sense should so give way to party!

Senator Grimes is ambitious, dissatisfied, always suspicious, and at times ungenerous. He is intelligent, has moral courage, but is not always bold to act. Beyond any other one man he is responsible for the present calamitous condition of affairs. Sumner and Stevens are open and undisguised in their hostility and without aid from Grimes they could accomplish little. Yet Grimes does not respect them or their motives and to me invariably condemns them. He knows his own ability and is vexed that Johnson, an old associate Senator but not a Radical, is in a higher position than himself. Fessenden and he act in concert, and Wilson of Iowa is stimulated, counseled, and controlled by him.

The course of the Radicals has received its direction more from Grimes than almost any other man, and yet others, for whom he has not high regard, instead of himself have the odium and the honor also of friends or opponents of the measure. This irritates and vexes him, but he would get angry with any one who should openly tell him the truth and give him his right position.

I regret that Admiral Smith should have informed him of what we know of his movements. I have hitherto got along very well with Grimes, for he has flattered himself that I was not aware of his operations and intrigues, because I have not put myself in his way. As chairman of the Naval Committee, with such a Congress as we now have, with such a chairman as J. P. Hale through the War, there has been no alternative but to submit in a degree to the disposition of measures which he might propose. By yielding to his suggestions I was sometimes able to modify his

JAMES W. GRIMES

opinions when we counseled together, if he was not publicly committed.

January 10, *Thursday.* The *New York Times* correspondent states, tolerably correctly, the position of General Grant on the suffrage bill of the District of Columbia. He condemned the Members of Congress for imposing negro suffrage on this District until their States had adopted the principle. The worst thing in the bill, he said, was that which violated the Constitution. Punishing Rebels by an *ex post facto* law was right; condemning them without trial he did not object to. Yet General Grant will very likely be the next President of the United States. I do not think he intends to disregard the Constitution, but he has no reverence for it, — he has no political principles, no intelligent ideas of constitutional government, and it is a day when the organic law seems to be treated as of less binding authority than a mere resolution of Congress.

Dined this evening with the President, the Cabinet, and their families, General Grant and the Tennessee delegation and their wives being present. Mrs. Taylor, wife of the Member from the Eastern District of Tennessee, says she buried her dresses to keep them from the Rebels, and the one she wore this evening she owned before the War and had buried it for over four years. Occasionally she unearthed her clothing, evenings, to air and preserve it. Colonel Hawkins said all his wife's dresses, save what she wore at the time, had been stolen from her, and what the Rebels could not carry away they had torn up and destroyed. Mrs. Taylor said she carried arms and was at all times "ready with her shooter." The people of Tennessee, particularly those of East Tennessee, were great sufferers during the Civil War.

January 11, *Friday.* Senatorial nominations were made last evening in several of the States. That in Pennsylvania, in place of Cowan, excites most interest. The competing

Radical candidates were Thad Stevens, Cameron, Governor Curtin, Forney, and Judge Kelley. The two latter withdrew some weeks since, and their combined strength was concentrated on Stevens. The Radical press in that State and throughout the country generally also favored him. Governor Curtin, however, had a distinctive and active newspaper and party support. Stevens, with some parade and an announcement of the fact on the floor of Congress, left his seat in the House and repaired to Harrisburg to superintend his own election. Forney left the Clerk's desk to aid him. Both Stevens and Curtin addressed a caucus of the Members.

A single ballot was taken, at which Cameron was nominated, getting 46 votes, Curtin 23, and the combined forces of Stevens, Forney, and Kelley but 7, — a few scattering. Forney last week made a violent attack on Cameron in his paper, the *Philadelphia Press*. The result surprises all, more in the fact that Stevens was so feebly supported than that Cameron succeeded. While I have not a high estimate of Cameron in many respects, I think him greatly preferable to either of his competitors. No worse man than Stevens could be elected. Curtin is limber, deceptive, and unreliable. Cameron is not great but adroit; his instincts are usually right, but he will sacrifice the right for selfish purposes. He is, however, equal to an average of the Senate. Is a politician of the second class.

In New York, Conkling is nominated to succeed Judge Harris, who has been sly and manœuvring and has defeated himself. Conkling is vain, has ability with touches of spread-eagle eloquence, and a good deal of impetuous ardor. He may improve and he may not. At present he is an intense Radical. If he has real sense he will get the better of it with experience. Conkling and Horatio Seymour are brothers-in-law, and either is a fair offset to the other. Both are ambitious and intense partisan politicians, but of opposing parties.

Little of interest at the Cabinet to-day. In a conversation with McCulloch he did not conceal that he was discouraged. The condition of the country is indeed deplorable, — that, I said, should make us the more resolute. But the great majority of the Radicals who are making war on his financial policy and striving to embarrass him, he says correctly, makes it a hard struggle. That the President is so slow in coming to a decision he feels to be a weakness in administration. The South is becoming rapidly demoralized. I expressed myself gratified that the President had, the other day, got Stanton unequivocally committed for the policy of the Administration and against the theory of territorializing the States. McCulloch says that Stanton, whenever it becomes an object, will deny this, or modify and change his views to suit his purposes; that S. is false and treacherous, and, he believes, a steady spy upon all of us. I apprehend there is much in McCulloch's suspicions.

Although the President has committed no act that can subject him to impeachment, and is in many respects one of the best and most single-minded Executives we have ever had, I have little doubt that the Radical leaders intend to try to get rid of him. This they feel to be essential to consummate their usurping schemes. There is a conspiracy maturing. How can they reduce the States to the condition of corporations, territorialize them, deprive them of their original, reserved, and guaranteed constitutional rights, without the aid of the Judiciary? How can they get control of the Court except by enlarging its numbers? If the number is to be increased, how can they get Radicals, except by displacing Johnson and getting Wade or one like him in his place?

January 12, *Saturday.* A law has passed the two houses convening the next Congress on the 4th of March. We have passed through the pressure and difficulties of the War without any such necessity, but Radicalism, which is striving to exclude certain States from participating in the government and to consolidate all power in Congress, like the

3

Rump Parliament, desires a perpetual session to override the Executive. We are living in a revolutionary period, and the character of the government is undergoing a strain which may transform it into a different character.

Erastus Corning writes me, earnestly, pressing that Captain De Camp may be made a commodore, and sends me the copy of a letter from Vice-Admiral Porter, stating that he ought to have that rank, that he (Porter) voted for him in the Board of Admirals and was disappointed he had not received it. This statement, if genuine, is a breach of confidence and of regulations; is unjust and unfair towards his associates; for the Board did not recommend De Camp; is, moreover, grossly wrong to the Department, and in every way unworthy of Vice-Admiral Porter.

De Camp is one of Porter's pets, — a trifling, disappointed, lazy officer, but popular good fellow with his cronies; ought to have been long since on the retired list and would have been but for some underhand intrigue.

January 14, *Monday.* It is given out that Senator Grimes intends making an assault on the Navy Department, or, in other words, an attack on the Secretary for dismissing Radicals from the Norfolk Navy Yard. His virulent and sectional hate, which has warped his better sense and led him to secretly push on others, compels him to now come forward, he being chairman of the Naval Committee, and show himself when one of his troop is removed. The man for whom he is interested went to Philadelphia to attend a sectional party convention; the money to pay his expenses was raised, or a part of it, in the Navy Yard, against regulations. Admiral Rowan suspended him, and I confirmed it, but being an intense Radical, Grimes would shield and sustain him.

January 15, *Tuesday.* The President submitted three bills, — one relating to suffrage in the Territories, one to the meeting of Congress on the 4th of March, and one covering the repeal of a clause in the amnesty law. This last was considered as of no moment, — it neither enlarged nor diminished the authority of the President. The second, although a mere party scheme, unwise and uncalled-for and of mischievous intent, was not such a bill as the President, under the circumstances, could very well veto. I suggested that no necessity for such an early session had existed during the War and there was certainly none at this time.

On the first proposition, or bill, there was considerable debate. Browning insisted it was operative no longer than the people of a Territory formed their constitution. I asked, if, in framing this constitution, they changed the principle and excluded the negroes, whether the application for admission into the Union would not be confronted with this law, and admission denied them because they disregard it. He thought not, because the people of the Territory would decide this matter for themselves. Stanton came to Browning's assistance and said the constitution of a Territory or State was no law until Congress had sanctioned it. I dissented from this doctrine. The people in their sovereign capacity framed their local organic law, and if they had the sovereign ability as well as the sovereign power, they might maintain their position. The Federal Government would refuse to admit such State into the Union, but if their constitution did not conflict with the Federal Constitution, they might, if sufficiently powerful, remain a State without the Union. Such a conflict was not probable, but should not be invited. The President did not commit himself, but was evidently not in accord with Browning.

The tone and language of the press and of considerate men are against the impeachment project; but the Radical leaders have a purpose to accomplish and intend to press the subject. Not to do so, after what they have said and done, would check the conspiracy and be a defeat that would in all probability injure them as a party. Whether it will not injure them more to proceed and fail, they do not pause to consider. They are vindictive and restless, regardless of right, and constitutional restraint and obligations. Thus far they have been successful in exercising arbitrary and unauthorized power, and they will not hesitate in the future, as in the past, to usurp authority, — to try without cause and to condemn without proof. Nor will they scruple to manufacture evidence if wanted.

There is nothing judicial or fair in this proceeding. It is sheer partisanism with most of them, a deliberate conspiracy with the few. The subject was taken up in caucus. A farce was then gone through with. A committee is sitting in secret, — a foul conspiracy, — trying to hunt up charges and evidence against as pure, as honest, as patriotic a chief magistrate as we have ever had. It is for his integrity they conspire against him.

I see by the papers this evening that the Radical legislatures of one or two States are taking the matter in hand, and urging impeachment without any facts, or fault, or specified crime, as a mere party measure, but it is all in character, — a conspiracy against the Constitution and the President for adhering to it.

January 16, *Wednesday.* An election of Senators took place in several States yesterday. Conkling was chosen in place of Judge Harris in New York. The Judge has been a cunning manager, as he thought; has, against his own convictions, gone with the Radicals and received his just reward. Conkling is vigorous and vain, full of spread-eagle eloquence and Radical violence. Time may temper his zeal and conduct, but this can hardly be expected under this recent success.

In Pennsylvania, Simon Cameron was elected in place of Cowan. The latter is a good lawyer and fair and well-meaning legislator. A man of talent and right instincts, a safe Senator, but not a politician or statesman of the first class. Until his election as Senator he had confined his studies to the law.

Cameron is an adroit and bold party operator. He does

not attempt to deny that he uses money, party influence, legislative abuses, and legislative grants to secure an election. In carrying his points, he is unscrupulous and cunningly audacious. His party tools he never forgets, so long as they are faithful in his cause and interest, and he freely gives his time, labor, and money to assist them. He is accurate and sharp, but has no enlarged view or grasp of mind; is supple as well as subtle and resorts to means which good men would shun. Against him were combined Thad Stevens, a man of as little principle as, but vastly more genius than, Cameron, and Forney, and Kelley, who support Stevens. The entire strength of this formidable combination commanded seven votes in the legislative Republican caucus. I have not thought Kelley corrupt, though a flaming and intense politician, but Stevens and Forney are infinitely worse than Cameron. Stevens has higher culture, more genius, learning, and education than Cameron, but less party tact and sagacity. He would sacrifice a principle, a constitutional question, for a joke, yet by his sarcastic power and the necessity of using him he is extolled in Forney's *Chronicle* and *Press* as the "Great Commoner" and controls the legislation of the country.

Trumbull was reëlected in Illinois after something of a struggle in the Radical Party. Trumbull has ability and culture, but is querulous, captious, and freaky. He has changed his principles within a year.

I had a long conversation with the President to-day and warned him that the leaders intended, if possible, to press impeachment, and inquired whether he had marked out the line of policy he should pursue; told him I thought it should be understood by the friends he could trust and that it should be bold and decided.

January 17, *Thursday.* In the Senate, Henderson of Missouri made his attack on me. It was based on a letter of mine to Rear-Admiral Rowan in command of the Norfolk Navy Yard, in which I informed him that the Department

gave no encouragement to disunionists, whether secessionists or exclusionists. Henderson had neither the manliness
nor the fairness to give the whole letter, but he may make
the most of the extract which he tears from the body of the
letter. The sentiments expressed I have always avowed,
and the doctrine I shall maintain so long as I live and there
is a Union. As to the employment of workmen, I have left
that to the officers of the yards. Before the suppression of
the Rebellion none who were Secessionists were employed
if their views were known. Many poor men who lived in
Norfolk and Portsmouth had worked to support their families and been pressed into the Rebel service, though neutral Unionists. Appeals in behalf of these poor men were
made to me by the best Union men in Virginia, and it was
on their appeal that the letter was written.

There was a pleasant reception this evening at the President's, which was very generally attended, except by the
more vindictive partisans in Congress who are conspiring
against him. I was glad to witness it, for the President is
vilely slandered and greatly misunderstood by many.

January 18, *Friday.* A fire early this morning consumed
the greater part of the conservatory building and destroyed
most of the plants at the Executive Mansion.

At the Cabinet-meeting the President submitted bills
which had passed Congress for admitting Colorado and
Nebraska with certain fundamental conditions as to the
qualification of voters. All the Cabinet, except Stanton,
were opposed to them, not only because they had not sufficient population, but because of the constitutional objection against the fundamental proposition. The want of
statesmanship and of intelligence with the demagogism
exhibited in these bills is lamentable. The population of
the Territories is not sufficient for one Congressional District, yet it is proposed to give them two Representatives
and four Senators in Congress. While they are doing this
for the sparsely peopled Territories on the frontier, the

same Members of Congress refuse to permit Georgia, with a million population, to have her constitutional right of representation; and so of other States.

A long discussion took place on the case of C——, a fraudulent contractor now in the penitentiary, having been confined nearly three years. The Attorney-General and the Secretary of War argued the case, the former for his release and the latter opposed. I think from the representation C. is a great rascal and so stated, but if he would pay the judgment I would leave the matter of clemency to the President, — merely as an act of clemency to an old man who had already been severely punished. The example had done its work, — the War is over. I would not be vindictive. Seward and McCulloch were for clemency; Browning and Randall, with Stanton, opposed. Stanton was ferociously vindictive; was for holding the prisoner the whole period, etc.

A letter to General Dix on Mexican matters, with documents, was submitted by Seward, and one on Indian difficulties by Browning.

I rode with Stanton back to Department. He said he wished this matter of vetoes might be over. I said it was unavoidable whilst Congress passed unconstitutional laws. Told him that in my opinion there must be equality of rights among the States, or we should have an unequal union or no union. He said he had no doubt on that subject as regarded the ten States, but he was not so clear on the question with Territories. I remarked that while Territories they might be governed, but that when they became States they were endowed with the same political rights as the other States. He replied that he had not given that question so much consideration as he desired, and for that reason had waived any expression of opinion on that point until he had examined the subject.

Sumner has been making a violent denunciatory speech against the President, which he will be ashamed of if he lives many years. It would hardly be excusable in a party gathering if made by a demagogue filled with whiskey, and is wholly unworthy of one of the pretensions of Sumner. Loon of Missouri has delivered himself of a counterpart in the House. Colfax, the Speaker, with his heartless, everlasting smile and slender abilities, decided Loon to be in order, and the House, of course, sustained the little demagogue. A more selfish and aspiring fellow is not to be found in either house, or one more unscrupulous, though always skulking from frank and open responsibility.

January 19, *Saturday.* The mails from the North are detained by a great snow-fall, which the high wind has drifted in places to the height of twenty feet.

I saw it stated a few days since that Senator Foster was to have the Italian Mission, and asked the President if such was the fact. He said it was the first time the subject had been mentioned to him and proceeded to say that some hasty and inconsiderate appointments had been made. The Chilian Mission he particularized as one of that character. I remarked that I was glad he had spoken of that, for it always appeared to me to be one of those unfortunate New York movements which were harmful. General Kilpatrick had that place given him by Seward at the instigation of Thurlow Weed, more to spite General Slocum, a true friend of the Administration, than to reward K.

Motley has tendered his resignation in a pet. One of Seward's spies had reported, it seems, that some of our foreign ministers and consuls were free in their censures of the President. Without going to the parties implicated, Seward appears to have forwarded extracts to all. Motley has evidently spoken freely and improperly and felt himself cornered, and, after a petulant letter, tendered his resignation. The President, *instanter,* as Seward closed reading the document, ordered the acceptance, without remark or word from any one.

Perry, consul at Tunis, sends his resignation under similar circumstances.

Seward stated yesterday that E. Jay Morris, our Minister at Constantinople, was at variance with Brown, Secretary of Legation, and called the attention of Attorney-General Stanbery to the subject, who, it seems, is an old friend of Brown. He (Stanbery) thought there should be no hasty action against B., who is a competent man, long a resident at Constantinople, had been the efficient man with all our ministers for years. Seward, with a manner not very unusual, but which is very offensive, said *he* had but one course to pursue in cases of this kind, and that was they must settle their difficulties or both quit. This was about what he had done with Hale and Perry at Madrid and had brought them to their senses very soon.

I remarked that I did not approve of the policy of putting the good and the bad on the same level; that one or the other of the parties in each of them, and in most other controversies, was chiefly in fault, and from my knowledge of the principals I should believe they were culpable; that Hale was notoriously unfit for his position.

The occurrences of the week have not improved the prospect of affairs. There is a wild delirium among the Radical Members of Congress which is no more to be commended and approved than the Secession mania of 1860. In fact it exhibits less wisdom and judgment, or regard for the Constitution, whilst it has all the recklessness of the Secession faction. By the exclusion of ten States a partisan majority in Congress, under the machinery of secret caucuses controlled by an irresponsible directory, has possession of the Government and is hurrying it to destruction, breaking down State barriers and other departments besides the legislature. Whether some of the better-disposed but less conspicuous men among the Radicals will make a stand is uncertain. As yet they have exhibited no independence, or political or moral firmness.

In the mean time the President, conscious of his right intentions and from habit, holds still and firm. Seward, relying on expedients, is dancing round Stevens, Sumner,

Boutwell, Banks, and others. Runs to the Capitol and seats himself by Stevens in the House and by Sumner in the Senate. This makes comment in the galleries, and paragraphs in the newspapers, and, Seward thinks, will, through their leaders, conciliate the Senators and Representatives towards himself, if not towards the President.

Sumner is easily and always flattered by attentions and notice, though he will not relinquish what he esteems his great mission of taking care of the negroes and subordinating and putting down the Southern whites. Seward is willing the negroes should have all Sumner would give them, for he sets no high estimate on suffrage and citizenship.

Stevens has none of the sincere, fanatical fervor of Sumner, nor much regard for the popular element, or for public opinion, but, having got power, he would exercise it arbitrarily and despotically towards all who differ with him. He has no professed respect for Seward, but feels complimented that the Secretary of State should come into the House of Representatives and sit down by and court the "Great Commoner." It is an observance that gratifies his self-esteem, a homage that soothes his arrogance.

Stanton continues to occupy an intermediate position on some important questions, differing with the President but almost obsequiously deferring to him. McCulloch says he is treacherous and a spy. He does not, however, I think, make regular report to any one. The Radicals receive his subtle advice and promptings and give him their support. The President understands him, but still consults him as fully as any member of the Cabinet. Seward and Stanton continue to coöperate together. Seward, I think, has doubts of Stanton's "divinity," yet, in view of his Radical associates, considers him more than ever a power and impresses the President with that fact.

Gradually the Radical Members are pressing on impeachment. Under the lead of the *New York Herald* and Forney's *Chronicle*, the Radical presses are getting into the movement. Yet the exclusionists, or centralists, have doubts if they can succeed, though earnestly striving to that end. Violent partisanship but no statesmanship, no enlarged or comprehensive views, are developed in either house.

The States which were in rebellion are each organized and in full operation as before the Rebellion, but Congress did not do this nor have any part in it. The people themselves in the respective States did it, and the lesser lights in Congress are told that they must assist in undoing the work which has been well and rightly done by the people interested, and compel the States to go through the process of disorganizing in order to organize.

The President remains passive and firm, but with no declared policy if the Radicals pursue their design to impeach and suspend him during trial. He said to me one day what he would do in a certain contingency, but it was rather thinking aloud what he might do than declaring a policy.

What General Grant and certain others might do, were Congress to proceed to extremities, neither the President nor any of his true friends are aware. I doubt if Grant himself knows. The Radicals, who distrust him, are nevertheless courting him assiduously.

January 23, *Wednesday.* The question of relinquishing the contract for the Dunderberg was to-day before the Cabinet. Seward brought it forward by request of Webb, the builder, who finds he has a losing bargain with the Navy Department and wishes to sell the vessel, he says, to Colombia. To this Seward states there is no objection, or violation of neutrality. If this is the case, the Secretary of State has nothing to do with the matter, though Seward introduced it with pomp and reference to the Attorney-General and myself.

I stated that I had on two or three occasions presented this subject to the President and Cabinet by request of Mr. Webb, who has proposed in various ways to repay the Government for all advances and take the vessel into his possession, with a view of reimbursing himself by disposing of her to some other government. No arrangement has ever been agreed upon, for he has wanted credit until he disposed of the vessel. But after advisement with our naval constructors, I would not object to receiving back our money and permitting Webb to take her. It is represented to me by our constructors and experts that there is much green timber and that there are other defects. I doubt if he can effect a sale, but would release him on return of the money which had been advanced.

Stanton objected to giving up the vessel. Was apprehensive that England or France would get her. One million and a quarter dollars was nothing, in his estimation, even if she had green timber and rotted down in half a dozen years. McCulloch thought best to keep the vessel, and Browning concurred. The President thought best to postpone the subject to Friday.

January 25, *Friday.* The subject of the sale of the Dunderberg, or the relinquishing of the vessel to the contractor, was considered. Mr. Webb had proposed to me to take her and refund to the Government the amount which had been paid, or, if that was not done, he desired that there should be a committee appointed to say what should be paid him on his losing contract. He called on me yesterday to converse on the subject. I advised him to put his views or propositions in writing, which led to the letter as above. As the contract with the Government stipulated the price, neither I nor the Administration could vary the contract, or authorize a committee to do so.

Stanton and McCulloch were very earnest and decided against selling, though each declared himself ready to defer to my opinion, which I had freely stated; but I requested that the subject should be disposed of by the Government in Cabinet. We could build a better vessel than this, but it would require time. Over three years have been given to the Dunderberg.

It was concluded not to sell, and I so informed Webb.

Letters from Admiral Goldsborough inform the Department that the Swatara left Nice on the 8th of January with Surratt on board. She may arrive at any time, but cannot reach Washington at present, the Potomac being closed by ice for forty miles below. Baltimore and Annapolis Harbors are also closed. It is urged by Seward and Stanton that the Swatara remain at Hampton Roads with Surratt on board until further orders or till the ice disappears from the river.

The House of Representatives has passed an act directing the Secretary of the Navy to receive the Idaho at $550,000. We have offered her to Forbes, the contractor, for $275,000. We could not get for her $150,000. Forbes sought this contract; said he could make a better and faster vessel than any in the Navy and in less time; guaranteed fifteen-knot speed; was to have delivered the vessel in about a year; was to have but $300,000 until completed. The vessel was not completed to time, cannot make over eight or ten knots; Congress long ago ordered $250,000 to be paid in addition to the $300,000 which had been paid. The whole is a failure, and Congress now steps in to relieve the contractor from the liabilities of his folly, error, and imprudence.

January 26, Saturday. Congress does not make much progress in the schemes of Reconstruction and impeachment. The Radical portion of the Republicans are as keen as ever and will continue to be so, especially on impeachment, but the considerate hesitate. It is a party scheme for party purposes, not for any criminal or wrong act of the President.

On Reconstruction, as it is called, there are differences and doubts and darkness. None of the Radicals have any clear conception or perception of what they want, except power and place. No well-defined policy has been indicated by any of them. Stevens wants a stronger government than the old Union.

Violence of language has broken out two or three times during the week. The Speaker, whilst ready to check the Democrats, permits the Radicals to go to extreme length. The President is denounced and vilified in the worst and most vulgar terms without any restraint or intimation of impropriety from the presiding officer, yet Mr. Colfax wishes to be popular. His personal aspirations warp his judgment, which is infirm, and, like most persons, in striving to reach a position for which he is unfitted he fails. Those who may be pleased for the moment with his partisan leanings will not confide in him beyond the moment.

January 28, *Monday.* The President sent in his veto on the Colorado Bill to-day, giving cogent and sufficient reasons why that Territory should not with the present population be admitted as a State. A veto on the admission of Nebraska will go in to-morrow. Both these vetoes have been looked for.

January 29, *Tuesday.* The Army desires to get possession of the Indian Bureau, and the Interior Department is not disposed to relinquish it. Stanton professes to care nothing about it, and thrusts forward Grant and other military men as the movers. I can perceive that they have in him a prompter and willing coadjutor. As the Radicals are in sympathy with Stanton and not with Browning, the question will be likely to go with the War rather than the Interior Department, whatever may be the merits involved.

It is a great mistake to change good Indian agents, if any there are. Political party adventurers and speculators, without conscience or principles, seek these positions to enrich and elevate themselves at the expense of the poor Indians. The old, single-hearted agents studied the character of the Indian, studied his habits, and interested themselves in his welfare. Military men are to a great extent natural enemies of the Indian, and if intimacy brings them into friendly relations, it can last only for a brief period, when they and their commands are ordered away to other duty. They are sojourners, not residents, and do not, like old and faithful agents, become identified with any Indian policy.

January 31, *Thursday.* The President sent for me this P.M. to call if convenient and when I could spare the time. When I met him, he inquired as to the arrival of the Swatara and Surratt and when they might be expected. I replied at any time, yet they might not reach Hampton Roads for ten days. At present the boat could not approach Washington on account of the ice, and she would necessarily be detained till it disappeared.

The President remarked that no good could result from any communication with Surratt, and that the more reckless Radicals, if they could have access to him, would be ready to tamper with and suborn him. The man's life was at stake, he was desperate and resentful. Such a person and in such a condition might, if approached, make almost any statement. He, therefore, thought he should not be allowed to communicate with others, nor should unauthorized persons be permitted to see him. In these views and suggestions I coincided, and told the President what Admiral Goldsborough had communicated and that the orders were stringent.

Passing from this subject, the President alluded to the condition of the country and the importance of bringing about an early reëstablishment of the Union. The Constitutional Amendment, which had been the policy of Congress, so far as they had a policy, was a failure, and something was now requisite to be done. He asked what I thought of a proposition from one or more of the excluded States for a compromise, — how would it be received?

I replied that would depend, of course, on the character of the proposition; but that I knew of nothing which was required of those States but submission to the Constitution, and *that* they had made. Individuals were amenable to the laws which they had violated, but I knew of nothing which the States were to do as States, beyond acquiescence, which they had already done.

The President assented, but asked whether, in the excited condition of the country and the party feeling which prevailed, it would not be well to take some steps which might be considered a compromise. Let the Rebel States themselves make a tender. Some Constitutional Amendment might be proposed which might be satisfactory and could, perhaps, unite all. In order to more clearly indicate his object, he wished to submit to me a paper which he had. This he brought from the library, and, sitting down together, he requested me to read it aloud.

It was a series of resolutions which the State of North Carolina proposed to adopt, and a committee, he said, was waiting to get from him an expression in regard to them. It was for this purpose he had sent for and desired to consult with me. The document had been prepared with some care, and there were interlineations in red ink which had been made. I do not mention the details of this paper because the President said, after having my brief criticisms, "To-morrow is Cabinet day, and likely the subject had then better be discussed. Moreover, if adopted, they will hereafter be published, altered and changed, perhaps, in some features or details."

In one or two suggestions made by me, one seemed to strike the President with force. A proposed Constitutional Amendment declared in effect that no State should retire from the Union and that the Union should be perpetuated. I proposed to amend by saying that no State should voluntarily withdraw or be *excluded* from the Union, or *deprived* of its constitutional right of representation, but that the Union should be perpetual. This was the idea; as regards the phraseology I was indifferent; but it seems to me, after past and present experience, and with the centralizing schemes and intrigues now upon us, that the organic law should not only be against the voluntary withdrawal of a State, but against its exclusion by the arbitrary desire of any accidental party majority in Congress. As the Radicals act from no fixed principles, but from party impulse and greed of power, they will object.

3

XLVI

The Circumstances attending Motley's Resignation discussed in Cabinet — The North Carolina Plan published in the Richmond Papers — The Matter of the R. R. Cuyler, bought by the Colombian Government and seized by the United States — Failure of the Samaná Negotiations — Thaddeus Stevens's Proposal to establish Military Governments in the Southern States opposed in the House — Banks leads the Opposition — Stanton's Sensational Report on the Enforcement of the Civil Rights Act — Plain Talk with the President about Stanton — Stevens's Bill passes the House — Sherman's Substitute adopted in the Senate — The House makes Further Amendments — Impeachment discussed in the Cabinet — The Tenure-of-Office Bill condemned in the Cabinet.

February 1, *Friday.* The President did not bring forward the document which he submitted to me yesterday, nor make any allusion to it. A number of gentlemen from the South, committeemen from their respective States, are here, or have been recently, many of whom have called on me, and each has had something to say on the unhappy condition of affairs. The Radical leaders look upon them and all the Southern people not as fellow countrymen, but treat them as though they had no rights and as if they did not intend they should be considered as equals, or as citizens who have, or are entitled to, a voice in the Government.

Seward spoke of the call which had been made or was being made on him for the letters and author of the accusations against Mr. Motley and others. He was, as usual when in difficulty and especially conscious that he may have made a mistake, very talkative, almost garrulous. The letters which passed between Seward and Motley, ending with the resignation of the latter, have been published, and very generally the Secretary of State has been censured and severely condemned. Men and papers of all parties are against him. Although his method and manner might have been different, I do not think this the most objectionable act which he has committed. His informant, who, he says, is an American gentleman traveling in Europe, told him that some of our representatives abroad are denouncing the Administration, particularly the President, and expressing views that are un-American and offensive. To have taken no notice of such a communication, coming from a person of position and character, would have been reprehensible, yet such it is generally claimed by his opponents would have been his proper course.

Senator Sumner, who has been conspicuous in this matter, is indignant that an obscure person, as he assumes this informant to be, should have received a moment's attention when making statements affecting Minister Motley, the historian. But if less notorious than Motley, he may be as intelligent, patriotic, and worthy, and entitled to as much consideration as the official who, in a foreign land, slanders the Government. "A cat may look upon a king," and a patriotic American citizen can hear and disapprove and make known the objectionable and offensive utterances of one of his countrymen who is officially clothed and recognized as a representative.

Mr. Motley denies a portion of the letters, and that part of it, if Mr. M. is one of the offenders alluded to, constitutes a question of veracity between the informant and the Minister. As Mr. M. disavows the opinions, he should have the privilege and right of relieving himself. If, however, he has been censorious or offensive, or careless in his language and utterances, why should not the fact be communicated? He speaks of his right to express his opinions within his own walls. Such would be the case undoubtedly were he a private citizen; but a public man with stranger guests, the representative of his Government at a foreign Court, is not to be justified in defaming before a miscellaneous company the public authorities at home.

This subject has not been, perhaps, managed discreetly and courteously, such as becomes the Secretary of State, but he could not have passed the matter without notice. Supposing the whole statement were true and admitted to be true by M. himself, would he be justified or excused because he is a writer and historian, and the informant an obscure man, as Senator Sumner declares? How was the Secretary to know without inquiry, and in what way so well as by direct application to Motley himself?

Seward says he shall answer the call of the Senate by giving the whole letter and the name of his informant. I said that was not, in my opinion, right unless his informant consented; that I did not like this tamely responding to calls which neither house had a right to make, if the communication was given in confidence. Seward, without stating whether his informant was or was not willing, replied that it was best to throw the whole matter before Congress; that, if we declined, it would only make them the more noisy and peremptory. I replied that I would act on no such principle. Some one interrupted by asking the name of the informant, and he said it was, I think, McCracken, a gentleman of character and large wealth, the former proprietor of Fort Washington, New York.

There may be circumstances and facts desirable to be made public, and the informant may consent to the surrender of his name, but I apprehend not, and if not, the disclosure is impolitic and wrong. I have so little confidence in the judgment, discretion, and courage of Seward that I shall feel uncomfortable until I know more. He is timid when cornered, and does many things that are strange. He stated to-day, among other things, that when he a few weeks ago brought forward Mr. Motley's letter of resignation, he had in his portfolio a soothing letter in reply, to the effect that his tender of resignation was perhaps made without due consideration, he would please reconsider, etc. This letter, he says, by some inadvertence had been sent off to Mr. M., the President, in the mean time, having accepted the resignation and nominated another person.

All this may be so, yet there is something in the management and way of doing things that is suspicious and strange, to say the least. Mr. Motley may, on reading this unauthorized letter expressing softly the sentiments of Mr. Seward, become reconciled to him personally and doubly vindictive towards the President.

February 5, Tuesday. Seward handed me in Cabinet a dispatch from Mr. Hovey, our Minister to Peru, inclosing correspondence with Admiral Dahlgren relative to Tucker, a Rebel deserter, formerly Commander in our Navy and now Admiral in the Peruvian Navy, and wished I would try to get the matter adjusted. It is a troublesome difficulty and not easy to dispose of, though not of great moment.

Seward also read McCracken's letter concerning Motley and other ministers and consuls abroad who are outspoken Radicals and, he says, objectionable and officious in other respects. I again asked if McCracken was willing to have his name given to the public. Without answering my question direct, he said if men wrote letters concerning public men and public business, they must take the risk of their being published. McCracken, Seward says, is a New-Yorker of wealth, a relative of Charles O'Conor, has influence, and if Sumner and his men want to fight the downtown bugs, damn them, let them. This is, I suppose, second-hand from Thurlow Weed.

The Richmond papers have the Southern proposed plan which the President showed me a few days since. It was not my suggestion to set off *exclusion* and *secession*. This, I think, shows want of judgment and tact on the part of those who have the subject in hand, nor do I think it wise to publish the plan before it has even been submitted to the legislature of any one State. There is an undercurrent in this, as in the Philadelphia Convention, that I dislike. As regards the project itself, I do not admire it as a whole, or as a compromise. In fact, I am not disposed to tamper with the Constitution at any time, but if changes are to be made, let the whole country participate, and let there be deliberation and consultation and comparison of opinions. I am apprehensive that we may be on the eve of great and serious movements which are to affect our government and institutions most deeply.

February 8, Friday. The Secretary of the Treasury brought forward the question of the seizure of the R. R. Cuyler, a steamer once owned by the Government, but which had been sold to private parties after the close of the War. Recently she has been contracted for by the Republic of Colombia, and was seized by our Government on the eve of sailing. It seems by the contract she was to leave under the American flag and that the transfer was to take place at a Colombian port. The Colombian Minister, Salanger, protests against the seizure and claims the transaction to be legal and in good faith. Seward says the sale is fictitious or a cover; that the vessel is to be converted into a privateer, or passed over to the Peruvians; and that no attention should be paid to Salanger, who is a weak man and can be easily imposed upon. He, therefore, justifies the seizure and proposes to turn the whole matter over to the Attorney-General and the courts.

I remarked that I had given the question no study, but from the statement of the Secretary of State I doubted the propriety of these proceedings. If the Colombian Government is not at war with any other power, she has an undoubted right to purchase; the acts of her representative, or minister, are her acts. These interpositions to check and embarrass the sale of vessels, on mere suspicion, would injure an important branch of industry, and our mechanical and business interests were already greatly depressed. Under the circumstances, I thought the Colombian Minister was to be respected and his Government must be responsible for his acts.

Stanton desired me to repeat what I said in regard to

shipbuilding and mechanics, which I did. He said he took an altogether different view. We had complained of Laird and the builders of Rebel vessels at Glasgow. But the English Government claimed their mechanics had a right to build and sell Alabamas. This was the very matter now in issue with that Government, and we must not embarrass the State Department, which had those negotiations, by committing a similar wrong.

I denied that the cases were parallel. The Rebels were belligerents, waging war against a Government in friendly relations with Great Britain; but Colombia was not a belligerent, and had as good a right to buy of us, and we as good a right to sell to her, as England or France.

The Attorney-General and Browning fully concurred with me, and in answer to a remark of Seward's that these South American states were poor and their ministers, some of them, indifferent men, Mr. Stanbery said we were not the conservators of those states. They are entitled to the comity of nations.

Stanton and Seward reiterated their claims, the former repeating that it was a question for the Secretary of State and that he would defer to him. Seward said it was a legal question and should be left to the Court; he therefore proposed to turn the matter over to the Attorney-General.

If there were legal points and nothing else, I said, that might be well, but I insisted this is a political question between us and a foreign government; that it devolved properly on the Secretary of State and should not be treated as a legal question.

Like many others, most men perhaps, Seward is disposed to evade responsibility when there is uncertainty and an impending storm. In this matter of the R. R. Cuyler, there is, in my opinion, no justifiable reason for her detention. Our shipbuilders and shipowners ought to be able to sell to a neutral government at peace; otherwise we shall drive all our customers away and into other markets. There is want of energetic national feeling in the State

Department which is emasculating the country of all vigor.

The subject of the R. R. Cuyler being disposed of, I brought up the case of the Dunderberg. Mr. Webb, the contractor, claims he can sell her at a great advance to a foreign government and wishes to refund advances and take her. To this, individually and officially, I would not object, but others of the Administration do. My own impression is that Webb will find difficulty in disposing of her, and if we refuse him the opportunity he will come back for a gratuity or advance award above the naval contract.

Mr. Seward brought his son Fred, Assistant Secretary, to state the result of his mission, which is a failure. The Dominicans are not disposed to sell. I am glad of it. We can, if at war with them, capture when there is necessity easier than we can purchase, or cheaper at all events. During the Civil War it would have been convenient to have had a station in the West Indies. But in case of a foreign war with England, France, or Spain, we can capture without difficulty one or more of these islands.

Seward and Stanton had made arrangements to send General Meigs to Denmark to purchase or negotiate for St. Thomas. I doubted the necessity; but the President ended the matter by saying he was opposed to the practice, which was being introduced, of sending officers on traveling excursions for their personal benefit at the Government's expense. General Meigs is a worthy man and a good officer, but a pet of Seward's and too much disposed to pander to him. I was, therefore, gratified at the prompt and emphatic decision of the President.

February 9, *Saturday.* The House has been excited for a day or two. A proposition submitted by Stevens from the Reconstruction Committee, proposing to establish military governments over the Southern States, meets with opposition from many Republicans who are not yet Radicals. There has been but little legislation this session in the [proper] sense of the word. A Radical party caucus decides in relation to the course to be pursued on all important questions. Two thirds of the Republicans and all of the Radical partisans attend. A majority of them follow Stevens and company. Those who hesitate or are opposed have neither the courage nor the ability to resist. The measure, however offensive or even unconstitutional, having the caucus sanction, is brought into the House, the previous question is moved and carried, and, without debate, adopted. But on the matter of these vice-royalties, a stand was made against Stevens, and the previous question was not sustained. Governor Banks appears to have been the leading man in opposition, but he had no plan or policy to propose. To-day, I am told, he introduced some rude scheme for a commission to take charge of each of the ten States which are under the Radical ban of exclusion. These commissions are to disorganize the States and then reorganize them.

There is neither wisdom nor sense in the House, but wild, vicious partisanship continues and is increasing.

February 11, *Monday.* Eliot of Massachusetts, chairman of a committee sent out by Congress to New Orleans, made a report for upsetting the State Government of Louisiana and converting the State into a province or Territory, over which there is to be a governor and council of nine, to be appointed by the President and Senate. These Radicals have no proper conception of constitutional government or of our republican federal system. On this absurd scheme of Eliot and Shellabarger, both centralists, the House has ordered, without debate, the previous question, — prostrating a State, tearing down our governmental fabric, treating States as mere corporations.

February 12, *Tuesday.* The subject of the R. R. Cuyler was reported upon by the Attorney-General, who thought the vessel should be surrendered to the parties, they giving bonds as required by statute. The conclusion was right, and Seward and Stanton acquiesced.

Webb, builder of the Dunderberg, called on me yesterday in relation to his vessel or contract. He wants more money. Senator Morgan was with him, and will, I suppose, introduce a resolution for a committee. Webb has thought I might exercise equity power, but this I shall not do, although the Attorney-General has given an opinion to that effect, for the power, I conceive, is not given me, but the law and contract must govern me. Equity power is with Congress.

February 15, Friday. A call was made, on the 8th of January, on the President for any facts which had come to his knowledge in regard to failure to enforce the Civil Rights Bill. When the resolution reached the President, he brought it before the Cabinet for answer, and it was referred to the Attorney-General on the suggestion of Stanton, that he should forward copies to the heads of Departments for answer. On receiving the resolution I answered immediately, without an hour's delay, and so, I think, did the other members, except Stanton. The subject had passed from my mind and I supposed had been reported until to-day, when Stanton brought in his answer to the President. It was a strange and equivocal document, accompanied by a report which he had called out from General Grant, and also one from General Howard. Grant's report was brief, but was accompanied by a singular paper transmitted to him by Howard, being an omnium-gatherum of newspaper gossip, rumors of negro murders, neighborhood strifes and troubles, amounting to 440 in number, — vague, indefinite party scandal which General Howard and his agents had picked up in newspapers and all other ways during four weeks, under and with the assistance of the War Department, who had aided in the search. There was but one sentiment, I think, among all present, and that was of astonishment and disgust at this presentation of the labors of the War Department. The Attorney-General asked what all this had to do with the inquiry made of the President. The resolution called for what information had come to the knowledge of the President respecting failures to execute the law under the Civil Rights Bill, and here was a mass of uncertain material, mostly relating to negro quarrels, wholly unreliable, and of which the President had no knowledge, collected and sent in through General Grant as a response to the resolution.

Two or three expressed surprise at these documents. Stanton, who is not easily dashed when he feels he has power and will be sustained, betrayed guilt, which, however, he would not acknowledge, but claimed that the information was pertinent, was furnished by General Grant. If, however, the President did not choose to use it, he could decline doing so. Subsequently he thought the Attorney-General should, perhaps, decide.

Seward undertook to modify and suggest changes. I claimed that the whole was wrong and that no such reply could be made acceptable under any form of words.

Randall thought the letter of Stanton and the whole budget had better be received, and that the President should send in that he knew nothing about them when this Senate resolution was passed, but that, having since received this information, he would have it looked into and thoroughly investigated.

Stanton, who showed more in countenance and manner than I ever saw him, caught at Randall's proposition. Said he would alter his report to that effect and went to work with his pencil.

Seward indorsed Randall. Said he thought all might be got along with if that course was pursued.

I dissented entirely and deprecated communicating this compilation of scandal and inflammable material, gathered by partisans since the action of Congress, and represented to be a matter of which the President had knowledge when the resolution was passed. It would be said at once

by mischievous persons that here was information of which
Grant complained, but of which the President took no
notice; that Congress had called out the information and
Grant communicated it, and that there is maladministration. [I said] that this was the purpose of the call; the
design probably of the Members who got it up.

Stanton looked at me earnestly. Said he was as desirous
to act in unison with the President as any one, no matter
who; that this information seemed to him proper, and so,
he said, it seemed to General Grant, who sent it to him;
but if others wished to suppress it they could make the
attempt, but there was little doubt that Members of Congress had seen this, — likely had copies.

Finally, and with great reluctance on his part, it was
arranged that he should, as the rest of us had done, give all
the information called for which had come to his knowledge in answer to the resolution, and that the reports of
Grant and Howard should, with the rumors, scandal, and
gossip, be referred to the Attorney-General for investigation and prosecution if proper.

It was evident throughout this whole discussion of an
hour and a half that all were alike impressed in regard
to this matter. McCulloch and Stanbery each remarked to
me before we left that here was design and intrigue in concert with the Radical conspirators at the Capitol. Stanton
betrayed his knowledge and participation in it, for, though
he endeavored to bear himself through it, he could not
conceal his part in the intrigue. He had delayed his answer
until Howard and his subordinates scattered over the
South could hunt up all the rumors of negro quarrels and
party scandal and malignity, and pass them, through General Grant, on to the President. It would help generate
difference between the President and the General, and, if
sent out to the country under the call for information by
Congress, would be used by the demagogues to injure the
President and, perhaps, Grant also.

Seward obviously saw the intent and scope of the thing

and soon took up a book and withdrew from the discussion. His friend Stanton was in a position where he could do little to relieve him. Randall played the part of trimmer to extricate Stanton, who availed himself of the plank thrown out.

Seward made allusion to the difficulty between our naval officers and Tucker, the unpardoned Rebel whom the Peruvians have made rear-admiral, and wished the members of the Cabinet, exclusive of him and myself, to consider and be prepared to act upon the subject at the Cabinet-meeting on Tuesday.

February 16, *Saturday.* Had a brief conversation with Browning, who was at my house at reception last evening, concerning the proceedings yesterday. He expressed his amazement at the course of Stanton. Said he listened and observed without remark till the close, and was compelled to believe that there was design and villainy, if not absolute treachery, at the bottom. It was with reluctance he came to this conclusion, but it was impossible to do otherwise.

I have been so disturbed by it and by the condition of affairs that I made it a point to call on the President and communicate my feelings. I told him that it was with reluctance I was compelled to express an unfavorable opinion of a colleague and that I would not do so except from a sense of duty. I adverted to the occurrences of yesterday and told him I had carefully and painfully pondered them, and my first impression was fully confirmed by reflection, that the details of Stanton's report, the introduction of Grant and Howard, with their catalogue of alleged murders and crimes unpunished, which had been industriously gathered up, was part of a conspiracy which was on foot to destroy him and overthrow his Administration; that it was intended the statement of reported murders should go abroad under his name, drawn out by Congress, and spread before the country on the passage of the bill establishing

military governments over the Southern States as a justification for legislative usurpation. That report was to be
the justification for the act. There had been evident pre-
concert in the matter, and Radical Congressmen were acting in concert with the Secretary of War. I alluded to the
manipulation of officers by the War Department, and mentioned how improper men had been placed at important
points, being first impressed with the views of the Secretary, which we all knew to be Radical and hostile to the
President's policy. I said that I could perceive Grant had
been strongly but unmistakably prejudiced, — perhaps
seduced, worked over, and enlisted, — and that gradually
the Administration was coming under the War Department.

The President listened and assented to my observations;
spoke of the painful exhibition which Stanton made of
himself; said he should, but for the rain, have sent for
Grant to know how far he really was involved in the matter, etc.; that as regards the military governments, they
were not yet determined upon, perhaps would not be.
He still hesitates, fails to act, retains bad advisers and
traitors.

February 18, *Monday*. The session of the Senate on Saturday continued through the night and until 6.30 yesterday morning. The subject under consideration was the
establishment of military governments over the Southern States. A bill to this effect was introduced by Thad
Stevens from the Reconstruction Committee, and was
carried under his management and dictation through the
House. Very few attempt to indorse or justify the measure, yet all the Radicals and most of the Republicans voted
for it. There is very little firmness or moral courage in the
House. The Members dare not speak nor act according to
their convictions. Indeed, their convictions are feeble and
there is little sincerity in them.

In the Senate, Wade, Sumner, and company undertook

to force through the bill at the Saturday's session. A stand was made by the minority against such precipitate and unreasonable legislation on so important a measure. Various amendments were offered and voted down, but at length, on Sunday morning, Mr. Sherman offered a substitute which was adopted. It is in one or two respects less offensive than the House bill, but is still an outrage upon the Constitution, the rights of the people, and the rights of the States. Sumner was violent, and Grimes tells me swore savagely when Sherman's substitute was adopted. He left the Senate in a rage. Grimes and Sumner, though both Radicals, are not friends or on speaking terms. Of course Grimes is enjoying Sumner's disappointment.

Stevens, Boutwell, and the extreme Radicals are as indignant as Sumner, and will make fight against the bill in its present shape and likely secure amendments. The Republicans, though disliking and mistrusting each other more and more each day, are not yet prepared to break. There is no shrewd man among the Democrats to take advantage of or to manage their rising differences or to lead his own party wisely.

Seward and Stanton confuse and bewilder the mind of the President, prevent him from pursuing a straightforward and correct course and from taking and maintaining a bold, decisive policy. They are weakening the executive power daily and undermining the constitutional fabric. Seward acts, as usual, from no fixed principles, but from mere expediency, his own self-wisdom, not with a design to injure the President or to help the Radicals. He tries to resuscitate, vitalize, and perpetuate the old Whig Party and to undo and destroy the Democratic Party, each for the glory of Seward. Stanton is deep in the Radical intrigues, but contrives to get along with and to use Seward and his superficial wisdom, and is so far successful as to keep his place, although the President knows his mischievous designs and purposes.

The country is in poor legislative hands and the prospect

is sadly foreboding. The Constitution and the great principles of union and free government on a federal basis are disregarded.

February 22, Friday. The politicians in and out of Congress have been busy for several days on the subject of governing the Southern States. Sherman's amendment went down to the House, was disagreed to, and some abominable additions were made. Partisans, and factions, and fanatics, and demagogues were each and all at work. Finally a bill was adopted establishing military governments and martial law in and over those States. Where Congress gets the power to do these things no one attempts to point out. The Members of Congress evidently confound martial law with military law, and know no distinction. Congress has the undoubted right to enact military laws for the government of the land and naval forces; but martial law exists and is in operation where there is no law. The will of the military officer in command is supreme. He can order courts martial or military commissions to try citizens as well as soldiers, but citizens cannot be tried by military law. Martial law abolishes jury trials; Congress cannot abolish them. Martial law may abridge freedom of speech and of the press, but Congress cannot.

When there is a congress or legislature to enact laws, there can be no martial law. It would be a solecism. Yet this Radical Congress has undertaken to enact martial law. In other respects the bill is subversive of government, destroys titles, and introduces chaos.

The President, as commander-in-chief of the Army and Navy, exercised the power, which devolved upon him when the Rebellion was suppressed, and the military forces occupied the Rebel States, and there was no law, and chaos reigned, of appointing provisional governors and ordering other measures to establish order and system and reintroduce law. Congress could not do this. It had no authority or power. All its powers are derived from the

Constitution, the organic law; but when martial law prevails, municipal law is suspended.

To-day the President laid this bill, and also the one respecting the tenure of office, before the Cabinet. The bill for the military government of the States was the only one considered. On this there was the usual uncertainty. No one of the Cabinet advised the President to approve the bill but Stanton. He said that, though he would have framed the bill differently and altered it in some respects, he should give it his sanction, and advised the President to give it his approval.

Following him, I wholly dissented, and plainly and directly advised the President to put his veto upon it.

Reverdy Johnson, the Senatorial trimmer, gave his vote in the Senate for this infamous bill. Stanton quoted him as an example and an authority. How long will the President be able to go on with such an opponent at his council board?

February 25, Monday. I read some suggestions on the Tenure-of-Office Bill to the President. They were prepared in response to an opinion of the Attorney-General some months since, but are applicable to the bill. The President was pleased with them. I also left with him some views on the bill for the military government of the Southern States. These views, which relate to the strange plan of enacting martial law by Congress, chimed in with his opinions.

On taking the paper, the President alluded to the Cabinet council on Friday and the pitiful exhibition which Stanton made of himself, and wondered if he (S.) supposed he was not understood. The sparkle of the President's eyes and his whole manner betokened intense though suppressed feeling. Few men have stronger feeling; still fewer have the power of restraining themselves when evidently excited.

I remarked that it was but part of the drama which had

3

long been enacting and asked what was to be the condition
of things, if impeachment were pressed and an attempt to
arrest him was made. This subject the President himself
had brought forward at the Friday meeting. Seward and
Stanton wished to give it the go-by, though each had his
own theory. Seward said it was not wise to anticipate such
a thing, — to discuss it even among ourselves, — had an
anecdote to tell, and his experience on the McCracken
correspondence. I differed with him, and thought it both
wise and prudent to be prepared for an emergency which
was threatened and had been undoubtedly discussed.
Others agreed with me and the President earnestly. Thus
pressed, Seward said it might be considered a law question,
coming particularly within the province of the Attorney-
General whenever it came up, but if the Attorney-General
should advise the President to submit to an arrest before
conviction, he would demand the immediate dismissal of
the Attorney-General. I asked if the demand would be
made on legal or political grounds. Stanton tried to evade
the matter; did not believe that impeachment would be
pursued; the session is near its close, etc.

The President was evidently not satisfied with this
treatment of the subject when we had our conversation on
Saturday, and was now a good deal indignant. But whether
he will make any demonstration in that direction remains
to be seen. I have little expectation that he will, although,
had I not previously had similar strong intimations without any result, I should from his expressive manner have
expected a change.

February 26, *Tuesday.* At the Cabinet the subject of
the Tenure-of-Office Bill came up. It had been postponed
at the request of the Attorney-General on Friday. He said
he had not read it until to-day, but he required no time to
express his unqualified condemnation of it. In this the
whole Cabinet were united. Stanton was very emphatic
and seemed glad of an opportunity to be in accord with his

colleagues. The President said he was overwhelmed with many pressing matters which must be disposed of, and he would be glad if Stanton would prepare a veto or make suggestions. Stanton asked to be excused, for he had not time. The Attorney-General said it was impossible for him to do the work. The President turned to Seward, who said he had not recently given these subjects attention, but he would take hold if Stanton would help him. The President suggested that both the War and Navy must help in this matter, and McCulloch expressed a special desire that I should participate. I saw that Seward was not taken with that proposition.

Some general discussion followed, and, before we left, Seward spoke across the room to Stanton and requested him to call and enter upon their duties; but no invitation was extended to me. The President turned to me and in an undertone remarked that I had given this subject a good deal of thought and he reckoned I had better prepare a paper. I told him I would have no objection to contribute to the document, but it had gone into hands that seemed willing to grapple with it, and I apprehended after what had been said that they would do it justice. If, however, anything was wanted of me, I would be ready to contribute at any time.

February 27, Wednesday. I called on the President to-day with a brief communication to the House of Representatives, declining to furnish certain information which had been called for at the instigation of a claim agent, which response I thought had better pass through the President. The anterooms were very much crowded. In the council-room, at the President's table, was a gentleman busily writing, who did not lift his head while I was in the room, but who, I am confident, was Judge Jeremiah Black. My interview with the President was necessarily brief, for I saw he was engaged and none were admitted. I have no doubt that Black is assisting in preparing the veto message on the Military Government Bill, stating some of the legal objections.

This evening, just before I left the Department, Seward's clerk Smith, his legal clerk, called and said Mr. Stanton was with Mr. Seward and they wished to know where they could get a copy of Mr. Webster's speech on removals from office, to which I had made reference in some of our discussions. I told him I could not get the volume at that time, nor did I know whether it was published in Webster's Works, but that it was in the great debate on Calhoun's resolution in 1834. He said that could not be, that the speech must have been in 1830; they had searched for it through 1830, 1831, and 1832. I told them they had not looked late enough, that Calhoun was then Vice-President and not a Senator.

No invitation came for me to participate. This is best. Our views are so different in many respects that it is well I should be absent. The principles of Seward and Stanton and their party education were different, and all may work out well, — better than if I were with them.

February 28, *Thursday.* Young Ruger, of Janesville, Wisconsin, who was nominated postmaster at that place, was rejected by the Senate and has come on here. In an interview with Senator Howe, that gentleman said to Ruger the Senate would confirm no man for any office who did not vote for Lincoln and Johnson. Mr. Randall, Postmaster-General, thinks it best to nominate only such Republicans as will be confirmed, and so told Ruger. Under such course and practice the President will have very little opportunity to strengthen himself or maintain his rightful authority. Randall was confirmed by the Senate under suspicious circumstances. There are many indications that he is under bad influences. Some of his associations are bad.

Sumner and Chandler made a gross and indecent attack on McCulloch in the Senate, and were rebuked by Sherman and Fessenden. The condition of the country is deplorable when such men, in such positions, thus exhibit themselves. Chandler's instincts are low and debasing, always. Sumner is domineering, arrogant, insolent, and presuming. He is angry because a brother-in-law was removed for malconduct. Chandler is mad because he cannot dictate all the Michigan appointments. High Senatorial duties are discharged by men who in their official acts are governed by narrow personal considerations. Little regard is felt for the country, while private resentments are all-controlling. I am not certain that judicious selections are always made, but I do know that good and judicious men are rejected for no cause.

XLVII

Seward and Stanton prepare the Veto Message on the Tenure-of-Office Bill — Vetoes of this and the Military Government Bill sent in — Reverdy Johnson's Extraordinary Course — Butler's Animosity towards Grant — The Chances of Impeachment — The Close of One Congress and the Beginning of Another — The Powers of the Military Governors — The President's Exclamation in regard to Impeachment — Ex-Congressman Law of Indiana on Andrew Johnson — The President's Reticence — Randall's Conciliatory Attitude towards the Radicals — Stanton apparently to select the Military Governors — Sickles among the Generals chosen as Governors — Wall Street's Influence in Congress — The Alaskan Purchase Treaty — Death of Charles Eames — His Career — Senator Foster and the Austrian Mission — No Opposition to the Russian Treaty in the Cabinet — The ex-Confederate Admiral of the Peruvian Navy to be saluted by American Officers — Indian Affairs — The President wishes to offer the Austrian Mission to General Blair — Judge Blair's Story of the Action of General Grant and General Dick Taylor against Seward and Stanton — Private Secretary Moore's Relations with Stanton — Congress refuses to adjourn — The Alaskan Treaty signed — Seward tells ex-Minister Bigelow how he shaped Lincoln's Cabinet.

March 1, *Friday*. Seward and Stanton have prepared and handed to the President the veto message on the bill for the tenure of office. They did not see fit to submit it to me, and I hesitated whether to inform the President of the fact. Amidst other multitudinous duties he supposes, I have no doubt, that I have participated in and revised the message. On the whole, concluded to say nothing unasked.

But little was done in Cabinet. Some little discrepancies between Stanbery and Black, who has been consulted, have delayed the veto on the Military Government Bill, which is the absorbing measure in this exciting time of extraordinary measures.

Business of importance has been as usual delayed to the close of the session. Office and place have been the engrossing subjects of the Members. Legislation by which the appointments may be transferred from the Executive to Congress, by which Radicals in office may be retained in place, or that will secure Radical appointments, has been a primary object. To break down State independence and State rights, to undermine and destroy the character of the executive and judicial departments of the Government, are great purposes with the Radical leaders. There is no doubt that the Government is to be subverted and constitutional limitations are to be swept away, provided the Radicals can succeed. Hate of the Rebels and of all whites, whether Rebels or not, if they lived in the Rebel States, with intense love for the negro, the "wards of the nation," for whom the rights and feelings of white men are freely sacrificed, characterizes Congress.

March 2, Saturday. The President is greatly pressed with business. Sent in to-day his two vetoes. That on the establishment of military governments over the ten States was received with deep interest. The opinions of a majority of the Republicans are undoubtedly against the principles of the bill, but they have not the independence and moral courage to act in conformity to their convictions and confront the Radicals. Party subjection overpowers them. Thad Stevens and the discipline of the caucus are potent.

In the Senate, as in the House, party dominates over country. Fear comes over the feeble-minded, who comprise nearly one half of the Senate. If two or three hesitated, the recent extraordinary course of Reverdy Johnson decided them to submit to the demands of party. Johnson knows and says the bill is unconstitutional and wrong, yet he violates his oath and votes for it. His justification is that the Radicals, in their fury, will impose harder terms if these are not accepted, and he wants the country should have repose. It is known, however, that his son-in-law is an earnest candidate for the office of District Attorney of Maryland, and he could not, under existing circumstances, expect to be confirmed by this Senate, were the President to nominate him. This apostasy of Johnson will insure the son-in-law's confirmation, provided he gets the nomination, and Reverdy, to say nothing of other malign influences, fancies that his position as Senator and one of the judges of the President in case of impeachment will secure the selection. I have no doubt this old political prostitute has been governed by these mercenary personal considerations. He has a good deal of legal ability, but is not over-burdened with political principles. This conduct occasions less surprise on that account. Sad is the condition of the country when such men influence its destiny.

March 3, *Sunday.* Spent two or three hours at the President's this morning. McCulloch and Browning called for me. Seward and Randall were there. The President was calm, but I thought more dejected than I had almost ever seen him. Not that he expressed himself despondingly, but his air and manner were of that appearance. Perhaps it was because he had had but little sleep, for he spoke of transactions past midnight.

While the President was absent for a short time in the library, Browning remarked that he felt disturbed by the state of things. "How," said he, "is Grant? Does any one know his opinions, and what stand he takes?"

Seward said he would know to-morrow at 2 P.M., or perhaps at 2 P.M. on Tuesday. Browning pricked up his ears and opened his eyes. "How," inquired he, "shall I know?" "Why," replied Seward, "Benjamin F. Butler will be sworn in by that time, and his animosity towards Grant is so much greater than it is towards the President that he will make his opinions known and understood upon the floor of the House. When that is done, you will all understand where Grant stands."

This was delivered very oracularly, and I have no doubt Seward has turned this matter over in his mind and come to the conclusion that the President will have a fast friend in Grant in consequence of the disagreement between him and Butler. Whether Stanton has helped to impress this on Seward is uncertain. I am inclined to think he has been instrumental in practicing on the too ready credulity of the Secretary of State in this matter. He is too ready to believe what he wishes, if he has even but slight authority.

Randall thought there was not much probability that the impeachment scheme would be pressed any further. Encouraged by this, Seward said nothing would be done. "But," remarked Browning, "provided they should go on, what have we to depend upon?" Seward evaded a direct answer; spoke of the discontent of the business men; said the Members were also disturbed. Randall took the same view; said Congress would not consent to this thing.

I said that was the common-sense view, and if there were any reliable intelligence and firmness in Congress there would be an end of the matter at once. But, unfortunately, there was neither good sense, ability, nor independence among the Radicals. There is no individuality among the well-meaning Members. A few leaders and the Radical cohorts had entire control of the whole mass of Republicans. Stevens, Butler, Boutwell, Schenck, Kelley, and a few other violent partisans led the positive element, and in revolutionary times such as these the positive and the violent always controlled. If the men I had named and a few others willed it, the House would unquestionably impeach, whether they found a reason therefor or not. I, therefore, thought Browning's inquiry pertinent and that the subject should receive attention.

Seward admitted that the positive element invariably bore sway, and told of some who had dined with him the past week and swore they would not vote to impeach, but he told them they would despite their assertions, if Stevens demanded it, — that they were drawn on step by step.

Randall made no further remark. I have a distrust of him that I can't remove. I regret it and hope I am mistaken. He is not treacherous, that I am aware, to the President, but he is on terms with the President's enemies and has bad associates. . . .

The President said he had last night, after one o'clock, a letter from Reverdy Johnson requesting that his son-in-law, Ridgely, might be nominated District Attorney. This, the President remarked, was about as cool a piece of assurance as he had ever witnessed. It does not surprise me. What will the President do?

March 4, Monday. Went at half-past nine to the Capitol. The President directed the Cabinet to meet at that time. I called at the Executive Mansion on my way and found the President very busy. He had signed all the bills sent him save three. One was the Army Appropriation Bill, the second section of which, as well as some others, was objectionable, — so much so that I could not advise him to sanction it. Another was the Woolens Bill, which I had not examined, but which McCulloch thought the President had better sign with a protest.

The two houses were in session until after meridian. Time was set back. The session was called as of the 2d of March, Sunday being *dies non*. The houses had each taken frequent recesses without adjourning. It was the only evidence of regard for the Constitution which I witnessed, and this was a fiction.

I looked briefly into the Senate, where the new Senators were being sworn in. It is the only time I have seen the Senate in session since I was there at the adjournment last July. I could not respect the body or many of its members. They are, in their intense faction hate of Southern whites and zeal for the negro, determined to pull down the pillars of the Republic.

Foster and I met in the passage as I was going into the Senate. He was looking disconsolate, but I wasted no sympathy on him, and in the few words which passed I was not hypocrite enough to express any regret that his term had closed. I was sorry that Cowan, frank and bold, honest as regards measures, though not always correct in his estimate of men, should leave. The Senate in its meanness did not act on his nomination to Vienna. It neither rejected nor confirmed him.

Reverdy Johnson's son-in-law was nominated and confirmed to be District Attorney for Maryland. So much for disregarding principle, conviction, and duty. Who influenced the President in this matter I know not. Seward, I am satisfied, assented to it, if he did not advise it. Johnson was frequently in and out, and I saw Cowan with him. Not unlikely the good-natured Senator was persuaded to appeal to the forbearing President.

I went with McCulloch to the House of Representatives, which was crowded. The Clerk was just commencing to call the roll for Speaker, and I left. Some changes take place in this body. Ten States are excluded and unrepresented, but the Radical fragment will press forward all all the more earnestly for mischief.

March 5, Tuesday. Some of the Radical revolutionary measures were discussed to-day in Cabinet. The legislation and action of Congress have thrown several hundred officers out, and the public funds are in jeopardy. Intent on office, place, and power, the real interests of the country have been neglected or not considered by the Radicals. Want of comprehension of consequences and a feeling of irresponsibility have been manifest throughout.

A question came up as to the power and jurisdiction of the military governors who were to be placed in charge of the Southern States. Stanton said they must be subordinate and accountable to their superiors who were in charge of the military departments. Stanbery doubted the correctness of this view. I put the distinct question whether, if there were conflicts of opinion between the military governor and his superior, — as for instance if the brigadier governor of Georgia and Alabama should take a position, or issue an order which was disapproved by Major-General Thomas, in command of that military department, would he override and annul the order of the military governor?

Stanton said General Thomas' order would control. I
questioned it and claimed that the special authority conferred by the act, if the act was of any validity, made the
brigadier independent of General Thomas in governing
the States to which he was assigned.

This seemed the prevailing opinion, but at Stanton's
request, decision was deferred until Friday, he promising
in the mean time to investigate the subject.

March 6, Wednesday. I was with the President on a
little business, and Stanbery was present at the early part
of our interview. The subject of yesterday's decision on
the powers of the brigadiers was introduced by S., who
said he had not a shadow of a doubt in regard to it; he
thinks Stanton and his friends have overshot the mark.

After Stanbery left, the President continued the conversation on the same topic, and if he intended to enforce an
unconstitutional law in regard to the importance of selecting the right men for military governors, I urged him to
be certain in regard to his men for those positions and
to have an interview with each before giving them orders.
He assented fully.

I then alluded again to the condition of things here in
Washington. In the event of the Radical leaders succeeding
in their intrigue to procure an impeachment, the first step
after impeachment should be voted would be to order his
arrest. If he was not prepared to submit to an arrest, was
he prepared to meet it? Whom could he confide in? Who of
the military men, or of the War Department, would stand
by him against an order issued by Congress, or the Senate
as a court, under the signature of the Chief Justice, commanding his arrest? I had on two or three occasions, I remarked, introduced this topic, not that it was pleasant or
interesting to me, but it was important to him and the
country. Once he had himself brought forward the subject, but a direct and positive answer by the Cabinet or
some of the Cabinet had been evaded by the Cabinet

or some of the members. The President said yes, he was aware of it, but he would bring the subject to a decision next Friday. I told him it was in my opinion due to himself, although Mr. Seward had said it was not best to anticipate.

But it has been the misfortune, the weakness, the great error of the President to delay, — hesitate before acting. It has weakened him in public estimation, and given the impression that he is not strong in his own opinions. Yet I know of no man who is more firm, when he has once taken a stand. But promptness, as well as firmness, is necessary to inspire public confidence.

March 7, Thursday. The Radicals are divided in opinion on the subject of impeachment, and also as to the adjournment. Some wish a continuous session, some wish to adjourn to May, others until October or November. The Senate seem determined to adjourn over until the fall, while the extreme Radicals wish to continue in session, although there is no business requiring their presence. But they desire to administer the government and impeach the President. Not that he has committed any wrong or that any offense can be stated; but they have had a committee searching the country to find, if possible, some mistake, some error, some act which can be construed into a political fault and thus justify his removal, because he is an obstacle in the way of Radicalism.

March 8, Friday. Very little was done to-day in Cabinet. It was expected, I think, by all that the President would bring forward measures in relation to the Military Government Act, and, therefore, they had omitted pressing any business except such as was absolutely necessary from the Departments. But the President made no allusion to the subject. He said he was very much engaged, as he must be, not only on that of the military government but other matters which should be immediately disposed of.

After the meeting, or the regular session, was over, Mc-Culloch reached over the table, at the end of which the President was sitting, I being as usual on his left, and Browning came and seated himself on the opposite side and said something in a low tone which I did not hear, or which passed out of my mind in consequence of what subsequently occurred. He said it — his suggestion, whatever it was — would check the impeachment movement. The President replied hastily: "I will do nothing to check impeachment, if there is any wish to press it. I am tired of hearing allusions to impeachment. God Almighty knows I will not turn aside from my public duties to attend to these contemptible assaults which are got up to embarrass the Administration. Let the House go forward and busy themselves in that matter if they wish."

There are rumors as to the persons to be selected as military governors, and I think the President is, unfortunately for himself, consulting with General Grant. How far Grant confers with Stanton, I know not, nor does the President, — if he confers at all. That Grant may be biased by Stanton and Holt, with whom he has constant, intimate intercourse is not improbable. However, my impression has been that Grant is himself rightly disposed, though there are some things which indicate subtlety and duplicity.

March 9, Saturday. Law of Indiana, who was a Member of the Thirty-seventh and Thirty-eighth Congresses, called on me, being on a visit to Washington. We have been good friends since our first acquaintance. He said he had just paid his respects to the President and reminded him of an incident. In the summer of 1861, he, L., was at the Burnett House in Cincinnati on his way to Washington in pursuance of the call of President Lincoln for an extra session. He had just finished his meal, — breakfast, I think, — and came out on the piazza, when a troop of horse, both riders and animals somewhat jaded, rode up, and opening in line, a citizen, in citizen's dress much dusted, came forward and dismounted. That man, exhausted and covered with dust, was Andrew Johnson, a Senator from Tennessee on his way to Washington under the call of the President, and the military authorities had dispatched a troop of horse to escort and guard him across the State of Kentucky. "I little thought," said Law, "that I should ever hear Andrew Johnson denounced as a Rebel, or a sympathizer with Rebels; that partisan malice would ever accuse him of want of fidelity to the Union; but God only knows what we are coming to in these Radical times. Such a patriot as Johnson," said Law, with tears running down his cheeks, "a man who has suffered and done so much, deserves better treatment from his countrymen."

March 11, *Monday.* Senator Morgan says Nye returns from Connecticut, where he has been making political speeches, very much alarmed at the prospect, and if extra efforts are not put forth, Deming will lose his election to Congress. Were the election to take place at this time, I am inclined to think the Radicals would be beaten, but much can be done in three weeks.

Stanbery and myself were with the President a short time this morning. Business disposed of, some conversation followed in regard to the selection of military governors. We both dwelt on the importance of judicious, good, reliable men. The President assented and said he hoped to finish up the matter to-day, but he made no intimation as to the persons whom he should designate. I had no desire to ask, and Stanbery seemed likewise disposed.

The President is without doubt too reticent with his Cabinet advisers, and perhaps with all his friends, although inclined to much public speaking and free utterance on matters that are public. From his silence on the subject of military governors I do not anticipate a judicious selection, and shall not be surprised if Grant, in whom he still has confidence, and possibly Stanton, are the only persons whom he consults. If so he will have trouble.

March 12, *Tuesday.* Current matters of no special interest to-day in Cabinet. Appointments and rejections were talked over. I do not learn that the President and some of the Departments have any system in this matter of appointments and removals. Randall equivocates, trims, and gives in to the Radicals. It is said he was confirmed with that understanding. He has no backbone or power. If the Senate rejects a good man because he is friendly to the President and adheres to the Constitution, Randall is content to present another of an entirely different character, a tool of the Senate, an enemy to the President, a wild Radical. Of course no party can succeed under such management, and the Administration is consequently making no headway. McCulloch is a different and much better man than Randall in every respect; but, overwhelmed with the financial difficulties of the country, he is for conciliating the Radicals, yields too much, and Randall and others increase that infirmity. The tendency is all wrong.

Nothing was said by the President in Cabinet on the subject of military governors. He took Stanton aside and had a conversation of some fifteen minutes with him, while the rest were waiting. At the close Stanton was unusually jubilant, had a joke or two with McCulloch and could not suppress his feelings. I shall not be disappointed if Stanton selects or controls the military governors, and I think Seward has advised that he should. These two men have contrived to break down the Administration, — Seward without intending it. Thurlow Weed has been in town for a day or two, almost as much at the War as at the State Department. His counsel is always pernicious.

March 13, *Wednesday.* Judge Field called on me to-day. He is very sound and correct on the great questions before the country. He concurred with me as to the peculiar characteristics of the President and the misfortunes which he has brought on himself and the country by failing to act promptly on his own convictions, and by listening to the advice of those who are not his friends.

Judge Field has no confidence in Stanton and fears he will influence bad appointments for military governors, and expressed a strong hope that General Sickles would not be selected.

The paper this morning announces the generals who have been designated, and Sickles is one of them. Sickles is a favorite of Stanton, who defended him for murdering Key. I do not think the selections in several respects judicious. That of Sickles accounts for Stanton's exuberant feelings yesterday and confirms my impression that he has been instrumental in selections, some of which will be likely to cause difficulty. It would not be easy, however, to go among the military men and choose five in whom to repose full confidence. In listening to Stanton the President has made no friends. The War Department has made itself felt in the appointments. "The slime of the serpent is over them all." General Grant has apparently borne himself under all influences as well as could be expected, yet I think he is to some extent affected and has been swayed by Radical influence.

March 14, *Thursday*. McCulloch spent some time with me this evening. He is a good deal desponding. Says Congress is very corrupt. Certain Wall Street operators know daily what is done in the Finance and Ways and Means Committees. He gets information of the transactions of that committee by way of Wall Street before the committee reports to or advises with him, and his own movements are also in that way betrayed. These Radical patriots are swindling the country while imposing on its credulity.

The want of prompt and decisive action on the part of the President, who is deceived by Stanton, aided by Seward, who supports Stanton, we both lamented. It has made the Administration a failure and transferred power

3

from the Executive to Congress, which is now omnipotent and unrestrained. On every hand the Executive has been hedged in and crippled. It annoys McCulloch that Stanton should have the ear and confidence of the President, while to him it is obvious that the President is betrayed; the rest of the Cabinet, who are faithfully discharging their duties, are assailed, while Stanton, who is faithless and treacherous, escapes, — has all the appropriations he asks.

But McCulloch does not realize what is obvious to me, — that Seward has the ear and the confidence of the President, and is the man who by his efforts and representations retains Stanton. These two men have sacrificed the President. He has permitted it and thereby made his Administration impotent.

March 15, *Friday.* Seward produced a treaty for acquiring the Russian possessions in North America. All assented to submitting it to the Senate.

The subject of naval courtesies with Tucker, the Rebel deserter, whom Peru has made admiral of her navy, came up. No one stood by me, of the Cabinet. The President patiently listened. Stanton declared his heart and sympathies were with me, but the question of international courtesies he thought should be left with the Secretary of State and Attorney-General. This lugging in the Attorney-General on international law and political questions and committing them to him I do not like. It is to enlist Stanbery and relieve Seward of responsibility in a matter which belongs to the State Department.

I could perceive that the Attorney-General had been consulted, and was prepared to give an opinion as the Secretary of State wished. As usual the Secretary of State disregards not only the national punctilio but the national points [*sic*], — surrenders all when the easy working of his own Department is concerned.

Stanton, who has heretofore, and, as he declared, deliberately, agreed with me, fell away at the crisis. This did not disappoint me. He always goes with Seward. They are one.

March 16, *Saturday.* Charles Eames died this afternoon. He was in many respects a very superior man, and, though a private citizen, his death is a public loss. I consider him to have been the best-read and most correct admiralty lawyer in the country, and the best authority on questions of maritime law. I have seen but little of him for a year past, — he has been so immersed in business, — but I have made it a point to get his opinion on important questions when I had doubts and when I differed with others whose opinions I thought of value.

Twenty years ago we became acquainted during Polk's Administration. He was a clerk for a short time in the Navy Department. Appleton was then Chief Clerk. Both, though my juniors, are now dead. Eames became editor of the *Union*,[1] was commissioner to the Sandwich Islands, Minister to Venezuela, etc. His attainments placed him, though unpretentious, high as a publicist and statesman. As a politician he lacked force, but was an excellent adviser. His politics were democratic Republican. As a critic he was acute and accurate. Marcy, Everett, and Guthrie submitted to him some of their most important papers before giving them publicity. He was the youngest and best scholar in the most renowned class which ever graduated at Harvard.

Buchanan treated Eames shabbily, and when I came here at the commencement of Lincoln's Administration, he was low in finance and business and somewhat dejected. We soon renewed our acquaintance, became social, and I was enabled to assist him. He was a politician in the best sense of the word and did not love the practice of the law, but necessity impelled him, and, being thrown out of public employment by the perverse action and

---

[1] A Washington newspaper.

opposition of Seward and the cold duplicity of Chase, he applied himself to the profession. The prize cases brought him forward, and the Treasury availed itself of his ability. Not endowed with a strong constitution, he broke down under the pressure of certain great cases intrusted to him. His physical system was not equal to his mental power and the demands upon him. Farewell, old friend! There is no one to supply your place to me.

March 18, *Monday.* Senator Foster called on me to-day to aid him in obtaining the mission to Vienna. Says Seward advised him to consult me. Seward knew that, though I had personal regard for Foster and appreciated his qualities, I did not think this a judicious appointment at this time and under existing circumstances. He assured me that nothing had, up to that time, been said to him by Foster, nor would he entertain the matter without consulting me. I have no doubt that he is turning his thoughts to Foster for this mission and has advised this call. I could give F. no assurance, nor yet was I prepared to tell him flatly I would oppose him. For Seward has, not unlikely, consulted and enlisted the President, and if the point is already determined, to resist it would be foolishness.

Foster, after recent occurrences, has certainly no claims on the Administration. He has not, it is true, been vindictive and acrimonious like some Senators, but he has been steady in his opposition, the slave of factious party discipline, often, as I have reason to believe, against his own conviction. He timidly threw away his own chance for reëlection and sacrificed those who stood by him.

March 19, *Tuesday.* Had the Russian treaty on the tapis. No division of opinion as to the measure.

The question of courtesy to Tucker, the Rebel deserter, whom the Peruvians have, discourteously to us, made admiral and consequently outranking his seniors in our service who were not Rebels, was brought forward by Seward. I stated that my opinion had undergone no change, but that I should, of course, although it might be humiliating to American officers, conform to the decision of the President and Cabinet. If, however, we yielded to the discourtesy, we should, besides doing an act tending to demoralize our Navy, be setting a bad precedent.

Stanton again repeated that his feelings and sympathies were with me, but as it was an international question, he should defer to the Secretary of State. Browning gave up the question without understanding it and was very earnest for Peru. Under the circumstances and with the united opinion against me, the President thought Dahlgren had better give up the point. I am, therefore, to inform him that the President has directed that Paragraph 96 of Navy Regulations, which I had authorized him to waive, would be hereafter observed by the South Pacific Squadron.

A long discussion followed between Stanton and Browning, growing out of the attempts of the military to interfere in Indian affairs. Browning claims that the agents, if respected and not interfered with by the army officers, will save us from an Indian war. Stanton thinks army officers are better judges as to the treatment of the Indians than the traders and agents. He protests against their selling arms and ammunition to the Indians. Browning says it is necessary for their existence that they should have firearms.

My views were and are with Browning. With firearms I believe the Indians are less furious than with bow and arrow and tomahawk. The attempt to prevent them from having arms they would naturally consider unfriendly and hostile.

Stanton attempts to fortify himself behind Grant.

March 20, *Wednesday.* In an interview with the President, after disposing of other matters, I read to him a letter from Connecticut on the approaching election, in which a very strong wish was expressed that Foster should not receive the appointment to Austria, as reported in the papers he had, — at all events, that it should not take place until after the election.

The President was much pleased with the tone and spirit of the letter and remarked that the writer might rest easy as regarded Mr. Foster. He said Seward had proposed Foster's name this morning, shortly before I called, and "I asked him," said the President, "what in God's name F. had done that we should select him. There are others, as good and as capable men as he who have stood firm and done service that should be remembered. Mr. Foster has no preëminent qualifications for the place; he has been here all winter voting for these abominable measures which we pronounce unconstitutional, and believe and know to be so, and so does he; and now, when thrown out of place by his own weakness, we are expected to take him up. What can be thought of our sincerity if we do this? If Mr. Foster is with us, why don't he go home and take a manly part in the elections? Why is he lingering here?"

"What," inquired I, "did Mr. Seward reply?"

"Not a word," said the President. "He took up his budget and left. I am sick of such things."

I informed him that Mr. Foster had called on me also and I could not otherwise than inform him of the object of Mr. F.'s visit; but after his remarks it was unnecessary to say more on the subject.

Some conversation as to the expediency of sending in General Blair's name followed.

March 21, *Thursday*. Wrote letter to Admiral Dahlgren on the subject of courtesies to Tucker in obedience to instructions from the President. Sent it to Seward for his perusal. Also sent him the correspondence which had passed between Admiral Goldsborough and E. J. Morris,

our Minister at Constantinople. The latter has been urging Admiral G. to send a ship to Candia to transport the
Cretans to Greece, — a direct infringement of neutrality.
Morris justified himself on the ground of assurance from
the Secretary of State.

March 22, *Friday.* There was no meeting of the Cabinet to-day. A severe snowstorm through the whole day.
The President on subject of veto of supplemental bill to
the military governments.

March 23, *Saturday.* Read to the President my letter
of instructions to Rear-Admiral Dahlgren relative to
interchange of courtesies with Tucker, the Rebel, late
Commander in our service, now Admiral in the Peruvian
Navy. Told him I had nothing to say after the discussion
which had been had. He remarked it was a matter which
he did not like, but the Secretary of State seemed to consider it important, and others coincided with him. I remarked that, as a general thing, I paid little attention
to what I called Mr. Seward's qualities. That his opinions
on international law had never impressed me; that the
national honor seemed of little concern to him and never
stood in the way of his schemes of expediency; that this
might be a troublesome precedent in the future. So far as
Peru was concerned, she had bestowed her highest honors
on a man who had been false to his country and flag.

We had a few words in regard to the Austrian Mission.
The President said he had sent in no nomination, that he
had sent to Judge Blair to advise with him in regard to
the nomination of General Blair, but the Judge had not
since called on him. I said if he was to communicate with
the General, it might be difficult, for he was in Connecticut.

March 25, *Monday.* I called this morning on Judge
Blair pursuant to an understanding with the President

on Saturday to ascertain if he had heard from his brother. He said he had not. I then expressed an opinion that the President had better nominate Frank and let the Senate dispose [of the measure. If they confirmed him and he refused to accept, it were better that he knew nothing on the subject, — if the Senate rejected, or adjourned without action, he would not be dishonored. The Judge agreed with me and I subsequently saw the President, who adopted the suggestion.

In my interview with Judge Blair he again expressed dissatisfaction with the President for retaining Seward and Stanton, and said some things were to him inexplicable. He informs me in confidence, that nearly a year ago General Dick Taylor [1] was in Washington and had spent some time with General Grant. The two discussed very fully the condition of affairs, and both concurred in approving the President's policy, but [thought] that to carry it out, he must rid himself of Seward and Stanton. With these views they saw the President and had a full and free interchange of opinion with him, and the President responded to them favorably, earnestly, and decidedly.

On the day following, Stanton called on General Grant, I think at his house, where he had never previously called, for he was not on intimate terms with the General; but on this occasion he opened his mind fully to Grant, and was ready to unite with him and Taylor in sustaining the President and his policy, even to the sacrificing of Seward. General Grant knew not what to make of this and communicated the conversation to General Taylor, who refused to have any connection with Stanton whatever, and immediately sought the President and told him that they had been betrayed, that Stanton had become possessed of their views and was ready to unite with them, provided he could retain his place in the War Department. But this,

[1] Richard Taylor, son of President Zachary Taylor and a lieutenant-general in the Confederate service.

Taylor declared, was out of the question, for he had no confidence in Stanton and would not be connected with him. The President, he said, seemed confused, but there the matter dropped. Blair thinks the President communicated the subject to Stanton, and it gives him distrust and dissatisfaction.

Revolving the subject in my mind, I question whether the President is in fault, yet there are some singular circumstances which seem to confirm it. Again my attention turns to Colonel Moore, the President's confidential secretary, who was turned over to him by Stanton, who is an officer of the War Department, and whose grateful feelings may influence him when Stanton is in danger. It is mere vague surmise on my part. I am and have been favorably impressed by Colonel Moore, who has appeared to me to be an honorable man in all my intercourse with him and who seems invaluable to the President. But there have been some singular things in the President's course which are wholly beyond my comprehension, and which I cannot reconcile or account for satisfactorily in any way except that he is betrayed.

March 29, *Friday.* Congress has been making itself a reproach to the country and to free government by its course in relation to adjournment, by its assaults on public men, by its rejection of some of the best men nominated for public position, and its efforts to invade and destroy the executive department of the Government. The lowest and most vituperative partisanship is exhibited, towards the President especially, who is denounced as a traitor and public enemy. One objection raised to an adjournment until next December is that the Radical majority *must see the laws executed.*

The Constitution makes it the duty of the President to see the laws executed, but the Radical majority openly usurp this power and propose a perpetual session in order to cripple the Executive and concentrate all power in

Congress. Propositions to adjourn from month to month, to adjourn and authorize the presiding officers to convene the two houses, or to adjourn them without meeting, have been made and supported by leading Radicals with a shameless disregard of their duty and oaths. If the public necessities require, the Constitution makes it the duty of the President to convene Congress in special session.

It is stated freely and without contradiction that Stanton and Grant both were on the floor of the two houses, beseeching the Members not to adjourn over to next winter and thus leave the administration of the government with the President. I was unwilling to believe this, particularly of Grant, but fear it is true.

The Senators show an unfriendly feeling towards army officers whom the President nominates for civil position, and Grant cannot have failed to see there is jealousy of the military among aspiring politicians. I am not sorry to see this, not that I approve of the proscription of men because they have been officers, or because they are friends of the President; but there is a disposition on the part of the military to be clannish and to grasp political office and power, which should not overshadow civil merit.

We had to-day a long discussion over Indian affairs. The military officers have assumed the control of matters which the law confides to the Indian agents, and have issued orders which conflict with and subjugate the agents. To this the Secretary of the Interior, who has charge of Indian affairs, objects and demands that the military orders be revoked. The Secretary of War thinks the officers are to be justified and brings forward Generals Grant and Sherman as his backers.

Seward is for compromising and after long discussion opposes the revocation of the order. McCulloch concurs with him because the army is there to protect the agents and settlers. Stanton is very emphatic the same way, of course. I dissented from the three who preceded me and took a different view from McCulloch. The military are there subordinate to the agents and the law, and should not control. All who followed me concurred with me. Stanbery made quite an argument.

March 30, *Saturday.* Dined with Seward to meet Bigelow, our late Minister to France. None present but Mrs. W., B. and wife, Senator Cattel of New Jersey, and Seward and family.

Congress adjourned to-day, until next July, when if a quorum is not present, presiding officers will adjourn then over to December, — a silly attempt to evade and get round the Constitution, which confides the subject to the President.

The President and Cabinet were at the Capitol at 10 A.M. and remained until twelve, when the adjournment took place.

Seward and myself were first on the ground. He told me that he and Stoeckel signed the treaty for the cession of Russian America at four this morning, having been up all night for that purpose. The consideration is $7,200,000. He had informed Sumner, and the treaty was to be sent in as soon as the President arrived. I suggested that Sumner might, as he was opposed to adjournment, avail himself of the occasion to delay adjournment. Seward was a good deal startled for a moment; said he hoped there was no need of prolonging the session. I asked what provision had been made for payment. He said that would not take place immediately, but could be made next winter.

He then called in, one at a time, four or five Senators and made special confidants of each, beginning with Cole. I was somewhat amused and not a little disgusted with the little acts and overpowering egotism he exhibited. The last is a growing infirmity.

Dining with him this evening, the whole time was spent in talking of himself and his doings, and his plans. Bigelow, I perceive, is very much taken with him and credulous in his belief of what he says, on all subjects. Attendance at Court has had an influence on B., greater than I should have believed.

Among other things Seward undertook to tell Bigelow how he had shaped the Cabinet of Mr. Lincoln, after it was formed. He commenced by saying that he had nothing to do with being brought into the Cabinet, of which, however, I knew more than he was aware. But, viewing the condition of the country in March, 1861, he perceived, he said, the necessity of entire unanimity and concert in the Cabinet council and his great object was harmonious action among all the members. This *he* succeeded in bringing about. Blair had sometimes been a little captious and Chase ambitious. The latter wanted to compete for the Presidency against Lincoln, which *he* (Seward) knew would not answer.

The truth is, no member was so meddlesome and intriguing as Seward; he was making more difficulties and committing more errors than all the others. They tolerated him because Mr. Lincoln did, and because it was necessary, as he says, in the then condition of the country.

He complimented the Cabinet as the ablest and best that the country had ever had; said that Jefferson and Hamilton, who were in Washington's, could never have carried the country through the War and the difficulties and the embarrassments we have had. The diary of Jefferson he condemned as unworthy. Bigelow says Jefferson's letters from France are infinitely inferior to Franklin's, who preceded him. He was astonished at the contrast.

XLVIII

Union Success in the Connecticut Election — Seward seeks to reward a
Political Trimmer with the Cuban Consul-Generalship — The President
receives Word that an Injunction against him is to be asked from the
Supreme Court — Conversation with General Butler on Public Affairs
— The Senate confirms the Alaska Purchase Treaty — Attempts to fill
the Cuban Consul-Generalship — Admiral Goldsborough seeks through
his Wife to be retained on the Active List — Senator Wilson electioneering in the South — Thaddeus Stevens denies Wilson's Authority to
make Promises — Governor English of Connecticut — Most of his
Message to the Legislature written by Secretary Welles — A Delegation
of Japanese visits the President — The House Judiciary Committee
seeking Evidence on which to impeach — McCulloch talks plainly to the
President about Stanton — The French buying War Vessels in the
United States — Seward considers acquiring Snake Island in the West
Indies — Wilkes Booth's Diary — The Price of the Danish West Indies
— Attorney-General Stanbery examining the Military Government Act
— The Indian Troubles — The Japanese conclude to buy the Ship
Stonewall — The President to visit North Carolina.

April 1, *Monday.* The annual election took place
to-day in Connecticut. It has been a severe struggle,
warmly contested on both sides. The issues were those
which the Radicals in Congress have forced on the country, and the importance of the result was generally felt.
In the selection of candidates the anti-Radicals showed
wisdom and shrewdness. There were old party organizations, and prejudices and impracticables to encounter,
but objectionable candidates were avoided and obnoxious
individuals were kept from the meetings. The few returns sent forward this evening leave no doubt that the
Union men, who support the Administration and disapprove the Congressional usurpations and innovations on
the Constitution, have been successful, electing English
and three of the four Members of Congress. In the last
Congress all were Radicals.

I went to the President with the first dispatch received

and told him I was satisfied the Radicals were defeated
in the State and three Congressional districts. He was
much gratified and said it was the turn of the current.

April 2, Tuesday. The Connecticut election creates
quite a commotion among the politicians. It is the first
loud knock which admonishes the Radicals of their inevitable doom. Seward attempts to talk sound philosophy
and to account for the result, which he says could not have
been obtained a month ago. I think, and so told him,
that we should have done quite as well a month ago.
The speech and vote of Reverdy Johnson, who had become a renegade, and the acquiescence of the South, or
their submission rather, had been discouraging and de-
pressing to the true Constitutional men in Connecticut.
Very little aid had reached them from without the State.

April 3, Wednesday. When at the Cabinet yesterday,
Seward informed me that the consulship at Panama is
vacant and asked if Earl Martin or some good Connecticut man did not want it. He felt anxious, he said, to give
recognition to Connecticut for the good work she had
done.

As I have no personal acquaintance with Martin, I could
not advise him, but said I did not feel anxious to send a
good man to a place where the yellow fever was raging
and which was always unhealthy.

This evening he called at my house with Senator Dixon
and said they had come to consult with me in relation to
the place of Consul-General to Cuba. Governor Minor
has sent in his resignation. Seward received it, he says,
yesterday afternoon, after seeing me, and, accidentally
meeting Senator Dixon, that gentleman had proposed
Gideon Hollister for the position, but he thought proper
before coming to a final conclusion that he should see me,
and had, therefore, got Mr. Dixon to call with him. Dixon,
being quite deaf and engaged in reading the Hartford

papers, did not listen or understand Seward's conversation, further than he knew its general purport, until I called him to listen. I told them I was not prepared to advise the appointment, that it did not strike me as particularly favorable in a political point of view, or that it would be received by the people who had elected English as a special compliment to them.

Our conversation was not very extended, but was such as led them both to suggest that the subject should be further considered, and Dixon is to call on me to-morrow morning in regard to it.

Hollister is a personal adherent and crony of Dixon, a sly and slippery partisan who has run himself ashore by little intrigues. Personally I have always been on terms with him, but the election of mere office-seekers who have no distinctive principle does not beget confidence.

The Democratic and conservative papers are jubilant over the election, and the Radicals are extremely bitter. Hawley vents his grief and disappointment in a rancorous article in his paper, denunciatory of me and spiteful towards Dixon.

April 4, Thursday. Dixon called this A.M., rather late, in regard to the consulate at Havana. I think he has in the mean time seen Seward.

I told him I had thought a good deal on the subject since last evening's interview and that my opposition to it had increased; that Hollister was in no sense a representative man of the party or people who had just achieved a victory in the State; that I had not heard of him through this hard-fought campaign; that I did not even know that he voted for the Administration, though I presumed he did for most of it, not from any deep conviction, but because he (D.) was for it; that the appointment would injure him (D.), for it would be at once said he had availed himself of the labors of others to get an important position for a personal friend; that the appointment would not strengthen the Administration or do it any good at home.

He was evidently impressed with my suggestions. Said he feared he had been hasty; that he supposed I had been consulted by Seward before he knew anything of the case; that Seward had sent for him and he met him after receiving the note, and at once and without much thought named Hollister; that Seward had replied, "Very well," but subsequently proposed that I should be seen. In the mean time, Dixon says, he wrote inconsiderately to Hollister that he could have the place, relying on what Seward said.

As it is, he thinks the appointment had better not go to Hartford, he has become so unfortunately complicated, but as Hollister may decline, the subject had better remain quiet for a day or two.

I was with the President in the course of the afternoon and introduced the subject of consul-general to Cuba, informing him, as I had Dixon, that a different man, like Judge James Phelps or Hovey of Norwich, would be a stronger and better appointment, and that English and others should be consulted. The President agreed with me, and said when Mr. Seward called on him to make the appointment he inquired what I thought of it, and said it would be proper to get my views.

All of this Seward has concealed from me, and strove to get Dixon committed with him without informing me. When the President sent him to me, he came with his story of accidentally meeting Dixon, but D. assured me, and twice repeated, that Seward had sent for him, — written him a note. Such is Seward. A great victory achieved by the friends of the Administration is perverted to personally enrich and reward a trimmer.

April 5, Friday. President called the Cabinet to a special session at 9 A.M., relative to notice given him of a motion which was to be made to the Supreme Court for an injunction on him and general order to stay proceedings under the military bill for constructing the Rebel States. Attorney-General was directed to object to the motion, — the President, as the representative of the United States, cannot be sued.

General Butler called on me yesterday, ostensibly on some little matter of business. When it was disposed of, he asked whether he was to congratulate or condole with me on the result of the Connecticut election. I replied that I was gratified at the result and, of course, had no need of condolence; that I congratulated myself and others on what had taken place. This opened the subject of our public affairs, on which we had a pretty free and apparently unreserved conversation, though he is neither frank nor reliable. He is not, I perceive, satisfied with his position, nor with his treatment by a portion of the Radicals. I spoke of the election as being favorable to the President, Mr. Johnson, whose policy I approved; the policy had commenced with Mr. Lincoln, and I believed it correct. I asked wherein he could except to it. He said that perhaps Congress should have been consulted, — he thought so. I inquired by what authority Congress could intervene. Congress was the legislative, not the executive, department of government, had none but granted powers, and where was the power conferred on Congress to construct or destroy a State? He answered there is no grant, but it grew out of the War; the Rebel States were conquered States; the President had no more power than Congress.

"Therein," said I, "we differ. I hold, as did Mr. Lincoln and as does Mr. Johnson, that when Lee and Johnston surrendered, martial law prevailed from the Potomac to the Rio Grande, and the President, as commander-in-chief, had the undoubted right under the war power to govern those States, temporarily, and to bring order out of chaos. He could have turned the matter over to General Grant and other military subordinates, but he preferred

3

to do it himself. He appointed a provisional governor, first in North Carolina and subsequently in other States, as you, General Butler, being in chief command in the Gulf, appointed Deming a provisional mayor in New Orleans. Mr. Lincoln had no intention of calling on Congress to assist in this matter. Every one knew this, who had any knowledge of Mr. Lincoln. Mr. Colfax was here on the day of his death to bid him good-bye, for he was intending to cross the Plains and be absent until October. As Speaker he would not have absented himself, had there been any intention of convening Congress.

"Then," said I, "these military despotisms over the States, — the assembling of the State Governments, — I don't see, General, how you, if a democratic Republican, can sanction such measures."

"I had nothing to do with them," said he. "They were enacted before I took my seat."

"But," said I, "you are identified with that party and those acts."

"Begging your pardon, I do not indorse those acts nor approve them. I am not identified with them, nor responsible for them."

I remarked that I was glad to hear him say so.

"Why," he asked, "does not the President test them? Why does he submit to such laws and attempt to carry them out? He declares them unconstitutional. If so, they are no laws. Why does he obey them?"

I called his attention to the constitutional requirement, that he should see all laws faithfully executed.

"But it is no law," said Butler; "the President says it is no law. He is one of the departments of the Government and must decide for himself. If, however, he wants to get a decision from the Court, there is no difficulty. Let a suit be instituted in Virginia and brought at once before the Supreme Court now in session."

He then went on to detail the *modus operandi*.

On the whole, I am satisfied that Butler is dissatisfied.

April 17, *Wednesday.* My time has been so occupied that I could make no record of daily occurrences in this book. Important events have occurred; some of the details should have been jotted down.

The Senate continues in session, rejecting the nominations which the President sends in, — not that the nominees are not competent and faithful, but because they are his friends and support his measures. Some of the Senators declare they will vote to confirm no man who is not a Radical. Dixon tells me that Sumner made his boast, in extra session, that he had allowed none but Radicals to be appointed to any office in Massachusetts, where the Senate has a voice. I have little confidence in Randall as Postmaster-General, under such circumstances. He gives in, trims, lacks vim and strength, if nothing else. I apprehend his course has some influence on McCulloch, who, loaded down with the financial difficulties, wants to conciliate. It requires some courage to meet a not overscrupulous body of men clothed with authority, and who can, if they choose, embarrass the Government without financial accountability. The President has held his own very well, considering his surroundings. Seward he probably consults most, and Seward has, as Mr. Clay said of him, "no convictions," — is an egotist and selfish aspirant. Randall, whose confirmation is understood to have been secured by pledges to Radical Senators, is greatly under Seward's influence, and the President cannot, with his reticence, avoid committing errors with such advisers. The result is the President is appointing more enemies than friends, and his Administration is thereby weakened. Seward seldom selects or makes a good appointment. He thinks he is helping himself and cares little about helping the President, except as it may ultimately benefit himself and his former Whig friends.

The treaty for the acquisition of Russian America was finally confirmed, only two Senators voting against it, though quite a number spoke against it. Some denounced it with violence, but voted for it at last, — mere partisans wanting in legislative wisdom and moral courage.

The *New York Tribune*, Mr. Greeley, made a ferocious attack on the treaty, ridiculed and denounced the acquisition, but found he had no influence where he thought himself all-powerful.

Dixon has urged me to unite with him in behalf of Gideon H. Hollister as Consul-General to Cuba. I have declined. Told him I was not aware Hollister was a representative of those who carried the late election; that I considered him a party trimmer without much regard for principle.

Dixon says he has become complicated. Repeats that Seward wished him to call and see him, asked him to nominate, and he supposed I had been consulted and was aware of the steps Seward had taken. Seward called with Dixon on me after all this had occurred, and opened the subject to me in confidence, wanted us to unite, etc. My views were fully expressed in his presence at that time, and it was subsequently that Dixon told me how Seward had first approached him. A day or two after the two had paid me a visit, the President spoke of the appointment, said Seward had brought him Hollister's name and he asked if I had been consulted. Seward said he had consulted the Senator from Connecticut, and the President desired that I should be seen. It was this order which had brought about the interview between S. and D. with me at my house.

I stated finally, after repeated calls from Dixon, who has behaved well enough so far as I am concerned, that I would give Hollister's true character to the President and there leave it, for he and I ought not to be in conflict.

The result is Hollister has been nominated. He is a hanger-on to Dixon, writes sonnets to Mrs. D., has a bad political record and no force.

April 20, *Saturday.* Hollister was promptly rejected. I then proposed Judge James Phelps, whom I had first named. Dixon assented, but afterwards suggested that Phelps' appointment would create a vacancy which the Radicals would fill. Ferry wrote Faxon a note that Phelps would be confirmed, but that Lippitt of New London, whom I had suggested with Phelps, would probably be rejected. On this state of facts, with a disposition to be kind to New London, where the people had been made sore by Brandegee and others on the Navy Yard question, I advised sending in Lippitt's name. He was at once rejected. The President then proposed to go elsewhere than Connecticut, and I could not object. Kilby Smith was nominated, and his name laid on the table.

So the consulate is not filled, nor is the Austrian Mission, and several other places.

. . . .

The Senate adjourned on Saturday, the 20th, at 9 P.M. From day to day, and on Saturday from hour to hour, the adjournment was postponed, in order to arrange for the offices. The President yielded to some extent as he has done before, which I regretted, for tampering with enemies and surrendering his constitutional prerogative weakens his position. In their usurpations, Senators claim the right to dictate in regard to appointments for which the President and not the Senators is responsible, and he, without acknowledging their right, yields to their usurping pretensions.

Rear-Admiral Goldsborough continues to press his claims for four years' addition to his time on the active list. He will in January have been an officer of the Navy fifty-five years, but as he did not from sheer favoritism receive orders for sea until four years after his appointment he now claims that those four years should not count against him. He has had the benefit of them for more than fifty years, giving him priority over others. Were he here to attend to his own case personally, I could get along, but, being absent, he stimulates and pushes forward his wife, the daughter of Attorney-General William Wirt, a very worthy woman and very devoted to him, and with her there is no reasoning. She is satisfied that her husband is the best officer in the Navy, has done more service than any other, and, being not only the wife of a Rear-Admiral, but the daughter of an Attorney-General, there is no convincing her. I do not controvert the facts which she assumes in regard to her husband. No one could. And her law is as good as his war statements.

She has consulted Chief Justice Chase, her former instructor and friend, Attorney-General Stanbery, and Reverdy Johnson, successor of Wirt, and some others, who all, without knowing the facts, assure her that her husband ought to be continued four years longer on the active list. Mr. J. P. Kennedy, late Secretary of the Navy, also favors Goldsborough, and has written a book, which has been printed, to prove that G. should continue to receive extraordinary favors.

April 29, *Monday.* The injunction cases in behalf of Georgia and Mississippi have been before the Court and are still pending. Attorney-General and Mr. O'Conor made arguments on Friday. The latter is evidently more of a lawyer than statesman, studies law more than constitutions, cases more than governmental principles. Nothing will be got from the Court, I apprehend, and there are embarrassments in the case. The Attorney-General's positions cannot be subscribed to in all respects. Why O'Conor and his associates make no use of the recent decision of the Court in Milligan's case I don't understand. Congress, under color of law, cannot invest brigadiers with power to abolish jury trial or to suspend the privilege of *habeas corpus* in time of peace.

Senator Wilson is electioneering through the Southern States, stirring up the blacks, irritating and insulting the whites, promising the people recognition and that they

GIDEON WELLES

may have their constitutional rights, provided they will submit to the unconstitutional and unwarranted dictation of the Radicals.

Thad Stevens has issued a card denying Wilson's authority to make promises for the Radicals. He, Stevens, intends to play the part of tyrant and dictator to the South for years, will not permit them to be represented, intends to exclude them and to confiscate the property of the Rebels. These differences among the Radical leaders may have the effect of bringing considerate men in the North to their senses, lead them to examine the principles on which the government is founded, and cause them to look again to the Constitution which they have thrust aside for some time past.

The North must retrieve itself from its errors growing out of resentment and evil passions, and in retrieving itself will extricate the country from the slough in which the Radicals have plunged it.

May 1, *Wednesday.* A delegation of Japanese have arrived here for some purpose. Seward sent Chilton, one of his clerks, to take them in charge, and they have been brought to Washington. Their arrival hastened Seward's return from Auburn, where he had gone to make his semi-annual visit and, it was said, to make his semi-annual speech. Happily the Japanese, or some other cause, saved the infliction.

May 2, *Thursday.* The new Governor of Connecticut, English, was inaugurated yesterday. His message is different in sentiment and principle from the views of his predecessor, Governor Hawley. I do not think, however, that H. has any well-defined opinions or convictions on great governmental or political questions. If so he does not consistently adhere to them. He began his career as an Abolitionist and was earnest and enthusiastic with probably more sentimentality than principle. As the cause expanded, he became bewildered, but clung to his humanitarianism as the Alpha and Omega of party. Since the emancipation and suppression of the Rebellion, he has floated with the current, impulsive by nature, yet Republican rather than Radical. . . .

The Radicals of Connecticut and of New England are narrow-minded party men of Puritanic-Calvinistic notions in politics and religion, intolerant and prejudiced in their opinions. Hate, revenge, and persecution enter largely into their composition. They think, — or believe, for they do not give so much thought as they should to the subject, — they believe that force, oppression, compulsion are necessary to govern the South and that the Radicals of the North should govern them; that the people of the South must be disciplined; that since the Rebellion they are without the pale of the Constitution and should be less tolerated than if they were aliens. These fanatics want a God to punish, not to love, those who do not agree with them.

May 3, *Friday.* The President compliments the message of Governor English, and the Radical editors, without controverting it, call it names.

Governor English has been a successful merchant in New Haven and represented his town and district in the legislature, without any marked distinction, but with a degree of fairness that led to his election to the Thirty-seventh Congress and his reëlection to the Thirty-eighth. His course in the national legislature had, of course, nothing brilliant, but he acquitted himself during that trying and turbulent period in a manner that was more acceptable to men of all parties than that of either of his colleagues. Although a Democrat, he supported the Administration in most of its War measures, and voted with the Republicans on some of the test questions of party without forfeiting the confidence of his associates, or political constituents. The good judgment he displayed rather

than any shining qualities or marked genius led to his
nomination and election as Governor. Most of the message
which the President commends, and which the Radicals
condemn, was written by me, but of this the President
knows nothing, and I apprehend English himself is not
fully informed. It was written with a view of calling
public attention to the vital political questions before the
country.

Senator Wilson extends his journey South, making offensive speeches, which are permitted, because the manliness as well as the haughty arrogance which once characterized the South is broken and completely subdued.
They seem to have no spirit in them. It can scarcely be
doubted, however, that the slumbering wrath will yet be
aroused. But Wilson's success has started out another
set of Radical orators, who are going South to enkindle
party animosity, arouse the ignorant blacks, and excite
them against the whites. This is the Radical process of
Reconstruction.

Seward had the Japanese to see the President to-day.
Spoke of them in Cabinet. Says they have not yet disclosed their object; supposes they wish to buy ships; likely
may want to make some inquiry about the two that were
built for them by Weed and Lansing, to whom they intrusted funds; but that all is friendly.

I hope that everything may prove satisfactory to them
and that they have not been wronged; but have my apprehensions that they have been cheated and swindled badly.
Seward knows that I have not fallen in with the course
he has pursued towards them. We could have their friendship and their commerce, — we may have it still, but it is
in jeopardy, for they have not been well and fairly treated
by us. I have already, and in former pages, made mention
of these circumstances, and my official letters to Seward
have expressed my opinions. He looks upon me, I think,
with some distrust in this matter. I know his friend Weed
does.

May 4, *Saturday.* I offered Commodore Lee to-day the Naval Observatory. He declined it. Said he had a house of his own and to take the observatory would lessen his percentage in consequence of the house there which he should have to take. I asked him if he would like the Norfolk Navy Yard. He said no, he would not, but he should be glad to have the Ordnance Bureau, which Wise was about leaving. I told him that I was not aware that Wise desired to relinquish that position. My impression was that he did not. Lee said that Mrs. Wise had given out that her husband was going to Europe and would give up the Ordnance. That, I remarked, was woman's talk. He said if Wise was not going to give up the bureau, he wished a day or two to think of the other matter, to which I assented. He is mercenary and avaricious to a wonderful extent.

The Judiciary Committee of the House has reassembled in Washington to pursue inquiries and see if they cannot obtain something on which to impeach the President. No facts, no charges, no malconduct are known or preferred, for the slip-slop of Ashley was long since discarded, but a standing committee is advertised and has assembled to ascertain whether something cannot be found which may be tortured or twisted against the President, whom they cannot induce to go with them in their revolutionary schemes, and who is, consequently, in their way. A more scandalous villainy never disgraced the country.

McCulloch tells me he has had a talk with the President and told him he had brought these troubles upon himself by the hesitating course he had pursued; that he had retained a man in his Cabinet who is notoriously opposed to his Administration, a man who, from the beginning, has been an embarrassment; that there was never any free interchange of opinion when that member was present, but there was reserve; yet in many of the important measures and movements that false member had a controlling voice and often was the only person consulted.

McC. instanced the appointment or selection of the military governors, which had been made without consultation with any member of the Cabinet, save the false and unfaithful one. The President listened and assented to the remarks, but having, under the influence of Seward, commenced in error, he will be likely under the same influence to continue in weakness, as regards Stanton.

I have seen all these errors, have adverted to them when opportunity presented, have had my opinions indorsed, but there the subject has ended. Seward, and Randall, whom he uses, are not elements of strength, but they are different from Stanton, for whom they apologize and whom they justify and sustain. They are weak; he is wicked. By weak I mean their course and counsel, politically, are worse than worthless. They have no sincere convictions, — no treacherous intentions, but are full of tricks and expedients, which accomplish nothing, while they beget distrust.

May 6, *Monday.* Dined at Seward's on Saturday with the Cabinet and the Japan Embassy. Senator Sumner and others were present, among them Madame Juarez, wife of the President of Mexico, and daughters. Each of the Cabinet and some others were introduced to them and to each of the Japanese. One of their number talked English, and others understood it.

To-day Seward called on me with some of the Japanese, who want to purchase naval vessels. A serious rebellion prevails in Japan. They profess to seek advice and assistance. Say they wish to act in good faith in carrying out the treaty.

Seward had informed them that we had various kinds of vessels. They wanted monitors, but had learned it was difficult handling and navigating them. I told them we could well spare some monitors, but it would be scarcely possible to get them to Japan. Any vessels which we could spare I would be glad to have them possess.

Seward and myself called on the President on their behalf, and I have detailed Commodore Jenkins to go with
the commission to Annapolis, examine the school and vessels, and have an interview with the superintendent.

May 7, Tuesday. Webb, builder of the Dunderberg,
informs me he has made sale of that vessel to an agent
of the French Government. And Quintard has also sold
that Government the Onondaga. Secor and Swift apply
to purchase five more monitors, doubtless for sale to foreign
governments. Their proposition is to resume or retake the
vessels, refunding to the Government the amount we have
paid.

Seward and the Cabinet were taken aback when I informed them that the French were purchasing our naval
vessels. Seward had stated that Berthémy, the French
Minister, had called upon him to remonstrate, or inquire
into the sale of war vessels to Prussia, and he had something of a querulous story to tell. When he had got through
and I told him what the French were doing, he stood in
amazement.

I submitted the proposition of Secor and Swift for the
five vessels. He seemed disposed to sell, but Stanton, who
objected, would sell none of these vessels. Others proposed to commit the whole subject to my discretion. I
informed them it was not a matter for me to decide, but
for the President, with the advice of the Cabinet, to dispose of. I was, however, individually decidedly in favor
of selling so far as I had a voice.

May 11, Saturday. Thomas Ewing called on me at the
solicitation of Mrs. Dahlgren, who insists on going out
to her husband in the South Pacific. She wants a public
vessel to convey her, her two infant twins, their nurses,
etc., from Panama. A great pressure has been made upon
me from the time Admiral Dahlgren received his orders,
and Mr. Ewing has on one or two former occasions spoken

on the subject. It has been before the Cabinet. At this time the matter comes up in a new form. The yellow fever prevails at Panama, and Mr. Ewing says that Admiral D. represents it is on board the packet ships. I asked if that was not an intimation that he deemed it inexpedient and ill-advised for Mrs. D. to leave the country with her infants. It has been the policy not to send women out in naval vessels, and I think it unfortunate that the ladies go abroad to their husbands on foreign stations. In this instance I remarked it appeared extremely injudicious, for Dahlgren had but a year and a half to serve. If Mrs. D. should be with her family at Lima it would, unavoidably, influence the movements of the Admiral and the squadron. Mr. Ewing assented to the correctness of my views, but said Mrs. D. was resolved to go if she had to take the sickly steamers.

Stanton yesterday made an exhibit of the requisitions for expenditures by the military governors, or satraps, in the territorialized States. They will draw largely on the Treasury. Sheridan especially "goes in with a rush" as they say. He is brave and patriotic, but not an administrative officer whom I should select for civil duties. But the officers are less blamable for this military government, whether well or poorly administered, than the Congress which passed the laws creating it.

May 13, *Monday.* Have talked with several naval officers on the subject of taking their wives on naval vessels, and found them generally opposed to it. There are, however, exceptions, and most of them admit there may be occasions abroad when it would be pleasant and excusable, perhaps, to give them passage, but it nevertheless disarranges and invariably causes discontent.

I have under the circumstances given a permit to Mrs. D. to go on a public vessel from Panama.

May 14, *Tuesday.* Attorney-General Stanbery read a

number of pages of his opinion on the subject of registration and suffrage, under what is known as the military
bill for governing the Rebel States. It is very elaborate
and has been carefully prepared. He promises the remainder at the next Cabinet-meeting on Friday. He will
give much more extended suffrage to the whites than was
intended by the Radical concocters of the law. Stanton
was somewhat annoyed by it, and I was satisfied from his
remarks that his intimacy with that bill has been early
and thorough. I have little doubt that he was consulted,
if he did not advise, perhaps originate, the measure.

May 15, *Wednesday*. Returning from the Department
this P.M., I met Seward, who was going with his sons to
call on me. I got into his carriage and rode with him, as
he had a matter to communicate. Some New-Yorker has
informed him of an uninhabited island, called Snake
Island,[1] near St. Thomas, which has a capacious and excellent harbor. His informant occupied the island prior
to the War and was engaged in making sugar-hogsheads.
The island, he says, is low and well timbered. I asked why,
if it had such excellent harbor, it had remained unoccupied.
Seward could not inform me, nor what nation claimed it,
but he supposed the Spaniards. I apprehend there must
be a want of water. Seward promises to send me the
papers.

I advised, if the facts were as stated, that his New York
friend should resume possession and that we would defend
him in his rights. If Spain should claim jurisdiction, we
must adjust the matter with her. I told him I much preferred this to buying St. Thomas.

May 16, *Thursday*. Was at the President's on a little
matter of business when the Metropolitan police came
for review. Randall and myself supported the President.

[1] The island of Culebra (Spanish for "snake") is between St. Thomas
and Puerto Rico and belongs to the latter.

Afterward Randall read to us his testimony before the Judiciary Committee.

The President submitted to us the letters of Judge Holt and Stanton in regard to Booth's diary and a copy of the contents, and inquired what we thought of its publication. I asked what objections there could be. It was a great mystery and was construed to mean whatever any diseased imagination might conceive. Randall thought as I did. The President said Stanton was violently opposed to its publication.

May 17, *Friday.* Seward had a long tale to tell in regard to his testimony before the Judiciary Committee. He makes himself, I perceive, the hero with Stanton of Mr. Lincoln's Administration. I shall be curious to see that testimony when published. Many things in regard to Reconstruction and organizing the provisional governments of the Rebel States occurred while he was sick and unable to attend to his duties.

May 21, *Tuesday.* Seward presents a telegraphic correspondence with Raasloff,[1] now at Copenhagen, and a memorandum given to Senator Doolittle relative to the purchase of the Danish West India Islands. Denmark wants $15,000,000 for the whole or $10,000,000 for St. Thomas, with consent of the inhabitants to the transfer. Seward sent a dispatch to Yeaman, our Minister, to offer $5,000,000, ultimatum $10,000,000. Any expression of inhabitants must be before treaty.

McCulloch and myself expressed surprise that more than $5,000,000 had been or should be offered. McCulloch said he believed something had been said about going up to $7,500,000 for the whole. I stated that I preferred not to purchase even at $5,000,000. At all events, would not go beyond that. During the War I had felt

---

[1] General Raasloff was Danish Minister to the United States. The negotiations for the purchase of the islands had been conducted through him.

that a station in the West Indies was desirable, but we should experience no such want again. We are now as well accommodated as if we owned St. Thomas. In case of a war with either of the great powers, — British, French, or Spanish, — we could seize one of these islands. In the condition of our Treasury I did not care to buy. Attorney-General Stanbery preferred to take Snake Island than to buy an inhabited island.

Seward is anxious to make a purchase somewhere. Has loose, indefinite, and selfish notions. It is more the glory of Seward than the true interests of the country, I apprehend. He craves constant notoriety, and the purchase of the Danish Islands for $15,000,000 or even $10,000,000 would, I think, give him more than he expects, or perhaps would want.

The Attorney-General presented another installment of his opinion on the Military Government Bill. Stanton criticized it closely, controverted some of the points, is friendly to the bill, and probably had much to do in its preparation if he did not originate the measure. He defended it with all the earnestness and tenacity of an author, and took ground such as would suit the strongest Radicals.

As the act and supplemental act are palpably and clearly unconstitutional, I see nothing substantial or valuable in the opinion which the Attorney-General has been, and is, elaborating, unless in the fact that he is giving a more liberal or enlarged scope to suffrage than the Radicals intended. More whites will be allowed to exercise their rights than was designed by the Radicals. All blacks, of course, are to vote, though they have no such right, nor has the Central Government authority to confer it. Hearing Stanton controvert positions, dissent from the opinion, tell what is the proper construction and meaning of an act which is no law, because unconstitutional, is highly absurd. Almost as absurd is the learned attempt of Stanbery to expound their acts.

I have asked what is the status of the people in the proscribed States. Are they foreigners? If so, not one of them can vote until naturalized. There must be a uniform system of naturalization. Are they citizens? They cannot be disfranchised nor their States overthrown, nor jury trials abolished, nor can they be tried and condemned by military commissions. No one answered my questions. The Attorney-General says the unconstitutionality of the law is beyond question. That point he does not touch. But that is the great essential, the foundation of all argument. If there is no foundation, how can he build? He has an insoluble problem and undertakes to give a result.

Stanton never touches the question of constitutionality, neither assenting nor dissenting, nor discussing it.

May 22, *Wednesday.* The Japanese have concluded to buy the Stonewall.

Webb wants me to let him have the Dunderberg on his depositing government securities, delaying payment for a year. He has produced an opinion from Lowry, indorsed by Evarts, that this is the intent of the law. When I declined considering the proposition, Webb became quite vexed and excited. He is selfish, jealous, and grasping. His object is to get the interest on a million and a quarter of dollars for a year.

May 23, *Thursday.* A special Cabinet-meeting. Seward submitted a modified proposition to Denmark for the purchase of her West India Islands, making $7,500,000 an ultimatum. McCulloch, Stanbery, and myself thought it best to guard the Treasury at this time; that we wanted money more than West Indian people. Seward was very earnest. It was necessary to get these islands, or a foothold in the West Indies, as a preservative measure, — as a means of security. It would insure peace. He had talked with the Senators. Grimes and Wade were earnest for it, and of course others were.

3

Stanton, Randall, and Browning went with him. I stated we had no need of a station in time of peace. We could take any of the islands from any power with which we might be at war.

A further installment from Mr. Stanbery was read on the Reconstruction or Military Government Act. Seward and the members generally expressed themselves as satisfied. Stanton dissented.

I thought Stanbery had done as well as one could who was compelled to try to make sense out of nonsense, law out of illegality. The act is admitted by everybody to be unconstitutional; of course, that being the case, it has no validity. It is a fraud perpetrated by a majority of a fragmentary Congress. I, therefore, cared not to comment on the opinion, and attempted practical workings of the bill. Why strive to solve an insoluble problem?

The Indian troubles were discussed at some length without coming to a conclusion. General Grant was sent for and was present. He and Stanton are in sympathy with the military men on the Plains, and there seems a determination to have an Indian war. Were there no troops there, or only a few at the posts to sustain the agents, we should probably have no war, but the military claim to supersede the agents and are sustained by the War Department and General Grant.

Letters were read from Colonels Wynkoop and Leavenworth, stating the destruction of three hundred lodges with all their contents,—tools, utensils, buffalo robes, etc., — constituting not only all the wealth of some fifteen hundred Indians, but the necessary means of shelter and subsistence for themselves, their women and children. The only excuse for this destruction which brings misery to so many is that the women and children fled from the lodges as the troops approached and could not be persuaded to return. Fear, it is admitted, influenced them in running away.

May 24, Friday. Jere Black, Buchanan's Attorney-General, called relative to the claim of Rear-Admiral Goldsborough for four years' additional continuance on the active list. After a pretty full and frank discussion, I think he became satisfied there was little law and merit in Goldsborough's claim.

We then had a long and interesting conversation on the condition of our public affairs. Our views in the main coincided. Some of my positions appeared to be new to him, or were presented in a way that seemed to impress him, I thought, with a stronger conviction. He said it would be well for the President to prepare a calm and considerate address to his countrymen, something in the character and strain of Washington's and Jackson's. I was not prepared to urge this or even adopt it. Had the President been more calm, made no speeches or harangues, it would be different. But his weak talk has weakened him, and his silence for the last five months leaves little doubt that he is aware of it.

May 25, Saturday. The Japanese conclude to buy the Stonewall. There will be trouble in getting her to them. The Navy Department will have to take the labor, care, etc., of all this, and the State Department will take credit, should there be any.

May 27, Monday. The opinion of the Attorney-General on Reconstruction is published and seems to stir up the Radicals, who know not what to say of it.

. . . .

May 28, Tuesday. The Indian matters occupied over two hours. It is evident the military intend to control Indian affairs to the annihilation of the whole race. Hancock admits the destruction of the three hundred Indian lodges and all the utensils and household gods and goods. His excuse is that the women and children fled when the chief said they should not; that they would not return, were afraid of the troops; all of which was in bad faith.

I listened to the numerous dispatches of the Indian agents to the Interior Department in behalf of the Indians, and those of the military to the War Department, and the discussion on both sides, with painful interest.

General Grant was present, and his sympathies and feelings were naturally with the military, but he was more reasonable than Stanton.

Seward was querulous and pointless and meaningless in some sprawling remarks intended to conciliate Grant and Stanton. Nothing patriotic, or humane, or just escaped him.

May 31, Friday. The President concludes to go to Raleigh, North Carolina, and will be accompanied by Seward. At one time it was understood he would be accompanied by some of the members of his family and one or two of his personal staff, but that none of the Cabinet would go with him. To-day it is stated that Seward will be his companion and that none of his family will be of the party. It is unfortunate for the President that he permits himself to be absorbed by Seward, who is, not without some cause, so universally distrusted and disliked. He is delighted with traveling, feasting, notoriety, and both he and Stanton make the President a convenience and help to themselves in all matters where they can.

XLIX

The President goes to North Carolina, accompanied by Seward and Randall — Chief Justice Chase to hold Court in North Carolina — The Judiciary Committee decides against Impeachment but reports a Resolution of Censure against the President — A Visit to the Naval Academy with Admiral Farragut — Parting with Farragut — Farragut the Great Hero of the War — Sheridan's Removal of Governor Wells of Louisiana — Stanbery's Liberal Interpretation of the Military Government Act— Talk with Governor Pease of Texas — A Faction in Colombia proposes to tax Foreign Residents — Seward's Presidential Ambitions and Craze for the Acquisition of Territory — The Attorney-General's Opinion on the Reconstruction Bills an Able Document — Mrs. Goldsborough presses the Admiral's Claims to Retention on the Active List — The President invites Secretary Welles to accompany him on a Journey to Boston — Cabinet Discussion of the Attorney-General's Opinion on the Military Government Law — Commander Roe's Action in seizing Santa Anna — The President starts for Boston — The Publication of Cabinet Proceedings — Sheridan's Insubordination — The President's Faltering Conduct — His Administration a Failure — General Sickles's Letter against the Secretary of the Navy — The President courteously received in New England — Grant's Probable Candidacy — Montgomery Blair's Opinion of Grant as a General — Admiral Farragut sails for Europe with two of the Secretary's Sons accompanying him — Conversation with the President on his Return from the South.

June 3, *Monday.* Admiral Farragut came on Friday and is stopping with me for a few days. I called with him on the President on Saturday and dined at Seward's that evening with him.

The President got off on Saturday. Seward and Randall went with him. McCulloch expressed his regret that any of the Cabinet had gone, but, as Seward went, was rather glad Randall had gone also. I take a different view, but it confirms my impressions of Randall and his affinity with Seward.

Chief Justice Chase told me Saturday evening that he intended going to North Carolina on Monday to hold court. Martial law being established by Congress and military governments in full sway, he can now, after evading and avoiding his duties for two years, hold court there. He is very aspiring and in some respects an unsuitable man for his position.

The municipal election was held to-day in Washington. It was an abuse and a farce. The negroes, under Radical training, have controlled the result, and negro votes will be sought and managed in the future of the South. All this strife, or usurpation, is in flagrant disregard of the principles on which our government and institutions are founded, as it is in disregard of and detrimental to intelligent citizenship and enlightened freedom. Under the pretense of elevating the negro, the Radicals are degrading the whites and debasing the elective franchise, bringing elections into contempt.

June 4, Tuesday. The Judiciary Committee have, by a vote of five to four, decided against impeachment, but by a strict party vote passed a resolution of censure against the President. A more shameless and disgraceful proceeding than this whole impeachment conspiracy has never been enacted. For many months a committee, composed mostly of extreme partisans, has been in session with extraordinary powers to send for persons and papers, and with the public treasury and an army of public scavengers to assist them, to find, if possible, some act or transaction or expression which would justify or excuse an arraignment of the Chief Magistrate. His public and his private acts have been scanned, his household affairs, his domestic life, his bank accounts, his social intercourse, as well as all his speeches, conversations, and doings as a man and President, have been scrutinized. Failing in their intrigue, scandal and defamation have been set to work to palliate these outrageous proceedings. Most of the members of the Cabinet and, I believe, all but myself, have been summoned before this committee, as well as his private secretaries and members of his family. Why I was spared, I know not. I have an impression and intimations in fact that Stanton proposed and ordered I should not be called. Both he and Seward, in a conversation which took place as to disclosing proceedings in Cabinet, thought the matter might be got along with by answering pretty fully all questions that were put without any allusion to the fact whether it was or was not a Cabinet subject. I doubted whether it was right to disclose what had occurred in Cabinet to such a committee, — perhaps to any one at present.

I went with Admiral Farragut, Commodore Jenkins, my wife and two eldest sons, and a few other friends to Annapolis to visit the Academy. The board of visitors now in session will probably close their labors to-morrow. The visit was gratifying in all respects. Vice-Admiral Porter, with some weakness, is in many respects a proper man for the position. No one appreciates it more highly than himself. In some respects he is a hard officer for the Secretary; his demands and requisitions are great and such as Congress might decline to sanction.

The improvements are very considerable, and the money spent to repair the waste and injury of the military and improve the place has been in the main judiciously expended.

The midshipmen are a credit to the country, and will do honor to it in the future, as they are a credit to it now. Foreign wars are likely to be in the future almost exclusively maritime, yet a large portion of the politicians and people seem not aware of it. There is, on the part of the more intense party men, a rigid parsimony and reluctance to make grants to the Navy, while appropriating immense sums to the military branch of the service.

I shall always regret that the naval school should not have been established at Newport News on the beautiful sheet of water at Hampton Roads. There would have been more ample accommodations and space, deeper water, — an abundance of it, — with every facility for such an institution. But Grimes and others, with a narrowness of feeling that surprised me, while admitting these advantages, would not consent to transfer the school so far South as Virginia. Porter first favored the measure, but was silenced by the Maryland authorities, deserted me, and helped to influence Grimes.

June 7, Friday. Admiral Farragut went home to-day. He has been my guest for a week. Gave him yesterday his orders to the European Squadron, and he expects to sail within a fortnight. In bidding him good-bye I was more affected than he was aware, and I perceived that he was to some extent similarly affected. We have both reached that period of life when a parting of two years may be a parting forever on earth. Circumstances have brought us together, and we are under mutual obligations. I selected him for important duties, and he proved himself worthy of the trust and confidence. In addition to his great service to the country, unsurpassed, he has given just fame to my administration of the Navy, and I honor him for his unassuming modesty as well as for possessing the heroic qualities which I expected. I trust we may live to meet again on earth and enjoy memories of the past. If not, God's will be done. I esteem the choice of Farragut to command the Gulf Squadron the most judicious and best selection which could have been made in the entire service. I consider him the great hero of the War, and am happy in the thought that I was the means of carrying him to the head of his profession, where he had an opportunity to develop his power and ability.

June 8, Saturday. The President and party returned to-day from North Carolina. All appears to have passed off well.

There is much talk and feeling in regard to Sheridan's movements, which are arbitrary, tyrannical, and despotic. His removal of Wells, the poor Governor of Louisiana, is justified by most of the Radicals, although it is an outrage

on our laws and institutions. The trimming course of
Wells and his want of honest character palliates Sheridan's conduct, which, however, is wholly indefensible.

June 11, *Tuesday.* Attorney-General Stanbery read
so much of his opinion on the powers and duties of the
military governors as he has written. It follows out his
former opinion and softens the hard features of the bill
in some respects in its execution. He claims that the
military governor and force are there to support order
and the provisional governments, not to destroy them,
etc.

Stanton dissented; claimed the governors were omnipotent, that martial law existed by authority of Congress,
which made the generals supreme

There is no doubt this was the intent of Congress, and
I have so construed the act, taking the same view as the
President in his vetoes. It is, however, a solecism for
the Congress or the legislature to enact martial law, but
the whole law is an absurdity, unconstitutional, abominable. If the Attorney-General can modify it and so con-
strue it as to make it less odious, very well.

June 12, *Wednesday.* Governor Pease of Texas called
on me. We had a very earnest talk on the condition of the
country. He attempted to justify or excuse the Reconstruction bills, but, finding he could not, threw himself
back upon the whole subject. He preferred despotism, if
it would give security to persons and property, rather than
a continuance of the condition of things which had existed in Texas for the last six years. The Union people
have undoubtedly suffered greatly. I asked if he could not
peaceably enjoy his property in Texas if he remained passive. He admitted he could, but said that was despotism.
He could not freely express his opinions and have open
discussion. I asked him if he could have that under a
despotism. The condition of the Unionists is undoubtedly

unpleasant in Texas, but time and forbearance will bring relief.

June 14, Friday. An extended Cabinet session. Seward read a long dispatch which he had prepared to the American Minister to Colombia in relation to a tax which one of the parties there propose to levy for belligerent purposes on foreign residents, as well as their own citizens. In his dispatch Seward says the citizens (American) must protest and that the naval authorities will see that our countrymen are not compelled to submit to exactions by either faction.

The Attorney-General asked what he meant by either faction, and which and what is the legitimate government. Seward said he recognized no legitimate government; that the President had usurped power and dissolved Congress, and that the opposing faction was going to war with him.

I inquired how naval officers could interfere. They could not go on shore and undertake to resist forcibly the civil authorities. Seward said things would never reach that point. We had only to let them know what we would do and that would end the difficulty. I expressed my dissent to such proceedings, to mere threats, and gasconading blasts to a weak government and people. The Attorney-General was very emphatic on two or three points. Stanton excepted to certain positions taken in regard to civil war.

No one seemed to second Seward, and he took back his dispatch to modify it. There was mischief under it. Seward has really the Presidential fever and flatters himself that he can swim on the current of acquisition of territory. The accession of Russian America, which is really not his work, although he has been the instrument, or agent, on our part in that transaction, has made him delirious. He is now crazy on the subject of obtaining territory, and his aim is to be a candidate on that specialty,

— the enlarging of our territory. The Isthmus of Panama, he thinks, may be obtained. The revolutionists have possession of the government in that State. He therefore proposes we shall resist them and at the same time refuse to recognize Mosquera, the President, whom he calls a usurper. In this state of things he himself disclosed his purpose inadvertently by saying there was a strong party there desirous of annexation to the United States, which, of course, will be likely to increase in numbers, if we make forcible and successful resistance against excessive taxes. If we relieve those who are under our flag, all will wish to come under it. There is no mistaking the design of Seward, who is not scrupulous where he has power and is without convictions or principle in such matters.

The Attorney-General read the remainder of his opinion on the Reconstruction bills. It is a document of ability and will cause the Radicals to resist. Not unlikely it may insure the assemblage of Congress, and an attempt to impeach the President if he carries into effect the policy marked out, — and I have little doubt he will. That is, he will disapprove the removal of the governors and judges, the prohibition against the assembling of legislators, the substitution of codes of law prepared by the military commanders, and ordered to go into effect as substitutes for the enactments and laws of the States, some of them in execution for more than two centuries. His efforts to preserve law and popular government will cause him to be denounced, and his impeachment will be demanded. The conspirators are watching their opportunity.

June 15, *Saturday.* Mrs. Admiral Goldsborough called on me to-day in great excitement and under much feeling, in regard to the retirement of her husband, which goes into effect next Tuesday, on which day he will have been fifty-five years in the service. It was a most unpleasant interview. She accuses me of cruelty and injustice, threatens that her husband will go to Congress, accuses me of prejudice against him for some cause she knows not what, says I have some favorite whom I wish to promote, etc. Until within a few months she admits I have been friendly and kind, but since this question has come up, I have been obstinate and unreasonable. She said she had been to the President and he told her I had never submitted the case to him, which she thought very cruel; that I had once or twice talked over the case with him, but had not submitted it for his decision. It was in vain that I tried to explain to her that there was nothing for the President to decide; that the law controlled in this matter; that these cases were never submitted to the President; that when an officer attained the age of sixty-two he went on to the retired list, unless he received the vote of thanks, in which case he was not retired until he had been fifty-five years in service; that Admiral G. would have been fifty-five years in service next Tuesday. She denied it, and under her strong appeals I told her I would present the case to the President, and I did so this P.M. In an interview of more than one hour I went over the case with him. He had evidently been seen.

Mrs. Goldsborough told me that Judge Beach, her attorney, had seen the President on the subject. Reverdy Johnson, she said, had failed her; some officers had influenced him, but she did not tell me who.

While we had the subject under discussion, Seward came in. He said Mrs. Goldsborough had been to him. He declined to act. She said it would come up in Cabinet, and he told her if so he would give it consideration.

The President asked what he had to do with the matter anyhow. I replied he was expected to reverse my conclusions if wrong, or if he supposed them wrong; that I had brought the subject to his notice by special request of Mrs. G. and because the Admiral himself was absent; that the law was to my mind clear and explicit, but that for myself, while I had no doubts on the subject, I should not feel aggrieved if overrode and my action set aside, farther than as it might affect the service. Personally I have none but friendly feelings towards Admiral G., but I do not think he is entitled to fifty-nine years, as he claims.

The President, as I was about leaving this long interview, spoke of his proposed journey to Boston; [1] asked how long since I had been to Connecticut, and intimated very strongly a wish that I would accompany him. I told him I should, of course, obey any order. He said he could give no order in these cases; he was invited and it would be pleasant to have me along as companion. Seward and Randall had volunteered to go to North Carolina with him. I told him I regretted it and would have preferred he should have gone only with his family and personal staff. I thought it would be much better if none of his Cabinet went with him to Boston. The Masons had invited him, but none of the Cabinet, and I thought we should be considered intruders. Besides, I believed the impression would be better if he went without any of us. I know the Boston Masons don't want Seward.

June 20, *Thursday.* The week has been one of incessant, unremitting labor. Cabinet-meetings of protracted length have been held daily, requiring constant and earnest attention in addition to current business. The chief subject of deliberation in Cabinet has been the Attorney-General's opinions on Reconstruction. The President, unfortunately I think, yielded to Mr. Stanbery, who naturally believes his professional children remarkable and worthy of universal nursing, and assented to a proposition to have a record of Cabinet proceedings kept and the vote of each member on each point recorded.

No one could object to this course, if the President required it, although I said to one or two that I preferred the old course, — let the President require in writing the opinion of each member. Then if either wishes to state

---

[1] President Johnson attended the laying of the corner-stone of a new Masonic Temple in Boston, June 24, 1867.

his reason for the opinion he entertains and expresses, he has the opportunity.

But Stanbery had another course. I think the plan was concocted by both. The President is nervous and apprehensive. He has, not without cause, an aversion to the reassembling of Congress during the regular vacation, for he knows the object is war upon himself. Striving to do right, intending to do no wrong, he is assailed and denounced for laboring to carry into effect the strange, wicked, abominable, unconstitutional Reconstruction acts, as they are called.

In a few conversational remarks on the introduction of the subject on Monday, I repeated what I have before said on one or two occasions, — that the Reconstruction acts were so abominable, so flagrantly unconstitutional, that I did not feel inclined to have anything to do with them; but the President had a duty to perform and it was a duty on our part to advise and act when he required us. The Attorney-General had labored to raise an edifice which has no foundation, had worked out a system which seemed consistent with itself and the laws, and I was willing to acquiesce in his opinion in the detail or the aggregate. He had done more for popular rights, under a law which despotically deprived the people of their undoubted guaranteed rights, than I had supposed possible, and, while I was opposed to the Reconstruction laws, I assented to his expositions if the law was to go into effect.

McCulloch said something similar. Seward said he did not know about giving the entire credit of the exposition to Stanbery.

During the discussion and criticisms and agreements which occupied us for four days, it was obvious to my mind that Stanton was an original adviser if not the originator of these laws. He may not have drafted them, but he, and probably Holt in consultation with him, devised the plan of military, despotic government to rule the South. It was equally obvious that the President was most solicitous to conciliate and bring Stanton into harmonious action with himself and the rest of the Cabinet. But for past observation and experience, I should have concluded that we had reached a crisis and that we should now be united, or we should part. Such may have been the President's thought and intention, as it has been before, but it will end in nothing.

Stanbery was chief fugleman. Submitted his summary, pioneered, advocated, controverted, and managed his case. Stanton was antagonistic. Seward was pliable, plausible, often querulous, sometimes sensible, seldom earnest. Randall followed Seward, of course, especially when he was in harmony with the President. The views of McCulloch and myself have been stated. We were, under the circumstances, for acquiescing in the opinion and propositions which Stanbery had elaborated, though they were not our views. Stanton took direct issue with Stanbery. Their differences were fundamental. On the second day Stanton brought in a paper defining his position. He claimed that the laws established military governments and invested the commanders with absolute power. That they could displace and appoint officers in the civil or provisional State Governments, etc. I shall not particularize the differences in detail. Stanton did not attempt to justify the laws or to claim they were constitutional, but was for rigidly enforcing them, and for maintaining the despotic authority of the military governors; denied that the President could control them, and claimed that Rebels were disfranchised without conviction and without a law condemning them to disfranchisement for treason.

I listened to these differences over laws that were in direct conflict with the Constitution and without warrant from it. At the close I stated to the President and Cabinet that I had listened attentively to the discussion, but I wished to be distinctly understood as in no way giving my sanction to the bill; that I considered him as placed in an extraordinary and embarrassing position;

that he had sworn to support the Constitution and also
to see the laws faithfully executed; that the two were
incompatible; that in appointing military governors the
President has done all, perhaps, that could be expected
of him. But the governors disagreed, were not united
in opinion, were embarrassed how to proceed, and had
applied to him for instruction. He had very properly
referred the subject to the law officer of the Government,
who had given a very elaborate and able opinion, which I
was willing they should accept and carry out. But I was
quite as willing the President should go no farther than send
it out as the opinion of the law officer of the Government,
his construction of the act, and leave the generals to carry
on their respective governments, for I concurred with the
Secretary of War in the opinion that the majority of the
fragmentary Congress which enacted these laws intended
to strike down popular or civil governments and establish military supremacy, had undertaken to enact martial
law, — an absurdity and a solecism. During the War,
extraordinary power had been necessarily exercised, and
what was a sad necessity then had begotten this mon-
strosity now.

The time has come when this defective, arbitrary, unconstitutional, impracticable law is to be put in operation.
The President may attempt it, but he cannot succeed.
The Attorney-General has presented his ideas, and they
are condemned. A reassembling in July of the Congress
which enacted these usurping laws, is demanded. We are
threatened with this, if the will of these military governors, — viceroys, — who cannot interpret the act alike,
is interfered with. I have little doubt that Congress will
come together, and am willing they should. Let them pass
a declaratory or explanatory law of their own act. There
can be no unity among themselves unless opposed. They
disregard or set aside all constitutional limitations or
landmarks, all constricted restraints, and have substituted
their own will as omnipotent and above and beyond the

Constitution. Let them carry out their weak and wicked enactments. It is as legitimate for them to execute as to enact such laws.

The President was, I perceived, impressed with my remarks. Seward looked at me, amazed and thoughtful. Stanton for the first time seemed troubled.

Stanbery said that matters were pretty much as I stated, but the President must act, — must see the laws executed, — there is no evading that. I replied I did not propose evasion, but the President could send his, the Attorney-General's, exposition for these generals; that the Cabinet had assented that the views taken by him should go out as the view which the law officer of the Government took.

McCulloch asked if we had not gone too far to stop now. I answered no; that my opinions and convictions had undergone no change in consequence of any action taken or argument presented. I considered the law unconstitutional, and therefore action under it nugatory. It is defective and impracticable, aside from its unconstitutionality. The Attorney-General, to whom the President properly referred the subject, has worked out a theory which I assent to, so far at least as to advise the President to send it to the military governors, in response to their inquiries, as the opinion of the law officer of the Government, and that there may be uniformity in their proceedings. Not that I cared to give the monster shape; no harm would follow conflicting action on the part of the governors under the bills, or difference of interpretation. The fact that there are differences — that no two of them can agree as to the meaning and proper construction of these acts — was a commentary on such legislation. Now let Congress convene and tell what they really do mean. I have no doubt they intended to give the governors arbitrary and absolute power, to give suffrage to the negro, to exclude and proscribe most of the white population, to authorize refusal of jury trials for alleged offense, all of

3

which are unconstitutional, revolutionary, and can have no sanction or approval from me. This being my position on the laws, I was willing the opinion and theory of the Attorney-General should go out as *his* exposition, but I did not wish the President to give his sanction to the law, or be committed to it.

Randall said he did not see why that might not be done; that it might be said, whereas the generals were embarrassed in executing these laws, and had asked for instructions, the President had referred the subject to the Attorney-General and taken advice of the Cabinet, and had come to the following conclusion.

Stanton and Stanbery each wrote a preamble. I objected to the word "conclusion" in Stanton's, which, after emendation, I thought preferable to Stanbery's, which was an executive order adopting his opinion and theory.

Seward, who seemed shocked when I said Congress would in my opinion assemble on the 3d of July, appeared relieved after Stanton's preamble was read. It was Randall's, he declared. It was able, just the thing. This matter would go over, and all come right, he had no doubt of it.

June 21, *Friday.* The President left this morning for Boston. Seward accompanied him, and Randall, who left last evening, is to join him in New York. The papers this morning contain a statement of proceedings, or rather votes, in the Cabinet on the several points embraced in the summary of the Attorney-General. I did not understand that publicity was to be given to our doings in detail, though I care nothing about it, personally. A record of Cabinet doings is, itself, a novelty. I cannot say that I am pleased with the innovation. I should have preferred that the President call upon the members to give each his opinion in writing, and then that he should decide for himself. In that way the position and reasons of each member would be stated by himself. This published record states correctly my votes, and the votes of others also, on Stanbery's exposition and theory. It may be the true and accepted interpretation of the law; nevertheless the men who passed it, intended differently. They designed to break down the State Governments, to divest the President of all power except that of designating the military commanders and passing upon the death penalty, of which the legislative majority could not deprive him.

I should have been willing to leave this bad law to its own working, without devising a plan or system to carry it into effect. This was my suggestion, and the President, perhaps, intends to leave the subject in the form presented in these publications.

It has, however, as the case now stands, an unfortunate aspect for the President, — indicating timidity, a desire to have others share the responsibilities which belong to him. All this impairs his strength before the country. The President should make himself felt and understood as a power, should stand out prominent above others. But Seward and Stanton have dwarfed him, I fear, — made him hesitate and doubt when his own nature is to be firm.

I wrote hastily, and when tired and exhausted, a sketch of Cabinet proceedings on the matter of the Attorney-General's opinion.

I took to the Cabinet and read a strange dispatch from Commander Roe of the Tacony, who, under the advice of the American and British Consuls, took upon himself to seize Santa Anna,[1] place him on the ship in which he came to Vera Cruz, escort him twenty miles to sea, and forbid his return. It was an extraordinary proceeding, and I made it a point to read the whole dispatch in Cabinet. Seward said, "That was all right," and asked me to send him the dispatch, or a copy, for he wanted to keep the record. No one else seemed to trouble himself about the matter, except the President, who remarked

[1] The well-known Mexican general and president, at this time a revolutionary against the French.

that the Mississippi and the levees were giving us much trouble by the overflow, and he thought it might be a blessing if the waters could go on and drench Mexico and wash out her faithlessness. I regret that Roe should have permitted himself to be a tool of the consuls, though I doubt not his intentions were right, but I apprehended that some exceptions would have been taken to Roe's conduct, and that I might have to recall and take action in the case. As it is, I think the Admiral must give his attention to Mexican affairs.

June 22, Saturday. The President and party got through very well to New York, and all passed off pleasurably by accounts on board the Franklin, Admiral Farragut's flagship, which he visited. He passed directly through or past Philadelphia without stopping, the city authorities having failed to extend to him an invitation. It is a specimen of the old Whig spite of former days. The Radicals are the baser materials of that bygone party. Their Reconstruction acts, their disregard of constitutional obligations and limitations, and the general demoralization and corruption crop out, — are parts and parcels of the old bank-debauchers of 1834, and the Hard-Cider politicians of 1840.

I cannot but regret that President Johnson is so much under the influence of Seward, who is a man of expedients and not of sterling, fixed principle. His publication of Cabinet proceedings amuses me the more I reflect upon it. McCulloch tells me that he was as much surprised as myself when he saw that record in print; that he had no conception the President intended to publish it.

On Thursday evening, as I was riding out, I met Seward near Columbian College. He called to me, I being on horseback, and said that he thought the President had better get out his paper to-morrow (Friday) morning. It had been understood and agreed that he would issue an order to the military governors, in answer to their call

for information, communicating the summary of expositions of the Attorney-General. This I had thought would
relieve him of embarrassment in consequence of his vetoes, in which he had taken different views. Moreover, as
he had pronounced the acts unconstitutional, and was
sworn to support and defend the Constitution, he could
send out the opinion of the Attorney-General, the law
officer, as a guide for the generals and as conducive on
their part to uniformity of action.

But this publication of Cabinet proceedings is a different phase and, I think, an unfortunate one. I am apprehensive that Seward, in his interview on Thursday evening,
achieved it, although he made no intimation to me of such
a purpose, farther than to speak of that "paper" instead
of that "order." Stanbery, who is a good lawyer, lacks
certain qualities as a politician. He sometimes wants tact,
and is too sensitive for a public man. It would be in character with him to advise the publication. His opinion
has been violently assailed, and it soothes him to find that
the Cabinet, with one exception, sustains, or more properly
submits to and acquiesces in, his exposition. He was advising to, if not the originator of the proposition of making
a record of the views of each of the heads of the Departments. The results he feels to be a relief, and persuades
himself, perhaps, that the publication will relieve him
before the public.

June 24, *Monday.* An impudent and disrespectful, if not
disobedient, letter of Sheridan's is published on the subject of registration, in which he puts himself in opposition
to the President and his order to keep open registration
till August. I am apprehensive that the President will not
promptly detach him. How Stanton and Grant will act
and advise, I shall be glad to know.

They cannot, it appears to me, do otherwise than recommend his removal. Grant thinks much of Sheridan
as a brave, dashing officer, but he is unfit for the delicate

duties of civil governor, nor is his judgment in civil
matters worthy of much weight. He, Grant, may, in his
partiality, think reproof and a peremptory order sufficient.
Stanton knows that, were he in the President's position,
a telegram for Sheridan's removal could not get to New
Orleans quick enough, but what he will do and advise
under the circumstances is a question.

For twenty months the President has submitted to
humiliation from the War Department, has been tame,
passive, and submissive under palpable wrong, has seen
the military officers and the Army gradually alienated from
him by intriguing and cunning manipulation. So far as
delicacy and propriety would permit, he has been warned
and advised, has many times determined that he would
act resolutely, but at the crisis has from some malign influence faltered and failed until his Administration itself is a
failure. The President is no longer regarded as a power,
the head of the Government, because he fails to exercise
his undoubted authority in vindication of what he knows
to be right, but defers, delays, and suffers.

The Army and officers generally were with him in his
Reconstruction policy at the commencement, as they were
with Mr. Lincoln, who initiated it. Stanton was not, and
Howard was not, — though the latter was not contumacious, — and Holt was not. Stanton and Holt were in
Buchanan's Cabinet; had been mixed up with the Secessionists for a time, and the hostility between them and
the Rebels became implacable. Hate was mutual.

Neither Stanton nor Holt desired immediate reconciliation or an early restoration of the Union, for that would
necessitate their retirement. Their policy, therefore,
never was and could not be the policy of the President,
for he desired speedy peace, harmony, and good will between States and sections. All their efforts, all their influence, has been in another direction. Yet the Secretary of
War, exercising this influence, using and abusing his power
and patronage, aided by Seward, has been able to hold his

place and so far to control, not only his Department, but in a great degree the Administration.

Seward, who has not been, like Stanton and Holt, opposed to an immediate restoration of the Union, has nevertheless been the constant supporter and friend of Stanton, has constantly impressed upon the President the necessity of retaining that gentleman in his Cabinet as essential to his Administration. The two — Seward and Stanton — have steadily played into each other's hands, Stanton all the time strengthening and fortifying himself and all the time weakening the President and bringing the Administration and its measures into disfavor.

June 25, Tuesday. The papers publish a letter from General Sickles to Senator Wilson, in which he says the Secretary of the Navy will do nothing in favor of the Reconstruction laws. Congress appropriated $500,000 to carry into effect Reconstruction; $5,000,000 will be required. Only a small appropriation was made to begin with, in order to delude and cheat the people into acquiescence, but millions will be expended. To make up the deficiency, money and means are to be stolen from other sources, other appropriations, and other Departments. Sickles sent to me for two steamboats to be placed at his service. I had neither boats, officers, crews, nor money for him. Congress had placed no appropriation at my disposal for such purpose.

June 26, Wednesday. The President has been courteously and properly received by the people of New England, — a striking contrast with some portions of the Northwest. None of the governors have run away, — absented themselves like Morton, Oglesby,[1] and others. Sumner and Wilson do not appear to have been present, or mingling with the authorities. The President has spoken less than when he went West. It would be better were he and all

---

[1] Governors of Indiana and Illinois respectively.

Presidents to avoid addressing miscellaneous public assemblages. And so of the Secretaries. Seward in his speeches indicates an intention of being a candidate for President and to run on the territorial acquisition claim. The purchase of Russian America has demented him in this direction, and he really flatters himself, though doubtingly, that the people will rally around him. He has, however, no party, no popular strength, and his retention in the Cabinet has greatly injured the President. It is unfortunate that the President does not realize this and that the constant companionship of Seward is a mistake for both.

A telegraph from Calcutta informs us of the wreck of the Sacramento in the Bay of Bengal, Collins commanding. This is a misfortune, but no loss of lives, thank Heaven. Collins is an honest, straightforward, patriotic man. He has not, I think, particular love or aptitude for the service.

June 27, Thursday. Montgomery Blair has become quite indifferent in regard to the fate of President Johnson. Says he is completely under the dominion of Seward and Stanton, who have demoralized him; that the President has listened to them until he has become nervous and apprehensive, without resolute courage to carry out or maintain his conviction, and that he is in constant dread of impeachment.

Blair is shrewd and observing, though of strong prejudices. He thinks it absolutely necessary to revive the Democratic Party and its organization in order to rescue the government from centralizing hands. This has been the policy of himself and some others for some time past. The policy has its disadvantages as well as advantages. One cause of the failure of the Union movement a year since was the attempt to bring forward as leaders and candidates those Democrats who had made themselves obnoxious for their extreme partisanship, and especially their opposition to the measures of the Government for the preservation of the Union. The people were not disposed to invest Copperheads, Rebel sympathizers, and Rebels with power while the soil was yet wet with the blood of patriots, and Blair and others injure themselves at this time in pressing forward prematurely that class of persons. In the conversation to-day we spoke of Grant in connection with the Presidency, and from present indications I expressed the opinion that he was disposed to be a candidate, and if so, he would probably be elected. Blair said he could not be if he was the Radical candidate. I said Grant would endeavor to be the Army and Union candidate; without much political intelligence or principle, he had party cunning and would strive to be a candidate but not strictly a party candidate; that the Radicals did not want him, but they could not help themselves, nor perhaps could Grant. They felt that they must nominate him in order that they might succeed; he felt that he could not reject their candidacy, if they took him up, but really prefers the Democrats to the Republicans.

Blair has been and still is friendly to Grant, but perceives that G. is becoming alienated from old friends and getting in with new ones, and it arouses his opposition. I asked whom he would have for a candidate in opposition to Grant. He said he cared not who it was. Nor I, was my reply, but whom can you present? He said McClellan. That, said I, insures defeat. The people will not, and I think ought not to, rally under him.

We then had some talk on the War and the generals. Grant, he said, was after all the only real general we had. Not that he had the genius and mental resources of Sherman, but he had dogged courage, unwavering persistency. No other general had these qualities. His remarkable conduct in the campaign, and the slaughter between the Wilderness and Richmond, Blair admitted were horrible. Still, Grant never flagged or doubted. Having got in the neighborhood of Richmond, he smoked his cigars and waited, until Sherman reached the seaboard and was

coming up through the Carolinas, when the Te Deum of
the nation, which was singing hosannas to Sherman,
roused Grant to the necessity of doing something lest
there should be another and greater hero who would
eclipse him. This led to Grant's final blows, for, Wilmington
having been captured, Grant could have remained quiet
and Sherman would have marched steadily up in the rear
of Richmond. In that event, it would have been Sherman's
name, not Grant's, and this, though Sherman's friend, he
would not permit.

Blair says he once inquired of Grant why he moved at
all when there was no necessity, and the final close was
inevitable. Grant was a little puzzled to answer for a
moment, but replied that he did it, not from military
necessity or any strategic purpose, but to suppress sectional animosity. All the hard fighting and successes had
been by Western men; the Army of the Potomac was distinguished for no great success; they had remained calm
before Richmond, having all in their grip, it was true, but
if the Western army, after marching to the sea, came up
and captured Richmond while the Eastern army was in
camp, there would have been jealousy and sectional feeling growing out of it. It was the selfish jealousy of Grant
himself, whose feelings towards Sherman exceeded those
of the sections in the West.

June 28, Friday. A committee to inquire into the ordnance transactions of the War and Navy Departments,
composed of as unprincipled a set of scoundrels, with
scarcely an exception, as is in Congress, is in session. I have
told Wise, Chief of Ordnance in Naval Bureau, to give
them every facility for inquiry; if he, or any one had done
wrong, I desired it should be exposed. This startles Wise,
who is nervously excitable, and not over-profound and
firm, and who, I have sometimes thought, was a little too
intimate with some of the larger contractors, — not that
I have ever believed him corrupt or pecuniarily interested.

How he will succeed before the committee, who will try
to confuse and bewilder him, is uncertain. He is pretty
sagacious, but mentally timid, though not, I apprehend,
wanting in physical courage. Of the transactions of the
Ordnance Bureau I have known less than of any others.
Their contracts are excepted from advertisements, their
business a specialty. President Lincoln busied himself
in that branch and Wiard and Ames, two disappointed
contractors whom he favored, are pets of the committee.

June 29, *Saturday.* Admiral Farragut sailed yesterday
from New York in the Franklin for Europe, to take command of the European Squadron. My two youngest sons
have gone with him. I know no better man to whom to
intrust them. One is his private secretary; the other is
clerk to Pennock, who is Captain of the Franklin.

The President and party are expected home to-day.
They have had, apparently, a pleasant tour. Too much
speaking, but less than in the Chicago jaunt last year.

June 30, *Sunday.* Called this morning on the President
and congratulated him on his safe return and in apparently
improved health. He was very cordial, disposed to talk.
Was not fully posted on occurrences and events of the
last ten days. Talked of Sheridan, of Congress, of Stanbery's opinions, etc. In regard to Stanton, he expressed
himself convinced that he had played a part for himself,
had an understanding with the violent Radicals, had embarrassed the Administration and thwarted its policy;
and he was surprised that Stanton should persist in holding on to his place, and mixing with us. I remarked it
was now of little consequence. He had so managed with
the Radicals as to cripple the Administration until it
was powerless, and he might remain on to the close, or
he might leave soon. The President assented; presumed
Stanton intended to be a candidate.

L

Seward proposes to purchase Two Islands from Denmark for $7,400,000 —
Cabinet Discussion of Sheridan's Letter to Grant — Maximilian shot in
Mexico — Congress meets in Extra Session — General Halleck proposed as Commissioner to go to Alaska — Seward justifies Commander
Roe in the Capture of Santa Anna — Stanton ignores the President in
addressing a Communication directly to the Speaker of the House —
Reconstruction Bill passed — The Influence of Seward and Stanton on
the Administration — Conversation with a Member of the British Parliament on Constitutions and Reconstruction — The President vetoes
the Reconstruction Bill without consulting the Cabinet — Congress
passes a Resolution of Sympathy with Cretan Insurrectionists —
General Banks calls to urge a Removal and an Appointment — The
President's Leniency in Matters of Pardon — Troops sent to Tennessee
— Grant's Change of Views — General Rousseau proposed for Sheridan's Place — Proposal to appoint Frederick Douglass to the Head of
the Freedmen's Bureau — The President receives Papers revealing a
Conspiracy to manufacture Evidence against him — Sheridan removes
Governor Throckmorton of Texas and appoints E. M. Pease in his Place
— McCulloch discouraged at the Political Outlook.

July 2, Tuesday. At the Cabinet-meeting to-day Seward
brought forward a proposition to purchase of Denmark
the two smaller islands in the West Indies for $7,400,000.
Stanton and Randall strongly supported him. McCulloch doubted; was willing the subject should be presented
and submitted to the Senate, though, if himself a Senator, would vote against it.

Stanbery claimed not to be sufficiently posted to act,
but his impressions were against it. I was perhaps strongest in opposition of any; stated we wanted these islands
for no present purpose; that, St. Thomas being a free
port, we had every facility we could have were these
islands ours; that the population is not American; the
possession would be costly to keep and maintain; that
the country was enormously in debt and needed the millions more than these islands; that in the event of a for-

eign war we could easier and at less expense capture one or more islands than hold them.

Seward, a little nettled by my views, said we wanted a station in the West Indies for naval coaling purposes, and we could not have Samaná, — that was ended. I said I was glad of it; I had never wanted Samaná, and I wished this Danish matter was ended also. Still, as the others assented, and the Secretary of State urged its importance for ulterior purposes which he claims the Senate will sanction with unanimity, I would not oppose its going to that body. McCulloch took much the same view.

The truth is, Seward has become almost a monomaniac on the subject of territorial acquisition, that being the hobby on which he expects to be a candidate for President. It shows itself in everything.

The subject of Sheridan's insulting and impertinent, disrespectful and disobedient letter to General Grant, which is in the newspaper, was brought forward by the President, who said he had received no official notice of the letter, — knew nothing of it save what he saw in the newspapers and the remarks of others.

The Attorney-General was emphatic against the letter; said it was insolent and insubordinate, and could not be passed without notice.

Stanton said the letter had not been communicated to him officially; that, if authentic, as he did not question it was, Sheridan had, perhaps, been rebuked already by General Grant for his impulsiveness; that the letter might have been stolen from the telegraph by some of the newspaper correspondents and published without the knowledge and against the wishes of Sheridan. He would advise that the matter should pass without producing any inquiry.

Seward said he had very little doubt that the matter had got into the papers as Stanton suggested, and probably without Sheridan's knowledge. It was published in the *Herald* on Sunday, and they had in some way got hold of it. He never noticed newspaper articles; would not notice this. I said it was not a newspaper article, but an official document from Sheridan's headquarters and signed by Sheridan himself. While I was not prepared to say what course had best be taken in regard to it, I by no means assented to the suggestion that the document had been surreptitiously obtained or that it was not written expressly for publication. No man could read it and say he believed it was a private, unofficial communication to General Grant. It was intentionally disrespectful to the President, and had been so received and considered by friends and opponents.

Stanton said it was an improper letter, and if it had been addressed to him, he should have rebuked Sheridan, not only for what he said of the President but for the allusion to the Attorney-General, the head of a Department.

McCulloch thought we had better get along without taking much notice of the letter, as the President had never received it officially. To move in it would stir up excitement without doing any good. I was aware from previous conversation with McCulloch that he wished to avoid collision with Congress, and that he had very little confidence that the President would take a stand against Sheridan and persist in it, backed as he would be by Stanton and Grant. He said to me that Stanton would control the President on this or any subject that had a military bearing or connection, sooner than the true men in his Cabinet. I was therefore more grieved than surprised at McCulloch's remark.

Randall said very little, but did not know what could be done, though the letter was very improper.

Stanbery and Stanton differed essentially and discussed some points. The President produced a dispatch from Sheridan of the 29th ult., stating he should continue registration until August as ordered. As the Secretary of War had not the correspondence between Grant and Sheridan, the President thought it best to defer the farther discus-

sion of the subject until it was procured, and he would
probably call a special Cabinet-meeting for its consideration.

Delay, of course, destroys the effect, if it does not prevent any action. I remained with the President to dispose
of some Department business after the others had left,
and said to him that promptness and decision were important in matters of this kind; that in postponing action
he was suffering before the country, and in a few days
nothing could be done. He agreed with me, and said he
would have sent for Grant when Stanton made known
that he had not the correspondence, but the session had
been so long that he could not have got him to the council
in season. Then, as regards Stanton's remark that he had
no copy of the letter,—that it had not been communicated to him,—"Do you suppose," asked the President,
"that there has been communication between Grant and
Stanton about that letter?" I replied that it could hardly
be otherwise than that they should have conversed and
interchanged views on such a paper which was before the
public, and probably there was an understanding between
them that it should be kept back and officially communicated. And that was the foundation of Stanton's proposition that the subject should pass without pressing any
inquiry.

The President's hesitating and irresolute disposition
and the influence of Seward and Stanton will be very likely
to prevent any special Cabinet-meeting, and perhaps any
farther steps in this matter. McCulloch is hopeless.
Randall will fall in with Seward. Stanbery feels wounded
personally, as well as being indignant that the President
should be treated with such disrespect. He may rouse the
President to vindicate himself and his office. I have said
in the Cabinet and in private all that is proper I should
say, without much effect.

July 3. On Sunday evening I received a dispatch from

Commander Roe that Maximilian, the *quasi* Emperor of Mexico, was shot on the 19th of June. It is one of the mistakes of that unhappy and distracted country. Apprehensions are entertained that the European powers will attempt to avenge his death, but I do not participate in those apprehensions. Europe has learned a lesson on the impolicy of interference in the fate of Maximilian and the results of French intrigues in that country.

Vera Cruz still holds out. No exceptions have as yet been taken to Roe's course in seizing Santa Anna. As he has been since taken from the Virginia at Sisal by the Mexicans, they may summarily dispose of him, though for a generation he has, like a cat, alighted on his feet when thrown, seemingly, down a precipice.

Congress met to-day. A quorum was present, though I am sorry to see many, perhaps most, of the Democrats are absent. There is, it is true, not only no public necessity for the meeting of Congress, but a public injury from its coming together. Still, as the majority had desired it, with them be the responsibility. Members individually should do their duty.

There is a malignant and revolutionary spirit among the leading Radicals, who continue to be reckless and utterly regardless of the Constitution. These men will desire to push measures to extremes, in the belief that they can thereby retain their party ascendancy. But it will not surprise me if the means to which they must resort shall react and overthrow them. Indeed, I expect it. They cannot go on with these violent and proscriptive measures without rousing indignation, and if any regard for the Constitution remains, the people, though strangely indifferent, will rally to its defense.

July 5, Friday. Yesterday, the 4th, was a quiet day, more quiet than Sunday. It was to me a day of rest, and I enjoyed it.

No matter of special importance was to-day before the

Cabinet. Seward and McCulloch arranged for a revenue cutter to Sitka. Stanton proposed that Halleck should be the Commissioner, and Seward concurred. I did not like it, for I do not like Halleck, but I said nothing. Neither did the President nor any other member of the Cabinet.

The President made no allusion to Sheridan's order and his correspondence with General Grant.

In Congress but little was done except to determine to reconstruct Reconstruction. Sumner and some of the extreme Radicals were not satisfied with this conclusion, and there is really so little sense and wisdom in Congress that there is no certainty they will adhere to their determination. They evidently know not what they want, nor how to do it.

On the 2d of March they passed their Reconstruction Bill, — their first step since the fall of Richmond. Two years were wasted in intrigues how not to reëstablish the Union. The succeeding Congress, which met two days after promulgating the Reconstruction Act, passed a supplemental bill to correct deficiencies and weaknesses, and another bill, limiting expenses to five hundred thousand dollars. Three bills in less than one month, and now Congress is again assembled to further legislate on the subject, and declare they will take up no other subject. They have no confidence in themselves.

Generals Schenck and Logan have undertaken to exclude all the Kentucky Representatives from the House because they are not Radicals. These two lawyer generals are Radical electioneerers. Schenck opposes Barnum of Connecticut, whose election is disputed because he used money. I have no idea that he used more if as much as his Radical opponent, and Schenck knows that Indiana and some other States have been secured to the Radicals by fraud and corruption. This move is to turn attention from their own villainies to another quarter, and to throw discredit on their opponents. The use of money is destroying confidence in our elections.

3

July 9, *Tuesday.* The dispatch of Sheridan was not alluded to. As Congress is in session, and calls for correspondence are made, the omission is not singular, but I apprehend the whole will be shuffled over.

The House of Representatives made haste, by a strict party vote, to pass a resolution of thanks to Sheridan for insolence and insubordination. No official communication, no report of any committee called for thanks, but his discourteous and highly improper letter had been published, — the publication being itself an act of insubordination, — and a vote of thanks is given him by the Radical legislators in the House of Representatives. The Senate has not sunk quite to the level of the House, and the resolution has been checked in that body.

Some differences are manifested among the Radicals in both houses. Some of the more intelligent and sagacious have mustered sufficient courage to oppose the extremists.

July 10, *Wednesday.* The loose, reckless violence and inconsiderate action of Congress make it irksome and painful for me to read their proceedings. How little regard have the members for their oaths and their country's welfare! The worst principles of tyranny and outrage they avow and encourage. The President is coarsely, falsely, and vindictively assailed by leaders as well as by followers, who are secretly prompted. The Constitution and its limitations are ridiculed and condemned.

Senator Wade equivocates and backs down from his recent aggressive speech. Instead of a step in advance, as he boasted, he takes a step to the rear.

A curious letter in the *New York Herald*, reciting a conversation and certain avowals of Thad Stevens, is attracting attention, and he to-day on the floor of the House made remarks on the letter. Almost all which this vicious old man does is premeditated, dramatic, and for effect. The letter was evidently carefully prepared by himself.

Not that he wrote it, but the correspondent had the catechism and answers furnished him. Stevens is perhaps a worthy leader for such a party, — the "Great Commoner."

July 11, *Thursday.* Some discourse in the House to-day, followed by votes, indicates a division in the House on the subject of impeachment. There is no cause, excuse, or justification for the long, labored, and shameful proceeding on this subject. The President differs with the Radicals, and justly and properly views their course with abhorrence. He sometimes expresses his burning indignation against measures and men that are bringing untold calamities upon the country.

July 12, *Friday.* Seward read a long document on the subject of the capture of Santa Anna, fully justifying Commander Roe, and approving his course and that of our consul at Vera Cruz.

Stanton presented two communications, which he proposed to send to Speaker Colfax, asking an appropriation of $5,000,000 for Indian wars and an additional $1,600,000 for Reconstruction. This latter was so worded as to create a false impression, leaving it to be supposed that this is the whole sum, whereas there was already half a million appropriated for the latter purpose, making over two millions. Much of this, a considerable percentage, will be expended in Radical electioneering.

I objected to the head of a Department addressing communications of this character to the Speaker and claimed that application for such appropriation should properly go through the President. No one differed from me but Stanton, who said very little. Seward saw that Stanton was vexed, and he put in a garrulous mess of pottage, about his always sending to Congress through the President, and believed it was proper for the heads of Departments generally to do this. But sometimes, he said, the Secretary of War had occasion to go direct to Congress, and on the whole, he thought it was well enough, — perhaps best; he approved of it. I insisted that it was neither respectful nor right to ignore the President at any time, and especially now, when Congress was trying to degrade and belittle the office. I thought no head of a Department should encourage the schemers by passing by the President.

The President, I saw, felt hurt, and made a remark or two, but concluded by telling Stanton that the Secretary of War would do as he thought best. "Then," said Stanton, "I will send both communications to the Speaker." "Very well," said the President. Pshaw!

This is the way things go on. Congress has got another edition of Reconstruction law about completed, which robs the President of his constitutional rights, transfers his powers to the General of the Army, the military governors, and the Secretary of War. Seward, who is chief counselor and Stanton's supporter, will not dissent from this, but, if he says anything, will advise acquiescence. Stanton is in concert with the Radicals in these aggressive matters, as the President knows, and has himself said to me. I do not expect, therefore, that any becoming stand will be taken to vindicate the executive prerogative, and it is perhaps too late, if there were energy and decision, to attempt it. Steady, constant aggression, and tame, passive yielding under the assuming and calculating Stanton and the pliant, flexible Seward have effectually broken down the Administration. I shall be thankful if it does not break down the government.

July 13, *Saturday.* Seward overtook me this evening as I was riding out on 14th Street, and says he has sent me a copy of his long statement in regard to the capture of Santa Anna. He evidently thinks it a great paper, and prides himself on its properties.

I understand the two houses have passed their Reconstruction Bill. Thad Stevens took occasion to sneer at those who still clung to the remnants of the shattered Constitution, which he ridiculed as a thing of the past. He is one of those who never regarded it as more obligatory than the resolutions of a last year's party convention. Its overthrow and destruction he would consider a party triumph. This is the spirit and feeling of the "Great Commoner," the Radical leader.

July 15. There is among the Congressional majority who call themselves Republicans or Radicals a wide difference, but there is want of patriotism with some, and of tact and talent with all. They are incompetent and vicious. The violent leaders are coarse and vulgar; the more conservative are weak and cowardly. The former defy, ridicule, and disregard the Constitution; the latter dare not defend it. Both can unite against the Administration, which adheres to the great principles of the fundamental law and maintains the rights of the States and the union of the States.

Unfortunately for the President, his chief adviser has no faith in the principles which the President most regards. Seward has no faith, nor has he any strength. To the President the Secretary of State is an element of weakness. The people have no confidence in him and they doubt and distrust the President, who has. His association with Lincoln weakened the power of the Administration. Still Seward does not oppose, resist, or attempt to coerce the President, but the latter knows he is from the great State and erroneously believes him the chief of a great party.

Stanton is more positive; but would often fail were he not aided by the sinuous, pliable, flexible Seward. The two hunt in couples, and, though of different temperaments, are both of them subtle and have a full understanding to stand by each other. Both are playing a game, and the cunning, wily Mephistopheles is outwitted by Mars. Stanton is treacherous. Seward is not, though a dissembler.

Stanton, while a part of the Administration, acts with the Radicals, and in a great measure directs their movements. They trust him; they hate and despise Seward.

To the President, Seward is always pliant and yielding, yet he contrives to do much towards shaping the President's course and often sadly misleads him.

Stanton sometimes plants himself in opposition to the President, and, when honest and sincere, not infrequently carries his point, though its rectitude may be questionable. When, however, he perceives that the President is resolute and determined, Stanton becomes as humble and obsequious as Uriah Heep. The President, who is courteous and attentive to all, is extra so to Stanton, — is more particular, I think, to salute him than any one else. This is more formal than earnest, and the politeness is reciprocal.

Stanton is sometimes more presuming because he knows he has a supporter or friend in Seward who will apologize for and excuse him. Between them the President has been prostrated and his Administration made powerless. From this, Stanton may, in certain contingencies, profit; but Seward cannot.

Both these men played a double part during the closing months of Buchanan's Administration. While ostensibly opposed, they had a secret understanding and were in constant communication. Stanton betrayed the South, and they know it. He knows that they know it, and hence he is not anxious that they should have power or influence in the Government whilst he is here. Whatever the President does, or proposes, to reëstablish the South is secretly, sometimes openly, counteracted and defeated; the measure is resisted, and he is denounced as a traitor to the party that elected him, — not to the country, — as sympathizing with traitors, because he strives to ameliorate the condition of the people of the South, to promote general harmony, and to reëstablish the people and the States that have rebelled in the Union.

July 16. The President is disinclined to appoint Otterbourg, the German, or German Jew, Minister to Mexico,
although Seward is very persistent for him. Randall originally proposed Otterbourg and would be pleased to have
him promoted, but, seeing the President's hesitancy, does
not press it. Seward, however, holds on vigorously.

Judge Chase has had it published that he has gone to
Albany to attend a wedding. It was a morning wedding
in the family of Judge Harris. This pretext of Chase is
to cover an electioneering tour. He still at times has the
Presidential mania.

Wade, who is also diseased with the Presidential fever,
has lost his vivacity and form, — is tame and passive; —
his "jump forward" in anticipation [?] has apparently
broken his knee-joints or backbone.

The Japanese indemnity was again up. They request
delay in last installment. Seward is not disposed to grant
it, and was anxious to push the matter by, without much
talk or explanation. Although unpleasant to always oppose, or to express dissenting opinion, I again spoke of my
regret that we were mixed up with England and France
in that matter, and thought we should suffer no wrong by
extending to them this favor which they asked.

I read my letter to the Speaker in answer to a resolution
introduced by Schenck, calling for information touching
the retention of Rear-Admiral Goldsborough on the active
list beyond fifty-five years. Schenck's brother, Commodore S., is, like other officers, affected, and dissatisfied that
my decisions and the usage of the Department are overruled. Seward, I saw, was disturbed; thought Stanton
should examine the letter and suggest alterations. S. and
I both declined.

In a conversation with Mr. Cave, a member of the British Parliament, who called on me with Chevalier Wykoff,
some conversation took place in regard to what is called
the British Constitution and our own, the two governments
and that of Mexico, France, etc. I remarked that the great

difference between the Teutonic and the Latin race consisted in the fact that the former had faith and the latter had not, — that Anglo-Saxons trusted each other, adhered to their traditions, observed and preserved the great principles of freedom; if there were abuses and departures from the great landmarks, a speedy return to first principles was required and exacted by the people; that these underlying principles were what was called the English Constitution, unwritten but understood, adhered to and loved by the English people, who had made them the basis on which their governmental superstructure was built. We Americans had embodied the great principles of freedom in a written constitution which all could read and understand, and from which those who were intrusted with legislative, executive, or judicial authority could not ignorantly wander. But, unhappily for us, our written Constitution is at this time no check or barrier against legislative abuse. The organic law is violated. A fragment of Congress has usurped the powers of government, trampled on the Constitution, and is exercising undelegated authority. This fragment had overthrown the constitutions of ten States and established military governments in their stead, had broken down the rights and power of the Executive and virtually declared themselves omnipotent and supreme.

In due time I trusted and believed these abuses would be remedied and the Constitution restored. A reaction usually follows excessive action, and our countrymen would before long correct Congressional errors and usurpations.

The Latin race, unlike the Teutonic, had not fixed, steadfast principles. Their changes are impulsive and revolutionary, and their governments are established and maintained by force. The popular element had no abiding faith, no well-recognized principles around which the people could rally. In other and plain words, they had no fixed principles embodied in a written constitution like the American, or unwritten but well-grounded and known law like that of England.

What is most to be apprehended among us, perhaps, is
a change in the habits, thoughts, and character of our people, brought about by a mixture of races, resulting from
emigration and from the present attempt to bring the negro
race into the government. Neither the emigrants nor the
negroes understand or can comprehend the foundation
principles of American and British freedom.

The Radical Party in their humanitarianism were striving to establish universal equality and individual liberty,
without conventional rules, and regardless of constitutional freedom and constitutional restraints and limitations. In order to promote, and with a view of exalting,
the negro, the Radicals did not scruple to trample on the
rights of the white men, rights inherent and secured by
all that was sacred and inviolate in the organic law.

July 22. Congress adjourned on Saturday. The President sent in his veto on the supplemental bill on Friday.
It is stated that all the Cabinet except Stanton gave
the veto their approval. For my own part, I neither saw
it, heard it read, nor knew its contents until I saw it in
the newspapers. McCulloch says the same, and I have
reason to suppose this of others. My opinion is that no
one but Stanbery was cognizant of it. He probably had
the principal preparation of it, though the President
himself does more in the preparation of these documents
than is generally supposed.

Stanbery is a good lawyer and takes a professional or
lawyer's view of questions rather than a statesman's or
politician's. Sometimes he is a little too technical, and too
much inclined to exhibit the attorney's knowledge and
capacity. Seward always defers to him. I do not remember
when he has dissented, though he may have been embarrassed and compelled to trim if Stanton arrayed himself
in opposition, as he often does.

The veto is, in its general features, essentially as I supposed it would be. Had I leave to advise, I would have

counseled brevity. There was no necessity of extended argument to such a Congress. No reasoning or truths, however cogently presented, would influence a single Member. The leading Radicals were predetermined, and their followers had not the moral courage to act out an honest, independent opinion. The bill, like its predecessors, is flagrantly unconstitutional, anti-republican and despotic, but there is the essence and spirit of Radicalism.

There is extreme bitterness among the Radicals, which manifested itself in the Senate and the House. Chandler, coarse, vulgar, and violent, assailed Fessenden, who was indignantly cowardly and apologetic to his furious antagonist.

July 23, Tuesday. Seward had a proclamation prepared against Mexican filibustering. The House had passed a resolution calling for it. I excepted to the paper, and especially to that part of it which said, "Now, therefore, I, A. J., being satisfied, etc., etc.," unless the President or Secretary of State had such information and was satisfied. If they had, or there was any necessity for a proclamation, I regretted that there should have been delay. . . . The President said he was aware of no reason for the step. Seward said there was nothing serious, nor did he suppose there would be, but he thought it prudent, under the circumstances, to send out the paper.

A more embarrassing subject was a resolution which had passed the two houses expressing sympathy with the insurrectionists in Crete, and requiring the Administration to communicate this fact to the Turkish Government. It was one of those loose, indiscreet measures which an inconsiderate Congress foolishly enacts. Seward had put his letter to the Minister in as unexceptionable a form as he could, but it can hardly be otherwise than offensive. The President regretted his attention had not been called to the subject, for he would not have signed the resolution. Seward said he knew not how the resolution originated. I told him that it originated with Morris, the Minister to Constantinople, and if it resulted in his recall or a request for him to leave, good might come of it. For months he had made himself busy in trying to induce our naval officers to break through neutrality and interfere in this insurrection.

July 24, *Wednesday.* General Banks called on me today with S. P. Hanscom in order to procure the removal of Mr. Hart, Naval Constructor, and the appointment of Isaiah Hanscom to the Charlestown Navy Yard. I told him I knew of no reason for a change; that Mr. Hart was discharging his duties faithfully and well, so far as I was advised. He said the people there were opposed to Mr. Hart, who was no naval constructor, but a mere boatswain, — that he governed the yard. I asked what he meant by saying Hart was not a constructor, but a boatswain. He had passed his examination first as an assistant constructor, and then as a constructor, — was educated a constructor. Hanscom was not. Well, he was unacceptable to the people. I asked wherein, — he was not a partisan as I had once heard. Banks said he busied himself in matters and things, and the people of the yard were against him. I said no such information had ever come to me; that Commodore Rodgers would have been likely to advise me if such were the case. He said Rodgers was under the influence of Hart.

"Am I to understand that you decline to remove him?" said B. in a loud voice.

"Certainly I do, as at present advised," I replied; "but I will inquire more particularly into this matter, and if you have any facts, — anything specific, — I should be glad to have you communicate them."

He said that was unnecessary; if I would not remove Hart, he must take other measures.

"Very well," said I, "a good officer cannot be removed

without cause. I regret the illness of Mr. Lenthall, Chief of the Construction Bureau, but I will myself look into this case farther. At present I shall not dismiss Hart."

July 25, Thursday. The President sent for me. He wished to dispose of the case of Major Field of the Marines, who was court-martialed last April and convicted, and was again subsequently court-martialed and again convicted. As the case is, in every view of it, bad, and the President has long hesitated, delaying from time to time acting, I had left the whole subject with him to dispose of when ready, expressing myself decidedly against Field. . . . Sam Randall has once or twice approached me, but I told him neither party nor personal feeling should be permitted to intrude; they would not with me; they ought not with the President.

. . . .

One of the greatest defects of the President, as Chief Magistrate, is a reluctance — an apparent incapacity — to discriminate in matters of pardon, or rather a failure to act on general principles. His sympathies for the criminal are easily enlisted in behalf of any man whom he has power to relieve. He lets off the drunkard, breaker of regulations, slanderer of the court, etc., etc., without reflecting on the demoralizing effect of his mistaken leniency on the service and the country.

July 26. The President showed me a telegram from Grant at Long Branch to Stanton. Grant says General Thomas has been ordered to Memphis; thinks it unnecessary for him (Grant) to go to Nashville; tells of troops that will be gathered at Memphis. The President said he was glad that regulars were moving into Tennessee, for it would have the effect of checking the movements of Brownlow's militia, who were striving to control the elections; but he compared the conduct of Stanton and Grant in the Tennessee election with that pursued by them in regard to Maryland. Last fall neither of them could get any armed force to Baltimore.

I recollect that Stanton was extremely sensitive at that time about overawing elections with troops. Grant, I think, had the impression that he, personally, could do better than soldiers, and deemed it more important that he should remain here and take charge of local elections than that he should go with Campbell to Mexico.

I remarked to the President that Grant had, unconsciously perhaps, very much changed his views within a year; that it was perceptible; that I had frequently alluded to this change; that Stanton, and Holt, and perhaps others had succeeded in twisting or modifying Grant's opinion and action. It had been with them a study, and he, the President, had permitted it to go on until they more than he were, in some respects, the Executive. The President recognized the truth of my remarks, and said, yes, Congress had conferred more power on the military governor than the President had ever exercised. "That," said I, "is but a part of the system. I know not that General Grant has been in the intrigue to cripple the President, though he has been, and is, used by the intriguers, — in my opinion, willingly used. You are advised to send General Halleck to Sitka. Seward has several times urged it. I do not think highly of Halleck, or his management, and do not wish the Administration to indorse him, or to give him additional reputation. He has got himself fastened on the Government for life, at high pay, without having rendered any valuable service."

In answer to the President as to who there had best be selected, I told him it was difficult to say, for most of the military officers had been gradually drawn into the Radical or Congressional policy through the manipulation of the War Department. But General Rousseau had been recently appointed, had borne himself well as a civilian, was, I understood, to go to Washington or Oregon. Why not let the transfer of Russian America be made to him?

The President hesitated a moment and said: "Rousseau is now at New Orleans. Here is a telegram from him, saying affairs are in a terrible condition there, and advising immediate correction. What would you, then, think of substituting him for Sheridan?"

"If Sheridan is to leave, my impression is that you cannot do better than select Rousseau, as things are. It is a pity, however, that this could not have been done earlier. The Radicals have been at great pains to enlist public opinion for Sheridan, in the full belief that he would, and conscious that he ought to, be removed. They have encouraged his insolence and insubordination in order to compel his removal, or to show that the Administration was too weak to vindicate itself. The managing Radicals know Sheridan's unfitness for administrative duties, but he is a brave and distinguished officer whom they are using, — availing themselves of his military reputation before the country. Had he been summarily disposed of when his insolent letter was written, or when he removed that trimming Governor Wells and the judge,[1] the people would have justified the act, and the Administration would have been strengthened for a righteous exhibition of energy. But the time has gone by for that display. There may be other causes."

The President again asked me what I thought of putting Fred Douglass at the head of the Freedmen's Bureau, instead of Howard. I said if he proposed to appoint negroes to any office, that perhaps would be as appropriate as any. Howard is a very good sort of man, but loose in taking and appropriating public property, and so intensely Radical that I wished him removed, and an overturn in the management of the Bureau.

But I was not prepared to appoint or recommend to be appointed to so responsible a position a person because he is a negro or a mulatto. Mr. Sumner and others have

[1] Judge Abell, who had declared the Louisiana convention of 1866 an illegal body.

expressed a hope that negroes would fill public and trusted positions, but I cannot. They may succeed, under their despotic and oppressive laws, in getting a few negroes into Congress, but there would, in all probability, be a sequence to this partisan negro philanthropy which would be calamitous to the poor negroes themselves.

July 30, *Tuesday.* But little of importance at the Cabinet-meeting. After we were through, the President requested me to remain for a few moments. Seward and Stanbery were not at the meeting, and are absent from the city. Mr. Hunter, who represented the State Department, was present for a short time, but had left, and Stanton was allowed to depart. McCulloch, Randall, Browning, and myself remained. The President said he had invited us to stop for a few moments, for some papers had just been placed in his hands of a character which seemed to him to deserve consideration.

It was, he said, proper for him to state that a woman representing herself as the wife of Conover,[1] now in prison, had called upon him, on, I think, the preceding Saturday evening, in behalf of her husband. She said promises and assurances of pardon had been held out to him by certain parties on condition he would do certain things, but he had been put off and tantalized until they (C. and his wife) knew not what to make of it. They had, however,

---

[1] Sanford Conover, *alias* Charles A. Dunham, convicted of perjury in connection with the trial of Jefferson Davis for complicity in Lincoln's assassination. The first communication referred to here, dated July 26, 1867, and received on Saturday, the 27th, was a petition for pardon accompanied by recommendations to clemency from Congressman Ashley, Judge-Advocate-General Holt, and A. G. Riddle, on the ground that while in jail Conover had disinterestedly aided in the prosecution of John H. Surratt. The communication of July 29, received on the 30th, was an extraordinary letter purporting to reveal a conspiracy into which Conover had entered with Ashley, Riddle, Holt, and B. F. Butler, to suborn testimony to show that President Johnson had been a member of the conspiracy to assassinate Lincoln. These papers were published on August 10, but they were regarded with some suspicion and Conover did not receive his pardon till February 9, 1869.

got a paper from Riddle,[1] indorsed by Judge-Advocate-General Holt, commending him to clemency. With this paper, there was, inadvertently, mixed up a note from Ashley, the impeaching Representative from the Toledo district, calling for the document. "Perhaps," said the President, "the best way will be to read the whole papers, but it will be proper to say that this note of Ashley led to further inquiry, which resulted in her bringing me this morning a petition from her husband and sundry papers, which I have detained for you to examine, and to give me your advice as to what had best be done with them."

He then called on Colonel Moore from the library with the papers, and directed him to read them. As they will doubtless be printed, I need say no farther here than that they furnish conclusive evidence of an atrocious conspiracy to impeach the President by manufactured testimony, which was to be furnished by this man Conover, *alias* Dunham, who was to be released from prison on condition he procured persons to testify as the parties desired.

When these papers had been read, and the surprise of all expressed, — not so much at the conspiracy, for none of us had any doubt of the villainy of the impeachment conspiracy (it is nothing else), but at the folly of Ashley and others in leaving traces of their intrigue and wickedness, — the President asked what should be done.

I advised that authenticated copies of the papers should be taken and lodged with different parties, and that the original should be carefully preserved. In this all concurred. The question then was as to disclosing the papers, — when and where. McCulloch and myself advised prompt publication. Randall advised delay to get other facts and testimony, — certain names and documents referred to. Browning hesitated, but was inclined to an early publication, and the President inclined to as little

[1] Albert Gallatin Riddle, an ex-Congressman, one of the counsel for the prosecution of Surratt.

delay as possible. Randall walked the room a few times and then came into that view also.

Conover, *alias* Dunham, after having been kept here by the court for months, had been suddenly hurried off to the penitentiary at Albany, so that he could not be seen. I told the President that was in consequence of Conover's wife having called on him, — that it satisfied me of what I had long believed, there were spies upon him and *in his household*. The fact that she had called on the President had been communicated to the conspirators, and C. was immediately hurried off to prevent him from having communication with any friend of the President to whom he might make disclosures.

It was concluded that we should meet again to-morrow, and in the mean time, each was to revolve the matter in his mind and bring the results of his reflections to the meeting. The President expected Mrs. Conover to call upon him to-morrow, and would ascertain if she had other papers or facts, but she would make no promises to procure them.

July 30. At the meeting to-day the President and the four members of his Cabinet who were together yesterday again took up the subject of the conspiracy and Conover's disclosures. Randall was again very earnest for postponing any publication until the names of the two witnesses referred to in Conover's petition could be ascertained and also the memoranda of the testimony which was wanted, and which they were to swear to, were procured. Ashley alluded to those papers in one of his notes, and is evidently anxious to get them. Randall says that as soon as it is known that C. has betrayed them, they will hasten to get these papers and to bribe these men. McCulloch gave in to these suggestions and was for delay, in order to make a perfect and complete thing of it. Browning was disposed to take the same view.

I suggested that a delay and failure to procure the

3

papers and names would weaken the case, and it would be well to look at all sides of the question. Would not the publication be likely to draw out other testimony and lead to these very disclosures which we wanted? A frank and prompt publication carried weight in itself. Delay and hesitancy, in the hope of something more, would be losing an opportunity. If Randall could be perfectly successful in his scheme, and get the names and papers, it might justify delay. Was it advisable to run this risk on such an uncertainty?

Randall proposed to go himself to-night to Kinderhook and there meet Reynolds, a lawyer friend of his in Albany, to whom he would immediately telegraph. Mrs. Conover should go on to-night also in order to see her husband, and get from him the names. R. would be his lawyer and perhaps see C. with his wife.

The plan appeared to meet with favor, and R. was so confident of success, and so ready to go and get his lawyer and detectives at work that one could not well object. I thought there seemed a little overanxiety on the part of Randall to figure and operate, but sometimes such men accomplish more than is expected.

General Sheridan has removed Governor Throckmorton of Texas and appointed my old friend E. M. Pease to be Governor of Texas in his place. This is a good selection, provided the change could be legally made; but I deny the authority of General Sheridan to do this, — deny that Congress can give him authority to do it. Pease was here two or three weeks since on his way to Texas, and I have little doubt that he was called thither for the purpose of receiving that office. It is a step in a conspiracy of which he is not cognizant.

In a contest between Throckmorton and Pease for the office of Governor some twenty months since, the people of Texas elected T. by a vote of six or seven to one over P. This was then the voice of Texas. This is probably about the present position of affairs with the legal voters.

In my opinion Pease is the best, wisest, and safest man, but the public whom he is to govern are of a different opinion. He has, from the Rebellion and the policy pursued, become warped in mind, and his principles are unsettled, but he will, I think, commit no imprudent or oppressive act. I regretted he was not elected, and regret the President did not originally appoint him provisional governor instead of Hamilton. He was presented by me at that time, but the President listened to bad men here, appointed one of them, who was the tool of the vicious gang who then were commencing an intrigue against him, and this appointee Hamilton became a traitor to the President and an ingrate. Stanton, who did not know Pease, I have no doubt took him up on my old recommendation, — a twofold object.

July 31. Had a short evening walk and talk with McCulloch, who is, not without reason, a good deal discouraged. A crowd of sharpers, mercenary party plunderers from Pennsylvania, — Flannigan, Sawyer, and others, — are crowding around the President, declaring their intention to so organize the Republican Party that it will not unite with Democrats. They all want offices for themselves or want to sell offices to their friends. The President has, McC. says, listened to these sharpers and thereby injured himself and his Administration in the estimation of good men. The revenues have been and are being defrauded by miserable partisan appointments, and the President sadly imposed upon. McCulloch proceeded to tell me how arrangements have from time to time been made by himself with the Radicals for dividing the offices, — a pernicious arrangement, — that sometimes they have in the Senate come up and confirmed appointments thus arranged, and the President has then failed to carry out the agreement.

I told him I should be sorry if the President ever broke faith, but I must frankly say to him I disliked the bargaining, — dividing with the trafficking, greedy, unprincipled

Radicals. McC. said it was necessary, we could not get along without it. The offices would not be filled.

I told him that a firm, steady hand from the beginning would have avoided this; there had been temporizing, conceding to factions, surrendering executive rights to the enemies of the President, mistaken arrangements, all of which had weakened the Administration and encouraged and stimulated the Radicals; that we could never make a stand, — have a policy, — nor could the Executive be the head, or a power in the Government, while we pursued such a course. This has gone so long and so far, however, that I know not that much can be done to retrieve the error and strengthen the Administration, but I would not divide nor surrender the executive power, patronage, authority, prerogative, rights, and duties to them.

LI

The President consults with his Cabinet as to the Advisability of removing
Sheridan — The Conover Allegations — McCulloch's Compromises —
His Great Ability as a Financier — Grant deprecates the Removal of
Sheridan — Grant going over to the Radicals — Conversation with the
President as to the Possibility of Stanton's Retirement — Postmaster-
General Randall asks for Leave of Absence — The President requests
Stanton to resign — Stanton refuses — The Tenure-of-Office Act in
Relation to the Question of Stanton's Removal — Randall's Shakiness
— Thurlow Weed's Attack on Chase — Secretary Welles advises the
President to remove Judge-Advocate-General Holt with Stanton and to
appoint one of the Blairs Secretary of War — The President discusses
the Matter with Montgomery Blair — The Jury in the John H. Surratt
Case disagrees — The President suspends Stanton and appoints Gen-
eral Grant *ad interim* — General Sickles prohibits Civil Process in his
Military Department — Alleged Conspiracy against Judge-Advocate-
General Holt — Stanton's Dismissal makes Little Commotion — Cor-
respondence between the President and General Grant relative to the
Removal of Sheridan — Conversation with Grant on the Subject of
Reconstruction — A Political Ignoramus — General Sickles announces
his Intention of obstructing the United States Court — Passage be-
tween Grant and Assistant Attorney-General Binckley in Cabinet —
Suspicions in regard to Randall — A Reorganization of the Cabinet
talked of in the Papers — Conversation with Montgomery Blair about
Grant — Grant, insubordinate in Cabinet, is rebuked by the President
— The President's Strength and Weaknesses.

August 2. After the adjournment of the Cabinet and
Stanton had left, inquiry was made of Randall if he had
been to Albany, or whether any steps had been taken in
relation to further developments of the conspiracy for
impeachment. He said no, that Conover's wife declined
to go, and wanted his pardon on the documents already
produced.

The President here remarked that as those of us who
were present could each freely speak his views, he wished
to know our several opinions in regard to the removal of
Sheridan.

McCulloch at once declared he thought it would be

injudicious, — would strengthen the extreme Radicals, who really wanted the President to take this step in order that they might make successful war against him. It would discourage the conservative portion, who were becoming much disquieted with the leaders, and who would, if not shocked by any rash step, defeat the impeachment movement. The Radicals were becoming divided among themselves, and if we abstained from any movement, they would hush up.

Browning earnestly pressed the last idea. Let them go on with their violent and obnoxious measures, — their usurpation and tyranny, — and it would break them down. The better portion of them were already sick of their measures. I asked, provided such were the fact, — which I did not believe, for the conservatives are cowards, — if it were proper administration to stand quietly by and permit such outrages upon the States and people to go on, or whether the Executive had not some duties to perform besides temporizing with corruption? We must not suppose we could escape responsibility. The idea of our doing nothing when great wrongs were being committed by the military governors would not answer. What have we done to prevent it? I think Sheridan ought never to have been put in such a position; I never advised it, nor that of Sickles, a different man. Being, then, in a responsible position for which he had no proper qualifications, I think he should have been promptly removed when he took upon himself to oust State officers and to appoint others in their places. I so stated on the day of their occurrence and had always regretted that he had not been at once displaced and sent the other side of the Mississippi after his insolent letter.

I have no animosity towards Sheridan, who is a brave soldier, and whose gallantry and services I honor, but he is unjust and made vain by his military successes, and absolutely spoiled by partisan flattery and the encouragement of the conspirators. The more he defied the President, and the greater the outrages on the people of Louisiana and

Texas, the more would he be praised by bad men who were imposing on his weaknesses.

From the tame, passive course which has been pursued, the Administration had lost confidence and strength. It has to-day no positive, established, successful policy; displays no executive power and energy; submits to insults; and we are now discussing no measure of the Administration, and it is assumed that we ought to have none, — that we must suppress our convictions, abdicate our duty, and in our helplessness trust to division among the Radicals, who have a policy, and who by their presumption and our submission have crippled the Executive, encroached upon his prerogative, and deprived him of his constitutional rights.

Randall became excited and advocated turning "the little fellow" out. The President warmed up under my remarks; his eyes flashed. "What have we to expect from long keeping quiet? Will the Republicans, the conservative portion of them, come into our views? They are always promising, but they never perform. It may be said this will enrage them and that they will then go forward and impeach me. If they would impeach me for ordering away an officer who I believe is doing wrong, — afflicting and oppressing the people instead of protecting and sustaining them, — if I am to be impeached for this, I am prepared."

I asked the President if he had any information from those States as to the sentiments and feelings of the people, — whether anything but the removal of the Governor of Texas and the overthrow of the municipal government in New Orleans had come to his knowledge. It would not be advisable to move in so important a matter without cause. These were sufficient. But weeks ago the same acts had been committed as regards the Governor of Louisiana, Attorney-General, judge, etc. The President said there was nothing additional now, but there was universal complaint of disorganization, confusion, insincerity, and oppression.

McCulloch said he should deprecate the removal of Sheridan, because he was exceedingly popular, and it would bring down violence on the Administration. He had a talk with Wilson of Iowa before he left for home, who said if the President did nothing rash, and — alluding to this very movement — would not disturb Sheridan, all would go along well, and the extreme Radicals would be defeated; a division would certainly take place.

"What," said I, "if Sheridan should proceed to hang some of the prominent and best men in Louisiana who differ from him? Would Wilson expect, or you advise, that he should still be continued?"

The President was called into the adjoining room, and McCulloch, turning to me, said he was afraid my remarks would produce great harm. "To do our duty will produce harm! How," I exclaimed, "are we subdued and humbled!"

On the subject of Conover's disclosures some further discussion took place. The President was inclined to pardon him on the application of Holt and Riddle, and let the reasons and documents follow which led to the pardon. But the rest of us were united in the opinion that the publication of the documents should precede pardon, and to postpone the pardon for a short time at all events.

It was also understood that Sheridan's case would be delayed for the present.

August 3, Saturday. McCulloch called on me early this morning. He was very much exercised in regard to the removal of Sheridan. It had disturbed him through the night, and as he was intending to be absent for a day or two, he besought me to see the President and prevent hasty action. The conservative and timid Republicans and some Radicals have been intimate with McCulloch and impressed him with their cowardly, shrinking views. He has been persuaded by them to compromise, and to bargain in regard to office. In all this he has been actu-

ated by good, though I think mistaken, motives. The bad
features of the Radicals may have been softened at times,
but their violence and strength have not been impaired
thereby. On the contrary, they have been fortified and
made more powerful by their success in invading the Executive, while the Administration has been weakened. It
has for the time being made matters more easy for the
Secretary of the Treasury, who has, indeed, a difficult task
to perform, but eventually these concessions to timid
men who sustain wrong acts of their leaders will be disastrous to the Administration, which has been putting
its opponents in place, — establishing, as it were, little
Radical fortifications in almost every Congressional district, to batter us down. They retain and exercise all the
powers granted them, usurp the powers of the Executive,
and we yield to them in fear.

I advised McCulloch to call himself on the President
and freely communicate his views. But he seemed to
think it would be of little avail. I sometimes am inclined
to believe the President does not so fully appreciate the
value of McC.'s services as he should, for I think him
the best financier we have had for years in the Treasury,
with a difficult part to perform were he supported instead
of opposed by Congress. If he possessed the firmness and
political experience of Guthrie, he would be his equal in
every respect. But he is politically timid and is wanting
in political tact, persistency, and force.

In this matter of Sheridan, I told him I could not answer
the President otherwise than I did when he put the inquiry to us whether Sheridan ought to be detached. There
is no question in my mind that it would be right to relieve
the people of Louisiana and Texas of an officer who has so
little discretion, such infirm judgment in civil matters,
and who knows so little how to exercise power. The law
itself is an outrage, a violation of the Constitution, and
Sheridan outrageously administers it, removing and making appointments at will. It cannot be otherwise than he is

secretly backed up and supported by some power, for he is accustomed to obey, not to disobey.

I called on the President, as McC. requested, and had a free conversation with him. Said to him that while Sheridan deserved rebuke and removal, I would not be obstinate but defer to him. It might, as things were now, be impolitic or inexpedient to make the removal; it would undoubtedly lead to a violent assault upon him; the conspirators — extreme Radicals — would avail themselves of the act to be more vindictive and ferocious, and the timid would be more cowed and submissive to them; while I had an inherent confidence in the great principles of right as the rule of action, there was no doubt it often tried the most resolute and required moral courage and steady persistency to make the right prevail.

"What," said the President, "have I to fear, what to gain or lose by keeping this man who delights in opposing and counteracting my views in this position? It is said that the weak Radicals — the conservative ones — will join the ultras to impeach me. If Congress can bring themselves to impeach me, because in my judgment a turbulent and unfit man should be removed and because I, in the honest discharge of my duty to my country and the Constitution, exercise my judgment and remove him, let them do it. I shall not shun the trial, and if the people can sanction such a proceeding, I shall not lament the loss of a position held by such a tenure."

I remarked that Sheridan was really but a secondary personage after all in the business. He would never have pursued the course he has if not prompted and encouraged by others to whom he looked, — from whom he received advice, if not orders. Little would be attained if only he were taken in hand.

The President said there was no doubt of that, and he was giving the subject attention. He said he had had a long interview with General Grant, . . . in which interview they had gone over these subjects, but Grant was hesitating. He then went to his desk and brought me a letter of Grant's, elicited by the conversation which had passed between them. Grant deprecated the removal of Sheridan, who, he says, possesses immense popularity; thinks it is not in the power of the President to remove the Secretary of War since the passage of the Tenure-of-Office Bill, and that it would be unwise as well as inexpedient to make these movements just when Congress has adjourned.

The letter was not such as I should have at one time expected from Grant, — was not discreet, judicious, nor excusable even from his standpoint. If not disingenuous, he has, without perhaps being aware of it, had his opinions warped and modified within a year. I remarked as I finished reading the letter, "Grant is going over."

"Yes," said the President, "I am aware of it. I have no doubt that most of these offensive measures have emanated from the War Department."

"Not only that," said I, "but almost all the officers of the Army have been insidiously alienated from your support by the same influences. If you had been favored with an earnest and sincere supporter of your measures in the War Department, the condition of affairs in this country would this day have been quite different. It is unfortunate, perhaps, that you did not remove all of the Cabinet soon after your Administration commenced; certainly some who have made it a business to thwart and defeat your measures ought to have been changed."

He assented, with some emotion, to the last remark, but expressed a doubt whether he could have got rid of Stanton. It would, he said, be unpleasant to make the attempt and not succeed. He presumed Grant had communicated the conversation which had taken place, and that the suggestion came from Stanton himself.

I doubted if Stanton would persist in holding on as an adviser when he understood the President wished him away, or he was requested to relinquish his office, although it was obvious he was very tenacious of his place, and clung to it from personal considerations. Yet I was not sure but things had about reached the point when he was prepared to leave. He was in close friendship with the Radicals who had the control of Congress; through that faction was as much a favorite of the conservatives as of the extreme Radicals. Congress having taken the whole government into its keeping, and he being a favorite, he might think it would conduce to his benefit to be dismissed, compelled to leave. They would be dissatisfied to have him retire; Seward and Holt would oppose it, and probably Grant also now, though he had at one time favored it.

The conversation on this point closed with his repeating the remark he had twice before made, — that he intended to bring this matter to a conclusion in a few days.

The President said he was annoyed by Randall's course. He seemed unsettled, anxious to be running about the country, leaving his duties to McClellan,[1] who was filling all the post-offices with Radicals, perhaps with R.'s consent, certainly without his opposition. Now he comes with a request to be absent and to leave the country for six weeks. "I told him," said the President, "it appeared to me no time to be absent, that he was wanted at his post now, if ever." But R. thought he could be absent; his wife was abroad; he could, having a free pass, go for her without expense; to send for her would cost him six hundred dollars. The President repeated to him that he thought his duties were here, but he should leave the subject with him after what had been said.

In the matter of Sheridan, I do not get any sufficient cause for moving now that has not existed for weeks and months. The removal of Throckmorton is following out the first step, the removal of Wells. The insulting letter has got cold. Still I have not a word for Sheridan.

August 5, Monday. I called on the President this A.M.,

[1] George W. McClellan, Second Assistant Postmaster-General.

and, after my errand, mentioned that no publication of Conover's case had yet been made. He said he had, after consideration, given that matter a different turn. It was an application for pardon, and he had passed over the papers to the Attorney-General, and given it the same direction as other applications for pardon. I inquired if Stanbery had returned. He said no, but the assistants were quite as competent for this case.

I asked about the Sheridan case, remarking that I was glad, as things are, that he was giving the subject deliberate thought. He said he had dropped Sheridan for the present and gone to the fountain-head of mischief, — that he had this morning sent a note to Stanton requesting him to resign. "It is impossible," said he, "to get along with such a man in such a position, and I can stand it no longer. Whether he will send in his resignation is uncertain. What do you think he will do?"

"I think he will resign," I replied, "and not intrude himself upon you, and longer embarrass you; yet his friends are the ones who have tried to tie your hands."

"Yes, and he instigated it. He has, I am satisfied, been the prolific source of difficulties. You have alluded to this, but I was unwilling to consider it, — to think that the man whom I trusted was plotting and intriguing against me."

"Well," said I, "it is better, if you are to act, that this course should be taken. Sheridan is only a secondary man in these matters, and to smite him would only aggravate and excite, without accomplishing any good beyond punishing insolence to you, and wrong to the people over whom he has been placed. He has been sustained and encouraged by other minds."

I do not see how Stanton can do otherwise than resign, and yet it will not surprise me if he refuses. Should he refuse, the President may be embarrassed, for Stanton has contrived, I suspect, to get a controlling influence over General Grant. Judge Cartter is a creature of Stanton, and his court is under subjection to the same influence. The President has, against all admonitions and warnings, been passive and impenetrable, until he is powerless. I do not perceive any benefit to himself by removing Stanton at this time. One year ago it would have been effective, and he would have retained Grant and the Army; he would have had a different Congress; the country was then with him, and would have continued so. But the conspirators and intriguers have bound him hand and foot; he has permitted his prerogative to be despoiled, the executive authority and rights to be circumscribed, until he is weak and powerless.

Stanton may defy him, and shelter himself under the Tenure-of-Office Bill, which contains a clause in relation to Cabinet-officers, introduced by his friends and for the special purpose of retaining him in place. When this subject was before the Cabinet, no one more strongly reprobated this flagrant abuse or more strongly declared that the law was unconstitutional than Stanton. He protested with ostentatious vehemence that any man who would retain his seat in the Cabinet as an adviser when his advice was not wanted was unfit for the place. He would not, he said, remain a moment. I remember his protestations, for I recollected at the time he had been treacherous and faithless to Buchanan. I knew, moreover, he had since as well as then betrayed Cabinet secrets.

August 6. Before the session of the Cabinet commenced this morning, the President invited me into the library and informed me that he had a note from Stanton refusing to resign. I was a good deal astonished, though since yesterday my doubts in regard to his course have increased. His profuse expressions of readiness to resign, declarations that any gentleman would decline to remain an intruder, etc., etc., when the Tenure-of-Office Bill was under consideration were mere pretenses to cover his intrigues. The President had requested Seward, Stanton, and myself

EDWIN M. STANTON

to prepare a veto on that bill. Neither of them consulted me farther than to send to me for information concerning the debates.

The President asked if he had better communicate the correspondence to the Cabinet at this time. I advised it by all means.

All the Cabinet except Stanbery were present. When the correspondence was read a good deal of surprise was manifested, and felt, not only with the invitation but the refusal. Stanton did not attend, and considers himself, it would seem, not of the Cabinet.

Seward immediately inquired when Stanbery would be back. The Tenure-of-Office Bill was examined and commented upon. Doubts were expressed whether the President could remove a Cabinet-officer. Seward thought it indispensable that Stanbery should be here. It was a question of law, and the law officer was the proper person to expound it.

The President seemed embarrassed how to act. As the law is, in the opinion of the whole Cabinet, including the Attorney-General, unconstitutional, I said this was a political as well as a legal question; that the Chief Magistrate could select and remove his advisers; that the legislative department could not take away the constitutional rights of the Executive; that the power of removal belonged to the President of right; that there has been too much concession to legislative usurpations. I do not consider that the President is under obligations to be an instrument in these violations of the Constitution, — to cripple the executive department by a fragment of Congress.

After an hour and more of discussion, the subject was postponed, and the Conover subject taken up. The Acting Attorney-General had embodied into a report, or opinion, the petitions of Conover, *alias* Dunham, the notes, etc. This it was thought ought to be printed at once.

McCulloch came to see me this evening. He is a good

deal disturbed. Laments that the President had not taken this step in regard to Stanton at least a year ago. Thinks it now too late to do any good, and fears Stanton, aided by the Radicals, will make successful war and overcome the President. Much will depend on the President himself, and he would come to right conclusions and carry them out but for Seward, who is bewildered and has not Weed here to advise him. If he listens to Seward, who has been taken by surprise, all will be frittered away, no decisive stand will be taken and held, but the honest purpose of the President will be defeated. Stanton, assisted by the Radicals in Congress, has been active in preparing himself for this event by crippling the President on every hand and in every way and by fortifying himself. He has got Grant and other army officers. He has got the court in this District. Judge Cartter, I am told, spent an hour or two with Stanton after he received the President's note, in the War Department. He is a coarse, vulgar Radical in the hands of Stanton; has complete control of his associate Fisher. Olin and Wiley are different men, but I know not how they would act at this time.

August 7. Nothing new has developed to-day. The Conover matter is not published, nor has anything been done with the Secretary of War. The present idea of the President is to suspend Stanton and order General Grant to take charge *ad interim*, but though Grant was willing and earnest when proposed a year ago, he would, I think, be reluctant now. I know not how he would disobey. Not unlikely Seward will try to patch up some sort of arrangement to gratify and soothe Stanton.

Herein is the President's danger. His strength, power, energy, and force are destroyed by Seward. He can do nothing to extricate himself while Seward has a directing influence. Stanbery, influenced by Seward, takes also a narrow view of things.

My own advice would have been, had the President

asked it, not to have executed the unconstitutional Reconstruction law, — to have assigned no military commanders to govern States in time of peace. If for this they attempted an impeachment, or sought by party drill to carry the unconstitutional law into effect, I would have gone to the people, appealed to them to uphold the Government and the Constitution, to stand by the Executive. It would hardly do for me, unasked, to suggest these things, to advise the President to offer himself a sacrifice, yet I wished it, — wished I could have been in his place in that emergency. It would have been a glorious privilege to have seized the horns of the altar, planted one's self on the Constitution, rallied the patriotism of the nation, immolated himself, if necessary, in defending the Government of his country and the integrity of the Union. But before asking the several opinions of his Cabinet, he announced that he should execute the law, and I saw it was under the advice of Seward, Stanbery, and Stanton, — for Stanton was then a busy counselor, directly and indirectly, through Seward, in all measures, insidiously working to destroy the power and influence of the President while professing friendship.

The President informs me that the Conover matter will be published and appear on Saturday. I saw Gobright, the general correspondent of the Associated Press, in the Secretary of State's rooms, and presume Seward has succeeded in procuring the document, which is quite long, to be sent forward to New York to appear simultaneously with its publication here. This was unnecessary, for these papers would readily have copied it. Now the whole thing will have something of the appearance of having been gotten up for effect, which is not true. Things may be overdone.

I met Randall at the council room. While waiting for the President, I spoke to him concerning certain changes, loudly called for, and which he had promised should be made, in a few post-offices. He said Dixon was urging

3

him to turn out some good men, friends of the President. I asked if he knew this to be so, — if he were acquainted with the facts and men personally. He said he knew they gave money freely for the organization. I inquired when and what organization. Did they assist in electing Governor English, and Hotchkiss Member of Congress, or did they oppose both? He confessed he did not know about that, which I told him was important, if support of the Administration was to be considered. I had no doubt that some changes should be made, as Dixon recommended, for other than party reasons. I saw that he did not like my comments, and he soon went out. Before leaving, he told me his wife was sick, and he thought he should have to cross the Atlantic for her, and it would be best for the President to fill his place. This was said half-slyly, half-earnestly, and satisfies me that he is shaky. I have been for some time convinced there is foundation in the rumor that his confirmation was received by pledges to Radical Senators, who do not like Dixon and would not strengthen him by appointments at home.

August 9. Stanton's course and what is to be done with him were discussed. Seward is extremely anxious to get the opinion of the Attorney-General, who is absent, before coming to any conclusion. Some one remarked that it was reported one of Mr. Lincoln's Cabinet, and who is now of Mr. Johnson's, sympathized with Stanton, and might resign if he did. I told them I had not heard the rumor, but they were at liberty to say to any one and to all that I was not the man to leave the Cabinet for that reason, but if the President ever invited me, I should not decline his invitation to leave.

The debates in the Senate on the Tenure-of-Office Bill and Senator Sherman's strong declarations were quoted. I remarked that they were not stronger than the declarations of Stanton himself to us at this board, as they would all remember. He had, with Mr. Seward, prepared the veto on the Tenure-of-Office Bill, but that was much milder than his declarations of the unconstitutionality as well as impolicy of that bill.

Seward said but little, and Randall was reserved. Perhaps there was no reason to sharpen my suspicion; but it is evident they are not forward in the measure or in efforts to encourage the President. The removal of Stanton was undoubtedly a surprise and disappointment to Seward, who has sustained him.

Weed has been making some more assaults on Chief Justice Chase, accusing him of getting rich while Secretary of the Treasury. I have heard these charges before. There were some strange proceedings in granting permits, and Chase had in Harrington and some others strange associates; but this charge, at this time, is, I have little doubt, in concert with Seward, who has been to Auburn and met Weed there. I am aware of no reason to suspect Chase of adding to his fortune after entering the Treasury. Weed has, I know, become wealthy since 1861.

Things have taken a turn which disappoints both Seward and Weed. Seward has thought of fishing for the Presidency and supposes Chase one of the obstacles. Neither of them stands any more chance of reaching the Presidency than of being created Sultan of Turkey. After the others had gone out, I had half an hour with the President, who requested me to stay. Advised him to remove Holt with Stanton. It would be more effective and proper to remove the two together. I looked upon both as conspirators, as having contributed more than any others to the embarrassments of the Administration. They had each a personal interest in preventing a restoration of the Union, for, having been associated in Buchanan's Cabinet, where one played, to say the least, an equivocal, and the other a treacherous, game towards the South, they dread a reconciled Union.

I suggested that the time was not inauspicious to strike an effective blow against Radical usurpations. The delay had, it was true, matured the plots, schemes, and intrigues of the conspirators, by which the South was prostrated and the whole country had become demoralized. But he could now in a measure rouse the South and the better portion of the country, and to some extent retrieve past error, by sweeping out the whole batch of generals who were governing the States of the South in violation of the Constitution and had made themselves part of the usurping conspiracy. There is a deliberate conspiracy to subject the executive department to the legislative. Congress has, in defiance of the Constitution, passed a law which is subversive of the States and the Federal Government, and they have designated the President as the instrument to destroy the Constitution which he has sworn to defend. Why consent to be that illegal instrument? He had endeavored to carry out the Reconstruction Act under the theory of the Attorney-General, whose construction of the law was that the military were a mere police force, subordinate to the civil authorities, or to act coöperatively with them; but since Congress, at its late session, had placed the military above the civil power, virtually assailed the State Governments, and openly trampled on the Constitution, he would be justified in refusing to be their instrument or to take part in that outrage.

They might in this Radical House, under their gag rules, prefer articles of impeachment; possibly the Senate might, in its partisan violence convict, but I doubted it. At all events, the great questions, involving the welfare of the government and the preservation of the principles on which it was founded, would be fully discussed, public attention would be drawn to the subject, and the danger understood. At present, the people seem dull, passive, and indifferent to what so nearly concerns them. At the worst he would be sacrificed for adhering with fidelity to the Constitution, but his historic record would be worth more than any office. If his appeal to the country could not be responded to until there was an election, he need

have no fear of the verdict which his countrymen would
ultimately render.

The President listened to me attentively, earnestly,
occasionally interrupting me with affirming exclamations,
and with expressions of contempt at impeachment threats.

I suggested the appointment of one of the Blairs to be
Secretary of War. Seward, Thurlow Weed, and his tribe
hated and had abused the Blairs and tried to get up a
prejudice against them, but they were bold, fearless,
honest men whom Stanton feared. Were Frank Blair
appointed, Stanton, who, though a blusterer, is a coward,
would fly out of one door as Frank entered at the other.
The President laughed and cordially assented.

August 10, *Saturday.* Gave the President some papers
left with me by Doctor Duhamel [1] and Captain Chandler
concerning Conover, *alias* Dunham. The *Intelligencer*
this A.M. contains the report of Assistant Attorney-
General Binckley and documents referred to him in that
case.

Talked with the President about the case, and also
the course of Stanton. Again repeated my wish that he
would not permit himself to be made an instrument to
break down the Constitution and destroy the character
of the government. If for this Congress would impeach,
let them. But in order to meet this question he would
need a new Secretary of War, one who is reliable and true.
"Who," asked the President, "is the man?" He read to
me a telegram from Senator Dixon, advising the removal
of Stanton forthwith, and the appointment of Steedman.
I asked if Steedman was better than Frank Blair. He
answered no, but hesitated, and looked inquiringly at me.
I comprehended his meaning and admitted there is a prejudice against the Blairs, created in a great degree by
Seward's man Weed, in which others of that school had

[1] Doctor William Duhamel, chief physician in the United States prison
in the District of Columbia.

joined and prejudiced the country. "But is it for you or me, to listen to, or be influenced by, this prejudice and injustice? Have you better, more reliable, and, in the main, more intelligent and trusty friends than the Blairs? True, they are party politicians, but they are politicians in the higher sense also." He said they were among the best and most sensible men in the country. "Then," said I, "they should not be dropped to gratify their enemies, who are not your sincere friends. I do not mean to press any one for the Cabinet, — no one should. The selection should be yours entirely, — men in whom you have confidence, — and the dismissal of any one should also be the President's own act."

"Where is Frank at this time?" he inquired. But I could not tell him, though I informed him it could be ascertained with little difficulty, for Montgomery had returned from Virginia for a few days.

The President said he would send for Montgomery, and began writing a note, when I told him I would do the errand. He might not be at his house, and it would be necessary in that event to look him up. He thanked me and wished me to find Montgomery and invite him to call at the White House. I went immediately to Blair's house; he was, fortunately, in and his father also. I told M. the President wanted to see him, and advised him to go directly, but did not disclose his purpose.

Later in the day, I saw M., who told me he had the interview but nothing definite had taken place. The conversation had been prolonged, and he, M., had been frank and free in his remarks. He says the President is intensely ambitious and all his thoughts are bent on a nomination and election; that Seward, having the same object in view for himself, was using the President, and creating enmity between him (the President) and General Grant.

The trial of Surratt terminated to-day, having been in hand about two months. The jury did not agree. This was expected. I have not read all the evidence. That Surratt was in the conspiracy to kidnap I have always believed, but I have had the impression that when the conclusion was to kill, he flinched, and his mother favored his absence, in order that he should not be under the influence of Booth. But this may be all a mistake on my part.

The judge was disgracefully partial and unjust, I thought, and his charge highly improper. The senior Bradley [1] was irascible, violent, and indiscreet, — some difficulty brought him and the judge in collision almost, — and the judge, at the conclusion of the trial, ordered his name stricken from the roll of attorneys, an arbitrary act.

August 11, *Sunday.* Saw the President this P.M. He tells me he has seen General Grant and had a pleasant, social, and friendly interview. They had come to a mutual understanding. The President wished to know if there was any alienation, or substantial difference, between them. Grant replied there was not, except that he had not last fall concurred in the President's opposition to the Constitutional Amendment.

The President assured him that Stanton must leave the War Department, and he desired him, *ad interim,* to discharge the duties. Grant said if Stanton's removal was decided upon he had nothing further to say on that point. As regarded himself, he always obeyed orders. He seemed pleased with the proposed arrangement and withdrew.

The President thinks he had better suspend Stanton without reference to the Tenure-of-Office Bill, and he perhaps is right under the existing embarrassments. He seemed anxious to have me satisfied on that point, and we talked over the whole subject in detail. I expressed a belief that it would strengthen the Executive were both Stanton and Holt to retire, for they have been willful, intriguing mischief-makers, and sectional exclusionists —

[1] Joseph H. Bradley, senior counsel for Surratt. His associates were R. T. Merrick and Joseph H. Bradley, Jr.

really disunionists — from the time the Rebels surrendered. Their study has been to produce hate and alienation, and beyond others they have prompted the violent Radicals, — conspired with them.

In talking of Stanton's course, the President expressed a desire that the fact that Stanton with Seward prepared the veto of the Tenure-of-Office Bill should be made public, and also Stanton's emphatic remarks against that bill, its principles, and its unconstitutionality. This desire he has before expressed.

McCulloch tells me he well remembers Stanton's opposition to the bill and that he quoted Buchanan.

August 12, *Monday*. Montgomery Blair called on me this morning and desired me to procure an interview with the President for his father. I assented, though just at this time, and with the President's peculiar temperament, it is a little embarrassing and will likely cause comment.

The President consented to receive Mr. B. at any time. He showed me the letters which he had prepared to Stanton, and also to Grant. They were decisive and proper. He said the question should be closed to-day. In our interview yesterday, he told me that Bingham[1] had called on him, very pleasant and friendly. Said he had, however, some of the facts of Conover's disclosures six weeks ago; that Matchett[2] was a suspicious fellow; doubted if much could be made of him. The whole of Bingham's talk was singular, and the President said he believed in his heart the fellow was sent by Seward to soften away the disclosures made. He expressed himself emphatically against S. as a weak, unsafe man, etc., etc.

Before leaving him this morning, Mr. Seward and General Rousseau came in with the instructions in regard to

---

[1] John A. Bingham, Member of Congress from Ohio, previously a special judge-advocate in the trial of the Lincoln conspirators.

[2] Rev. D. F. Matchett, who, according to Conover, was Ashley's "man Friday" in the negotiations.

the duties of General Rousseau as Commissioner in effecting the transfer of the Russian territory. They wished me to remain, but after a little talk it was concluded best that the Secretary of the Treasury and General Grant should also be present, and we left, agreeing to come together at 1 P.M.

After the consultation with those gentlemen, and Seward and General Grant had withdrawn, the President handed me Stanton's letter. He is furious, blustering, denying the President's authority to act without the consent of the Senate, but as General Grant had accepted, he had withdrawn with a protest.

August 13, *Tuesday*. General Grant attended the Cabinet-meeting, also Assistant Attorney-General Binckley. I can perceive that Grant is not at all displeased with his new position; on the contrary there is self-satisfaction very obvious. Stanton is disappointed in him; I doubt his sincerity to the President. He is braced up, I perceive, and committed to the unconstitutional law of Reconstruction, has been persuaded it is his duty, and feels that he must stand by the military governors. All this does not disappoint me. He will be likely, however, though not very intelligent on civil matters, to exercise some common sense, which will modify action; at all events, being a soldier, he will not foment Radical intrigues.

I am at a loss as to the policy of the President, and have some doubts if he has finally determined in his own mind what it shall be. On some minor questions that came up to-day, Grant was very prompt to express an opinion that the law must be executed. If, said I, the law is *palpably* unconstitutional and destructive of the government and of the Constitution itself, and if a part of that law makes the President the instrument to destroy the Constitution, which he has sworn to protect, how is he to act? "Who," said Grant, "is to decide whether the law is unconstitutional?" I replied that I had said *"palpably* unconstitutional," and I answered by saying the Executive is as distinct and independent a department of the government as Congress, and if compelled to act, he must decide for himself on so grave a matter whether he will permit himself to be coerced into a conspiracy against the Constitution.

Here the subject dropped. An order of General Sickles, prohibiting civil process in his military department has been construed by some of his subordinates to authorize them to interpose and prevent the United States Marshal from discharging his duty. Sickles has been written to, to explain his order, but fails to answer. Grant said, clearly he had no authority to do this, and he would immediately instruct him on the subject. He accordingly wrote the substance of a dispatch, which he read, but, it being a little rough, said he would complete it at the Department. Sickles has no more power to prevent civil processes in the State Courts than in the United States Courts.

Mr. Seward handed a communication from Mr. Riddle, implicated in the Conover matter, to the Assistant Attorney-General for him to file or dispose of as he thought best. He said Mr. R. wished to have it published or to publish it himself, and the Attorney-General could do what he pleased. I inquired why such a paper should be brought here? Mr. R. could, if he pleased, publish any document, without asking permission of the Administration.

Seward was disconcerted, — told how he did with papers and acted queerly. The President and most of the Cabinet thought the paper out of place. Seward was persistent, and the President ordered the paper read. This, I saw, annoyed S. still more. It was a curious document in some respects, and disclosed the fact that R. had been employed by Seward to hunt up, or manufacture, testimony against Surratt. Why the State Department should busy itself in that prosecution is not clear. Riddle, in this letter, says he never saw Conover but twice, that Conover never gave him the name of a single witness, never furnished him a solitary fact. Why, then, did Riddle apply to the President for a pardon for C., and base his application on the ground of service rendered in the Surratt trial?

The President expressed to me a wish that the statement of a correspondent of the *Cincinnati Gazette*, who proposes to give details of a Cabinet-meeting when Stanbery's exposition was under consideration, might be corrected. I and others were misrepresented and misstated. He also repeated a wish, often made, that the fact that Stanton prepared, with Seward, the veto message on the Civil Tenure-of-Office Bill might be made public. I advised that he had only to indicate his wish, or direct publication, and it would be made.

August 14. The President called my attention to the different laws creating the office of Judge-Advocate-General and the Bureau of Military Justice, with a view to the removal of Holt. I remarked that both Holt and Stanton had early anticipated their probable removal, and each had endeavored to fortify himself in place by special legislation. That, in my view, Congress had not the constitutional power to make public officers independent of the Executive. The Constitution had specified what officers should be independent, viz., the judges, but all other officers held their places at the will of the President. To make them otherwise would be to make a multiplicity of executives, each independent of the other. But the President was, by the organic law which controlled the different departments of the Government, made responsible for the due execution of the laws, and he could not be held to that responsibility if his subordinates and agents were independent of him.

The President apparently acquiesced in this, but I perceive he hesitates about acting on that principle, which will bring him in conflict with the Radicals in Congress, and seeks, therefore, some other method of getting rid of an obnoxious officer, who, he is satisfied, is conspiring, intriguing, and using his official position to injure the Executive and weaken his influence and authority. This reluctance to act in defense of a high and undoubted constitutional right is weakness and impairs his strength. If Congress were disposed to impeach him for maintaining the prerogative of the Executive, let them do so, or try to do so. These Congressional usurpations must be stopped, or the government will undergo a radical and fatal change.

August 16, *Friday.* At the close of the Cabinet session to-day, Mr. Binckley, the Acting Attorney-General, submitted a copy of the *New York Times* of yesterday, containing a statement and sundry affidavits of parties who swear they have been bribed or suborned by Roger Pryor, Ben Wood, and others, to destroy the character of Holt. These affidavits, it is said, are filed in the office of the Attorney-General or War Department and office of Military Justice.

General Grant hastened at once to oppose any call on Judge Holt for either an avowal or disclaimer of any such files as Mr. B. requested. He said no head of a Department could know all the papers which were filed in his. He knew of no such files in the War Department. B. explained that this was not the point, — he had furnished a statement in which he declared that all the papers in the Attorney-General's office relating to that subject were produced. Here was an attempt to impugn him and his veracity.

Seward attempted to enlighten the subject, but only confused it. He saw, as all did, that Grant was unusually earnest, without fully understanding B.'s object of tracing these documents to the Bureau of Military Justice.

I proposed that an inquiry should be first made to ascertain whether the papers were in Judge Holt's office before proceeding farther. This did not suit B., who said Holt would abstract papers were he not instantly removed. "Suppose," said I, "that on inquiry it is ascertained there are really no such papers in any office or bureau, — that the whole is a fiction, got up by the newspaper correspondents or other mischievous persons."

This suggestion seemed to strike Grant favorably, and all fell in with it except B., who said he had no doubt where the originals were, and as little doubt that others could be manufactured or abstracted, as Holt felt would be for his interest.

Browning read a letter from Stanbery, received this A.M., expressing gratification with what had been done with Stanton, which should, however, he says, be soon followed by removal. This is sensible and positive. I like it.

August 17, *Saturday.* The dismissal, or suspension, of Stanton creates no commotion. None but certain Radical politicians regret his expulsion. The President seemed surprised that so few cared about him. One would have supposed from the Radical press that an earthquake would follow Stanton's retirement, and he undoubtedly expected a sensation. The truth is that Stanton, whose manner is brusque and ways subtle, is generally disliked by the best men of the Army, — is hated and detested by many of them. The people have little regard for him anywhere. Certain conspiring politicians, in Congress and out of it, with Forney and a few others connected with the press, have puffed and extolled their coadjutor in the Cabinet to give him power and influence. With his accustomed duplicity he has managed to deceive both the extreme and conservative Radicals, the latter especially. Fessenden, in particular, has been his dupe. Horace Greeley, so often misled, for a wonder has for some time past appeared to have a little insight into Stanton's true character, but whether it was from sagacity as regards the man, or from opposition to Weed, who, as well as Seward, is devoted to Stanton, I am not able to say. Probably the latter. The President has been made to believe that the removal of Stanton would break down his Administration.

August 19, *Monday.* A long letter from Viceroy General Pope to Grant shows the progress of despotism. If men will neither talk, write, nor think different from Pope and the Radicals, he is sure all will go on well in Reconstruction as Congress wishes. But there are certain "pestilent fellows" who will not hold their tongues, and "banishment" seems to be Pope's remedy in their case. Get all who differ from him out of the way, and all will go well enough.

The affidavits which have been published implicating Pryor and Ben Wood are undoubtedly false and fraudulent. Whether gotten up by Holt himself, or by some one in his interest, is not yet ascertained. Holt publishes an adroitly worded letter, which, in its cunning, discloses the rogue, and leaves little doubt who is the real originator of these fraudulent affidavits.

August 20, *Tuesday.* The President showed me the correspondence between himself and Grant relative to the removal of Sheridan. Grant objects to the removal, — thinks it contrary to the wishes of the American people. The President responds, compliments the soldierly qualities of Sheridan, but thinks he has not the calm judgment, civil qualities, and ability of General Thomas for such a position, and as to the wishes of the people, he is not aware that they have been expressed.

There is no doubt but that the Radical politicians will bellow loud over the removal of Sheridan, whose fighting qualities and services are great. Their editors and speakers have undertaken to control the course of the Government as regards Sheridan, and Grant, if not a participant with, has been led away by, them. Undoubtedly many people have read the papers and come to the conclusion that the President could not — dared not — remove Sheridan, and his insubordinate and rash conduct has been commended for its ability.

General Grant has, not without reason, personal regard

for Sheridan, though the judgment and administrative qualities of this cavalry officer, Grant does not, or did not, think of a high order. But the successes of Sheridan's government, the hurrahs and applause with which his arbitrary and violent conduct have been received by the boisterous Radical press, have made Grant doubt whether, after all, Sheridan has not greater capacity and executive ability than he supposed.[1]

The decision and promptitude of Sheridan, even though wrong, have made him strong with the people, who love bold and resolute action. Were the President to display more of these qualities, he would be more popular, but he is accused of rashness when he delays. On the whole, I think the President appears to advantage in this cor-

---

[1] At a later period I became satisfied that Sheridan had been secretly prompted and influenced by Grant in his reprehensible course in New Orleans and Texas. Most of the viceroys, or military governors, had secret telegrams, or oral instructions from the General-in-Chief, who was in collusion with Stanton (whom, however, he disliked) and the chief Radical conspirators. In all this period, Grant with great duplicity and vulgar cunning succeeded in deceiving not only the President but the rest of us. Sheridan was flattered by the confidential communications, and encouraged in his insolence and insubordination towards the President by his superior officer, who had become enlisted in the conspiracy against the Chief Magistrate. Grant until the fall of 1866 was a decided and avowed supporter of the Administration and of the Lincoln-Johnson policy of reëstablishing the Union, but, flattered by attention, he began to have aspirations for political promotion, with very little political intelligence and no political experience. Some men of both parties, though aware of his incapacity and unfitness for the performance of civil duties, thought his military éclat might make him available as a candidate for President. Sensible men who came in contact with him were aware that he was destitute of all aptitude and experience to qualify him for the position, and declined committing themselves to the intrigue for his elevation. But the Radical conspirators were desperate, and in the belief that they could mould him to their wishes and views, his ignorance of and indifference to political and civil affairs made him more acceptable. Grant, however, hesitated for some time before he openly deserted the Administration, and contrived, even after he was secretly acting in concert with the Radicals to deceive and beguile the President, to receive his confidence and office at his hands. It was at this period, and while the President was in daily communication with him, advising with him as freely as any of the Cabinet, that Grant was writing secretly to Sheridan and to the viceroy generals, counteracting the measures of Administration. — G. W.

respondence, because it displays energy as well as correct intentions. The removal of Sheridan will break no bones; had it been earlier done it would have been more popular. He ought never to have been detailed to command that department and govern those States in the first place, but, having been detailed, should have been removed on the first exhibition of his unfitness. Sickles should also have been cleared out some time since. The President showed me after the Cabinet adjourned an impertinent and presuming letter from King Sickles, who insists on obstructing the Federal Courts and setting them at defiance, because if he and the other four viceroys, or little monarchs, cannot set the courts aside, the courts will set the little monarchs aside. I advised the President to make short work with King Sickles.

August 22, *Thursday.* Had this A.M. an hour's conversation or more with General Grant. It was the first time I had met him in the War Department since he entered upon the duties of Secretary, and I congratulated him on his new position. He thought he ought to decline receiving congratulations on that account, but they were obviously acceptable. I begged to differ from him and inquired why he should decline congratulations on a change which had been so well and favorably received by the whole country. "Well," he said, "I do not know about that; these changes that are going on, striking down men who have been faithful through the War, I do not like." "So far as the War Department is concerned," said I, "the country on all hands believe that as good and faithful a War man is in the place as we have had at any time." He disclaimed alluding to that change. "If," said I, "you have Sheridan and Thomas in your mind, there is no denying that Thomas is in every respect as good a War man, with better administrative powers than Sheridan, whom I would by no means disparage."

With this opening, we went into a general discussion

of the condition of the country and the affairs of the
Government. It pained me to see how little he understood
of the fundamental principles and structure of our Government, and of the Constitution itself. On the subject of
differences between the President and Congress, and the
attempt to subject the people to military rule, there were,
he said, in Congress, fifty at least of the first lawyers of
the country who had voted for the Reconstruction law,
and were not, he asked, the combined wisdom and talent
of those fifty to have more weight than Mr. Johnson,
who was only one to fifty? Congress had enacted this
law, and was not the President compelled to carry it into
execution? Was not Congress superior to the President?
If the law was unconstitutional, the judges alone could
decide the question. The President must submit and obey
Congress until the Supreme Court set the law aside.

I asked him if Congress could exercise powers not granted, powers that the States, which made the Constitution,
had expressly reserved. He thought Congress might pass
any law, and the President and all others must obey and
support it until the Supreme Court declared it unconstitutional.

"You do not mean to say, General, that Congress may
set aside and disregard all limitations, all barriers that are
erected to guide and control their action?" He did not
know who could question their acts and laws until they
came before the Court.

"The Constitution," said I, "prescribed that the President and Senate shall appoint ministers, consuls, etc.,
but Congress may, by law, confer inferior appointments
on judges, heads of Departments, or on the President
alone; but it nowhere authorizes Congress to confer on
generals the appointing power."

"It authorizes Congress to confer appointments, you
say, on the heads of Departments. Are not those districts
under General Sickles and other generals Departments?"
said Grant.

3

"Not in the meaning of the Constitution," said I, "and you can hardly be serious in supposing the provision of the Constitution alluded to, had reference to military districts, or any particular territory parceled out and called Departments."

He did not know, he said, he was not prepared to say about that. The will of the people is the law in this country, and the representatives of the people made the laws.

"The Constitution gives the pardoning power to the Executive. Do you suppose that Congress can usurp that power, and take it from the President, where the Constitution placed it?"

To this he replied that President Johnson once remarked in the Senate, in regard to talk about the Constitution, that it was well to spot the men who talked about it. It was, he said, just before the War, when the Secessionists talked about the Constitution.

"The remark," said I, "was opportune, and well put at the men and the times. The Secessionists claimed, and many of them honestly believed, that their States had the right to secede, — that there was no constitutional power to prevent them. So feeling and so believing, they searched the Constitution and appealed to it for any prohibition against secession. The appeal was absurd, according to your and my views, because the Constitution would not and could not have a clause empowering a fragment, a single State, to destroy it. Secession was a delusion which had its run, yet the men were generally scrupulous to observe in other respects the organic law, and, while meditating and preparing for the overthrow of the Government, their persistent appeals to the Constitution provoked the remark of Mr. Johnson to which you allude. While, however, the Secessionists professed to, and generally did, regard the Constitution, the Radicals openly trample upon it, and many express their contempt for it. The Secessionists claimed that they violated no principle or power or limitation in their act of secession. The Radicals do not claim, or pretend, to regard any principle or power or limitation of the Constitution when they establish military governments over States of the South and exclude them from their rights. When President Johnson made his remark, it was to contrast their appeals to the Constitution in all other respects, while Secession itself was destructive of the Constitution which they held in reverent regard."

"Would you," said he, "allow the Rebels to vote and take the government of their States into their own hands?" I replied that I knew not who were to take the government of those States in hand but the intelligent people of the States respectively to whom it rightfully belonged. The majority must govern in each and every State in all their local and reserved rights; other sections are not to govern them. A majority of the voters — and they decide for themselves who shall be voters — is the basis of free government. This is our system. Georgia must make her own laws, her own constitution, subject to the Constitution of the United States, not to the whim or will of Congress. Massachusetts has no power to prescribe the form of government of Georgia, or to govern the people of that State as a State. Nor is Georgia to give government to Massachusetts.

Grant said he was not prepared to admit this doctrine; it was something of the old State-Rights doctrine, and he did not go to the full extent of that doctrine. He looked upon Georgia and the other States South as Territories, like Montana and other Territories. They had rebelled, been conquered, and were to be reconstructed and admitted into the Union when we felt that we could trust them. It was for Congress to say who should vote, and who should not vote in the seceding States as well as in a Territory, and to direct when and how these States should again be admitted.

That I told him was not only a virtual dissolution of

the Union, but an abandonment of our republican federal system. It was establishing a central power, which could control and destroy the States, — a power above and beyond the Constitution, and I trusted he was not prepared to go that length, but if he was, I hoped he would avow it. For my part I clung to the old system, the Constitution and the Union, and favored no Radical theories of central power.

"Well," he said, he did not believe we could either convince the other, and we had better dispose of our business. I remarked that one of us was right and one wrong, and that it should be the object of each to put himself right, regardless of all partisanship, commitments, or preconceived opinions. This he admitted most fully.

There were other points which in this hasty memorandum, written immediately after its occurrence, I have not penned, but the essential points I have sketched, and have, as far as I could, used the very words. On the whole, I did not think so highly of General Grant after as before this conversation. He is a political ignoramus.

General Grant has become severely afflicted with the Presidential disease, and it warps his judgment, which is not very intelligent or enlightened at best. He is less sound on great and fundamental principles, vastly less informed, than I had supposed possible for a man of his opportunities. Obviously he has been tampered with and flattered by the Radicals, who are using him and his name for their selfish and partisan purposes.

In our conversation, when I asked if our Government and Union were to be maintained by force, his only answer was the Rebels must be put down and kept under. "Will that," I asked, "make friendship and unity? Must we not, in the different States, be equal in political rights? Is not our governmental system voluntary and not compulsory? Can we have a reëstablished Union, and be one people by enforcing, under the bayonet, upon certain sections and an unwilling people (who are our countrymen, our equals, and who have their own laws and institutions), governments and laws not of their own choice and which are repulsive? Proscription, alienation, exile will not promote reconciliation and harmony. The Radical policy is to proscribe the intelligent, the wealthy, the moral portion of the South, and to place over them the ignorant and degraded and vicious." He said he did not think Jeff Davis and Benjamin ought to be put on the same footing and have the same voice and influence as those of us who had maintained the Union. I replied they had not so good a record, and their influence and success in future would depend on their own acts. We might lessen ours; they might improve theirs. As we now stood, I thought we had nothing to apprehend.

It appears to me he was somewhat excited and stirred up by appeals of the Radicals and fears that he might lose their good will. None but Radicals, and the most mischievous of them, are hounding and stimulating and cautioning him. Anxious, as I am satisfied he is becoming, for the Presidency, he fears to fall out with them. Hence, believing, as he does, that a majority of the country which is represented is with Congress, he is rather vexed, dissatisfied, and somewhat confused, has listened to Radical fallacies and is strangely ignorant of the true character of men as well as the real principles in issue.

I went over and saw the President, and stated my interview, and my apprehensions that Grant was weaker and a little farther astray than I had apprehended. [I said] that I thought our conversation would perhaps do some good, — enforce some ideas which he had not previously entertained, and perhaps correct some that were in a measure erroneous. He is, however, a man of little reading or reflection.

I also called on Judge Blair, and requested him to see Grant, talk with him, get others who are right-minded to talk with him also, and write him, — enlighten him. He needs instruction.

August 23, *Friday*. Have dispatches to-day from Admiral Bell of the Asiatic Squadron, detailing the attack on the natives of Formosa. Also a long statement from Carter, reporting affairs at Borneo, and the burning of the house of the consulate, which I think was set on fire by the consul himself.

At the Cabinet quite a discussion grew out of a dispatch of an extraordinary character from General Sickles, insisting he would obstruct the power of the United States Court, and, alleging, as a reason, that if he did not, the Court would soon pass on the Reconstruction acts and pronounce them unconstitutional.

Mr. Binckley, the Assistant Attorney-General, said that it had been his intention to present a written opinion on this subject, and he should not have attended the meeting to-day had not the President sent for him. He expressed his surprise that General Sickles, who is a lawyer, and could not be ignorant of the consequences that must follow an attempt to make the civil power subordinate to the military, should put himself in opposition to the Chief Justice and resist the processes of the Court.

General Grant said he had sent an order to General Sickles not to obstruct the United States Court, as he promised he would, but, after thinking of it, he had come to the conclusion that General Sickles might have his reasons for what he was doing, and as there are always two sides to a question, he had countermanded his order, that Sickles might have an opportunity to be heard. Congress had put in his (Grant's) hands the execution of this law, and he intended to see it was executed, but he was willing to hear, or see, Mr. B.'s written opinion, when it was made out.

There were some rather flippant, overbearing, and ungenerous remarks of Grant towards Binckley, which were unworthy of him, when the positions of the two men were considered. Binckley, though a little excited, was more than a match for the General in such a discussion, and did not allow himself to be put down by what was really arrogance and intentional insult.

I am glad that I made no remark on the subject of Grant's declaration that *he* should see the law executed, for Congress had put it into *his* hands. He evidently supposed that it was *his* province, exclusively, to decide in regard to this whole subject, but B. coolly said he supposed the General expected to execute it in subordination to law and authority.

August 24, *Saturday.* I inquired by way of suggestion, or I, more properly, suggested by way of inquiry, of the President the subject or expediency of general amnesty. There might be individual exceptions, but it seemed to me it would be well, before voting commenced in the proscribed States, that the people should have amnesty. He said he had thought much on the subject and should before long have something definite to say in regard to it.

Alluding to the discussions yesterday, he complimented Binckley, but he inquired what I thought of Randall, and if his conduct was not somewhat singular of late, on some of these important questions. I had noticed that Randall said but little, and that little was evasive, but the President saw and noted more in that quarter than I did.

In submitting a certain document, Seward said he had desired to bring it before the Cabinet, in order that it might be borne in mind, should he not be here to explain. There was, I thought, something significant in the remark under the circumstances. I also observed that he very much wished Randall to take an excursion of a few days with him on the river and coast. R. could not go, however, but no other one was invited to supply his place. Seward evidently feels the absence of Stanton.

The papers speak of a reorganization of the Cabinet. This has not been unusual but is periodical. Just at this time it has more than ordinary significance, and the *Intelligencer*, which I know speaks not unadvisedly, had one or two

emphatic articles on the subject of an entire change. The
fire has been more particularly directed to Seward, though
McCulloch has been attacked by harpies. The rest have
come in for slight attacks, but all except Mr. Stanbery are
named to go. It may be best.

August 26, Monday. Montgomery Blair called to suggest the name of D. D. Field for Secretary of State, should
Seward resign, which he seems to suppose a fixed fact.
I gave him to understand that it did not strike me with
particular favor. But Blair knows Field to be very right on
present questions, — is from New York, was a Barnburner
in 1848, something of a favorite, etc., etc., and he is recommended by William B. Reed. This last information did not
strengthen the matter in my estimation. Reed is a man of
talents but impracticable, and of erratic principles and
politics. Blair tells me he has sent Reed's letter to the
President.

In all my conversation with Blair he has been persistent
in pressing General Grant as a man of shrewdness and of
unusual popularity. He urged, I know, G.'s appointment
to the War Department, and told me last week he was preparing an article for the *New York World* in favor of Grant
for President. I have not been hasty to commit myself to
this suggestion, for, whatever may be Grant's popularity,
growing out of military successes and services, I see no
evidence of civil capacity, administrative ability, or general
intelligence. He is stolid and stubborn, but has been tampered with, and I believe seduced, by the Radical conspirators, who have the start of Blair in this idea of availability
and mean to use him as their candidate. He has been willing to be courted, but is not quite prepared to have it
published that the parties are engaged and to be married.
The President is still reluctant to believe that Grant is
unfaithful. I have uniformly stated that Grant, while
apparently simple-minded and perhaps honestly disposed,
— though I have misgivings on that point, — has fallen into

the hands of Radical rogues, who are imposing upon him,
not unwillingly. They have him in their keeping, I fear.
I spoke of these matters to Blair; asked what could be said
or thought of Grant's course in regard to Sickles' Order
No. 10, proclaiming a stay-law in the Carolinas, and obstructing, by military force, the judgments and processes
of the courts. Grant himself has said he thought this
wrong as regarded the United States Courts, and has
issued an order annulling so much of the Order No. 10
as applied to the United States Courts. Within two days,
however, he countermanded his own order and permitted
Sickles to go on in his lawlessness. Of course Radical advice
and intimacy had overcome his own better judgment.
Grant is an insincere man, I fear, very ambitious, has low
cunning, and is unreliable, perhaps untruthful.

I gave Blair to understand that my confidence in Grant,
in his intelligence and even honesty, was less than his, —
that it was, indeed, very much shaken. I am not prepared
to condemn him as a bad man, but I consider him an insincere one. He has no political experience, has not
studied, nor made himself familiar with, our Constitution
or the elementary principles of civil government even, but
has permitted himself to be flattered, seduced, and led
astray by men who are bad. Unless he can be extricated
and that soon, he will, because he has a War record, be
made an instrument of evil. The people admire military
men, and are grateful for military services. Grant has
power and position without the knowledge to use them
properly. I instanced several matters. Blair heard me and
frankly admitted that with these facts he gave Grant up,
— that he had gone over to the Radicals, and we could
hope nothing from him. I am unwilling to give him wholly
up if there is any good in him. Let him have a chance to
retrieve himself if he will, — not that I would make him
President.

August 27, Tuesday. The correspondence between the

President and Grant in relation to the removal of Sheridan has been published. There has not yet been time to get response. Of course the Radical press will indorse and extol Grant, but he certainly does not in this matter appear to advantage. His letter is weak, his logic is weak, the thing is feeble. The letter was written plainly for publication, but the President's reply is dignified and conclusive.

At the Cabinet to-day, a question came up respecting the Governor of Idaho, who is represented as a cheat and swindler. Another was nominated and confirmed as his successor at the last session, but the Senate reconsidered the vote, and the subject remained unacted on. Over two hundred thousand dollars of Indian amnesties are due, but the Secretary of the Interior declines putting the money in the swindler's hands.

The question was raised whether a successor could be appointed under the Tenure-of-Office Bill. If G. is appointed, and B., the incumbent, refuses to give up the office, what is to be done? Should B. resist by force, McCulloch said, call on the military. General Grant said in that case the military would not respond. They would sustain the Tenure-of-Office Bill, which Congress has enacted, until the judges said it was unconstitutional.

General Grant addressed the President, remarking that he had received his order directing General Sheridan to proceed forthwith to Kansas and relieve General Hancock. In the mean time the duties of the office would devolve on the next in command. But that officer was sick. No word had yet been received from General Thomas. It was known, however, he had gone to the Springs for his health. But he thought it would be injudicious to take General Hancock from the Plains, where he had varied duties. It would be better to carry out the original order. Let Sheridan remain, therefore, until General Thomas can relieve him. When Sheridan is relieved from his present command, Grant wished him to have leave and visit Washington. He had hardly been home since he graduated, and it would be well to have him come here. Furthermore, the law placed the execution of the Reconstruction acts in his, Grant's, hands. He had not been consulted when he received orders, and those orders counteracted, in their terms, some of his orders. While he had no wish to come in conflict with any one, he had a duty to perform. He must see the Reconstruction law executed.

The President was very cool, calm, and deliberate in his reply to this studied and premeditated speech. He reminded General Grant that he himself had brought the surgeon's certificate in regard to General Thomas' health, had stated it was such that he thought it imprudent for General T. to go at this time to New Orleans, and had asked to have the order suspended. That, as regarded a leave to Sheridan, that could as well be granted after he reported on the frontier as before. Let him repair to Leavenworth or Denver and relieve General Hancock, then, if he can be spared for a visit, he can take his time and the several orders would be carried into effect. "General Grant will understand it is my duty to see the laws are executed, and also that when I assign officers to their duty my orders must be obeyed. I have made this arrangement and performed this work deliberately, and it will go with as little delay as possible."

Grant was humbled by this great rebuke and changed the subject. He said if General Sickles was to be detached, no better man than General Canby could succeed him. Canby could not, however, be very well spared from here, where he was familiar with details, and above all his services were important on the Board of Claims. As regarded General Sickles, two of his orders, the one intended as a stay-law and one establishing a code, were unauthorized. Both were good in themselves, but General Sickles had no authority to issue such orders. There might also be other objectionable orders.

The President said he was glad there was concurrence of views in regard to the future of General Canby, and as for the matter of his being one of the Board of Claims, it would not weigh a feather. The board itself was of little importance, — had no final action.

General Grant also remarked, in a subdued manner, that he wished to say that while it was proper he should discharge the duties *ad interim* of Secretary of War, he was no politician and preferred not to be mixed up in political questions. He would, therefore, prefer not to sit at the Cabinet consultations and pass opinions on the subjects which came up for consideration and decision. The President told him that was at his own option.

The General said he would wish, then, to be excused, for he had much to attend to at the Department; and he accordingly withdrew.

August 29, *Thursday*. The President narrated the particulars of proceedings and consultations between himself and General Grant. He says that G., after stating on Tuesday that he wished to discharge his duties as an officer, but wished to be excused from taking any part in, or expressing any views or opinions on, political subjects, proceeded to write a long and very weak letter to him, most of it on matters purely political. It was such a letter as he would wish him to write, if he was disposed to pursue a course that would embarrass the Administration, for he could be annihilated by a reply.

Under the circumstances, however, he thought it best to send for Grant. The President was frank and blunt with him, — told Grant he should speak without reserve, but intended no offense. He then took up each position in the letter, pointed out his errors and fallacies, and so satisfied was Grant himself of his untenable positions, and the mistakes of his letter, that he asked to withdraw it. The President told him he might do as he pleased about it, but continued the conversation, during which Grant reached over, and, folding down the letter, took it and said he would send a note withdrawing it, but desired to take it personally. Grant had persisted in his old error that Congress had superseded the President and conferred on him (Grant) executive authority over the ten Southern States. He had, therefore, in this letter taken exception to the President's order detaching Sheridan and ordering Hancock to the Fifth District; supposed he could originate measures and rules for those States, make appointments, etc., instead of the President. The Constitution, as well as the President, was suspended by Congress. But he was soon satisfied, after having seen the President, that he had mistaken his duties, — that he was not the officer he supposed himself to be, and that he must back down.

The President called my attention to an article in this morning's *Chronicle*, showing that the writer of the editorial was aware of the contents of Grant's letter, — that there had been consultations in its preparation and that the commencement of the awkward withdrawal was also corrected. I am glad that Grant has permitted himself to be convinced to the extent mentioned, for he is, to use a vulgar phrase, somewhat pig-headed, having in his ignorance been inspired with certain strange notions by the Radicals, without resources of his own to correct them, or the intelligence necessary to carry him through. He would not have allowed himself to be convinced by any other person of the Cabinet, — probably by no supporter of the Administration, — but respect, deference, discipline made him listen to the President, his superior, and, listening, his faculties were stimulated and he comprehended the fact that he was making a sorry exhibition of himself.

In the course of their conversation, the President informed Grant that he (Mr. Johnson) was not a candidate for the Presidency. Grant replied that he was not. I bowed acquiescence and neither expressed regret nor a wish, that he, the President, should be a candidate. Perhaps he was disappointed that I did not.

August 30, *Friday.* There was a pleasant Cabinet-meeting to-day. Stanbery and Browning were absent. Grant was present and communicative, with a mind much softened, and more disposed to fellowship than at some recent meetings, particularly at the last. He has wholly revised his stand in regard to Sickles, and is decided against his Order No. 10, and also the order relating to the code.

August 31, *Saturday.* Had a pleasant talk with the President this evening. He has great capacity, is conversant with our public affairs beyond most men, has much experience, possesses great firmness, sincere patriotism, a sacred regard for the Constitution, is humane and benevolent. Extreme men and extreme measures he dislikes; secession and exclusion are alike repugnant. The Radicals accuse him of being irritable and obstinate, but the truth is he has been patient and forbearing, almost to an infirmity, under assaults, intrigues, and abuse. Had he been less yielding, less hesitating, more prompt and decided, met Radical error and misrule at the threshold, checked the first innovations on his prerogative, dismissed at once faithless public officers, he would have saved himself and the country many difficulties.

It is one of his greatest weaknesses that he has no confidants and seeks none. No man should hold such a position without tried and trusty friends to whom he can unbosom himself, and with whom he can consult and advise freely on all questions. To me, perhaps, he has been as free and as communicative as to any one, and yet there has been constant reserve. Many of his most important steps have been taken without the knowledge of any of his Cabinet, and I think without the knowledge of any person whatever. He has wonderful self-reliance and immovable firmness in maintaining what he believes to be right; is disinclined to be familiar with men in prominent positions, or to be intimate with those who fill the public eye. There are

around him too many little busybodies, almost all of whom
are unreliable, and often intentionally deceive him. It is a
misfortune that he permits them to be so familiar; not that
he means they shall influence him on important questions,
but in appointments they sometimes have influence and
mislead him. He does not make these fellows his confidants
any more than greater men, but they are intrusive, glad to
crowd around him, when men of mind and character will
not intrude uninvited, — and he invites none. Yet he willingly listens, receives information and suggestions, but
without reciprocating.

Coming into the Presidency under peculiar circumstances, he has hoped to conciliate Congress and those
who elected him, without making proper discriminations
as regards men and the conflicting views of his supporters
on fundamental questions. Many of the Republican Members were kindly disposed towards him and believed in the
Lincoln policy, which he adopted. These he could and
should have detached from the extremists. They were not
leaders, — not Radicals at the beginning; like himself, they
were sincere Republicans, but, not having the faculty of
receiving and giving confidence, these passive men were
treated coolly, as were the Radicals who constituted the
positive element opposed to him as well as to Mr. Lincoln
before him. Stanton, who conformed to this policy in
Mr. Lincoln's time, has been in constant intrigue with the
Radicals to thwart the President. Seward and Weed undertook, with Raymond and partisans of this school, to make
a division, but Raymond was so fickle, wavering, uncertain, and unreliable, that the really honest and worthy
men, while acknowledging his genius, despised his pusillan-
imity. Like Seward himself, Raymond became a source
of weakness, a positive injury. For a time he assumed,
under Seward's management and givings-out, to be the
organ of the Administration on the floor of the House, but
under the irony and sarcasm of Thaddeus Stevens, who
ridiculed his conscientious scruples, he soon stood alone.

The President really had no organ or confidential friend in the House, no confidant who spoke for him and his policy among the Representatives. Seward and Weed, to whom he listened, alienated the Democrats and almost all of his friends.

LII

Grant's Insubordination — Form of a Proclamation of General Pardon —
Newspaper Rumors of Differences between the President and Grant —
Amnesty proclaimed — Newspaper Reports of an Intended Prorogation
of Congress in case of an Attempt at Impeachment — Exercises at the
Antietam Battle-Field — Governor Geary's Followers try to turn the
Affair into a Radical Demonstration — Death of Sir Frederick Bruce —
The President consults with Lewis V. Bogy of St. Louis — Jeremiah S.
Black as an Adviser of the President — The Case of Paymaster Belknap
— The Sale of Ironclads discussed in Cabinet — General Sickles asks for
a Court of Inquiry — The Question of the Power of State and Municipal
Courts to discharge Men enlisted in the United States Service — The
Attorney-General consulted on the Subject — The Matter discussed in
Cabinet — Stanbery's Views as to the Habeas Corpus Writ — Admiral
Godon on the Naval Battle at Port Royal.

September 2, *Monday.* General Grant has issued an
order forbidding the district commanders from appointing, in other words reinstating, any of the removed civil
officers displaced by themselves or their predecessors. This
order is in bad taste and in a bad spirit, prompted, without
doubt, by Radical advisers. The manifest intention is to
keep Sheridan and Sickles appointees in place, to defy his
superior, to antagonize him, to defeat his intentions, provided he (the President) thinks it proper and correct for
the public interest to reappoint one or more of the local
State officers who may have been unfairly displaced. It is
the essence of insubordination by the General of the American armies, who should be an example of obedience.
General Grant is more intensely partisan than I was aware,
or perhaps than he himself supposes. One of these days,
when he calmly reviews his conduct, he will, if honest, be
ashamed of this order and of the spirit which prompted it.
I read to the President the form of a proclamation of
general pardon to the Rebels. He was pleased with it,
and requested a fair copy to be made, and at the same

3

time showed me the draft of one already prepared. It takes milder ground than the one I presented, and I am apprehensive he will not make his work as effective as I wish. He too often fails to come full up to the occasion. In our conversation he did not dissent from my views and positions in any respect, and persons not acquainted with him would have supposed he adopted them all; but this is not his way. He listens, but, unless he squarely and emphatically disapproves, is disinclined to controvert. This trait has led many to misunderstand and to misrepresent him. They make statements themselves which he does not deny or dispute, and he is consequently represented as entertaining the views of his auditor or adviser.

September 3. Received dispatches to-day from the commanders of all our squadrons except the South Pacific, — all satisfactory.

General Grant did not attend the Cabinet-meeting to-day. There was not much of special interest before it.

McCulloch presented the case of a Collector and Assessor in Virginia, and recommended that they should be suspended. They have received repeated bribes to the amount of over thirty thousand dollars. I inquired why they should not be *removed*, and he said the Tenure-of-Office Bill interposed. I thought, and so stated, that removal in such flagrant cases as these was not only justifiable but proper, and if Congress, or the Senate, took exceptions, let the facts go before the country. The people will judge and decide rightly in such an issue, and better understand the value of present legislation. The President, I see, concurs with me, — is pleased with my views, — but I am not certain how he will do when compelled to act. His opinions and mine of the Tenure-of-Office Bill are alike. I hope he will not surrender the right but will act upon it. He would but for wrong influences and an attempt to reconcile contradictions. His faith is sound; I wish his works were in accordance with his faith on these constitutional questions always.

If Congress wish to impeach him for opposing unwarranted innovations on the Constitution, for firmly and fearlessly maintaining the constitutional rights of the Executive, they will injure themselves more than him. It is not for me to urge him to be a martyr, if he is disinclined to encounter the warfare that will be waged by Radical partisans; but had he at the beginning resented these encroachments and innovations, the war would have been avoided that he now must encounter if he resists.

September 4. Montgomery Blair called to tell me that he had a long talk with the President. He was at my house Monday evening, having returned from Virginia that day, and was disturbed to find no farther changes had been made, — that things seemed at a standstill. Said nothing could be done for the President and Administration if Seward remained in the Cabinet. Showed me a dispatch from California and his reply. While Seward has very little personal popularity, and his advice and influence are often harmful, the President considers him the head of a powerful party — old-time Whigs — whose support is necessary for the success of his Administration. Seward has impressed him with this, but I cannot take part against him. There is very little sympathy or confidence between us as politicians or party men, and has never been. We have different temperaments, different principles, different associates and lines of action, but seldom, and never of late, any controversy. So long as the President yields to Mr. Seward's views and schemes and chooses to continue us as colleagues, I cannot personally oppose him. Blair knows my estimate of Seward; knew it when we were all associated in the Cabinet of Mr. Lincoln; would be glad to have me take an active part against Seward now, but I cannot.

To-day he sent his California dispatch to the President

and had quite an interview. He says he talked plain and blunt to the President; showed him a letter from Cassidy, of the *Albany Argus*, denouncing Johnson, declaring the Democrats could not and would not be identified with him so long as he retained in his counsels their avowed opponents. He says the President was equally frank and blunt. Said too many changes — too much yielding — would cloy the Democrats. They did not elect him, and though on principles of government and administration agreeing with him, they were reluctant to support him, etc., etc.

September 5. There is rumor of sharp differences between the President and Grant in an interview yesterday, and the sensationalists have got it in the papers. I should not be surprised if there were decided differences between them on some points, but nothing which has a semblance of altercation. They are not men for such scenes.

Grant has less intelligence and comprehension on political and civil matters than is generally supposed, and is more in the hands and under the control of active Radical party managers than he or the country is aware. Hence he is misled, blunders, misconceives, and takes feeble positions. I think he is committed to the Radicals and is prompted by them, but gets his lessons imperfectly. Not unlikely the President may have exposed his infirmities to him, told him his errors, and with his natural perversity, and ignorance, Grant may have been pig-headed and resisted the attempt to beat or screw intelligence into him. When he got back to the Department, or to his house, and was listened to, and schooled and drilled by Schenck, Cook, Shanks, and others, he recounted to them what had taken place at the White House, and it was in a few moments repeated with exaggerations at the hotels and in the papers. Grant was willing, probably intended, it should be understood that he and the President differ.

It is Grant's cunning; he has sly cunning, if but little knowledge.

September 6. Most of the time of the Cabinet was taken up with the subject of amnesty and pardon. The two forms of proclamation were submitted and discussed. Seward's was approved by all, and no exception taken to the paper which I presented, but it was more decisive and presented certain impregnable points, which milder men would rather avoid. The drafting of a proclamation is more especially the province of the Secretary of State. I therefore presented a paper to the President at his own request, as I suggested, for him to adopt or reject, in whole or in part.

September 7, *Saturday.* Was at the President's this P.M. Seward was about leaving. Colonel Moore, Private Secretary, was transcribing the Proclamation, which the President had remodeled, and Seward was criticizing. Some of my suggestions were incorporated; some which I think would have given it more character and popularity were omitted. The subject of relieving from *disfranchisement* was incorporated. It was one of the points urged by me as important, before the Proclamation was decided upon. In the document read to me this P.M., the subject of personal rights was omitted, while the rights of property had received special attention. I mentioned the omission, and the President thanked me, said immunities were intended. In the discussion yesterday, I noticed that the lawyers dwelt on the rights of property, but gave little heed to the rights of persons.

I would in the proclamation have alluded to the report of General Grant in December, 1865; would have brought out the fact of Congressional amnesty which was on the statute-book at the time the Rebels surrendered, and which they received and we in good faith promised, though Congress has since in bad faith repealed; would also have

more pointedly and distinctly brought out the divine
attribute of mercy. But the document is the President's;
I had made my suggestions; he knows my views; I would
not urge them farther. Seward would not, of course,
favor them, for they had not occurred to him, and he
would not willingly admit that I should prompt or correct him in a matter which belongs peculiarly to the
Secretary of State. Further he prefers what he believes
to be expedient to what he knows to be right.

September 9, *Monday*. The Proclamation is printed in
this morning's papers. Some modifications have been
made since Saturday. There is a little obscurity, perhaps,
on the subject of amnesty and pardon, of which the Radicals will try to take advantage. I endeavored that this
difficulty should be avoided. The President has the power
by the Constitution to grant pardons, but not amnesty.
In Great Britain, to whose laws and usages we look for
precedents, the King grants pardons to individuals, the
Parliament grants amnesty or general pardon to the masses.
Here no such distinction exists. The entire pardoning
power is with the Executive; none is conferred on Congress.
But that body of lawyers is so imbued with British law
and British precedent that it assumes for Congress the
powers of Parliament.

As regards amnesty, or oblivion, there is no such action
adapted to our government. Here we have no attainders,
forfeitures of blood, successions to the crown, requiring
oblivion; hence it does not properly enter into our
system.

September 10, *Tuesday*. At the Cabinet-meeting some
discussion took place in regard to certain removals and
appointments necessary to be made, but any action that
may be taken brings the Executive and all concerned
within the penalties of the unconstitutional Tenure-of-
Office Bill. The Senate having refused to confirm, or to

act on certain appointments, the functions of the government seem in those cases to be suspended.

The partisan, reckless, unauthorized legislation of the last and present Congress is hurrying the country on to anarchy. I was glad General Grant was present at the discussion. It seemed to impress him in a degree with the folly and wickedness of Congress.

September 11, *Wednesday.* The Radicals are full of sensation and malignity over the "Amnesty" Proclamation. They see in it incipient monstrosities, and the leaders declare that the President shall now certainly be impeached. He has pardoned Rebels, as he had the undoubted right to do, and this will allow them to vote, which Congress has no authority to prevent. General Butler is here. I saw him at the War Department, but he avoided General Grant. General Banks has been here on the invitation of Seward, who is very apt to get up little by-plays for his own ends. In this instance he is posting Banks on the purchase of the Danish islands.

September 12, *Thursday.* The *New York World* to-day has a very ungenerous and in a political view I think injudicious article, casting off President Johnson, for whose acts, they claim, the Democrats are not responsible, declaring he is the Republican President, etc., — all for party, nothing for country.

Such a course is calculated to and ought to injure any party. The repelling principle is not a wise one for minorities to act upon. The Democrats in New York and everywhere else should strive to recruit, and not drive off, forces. But the New York Democratic leaders of these days are small men with slight patriotism and have but little sagacity. The election this fall may be carried in spite of their folly, the good sense of the people is so shocked with Radical misrule; but the policy and views of the Democratic leaders, whose selfish anxiety for power and place is so perceptible, may continue the Radicals in power.

The President may not have been as discreet, wise, and decisive in some respects as he should have been. He has thrown away opportunities, neglected to strike at the right time, often has omitted — strangely omitted — to strike at all. Thus he injured himself and strengthened his opponents.

I met to-day, as I was going to the Treasury, several Pennsylvanians, — Packer, Campbell, Judge Patterson, etc. These men, McCulloch informs me, came to Washington expressly to see the President, had waited two or three hours in the ante-chambers, had seen a number of little, busy, partisan letter-writers admitted, and finally left in disgust, but he, McC., had persuaded them to return. McCulloch besought me to stop and see the President and procure them an interview. This I did without any inquiry into the object of their mission. They are men who should be treated with consideration and respect. The President remarked, when I spoke to him, that he had sent out for them, but was told they had left; that persons must have their time, etc. These are, however, men entitled to consideration, who should not be postponed for letter-writers and newspaper correspondents.

September 13, *Friday*. General Grant was not at the Cabinet-meeting. Stanbery was present, — the first time in some six weeks. Very little was done; the session was brief.

September 14, *Saturday*. The *New York Herald* and some other papers have Washington letters stating the design of the President to prorogue Congress, etc., in case that body undertakes to proceed with impeachment. I think from certain indications that the writers of those letters had some authority for their statements. I therefore made it a point to call attention to the *Herald's* letter, after concluding a little matter of business. The President said, with a laugh, he had seen the letter and there were some good points in it. I spoke of the prorogation. He remarked it was difficult to tell what might take place.

September 18, *Wednesday.* Went yesterday, the 17th, with the President and others to the battle-field of Antietam, it being the anniversary of that battle, fought five years ago. It was an interesting time, and we had a pleasant miscellaneous company, of politicians and military, — the latter much given to politics, — foreign legations, etc.

Not having been absent from the District for a year, excepting the single occasion of going over to Annapolis, part of a day, on an official visit, and never having passed over any part of the Baltimore and Ohio Railroad west of the Relay House, and never having visited any battle-ground east of the James River, I very willingly accepted the invitation to be present. The route up the Potomac is not interesting. At the Point of Rocks, where the canal and railroad crowd in under the ledges upon the river, there is local interest, — the naked stone piers which stand as monuments of the Rebellion, the wooden superstructures having been burnt, are there.

The Monocacy battle-field, of which we once heard so much, and other points still have evidence of the ravages of the War.

We reached Keedysville, where we left the cars, soon after noon. At the time it began to rain, which continued until we nearly reached the place selected for the occasion. This was on one of the highest Antietam hills, the place where Lee had his headquarters during the battle.

As the papers contain the proceedings, no record is necessary here. There was a large gathering of well-behaved and well-appearing people, who listened attentively to the proceedings. After the close of the oration of Governor

Bradford,[1] a loud and evidently preconcerted and pre-arranged cry went up for "Geary, Geary," from fifty or a hundred voices. Governor Swann, the President of the Day, attempted to be heard so far as to assure them that when the programme was completed, Governor Geary [2] and other men should have an opportunity to address them. But this did not satisfy the rude, ill-mannered fellows who had accompanied Geary from Penn-sylvania for the purpose of making a Radical demonstra-tion. As Geary sat near me, I saw that he was by no means dissatisfied with this disgraceful scheme to interrupt proceedings, but that he well understood and approved the row. At length he stepped forward, and informed his boisterous followers that he and others would address them when the "*programmatical*" order was completed.

We left as soon as the "*programmatical*" proceedings closed, and, being delayed in getting the cars started, which were detained for those engaged in the party har-angues, we did not get home until nearly two o'clock in the morning.

The Governors of Maine, Connecticut, New York, New Jersey, Pennsylvania, West Virginia, and Maryland were present. With the exception of English[3] and Swann, these are Radicals, and some of them small, very small, party politicians. Geary was on the ground with party designs and made a Radical partisan's speech in a national grave-yard. Fenton,[4] slow, deliberate, affected, and light in mental calibre, was far more decent in his bearing.

He, Fenton, called on me to-day and was quite civil and patronizingly *condescending;* wanted to patronize me by asking an office for one of his staff. Governor English, with Ingersoll, Adjutant-General, and one of his staff, called. He has no confidence in Postmaster-General

---

[1] Augustus W. Bradford, the War Governor of Maryland. He was succeeded by Thomas Swann, 1865–67.
[2] Of Pennsylvania. He was a brigadier-general of volunteers in the War.
[3] The Governor of Connecticut.
[4] Governor Reuben E. Fenton of New York.

Randall, and would be glad to have Seward a permanent resident in Auburn. Rejoices in Stanton's removal, but would be particularly pleased if Randall were also removed.

September 19, *Thursday.* Sir Frederick W. A. Bruce, the British Minister, died this A.M. in Boston, of diphtheria, or something else. A fortnight since, I saw him in apparently full and vigorous health. He told me he was going to take a little run for relaxation, and quietly urged it upon me also as a necessity. It was the last time I saw him. He claims to be a relative, perhaps a descendant, of *the* Bruce. Was a pleasant, fine-appearing man of popular manners. A much more sprightly and affable man than Lord Lyons, his predecessor, but of less mental strength.

September 20, *Friday.* Weather has been excessively warm the last two days. Many persons in town. The approaching elections excite much interest. There are vague and indefinite rumors of changes. Blair informs me that the President has invited Bogy [1] here from St. Louis for consultation. I think it singular. Bogy was rejected by the Senate last winter or spring as Indian Commissioner, — a position which he filled very creditably. He is earnest and apparently sincere, — not always judicious and discriminating, nor does he always read men and movements correctly. He tells Blair that the President assures him he intends to remove Seward, McCulloch, and Randall; intimates that he shall perhaps make Horatio Seymour Secretary of State. This is, or would be, a strange movement, — a specimen of New York partyism which is about played out. Blair is probably right in imputing the intrigue to Seward. I trace it to Weed, but the two go together, and the present great object of the master spirit, Weed, is to defeat the New York Democrats. The movement would injure the President, and it would assist the Radicals. I can hardly believe he will commit so grave a mistake.

[1] Lewis V. Bogy, afterwards a Democratic Senator from Missouri.

In view of this information, I remained after the others left the Cabinet-meeting, and in a desultory conversation cautioned the President against the intrigues of Weed, who I assured him was laboring to defeat the Democrats in New York, regardless of any effect it might have on the Administration. He said Weed would get nothing farther here. Thought Wakeman ought to be removed. I reminded him that Weed and Seward were one. I reminded him that Kilpatrick was still holding two offices, — Minister to Chili and a commission in the regular Army. At all events I had never heard that he had relinquished either place, though I had understood it had been ordered. He said that should be done, — should not pass the next Cabinet-meeting.

I told Blair that I questioned the expediency of removing McCulloch, which some were urging; that I could not only advise, but should object, if I was allowed to know before a movement was made or attempted. Blair says McCulloch has fallen under Seward's influence. I should not be surprised if that were so, to some extent, yet I cannot think it very great. He feels it necessary to carry on his Department, and is glad of help from any quarter. McCulloch may be imposed upon, — the victim of Seward's and Weed's New York superfine party management, — but if so, it is because he does not understand the intrigues and their object. Blair says Bogy told him the President did not express himself satisfied with any of his Cabinet but me, but that he complimented me.

I yesterday dined at the President's with General Hancock and General Mitchell, his Chief of Staff, Jere Black, and Colonel Cooper [1] of Tennessee. General H. talks very well, and I hope will act sensibly in Louisiana. The Radicals are a little disconcerted on account of his being here when they wish to make a partisan demonstration for Sheridan, whom Hancock supersedes. At the theatre

[1] Edmund Cooper, who represented a Tennessee district in the Thirty-ninth Congress.

on Saturday evening the audience cheered Hancock, while Sickles and Forney were in an adjoining box unbeknown to H. General Mitchell is a Mifflin County, Pennsylvania, boy, known to our relations there.

Jere Black is spending much time with the President of late. He was Buchanan's Attorney-General, and Secretary of State after Cass resigned. He has legal ability and is a politician of more than ordinary power, but I distrust that class of politicians who really promoted rebellion when they declared themselves paralyzed and unable to coerce a State. I do not consider him a good and sound adviser for the President, and am sorry that he is so much consulted and deferred to, when there are sound and good men outside of the Cabinet — if he is driven there — whom he might consult. I shall not be surprised if there are some changes of an important character in contemplation and strong measures taken. The President, I know, has such intentions, but he hesitates, — delays executing his good intentions. Whether Black's advice will be judicious if it is sought, is questionable, yet he has a good deal of sagacity and shrewdness.

Colonel Cooper was a member of the last Congress, but was defeated by the negro vote in the recent election. He thinks Brownlow will be elected to the Senate, and both he and Patterson [1] think him, with all his coarse roughness, a better and honester man than Maynard and Stokes.[2]

Senator Thomas [3] of Maryland and ex-Mayor Berrett [4] made a formal call to-day in behalf of ex-Paymaster Belknap, who was dismissed, or went out of the service, several years since as a defaulter. There was a mysterious robbery

---

[1] David T. Patterson, one of the Senators from Tennessee.

[2] Horace Maynard and William B. Stokes, Representatives from Tennessee.

[3] Philip Francis Thomas was at the time Senator-elect from Maryland, but in the following February he was refused a seat on the ground of "having given aid and comfort to the Rebellion."

[4] J. G. Berrett, Mayor of Washington, 1858–62.

of some hundred and thirty thousand dollars in the Brooklyn Navy Yard, when he was Paymaster of the Yard, for which he could not account, and after some two years or more ... he was dismissed, having in the mean time, through the influence and activity of powerful friends, had opportunity to go before Congress. A few months since, Marshal Murray and a Treasury detective brought a parcel of thieves and burglars here, who, they said, confessed themselves to be the robbers. But as the case was outlawed by lapse of time, no punishment could be inflicted on the wretches if actually guilty, which is questionable, to say the least, and as they had no characters, their acknowledgments I consider unreliable and unworthy of credit.

In bringing up the case to-day, Mr. Berrett said one reason for the delay in pressing the subject before Congress was the difficulty which he experienced in getting the act of March 2, 1865, through Congress. This act says, if an officer is dismissed by the President, he may demand a court martial, and if not granted within six months, he shall be reinstated. I asked if Belknap procured that law to be passed, and he said he with others did. "Then," said I, "he expected after leaving the service that a court martial could reappoint him. The Constitution gives all appointments to the President and Senate, but Congress *may by law* give inferior appointments to the President alone, heads of Departments, or judges. It does not confer this authority on courts martial, and as Belknap is out, and has been out for several years, I am not prepared to say that he is restored because there has been no court martial in his case." Senator Thomas said this was a new view of the case, and the two left, Berrett saying the case should be submitted.

September 24, *Tuesday*. At the Cabinet-meeting Seward proposed that it should be understood that we had no more ironclad or naval vessels to sell. He said the Turks were making application and it would be annoying. I said more annoying to me than any one else, for the Greeks were also applying. The Greek Minister has called on me; wanted to get the small ironclads for about three hundred thousand dollars, and wished credit for one half until May next, perhaps longer. I told him to put his proposition in writing and I would give a written answer. One thing he might understand at once, — that we could sell no vessel elsewhere than in the United States.

McCulloch thought it not advisable to refuse to sell any of our vessels, particularly ironclads. I said we might sell and ought to sell if we had an unobjectionable purchaser, but that we were not in the market. I so said to the German Minister. The truth is they are expensive to keep and will soon go to waste unemployed on our hands.

General Grant presented the case of General Sickles, who asked a court of inquiry. Some discussion followed. Stanbery seems not to understand these matters. Grant thought an officer could demand a court of inquiry. I queried whether he could have one unless the President deemed it advisable. In this instance the court was asked, not for military, but civil reasons. General Sickles disliked the views of a civil officer of the Government, and disliked the act of the President detaching him. For these reasons he wanted a court of inquiry, — in other words, wanted to try the President and Attorney-General for disapproving his conduct.

The President suggested that the elections in the proscribed States should be upon the same day. Grant interposed difficulties. Some of the States had closed registration, fixed the day of election, and could not well go over the process. Thought it would cause difficulty. I perceived that he and the President had conferred on the subject, and I also perceived that others had had some conference with him.

I went to a party at General Grant's this evening, given in honor of the generals now here. There was quite an attendance of army officers and others, and also of most of the Cabinet. I went early and left early, — as soon as I could see Sheridan and Sickles. If Hancock came, it was after I left.

September 25, Wednesday. Had a long interview with Rear-Admiral Godon, who gave me at great length his troubles with our Ministers in South America, particularly with General Webb.[1]

Mr. Roselius of New Orleans called on me this evening. Deplores the condition of affairs in Louisiana and through the whole South; is ready to submit to any government that will give security to person and property. This will become the general cry and petition there and elsewhere if the mad partyism of the Radicals is not checked, as I trust it will be. There are indications that the sense and reason of the people are moving in the Northern States, I trust in the right direction, but partyism is stronger than patriotism. The extreme Democrats seem to consider their obligations to party greater than to their country. In this respect they are surely better than the Radicals, who are partisan in the extreme. The Democrats do not, however, in all their excitement, ignore or trample on the Constitution, as the Radicals do, in order to attain party ends.

Received a telegram from Commodore Selfridge, asking that instructions be sent District Attorney in relation to refusal to submit to *habeas corpus* in State court, or to be arrested for such refusal. There has been a difficulty arising for some time past in relation to enlistments, — various contrivances to withdraw the enlisted party from the custody of the United States Government and Courts. There are, I believe, two or three naval cases and one army case pending, the latter being first to be tried. Commodore Smith came to me a few days ago with a telegram from Selfridge, asking what should be done when the writ was served, supposing it related to one of the recruits on

[1] James Watson Webb, New York journalist, Minister to Brazil, from 1861 to 1869.

the receiving ship. There are many whom a ring of petti-
foggers are constantly striving to retain after they have
drawn advanced pay. I said he must not let the officer
come on board to serve the writ. Faxon, who was present,
said, "Resist him by armed force." I told the Commodore
to call on the legal officer, who had charge of these matters
and would advise him how to proceed; that we had written
to the District Attorney some months since, anticipating
this trouble, but had received no answer; that he seemed
timid, afraid to meet the case, or did not know how to act.
This telegram shows that the trouble has commenced.
The question whether the State or municipal courts can
interpose and discharge men enlisted in the United States
service should be settled, and if I had confidence in the
energy and ability of the District Attorney at Philadelphia,
I would as soon have it disposed of now as ever. Were the
Attorney-General a firm, decided man, less a technical
lawyer and more of a statesman, so as to instruct and
inspire Gilpin, I should feel more assured.

September 26, Thursday. Presented Admiral and Mrs.
Godon to the President this morning, and took a long ride
with them this evening. The Philadelphia papers this
morning have a report of the proceedings before Judge
Pierce in the *habeas corpus* case, George Gormel, all of
which was discreet and proper, save the coarse and vulgar
speech of Mann, the District Attorney. A dispatch from
Selfridge also asks instruction. My first thought was to
send a letter of instructions to Commodore S., but when
it was prepared, I thought it better to submit it to the
Attorney-General and get his opinion whether it was
proper and correct, and also get from him an opinion concerning the case,—whether a body of troops on the march
or a naval vessel getting under weigh could be stopped by
a local municipal judge. I had very little confidence that
I should procure anything definite or satisfactory, and was
therefore not disappointed when he began to express doubts

3

and to hesitate. "It is a great writ, Mr. Secretary," he repeated half a dozen times at least. I did not controvert this, but told him this was a great country, that we were a great people, and the naval service itself was something; perhaps all could be checked and thrown out of gear by a person holding office under a different jurisdiction than that of the United States. I called his attention to the Booth case in Wisconsin, where the Supreme Court said the marshal should not give up a prisoner who was in the custody of the United States. Referred him to Judge Holt's book. After reading twice the article on *habeas corpus*, he looked more wise and unbent a little, — inquired about the case. Who sued out the writ? Was he accused of crime? He must know the particulars. I told him that it did not seem to me necessary, — no particular case was the subject of my inquiry. The question is, can the Government — can the United States — be impleaded? Can a State court require the United States to show cause why it has a person in custody, — inquire into the validity of an enlistment? In answer to his question, however, I stated I supposed the writ was sued out in this instance by the father of the enlisted man. "Yes, this is a great writ, Mr. Secretary, a great writ. If he were a murderer, or criminal, the State would demand him." "That," said I, "is not denied or questioned; he is neither. But if the writ can be sued out in this way, great public injury may follow. A vessel on the point of sailing — going, perhaps, on an important errand for the Government, one affecting peace or war — may in this way be stopped by factious parties and detained for days and weeks. The Government is powerless, if it has not the control of its enlisted men. Such an abuse is not to be thought of."

After rubbing his face and hands, looking up, and then at the fire, he said the question was important, required time. I said that was not allowable, for the judge had delayed the matter only until the 28th, Saturday, and I wished to answer Commodore Selfridge to-day, and

I desired the District Attorney, or his assistant, Mr. Valentine, who appeared to manage the case, might be advised. He then asked for the proceedings, — the steps which have been taken, — and I told him I would send over the correspondence and some suggestions. He desired I would do so and said he would give the subject prompt attention.

On getting the correspondence from the Bureau, I find it pretty taut, — a little more belligerent in some respects than it would have been had it been submitted to me, — but Commodore Smith says his letter of instruction was obtained from the War Department. In so important a matter I should really have been more consulted, as things turn out. It is unfortunate that he went only to the Solicitor or Judge-Advocate of the War Department. The truth is none of these telegrams and orders have been submitted to me until the conflict came on, except in the single instance when I referred Commodore Smith to the law office for advice as to the usual form and course of proceedings in similar cases.

September 27, Friday. The apprehensions of a collision at Nashville was the principal topic of discussion in the Cabinet. The municipal authorities claim the right of conducting the election under their charter, which has not been altered. Brownlow, the Governor, insists they shall not, but that negroes and others shall vote and that the polls shall be opened and conducted by his instruments. He has called out the militia to enforce his plan. The city authorities have organized an armed police to maintain their rights.

The President directed General Grant to order General Thomas with regulars to Nashville that he might assist in preserving the peace. General Grant read to-day the correspondence between himself and Thomas, which will probably result in giving the whole question to Brownlow. The regulars are not to interfere, and probably could not, except upon application of the Governor, and he will not make that application if he can succeed without. If he cannot succeed, then he will take the necessary steps to call General Thomas and the United States troops to his aid, if the President, to whom B. dislikes to appeal, will permit. Thomas inclines to the Radicals; at the beginning of the Rebellion he inclined to the Secessionists. These people, the Radicals, will not regard the rights of Nashville if they conflict with the negro.

I brought up the subject of a conflict of authorities at Philadelphia, and remarked that I had placed the subject in the hands of the Attorney-General, who would, perhaps, state the case.

With a wave of the hand and a shake of his head he said yes, I had called on him, but had not fully informed him as to the particulars, and until he had all the circumstances he would not undertake to give an opinion. The writ of *habeas corpus* is a great writ, and there was but one course that he was aware of, when it was sued out, and that was to produce the body.

"What," said I, "if the judge or court has no jurisdiction?" "But," said he, "the court has jurisdiction; the body must be produced in all cases." I replied this was not done, and could not be done without bringing the Federal authority into contempt, and discouraging and demoralizing the service.

"What," said he, "if the *habeas corpus* is for a murderer?" "Then," said I, "the man would be given up to be tried, and so would any man charged with crime without the *habeas corpus*. When, however, there is no crime, but a question of the validity of an enlistment, I apprehend a local State judge cannot interfere. The United States are not servable, and if not servable, how are enlisted men to be brought before a Pennsylvania judge, for him to decide whether the contract is proper and acceptable?"

General Grant remarked that this question had given the Army great trouble, but he believed the question was pretty well settled, though there was just now a little fuss

in Philadelphia with one of their officers. It would not do,
however, to have petty courts setting the soldier free.

"But," said Stanbery, "they must reply to the writ of
habeas corpus and produce the man." Grant said he
thought the Army was not doing this to the State judges.

Seward told Stanbery he did not believe he could get off
from this question without investigating it; that the writ
was a great one, but great questions were involved which
could not be set aside by mere remarks that the body must
be produced. McCulloch, Randall, and Otto,[1] all maintained that they thought the Federal authority should be
maintained.

Finding himself sustained by none and that the question was not to be evaded, the Attorney-General said he
was willing to look into it, but he must have time. He
wanted to know all the facts and circumstances, and
wished I would let him have them. I told him it had never
appeared to me necessary to travel over the details of any
particular case. We wanted a principle settled. The question is, Can the United States be sued in the State courts?
Will the *habeas corpus* lie against an officer acting under
orders, who returns that the prisoner or person is in his
custody by authority of the United States? I had given
him the respectful answer of Commodore Selfridge to the
writ, and had also sent him the correspondence. He said
he had not seen this; his clerk having lost a child, his
papers were behindhand.

I remarked that the case was adjourned until to-morrow
and Commodore Selfridge was expecting and entitled to instructions. He wished me to inform the Commodore that he
was investigating the case and would give an answer at the
earliest moment possible. I declined; told him that would
not be satisfactory; that, the case having been put in his
hands, it was for him to make that application or request.
He hesitated, — demurred a little. I told him I would,
if he wished, forward it; that he might address a line to me,

[1] William T. Otto, Assistant Secretary of the Interior.

expressing his wish for time, and I would send that. He assented and wrote the note. "What," said I, "if this is unavailing, and the judge refuses, as I think likely he will, to postpone?" He said he could not, in that event, advise. "But," said I, "I must,—advise and dissent."

September 28, *Saturday.* I called on the Attorney-General tolerably early and found him and his clerk busy hunting up authorities for the *habeas corpus* case at Philadelphia. We had pretty earnest talk on two or three points. Like all lawyers, he is stuffed full of English law and English precedents, and most of his books were English authorities. He read to me from several volumes regarding the writ. I told him I was not ignorant of its importance, especially in England at an earlier period than the present, and that it was not without value in these days and in our own country, but was now and here perhaps overestimated.

"This case," said I, "could not come up in this form in England, to which country you are so intently looking for authorities, for they have not, like us, two sovereignties. Here there are two jurisdictions, and the lesser assumes to pass judgment on the superior in a matter affecting the latter. Commodore Selfridge, under direction from the Navy Department of the United States, and, for that matter, under the President himself, denies jurisdiction, has returned a respectful answer to the writ, and his action is to be approved or disapproved. If his return is imperfect, let us perfect it; if in error, let us put him right; but I deny the jurisdiction of the quarter-session court of Philadelphia to pass judgment on the United States."

He admitted the correctness of my suggestions; said he had thought of most of them himself, but we must, just at this time, move very cautiously. Our opponents were charging us with taking too much power now. I told him that he and I knew how false and groundless these charges were. The error had been in the opposite direction. "I am a State-Rights man, and I am also for Federal rights. The

authority conferred by the Constitution on the Federal
Government I shall assert and maintain as sacredly and
inviolably as the rights of the States which are reserved.
But the error of this Administration has been that it has
dwarfed, belittled itself, — failed to exercise the authority
conferred by the Constitution on the executive department. We have been passive and shrinking, — have not
maintained the national rights and authority intrusted to
us by the Constitution. It is not for me to say who have
been advisers of this policy, or who have opposed it. I, as
a Federal officer, support without transcending Federal
authority. In the matter now before us, my Department
is involved, and I have thus far sustained, and so far as
I have a view I intend to sustain, the authority of the
Department and the Government against encroachment.
I deny the jurisdiction of the State courts. I deny that the
United States are suable in those courts, and the time
must come when the Administration must declare and
maintain its authority. On you, Mr. Attorney-General,
much depends."

He answered me that he should thoroughly look into
this question, and believed he should give an opinion that
would be satisfactory to me. "But the fact is, in this great
writ one thing is always and forever essential, — the
person must be produced in court. He may be at once
discharged by Judge Pierce, and that would end the
controversy."

"Suppose he is not discharged," said I, "what then?"

"Ah! well, that to be sure; then we should have to carry
the case up," said he.

"Has Judge Pierce any business with this case?" I
asked. "Can he try it? Was it not his duty, when application was made to him, to have said to the parties he had
no jurisdiction, — that they must go to the United States
judge?"

Without answering my question, he said, "Supposing
Commodore Selfridge had seized a citizen of Philadelphia

and confined him in the Yard, — a person who had not enlisted, — could not Judge Pierce grant a writ of *habeas corpus* for the production of that citizen?"

"Most certainly he could," said I, "but that is not the present question."

"Then," said he, "supposing Commodore Selfridge had returned that the man was enlisted, when he was not enlisted?"

"In that event, Selfridge himself would have been liable. It would have been a wrong of T. O. Selfridge individually, —not the Commodore officially, —for which he would have been personally responsible. He would in such case be no more acting for the United States than if he had stolen the man's watch and denied the theft."

These are some of the points which passed between us, and I think the discussion had a beneficial effect. The Attorney-General started wrong; he intended to have put aside the great question; he is a little professionally conceited, but means to do right, — is a little annoyed when I raise points, or controvert his positions, as I sometimes do. Often, without arguing the question, he resorts to technicalities, subtleties of the law, pleadings, etc., as if great truths can be hidden or disposed of by such means. He really injures himself by these devices, — I will not say tricks, — the lawyer rather than the statesman appears at such times. His *habeas corpus* ideas are purely English, not American. But the structure of the two governments are different, — one central, the other federal. It will be a little mortifying to him to come over entirely on to my ground, and I ought not, perhaps, to expect it; but I think his views on the subject of *habeas corpus* have been modified, and as he has a good deal of ability, with his pedantry, I hope he will give us a fair opinion.

September 30, *Monday*. Admiral Godon and wife dined with me yesterday. They have been some days in W., have driven out with me, etc., etc. Godon tells me some facts in relation to Du Pont of which I had not previously been informed. They had been intimate and particular friends, but Du Pont evinced the little jealousy which was one of the banes of his life. At Port Royal, Godon placed his vessel, the Mohican, in a position where she enfiladed the Rebel batteries and literally drove them from their guns. Du Pont, instead of thanking, he says, insulted him for it. The attack by sailing in a circle was, Godon says, not part of the original plan but an expedient, an afterthought, when it was found more convenient to move from under fire than to remain. This movement was made by Stringham at Hatteras, and I have no doubt that steam vessels, which can be always in motion, prompted the idea. Little credit is due any officer for originating what would have been a culpable piece of stupidity to have omitted.

I called on the President and showed some of the authorities and stated some of my reasons in the Philadelphia *habeas corpus* cases. He appeared to enter into my views, and I am in hopes will encourage Stanbery in the right way.

The court at Philadelphia postponed the hearing until next Saturday, in order to give the Attorney-General an opportunity to investigate the case. Mr. Courteney, District Attorney at New York, has written a pretty smart letter in reply to Mr. Mann, the Philadelphia lawyer in this case, a copy of which he sent me.

LIII

Attorney-General Stanbery reads his Opinion on the Habeas Corpus Case — The President calls General Sherman to Washington — Colonel Cooper on the Political Situation in New York State — A Sketch of Party Politics in New York — James A. Seddon's Application for Pardon — Governor Cox of Ohio mentioned for the War Portfolio — General Blair's Qualifications for the Position — Sherman's Relations with Grant — Election Returns from Pennsylvania and Ohio indicate an Overthrow of the Radicals — The President has a Frank Talk with Grant, who assures him he should expect to obey Orders — Boutwell disavows any Intention of attempting to arrest the President.

October 1, *Tuesday.* Full attendance at Cabinet. Judge Otto appeared for Browning, who is still at the Virginia Springs.

Some appointments being under consideration, there was little inclination to move in them by reason of the Tenure-of-Office Bill.

I had a talk with Stanbery on the *habeas corpus* case. He is still hesitating and uncertain. Thinks the body must be produced in court, even if the court has no jurisdiction. Is overwhelmed with English law and English precedents, though our system of general and State governments is fundamentally different from theirs, and consequently a different rule must prevail. I have reverence for the privileges of the writ of *habeas corpus* and am for the sacred observance of the rights reserved to the States, but I am also for maintaining Federal rights and Federal authority unimpaired. There are difficulties in this case, — an apparent conflict of jurisdiction.

It would have been well to have made a specific concession in the Constitution that the *habeas corpus* should not be issued by State authorities to persons in the military or naval service of the United States. But this was not done, and it is now a question to be met, and I assume

that it is incidental and essential to the sovereignty of
the Federal Government that it should have full and absolute control over the military and naval forces; that
there would not be that full power, if the local State and
municipal judges can interpose and decide on the validity
of enlistments and set soldiers and sailors at liberty.
Demoralization and weakness would follow from such a
state of things. A person in the service who claims that
he is improperly detained is not without remedy. The
courts of the United States are open to him and to his
friends. They have undoubted jurisdiction, and they
alone. These are my conclusions, and I think without
prejudice.

At this time, when the Radicals are breaking down all
constitutional barriers, — confounding and ignoring all
rights, State, Federal, Departmental, and individual, —
it is the duty of those who are in position to be cautious
but courageous, to abstain from assumptions, but to fearlessly assert the powers with which they are invested.

Congress is disposed to usurp all the powers of government, and take into its own hands not only the making
but the execution of the laws, — to adjudicate and carry
into effect its judgments. The President has passively
submitted to have the executive department step by step
encroached upon and crippled. Concession and submission have been advised, until the Government is a mass
of weakness, losing its character. If Stanbery fails me,
I shall have none to stand by me in the Administration.
Sam Randall and some of the politicians have been here,
fearing a decided course may affect the elections. The
case is a Radical trick.

October 4, *Friday.* The Attorney-General to-day read
his opinion, prepared with much labor and at great
length, on the *habeas corpus* case. I was not disappointed,
though somewhat annoyed, with his conclusions, — that
the prisoner or enlisted man must be produced in court

and that the Commodore must not resist the decree if
the prisoner is discharged, that the local court has jurisdiction, etc. [He said that] if discharged, he, the Attorney-General, should instruct the District Attorney to
carry the case to the Supreme Court.

I inquired why he would carry it there, if the local
courts had jurisdiction; and if their decision was not final.
And I asked how he was to get the case before the Supreme
Court? He replied that he had not much doubt that G.
would be retained and remanded to custody, but if not,
he should have no difficulty in getting the case to the
Supreme Court, though he knew not the precise features
of Pennsylvania law. He went on to say, in answer to my
former inquiries and remarks, that it was time this question should be settled by the highest judicial tribunal,
because, if the local courts could interfere in military and
naval cases, some immediate legislation would be necessary.

I asked if Congress could legislate away a constitutional power. The local courts either have or they have
not the right to issue this writ calling for the production
of enlisted persons. If they have this right under the
Constitution, Congress cannot deprive them of it; if they
have not this right, I cannot see how they can demand
the production of this person.

Without meeting the points, he went off into a disserta-
tion on the distinction between the custody of a prisoner
under judgment of a court and custody under an enlistment in the Army and Navy.

I asked if an enlistment was not a contract to which
the United States is a party. He admitted such was the
fact. I then inquired whether the United States was
suable. He said no, but a judge in Pennsylvania had,
under the laws of that State and under the *habeas corpus*
provision, authority to demand the production of the
person enlisted, until Congress passed laws prohibiting
State interferences.

Seward and Randall each thought there should be immediate legislation since hearing this opinion.

The Attorney-General produced a telegram which he had prepared for me to sign to Commodore Selfridge.

The President remarked, if this, which was the first business of Cabinet, was disposed of, we would proceed to other matters.

I was sorry that so important a question should have passed off without a more full and general discussion, and expression of opinion by others. Important principles are involved which should not be thus lightly disposed of. The liberty of the citizen, and the rights of the Federal and State Governments are involved, but no disposition was evinced to defend, discuss, or touch them. There was no favoring response to the Attorney-General, whose argument, I thought from his single reading and from what passed between us, is narrow, without original thought, power, or grasp, — a skulking from the real question under the precedents of local courts. That Mr. Stanbery is a lawyer of acquirements and ability may be admitted, while denying him the higher and nobler qualities of a statesman. He is, moreover, timid and shrinks responsibility.

Colonel Cooper informs me that he is to remain in Washington as a companion and friend to the President. It is well. The President needs such a friend, and it is to be regretted, if Cooper is such, he was not invited earlier. I fear it is now too late, and so told Colonel Cooper.

He says General Sherman has been called to Washington by the President and will be here by Sunday next. Both the President and he think Sherman may influence Grant by reason of their intimacy. There is no doubt that Sherman has more general intelligence and knowledge of the government than Grant, but he is sometimes erratic and uncertain, whilst Grant is prejudiced, aspiring, reticent, cunning, and stolidly obstinate in his ignorance. The two men will work well and advantageously together

when they agree, but when they differ, the stubborn will
and selfishness of Grant will overpower the yielding genius
and generous impulses of Sherman. These are my views of
the two men, and I so told Colonel C. That Sherman
has a mortal antipathy to Stanton and is really in sympathy with the President, I can well suppose, but when
he associates with Grant, I apprehend from what I have
seen and understood he will be powerless. Had he been
here for the last fifteen months, his influence upon Grant,
who is subordinated by Stanton, whom he dislikes, might
have been salutary. He can now do but little.

October 7, Monday. The opinion of the Attorney-General in the *habeas corpus* case does not appear to have
been welcomed by any portion of the community thus far.
It has not, however, been much criticized, but has been
received indifferently, without comment or respect. On
reading it, my impressions of Friday are confirmed. It is
a mere lawyer's brief, not a statesman's views. He and
I have had the misfortune to differ several times on fundamental questions, and this fact may have had its influence
upon him.

Colonel Cooper called again to-day. He has seen General Sherman, and so has the President. Colonel C. says
S. feels and talks well, but the suggestion that I made that,
in any difference between the President and Grant, Sherman would yield and go with the latter impresses him
strongly, and he so said to the President. Though naturally sanguine and hopeful, C. is a good deal despondent.
Says the elections to-morrow will decide the matter.
What he meant by this I could not comprehend, and so
said to him. To me it is uncertain how the Radicals will be
affected, whichever way the elections may terminate.

If the Radicals are defeated, they may feel discouraged
and change their tactics, or they may be more vindictive
and spiteful than ever. If they are successful, they may
be content to let what they deem well enough alone, or

they may recklessly push on their usurpations and assaults upon the President still farther. What then, I asked C., could the elections of to-morrow decide? He admitted it was difficult to tell what would be Radical action in either event; but there was evidently something which had been discussed which he did not disclose.

In our conversation on Friday, he expressed his great disappointment over the condition of things in New York. He has just been there and mixed in freely with their leading men. Saw Tilden, who showed him my letter. Tilden talked well, but the tendency was to maintain a New York party organization and to cut clear of the Administration. It is a party, not a patriotic, scheme, and will fail. Tilden's partyism is weakness and does not surprise me so much as it does Cooper. The President is too much identified with Seward, has been too much advised by him, to gain the affections or even the good will of the New York Democrats. There was intentional rebuke of the President by the managing New York Democrats — Seymour, Tilden, etc. — in omitting the President's name in their late State Convention, or any allusion to him. In this they were ungenerous and committed a mistake which they may regret. Their selfish ambition is overleaping itself.

The political organizations of New York from the foundation of the government have had an important influence on public affairs in that State and the country. Hamilton and Burr, in the early days of the Republic, were antagonistic and shaped parties. The break-up and dissolution of old parties, which began in that State in 1812 under the lead of DeWitt Clinton, who became a candidate for the Presidency against Mr. Madison, was completed twelve years later at the close of the Monroe Administration. Adams, Crawford, Jackson, Clay, and Calhoun were opposing candidates in that election. Crawford was the candidate of the large fragment of Republicans who adhered to the Republican organization, but Adams was successful.

A new organization of parties, based on new issues, which the decadence of old parties and the growth and progress of the country rendered necessary, was instituted.

There was, at that period, a combination of powerful minds associated in the government of New York, who were Republicans of the Jeffersonian school, but anti-Clintonians, although Clinton was of the same school. This combination was stigmatized as the Regency, and their party was called Bucktails, from the fact that they for several years went to the polls wearing in their hats a buck's tail to distinguish them from the Clinton Republicans, who had been their party associates prior to 1812, but who subsequently coalesced and voted with the Federalists in support of DeWitt Clinton.

The Regency and the Bucktail Party very generally supported Crawford for President in 1824, but a union of the friends of the other candidates against them caused their defeat, and eventuated in the election of J. Q. Adams, whom they had opposed. Although Mr. Adams was successful in obtaining a large portion of the electoral vote of New York, he was not a favorite with a majority of the people of that State.

The Federalists who supported Clinton were gratified with Mr. Adams' election, but the Republican Clintonians and Clinton himself were not satisfied.

In the general chaos of parties that prevailed during the first two years of the J. Q. Adams Administration, the Regency was not idle, but in the midst of their operations a new party organization sprang up which sunk all other party ties, principles, and distinctions in its opposition to any candidate for any office who was connected with the Masonic institution. Governor Clinton was a prominent Mason, and the anti-Masonic movement took from him a large portion of his supporters.

It was at this juncture that the Regency exercised and developed its ability, tact, and sagacity in organizing from fragmentary and opposing elements a party which for many years controlled and possessed the government of New York, had deservedly the confidence of the people of that State, and exercised a powerful influence for more than twenty years in national affairs. The men comprising the Regency and who were the leaders of what became thenceforth the Democratic Party were Van Buren, Marcy, Flagg, Sam Young, and Wright.[1] At a later day, Dix and others of less vigor and power succeeded the original Regency, but they had not the ability to combine and maintain the organization of their predecessors. New questions arose which they could not successfully grapple, lax principles, abuse of power, devotion to party and adherence to it right or wrong; a decreasing political morality weakened public confidence and ultimately caused their defeat. But the Regency, which organized the party to victory in 1828 and success for many succeeding years, was an association of politicians and statesmen of wonderful mental capacity, whose integrity is unquestioned and who, while maintaining ascendancy, exerted themselves to administer the government for the good of all.

Van Buren was the acknowledged and admitted chief of that Regency, and his sagacity, shrewdness, judgment, and forecast probably entitled him to be so considered. He was calm, self-possessed, and deliberate in the most trying emergencies, cautious and prudent almost to timidity, always safe as a projector and counselor, never impulsive, with admirable self-control on all occasions.

Marcy, with less reserve and with a more rugged intellect, had greater courage and daring than Van Buren, but was always not so politic. He had the excellent, though rare, quality of frankly and boldly expressing his opinions to his friends when he thought they erred, and telling them wherever he dissented from them. This made him a valued and inestimable critic and adviser in that circle of which Van Buren was chief. Later in life and after considerable

[1] Martin Van Buren, William L. Marcy, Azariah C. Flagg, Samuel Young, and Silas Wright.

3

experience, Marcy, in public and as a public man before his countrymen, was not so bold as he had been with the friends who knew him and could make proper allowance for his sometimes rude speech. It was Marcy who, in the Senate of the United States, said, in the matter of appointments and removals, "To the victor belong the spoils." No man was more unsparing and unrelenting in his party action and exactions than Marcy.

Flagg, who was of similar temperament and a rigid party disciplinarian, permitted no party dissenters, and avowed as a rule of political action that he would "shoot all deserters." Both he and Marcy were intolerant in their party discipline and management. Near the close of their united action at Albany, Marcy, who, with his father-in-law, Knower,[1] Treasurer of the State and a minor appendage of the Regency, became pecuniarily embarrassed by injudicious speculation and wavered in his principles and party fidelity, — flinched in his support of the national administration, Mr. Van Buren being President, — had failed in rigidly maintaining, if he did not openly oppose, the "independent Treasury" and financial measures of the Government. Coolness, if not alienation, followed, and the cordial intimacy which had previously subsisted was never again fully restored.

Sam Young, more radical and more rash, was less reliable and had less influence than the others. Wright, the youngest, had the best qualities of all and the confidence of all and was most esteemed and regarded by men of all parties. In the highest sense he was a politician, statesman, and patriot. Commencing public life at the formation of the Democratic Party, trained and disciplined by his seniors in the severe requirements that the period called for, he may sometimes have yielded too much to the demands of party, but he was catholic, generous, and tolerant in his views, and would not permit himself to knowingly do wrong or depart from what he believed to be right.

[1] Benjamin Knower.

Such were the components of the famous New York Regency. Before the death of Mr. Wright, who though the youngest was the first to die, the members of the Regency no longer concentrated at Albany; the organization instituted in 1828 had become enfeebled, divided, and lost character.

The National Republicans, or Whigs, of New York soon began to imitate the Democrats and attempted a similar organization for party ascendancy with little regard for principle. Thurlow Weed, the master spirit, had been a conspicuous anti-Mason, and, finding success impracticable on that narrow and proscriptive basis, he and most of his anti-Masonic associates coalesced with Masonic Federalists and other cliques, and, by the free use of money, which was obtained in abundance from the merchants, manufacturers, and others in the city of New York, made themselves a formidable though not a compact nor, until the Democrats began to fail, a successful party. But the central directing power, a Regency composed of several superior minds combined and united in the government and possessing the confidence of the people, was wanting. Weed, whose mental strength and power compared with Marcy and whose energy and industry were unsurpassed, removed to Albany and established the *Journal*, a paper in opposition to the *Argus*, the recognized organ of the Regency. Both papers were conducted with ability. Weed was almost alone in his political operations, while the editor of the *Argus*, surrounded and guided by others, became loose in his politics, and, like Marcy, indulged in pecuniary speculations that were unfortunate, enlisted, as did his antagonist Weed, in corrupt schemes, was a legislative lobbyist, lost confidence, and by his mismanagement contributed to the defeat of his party. Weed had no such backers and associates as the editor of the *Argus*, but he found a ready and able coadjutor in Mr. Seward, who just at the period of his removal to Albany entered upon his public career. There were men of intellect and ability in other parts of the State associated with them, but they were not of Albany nor at Albany, and a mistrust and distrust of Weed which was general, the odor of corruption attending his acts, his trickery and deception, made him suspected and failed to win confidence. But similar infirmities in the *Argus*, the frailties of its editor and the failure of Marcy on the financial measures which were then the absorbing and test questions of party, enabled the conglomerate of anti-Masons and Federalists under the name of Whigs to triumph.

Mr. Seward was elected Governor and with Weed and some newer personages established a sort of Whig Regency, where Weed was both corrupt and despotic and governed the heterogeneous organization with almost arbitrary power. Successive defeats and successes followed. Dissensions and enmities prevailed in each of the parties, which each constantly labored to reconcile and conceal.

Marcy's defection did not cause immediate and entire estrangement, but it was instrumental in the defeat and ultimate prostration of Van Buren and his friends. Wright was sacrificed, and for a time implacable and violent hostilities existed. Marcy, though in a small minority of the Democrats, did not identify himself with the Whigs and by an adroit and skillful intrigue was brought into Polk's Cabinet, where he in a measure regained strength, and by similar services under Pierce became again a prominent but not fully trusted leader.

In the mean time Seward, pressed forward by Weed and his associates as the ostensible chief of the Whigs, became conspicuous in national politics as a Senator and representative of that party in the great State of New York.

Tilden in these movements was, although a younger man than Wright, a very active and sincere friend and supporter of Van Buren in the Regency, went with the Barnburners or Free-Soilers in the great break-up, and opposed Marcy and the Hunkers, as that branch of the party was called. It was a contest of great acrimony, in which both factions suffered, and the effect on the leading politicians when they finally effected a reunion was to make them more intensely partisan and warmer adherents to organization.

To maintain the ascendancy in national affairs and regain influence at the South, the Democrats of New York, who clung to the organization without planting themselves firmly on immutable principles, became the apologists of the Secessionists, without, however, to any considerable extent adopting that theory. The consequence was the overthrow of the Democratic Party when Lincoln was elected, but the extreme men, determined to preserve the organization, while they did [not] subscribe to Secession, opposed the Administration, which struggled to put down that heresy and maintain the national existence.

When the War was over, and the question [arose] of reinstating the States which had undertaken to secede in the Federal Union, with harmony and fraternal feeling, a Radical faction sprang up among the Republicans to prevent it, who taking "stand outside the Constitution," denied the equal political rights of the States and put under the ban of proscription the whole people of the South. President Lincoln, and President Johnson, who succeeded him, were Union men, but the former was assassinated early in that contest. President Johnson, an original Democrat, enforced the doctrine and principles which Lincoln had initiated. They were the views of the Democrats everywhere and of all Republicans who were not of the Radical faction; but the Democratic organization, with Seymour and Tilden as leaders, failed to support and identify themselves with the Administration. Party was with them paramount to country. They did not oppose President Johnson, but they held off and declined to be recognized as his supporters. They approved his views and principles, but they had not voted for him and their opponents had.

October 8, *Tuesday*. In a dispatch to Van Valkenburg, which Seward read to-day in Cabinet, he instructed the

Minister to remonstrate with the Japanese Government in regard to their treatment of Christians. The sentiment was well enough as a sentiment, but I asked if there was any improper treatment of our countrymen or foreign Christians or whether it referred only to their own people. He said it was only the Japanese Christians that were harshly treated, and they not so severely as formerly. I questioned the propriety of pressing upon that government too far in a matter which belonged exclusively to themselves, — we as a government and people are not religious propagandists. They may have a national religion, and if so, might deem our interference in their domestic affairs impertinent and offensive. As his letter was a remonstrance, I suggested that it might be well to cite our noninterference and our tolerance of all religious beliefs as an excuse for presenting our views. Seward, who dislikes prompting, perceived the applicability of the suggestion, said he should have introduced that point but for the fact that Van Valkenburg had made mention of it.

An application from Mr. Seddon [1] of Richmond for a pardon was presented by the Attorney-General. Seddon says he had opposed extreme measures, was in retirement when invited to the War Department of the Confederacy, did what he could to mitigate the calamities of war whilst in that position, made himself unpopular thereby, had taken the Union oath, etc., etc. Seward thought it best to postpone the subject until after the election, when it might be well to grant the pardon, for Seddon was a harmless old man [2] and undoubtedly true to the Union.

I said that I had no spirit of persecution in me; that two and a half years had passed since the Rebellion was suppressed, and I thought it unwise and unjust to continue this proscription; I was, therefore, ready at any time to consider favorably such an application as Mr. Seddon's.

[1] James A. Seddon (1815–80), Confederate Secretary of War.
[2] Mr. Seddon was only fifty-two at this time, but he had been in feeble health.

General Grant said very curtly and emphatically that he was opposed to granting any more pardons, for the present at least. This seemed to check the others, who expressed no opinion. I remarked, if as a matter of policy it was deemed expedient to delay three or four weeks until the November elections had passed, I would not object, but I thought the time had arrived for the display of some magnanimity and kindly feeling.

A year since, General Grant expressed to me very different views from those he now avows. Said he was ready to forgive the Rebels and take them by the hand, but would not forgive the Copperheads. He is pretty strongly committed to the Radicals, — is courting and being courted.

After the Cabinet adjourned, Stanbery, Browning, and myself remained with the President and had twenty minutes' talk on the condition of affairs. Browning said that Governor Cox [1] was spoken of as a suitable man for Secretary of War, provided he would take the place. Stanbery said he had not before heard Cox's name, but he thought it would be an excellent selection. Grant being *ad interim*, it was important the change should take place and Stanton be removed. Cox would hold on to the close of the session. I inquired if he was firm and reliable, and if he would stand by the President against Congress and General Grant if they resorted to revolutionary measures, which from certain indications are not improbable. On that point neither of them was assured. I named Frank Blair as a man whom Grant respected and Stanton feared, who, with some infirmities, had courage and energy to meet any crisis, and who would be a fearless and reliable friend of the President and of sound constitutional principles. Browning responded favorably; Stanbery said nothing.

The President, after the others left, expressed himself

---

[1] Jacob Dolson Cox, Governor of Ohio (1866–67) and afterwards Secretary of the Interior under Grant.

favorably to Blair. I urged the point farther. Told him
Seward would be likely to object, but that, I thought,
ought not to influence his action. I did not hesitate to
tell him my apprehensions of Sherman, — that if Grant
opposed the Administration, Sherman would be likely not
to support it. Something had been said of Tom Ewing,
senior, for a Cabinet officer, but he is too old and clumsy
for such a period as this; but I thought him right on
present questions, and if here, he might have influence
with Sherman, who had been his ward and who married
his daughter. I doubted, however, whether he would detach Sherman from Grant. The President spoke of Sherman's superior intellect to Grant. I acknowledged that
he had more genius and brilliancy, but had not the firmness, persistency, and stubborn will which are the strong
points of Grant, who is not a very enlightened man. Whenever the two are associated, Grant's obstinacy will make
his the master mind, and if there were to be antagonism
with Grant, the President might have to depend on some
other man than Sherman.

The President said that Grant had gone entirely over
to the Radicals, and was with Congress. I told him that
was my opinion, and I was fearful he was so far involved
that he could not be withdrawn from mischievous influences. The elections of to-day may have their influence,
however, in this matter.

October 9, Wednesday. The President showed me to-
day General Sickles' letter demanding a court of inquiry,
with Grant's favorable indorsement and the draft of a
reply. The latter did not suit me, and I suggested
changes.

The returns of the Pennsylvania and Ohio elections show
most extraordinary results, and indicate the overthrow
of the Radicals and the downfall of that party. The
reports are hardly credible.

Montgomery Blair called this evening and is jubilant

over the election news, but expresses his mortification and chagrin that the President should have called Sherman home, whom he denounces as a Radical, — treacherous, ambitious, and no friend of the President. Blair's prejudices are deep and often mar his general good sense.

October 10, *Thursday.* I wrote the form of an indorsement to be put on Sickles' application, or demand, for a court of inquiry, which I handed to the President. He was pleased with it, and it was certainly preferable to his extended document.

I took the occasion to again express my distrust of Sherman as his reliable friend for such an emergency as was anticipated; and advised most earnestly that he should, if he had not already, have a frank and unreserved conversation with Grant. The time, I assured him, had arrived when this subject should receive prompt and decisive attention; there could be no impropriety, but it was a matter of duty on his part, to have a thorough understanding with his immediate friends, and especially with his Secretary of War and General-in-Chief; that I knew not how freely he had communicated with Grant, but I thought G. loved office and was pleased with his position, was gratified with confidence and attention. There are indications that he is under Radical influence; if committed to these, we should know it. I reminded him that on one occasion he had persuaded, or convinced, Grant that he was wrong, and caused him to recede and withdraw his letter.

I reminded him also that Grant occupied, after himself, the most important post in the country; that he was and would be a tower of strength to any party; that without him the Radicals and Congress could do nothing. I admitted that he had not as enlarged and intelligent views as was desirable on political and governmental questions, that he was too much under the influence of little and unworthy men, but I trusted, though selfish, he was at heart honest, patriotic, and desirous of doing right. If so, and his views were correct without political aspirations, kind attention, persuasion, argument, and truth from the President would not be lost upon him.

The President listened attentively, received my suggestions kindly, thanked me for them, and assured me he would have an interview with Grant, — to-morrow, if possible, though to-morrow is Cabinet day.

October 19, *Saturday*. Time has been wanting for some days to enter occurrences. The President informs me that he called on General Grant in pursuance of my advice. He went to the War Department last Saturday, a week to-day, and consulted in a friendly way with General Grant; told Grant he could not be ignorant of the schemes and threats that were made, and must be aware that it was his (the President's) duty to be prepared to vindicate the rights of the Executive and maintain the Constitution, and resist invasions and usurpations. Should an attempt be made to depose or arrest him before trial or conviction, — if impeachment were attempted, — he desired to know if he would be sustained and whether officers in high position would obey his orders.

He says Grant met him frankly, seemed to appreciate fully the question and the object of his inquiry; said he should expect to obey orders; that should he (Grant) change his mind he would advise the President in season, that he might have time to make arrangements.

Under these declarations the President thought he might rely on General Grant. He could, after this avowal, press the point no farther.

In this I think he was correct. Grant will make good his word, and act, I have no doubt, in good faith. I so said to the President, and expressed my gratification that the interchange of views had taken place. At the same time I requested him to continue and increase his intimacy with Grant, who is not intelligent, — seems to be patriotic and right-minded, but the Radicals of every description are laboring to mislead him. Defeated in the recent elections, and with public opinion setting against the obnoxious measures, the scheming intriguers begin to rally around Grant, — speak of him as their candidate for President, — not that they want him, but they are fearful he will be taken up by the Democrats.

October 23, *Wednesday.* Randall says that Boutwell disavows any intention of arresting, or attempting to arrest, the President before impeachment and conviction. Says it cannot be done, and does not favor the scheme of Stevens to that purpose. If this is so, the conversation of the President with General Grant is already having its effects. Boutwell is a fanatic, a little insincere, violent, and yet has much of the demagogic cunning. He has been, and is, for making Grant the Radical candidate for President. He has the sagacity to see that with Grant opposed to them the Radicals would be annihilated. Grant had therefore, I infer, admonished Boutwell that he cannot be party to any movement for arresting the President before trial and conviction, and will not be an instrument in such a work. This accounts for Boutwell's declarations to Randall. I so stated to the President this afternoon, and he seemed struck with my explanation.

When the Cabinet adjourned yesterday, the President requested me to remain, and submitted to me a letter of some length addressed to the heads of Departments. It made mention of the condition of public affairs, the attempt that was to be made to arrest him, etc., etc., and concluded with requesting of each member his opinion on the subject, and in what manner each would advise him to proceed. I told the President the subject was important and that I thought he would be justified in ascertaining the opinions and views of his Cabinet fully and explicitly, especially if the subject was pressed. I suggested that in this stage of the proceedings, it was perhaps better to put the subject hypothetically than to make a positive assertion of what the Radicals intended. Their intrigues may be checked or modified, or abandoned. He concurred, and will hold the matter under consideration.

LIV

Cabinet Discussion of the Question of Arrest — The President's Message —
The Judiciary Committee of the House reports in favor of Impeachment
— The President's Message to the Senate giving Reasons for suspending
Stanton — The Alabama Claims discussed in Cabinet — A Complaint
from Alabama against General Pope's Oppression — Grant's Presidential Aspirations — Senator Nye introduces a Bill to establish a Board of
Survey to supervise the Naval Bureaus — Admiral Porter thought to be
behind it — Porter's Services and Ambition — Thurlow Weed moving
for Grant — The Retirement of Captain R. W. Meade, U.S.N., called
up for Revision — Raymond and the Philadelphia Convention.

November 30, *Saturday.* A long and serious illness has
prevented me from recording some important events.
Yesterday, though weak and debilitated, I for the first
time in four weeks attended a Cabinet-meeting. When last
at the council room I was quite ill; came home and went on
to my bed, which I did not leave for twenty-one days,
except once, on the seventh, for a few moments, which
did me no good. Thanks to a good God, my health is
restored, for which I am indebted to the faithful nursing
of the best of wives and the kind attention of my physician.

Little of interest was done in Cabinet yesterday. The
President and all the Cabinet manifested great pleasure
on seeing me. Each of them has been friendly in calling
during my illness, the President sometimes twice a day.

To-day the President laid before us his Annual Message.
A sound, strong, good document. After its perusal, and
running criticism, he submitted a letter addressed to the
Cabinet, stating the condition of affairs, — the proposed
impeachment and the proposition to suspend the President,
or any officer when impeached, until after his trial, and
judgment by the Senate. There was great uncertainty
of opinion on the subject in the discussion.

That the President should submit to be tried if the House

preferred articles was the opinion of all. That he should consent to, or permit himself to, be arrested or suspended before conviction was in opposition to the opinion of each and all.

General Grant said it would be clearly *ex post facto* to pass a law for suspension in the case of the President, and, unless the Supreme Court sustained, it ought not to be submitted to. If Congress should pass a law directing that officers should be suspended whenever the House impeached the officer, that would be a different thing. Then it would be the law, known in advance.

I agreed with General Grant that a law in the President's case would be *ex post facto* and therefore to be resisted, if attempted. But I went farther and denied that Congress had authority to suspend the President, — the Executive, a coördinate branch of the government, — on the mere party caprice of a majority of the House of Representatives.

Mr. Randall was very emphatic in denouncing such a movement as destructive to the government.

General Grant said he thought a mere law of Congress would not justify suspension or authorize it, but that there should be an amendment of the Constitution to effect it.

We all assented that if the Constitution so ordered, submission was a duty, but not otherwise.

A few days since, the Judiciary Committee, who have been engaged by direction of the House to search the Union, ransack prisons, investigate the household of the President, examine his bank accounts, etc., etc., to see if some colorable ground for impeachment could not be found, made their several reports. A majority were for impeachment. Until just before the report was submitted, a majority were against, but at the last moment, Churchill, a Member from the Oswego, New York, district went over, without any new fact, to the impeachers. Speculators and Wall Street operators in gold had expected that a resolution for impeachment would cause sudden rise in gold.

Unfortunately for them, no rise took place, but there was a falling-off. If Churchill was influenced by the speculators, as is generally supposed, his change did not benefit them, and in every point of view was discreditable to him.

Boutwell, who made the report to the House, is a fanatic, impulsive, violent; an ardent, narrow-minded partisan, without much judgment; not devoid of talents, with more industry than capacity, ambitious of notoriety, with a mind without comprehension nor well trained; an extreme Radical, destitute of fairness where party is involved. The report was drawn up by Thomas Williams of Pittsburg, a former partner of Stanton's, a rank disorganizer, a repudiator, vindictive, remorseless, unscrupulous, regardless of constitutional obligations and of truth as well as fairness, who was put upon the Committee because he had these qualities. The other three gentlemen of the majority may be called smoothbores, — men of small calibre but intense partyism. The report and its conclusions condemn themselves, and are likely to fail, even in this Radical House. Whether such would have been their fate had the elections gone differently is another question. The voice of the people has cooled the Radical mania, and checked their wild action.

December 3, *Tuesday.* There was a brief session of the Cabinet to-day. The Message is generally well received notwithstanding its decision and firm tone. Some of the extreme Radicals are angry and excited by reason of the calm and unanswerable argument of the Democrats. I have been surprised that some of the Radical journals have received the Message so meekly. They try to excuse or relieve themselves by declaring that the President is irritable, ill-tempered, and that in opposing the military governments and schemes to establish negro supremacy he is putting himself in antagonism to Congress.

December 10, *Tuesday.* Am slowly recovering strength.

Little of special interest was done in the Cabinet. We are receiving shocking accounts of earthquakes and storms in the West Indies. Two of our naval steamers, the Monongahela and the De Soto, are reported to have been wrecked, — thrown ashore and left high and dry by the receding waves. Over a hundred shocks of earthquakes are said to have taken place. Our accounts are by telegraph and not entirely reliable.

December 12, *Thursday.* The President requested me by note to call on him at eleven to-day. Stanbery and Browning were also there by invitation. The President submitted a message to the Senate, communicating some of his reasons for suspending the Secretary of War. (No removal has yet taken place.) It is an able document. He first asked my opinion, and I so stated, but in view of the traits and peculiar attitude of Grant, in whom the President had not lost all confidence, suggested that it would be well to inform the Senate that the Secretary *ad interim* had performed the duties acceptably, and that the reforms he had made and the economy he had practiced were of benefit to the country. He says he has dismissed some forty supernumerary clerks. Both S. and B. concurred in the suggestion. S. said it was a wise suggestion. A brief statement was accordingly added to the close. I should have made it more full and declared that General Grant had my confidence thus far in administering the office, if such is the fact, and thus have hitched him to the Administration. It would have made an issue between him and the Stanton Radicals.

Governor Dennison, who is here, tells me that when Stanton was suspended, he coaxed and wheedled the commendatory letter from Grant, when taking possession of the Department, but did not make the return which Grant expected.

December 13, *Friday.* After disposing of business in the

Cabinet, spoke to the President in regard to the communication to the Senate concerning Stanton's refusal to resign. He said he by no means intended it should be withheld from the public. I suggested that the Radicals did not intend his communication should appear until Stanton could reply and in some way weaken or stave off the effect of his statement.

Some days since, Seward submitted his last correspondence with Lord Stanley relative to the Alabama claims. Stanley declines to submit the action of the British Government to arbitration. Seward insists that everything shall be included. Mr. Stanbery inquired whether we had not a case strong enough without insisting on the second point. Seward said, whether we had or not, he wanted that point should go with the other. Stanbery asked if we were not weak on the second point. Seward thought not. Some discussion took place in regard to the Queen's Proclamation and the recognition of belligerent rights, which Seward denounced. Stanbery could not recall the facts. I stated that the declaration of blockade, which was an international question, instead of a closure of the ports, which was a domestic question, was claimed in accordance with the views, and a justification of the action, of the British Government. "That is the distinction," said Stanbery, "the point that was in my mind."

December 17, *Tuesday.* The President to-day read a communication which he proposed to send into Congress, commending Hancock for the views expressed in his general order and his deference to the civil law. Should he send it in, he will exasperate the Radicals, but it may have the effect of inducing a contrast between the action of Hancock and the other military generals now at the head of departments.

December 19, *Thursday.* Having dispatched some business to-day with the President, I was about leaving, when

3

he requested me to remain. He had, however, nothing special to communicate, but evidently desired a few moments for conversation. We ran over several subjects. His communication respecting the suspension of Stanton, I took occasion to compliment, and [I said I thought] that its effect on the public mind was good. He spoke of his message in regard to Hancock, which he evidently thinks is a skillful movement. I spoke of it as less effective than the other, and [said] that the Radicals, finding themselves weak with Stanton, would make fierce attack on this; but that would lead to criticism on the other viceroy generals to their disadvantage.

Yes, he added, and would bring out before the country the weakness of General Grant, who, he was sorry to perceive, was becoming identified with the tyrannical and oppressive measures of the military commanders. This is true, and I have no doubt that this consideration had its effect in producing the Hancock Message. He told me, what he has before repeatedly said, that Grant had expressed his dislike of Stanton, yet he had been induced to write him (the President) that improper letter, which has just been published. I informed him that I was satisfied that Grant had been seduced by Stanton to write that letter. Governor Dennison had told me of the letter and of Grant's regret that he had been persuaded to write it, — a fact which had reached him through some of Grant's staff by way of Garfield. In no other way could D. have known of such a letter, for he gave me this information some time before Grant's private letter was published.

December 20, *Friday*. Whilst in Cabinet-meeting, the President handed me a letter from Forsyth of Alabama, imploring him to grant and extend to the people of that military district relief from the malgovernment, oppression, and outrage of General Pope. He subsequently handed the letter around to some others. I heard Stanbery say to Browning he was glad to see this; that the true course was to let it go on; that the country would overwhelm Radicalism as soon as it could be reached. Seward, Grant, and Randall left immediately on the completion of the necessary official business. Stanbery and Browning had put on their overcoats and taken their hats to leave, when I felt that there really should be something said respecting the condition of things in General Pope's dominions, and asked the gentlemen if they had read Forsyth's letter. Stanbery promptly replied that he had; that everything was working well; that the President must not move a finger; let the Radicals have their own way, they are killing themselves, etc. To all this Browning assented. I inquired what in the mean time was to become of the people of Alabama. *We* were not bearing *their* suffering. Is the President discharging his duty, and we ours, if we quietly witness these wrongs, these palpable violations of constitutional rights, and the subversion of society and government, without trying to prevent it? Both S. and B. insisted that it was best and most politic to let these enormities go on; the indignation of the country was rising. I said the indignation of the suffering South, but the non-suffering Nor h were not indignant.

McCulloch said there were two sides to the question. He had his doubts whether the President should remain passive, and, alluding to a remark of mine that the President should always do right, — that he must not permit or do evil that good might come, — McC. said he had been alarmed when the President removed Sheridan, a measure which I advised but which he and others opposed; that he had apprehended the measure would be disastrous to the Administration, but it had not injured, it had strengthened, the President and damaged the Radicals. In view of the effect in that case, he was not prepared to say it was not best to deal in like manner with Pope. Stanbery and B. were vehement and earnest in their protests; claimed the responsibility and odium was wholly on the Radicals. I again asked, if the President could relieve them and did not, if he was released from responsibility. What would be the judgment of the people and the record of history, if the President, knowing these wrongs and having it in his power to remove the tyrant, failed to do it? As a political move, they said, it would be injudicious, and left, I have no doubt, with the belief that I am a rash and injudicious adviser. It is, however, the old difference. They are Whigs; I am a Democrat. They are afraid to trust the people on a question of right; I hold it our safety and strength.

December 24, *Tuesday.* A few Members of Congress remain in the city, but most have left for Christmas vacation. The adjournment and an interview with their constituents may do them and the country good. The elections of the year and the unmistakable evidence of condemnation by the people have annoyed them, but there is not among them the patriotism, ability, and independence to extricate themselves from the control of intriguing conspirators, who by secret caucuses have made it impossible for them to retrace their steps, and try to do right. Among the Radicals there is little statesmanship. They are striving to retain their usurped power by outrageous measures and violence.

Chief Justice Chase still aspires to be the Radical candidate for President, but few, however, of the Radicals are disposed to gratify his aspirations. Among bankers, speculators, and a certain class of capitalists he finds supporters, and he has a *quasi* strength among the Southern Radicals and negroes. The Republicans, or the conservative element of what was the Republican Party, are favoring General Grant. Comprising the largest segment, they will be likely to control party action to the disgust of the earnest Radicals, who, however, dare not oppose the movement. Grant himself is not only willing but grows daily more and more anxious; his aspirations, although he strives to conceal them, are equal to and even surpass those of the

Chief Justice. His reticence is all a matter of calculation; he fears to commit himself on anything lest he should lose votes. But popular opinion moves him. A year since he believed that the country was fully committed to Radicalism, and under that conviction he became identified with the Radicals, changing his previously expressed opinions and acting with them until the recent fall elections. Those results astonished no man more than Grant, and he has felt uneasy under his hasty committals, while striving to be reserved. Stanton, whom he dislikes, has managed to get him committed, which he would not have done had Grant better understood public sentiment. But in Washburne and other little Radicals he has had surroundings that controlled him.

I am becoming impressed with the idea that Grant may prove a dangerous man. He is devoid of patriotism, is ignorant but cunning, yet greedy for office and power. In discussion, from time to time in Cabinet, when he has been necessarily to some extent drawn out, this shadow of military absolutism has crossed my mind. It struck me more forcibly to-day when the military government of the South was under consideration. General Hancock thinks he shall want another regiment or battalion of white troops. General Canby writes a doleful account of destitution and need of help for the poor. General Ord wishes to be relieved. I could see that Grant was not displeased that Hancock called for more troops, and also that the wish of Ord met his approval. He gave Ord the credit of being very honest, but unsteady and fond of change. Thought it best to send him to the Pacific and recall McDonald to supply his place. In the mean time, General Gillem would discharge the duties. The President asked if Gillem could not as well fill Pope's place as Ord's. Grant, who knew the President's purpose, grinned and said he did not know how that was. On the necessity of feeding the freedmen, especially referred to by Canby, and alluded to by the others, with a very telling letter from General Gillem on the condition of affairs, there was much said, a good deal of which was not pertinent. Grant remarked he had seen General Howard, who had some funds which would hold out until Congress came together, when, undoubtedly, provision would be made. Stanbery said the people of the South were in a deplorable state, and he could see no permanent relief for them except from the Treasury, which the people would not long stand.

Seward said there were always disturbances in times of scanty provisions; that this was always felt most in the cities and often ran into riots. He told a story of a man who wished on a stormy night to send a message and proffered a guinea, the usual fee, to the messenger, who wanted two. This he refused to give, and the two parted in high anger with each other. After several hours the gentleman gave in, tendered the two guineas, and the messenger, who wanted the money, accepted it and did the duty. The planters and negroes, he guessed, would after a while feel the need of each other and come together.

I expressed dislike of the views taken, for only temporary and superficial relief was talked of, or proposed, for an enduring evil. The whole fabric of civil government, industrial employment, and social society has been overthrown, upturned, and prostrated by the penurious, partisan legislation of Congress, and the talk of relief by feeding the lazy and destitute negroes for a few weeks was an absurdity. There was no probability that the planter and the negro would come together and act harmoniously while the Federal Government was exerting its power to make them antagonistic. Grant once or twice interrupted me, and I could see did not like my remarks. So also with Seward, who is always a temporizer, but Grant is acting with a purpose, and in concert with Radicals and the military.

I see by the paper that Stanton has returned. He has been in Washington but little since his suspension. It is said he fears personal chastisement from persons whom while in office he has insulted and wronged. This, I think, can hardly be the case, for he knows himself to be still in office. He cannot do otherwise than make some answer to the President's communication respecting him.

The President informed me a few days since that Stanton's bull against Sherman for the treaty with Johnston was without his authority or knowledge. That being the fact, it was a piece of arrogance and impudence which at the time ought to have been rebuked. Supposing it to have been issued with the sanction of the President, I had with others submitted to it as an administrative measure and attempted to justify it.

The House of Representatives soon after Congress met passed a resolution to curtail work at the navy yards. It came opportunely, for we were about issuing orders to reduce work, which always creates distress at this season. I was not unwilling that Congress, which is captious towards the Department, should take its share of responsibility when its resolution was uncalled-for and passed for self-glorification. As I expected, the dismissed workmen are full of complaints and suffering, and to some extent have annoyed the Members.

Senator Nye introduced while I was sick a bill to establish a Board of Survey, in other words a Board of Admiralty, to be composed of the Admiral, or Vice-Admiral, as president, and two rear-admirals. This Board is to supervise and control the bureaus, and virtually supersede the Secretary. It is to perform no labor and to be exempt from all responsibility. I have no difficulty in tracing the origin of this bill to Vice-Admiral Porter, who is uneasy, scheming, ambitious, wasteful in expenditure, partial and prejudiced as regards officers, a most unfit administrator of civil affairs, though brave and full of resources as a commander. For two or three weeks he had charge of the Bureau of Detail, and his action was demoralizing and injurious.

As Superintendent of the Naval Academy he has been efficient, because there has been much to do, and he has been enabled to make large expenditures. But I have been compelled to check, limit, and to some extent regulate these matters. I am held accountable for expenses; he derives credit for whatever is done. This is right enough, if rightly understood. I have allowed him to have his selection of officers, almost without restraint, and cliquism is the result. His officers are, in his opinion, the only good officers in the service, and those who have been associated with him and under his immediate command he commends indiscriminately; and, in violation of regulations, he gives them individually, one and all, indorsement, to the great embarrassment of the Department.

In war and afloat, Porter is, though always presuming, one of the best officers in the service and gallantly won his position. I have always given him full credit for his services and shown my appreciation of him as an officer. At the Naval Academy he has done well because there has been much to do, but, as the work is being completed and he is relieved from employment, he grows restless and desires action in a sphere to which he is not adapted. This crude bantling of his, which Nye has introduced, is a miserable contrivance to get place and power for himself at Washington. During the War, when we were building a hundred vessels yearly, had five hundred vessels in commission, and fifty thousand seamen in service, no such board was needed; they would have been a positive drag and hindrance. Now, when we are building no new vessels, launching but two or three a year of those commenced and on the stocks, the idea of such a board is absurd. Our Admiral and Vice-Admiral will be wanted on active duty in war, when such a board, if of any use, would have most to do. It is *bureau*, not *naval*, service that is sought.

December 27, *Friday*. Great complaints of distress and suffering at the South are made, not without cause. General demoralization is the result of vicious partisan legislation. There can be little doubt that General Grant, though secretive, is fully, and probably irretrievably, committed to the Radical policy, and there are unmistakable indications that he was in the original movement to overthrow the States and establish martial law by Congressional enactments. General Ord asks to be relieved from his place in Mississippi and Arkansas. General Grant says he has asked this repeatedly for four or five months past, and he, Grant, now advises and urges that he may be relieved. Why Grant should be so extremely urgent now, while he has never before mentioned it, I cannot tell. The President, while he seemed not anxious to relieve Ord, who appears to be conscientious, said he must get rid of Pope. This Grant did not oppose, but he did not readily concur in or advise.

J. F. Babcock of New Haven gave me some days since an account of an interview he had with Thurlow Weed on the day preceding the Grant meeting at the Cooper Institute. Babcock and Weed have been old friends for more than thirty years, personal and political. The two met in New York, and W. asked B. to call upon him, which he did, and found W. busy giving directions to persons in regard to the meeting, enjoining the necessity of having Stewart to preside, — that it must be personally seen to, etc., etc.

After the others had left, the two entered upon political matters, — the Grant movement, the meeting, etc. Weed said *he* had taken up Grant as *he* did General Taylor; had told him, as he told Taylor, to make no declarations, to write no letters, and, if he strictly followed his advice and directions, *he* would elect him. B. asked if the country was not getting tired of the military, — if the military governments of the South were not sickening the nation. For his own part, B. said, he was tired of generals for civil service, — wanted some other material for President. Weed became excited, accused him of being misled, etc., etc. I am reminded of this by seeing a call for Grant meetings by Stewart and others of the Cooper Institute meeting. The call says they wish to take the Grant movement out of the hands of politicians. Yet the whole proceeding is commenced, fed, and carried on by the most scheming, intriguing, and unscrupulous partisan politician in the country, who has cunningly contrived to persuade Stewart, Vanderbilt, Moses Taylor to be used without their knowing who used, or is using, them.

December 31, *Tuesday.* The retirement of R. W. Meade [1] was called up to-day for revision. The Attorney-General had his law-books and documents, was anxious to find some book or authority to justify the President if he would order a review or reëxamination of the case. He made quite an argument; went into specialties on certain sections of the acts of 1862 and 1864; thought the President could exercise authority, etc., etc. I could perceive from certain promptings and suggestions of the President that he and the Attorney-General had been in consultation on the subject, having been urged thereto, not only by Captain M. and his family, but by his brother-in-law, Judge Meigs, and especially by his brother, General Meade.

It was the old question over again of favoritism and family influence at the expense of good administration and established usage. I told them that Captain Meade was retired by law; nevertheless the President could, if he chose, order a reëxamination, but after all I did not see how it could affect the case, or how it would if another board had immediately been ordered. Should we now have another board, let the result be as it might, whether like that of the former board or opposed to it, a commodore is to be appointed, for there is a vacancy. Meade is not at the head of the list. The President must either nominate him in opposition to the report of the board or he must override their report and pass Meade for the next man. The Senate is to act on the case, and I have little doubt what would be its action. I should be sorry to see the usage of the Department set aside in any case, very sorry to see

[1] Captain Richard Worsam Meade was a brother of General George G. Meade. He had been retired on December 11.

it in such a case as this, which has really no merit or claim whatever. It would be a bad precedent, which the President would have cause to regret. These exceptional cases, whatever might be the influence of family or friends, should not be permitted.

But the result, which I foresaw from the first was to be the case, was a reëxamination by order of the President. The Attorney-General, instead of rightly advising the President, has been flattered by General Meade's attentions and solicitations and those of others. So it was in Goldsborough's case. The Administration loses respect by giving way when its duty is plain to stand firm.

After Cabinet-meeting, the President intimated a wish that I would remain. The subject of the removal of Pope and the manner in which it has been received was talked over.

I asked the President if he had seen Raymond's letter in regard to the Philadelphia Convention and his subsequent action. He said he had. I remarked that it did not, as he knew, disappoint me to learn that Raymond had helped destroy the good effects of that convention and that he relapsed into Radicalism.

Doolittle and others were deceived in that matter. I was satisfied of it when the call was issued. Postmaster-General Randall was the tool of Seward, who was himself influenced by Weed, to mislead those who commenced in good faith. Cowan and Doolittle were with me in their convictions. But Randall, with a set of fellows, tools of Seward and himself, whom I never before or since met with in any consultation, carried their point. Doolittle thought it a great thing to secure Raymond and the *New York Times*, and, to get him enlisted, the call was softened, principles were omitted, and in the end Raymond and the *Times* directed us, having first duped men who should not have been deceived.

LV

Senator Grimes wishes to reorganize the Engineer Corps of the Navy —
Jealousy between the Line Officers and the Engineers — The Indian
"War" — Stanton's Case in Congress — Charles Francis Adams re-
signs the Ministry to England — The President considers appointing
General McClellan to the Place — John Sherman's Instability — Grant
leaves the War Department — His Explanation of his Course, made in
Cabinet — Will Stanton resign? — The Naval Estimates and the House
Committee on Appropriations — Grant keeps away from the White
House — Mrs. Welles's Reception — Grant's Interview with Stanton —
The Political Situation in Connecticut — Grant writes the President
denying the Reports of his Action in abandoning his Position as Secre-
tary of War *ad interim*.

January 1, 1868, *Wednesday*. Mrs. Welles and myself
paid respects with the rest of the Cabinet and the Judiciary
to the President at eleven this morning. The arrangements for reception at the Executive Mansion not very
well systematized, but better, I think, than last year.

The morning was unpleasant, and after the severe snowstorm of yesterday, the streets were not in good condition.
About noon the weather came off pleasant.

Received company until nearly 4 P.M., commencing at
twelve. Some four hundred calls. Found myself very tired
and exhausted at the close, not having fully recovered
my strength after my recent illness.

January 2, *Thursday*. Some talk with Senator Grimes
of a general character concerning naval matters. He is intensely hostile to Isherwood and the whole Engineer Corps,
being stimulated by Porter, and has in view the preparation of a bill for the thorough reorganization of the corps.
I do not find, however, that he has any well-defined plan.
Thinks there are too many engineers. Says there are fewer
in the French service; but the French have an auxiliary

force called mechanicians who answer the purpose of our second and third assistants.

Grimes has imbibed all the prejudices of certain line officers against the engineers, who are becoming a formidable power and rivals with the line officers in the service. His nephew Walker, now attached to the Naval Academy, influenced by Porter, is the moving spirit with Grimes. The differences which are growing up between the line officers and the engineers, fostered by Porter, who has but little administrative capacity or sense, can be prevented in but one way, and that I have suggested in my reports two and three years since. The officers must themselves become engineers as well as sailors, — be able to direct the motor power below as well as above the deck.

This proposition did not meet with favor on the part of most of the line officers. I hardly supposed it would, for they had become too old to learn, or had no talent for mechanism or learning. Still, the necessity of the case I hoped would lead to sensible conclusions. The engineers were as averse to being absorbed as the officers to absorbing them.

It is, I think, the only true solution of a great difficulty, but to accomplish it time, energy, perseverance, and will are requisite, backed and sustained by Congress and by better counsel than Porter's among naval men. A younger man than myself must embark in this conflict, and the policy, once commenced, must be carried forward by succeeding Secretaries. I should have pressed the subject, which I had initiated, but, besides encountering the opposition of officers and engineers, Congress became so constituted and other questions so interwoven, that the subject could not at this time be successfully carried forward.

I have no idea that Grimes can present a successful plan. He may reorganize the Engineer Department, sift it of some of its old and trashy members, but he cannot have a steam navy without engineers, and they are, and will be, a body to be in constant rivalry and collision with the naval line officers.

January 3, Friday. Little of interest in Cabinet. Dined with Mrs. W. at the President's. The dinner was complimentary to General Sherman. Only he and his daughter, his father-in-law Thomas Ewing, Stanbery and lady, who were old township acquaintances of Sherman's, were present, except the President and his daughters. It was a pleasant party. General Sherman says it is the first time he has ever dined at the Executive Mansion. The President is desirous of making close friendship with Sherman, and may succeed, but he cannot detach him from General Grant, even if disposed. Although the two men are unlike, there is between them close identification.

January 7, Tuesday. After council, at which nothing of special interest occurred, some conversation took place relative to the banquet to-morrow evening. The Attorney-General concludes to go and come out squarely. I had previously advised it, and told him I made no secret of my position. He said, "We are all aware of that."

I have this evening written a brief letter to the banquet. These letters are always troublesome, but the committee made special request, and I perceived that the President wished it.

January 10, Friday. Browning submitted and read extracts from the report of the Indian Commission, which has been in session, composed of Generals Sherman, Harvey, Terry, etc. It shows that the Indian war was no war at all; that our people, not the Indians, were in fault; that in the struggle which took place in the Cabinet months ago between Stanton and Browning, the latter was right, — that Stanton really desired an Indian war. After aggressions on the part of the whites, the Indians killed a number, and our army succeeded in killing six Indians.

This war will cost the country scarcely less than fifty millions. The people will in due time learn the value of "Carnot," the divine Stanton. Senator Howard has prepared an elaborate reply to the President's communication stating the reasons for removing Stanton, which he calls a "Report." This he has given to the public before either the Senate or his committee has seen it. He now complains that certain newspaper correspondents have been guilty of breach of confidence. But he is the first and chief criminal in this matter. His argument states a falsehood in relation to the New Orleans telegram. He asserts that "at once" was interpolated. This is not true; I have seen the telegram which Stanton sent the President, and it contains these words.

January 11, *Saturday.* Senator Doolittle called at my house early this morning and says the Radicals are determined to press a vote in Stanton's case to-day. The Committee, except himself, adopt Howard's argument, and exhibit an unwillingness to give him an opportunity to reply or permit a minority report. He asked me to go with him to the President and have an immediate interview. The President promptly received us and heard D.'s statement calmly. I thought he did not seem displeased that the Radicals were hasty and violent. "But," said he, "does the Senate propose to proceed in this matter without submitting the argument and statement of Senator Howard?"

I suggested to D. that he had best present a resolution that Howard's document, or a copy, should be sent to the President for any comment he might be pleased to make. This both considered proper. D. says that they have struck out that portion which related to the mutilation of the New Orleans telegram; but they must not be let off so. Howard's falsehood has gone abroad to the country, and should be officially corrected. The President brought forward the original telegram given him by Stanton, and also a certified copy of what was received at the War Department, containing the words alleged to be interpolated.

Doolittle had to hurry away to meet his committee. McCulloch came in just before he left, and while we were there a telegram was recieved by the President from Governor Jenkins of Georgia to the effect that General Meade had *ordered* him to issue a warrant on the Treasurer of the State for the payment of the bogus Convention, and threatening the Governor with removal in case he refused. I expressed my astonishment and a hope that Meade would be asked to show by what authority he issued such order and by what authority he assumed to depose the Governor of a State. McCulloch said nothing. The President was mortified and chagrined that he should have been disappointed in Meade, who follows in the wake of Pope. These generals show their unfitness for civil position, and their ignorance and disregard of constitutional obligations and civil and individual rights. This is, I am satisfied, current among these generals and a secret moving power behind them.

As McCulloch and I were leaving, the President requested me to remain. He said he wished to inform me that Mr. Adams had sent in his resignation as Minister, to take effect on the first of April, or May, he was not certain which, and asked me who I thought would be a proper person for the place. He had, he said, an individual in his mind, and his object was to see whether my mind took the same direction. I remarked that the subject took me by surprise, but his intimation that he had a person in his mind made me think of Mr. Seward. Not that Mr. Seward would be my selection were the field open, but, talking with him frankly and without reserve, we both knew that Mr. S. was a weight upon him, and that the Democrats would not give their confidence to an Administration which retained him in the Cabinet. As a political move, I thought it might be effected, provided S. was willing to take it, which was, perhaps, uncertain.

Before I had concluded, I saw by the expression of his

face and by his manner, that our minds were not in accord, — that Seward was not the man whom he proposed
to appoint; and he said S. was not the man whom he had
thought of. Running hastily over prominent characters,
no one struck me as particularly fit, whom the President
would be likely to appoint, and I so told him.

He asked me what I thought of General McClellan.
I told him I had not had time to consider the subject in
all its bearings, but it appeared to me a bold stroke and
perhaps an effective one. [I said that] he had received the
votes of nearly one half of his countrymen for Chief Magistrate, which was an indorsement not to be treated lightly;
that he had the affection of the Army at one time more
devotedly than Grant or any other officer; that he had
education and ability; that his nomination, whether confirmed by the Senate or not, would be conciliatory and
particularly acceptable to a large portion of the people who
were now on the Union side. His dilatoriness as a general
would, perhaps, commend him as a diplomat, but it would
be urged against him; and his unfortunate letter from Mal-
vern Hill to Mr. Lincoln was not to be excused; but none
are exempt from error. I then told him of a conversation
I had with General Sherman at Admiral Dahlgren's
nearly two years ago, which I noted in my journal at the
time, and which was an extenuation of McClellan's tardy
movements. The President said he had mentioned the
subject of Adams' resignation to no one. Mr. Seward
knew it. The resignation came through him, and he had
named two or three for the place, the most prominent of
whom was Hamilton Fish. I told him such an appointment would not be objectionable, but would have no
significance except for Mr. Seward, who was willing from
personal considerations to honor Mr. Fish.

The President wished me to consider the subject of
McClellan's appointment, and communicate with him soon.
In the mean time he wished it a confidential matter be-
tween us, for he had not named McC. to Seward even.

3

Some farther communication took place in relation to J. P. Hale, Cassius M. Clay, Burlingame, and others, who he said had all better come home.

January 13, *Monday.* The Senate did not get to a vote on Stanton's case on Saturday, but they doubtless will to-day or to-night from what I learn. There is little doubt the whole subject is concocted and understood by the Radicals. Some of them may dodge, like Sherman and Williams,[1] who are committed by speeches which they made on the Tenure-of-Office Bill. It would matter little with Sherman, however, who often makes an argument and votes against it, is not steadfast in principle, lacks stability, and is unreasonably partisan in his votes.

In the House, under the discipline and stimulation of the Radical leaders, there is manifested a revolutionary and violent spirit. Part of the conspiracy is a scheme to change the character of the Supreme Court, which Stevens and his fellows find is against them. A new Reconstruction bill, an act to legislate Hancock and Rousseau out of office, is among the topics which were before that body. Strict party tests were applied and enforced, and from this I have little doubt that Stanton will have every party vote of the Radicals in the Senate. I cannot but think, from what I see and hear, that General Grant is acting in concert with them, though the President on Saturday was unwilling to believe that Grant was false and was deceiving him. McCulloch expressed his belief on Saturday that Stanton, if reinstated, would immediately resign. I took issue with him, for I have no doubt Stanton will strive by every means in his power to retain the office. He may get up some hollow pretext of willingness to resign, but it will be untrue, a mere pretext. Stanton wants the office, which he will recklessly and unscrupulously use, to keep himself in power. And the funds of the nation will enter largely into the elections. Had Stanton been in the

[1] Senators John Sherman of Ohio and George H. Williams of Oregon.

War Department last autumn, election results would probably have been materially different. Grant did not, and would fear to, use money that Stanton would use without hesitation.

January 14, *Tuesday.* General Grant attended the Cabinet-meeting to-day, but stated it was by special request of the President. The Senate had notified him last evening that the reasons for suspending Mr. Stanton were insufficient, and he had therefore gone early to the War Department, locked the doors, and given the keys to the Adjutant-General. Subsequently he had sent General Comstock to the President with a letter and a copy of the resolution of the Senate, and had received a request through General Comstock when he returned to be present to-day, and had therefore come over, though he was now at the Headquarters and considered himself relieved of the duties of Secretary.

The President asked if this proceeding conformed to previous understanding, etc. General Grant, without answering directly, said he had promised sometime ago that he would give the President notice before relinquishing the office; but that he had not then examined closely the second and fifth sections of the Tenure-of-Office Bill. He was not willing to suffer five years' imprisonment and pay ten thousand dollars fine, but preferred to give up the office.

The President asked why, when he had read the sections and come to the conclusion to leave he had not informed him as agreed and remarked that he would undergo the whole imprisonment and fine himself, which might be adjudged against General Grant and said he so told Grant on Saturday when he spoke of apprehensions.

The General said he was not aware of the penalties in the Tenure-of-Office Bill, until he saw the discussion in the papers; did not know when he had his first talk with the President; and he came over on Saturday expressly to take up this subject. Had spoken of these difficulties at that time, and expected to see the President again on Monday, but he was busy with General Sherman, and had a good many little matters to attend to. He did not suppose the Senate intended to act so soon.

" Was not our understanding — did you not assure me some time ago, and again on Saturday, that if you did not hold on to the office yourself, you would place it in my hands that I might select another ? " said the President.

"That," said Grant, " was my intention. I thought some satisfactory arrangement would be made to dispose of the subject. Mr. Johnson (Reverdy) and General Sherman spent a great deal of time with me on Sunday. Didn't Mr. Johnson come to see you? I sent General Sherman yesterday after talking the matter over. Didn't you see Sherman?"

The President said he saw each of them, but he did not see what the interview with either had to do with giving back into his hands the place agreeably to the understanding. "Why did you give up the keys to Mr. Stanton and leave the Department?"

General Grant said he gave the key to the Adjutant-General and sent word to the President by General Comstock.

"Yes," said the President, "but that, you know, was not our understanding."

Grant attempted some further apologies about being very busy, stammered, hesitated, said Sherman had taken up a great deal of his time, but he had intended to call on the President on Monday; asked to be excused, and left.

This is, as near as I recollect, the substance of the conversation as it occurred. I do not claim to give the precise words, though in many instances I probably have done so. My intention and wish is to do injustice to neither, but fairly present what took place and the remarks of both. I write this on the evening of Tuesday, the 14th, while the subject is fresh in my mind.

ULYSSES S. GRANT

The President was calm and dignified, though manifestly disappointed and displeased. General Grant was humble, hesitating, and he evidently felt that his position was equivocal and not to his credit. There was, I think, an impression on the minds of all present (there certainly was on mine) that a consciousness that he had acted with duplicity — not been faithful and true to the man who had confided in and trusted him — oppressed General Grant. His manner, never very commanding, was almost abject, and he left the room with less respect, I apprehend, from those present than ever before. The President, though disturbed and not wholly able to conceal his chagrin from those familiar with him, used no harsh expression, nor committed anything approaching incivility, yet Grant felt the few words put to him, and the cold and surprised disdain of the President in all their force.

After Grant had left, the President remarked that it had been said no man was to be blamed for having been once deceived, but if the same person a second time imposed upon him the fault and folly were his.

He said that Reverdy Johnson and General Sherman had called on him, after the consultation with Grant alluded to, and wanted him to nominate Governor Cox of Ohio, whom *they* had selected to be *his* Secretary of War. They thought the Senate might be induced to *consent* that he might have Cox, and in that way dispose of Stanton.

There is no doubt that Grant has been in secret intrigue in this business, acting in concert with and under the direction of the chief conspirators. He did not put the office in the President's hands on Saturday, because the Senate had not acted, but he anticipated, as I and others did, that they would. If, therefore, the subject was delayed until Monday it would be too late. But the Senate came to no conclusion on Saturday, as he expected; he therefore avoided seeing the President on Monday, as he promised. On Tuesday he yielded to Stanton.

All the members of the Cabinet present were astonished and declared themselves unqualifiedly against both Grant and Stanton, except Seward, who was very reticent, but expressed an opinion that no action should be taken hastily. On grave and important questions he always preferred to take a night's sleep.

January 15, *Wednesday.* The President informs me that Grant and Sherman called on him this morning. Grant is disturbed with an editorial in the *Intelligencer* of this morning, which describes occurrences of yesterday and the equivocation and bad faith he exhibited. He attempted to explain, but, the President says, only reaffirmed the fact that he had not been true to the understanding and his pledged word.

January 17, *Friday.* No allusion was made to Stanton or Grant during the session of the Cabinet. After it closed, some general conversation took place. Seward hastened away. I had put on my overcoat to leave, when Colonel Moore brought in a scrap-book and whispered a word to the President, who requested us to be seated. He desired to ascertain if the recollection of the members of the Cabinet in regard to the interview between himself and General Grant on Tuesday corresponded with his own. His impressions were embodied in an article in the *Intelligencer* of Wednesday, which he requested Colonel Moore to read from the scrap-book. Each of the gentlemen present — McCulloch, Randall, Browning, and myself — concurred in the correctness of the statement, which was a compend rather than detail. Browning said he had a more full report, which, however, corresponded with the statement in the *Intelligencer*. He farther volunteered to remark that he was accustomed to make a record of what occurred in Cabinet-meetings. I stated I had also a memorandum of what took place on Tuesday, made that evening.

January 18, *Saturday.* The proceedings of the Senate in reinstating Stanton, Stanton's obtrusions, and Grant's conduct are none of them well received by the country, and I think all concerned in the company are dissatisfied.

There appears to be a general belief and expectation that Stanton will resign. To this I am not a convert, unless he becomes convinced that the Radical Senators will not sustain him. They will come to no such conclusions. Morgan, Fessenden, the Morrills, Patterson, and other limber-backed Senators have not the independence to demand such a step. Senator Sherman, whose brother, General Sherman, has been insulted and wronged by Stanton, has not self-reliance, self-respect, and strength of mind sufficient to do his duty.

It is reported that Generals Grant and Sherman have said to Stanton that he must resign. They may have done this together, but I doubt if Grant has taken such a stand by himself, for he is cowed and submissive before Stanton. Sherman, if he has had an interview, would· be likely to have expressed himself with some freedom and boldness.

The President told me on Wednesday that Seward said to him: "You observed my reticence yesterday. I was silent because I believed you would before this [Wednesday noon] have had Stanton's resignation." This remark of Seward has, I think, an influence on the President, who is daily looking for a fulfillment of Seward's prediction. Seward probably wishes Stanton would take himself out of the way. He may say as much to Stanton, but if the latter bluffs him with an oath and rough expression, there will be no further remark, for Seward droops at once under rebuff from the "divine Carnot." Yet the President relies much on Seward; is inflamed by his *ad captandum* assertions and flippant prophecies, which are blundering guesses and mistakes. It was an error to suppose Stanton would resign, cowardly to keep silent.

January 20. Doolittle called last evening and read me the concluding portions of a speech which he proposes to deliver on Wednesday if he can or soon thereafter. The speech is very well got up.

Colonel Babcock called a little later and spent two hours on various matters. Wanted my views on the subject of Senator. Says Dixon is anxious. I advised that the subject should not be agitated until after the election.

I said the same to A. E. Burr yesterday. Burr is here, and speaks confidently of carrying Connecticut for the Democrats by an increased majority, and of securing a majority of the legislature. Others are alike confident, and I trust their expectations may be verified, for our country is in an unhappy condition, and I am not without apprehension of a civil convulsion. There is among the Radicals neither statesmanship, sagacity, nor sense. Hate, revenge, thirst for power govern them. To oppress and persecute the white population of the Southern States is their delight; to place negro governments over them by the aid of the military is their intention.

January 25, *Saturday.* The week has been a busy one, and I have found little time and less inclination to open this book. A venomous and malignant spirit actuates certain of the Radical leaders, and I and the Navy Department come in for our share of their spite. The naval estimates, made out when I was sick in bed, for the ensuing year are large, unusually large; but when submitting them I had no expectation that the appropriation would reach the amount of these estimates, nor would I have advised it. But the Bureaus really in that way made their suggestions for improvements as well as for current expenses, and I, erroneously and sick, allowed their presentation to go forward without curtailment, expecting to review the whole when well with the Naval Committees. The estimates for men and supplies were larger than is required, and I intended should be reduced in the appropriations;

but I was sick and confined to my bed and thought best to submit the whole to Congress. In so doing, however, I gave the petty demagogues an opportunity to attack and misrepresent me, and it is right I should be rebuked even by them for putting myself in a false position.

The House of Representatives in November passed a resolution to stop work on the vessels which are building. The Naval Committee informed that the force would be limited to 8500 men, — a reduction of nearly one half, — that they are opposed to farther improvements in the navy yards, etc. Under these circumstances I have reviewed and reduced our estimates nearly one half, and have sent in this revised estimate with a letter to the Speaker. It seems to have caused E. B. Washburne great unhappiness. He had been at work, without data or facts, slashing our original estimates, but had not perfected his onslaught when our revision went in. A day or two later he presented his proposition, or report, in the form of a bill from the Committee on Appropriations, and in doing so let off a little pent-up self and party glorification as to what a Republican Committee of a Republican Congress had done when compared with a Democratic Secretary of a Democratic Administration. Spaulding of Ohio, a Republican member of the Appropriation Committee, corrected and quietly rebuked him for his injustice to the Department.

Went one evening for an hour to Mr. J. A. Griswold's, there being a gathering by invitation to witness the presentation of a watch which belonged to Roger Sherman to General W. T. Sherman. It was, in a measure, a Connecticut affair, and all passed off very well. General Sherman was not very near kin to Roger Sherman, who was a third or fourth cousin of Daniel Sherman, the grandfather of the General. It was the first time I had gone out of an evening since my illness, or since October.

January 28, *Tuesday.* After close of official matters in

Cabinet, and some little conversation of a general character, Mr. Seward remarked to the President that if there was nothing further he would leave. I suggested that he had better remain until we all left, for, having gone a little in advance of the others a few days ago, he failed to get his name into a discussion when he as well as the rest of us was cognizant of the facts. "Ah, yes," said he, "I read in the papers that there had been consultation here when I was not invited." "Well, then," said I, "remain now. I wanted you to bear testimony to the interview which we all witnessed, and as you have read the statement, to affirm whether it is, or is not, substantially correct." He evaded a direct answer, hoped he should be present when the subject was again discussed. I told him this would not answer, and unless he controverted, or questioned, the statement or some part of it, he must be considered as affirming it. Without making any reply, he went for his overcoat. The President remarked with a smile, after Seward left, that I was not inclined to let Seward go without showing his hand with the rest. He said he had not seen Grant since he returned from Richmond. Whether he felt that he had not done exactly right, or that he did not want an interview until he advised Stanton to resign, or from what cause, he could not say, but he had absented himself. The President then related the interview between himself and Generals Grant and Sherman, also produced a letter from the latter, apologizing for not having seen Stanton as promised, because he was obliged to go to Annapolis to fulfill an engagement and Grant was obliged to go to Richmond, but the subject should receive attention when they returned.

.   .   .   .

January 29, *Wednesday.* The first general reception of Mrs. Welles took place last evening. There was a large and pleasant company. All appeared to enjoy themselves. The President and his daughter, Mrs. Stover, with ladies visiting at the Executive Mansion, were present. Foreign Ministers, Senators, and Representatives, as well as Cabinet Ministers, were among the crowd with ladies, comprising the *ton* of Washington society. All seemed and declared themselves pleased, which made the occasion pleasant to us, who wished to entertain them.

January 30, *Thursday.* Congress is malignantly Radical. The party-servers are all-potent. Not a man of the party has sufficient independence to act on his own individual opinions and convictions. Some of them will whisper in confidence their disgust and dissatisfaction, but yet when the test is applied they succumb.

Senator Doolittle's speech has greatly disturbed the whole Radical nest, who are hissing and snapping like vipers. Evidently they are not satisfied with themselves. I hear that some of them are incensed with Stanton because he does not resign. They expected he would at once leave on being reinstated.

General Grant is disturbed; feels bad; has made a fool of himself; is afraid of Stanton and overawed by him. He wishes Stanton out of the way; dislikes him; has promised to see him and advise him to resign, but there are yet no evidences that Grant has fulfilled his promises in this respect. Am told he went to see Stanton; that S. had some information of his intention, and was in apparent rage when Grant called. After waiting some time for Stanton to subside, Grant left without daring to make known the object of his mission.

The State Convention yesterday in Connecticut renominated the present ticket and passed some pretty good resolutions. Governor English made, or read, a good speech, which some one has prepared for him. Affairs are looking very well in Connecticut.

January 31, *Friday.* After the close of the Cabinet-meeting the President submitted some letters from Gen-

eral Grant which confirm more fully his duplicity and subserviency to Stanton and the small politicians. He wanted
a verbal order of the President reduced to writing, but when
he received it, cavilled and said Stanton had not been notified. He also wrote a long letter to the President, denying
his words and acts in abandoning his position as Secretary
ad interim. To this the President had prepared a reply
which was in its rough state a recitation of the facts. Some
suggestions and modifications were made by the members
severally, and Seward indorsed the whole, making the five
Cabinet members who were present at the interview with
the President united. There was no mistake as regards the
conversation. Grant was confused and embarrassed, hesitated, and was conscious of his bad faith towards the President, — which perhaps caused him to disremember. This
is the most charitable view.

LVI

Grant's Treachery — Conversation with the President on the Subject of
Preparation for an Emergency — Proposal to make Washington a
Military Department and order Sherman to it — Excitement over the
Correspondence between the President and Grant — Grant's Account of
his Interview with Stanton — Grant's Dislike for and Subjection to
Stanton — His Indifference to Human Life — Stanton goading the
Radicals to Impeachment — He dreads being out of Place — The
President sends to the House the Account of his Interview with Grant,
with the Statements of the Cabinet Members — Hancock remonstrates
against an Order of Grant's — General Lorenzo Thomas ordered to re-
sume his Duties as Adjutant-General at Washington — A New Military
Department created at Washington and Sherman placed in Command
— Sherman asks to be excused from coming to Washington — The
President removes Stanton — McClellan nominated as Minister to
England — Excitement in Congress over Stanton's Removal — Ad-
jutant-General Thomas arrested — The President nominates Thomas
Ewing Secretary of War — Stanbery an Honest Lawyer and Faithful to
the President, but too Dependent on Precedents in an Emergency —
Jeffries, Register of the Treasury, advises the President to use Strong
Measures — Officers summoned from an Evening Party — General
Thomas's Unfitness for the Place of Secretary of War *ad interim* — The
Question of the Tenure of the Four Hold-over Members of the Cabinet
— The House votes to impeach the President — Conversation with John
Bigelow on the Situation — Repugnance of the Conservative Senators
to the Possibility of Wade's becoming President — General Lorenzo
Thomas arrested and then discharged — Suggestions as to the Demo-
cratic Candidate for the Presidency — A Nitro-Glycerine Scare in Con-
gress — Stanbery considers resigning to devote himself to the President's
Cause.

February 4, *Tuesday*. A resolution was introduced yesterday by Hubbard of West Virginia, calling for correspondence between the President, Secretary of War, and
General Grant. The resolution was introduced about an
hour before the last letter of Grant reached the President.
The whole shows an intrigue and conspiracy on the part
of Stanton, Grant, and certain Radical leaders. The President to-day submitted to the Cabinet the correspondence.
It is throughout highly discreditable to Grant's integrity,

honor, ability, and truth. He is in this matter the tool of Stanton and the victim of his own selfish aspirations. He has vulgar cunning, is deceptive and unreliable. . . .

The correspondence shows that he played a false and treacherous part with the President throughout. From the first, he has studied to deceive the man who trusted him. This he virtually admits; says he was afraid the President, in selecting his military adviser, would choose a man not acceptable to the Army. Denies that he agreed to see the President on Monday, the 20th, although he twice admitted it on Tuesday in Cabinet-meeting and made his excuses and apologies for not fulfilling his promises. Prevarication and downright falsehood, with deception and treachery towards his chief, mark the conduct of U. S. Grant.

These things and other occurrences fully convince me that there is a conspiracy maturing for the overthrow of the Administration and the subversion of the government and our federal system. The Radicals are using Grant as their tool; he is prepared to use them for his purpose. As a general he was reckless of human life and witnessed the slaughter of his countrymen with composure; he is equally callous as to all the sympathies and moral and friendly obligations which endear man to his fellow man, and make society dear. It will not surprise me, should circumstances favor him, if at no distant day he strives for military dictatorship and empire.

February 5, Wednesday. The President showed me this P.M. a reply to Grant's last impudent and insubordinate letter. It was very well, provided he thinks best to continue the correspondence. I so said to him, reminding him at the same time of what I had said yesterday, viz., that I would direct the Private Secretary, Colonel Moore, to inform General Grant that his last letter was of such extraordinary tone and character that no further communication or correspondence could be had with him on that subject. The President said he thought it best on the whole to reply. He also deemed it advisable that all the members of the Cabinet who were present at the last Cabinet interview with General Grant should state their own impressions.

Colonel Moore called at my house this evening with a note from the President to this effect. I asked if he had called on the other members of the Cabinet. He said he had; that he had just come from Mr. Seward, who had detained him long and dictated an answer while he was there. I asked to see it, but Colonel Moore said Seward was to have it copied and sent to the President. McCulloch and Randall, he said, would make brief replies; Browning would probably answer at length. I doubt if he has got anything definite from Seward; shall not be surprised if Seward persuades the President to give up these answers. In some way he will be likely to evade and get rid of a frank and explicit statement, or I shall be mistaken; although he is fully and unequivocally committed, orally, to the President's statement of the conversation.

Saw the President this evening; told him I would make my reply to his note brief, or detail my recollection. He told me to do as I pleased, but a short reply would be sufficient.

I took occasion to express my apprehensions of public affairs, and of threatening impending calamities which were to be met. I reminded him that it was a duty for us all, and particularly for him, to be prepared for approaching extraordinary emergencies; reckless, unprincipled men in Congress had control of the government, were usurping executive authority, and would exercise these powers to extreme, and evidently beyond constitutional, limits. They had contrived to get General Grant, not unwilling, I apprehend, in their interest. He had entirely changed his ground. Having been suddenly elevated to position without much culture, with no experience, knowledge, or correct information of the principles of government, Grant was intoxicated with his success and beginning to believe that with the Army he could make himself permanently supreme. The Radicals consider him an instrument in their hands. He thinks they are puppets in his. They are acting together, however, at this time, and will until the crisis comes.

I asked the President if he was prepared for that crisis. Should they attempt to seize the government, — to arrest him, — had he determined the course he would pursue? Such a step is, I know, meditated and discussed by some of the extreme Radicals. They have intended, by any measure, no matter how unprincipled and violent, to get possession of and to exercise the executive authority. Grant would help them. Congress, unmindful of the Constitution, will place the Army at his disposal instead of the President's. Who, I asked the President, had he got in whom he could confide, if a collision took place?

The President became somewhat excited, arose, and walked the room. I had evidently touched on topics which had been in his mind. He spoke of Sherman as having been more emphatic in his language before he left, and suggested that Washington might be made a military department and Sherman ordered to it. Sherman, he knew, would take it.

I expressed misgivings as to Sherman if Grant were to be his antagonist. He is friendly disposed, but would yield, I feared, and follow Grant rather than the President. I admitted that he was a man of superior intellect and of a higher sense of honor than Grant, but their military association and the ties and obligations of military fellowship and long personal intimacy and friendship would attach him to Grant, though I hoped not to the overthrow of the government.

February 6, Thursday. Gave the President my answer to his note about eleven this morning. It was brief and direct. I again told him I would make it more extended if

he wished, for I had pretty full notes; but he was satisfied
with this. I asked if any others had sent in their answers.
None had yet been received. Seward had promised, and so
had the others. I shall not be surprised if Seward prevails
on the President to omit signed testimonials from the Cabinet. If not, he will be likely to have a diluted and indirect
reply, with many words and inoffensive and guarded committals. Browning will, the President thinks, give a detailed statement. Says he made a full record of what took
place at the time.

February 7, Friday. The Cabinet-meeting was brief.
Stanbery and McCulloch were not present. After business
was over I asked the President if he had answers from the
five gentlemen relative to Grant's conversation. He said
he had, from all, but as he did not continue the conversation or offer to submit them for perusal, I made no further
remark. Browning asked me before I left if I had seen the
letters. I replied I had not. He said that was the case with
himself, but he thought we ought to see and compare
them. He remained when I left, and may then have seen
them.

February 8, Saturday. There has been, and is, and will
continue to be much excitement over the correspondence
between the President and Grant. In reading it, my apprehensions and suspicions of Grant's duplicity and full com-
mittal to the conspiracy are confirmed. . . . It is evident
he has been in collusion with the Radicals, intriguing with
them, and false to the President who has trusted him.
Stanton he does not like, but yet, in the plot or intrigue
against the President, he is Stanton's instrument and tool.
Stanton's manner — bluffness and arrogance — subordinates Grant, who fears him, — dreads him.

Randall said, a few days since, that Grant went to see
Stanton and try to have him resign, but Stanton, knowing
his object, put on an imperious and angry look, and spoke

3

loud and violently of some matter that offended him, which completely awed Grant, who sat and smoked his cigar, but preserved his remarkable quality of reticence for half an hour, when, without saying a word, he quietly left. I did not give much heed to the story until I saw the correspondence, and find that Grant states he "did have an interview alone with Mr. Stanton, which led me to the conclusion that any advice to him of this kind [resigning] would be useless." He was, as usual, speechless.

While Grant dislikes Stanton, he is subjected to and controlled by him, — more overawed through others than directly, perhaps, for Stanton understands his man. The Radical politicians, some of them very small ones and others sharp and cunning, if not great, are Grant's advisers. These Stanton uses. Washburne, who is godfather to Grant and for his own selfish purposes has constantly pushed him in Congress, has narrow, contracted, and grovelling ideas and is reached by Stanton through others, which throws off suspicion on the part of both Grant and Washburne. Bingham, a shrewd, sinuous, tricky lawyer, Stanton has extolled to Grant as an extraordinary legal mind, and of course, what is said by B. is received as conclusive by Grant.

The resolution calling for this correspondence was offered by an obscure and dummy member, Hubbard of West Virginia, an old lawyer acquaintance of Stanton when he practiced in that section. How comes he to know anything of a correspondence with the President and Grant? How came Stanton or any one acquainted with the fact? Grant had intrigued with the Radical Members and with Stanton, had tried to entrap the President under their direction, and wrote his insolent letters at their instigation, to irritate and provoke, if possible, the President into the commission of some rash or indiscreet act.

. . . Grant . . . is destitute of the feeling of real friendship; is wanting in sympathy and the finer sensibilities. The slaughter of his soldiers he viewed with indifference, and the suffering of our men in Southern prisons did not excite his compassion. Mr. Fox, Assistant Secretary, reported to me three years ago that Grant made use, to him, of the inhuman expression that we could not afford to exchange healthy Rebel prisoners for the skeletons at Andersonville, etc. His march from this [city] to Richmond was really a succession of defeats, and has been characterized, indeed, as a bloody swath. It has been said he made a macadamized road from Washington to Richmond, which he paved with the skulls of Union soldiers. In a conversation among the Cabinet officers one day before the session commenced, on the subject of population, he asserted that the country had lost no population in consequence of the War, — that many were killed, but others had come forward to supply their places, so that there were as many lives to-day in the country as if there had been no war. Whether the assertion be true or not, I stop not at this time to discuss, but the positiveness and indifference to life with which the remark was made, struck me at the time most painfully. I thought of the charge that he was a butcher, which had been so freely made. So far as my observation extends, there was among the soldiers none of that enthusiasm or warm attachment for Grant that was shown towards McClellan, Sherman, Sheridan, and other generals. The feeling was less marked as regards the officers.

February 10, *Monday.* The Radicals continue vindictive and are beating about without aim or intelligent purpose to get rid of the President. Their great object is, and has been, from the time they found that President Johnson would not give up his conviction of duty to the demands of party, to possess themselves of executive power, and they are not scrupulous as to the means by which to obtain it. Stanton is goading them on to impeachment, but quite a number still hesitate. They have constituents behind them; he has none. His past violent and arbitrary conduct has made him enemies everywhere, and he dreads being out of place. In place he is tolerated, courted, and extolled in a measure by many who hate and detest him, while the extremists applaud and encourage him as "Carnot," the *great War Secretary*.

February 11, Tuesday. The President this day sent in his letter with the statement of the members of the Cabinet, to the House, in answer to a call. My letter was the first reply, and appears first of the list. It is the most brief and direct, and on the whole I am most pleased with it. McCulloch's is almost as brief. Randall's is direct, but recapitulates, which I thought unnecessary. Browning's is full and explicit. He made memoranda at the time. Seward has a great many words, is diplomatic and ambidextrous, and, on the whole, weakens rather than strengthens by trying to steer between parties. As we all had the letter of the President to Grant read to us twice when together, and each and all criticized, suggested, and assented to the statements, it is ungenerous and almost untruthful on the part of Seward to now equivocate. He distinctly, emphatically, and unequivocally declared on the 31st ult. that he recollected the remark of General Grant that he "did not expect the Senate would act so soon." I *know* that remark was made. The others recollect it. But Seward says in his letter that he is not certain whether Grant made the remark or he (S.) had it in his own mind. Pshaw! the doubt is put to conciliate Grant, and help himself. It is characteristic. He is never reliable in a crisis, and is not always as direct and truthful as he should be.

Grant has written a letter which came while we were at the President's, in reply to that part of the President's letter which speaks of his insubordination, disavowing such intention, etc. I presume he is surprised at his own folly and errors, and will, if he does not already, regret them. But he is now under the management and control of vicious and very bad men, who are using him for vicious purposes, and he assents with bad intent.

February 12, *Wednesday*. Mrs. Welles has had her last reception for the season. It was largely attended by the notables and the fashionables, the old and young. It is spoken of as the largest and pleasantest party which has yet been held this season, except perhaps the President's, which exceeded ours in numbers, and probably General Grant's, which were publicly advertised, and the whole public were invited through the papers without cards of invitation.

The tone and excitement of the Radicals have moderated. They are less boisterous and they evidently find difficulty in rallying their men to extreme measures.

How far Grant's prospects as a candidate will be affected by recent developments and publications remains to be seen. With candid and thinking men he has sunk immeasurably, but partisans do not think, and have not candor. An acknowledgment on the part of the General of our armies, who should exhibit all the better qualities of the soldier and be the soul of honor, that he had deliberately and purposely deceived his superior, and accepted place, and imposed himself on the confidence of the man who trusted him, in order to cheat and deceive him, that man being the President of the United States, is humiliating and demoralizing.

The President showed me to-day a telegram from Hancock, who has dismissed some negro aldermen in New Orleans who were elected under an improper and illegal order from Sheridan. General Grant has ordered Hancock to restore these negroes, — which he [Hancock] mildly remonstrates against, and if the order is persisted in, requests to be relieved. I apprehend that Stanton is in this thing. It is a Radical movement. But Stanton means evil, and, while pushing Grant forward, intends to profit himself by the General's weakness and baseness. I can hardly suppose that Grant can rouse himself and recover from the delusion under which he now labors and which exhibits traits as bad almost as Stanton. Both have been treacherous.

February 13, *Thursday.* There is an attempt to establish a Radical *ton,* or condition of society, in Washington. General Grant, Stanton, Colfax, and others have shown signs of this. As Stanton is tabooed by the President and Cabinet, he is excusable in tabooing them in return. Perhaps Grant has something of the same ailment since the letters of the President and Cabinet were received, but his position is really unlike Stanton's, and he lets himself down by imitating him. The two attended the last weekly reception of Colfax; the two were last night at Senator Chandler's. Neither of them attend receptions at the President's or members of the Cabinet. Stanton cannot, for he is not invited. It is different with Grant, though I have attended none of his receptions, and could not with my lame knee and restrictive orders of my physicians in regard to evening exposure. I have only been to the President's this season. But were it otherwise I would not go to the publicly advertised jams of Grant. As regards Colfax, he is light timber and would be glad to be sociable. If I went out to general gatherings, I might and probably should have called upon him, though I do not subscribe to Seward's dictum that he is the third officer of the Government. I know no such officer.

I am told Grant looks dejected and dispirited. I have not seen him for a fortnight. His course with the President I cannot reconcile with my previous opinion of him. I thought him truthful and as unselfish as could be expected, — though somewhat coarse, low-mannered, and devoid of very refined feelings, — but he confesses himself to have been false and faithless to the President. He has not a high appreciation of public intelligence; has no deference to, or regard for, the Constitution, which he considers less obligatory than legislative enactments; has fellow-feeling with the factious majority of Congress because he considers them with him.

I suggested to the President on Tuesday that it would be well to have a gentleman in the Adjutant-General's office who is true and faithful to him and not in fear of, or under the control of, Stanton. General Townsend, the Assistant Adjutant-General, is a worthy and estimable man, but stands in dread and awe of "Carnot," who domineers over him. In fact, Stanton has taken all manhood out of Townsend, and I have often been pained to see with what humility the subordinate stood before the imperious tyrant. I spoke to the President of the importance of the office, through which military orders of the Department passed. He caught promptly and at once to the suggestion, and said General Thomas[1] should be ordered to his old position. I asked if he had not better see him before giving the order. He said he probably should, but he knew Thomas to be right-minded. That is my impression; he is right, but not strong, and there are so many who wilt down in these days, or whom we misunderstand, or who are weak or unreliable. Between Stanton and Thomas there has been a difference for five years. General Fry[2] is another under the power of the great intruder.

To-day I learned that orders were yesterday issued for General Thomas to resume his position and duties as Adjutant-General. Orders have also been issued to establish a new department. Sherman has been nominated Brevet General. The President has two or three times spoken to me of creating a new department and putting Sherman in command. I have always asked if Sherman could be depended upon in opposition to Grant. In other respects I consider him right. The President thinks he can rely on him. He can, doubtless, if Sherman enters upon the subject understandingly, but unless he fully

[1] General Lorenzo Thomas.
[2] General James B. Fry.

consents and agrees in advance, he will be likely, from old military associations, to cling to Grant.

February 14, Friday. Some conversation took place in Cabinet to-day on the subject of communications to the Secretary of War. I asked, "Who is Secretary of War?" The President looked at me significantly and said, "That matter will be disposed of in one or two days."

He then brought up the subject of removals and of authority on his part to assign the duties of one Cabinet officer to another. I asked him if he had seen a bill reported by Senator Trumbull on this subject, which was before the Senate yesterday and, from indications, I thought would be rushed through Congress. Of course, there is an object in this bill and this haste. None had seen the bill, which was published in the *Republican,* and on getting the paper and scrutinizing its provisions and preceding laws, it was evident it was another hedging-in of the President, which I should hardly have expected of Trumbull, though he is becoming extremely partisan.

I think the President is prepared to take decided action with Stanton, and if he will do it promptly, all may yet be well. He should have removed Stanton before this, since his last intrusion.

February 15, Saturday. Dined with the President yesterday. The Cabinet were all there with their families, and several Senators and others. It was a pleasant meeting, and the first state dinner-party of the season. All was pleasant and passed off cheerfully.

Many calls to-day. Got off an elaborate letter to Pike and the Naval Committee, on the subject of appropriations, and, incidentally, of estimates and the Navy generally. In the hands of a good chairman of the Committee the paper would be effective, but Pike is lazy and uncertain. Tries to be shrewd; is devoted to party more than to the service or the country; and there is consequently no certainty how much he will do. I intend, however, if the Navy is broken down, or impaired, that Congress shall be responsible for its acts.

February 17, *Monday.* Senator Doolittle called at my house last evening and read me a prepared speech which he proposed to deliver on Reconstruction. It is well calculated for effect among the people, and will be a little annoying to some of the Senators, who have changed their votes on this subject and on negro suffrage.

Attended reception at the President's this evening. A very full and general attendance, except of ultra Radicals, a few of whom were there. There is much spitefulness and hate among these men.

February 18, *Tuesday.* No great matters of interest were to-day before the Cabinet. I did not know but that the President might communicate something in regard to the conferring of a brevet appointment on General Sherman and assigning him to the command of this department, but nothing was said. It is rumored that Sherman refuses the brevet, and that he has written his brother, Senator Sherman, if it is insisted upon, he will come to Washington and throw up his commission. I do not credit this, but he is erratic and uncertain. Not unlikely he declines the brevet, for he expects, if Grant is elected President, to be made his successor; probably he may also wish to have duty elsewhere than here, because, as a friend of Grant, he wishes to avoid any conflict; but I shall be disappointed if General Sherman has, as the Radicals represent, committed anything approaching incivility towards the President. In any matter personal between the President and Grant, Sherman will endeavor to stand aloof, for he respects the President, while intimate and friendly with Grant; but, if compelled to take part, his leanings will favor Grant. The President flatters himself otherwise, but he is, I think, mistaken.

In their war upon the Court, the Radicals, under the
lead of Trumbull, have under consideration an act prohibiting the Court from passing judgment on political questions, and they have now a bill declaring what are political
questions. These usurpations and intrigues strain our
government.

February 19, *Wednesday.* The President informs me
this P.M. that he received this morning a letter from
General Sherman which was sent to him through Headquarters, where it has undoubtedly been read. He says
the letter is friendly and respectful, but he (S.) wishes
to be excused from Washington, and if he is detailed to
command this department, asks that he may be permitted
to have his headquarters in New York.

In view of all the circumstances,—the rumors, which
were not without some foundation, of his having telegraphed his brother Senator Sherman, his corresponding
with the President, who is Commander-in-Chief, through
General Grant, and his disinclination to come here, — the
President says he telegraphed to him at once, relieving
him of the order and directing him to remain in his present
command. The President thinks that, in communicating
with him through Grant, Sherman aims to keep in with
both sides and that he cared more to conciliate Grant than
anything else.

It is well these matters have taken this shape, perhaps,
though it is difficult to come to any satisfactory conclusion in regard to the President's movements and intentions. Indeed, he does not declare his intentions, and therein fails, I think, in sometimes coming to the best decision
that is to be attained. Perhaps the impeachment movements and threats are over, but he certainly was not well
prepared for a crisis such as some of us apprehended and
some of the extremists intended. He could not, it is now
evident, have relied on Sherman, had there been a necessity to resort to military measures. Yet he has persuaded

himself that Sherman would be his staff and reliance if Grant failed. How far he could have relied on General Emory as military commander of the district, I do not know; nor does the President, I apprehend. My impression is that E. is not to be depended on in civil matters, but he will be found where he thinks the power is.

February 20, *Thursday.* The reports of the Commander and the Engineer of the Wampanoag are gratifying. Isherwood has exerted himself wonderfully to make his engines a success and has been sustained by the Department in that effort. On the other hand, he has been vehemently and persistently opposed and denounced by a clique under Porter. There have been doleful predictions of failures of this vessel, but the predictions have proved false. I am glad, on Isherwood's account as well as on my own and that of the service, of this favorable result.

Vice-Admiral Porter is indulging in many intrigues against Isherwood and the engineers and staff generally, and is scheming in a way that is not creditable to bring himself into position in Washington. With some good qualities as a naval officer, he has some great faults and is wholly unfitted for administrative duties or place here. In his restless, suggestive nature, the Department would experience detriment and the country infinite evil. He should be kept afloat and in active service, but with a taut rein.

February 21, *Friday.* Seward read a letter to-day in regard to the employment of O'Conor or Brady [1] to go out to England to defend the Fenians. He and the President have had an understanding on the subject, which has been up once or twice before. I question the propriety of sending out counsel in these cases. Still, there may be justification.

[1] Charles O'Conor, who had been counsel for Jefferson Davis, and James T. Brady, who had defended General Sickles in his trial.

After disposing of regular Cabinet business, as we were about rising, the President informed us he had this morning removed Mr. Stanton. He had, he said, perhaps delayed the step too long. At all events, it was time the difficulty was settled.

Some one, I believe myself, inquired who was to be his successor. The President said General Thomas, Adjutant-General, would officiate *ad interim* and until a regular Secretary was appointed.

I asked if Stanton had surrendered up the place and General Thomas taken possession. The President said General Thomas had called on S. and informed him of his appointment; that Stanton seemed calm and submissive; that some little conversation had passed between them as to removing his books and papers, and S. was willing that Thomas should act his pleasure.

Browning said he had been informed that Stanton intended sending in his resignation to-day or to-morrow. A few remarks took place on this subject. I wholly discredited it, and expressed the belief he would under no circumstances resign, except on the single contingency of an assurance that he would not have Radical support. I was surprised to hear that he had quietly surrendered to General Thomas, and should be glad to hear that he had left and that General T. was in the rooms, in possession.

McCulloch said he doubted if Stanton had resigned, or intended to. He and I had once differed. He had thought Stanton would resign as soon as reinstated. I then said he would not. The result McCulloch said had proved that I was right and he was wrong. He now concurred with me. Browning said he gave no credit to the rumor which he had heard. It came to him through Cox, his Chief Clerk, who caught everything afloat.

The President said he had also brevetted Major-General G. H. Thomas to be Lieutenant-General and General, or rather that he had sent in these brevets to the Senate.

He had also nominated General McClellan as Minister to England, in place of Mr. Adams.

These acts of the President will excite the Radicals, and the violent ones will undoubtedly improve the opportunity to press on impeachment. Impulse, rather than reason or common sense, governs them. The President is vigorous and active, but too late, and has attempted too much at once.

February 22, *Saturday.* There was great excitement and many rumors last evening in regard to the President and Congress and others. Stanton, on getting notice of his removal, immediately sent it to the House of Representatives through the Speaker, and fire and wrath were exhibited. The movement was not unexpected. The communication was at once referred to the so-called "Reconstruction Committee," with a resolution from cunning but illiterate old Covode to "impeach the President."

The Senate were promptly informed by the President himself of the removal of Stanton, and the appointment of Thomas *ad interim.* That body at once stopped all business and went into executive session, where a fierce and protracted debate took place, extending far into the night. A resolution was finally adopted by a strict party vote, except Edmunds, who, though a central partisan, has a legal mind, that the President had no constitutional or legal power to remove the Secretary of War and appoint another, thus giving an opinion in advance of impeachment on a point for which the President may be presented to themselves for trial.

A committee of Cameron, Cattell, Conness, and Thayer was appointed in a Radical caucus, hastily convened while the Senate was in session, who proceeded to the War Department, and counseled and conspired with Stanton, how to resist the Executive, and they afterwards called on General Grant, who was inclined to be "reticent."

This morning General Thomas was arrested, on a writ

issued by Judge Cartter, a tool of Stanton, on a complaint
by Stanton that General T. had violated the Civil Tenure
law in accepting office against requirements of that law,
which he, Stanton, had himself emphatically declared as
unconstitutional.

General Thomas readily submitted to the arrest and
gave bail to appear next Wednesday. Stanton remained
at the Department all night with a parcel of Radical Senators and Representatives, and is there now and has been
all day, most of the time locked up.

It was impolitic for Thomas, who is a subordinate and
not an independent or self-reliant man, to have given
bail. Better to have gone to jail and sued out a writ of
habeas corpus. Better still, it seems to me, if he had first
got out process against Stanton. The people still have
great deference to law and to legal proceedings.

I called about noon on the President. He was in the
library with the Attorney-General. We had a brief conversation on affairs, when the Attorney-General proposed
to the President to ask my opinion on the subject they were
discussing when I entered. The President said that was
his intention, and I was asked what I thought of Thomas
Ewing, Sr., for Secretary of War. I asked if a person of his
years was the man for the occasion, — the crisis was important. The President said he was sound and right on the
questions before us, trustworthy, and, he believed, reliable.
I still hesitated and debated the subject, — his former
standing, his relationship to Sherman,[1] his great age, etc.
Stanbery said McClellan had just been nominated Minister to England from the Democratic side, if we now name
Ewing from the old Whig ranks the two will go well
together. The President smiled assent. I remarked that I
thought it would be well to get a nomination in early. The
President said if we two approved, he would send in Mr.

[1] Thomas Ewing was both adopted father and father-in-law to General
Sherman. He was seventy-eight years old at this time and he had been
Secretary of the Interior under Taylor and Fillmore.

Ewing's name at once. I said if that was his view, I should acquiesce cheerfully; he was unquestionably the man who should select his own advisers.

The President directed Colonel Moore to immediately write a nomination, which he at once signed and sent to the Senate. But the Senate, although it had assigned this day to a speech from Senator Doolittle, met and adjourned without doing any business, so that when Colonel Moore reached the Capitol the Senate was not in session. The day, I understand, was consumed by the Radical Senators in *secret caucus*. The Attorney-General, although a very good lawyer, is not the best adviser for administrative and executive service in such a time as this. There is a conspiracy against the Executive by Senators who are to adjudge him, and he, the Attorney-General, searches for precedents and authorities, when action, decision, and novel questions require a stand to be taken and a path to be stricken out with promptness. In the little conversation we had, and so on some former occasions, he seemed bewildered for precedents and undetermined how to act from the absence of previous authorities. In the mean time, whilst he is hesitating and groping around among the books for precedents, the Radicals are acting regardless of precedents or law.

The President needs, at this time, resolute and energetic surroundings, — men of intelligence and courage as well as of caution and prudence. With them he should counsel freely and without reserve. I apprehend he has not sufficiently fortified himself with such men. In his Cabinet, he has an honest lawyer in Mr. Stanbery, who will be faithful to him so long as he has law and precedent, but when new questions arise he is at sea and knows not how to steer. He is not, like Seward, calculating, unreliable, and selfish, but he will take no new step, nor enter into any untrodden path. In the mean time the Radicals are breaking over constitutional law and all legal restraints, and will, if they dare, arrest the President and his principal friends and imprison them. I do not anticipate this, yet the scheme is agitated by leading conspirators and I shall not be surprised at any movement they may make.

Returning from an evening ride, I called upon the President, hoping to find him alone, but McCulloch and Jeffries [1] were with him. Jeffries was advising strong measures. Thought if the President were to send a communication to the Senate, or to Congress, saying he wished the constitutionality of the Tenure-of-Office Bill and the Reconstruction acts decided by the courts, — that he would submit the laws to them, and if they should decide against him, or that the laws were constitutional, he would resign, — such a proposition, J. thought, would carry the country with the President. If Congress would not acquiesce in such a submission or reference, but were to proceed to extremities, then resist, seize the principal conspirators, etc. Fifty armed men would be all that were necessary. The President made no reply, nor did he enter into any conversation with J. on the subject. I merely observed that these theories would not be carried out, however plausible they might seem when not commenced. Congress would consent to no reference of their laws and proceedings to any court. That would be a trial of the Legislature as well as the Executive by the Judiciary; it was the purpose of the Legislature to try the Executive themselves. And then, as to the fifty military men, what could they do? Here was the General of the armies in the conspiracy, secretly urging it on. He might be arrested if insubordinate, but who was to do it? Emory is in command of the District. Can the President depend on him in an emergency? I have but little confidence in him, but the President ought to know him, and I presume does. He should have the best friend he has got in the Army in that place.

On asking the President in regard to Emory, he gave no satisfactory answer, but it was evident he did not fully confide in him. Jeffries, though a Marylander, knew little of E., but said Colonel Bowie, a true man, has great faith

[1] Noah L. Jeffries, Register of the Treasury.

in him, believes him true, etc., etc. I remembered he was false to the Union and pursued an equivocal course at the commencement of the Rebellion, and though there was entreaty and importunity to reinstate him, with many statements and explanations of his error and pledges of his future fidelity, I had little faith in him then, nor have I much now.

I called on the President this morning in consequence of an incident which took place at a party given by Mrs. Ray last evening. After the company assembled, an orderly appeared, requiring all officers of the Fifth Cavalry to appear at Headquarters. Shortly after, another orderly, requiring all officers under General Emory's command to appear at Headquarters. Both orders came from E. I asked the President if he had made preparations, — had issued orders to E. He said he had not. "Some one," said I, "has. Who is it, and what does it indicate? While you, Mr. President, are resorting to no extreme measures, the conspirators have their spies, — have command of the troops. Either Stanton or Grant or both issued orders which were proclaimed aloud and peremptorily at this large social gathering."

The President was disturbed, but said very little. It is an error with him that he does not more freely communicate with his Cabinet and friends. This whole movement of changing his Secretary of War has been incautiously and loosely performed without preparation. The Cabinet was not consulted. His friends in the Senate and House were taken by surprise, and were wholly unaware of the movement.

General Thomas proves himself unfit for the place of Secretary of War *ad interim*. He is like a boy, ready to obey orders, but cannot himself act with decision or direct others, — is a mere child or worse in Stanton's presence. Instead of taking upon himself the duties of Secretary of War and commanding Stanton, he submits to Stanton's orders, and is locked out of the Department, laughed at, and treated with contempt.

3

I am told he was weak and foolish enough last evening to attend a mask ball; was at Willard's Hotel, . . . that he talked openly and loudly of his being Secretary of War, — that he should to-day take possession, open the mails, etc. But he is snuffed out.

February 24, *Monday.* Senator Doolittle and Attorney-General Stanbery called on me last evening. Their object was to ascertain my recollection of what took place in the Cabinet when the Tenure-of-Office Bill was under consideration, especially on the point which related to the four first secretaries, who were appointed by Mr. Lincoln. I recollect that they were considered as holding office by a different tenure than the others, who were appointed by Mr. Johnson, but the remarks of the several members I could not recall. There was entire unanimity as regarded the unconstitutionality of the bill itself, and this absorbed the minor questions. The distinctive point now alluded to was, I remember, discussed. Mr. Seward, I think, alluded to it, and I well recollect that Mr. Randall made remark to the effect that the law appeared to carry out the four members by legislation, or there was a question if it did not. The Attorney-General said it could have no such retroactive effect, even if the law was good for anything, but he was emphatic and decisive in pronouncing the law absolutely and beyond all question unconstitutional. Stanton was quite as emphatic, and I think every member declared his readiness to surrender his place, whenever the President should express a wish to that effect.

Each of these gentlemen, as did also McCulloch, who called on me earlier in the evening, regretted that the President had not in this and other instances been more free and communicative with his friends, and advised with them without reserve. While reticent towards those with whom he should be most intimate, he has been holding free conversation with newspaper correspondents, and giving them his opinions, and an account of his actions on the most important subjects of administration. I have long lamented this condition of things, but I know of no remedy. The President has his peculiarities in this respect, as he had in speechmaking when "swinging round the circle."

I have sometimes been almost tempted to listen to the accusation of his enemies that he desired and courted impeachment. Yet such is not the fact. He is courageous and firm, with great sagacity and wide comprehension, yet is not in many respects wise and practical. It may be that he is willing the Radicals should make themselves ridiculous by futile assaults, but he hardly could have expected this flurry for so peaceful and justifiable a movement.

The Radical leaders have for some time striven to alarm and agitate the country by whispers and insinuations that the President was intending to make himself dictator, and Senator Thayer [1] pledged his honor as a Senator that the President was about to assume regal power or something of the sort, in a public speech last summer or autumn at Cincinnati. Forney, Secretary of the Senate, as deep in the conspiracy as the chiefs will permit, in his paper the *Chronicle*, which is the Radical organ, gave out that the President, with Governor Swann, was organizing the militia of Maryland to secure for himself absolute power. Others have tried to alarm the popular mind by similar silly and absurd falsehoods.

I this morning called on the President. There were many waiting. Randall and Mr. Ross were with him, but both soon left. Stanbery was in the library, writing and revising a message, which the President sent to Congress in a few hours, vindicating his course and removing Stanton. I had called because Mr. Stanbery and myself had an understanding to that effect last evening, believing it best the President should see all his Cabinet on the subject of his message or communication. But the President

---

[1] John M. Thayer, of Nebraska.

said he thought it unnecessary to see any others than Stanbery and myself.

The House this afternoon decided by a vote of 126 to 47 to impeach the President. The alleged cause of impeachment is the removal of a contumacious, treacherous, and unprincipled officer, who intrudes himself into the War Department under the authority of a law which he himself denounced as unconstitutional, a law to fetter the President and deprive the Executive of his rights.

The impeachment is a deed of extreme partisanship, a deliberate conspiracy, involving all the moral guilt of treason, for which the members would, if fairly tried, be liable to conviction and condemnation. If the President has committed errors, he has done no act which justifies this proceeding. The President is innocent of crime; his accusers and triers are culpably guilty. In this violent and vicious exercise of partyism I see the liberties and happiness of the country and the stability of the government imperiled.

The President has a reception this evening, and though neither my wife nor myself are well, and the night is inclement, we shall, with all the family, be present.

February 25, Tuesday. There is, I think, less excitement to-day. The weather, which is damp and dreary, perhaps contributes to it. A feeling of doubt and sadness pervades the minds of sensible men. Some of the less intense Radicals are dissatisfied with their own doings. A little routine business was transacted in the Cabinet, principally from the State Department. The President, though calm, is not without sensibility and feels the wrong and outrage of the conspirators, although he makes no complaint.

The debate which has taken place on the subject of impeachment is disgraceful, wicked, and malicious. E. B. Washburne, the . . . man of little work for Grant, was mendacious and villainous. . . .

John Bigelow, late Minister to France, spent an hour with me this P.M. He has been here some ten days, a looker-on, and is a good and honest observer. The proceedings at the Capitol have greatly interested him. He complains, and perhaps with reason, that the President was in fault in not communicating to his friends in Congress his purpose in removing Stanton, that they might have been prepared for the contest. The President's measures, he thinks also, should have been taken with deliberation; he should not have permitted himself to be foiled by Stanton; Thomas, or the man who was to take the place of Stanton, should have ejected him at once. All this is very true. It is easy, now that the matter has passed, to say, that so great a scoundrel, so treacherous, false, and deceitful a man should not have been treated like a gentleman. The President has, from the first, extended to Stanton a consideration and leniency that has surprised me, for he knew him to be false, remorseless, treacherous, and base. I expressed my disbelief in his quiet retirement last Friday, when the President announced his removal and T.'s appointment.

Bigelow is confident, or rather has high hopes, that impeachment will fail in the Senate. Says that the large conservative force in the Senate, with the Chief Justice, look with repugnance and horror to the accession of Wade,[1] and would prefer to continue the President. Unless, therefore, Wade will resign and allow some good conservative Senator to be made President of the Senate, he thinks impeachment will be defeated.

I encouraged his hopes, while I have very slight expectations. This is a party scheme, a conspiracy on a large scale, more offensive and reprehensible than that of secession, but the conspirators, having taken the fatal plunge, cannot recede. There are Representatives who have qualms, but these very men will stimulate hesi-

[1] As President *pro tem.* of the Senate, Senator Benjamin F. Wade of Ohio was next in line of succession to the Presidency.

tating Senators to do as they have done, — get into the same boat with themselves. Radicalism will not only be dead, but will rot if they fail. They know this as well as we know it, and, knowing it, they "give up to party what was meant for mankind." I fear no moral courage will be found among the Radical Senators, no individual independence; but shall wait events, calmly I hope, though it is difficult to restrain giving utterance to one's indignation at deliberate villainy.

February 26, *Wednesday.* General L. Thomas was arrested last Saturday morning at the instigation of E. M. Stanton, on a writ issued by Cartter, Chief Justice of the District Court. General T. gave bail in $5000, and the case came up to-day, when he was prepared to submit to imprisonment, with a view of suing out a writ of *habeas corpus* and getting a decision from the Supreme Court on the constitutionality of the Civil-Tenure Bill. This the Radicals and Stanton dreaded, and after various twistings and turnings, General T. was discharged.

Cartter, in this whole proceeding, from its inception to its close, showed himself a most unfit judge. He has secretly visited Stanton at the War Department, and his associate Fisher has spent much of his time since Thomas' arrest, with Stanton.

A summons was issued for Stanton to appear as a witness for Thomas to-day, and to produce his commission, but the quondam Secretary refused to appear.

I, yesterday, and again to-day, suggested, not to say urged, that Judge Curtis [1] should be one of the President's counsel in the impeachment. The President assented to my suggestions, but whether he will engage C. is another question. Something will depend, without doubt, on the disposition of the Attorney-General, and perhaps Black will also have a voice.

The Democratic National Committee has been in

[1] Benjamin Robbins Curtis.

session here, and, from what I learn, have not been over-
wise, but somewhat conceited and weakly and foolishly
partisan. Bigelow tells me that the intention is to make
Horatio Seymour the Presidential candidate. Tilden thinks
Seymour will run stronger than any man in New York,
and that is a great State, — he does not look beyond it.
I said to B. that it was important that Democrats should
have a ticket which would draw recruits and not repel
them; that Seymour was not an acceptable candidate out
of the pale of party and not strongly popular within it.
It might be possible, under the mad conduct of the Radicals, to elect a strict party candidate, but not certain. He
asked who there was that could be taken up. Said that
Tilden assured him Doolittle would not be acceptable
in New York. I named Hendricks, Hancock, or, if they
would go in for a man for the country, and relax as regards party, there was Charles Francis Adams. He would
be the third of the name and family, and would be attacked for that reason, but the fact had also its strong
side. There would be many who would, especially in these
turbulent times, be glad to have peace and stability, such
as the country had forty years ago under his father. He
has not the popular element, would not be acceptable
to the Fenians, and therefore would not be a party candidate; but the country would have in him a *good president*, but with some family infirmities. There is some
military feeling which might be made available for
Hancock, who is better liked than Grant.

February 27, *Thursday.* The feverish excitement has
abated. Impeachment as a sensation has had its day.
When the trial comes on in the Senate, it will be revived,
perhaps, but with less intensity.

Woodbridge of Vermont, one of the Judiciary Committee, who always opposed impeachment, came to see me
to-day. He spoke deprecatingly of the movement; regretted that he was compelled to vote for it under party

demands, but his colleagues from Vermont all went for it, they and the party at home were violent, and it would have been death for him to have resisted. He voted with reluctance and against his wishes and convictions, for the President he knew to be honest and patriotic; and he so said to me. It is melancholy to witness such things. Woodbridge is but one of many who are guilty of this wrong. A moral infirmity or weakness. They dare not act in accordance with their convictions. A fear of party ostracism controls them. But their acts forfeit their self-respect for the time, and sooner or later will lose them the respect of others.

The whole impeachment scheme is a piece of party persecution, which, if successful to party, will be ruinous to the country. It is a deliberate and wicked conspiracy from its inception.

February 28, Friday. Mr. Seward read to-day one of his strange, unstatesmanlike, and improper dispatches. It was addressed to Mr. Stillwell, our Minister at Venezuela, in relation to certain of the crew of the Hannah Grant, a whaling-schooner, who were unlawfully detained in that country. The dispatch was objectionable as a state paper, and was offensive because wanting in proper courtesy to the naval officer who might be ordered to La Guayra. Mr. Stillwell was told that a naval vessel would be sent (without any reference to the Secretary of the Navy), that the naval office would be directed to commit no hostile act without his (Stillwell's) direction, etc., etc. In other, or plain, words, the Minister and naval officer were authorized at their discretion to declare war, or make war, on Venezuela.

Mr. Stanbery took exception to this part of the dispatch, in which I joined. Seward was annoyed by the criticism and objection, but finally professed to put in some pencil alteration. He would not presume to send a dispatch of this nature to Russia in regard to the recent outrages in the

Sea of Okhotsk [1] nor to England in regard to the Fenians, nor to France, but he can be arrogant to feeble Venezuela.

I am inclined to think that a claim which his pet Sanford, our Minister to Belgium, has against Venezuela may influence him in asking for a man-of-war at Curaçao, as much as the seamen of the Hannah Grant.

Some laughter took place, after Cabinet council, over the fortification and intrenchment of the War Department, and the trepidation of Stanton, who has this morning doubled his guard. Kennedy, Chief of New York police, sent a letter to Speaker Colfax, that some nitro-glycerine had disappeared from New York, and that shrewd, sagacious, and patriotic functionary knew not where it had gone, unless to Washington.

The chivalrous and timid Speaker at once laid this tremendous missive before the House, and the consternation of the gallant band of Radicals became excessive. A large additional police force had been placed around the Capitol, but as it was still considered unsafe, an immediate adjournment was called for. Stanton, unfortunate man, could not adjourn. There was no refuge for him, save in the War Department, which is surrounded and filled with soldiers to protect against an inroad from old General Thomas. As Stanton, Grant, and the Radical Congress have assumed the entire control of the military, to the exclusion of the President, who is Commander-in-Chief, the apprehension seems to be that the Adjutant-General and his friends have resorted to nitro-glycerine.

Browning inquired whether there should not be more free communication and interchange of opinion among the members of the Cabinet in regard to the measures before Congress. Seward promptly and in a manner that was intended to put a stop to this said the President would, he suppose, consult any member he pleased on any subject; that this matter of impeachment belonged more particu-

---

[1] A Russian sloop-of-war fired on an American vessel in the Sea of Okhotsk in December, 1867.

larly to the Attorney-General, and he proposed they (the President and the Attorney-General) should do what they thought best; he might, he continued, be called as witness, and it was best to ward off any charge of conspiring, etc., etc. I dissented wholly from this view, as did the Attorney-General and indeed every other member. I regretted that we had not been more free in expressing our views to each other at all times, — though it was felt we could not, so long as Stanton was with us, be frank and friendly. McCulloch took the same view. Browning said he had, perhaps, done wrong in bringing the subject forward; it was not his intention to intrude on the President, but the times demanded the united counsel of all. Seward, after remarking that "too many cooks usually spoiled the broth," expressed his readiness to meet and consult at all times.

The subject of counsel in case of a trial was then introduced. Every man advised the retention of Judge Curtis. O'Conor was mentioned. McCulloch objected that he was counsel for Jeff Davis, and that party antipathy would counteract his ability. Evarts was mentioned and rather pressed. I admitted his ability, but feared his want of heart in the measure. He had united himself with the Radicals when their cause seemed strong; it must have been from no mental and moral workings of such a mind as his; in that act he was not true to his nature and to what he knew to be right.

Seward, who has always heretofore been steadfast for Evarts, gave in to the correctness of my remarks, but said he knew not how far he had gone with the Radicals. He was a very cold man. After further talk it was agreed we would come together on Saturday evening at half-past seven.

Grant has overruled General Hancock, and reëstablished, or reappointed the negro aldermen in New Orleans. He is implicated in the conspiracy against the President, — a willing party to it. . . .

February 29, *Saturday*. The impeachment committee have printed ten articles. Nine of them contain a mountain of words, but not even a mouse of impeachment material. The tenth is even weaker than the other nine, and has a long tail from General Emory. I never had faith in the firmness and honest stability of this man, who was false in 1861, and whimpered back into the service which he had deserted. His willing, volunteered testimony has been evidently procured and manufactured, and yet is nothing. The President had sent for him on the 22d in consequence of information and suggestions from myself, and questioned him. Emory puts the *questions* in the form of *averments* by the President, and throughout exhibits himself a Radical partisan for the time being.

Mr. Stanbery says that Judge Curtis will be here on Tuesday evening next. There is, Stanbery thinks, an intention on the part of the managing Radicals to exclude him from taking part in defense of the President before the court of impeachment because he is Attorney-General. He queries whether he had not better resign forthwith, and devote his whole time to the case. To this we were each and all opposed, or to any resignation unless he were compelled.

A writ of *quo warranto* is to be sued out, but with the Court in the District wholly under the influence of the Radical conspirators, action will be delayed as long as possible, for there is nothing they so much dread as a decision of the Supreme Court on their unconstitutional laws.

There is no "high crime or misdemeanor" in these articles that calls for impeachment, and those who may vote to convict upon these articles would as readily vote to impeach the President had he been accused of stepping on a dog's tail. But any pretext will serve unprincipled and unscrupulous partisan vengeance. He would not lend himself to a series of unconstitutional measures and to get rid of him is imperative.

LVII

Preparations for the Impeachment Trial — The Notice of Impeachment served on the President — Selecting the President's Counsel — Stanbery determines to resign his Cabinet Position before undertaking the President's Case — Stanton fortified in the War Department — Radical Victory in the New Hampshire Election — A Sketch of New Hampshire Politics — Stanbery hands in his Resignation — The President's Ill-considered Talks with Newspaper Men — Senator Sherman wishes a Naval Lieutenant court-martialed for using Disrespectful Language of Congress — The President's Uncommunicativeness — Judge Black on Seward's Handling of the Alta Vela Affair — The Impeachment Proceedings open with Little Excitement — Judge Black withdraws from the President's Case — Probable Reasons for his Course — A Spirit of Mischief in the Hawaiian Islands — Black's Letter to the President withdrawing from the Case and denouncing Seward's Conduct in the Alta Vela Matter — Wilson and Sumner and the Naval Appropriation Bill — General Butler's Opening in the Impeachment Trial.

March 3, Tuesday. The journals of the day and published proceedings will be a record of what occurs in matters of impeachment. I do not, therefore, record details of official transactions, but such only as seem to me proper with individual movements. The spirit which has led to the impeachment movement and its consummation in the House is strange and various. A considerable portion of those who voted for it did violence to their own convictions. There is another large element which had no convictions, but are mere shallow, reckless partisans who would as readily have voted that the President should be hung in front of the White House as that he should be impeached in the Capitol, provided their leaders — Stevens, Boutwell, and others — had presented papers in form for that purpose. Another and different class, like Boutwell, seek and expect notoriety and fame. They have read Macaulay's interesting history of the trial of Warren Hastings, and flatter themselves they are to be the Burkes and Sheri-

dans of some future historian. Malignant party hate and
unscrupulous party thirst for power stimulate others.

A shameless, brazen effrontery and villainy mark certain
Senators. Howard and Chandler of Michigan, Sumner,
Cameron, Conkling, and others have already made themselves parties against the man whom they are to adjudge,
— have some of them, if not all, connived in secret to urge
on impeachment. They have broken down the barriers
of the Constitution, while the President has striven to defend them, and for his defense he is to be tried and condemned by these violators, conspirators, and perjurers.

March 4, *Wednesday.* Chief Justice Chase has sent a
letter to the Senate which disturbed the Radicals. It was
not of great moment, and will be swamped by leading impeachers who are anxious to hurry on their work. Stevens,
with his arrogance, insolence, and vicious despotism,
threatens every Senator who shall dare to vote against
his party; tells them they are committed by their votes.
It must shame and mortify some of the intelligent minds
in the Senate to be held in subjection and compelled to
receive the excoriations and threatenings of this wicked
and bad man, but it is questionable whether they have the
moral courage and independence to do right, when the
terrors of this party tyrant are before them.

Seward and I met in the council room, and, while waiting for the President, allusion was made to our meeting
seven years ago yesterday, and of events which have since
transpired. He says it is nineteen years this 4th of March
since he entered the service of the United States, seven
years since he became a Cabinet Minister. "How few of
all the men," said he, "with whom we have been associated,
have proved faithful! — how many have disappointed us!"
This was said in connection with present transactions,
and had particular reference to Stanton.

The Cabinet met last evening at half-past seven instead
of at noon. But little official business was done. We had

a two hours' talk of the condition of public affairs, and
especially of the great question now before the country.
Judge Curtis was expected to-day. He is associated with
Mr. Stanbery as one of the counsel of the President. Other
names were talked of, but no conclusion come to.

McCulloch expressed a hope that the President would
go to the Senate on the first day, but not afterwards.
Seward said if he went the whole Cabinet ought to accompany him. I objected to either. It would give dignity
and imposing form to the proceedings, which the conspirators wished, but we did not. The managers undoubtedly
desired that the President should exhibit himself there,
and if surrounded by his advisers it would make the scene
more imposing. Men, and women too, would come from
a distance, and gather at the Capitol to see the victim,
if he should consent to gratify them.

March 5, Thursday. The Cabinet met this evening.
Seward brought forward the removal of Timothy Pickering from the office of Secretary of State in May, 1800, by
John Adams, as a case in point. His clerks had hunted up
this precedent, and if Congress was in session, as Seward
says, it is in all respects like the present case, except that
the Tenure-of-Office Law had not then been enacted.

The movement which had been made by the Republican
Senators in 1862 to procure the removal of Seward was
brought under discussion. At that time, these Senators
called on President Lincoln to make his Cabinet a unit
by removing an objectionable minister, as they considered
him.

Judge Curtis has arrived. When I went to the President's this evening, no others of the Cabinet were there, but
I found Mr. Groesbeck [1] of Cincinnati with him. He was
and is most earnestly opposed to this conspiracy and with

[1] William Slocomb Groesbeck, a liberal Republican who had been a delegate to the Philadelphia Convention. He was retained as counsel for President Johnson.

the President, and there has been mention of his name as one of the junior counsel for the President. His being here, however, at this time was accidental, — was for other and business reasons.

David D. Field was spoken of complimentarily by Browning from the representation of others. Seward did not concur; said Field was the greatest small man he had ever known.[1] Stanbery thought he spread himself too largely, had too many points, was a book man, not an original.

March 6, Friday. A brief Cabinet-meeting. Browning brought his diary, detailing occurrences and remarks in the Senatorial Republican Caucus of 1862 for removal of Seward, he being at that time a Senator from Illinois. General Thomas was present at the Cabinet-meeting this evening, but no business was transacted, nor was there a disposition to have much free discussion while he remained. I was sorry the President invited him, unless it is necessary to carry out explicitly the *ad interim* appointment.

March 7, Saturday. The President was served with notice of impeachment this evening. I was at the White House a few moments after the copy was left. We had a Cabinet-meeting this evening. I was the first who arrived. The others came in soon.

Mr. Stanbery is sensitive on the subject of retaining the office of Attorney-General while defending the President. Thinks exception may be taken to his appearance by extreme partisan Senators, and proposed to anticipate their movement by a resignation. Says that it will involve the necessity of wholly giving up all attention to official business during the trial, for that and that alone shall occupy his mind. But this can be got along with by turning over

---

[1] David Dudley Field, the eldest of four distinguished brothers, was a very large man physically.

current official matters to his Assistant. He is, however, sensitive to any imputation from any quarter, and is pretty much determined to resign. All the members preferred he should not. I think, and said, if he found it a point to be met, he could, when challenged or when decision was had by the Senate, present his resignation. The effect, it seems to me, would be good, if so presented. Let the Radical Senators sitting as judges hound down the President, — object, if they please, to his having one of his political family, his legal selected adviser, to defend him.

In the consultations which have been had by the counsel thus far, Stanbery, Curtis, and Black have participated. At the last meeting, Stanbery says, Black suggested that his (B.'s) appearing might prejudice the case, and while he was extremely solicitous to participate he would by no means act if it were supposed his doing so would be injurious to the President. Both S. and C. had apprehensions it might be unfortunate, but desired the Cabinet to express their views, and, above all, that the President himself might decide on this subject.

McCulloch promptly expressed his opinion against the retention of Black as one of the counsel. Said that Senator Hendricks had said to him it would be injudicious; that the Democrats in the Senate would all be right, he had no doubt, but that the Republicans were hostile to Black.

Seward was inclined to believe that this was the case, and perhaps some one as capable and not so obnoxious might be found. Several names were suggested.

I asked if it would be wise or politic to exclude from the managing counsel any pronounced Democrat whatever. It appeared to me important that there should be one such lawyer among them, and while I had no great intimacy with, or partiality for, Black, I knew of no one who was, under the circumstances, in all respects his equal. We wanted something more than a mere lawyer for such a case as this, — a politician and statesman, one who made the Constitution and public affairs a study. Still, if Black was personally or by reason of his party entanglements and associations so offensive as to alienate any of these Senatorial judges, I would not press him. But no man was fit to be a Senator or a member of the court, whose judgment would be biased by his personal or party dislike of counsel. I cautioned them to remember, however, that the friends and supporters of the President were almost all Democrats, and the ground-swell of public opinion would have its influence on the Senators.

There was a general opinion that the third man should be a Democrat, and Thurman of Ohio was named. Seward favored him, and McCulloch also. Stanbery complimented him but did not explicitly commit himself for him. Browning inclined to Black, if not so objectionable as to injure the cause before the Senate. I stated my opinion of Thurman was favorable from what I had heard of him, but he had no such national reputation as Black.

March 9, *Monday*. I called on the President this morning and informed him I had reflected much on the subject of his counsel, and although there was opposition to Black, it appeared to me he ought not to give way to it, provided B. had his confidence. He thanked me and said the retention of Black was not an open question and he had so informed Mr. Seward who called last evening and wished to dissuade him. The President attributed the hostility of Seward to the fact that Black had been opposed to Seward in the Alta Vela matter.[1] I have understood that Thurlow Weed was interested in that question, and his interest in that questionable transaction was in consequence of his intimacy and well-known influence with the Secretary of State, and I so informed the President. For

[1] This was the claim of Patterson and Murginendo for damages on account of the seizure by the Dominican Republic of Alta Vela, a guano island off the coast of the island of Hayti. The island was occupied in 1859 or 1860 by United States citizens and taken possession of in the name of the United States, and the seizure was regarded by some as a *casus belli*. The claim was finally dismissed.

3

a little matter, Seward has manifested the deepest anxiety in the Alta Vela business. I do not think he has any pecuniary interest in it, but he is solicitous for his friend Weed, who has. The President asked me if I knew Swett[1] of Illinois. I do slightly, but am not particularly favorably impressed with the idea of his being one of the counsel. I thought neither his abilities nor standing in the country would justify such a selection. The President said he knew very little of Swett, but Seward urged him because he was the special friend of Mr. Lincoln, and to retain him would gratify Mr. L.'s friends. I besought him to be influenced by no such representations, and expressed my regret that they had been made.

We had a Cabinet-meeting this evening. In a desultory conversation at the beginning of the session, some one, I think Browning, stated some fact in regard to Chief Justice Chase which indicated his opposition to impeachment, and that his influence would be against it. Seward denied that Chase had any influence; there was not, he said, a Senator, or a press, or a community where his opinion weighed a feather, or was of the slightest consequence. He went on in one of his rambling, dogmatic dissertations, which seemed to astonish and awe Browning. I took exceptions and insisted that Chase had official, political, and moral influence, that should not be lightly thrown away. Seward became excited. "Name a man — name a Senator — whom he can influence." I mentioned Fessenden, at which S. phewed, — said he had more influence with F. than Chase had. I congratulated him on his good opinion of himself with F., but assured him that *I knew* he was mistaken. The truth is, Fessenden has great admiration of Chase, but very little respect for Seward. No one sustained Seward, who went on dogmatizing and prophesying. He claims to know how both the New York Senators feel on the subject of impeachment.

[1] Leonard Swett, an intimate friend of Lincoln's and during his Administration employed on government cases.

The question of the counsel of the President was discussed. Stanbery, Black, and Curtis were decided upon favorably. Seward informed the President that he had telegraphed for Evarts, who would be here to-morrow morning. The President looked at me, and saw perhaps that I did not respond to that selection with alacrity, and said to Mr. Seward, "His coming here does not insure that Mr. Evarts will be retained." "No," said Seward, hesitating, "but you cannot do better." All concurred in that opinion but myself. I admitted his high standing as a lawyer, his intellectual capacity, his fidelity, if he engaged in the cause, but this cold, calculating, selfish man was destitute of enthusiasm, magnetic power, or political influence; had abandoned the Administration with which he had been associated without cause and gone over to the Radicals. Ought such a man, though unsurpassed as a lawyer, technical, legal, but in his politics a mere calculator, to be selected in such a case as this? In deserting the Administration when he did, he exhibited weakness, — with all his legal lore, — want of conscience, want of fidelity to principle. Seward admitted Evarts had taken a strange course. I named Samuel Glover, of St. Louis, as a lawyer and orator, if the President was intending to select another Western man. He said Mr. Seward had named Swett, and others had spoken of him. I asked Browning, who knew them both, as to the two men. He said they were not to be named together, — that Glover was incomparably superior. I asked Seward what were the particulars of Swett's California transactions, — there were imputations upon him coincident with those matters. McCulloch said Blair told him that Swett was a tool of Stanton's. Seward denied this, and said the hundred thousand dollars which Swett obtained was his (Seward's) doing; that Swett was such a man as the President wanted; everybody knew of his intimacy with Lincoln, and it would bring them into good relations with the President were he to retain Swett.

No one seconded Seward in this matter. He evidently is using the occasion for his own personal benefit more than the President's. I should almost think he is in Stanton's interest. Evarts and Swett he has imposed on the President in sly interviews.

After an hour and a half's discussion, we went below to the President's evening general reception, which was well and fashionably attended.

March 10, *Tuesday.* At the Cabinet-meeting this noon, Mr. Stanbery named, as the counsel who would probably be retained, himself, Black, Curtis, Evarts, Groesbeck, and Nelson of Tennessee, whom the President has invited here, and who was introduced to us. Field seems to be excluded, which is Seward's doings, and will be a disappointment to many, — as much as the retention of Evarts.

I spoke freely of Evarts, and the objections to him. It may be, however, that he will acquit himself with credit. I shall be disappointed if he does not, for he has abilities and the occasion is a great one.

Mr. Stanbery says he must resign his place as Attorney-General in order to devote his whole time to this case. He is unwilling to be trammeled, or have his mind disturbed by any official duties, obligations, or embarrassments, and says it will undoubtedly be urged against him that, as the prosecuting officer of the Government, it is his duty to sustain rather than oppose the articles of impeachment. I am not impressed with his views. As the constitutional legal adviser of the President, — one of his civil household and officially and personally a part of the Government, — I think he would find no difficulty in sustaining himself before the Senate, and the very fact of opposition to him on account of his being a member of the Cabinet, the legal adviser of the Administration, would have a good influence before the country. I so expressed myself. But Mr. Stanbery is sensitive and timid. Herein, I fear, he will fail before the insolent, reckless, and audacious

WILLIAM M. EVARTS

Radical Managers and conspiring Senators who are to sit in judgment. Stevens and Butler will take pleasure in bluffing and insulting, and he is too courteous, gentlemanly, and dignified to meet and boldly rebuke them.

Stanton is still making himself ridiculous by intrenching his person in the War Department, surrounded by a heavy guard. This is for effect. He is, it is true, an arrant coward, but can have no apprehension of personal danger requiring a military force to protect him. Some of his *wise* Senatorial advisers, doubtless, in their conspiracy to defeat executive action, counseled and advised the redoubtable Secretary to hold on to the War Department building, and to fortify himself in it. Thayer, Conness, and Cameron would have minds for such work.

March 11, *Wednesday.* The election in New Hampshire yesterday resulted in the success of the Radical ticket by probably about the same majority as last year, on a great and unaccountably increased vote of both parties. The effect of this will be to elate the Radicals, far more than it will discourage the Democrats, for the former have no faith in their cause while the Democrats are full of confidence in the rectitude and ultimate triumph of their principles.

The popular element in New Hampshire is pretty stable and fixed. People do not easily change their party relations. For a long series of years the men of the Isaac Hill class of politicians had a controlling influence in the Granite State. Their principles were sound, and the management of the State was judicious. A younger set of men of the same politics came forward and took and were awarded high official position by the country in consequence of the firm and persistent political character of the State. But they have not the qualifications of their predecessors and seniors. The firm foundation laid by Hill, Harvey, Woodbury, and others continued to uphold the party for years; but at length it was undermined and gave way.

Pierce, Atherton, and Burke were mere politicians, wholly incapable of building up or maintaining a party. Their weakness and impracticability led to vigorous antagonism, and events favored their opponents, who had been schooled in adversity. Pierce, a vain, showy, and pliant man, was made President by Jeff Davis, R. J. Walker, Gid Pillow, and others, and by his errors and weakness broke down his Administration, and his party throughout the country. How could such a man and his associates impart strength and vigor to any party anywhere?

In the mean time, a set of younger men of opposite politics came forward and established an efficient and energetic organization in New Hampshire, which swept the State. The repeal of the Missouri Compromise, the swindling villainies in Kansas, the flagrant disregard of the principles of their party, their debasing subserviency to the arrogant and insolent assumptions of the imperious Southern leaders — even to countenancing and affiliating with the Secessionists — demoralized and broke down the Democratic Party, which for a quarter of a century had held supremacy in New Hampshire. The rising young politicians of the opposite party assimilated with those Democrats who opposed central aggressions and availed themselves of the advantages which the feeble and weak Democrats who clung to organization regardless of principle threw into their hands.

Chandler, Assistant Secretary of the Treasury; Rollins, Revenue Commissioner; Rollins, Member of Congress; Ordway, Sergeant-at-Arms of the House of Representatives; Fogg, late Minister to Switzerland, and others have, for the last dozen years, been as efficient and powerful as Isaac Hill and his associates in other days. Their organization and the discipline of party have prevented the State from securing its rightful position at this time; but the change is upon them. The Radicals are extremists or disunionists, and as much in fault as the Secessionists, and the rising young Democrats will take advantage of their centralizing and disunion heresies to overthrow the Republican Party.

March 12, *Thursday.* At a special Cabinet-meeting the matter of Stanbery's resignation was considered. The general wish was that he should retain the office and act as counsel; but he prefers to be untrammeled, and has his heart much set on the trial. The President has recently had a conversation with a newspaper correspondent (the *World's*) in which he disclosed Pickering's case, who was removed by John Adams, — a point on which the counsel were relying and which we all had studiously kept secret.

Stanbery, having presented his resignation and the matter being adjusted, was about leaving, when he stopped, addressed the President, and resumed his seat, "You are now, Mr. President," said he, "in the hands of your lawyers, who will speak and act for you, and I must begin by requesting that no further disclosures be made to newspaper correspondents. There was in the papers, yesterday or this morning, what purported to be a conversation between the President and a correspondent, in which the Pickering correspondence was brought out and made public. This is all wrong, and I have to request that these talks, or conversations, be stopped. They injure your case and embarrass your counsel."

Mr. Browning followed in the same vein and more at length. The President was taken aback. He attempted some apologetic remark. Said the correspondence was in the books, accessible to all, etc. But no one justified, apologized for, or attempted to excuse him. He saw that there was general disapproval.

Some of these proceedings of the President are unaccountable and inexcusable. He seems to take pleasure in having these "talks" of the President with this or that correspondent published. It is in his position hardly a pardonable weakness.

Seward has gone to New York and will visit Albany and Auburn before he returns. Why he selects this time to be absent, I cannot tell. It is not unusual for him when some crisis, some development, some of his own intrigues are about ripening to leave Washington for a few days. The impeachment hearing comes on to-morrow, and, though a postponement will take place, I know not why he should be away. He says he will see friends in New York and can help the President more there than here.

March 13, *Friday.* Impeachment was the order of the day. The reports render description and detail unnecessary. Of course the President was not there, nor were any of his Cabinet. The hollow farce has no friends, — hardly any with the Radicals, beyond mere pretense. An attempt to proceed forthwith to trial was made, and the Senate had a Star-Chamber sitting on the measure, from which all but Senators were excluded. Little of interest took place at the Cabinet-meeting.

Senator John Sherman sends me three affidavits, stating that Lieutenant Day used very improper and disrespectful language against Congress and General Grant, and demands that he shall be court-martialed. Day is off duty — on leave — at home among his friends — and in some discussion at a gathering, cross-roads, or railroad depot, expressed himself strongly and unbecomingly. Others may have done the same. Whilst this was reprehensible, and perhaps may justify admonition and reproof, since attention is called to it by a Senator, I do not consider it a military offense requiring a court martial. If all officers are to be court-martialed for expressing their condemnation of Congress, or any department of the Government, we shall have our hands full. It is bad enough to bring them before a court for too free utterance against their superiors when on duty, but to attack them for free, though erroneous and improper, speech at home, when off duty, in regard to the Government or any department, is hardly to be thought of. Senator Sherman would revise the sedition law and put a gag in the mouths of his countrymen — especially its naval and military men — who should venture to give free utterance to their opinions of the bad acts of himself and associates. But neither Congress nor General Grant are above or beyond criticism.

March 14, Saturday. I was confined to my house by order of Doctor H[orwitz] in consequence of a severe cold which threatened congestion of the lungs, but went a short time this evening in a close carriage to the President. Browning and Randall were there; no others. The President indicated more uncomfortable and uncertain feeling than I had before witnessed. He has great calmness, great fortitude, great self-reliance, but it is evident these qualities are put to a severe test by late proceedings. Browning is also disquieted, though not prepared to confess it. Randall, who mixes more with all classes and has better opportunities of feeling the pulse of the public here in Washington than others of us, expresses the strongest conviction that the President will be sustained and that the impeachment will fail. I should have no doubt myself of such a result in an ordinary case in ordinary times, or were the Senators above fanatical partisan prejudice and influence, — were they statesmen and independent patriots. But, I am sorry to say, I have so little confidence in a majority of the Senators that I make no reliance upon an acquittal. Should a sufficient number evince moral principle and independence to discharge their duty honestly, he may not only be acquitted but have a majority in his favor.

I have seen none of the counsel since the session of yesterday. They asked for forty days to prepare. The Senate went into secret session and gave them nine. This has a bad look. Only nine days for so great a cause, affecting the Chief Magistrate and the Nation itself! Men who would so limit time in so grave a matter, even under secret caucus stimulant, can scarcely be considered worthy to

sit in judgment in such a case. The charges are indeed
frivolous, contemptible, but, the House of Representatives
having preferred them, the President should have been
allowed ample time for his defense. But a majority of the
Senators have prejudged the case, and are ready to pronounce judgment without testimony.

It is evident that the Radicals in Congress are in a conspiracy to overthrow not only the President but the government. The impeachment is but a single act in the drama.
Alabama is to be admitted by a breach of faith and by
violence to honest, fair legislation. By trick, imposition,
and breach of courtesy an act was slipped through both
houses repealing the laws of 1867 and 1789, the effect of
which is to take from the Supreme Court certain powers,
and which is designed to prevent a decision in the McCardle
case.[1] Should the Court in that case, as it is supposed they
will, pronounce the Reconstruction laws unconstitutional,
the military governments will fall and the whole Radical
fabric will tumble with it. Only one course can prolong
the miserable contrivance, and that is a President like
Wade, who will maintain the military governments regardless of courts, or law, or right. Hence I have very
little expectation that the President will escape conviction.
His deposition is a party necessity, and the Senators have
not individually the strength, ability, nor honesty to resist
the Radical caucus decisions which Stevens, Ben Butler,
and other chief conspirators sent out.

March 17, Tuesday. The Cabinet met in the library, the
council room being occupied by the President's lawyers

[1] This was a *habeas corpus* case alleging unlawful restraint by military
force, appealed by William H. McCardle from the Circuit Court for the
Southern District of Mississippi. The act referred to repealed so much of the
Act of 1867 amending that of 1789 "as authorized an appeal from the judgment of the Circuit Court to the Supreme Court of the United States, or the
exercise of any such jurisdiction by said Supreme Court on appeals which
have been or may hereafter be taken"; and the Court accordingly dismissed
the case for want of jurisdiction.

preparing for the impeachment trial. There was little of interest. General Thomas was present as the *ad interim* Secretary of War. The President is anxious and more than usually abstracted. I trust he communicates freely with his counsel, though always inclined to be reserved. It has been, and is, his misfortune that he has tried, and still does, to carry on this great government without confidants, — without consulting or advising, except to a very limited extent, with any. It wears upon him, and his measures are not always taken with the caution and care that wisdom dictates.

In his movements the President is irregular. Sometimes he is inexcusably dilatory; sometimes he appears to act from impulse. His best friends expected the removal of Stanton two years earlier than it was made. So far as he communicated anything on the subject, I supposed on several occasions that change would take place. But he delayed until Congress passed a law to prevent Stanton's removal and the President from acting.

The conduct of Stanton was not gratifying to the Radicals, or to one wing of the Republican Party, the more moderate. They were becoming tired of him. A little skillful management would have made a permanent break in that party. But the President had no tact himself to effect it, he consulted with no others, the opportunity passed away, and by a final hasty move, without preparation, without advising with anybody, he took a step which consolidated the Radicals of every stripe, strengthened Stanton, while it weakened his supporters, and brought down a mountain of trouble on himself. Had he unbosomed himself to his Cabinet, received their suggestions, and canvassed fully and deliberately the subject, results would have been different.

March 18, *Wednesday.* There is a strange, dull apathy in the public mind, when measures of great moment are so imminent. The proposed impeachment of the President creates but little excitement, nor does the wild, heedless, partisan legislation of Congress appear to disturb even the commercial interests. The Radical press is vociferous for impeachment, not because the President has committed any crime, but for party considerations. The Democratic press is cool and comparatively indifferent, because they apprehend that impeachment will ruin Radicalism. The welfare of the country, the true interests of the government, the salvation of the Union, the stability of our institutions, do not affect seriously the discipline of the two great parties. Neither party means to abandon its organization, but neither of them realizes the terrible consequences that must result from the extreme and revolutionary proceedings of the conspirators.

At a brief Cabinet-meeting this evening, nothing was done. The President was calm and uncommunicative as usual, — perhaps with more than usual reason.

Judge Jere Black called on me this morning and had a strange talk about Alta Vela. Represents Seward as behaving badly and to the discredit of the country in that matter. Told him I knew little of it, that I had been the confidant of neither party. Black inquired in regard to the naval vessels, — whether there was not one or more at St. Thomas which could be ordered to protect American interests, which Seward was abandoning. I did not like the direction which Black seemed disposed to give the affair, — the half threat of making the President accountable and responsible for Seward's errors or mismanagement just at this time. It would be deplorable, Black said, and I would undoubtedly have an interview with the President in the course of the day on the subject. I remarked that nothing would be done, of course, until Seward returned, as it was a subject within his Department, and he had studied it thoroughly, whatever might be his views. This, I saw, did not suit Black.

March 19, *Thursday.* The President is making some

movements, but the scope and object he keeps to himself. Perhaps it is best, if he intends extreme measures with the conspirators. General Hancock is expected this evening. He has not been treated as he should have been by Grant.

There is a rumor that Hancock will be assigned to this military department and that Gordon Granger will take the place of General Emory here in Washington. If such be the fact, I know nothing of it, nor, I apprehend, do other members of the Cabinet. The changes, if made, will be likely to stir up the conspirators, and are made too late to be effectual. These precautions should have been taken long ago, if taken at all. I do not believe that the President, unless personally assailed, intends seriously to resort to military assistance to maintain his position; and military officers who are his friends can now do little for him, if he even wishes it. The President has a policy known only to himself. Honest, patriotic, devoted to his duties, he has failed to attach to himself a party. He would not lend himself to the Radicals to exclude the States, nor to the Democrats to secede from the Union, but has stood as it were alone on the constitutional policy of Lincoln and himself. I hope he is frank and confiding with his lawyers; he has not been sufficiently so with his Cabinet.

Black called on me again this morning and inquired if the President had given me any orders in relation to Alta Vela. I told him no order had been received. He inquired if I had seen the President since his and my interview yesterday. I replied that I had, but nothing had been said to me concerning Alta Vela. Black expressed astonishment, appeared vexed, said the President could not go on in this way, yet he was sorry to leave him just at this time. I remarked that he would not. But he turned short and left. His son was with him. An hour or two after, S[imeon] Johnson, who writes for the *Intelligencer*, but who is a special friend and admirer of Black's, called on me in alarm on account of a disagreement between the President and Black. Says the President has not kept his

word with Black, and the latter has told him so. He says
Black will not go on with the trial if the Alta Vela matter
is not arranged. I discredited this and so told Johnson.
The thing looks to me very suspicious. If Black is interested, as I suppose he is, largely, in the Alta Vela affair
and thinks to take advantage of the President's necessities
to effect an object, he is mistaken in his man. The President is about the last man who would be moved under
compulsion of such circumstances. That Black is deeply
interested and has a large pecuniary stake in the results of
the Alta Vela affair I am compelled to believe, and there
is something that indicates a like deep interest on the part
of Seward. I have supposed it was Weed who was interested and who influenced Seward.

March 20. No matters of great moment before the Cabinet. Seward is still absent, but Fred represented him.
This is always persistently and particularly done. Fred
is the first on the ground at Cabinet-meetings and the last
to leave. He hears, sees, watches, and catches all. Bringing his assistant did much to impair the efficiency and confidence of Mr. Lincoln's Cabinet, and so of Mr. Johnson's.
Stanton told me he would never bring forward an important
matter when an assistant was present.

The President has a severe cold and is, I see, affected
by the impeachment. How could it be otherwise? I had
a little talk with him, which gratified him. He asked me
if Black had been to see me. I told him he had, twice.
"Yes," said the President, "he seems to be absorbed with
Alta Vela. Seward has also been devoting a good deal of
time to it." I remarked I had never investigated it
or been asked to. When the subject was up some time
ago, Seward had politely informed us that he required
the attention of no one but the President and Attorney-
General, and I had therefore made it a point to avoid the
question. Here the subject was dropped by the President,
and I left.

March 23, Monday. There was some effort for dramatic effect and crowded galleries to-day to witness the impeachment trial. But there was no great excitement nor intense or absorbing interest in the subject. It is one of the remarkable and sad events of the times that a subject of such magnitude, an outrage so flagrantly and vindictively partisan, a deliberate conspiracy against the Chief Magistrate of the nation, should be treated with such indifference here and elsewhere. There is idle curiosity with many, some of the busy actors fancying they will be the Burkes and Sheridans at this trial. The Radicals are so demoralized and depraved, are so regardless of their constitutional obligations and of their oaths and their duty, that nothing good can be expected of them. But there are unmistakable indications that the Democratic leaders — a set who think more of party than of country — secretly desire the conviction and deposition of the President. Not that they are inimical to him, not that they believe him guilty of any crime deserving of impeachment, not that they will vote against him, but they look upon the act as perfectly suicidal to the Radicals. They seem not aware that their own unwise conduct is scarcely less suicidal and may save the Radicals from annihilation.

The President's defense is a studied and well-prepared paper, wanting, perhaps, in power and force in some respects. There was, I am told and from what I read, a great contrast between the attorney for the President and the Managers. Black, I perceive, did not appear, and I judge has abandoned the case. If so, there is something more than is apparent in his course. Alta Vela is the pretext, but there is perhaps a deeper cause, a selfish or a party one. Black has been named as a Democratic candidate for President, and this may have influenced him. Blair said to me early that Black was strong and ought to be one of the President's counsel, but that he was in collusion with Stanton, and could not be relied upon to bring out Stanton's villainies, for he fears Stanton.

The Judges of the Supreme Court have caved in, fallen through, failed, in the McCardle case. Only Grier and Field have held out like men, patriots, judges of nerve and honest independence.

These things look ominous, and sadden me. I fear for my country when I see such abasement. Fear of the usurping Radicals in Congress has intimidated some of these Judges, or, like reckless Democratic leaders, they are willing their party should triumph through Radical folly and wickedness.

These are indeed evil times! Seward has on more than one occasion declared that he controlled Judge Nelson. Whether he is, or has been, intriguing in this matter, or taken any part, is a problem.

The *New York World* of to-day has not a word in its editorial columns on impeachment, — a question of momentous importance to the country. It has a variety of articles on light and insignificant subjects. But the *World* has more than once proclaimed that it was in no way identified with the President nor responsible for his election. They approve his principles, but he is not their man nor of their organization. Its editors fear that, if they were to become the vigorous champions of Johnson against his persecutors, the people would compel his nomination. Hence they are putting their cause and professed principles in jeopardy by failing to do right.

But the most deplorable, or one of the most deplorable features in all these proceedings is to witness party assemblages, conventions, and legislatures in distant States passing resolutions approving of the impeachment of the President and urging his conviction, without any fact, or specification, or alleged crime, or any knowledge whatever on the subject. Some of these proceedings are sent to Congress and received by the Senate, which sits in judgment. It is not difficult to see the near downfall of a government which shall long pursue a course such as the Radicals are initiating for mere party purposes.

March 24, Tuesday. The impeachment movement was again before Congress and the Court. The Managers on the part of the House were ready with their replication, and there is reason to suppose it was prepared before the President's reply was received.

On the part of Butler and some others there is an inclination to play the part of buffoons, and display levity in a matter of the gravest importance to the nation. Sumner and certain Senators do not conceal their readiness to proceed at once to judgment and condemnation without proof or testimony. In their unfitness and vindictive partisanship and hate, they would not award the President rights or privileges granted criminals for the court of errors or give him time for preparation. They are really unwilling to allow him to make defense.

These usurpers and conspirators — for they are such, truly and emphatically, having arrogated power without authority, excluded States and people from their constitutional rights of representation — are now deliberately attempting the destruction of another department of the government by the unlawful exercise of these usurped powers. Were all the States represented, as they should be, and would be, if not wickedly and wrongfully excluded by an arbitrary, usurping faction, there could be no conviction, and would have been no impeachment. But the President is arraigned for doing his duty and striving to defend the Constitution in conformity with his oath. The Constitution-breakers are trying the Constitution-defender; the law-breakers are passing condemnation on the law-supporter; the conspirators are sitting in judgment on the man who would not enter into their conspiracy, who was, and is, faithful to his oath, his country, the Union, and the Constitution. What a spectacle! And if successful, what a blow to free government! What a commentary on popular intelligence and public virtue!

Mr. Seward, having returned after a strange absence at this critical period, was present at Cabinet-meeting, as were

3

all the members, including General Thomas, *ad interim* of the War. Among the matters submitted by Seward was a long dispatch in relation to Captain Reynolds and the Lackawanna, addressed to the Hawaiian Minister. The positions taken were, I thought from the reading, very well. There is a spirit of mischief among those Islands, aggravated, I have little doubt, by Reynolds, and they have sent here a thick-headed, garrulous Minister who has no clear and distinct opinions, and who is obviously the tool and instrument of the English and French intrigues at the Sandwich Islands.

After the Cabinet-meeting, had some conversation with the President on the impeachment. Suggested the *ad interim* appointments of Mr. Lincoln when Chase resigned, and also when Fessenden resigned, Congress being in session on both occasions; but an *ad interim* appointment became necessary until a permanent appointment was made, in order that the current business of the Department and Government might go on.

I then remarked that Black did not appear among the managers and asked if he was behaving badly. The President said he had withdrawn from the case, and he thought was behaving very badly indeed. [He said] that he had a letter from B. which he wished me to read. It announced his withdrawal in justice to his clients in the Alta Vela case; regretted if it should injure the President, whose course he justified and approved in these persecutions; denounced Seward's conduct in the Alta Vela matter, whose little finger was more potent with the President than the loins of the law, etc., etc. I said that from the letter and Black's career I judged he had undertaken to compel him (the President) to make himself a party in a private suit, and because he would not, he had lost the service of Mr. Black, and was also so far damaged as the withdrawal of one of his leading counsel at a critical moment might injure him in public estimation. The President said that was true, but if Mr. Black had for a moment deceived himself by supposing that he would deviate a hair's breadth from his duty in order to retain his services or prevent conviction even, he was a sadly deceived man. As regarded the Alta Vela, he had not decided against Black's clients; he had thought there might be merit, or the color of merit, in the claim. The Secretary of State, whose special duty it was to look into the question, had investigated it and was against Black, whether rightfully or wrongfully he could not say. The whole subject, however, had been called for by Congress, and at this time and under present circumstances he could not take any step, nor was he inclined to make himself a party in the matter.

I doubted if Black's withdrawal and non-appearance would operate injuriously to the President before Congress or the country, — certainly not if the facts were known.

We both thought that Black's political aspirations might have influenced him in this step. He is very ambitious, and, as is often the fact, not the best judge in his own case, though undoubtedly a man of great legal ability and of strong mind and power. I think Stanton controls him.

March 25, Wednesday. The *Cincinnati Gazette*, an extreme Radical paper, has a letter from its correspondent, Reid, from Washington, imputing to General Howard the scares and alarms which have terrified Stanton and led Emory to extra vigilance in his commands. He has been filled with suspicions and frights, which he has communicated to Stanton, who is easily alarmed. Howard, at the beginning of the War, was a religious man of small calibre, but has become a pious fraud.

March 26, Thursday. The action of Congress and particularly the Senate in taking from the Supreme Court certain powers to prevent a decision in the McCardle case is shameful, and forebodes an unhappy future to the country. There is no exercise of reason, judgment, intelligence, or patriotism by the Radical majority on any subject whereby their party is liable to be affected. Truth, justice, right, law, and Constitution are broken down and trampled under foot by Senators. I say this in sorrow.

March 27, *Friday.* Very little of importance at the Cabinet. Every member, I think, considers conviction a foregone conclusion in the impeachment case. The Senate seems debauched, debased, demoralized, without independence, sense of right, or moral courage. It is, to all intents and purposes, a revolutionary body, subject to the dictation of Sumner, who is imperious, and Chandler, who is unprincipled, — both are disliked and hated by a considerable portion of the Republicans, who nevertheless bow submissive to the violent extremists.

I cannot come to the conclusion that the Senate, feeble and timid as it is, will convict the President of high crimes and misdemeanors and depose him, yet I have no confidence whatever in the fairness or justice of that body. There is a party necessity to obtain possession of the executive, in order to put a Radical in the office of President next year. Fraud and force will be resorted to, if necessary, to accomplish this end. Hence impeachment is a necessity. Johnson must be removed, for he will countenance no fraud or wrongdoing. And men will surrender their consciences, violate their oaths, be recreant to every honest principle and instinct, and make a victim of an honest man for doing his duty. It is like slaughtering, shooting down, the faithful sentinel because of his fidelity in standing to his post.

We are, in fact, in the midst of a revolution, bloodless as yet, a revolution not of arms but of ideas and government, more effectual and complete than that of the armies of the Rebellion. It is a question whether the Union and the Constitution can be retrieved and restored, though I do not yet permit myself to despair of the Republic. I have not faith in the Senate, yet if the President should be convicted and deposed, the names of those Senators who shall declare him guilty will go down in infamy, and be recorded in history as the betrayers of truth and traitors to justice and freedom.

March 28, Saturday. The Senate yesterday had under consideration the Naval Appropriation Bill. Unfortunately, Grimes, the Chairman of the Committee, and Anthony, the only two men familiar with the subject, were absent. Wilson and Sumner betrayed gross ignorance as well as malignity in the debate. The latter I expected, but there is no excuse for the former. Both of them and the New Hampshire Senators professed to be actuated by disinterested and proper motives and were profuse in their denunciations of party appointments, yet those Senators have done and said more, and importuned me harder, than any and all other Senators to make party removals and appointments. Wilson represented that the masters whom I appointed were all from the Navy, — old salts, who knew nothing of the trade of mason, blacksmith, etc., placed over civilians who were unfit for the duty. Notwithstanding this assertion, no such appointments have ever been made; the statement is false. In order to prevent any abuse of that kind, which I have understood sometimes has existed, I established a regulation that no person should be appointed until after he had passed an examination before a competent board.

In giving expression to his party malignity, Wilson said the administration of the Navy Department for the last two or three years had been wasteful and extravagant beyond any other Department of the Government. This from the Chairman of the Military Committee, where millions upon millions have been profligately wasted, while I have been accused of miserly economy in expenditures. But this is only a specimen of Radical truth and fairness.

Wilson and Sumner are put up to this by General Banks and his creatures, the chief manager being Simon P. Hanscom, an office-broker, who professes to, and I believe does, act with the Democrats, and who whispered in my ear a

few months ago, while coöperating with Banks, that the
scheme was Democratic, but that Banks did not know it.
The Natick cobbler is a dupe as well as an ignoramus and
falsifier on naval matters.

Blundering, plundering Nye,[1] without honesty or integrity, but who has some pretensions to coarse humor, got in
a fog and bellowed about the engineers and their rivalry
with the officers. The poor fellow knew not the difference
between the *civil* engineers of the yard and the *steam*
engineers.

March 30, *Monday*. The opening speech of General
Butler in the impeachment trial is variously spoken of.
As he has talents of a certain kind and has prided himself
in getting to be one of the Managers, where there is rivalry,
and as he wants notoriety, he cares but little of what kind,
and as he has impudence and audacity and the employment is familiar, I presume he made a speech with some
strong and forcible language. As to his facts, his history,
his law, and correct application of principles, there is room
for criticism and doubt. Though a Radical favorite, he is
an unscrupulous and, in every respect, a bad man. The
intelligent Radicals do not seem to be satisfied with his
performance, while the Democrats do not feel that Butler
has made much headway against the President.

March 31, *Tuesday*. Nothing but current business at
the Cabinet. The President requested us to meet him and
his counsel this evening at eight. Just before leaving I was
subpœnaed as a witness to appear to-morrow at twelve
before the court of impeachment. Seward, after getting at
the President's, said that it was Mr. Stanbery's summons
for myself and others of the Cabinet.

Mr. Stanbery, Evarts, and Groesbeck met us at the President's. Talked over certain circumstances and incidents
in the past. Seward said he knew nothing of Stanton's

[1] James W. Nye, Senator from Nevada.

suspension, was absent at the time. Had early seen disagreement between the President and Stanton, and had exerted himself to prevent a rupture. This had been his course, he said, with each and every member of the Cabinet from the time he became connected with the Administration in 1861. He supposed the President had avoided consulting him, because of his earnest efforts to retain Stanton. Had never asked the President before, but did now. The President did not give a direct and explicit answer, but yet it was essentially affirmative.

A difference occurred in the Senate to-day, involving the power of the Chief Justice and his right to decide on questions subject to the decision of the Senate, in which he was sustained by ten majority. The extreme Radicals are greatly incensed, and have mutterings against Chase.

There are growing differences between the Radical and Conservative Senators. The latter lack courage; the former lack sense.

LVIII

Gloomy Political Outlook in Connecticut — English reëlected, however, by an Increased Majority — Curtis opens for the President in the Impeachment Trial — Consultation as to the Introduction of General Sherman's Testimony — The Need of a Lawyer who can meet Butler and Bingham on their own Ground — Sherman's Testimony admitted — Secretary Welles on the Stand — Manager Wilson's Elaborate Speech interjected into the Proceedings — The President nominates General Schofield as Secretary of War — Senator Grimes on the Impeachment Trial — Surmises as to the President's Reasons for nominating Schofield — Vice-Admiral Porter said to be fishing for the Secretaryship of the Navy — The Speeches of Thaddeus Stevens and Thomas Williams — Stanbery, though ill, is confident of Success — Evarts's Speech.

April 1, *Wednesday*. The aspect of the campaign in Connecticut does not suit me. Burr writes that we will carry the State ticket, but probably lose the legislature. This is a let-down from all previous statements, and I am apprehensive there may be a further let-down in the result. The *New York World*, the Democratic organ in that city, has hurt the Democratic Party and cause in Connecticut. When it declared Johnson was not elected by the Democratic votes, that the impeachment was a controversy between the President and those who elected him, etc., etc., it damaged the cause and may have lost us the State. It is easy to perceive that they would not grieve to have the President convicted, because they believe it will ruin the Radicals and dispose of Johnson. While if they made fierce and just war against this Radical outrage and persecution, it would, in their apprehension, enlist public sympathy for the President, who, they fear, may be a candidate.

Sumner attempted to get a rule established that the Chief Justice should not vote or give an opinion, but was voted down by six majority.

April 2, *Thursday*. Impeachment progresses, but I do not see that the impeachers have yet made an impeachable case. Still it is a question whether there is sufficient courage in the Senate to do right, under the threats of the Radical papers, party meetings, etc.

April 3, *Friday*. My brother, Colonel Babcock, and John Cotton Smith write me with confidence in regard to the election, yet each speaks of the closeness of the contest, and the efforts being made by each party. The Radical papers speak with much more confidence than last year, and the editors have, I think, persuaded themselves they will win. This confidence is in itself strength. . . .

April 7, *Tuesday*. Am pressed for time. The Connecticut election has resulted in the reëlection of English by an increased majority, but the Radicals have both branches of the legislature, which will give them a Senator in Congress in place of Dixon. It will be a great political battle, and has cost the Radicals a great amount of money for speakers, to say nothing of corruption expenditure. The result is a great disappointment to the Radical leaders here, who had persuaded themselves they should carry Connecticut. On the whole, the battle has been hardly and skillfully fought on both sides. Michigan has gone, unexpectedly, against negro suffrage by an overwhelming majority.

Mr. Stanbery came upon us while in Cabinet-meeting, and questioned us on many points, and brought his own recollection and ours to bear on matters relating to impeachment.

April 10, *Friday*. Many occurrences pass which I have not time to note down. Am busy till late at night.

Seward gave me, in Cabinet-meeting, papers from Honolulu, forwarded from that Government, exposing a spy on board Reynolds' vessel, the Lackawanna. The spy is his own private secretary.

Mr. Curtis opened the case yesterday for the President and finished to-day. A very finished legal argument, but I doubt if as effective as might have been made by some others. Perhaps it is because I am more earnest and indignant over this infamous and infernal villainy, which is treated so gingerly by the professional friends of the President, and so infamously and audaciously by his opponents.

April 13, *Monday*. Mr. Stanbery sent me word to meet him last evening at the President's at eight. Was punctually there and found the President's counselors in impeachment matters there except Mr. Stanbery. His wife had been taken suddenly ill, and he was thereby detained. Having no occasion to remain, I was about leaving, when the President invited me to wait. The lawyers were examining documents most of the time. Judge Curtis and Evarts read over the letters of General Sherman with great care. Groesbeck examined certain Department documents. Nelson sat quietly by, saying little and doing nothing.

The conversation was chiefly on the point of pressing the further introduction of Sherman's testimony, and especially the letters which they had just examined. These letters contained some expressions which they, Curtis and Evarts, thought would do as much harm as the letters themselves would do good. Both these gentlemen thought the President had a perfectly good case as it stands, without farther testimony. Judge Curtis said he feared every new witness; that the other side were fishing for evidence. Evarts concurred.

I was not altogether satisfied with their reasoning or conclusion, but I am not, of course, as capable of framing an opinion as these legal gentlemen who are in the case. It is not, however, a legal but a political question, and the conspirators are the triers. The Managers have a feeble case or no case at all. There are no grounds for impeachment; there were none from the beginning, yet every Rad-

ical in the town voted for impeachment, and a large portion
of the Senators are ready to-day to vote to convict. They
were as ready to give the same vote when the trial, as it
is called, commenced. They had caucused on the subject
they were to adjudicate and are still caucusing. The Senators are many of them incapable of candid judgment, or
intelligent judgment. Judge C. makes a mistake, I think,
in resting where he is. Were they, the Senators, as good
lawyers as the Judges of the Supreme Court or governed
by any rules, the case might be considered safe. But
Butler gives rules to the Senatorial judges, and tells them
how to vote, and they obey. Unfortunately they are not
legally wise, nor honest, nor candid. They are less safe as
triers than an ordinary intelligent jury. The latter would
give heed to the clear mind of an intelligent and impartial
judge. These Senators are judge and jury in a case of their
own, prejudiced, self-consequential, and incompetent.
Such a tribunal, it appears to me, is to be treated peculiarly, and not upon trust. They must have it made to
appear to them that they are in the wrong. Earnest,
vigorous, unwearied efforts are wanted. Scholarly, refined, legal ability are not alone sufficient with men who
were tested before trial was ordered and who meet in
secret caucus daily.

I made a few suggestions to this effect after the others
left, and stated a few points that appear not to have been
touched upon. One was that Stanton, for whom the conspirators were contending, never had called on the President, met at his council-board, or consulted with him or
others of the Cabinet, since last August, — had been useless as an adviser, head of a Department, or executive
officer.

On the suggestion of Judge Curtis, I called this morning
on Mr. Stanbery at his rooms in the Metropolitan, and
Judge Curtis was there. He, with Mr. S., went over the
same ground as last evening in regard to General Sherman;
but Mr. Stanbery dissented from his associates and thought

with me they should, at all events, try to get the General's testimony. If refused, let the consequences be with them, and the refusal go out to the country.

Mr. Stanbery questioned me on one or two points; thought he should not want me for some two or three days, and said Edgar could go to New York.

I feel the want of a man of different metal from either of these lawyers on the part of the defense,—one who has audacity, can meet Butler and Bingham [1] on their own ground and with their own weapons. Still the courteous and accomplished attorneys may fight the battle, but before this tribunal different metal is also wanted.

April 14, *Tuesday.* There was an interesting time yesterday in the Senate, and that body, after vacillating, finally admitted General Sherman to testify in answer to Senator Reverdy Johnson, as to the object of the President in tendering him the appointment of Secretary *ad interim.* The remark of the President that he, General S., need have no apprehension of or from Stanton, who is cowardly, came out. Mr. Stanbery is sick to-day, and the Court adjourned over until to-morrow in consequence. Seward and Randall spent last evening with him, when, as they report, he appeared to be well, but his brain was active and excited. Browning called at my house this evening and says Stanbery is better.

It appears to me impeachment has lost ground in public estimation during the last few days; still I have no confidence in the partisan Senate. There are men there of ability sufficient to know what is right, to act independently, and who should have enough honesty and moral courage to do right. I trust they will, yet I do not rely on them in this excitement. As for the crowd of little creatures who are out of place in the Senate, and who ought never to have been there, — like Chandler, Thayer, Morgan, Nye,

---

[1] Congressman John A. Bingham of Ohio was one of the Managers of the trial on the part of the House.

Conness, Cameron, and others, who are neither statesmen, enlightened legislators, nor possessed of judicial minds, — no one expects from them justice or any approach to it. But the question is whether the abler minds will be wholly carried away by chief conspirators who hold in their hands the great amount of partisan small trash.

April 16, *Thursday.* Was subpœnaed to-day as a witness before the high court of impeachment, and attended about 1 P.M. I was not, however, placed upon the stand. Cox and Merrick [1] were examined, and cross-examined by Butler. More time was consumed by the Managers in objections to exclude the truth than by witnesses in testifying to facts. At a late hour Butler made a violent, indecent party harangue, which disgraced the Senators who failed to call him to order and listened to his tirade with satisfaction.

April 17, *Friday.* At the court of impeachment most the day and for two or three hours on the stand. Nearly every question put was objected to and discussed. The Chief Justice presided with fairness, and the Senators, in most cases by a majority, voted against the Managers. About twenty are violent partisans, as much interested in the prosecution as the Managers, and some of them taking an active part with them. Cameron, Conness, Howard, and others manifest this. There is another set of stupid, stolid creatures, like Morgan, Chandler, etc., — the latter violent, the former time-serving, — who vote uniformly and always to exclude all testimony for the President, and are, and have been, ready from the first to vote to convict. In point of morality, I put these fellows on a par with the thief and the murderer. The fear of punishment and

---

[1] Walter S. Cox, a lawyer of Georgetown, District of Columbia, who had been consulted by the President in connection with General Lorenzo Thomas's appointment, and Richard T. Merrick, a Washington lawyer, who had been employed by General Thomas.

the opinion and judgment of others will restrain them from committing those crimes, not any sense of moral justice or obligation. Morgan has become debased, and, after first taking a manly stand, has become dragooned by leaders, fears his associates, whom he now follows like a whipped spaniel. Chandler is more coarse and free-spoken than Morgan, but quite as contemptible. . . .

As my testimony will appear in the proceedings, I shall not attempt to here recapitulate it. Should have been glad to have been permitted to state my knowledge on the points, without being restricted to narrow questions and answers.

I perceived that the Radical leaders, as well as Managers, were becoming disturbed and discontented by the course things were taking, and, under apprehension that a pending question might go against them, there was a concerted movement to adjourn. A caucus and discipline were necessary. The Managers directed it. I saw it whispered and passed from one to another. Judges! O what judges!!

April 18, *Saturday.* The court of impeachment opened this morning with an elaborate speech from Manager Wilson,[1] crowded in on an interlocutory question, which consumed over an hour and was read from a carefully prepared manuscript. This, I soon perceived, was the speech which he had been weeks preparing and hoped to deliver at the close of the trial, but, being denied the opportunity by the secret caucus arrangement and decree last evening, it was here injected into the Senate, or court, proceedings. My suspicions were at once aroused that there had been caucusing, or both caucusing and drilling, overnight, to exclude, after listening to all hearsay evidence and scandal against him, the President's testimony refuting the lies and manufactured evidence. The suspicion was fully confirmed by the day's action.

Nothing from any member of the Cabinet was permit-

[1] Representative James F. Wilson of Ohio.

ted, from a conviction evidently that it would exculpate and exonerate the President. Sumner, therefore, who has to this time voted to admit all testimony, because he was predetermined to convict, absented himself now when votes intended to cut off evidence were to be taken. Morton was not present at all. Sherman, Frelinghuysen, and the equivocal men had been last night whipped in.

I was put forward by the counsel for the President to receive and answer the test questions, or to be opposed and rejected. This relieved Seward and yet annoyed him. It did not displease him that the testimony of Cabinet officers was prevented. He had, he said, been on friendly terms with Stanton, and for that reason President Johnson had not consulted him so freely as others. He claims he was the confidant of President Lincoln, and advised with him in certain removals. For these reasons, he declares, he did not wish to be placed on the stand, though Judge Curtis and Evarts apparently wished it. When the Cabinet was in consultation with the counsel a few mornings since, I mentioned the particulars under which the President announced the removal of Stanton and appointment of Thomas. Seward undertook to say he was informed before we met, but T. went to the War Department just as we met, and returned while we were in session. It was not a judicious appointment, whether advised by him or not.

April 20, *Monday.* I did not attend the Senate. The session of the court of impeachment was brief. The factious Radical majority, regardless of law, justice, and right, having decided on Saturday to exclude all testimony for the President, there was little to be said or done. I remarked to the President to-day that I thought it would have been well to place Seward on the stand, that he might at least testify in regard to the preparation, by him and Stanton, of the veto message on the Tenure-of-Office Bill, and that he counseled the selection of General Lorenzo Thomas to take the War Department, if such was the fact.

He said he regretted that evidence had not been introduced respecting that message and that there were several things which he wished were different. Strange that he should permit himself to be misled and deluded!

April 21, Tuesday. Little of interest in Cabinet. There is no disposition to press forward matters just at this time. Congress neglects and abandons all public business in mere party tricks and intrigues. No case has been made against the President; therefore it would seem the greater necessity for the conspirators to disregard decency and resort to false and infamous means and statements.

It is easy to perceive that the constitutional plan of impeachment will be a failure in revolutionary times or in periods of high factious and party excitement like these. Perhaps any plan would be, when a corrupt faction, led and managed by such men as Stevens and Butler, etc., gets in power and conspires to overthrow the Constitution. It is melancholy and ridiculous to see such men as Morgan, Chandler, and other small lights sit in their seats and overrule the Chief Justice on law points and questions essential to develop truth.

Seward says Morgan got off soundings when he left him and Weed; that he has been floating about ever since without chart or compass, in a very uncomfortable condition. He (Seward) represents that he made Morgan. No doubt Weed contributed much to his election, and Morgan has broken away from his creators when they were right.

April 22, Wednesday. When I was coming up H Street this evening, between 4 and 5, I came upon Conkling and Benjamin F. Butler, who were in close conversation on the corner of 15th Street. It was an ominous and discreditable conjunction, — the principal Manager, an unscrupulous, corrupt, and villainous character, holding concourse with one of the Senatorial triers, a conceited coxcomb of some talents and individual party aspirations. They both were, as Jack Downing says, stumped, and showed in their countenances what they were talking about and their wish that I had been on some other street, — or somewhere else.

I am, among other matters, getting up an answer to a resolution of inquiry presented by Starkweather [1] in relation to the alleged detention of the apprentice-ship Sabine at New London. Such little things are often annoying and require considerable labor to answer. To recall trivial and almost forgotten incidents and to analyze the subject correctly makes a demand on one's time, and taxes his recollections. I think Mr. Starkweather, who is a petty partisan, may wish he had not offered this resolution. He has got on a false scent and discovered a mare's nest. Things are blended in his mind, and have been mixed up and become confused and foggy in the party excitement, local interest, orders to the Sabine, detailing her commander, and the elections.

April 23, *Thursday.* Made a selection of seven or eight youths for midshipmen with the President, and afterwards had a long talk on public affairs. Suggested to him the propriety of an address from some one or more of his counsel or from some other, setting forth the facts he and they were prepared to present, which the Chief Justice has decided were relevant and competent, but which the Senate refused to hear or receive.

April 24, *Friday.* No Department business in Cabinet. General conversation on current topics. Seward professes to have knowledge that the President will not be convicted. I place little dependence upon it, for his judgment is good for nothing in such matters. Nevertheless, it is his nature to pry and set machinery to work to get at the designs and purposes of men and tribunals.

After the others, except McCulloch, had left, we had twenty minutes with the President. He showed us an

[1] Henry H. Starkweather, Member of Congress from Connecticut.

3

order from Grant to Emory, issued by request of Stanton, for a guard at the War Department to preserve documents, etc., issued on the 22d of February. These conspirators will have their works uncovered sooner or later. The President yesterday, and again to-day, said this man Emory ought to be removed from the command of this district. I said that he ought some time since to have left, but it might not be judicious at this moment. McCulloch to-day took the same view.

April 25, Saturday. The argument before the court to-day by Mr. Groesbeck is highly spoken of by all. The President yesterday sent in the nomination of General Schofield for Secretary of War in place of Stanton. I knew nothing of it until I saw it in the papers, nor do I think more than one, and perhaps none, of his Cabinet knew of it. This movement is a concession, and I apprehend has been prompted from a friendly quarter, but I am not sanguine that it will be successful.

When Fox was here ten days or a fortnight since, he informed me of a conversation with Grimes, who was to him outspoken in his disgust at the impeachment. There are several Senators who revolt at the intrigue, but, from party faction at home, Grimes said that there was, however, much embarrassment on the part of conservative men what to do. Their political friends expected they would vote to convict, regardless of the merits or demerits of the question, but if any should not, and were to give an honest, judicial vote to acquit, they might be overwhelmed by the President's subsequent acts. Could they be assured that the President would be guilty of no indiscretion, that he would commit no rash act, would consult with and listen to the advice of his Cabinet or a portion of it, he thought there would be little doubt he would be acquitted.

Whilst I am convinced the President would have saved himself much trouble, and the country also, had he more freely consulted with reliable friends, — communicated and received opinions, — I nevertheless think his impetuosity or rashness is much exaggerated. He has good judgment and honest intentions, although subjected to great misrepresentation. His indiscretions and errors I do not conceal, but they are venial.

This movement for Schofield, or the movement which has resulted in his nomination, has its origin, I conclude, in some such prompting as that suggested to me through Fox. Seward, or Randall, probably the former, were more ready than myself to make an effort, and the President has yielded. His doing so may bring a friendly return, and it may not. It is going far on his part, for it is not a week since he spoke to me of the Radicalism of Schofield, which, if not as offensive as that of Sickles or Sheridan, was bad enough.

April 27, Monday. As I was about getting on my horse yesterday P.M. for my daily evening ride, Senator Doolittle called, and, after a brief conversation, proposed we should go to the President. We found him alone and had about an hour with him. Had either of us been alone, he would doubtless have been more communicative. Certainly he would have been with me. On the subject of General Schofield's nomination he talked pretty freely without communicating particulars or motives beyond a desire to relieve himself of Stanton. Schofield would not have been his choice if he could have made a free selection, but Schofield, besides being a military man, occupied that peculiar position which would be likely to .secure a confirmation. I cannot suppose, however, nor can he. that the Senate will act whilst impeachment is pending.

I inquired if he was satisfied Schofield would stand and not decline the nomination. The President said he apprehended no difficulty in that respect, — that he felt assured there was, on Schofield's part, no partiality for Stanton. General Grant wishes Stanton out of the way, and will so differ from his associates as to acquiesce in, if he is not gratified with, Schofield, although the latter is not specially devoted to Grant.

For my own part, I have little confidence in any of the military governors. This movement is one of that singular class that has sometimes astonished me, as exhibiting a want of administrative ability when I should expect entirely different qualities. It is Sewardism in all its aspects, whether Seward is in it or not.

Doolittle and myself visited Governor Randall after leaving the President. If R. has had any knowledge of Schofield's nomination he did not disclose it. I judge he is as ignorant as myself, but his conclusions are like mine. He is confident the President will be acquitted, and says the Radicals are becoming afraid of that result. I have not that confidence, for a majority of the Senate is composed of very indifferent men, who will, under caucus dictation, vote as partisans, not as judges. He thinks the Senate will not come to judgment until after the Chicago Convention, but this, I take it, is mere conjecture. There may be some talk among party men to that effect, but no such conclusion. Washington is great for rumors at all times, and the credulous and interested listen.

Vice-Admiral Porter has been here several days, the guest of General Grant. Rumor says he is fishing for the place of Secretary of the Navy. This is likely to be the case, for he is ambitious, restless, and intriguing. He is a very unfit man for Secretary, and would soon turn things upside down and destroy all unity and disregard systematic and practical economy.

April 28, *Tuesday*. The speech of Thad Stevens yesterday was characteristically abusive, but displayed less ability than I expected. I do not think he has injured the President so much as he desired, though he has spent great labor and time on his speech, which has been three times rewritten and revised. His nephew, who boards at Willard's with Faxon, told the latter that he was assisting his

uncle in reading his third printed proof of what he intended
to say.

Thomas Williams,[1] who followed, is prolix, a poor
reader, and will not make a favorable impression. . . .
He was, I have understood, a *quasi* partner of Stanton in
Pittsburg, and has been much devoted to and much used
by him in Congress.

Only necessary current business done in the Cabinet.
Seward, Randall, and Browning expressed great confidence
of the acquittal of the President, but gave no particulars.
McCulloch is more hopeful than I have seen him since the
impeachment movement commenced. I called last evening
on Mr. Stanbery. He is very feeble. Says he has completed his argument, but I advised him not to undertake
to deliver it, and I think he will not. He expresses great
confidence of acquittal, and so, he says, does Evarts.
There could be no doubt of it, were the triers uncommitted,
— honest, candid, and capable men. All depends on the
fact whether there are a sufficient number of such independent Senators.

Poor E. B. Washburne cannot sufficiently vent his spite
and venom against the Navy Department. My reply to
Starkweather's resolution disappointed him. He found
a mare's nest and set Starkweather cackling, but the eggs
were addled. To-day he introduced a resolution of inquiry
into the corrupt sale of ironclads. He will find his head in
a bag, or against a stone wall in that matter. I presume
Washburne has heard of my contempt for him and his
mock economy, — his proverbial meanness and the way
in which he lives off Grant, to whom, and for whom, he
toadies. He partakes of Grant's dinners, swallows his whiskey, smokes his cigars, rides his horses, travels as a dead-
head, and eats and drinks every day of his life at the public expense. I have seen and sneered at his penuriousness
and meanness, his little regard for truth, and his many
infirmities. Some Radical go-between has informed him,

[1] Of Pennsylvania.

I have no doubt, of my expressed and real contempt and disgust of him, and of his shallow pretensions, and he means to show proper resentment by lying statements in resolutions concerning Navy management. If the reply shows its falsity, his misstatements have nevertheless gone out ahead. The lie will travel some distance, and get in some corner where it will not be exposed.

April 30. There is but little doing by Congress. Impeachment is the question. Mr. Evarts' speech is interesting and able, and men and women of all parties are greatly interested in it. There is an impression that the Radical cause is growing weaker, and indication that the Radical leaders have apprehensions. The arguments of the President's lawyers have alarmed them, have shown them they have no case, that though they have deceived themselves into the belief that they can deceive the country, there are truths which cannot be covered up and will endanger their future. The conspiracy — for it is nothing else — is an excess of party zeal and hate, without any foundation whatever. It will overwhelm them with infamy. In their present state of party discipline, party power, and party terror, votes may not be changed, but conviction has struck some of them. Grimes says there will be no conviction, and he is one of the best judges and most sensible men in the Senate. But Fox, who is here for a few days, says that in circulating around among Senators and others of all parties, he finds the prevailing opinion seems to be that the President will be condemned.

LIX

A Visit to Mount Vernon — The President's Disappointment at Black's
Desertion — The Outcome of the Impeachment hanging in the Balance
— The Doubtful Senators — The Carpet-Bag Constitutions of Arkansas
and South Carolina transmitted to Congress — Bingham's Closing
Speech for the Prosecution — Congressional Inquiry into the Sale of the
Ironclads Oneota and Catawba — The Case of the Hannah Grant —
An Exciting Afternoon and Evening in the Senate — Speeches of Sher-
man, Grimes, Trumbull, and Fessenden — Hopeful Outlook — The
Vote on Impeachment postponed — Illness of Senator Grimes — Public
Opinion manufactured in Washington by the Radicals — The Vote on
the Eleventh Article fails to convict the President — A Call on Senator
Grimes — Attack on Ross of Kansas for his Vote in favor of the Pre-
sident — The Candidates before the Republican Convention at Chicago
— Grant and the Radicals — Rumors of Cabinet Changes — Japanese
Affairs — Grant and Colfax nominated at Chicago — The Acquittal of
the President — The News comes to the Cabinet in Session — Charges
of Corruption — Stanton leaves the War Department — His Character
and Abilities and his Administration of the Department — Schofield's
Appointment as Secretary of War sticks in the Senate — A Seminole
Chief on the Written Constitution.

May 1, *Friday.* I went with my family, a few visitors,
and a small party of friends to Mount Vernon. It is the first
time I have ever landed there, though I have often passed
the place, and have always intended to perform a pilgrimage to the tomb of the Great American Patriot.

We had a pleasant company, and the day was pleasant.
I enjoyed the excursion as an excursion, but it was not the
way and manner that would have suited me to discharge
a duty. Alone, or with my wife and children, or perhaps
three or four chosen friends, not more, I should have felt
a melancholy pleasure in such a pilgrimage.

May 2, *Saturday.* A short interview with the President.
Completed selections to Naval Academy, — always an unpleasant and unwelcome duty. After this was disposed of,

had a little talk on general subjects. He says the Alta Vela letters of Black were not obtained from him or any one at the White House. They must have been furnished by Black himself, perhaps through his son or partner. The conduct of Black has surprised and affected him more than that of almost any other person. It was unexpected, ungenerous, and a betrayal or desertion at a critical period, and when the President was relying more on Black than any one else as a counselor, confidant, and friend.

The President is by no means desponding. I think his faith is in an honest and sincere consciousness that he has been, to the best of his ability, faithful, that he has done his duty, and that a good Providence will not permit him to be sacrificed under these circumstances.

While I am reluctant to believe in the total depravity of the Senate, I place but little dependence on the honesty and truthfulness of a large portion of the Senators. A majority of them are small lights, mentally weak, and wholly unfit to be Senators. They are neither intelligent legislators, wise statesmen, capable judges, nor good patriots. Some are vulgar demagogues . . . some are men of wealth who have purchased their positions . . . men of narrow intellect, limited comprehension, and low partisan prejudice. . . .

With the party appeals and party demands from the Radical press and Radical leaders throughout the country, the narrow views and inexcusable ignorance of Radicals generally in regard to our government, its structure and scope, their readiness to sacrifice the government and country for mere party ends, I have but slight expectation of an acquittal.

May 4, *Monday.* On Friday and Saturday there was a disgraceful but characteristic exhibition of Radical notables in the House, — Butler and Logan on Friday, and Donnelly of Wisconsin and Washburne of Illinois on Saturday.

Butler was exposed and flogged by Brooks severely. Washburne was more coarsely and frankly punished by Donnelly, a brother Radical. Had he been less loose and vulgar, his speech would have been more effective. Washburne, though the oldest member, is more universally detested for his supercilious pretensions, manners, insolence, disregard of truth, and malignity than any man in the House, and all enjoyed the infliction he received. Bingham commenced the closing argument in the impeachment case to-day. It does not appear to have excited much admiration, although there is reported to have been a large attendance.

May 5, Tuesday. In general conversation before business commenced at the Cabinet, Seward taunted Browning for being shaky on the question of impeachment. Browning confessed his doubts, said he had expressed them to confidential friends and thought it best to do so. Seward did not agree with him as to his policy, but said he had no doubts as to an acquittal, and wished to wager a basket of champagne, which B. declined, and S. then offered two to one. McCulloch, who came in just at the close of the banter but did not hear it, was as decided in his opinion of an acquittal as Seward, and offered to bet a bottle of wine with B. I could, however, get no facts to justify the confidence of the State and Treasury, farther than that they have talked pretty freely with Members.

It seems to be generally conceded that Fessenden will oppose impeachment. McCulloch has hopes that Morton will do the same. I have little expectation in that quarter, though the hypocrite has sagacity enough to see that a mistake is made.

Seward quotes Banks for authority, who says Fessenden and Morrill of Maine have each written arguments, have had one interview and are to have another with their written documents. Much of this Banks gets from the Maine Members who have tried to influence F. but without success. There may be something to base this upon, but I do not give it the credence which Seward does. Until the argument is closed and the whole case committed, F. would not be likely to declare his opinion. I have supposed he would vote against conviction, although a decided Radical, for he has intelligence and a character which he wishes to preserve. I have had the same opinion of Trumbull for the same reasons. Both are crotchety and uncertain, and I therefore do not consider it sure by any means that they will go for acquittal. Other Senators, like Frelinghuysen, the Morrills, and others, should vote for acquittal, but it is most likely, from all I hear and see, that they will abase themselves.

I therefore am less sanguine than either Seward or McCulloch. The last has, until recently, believed that conviction was probable. What facts have changed him I fail to learn. Seward is not to be relied on for accuracy in such matters; he catches at shadows. Grimes is chairman of the Naval Committee and strong in his political views and prejudices, but he has a legal and discriminating mind, and sincere respect for the President's honesty, though very little confidence in his tact and judgment. He will not commit so unjust an act as to vote to impeach, and Fessenden usually goes with him. Neither of them has much love for Sumner or regard for Thad Stevens, which will strengthen them to act right when others fail. I should have no doubt of Trumbull if he had not done himself and his principles injustice on certain test questions. The Radical Senators continue to hold their secret meetings at Pomeroy's to discipline and strengthen each other to do an illegal and wicked act, while sitting as judges in the high court.

Seward says Morgan will go for acquittal, provided it is clearly ascertained in advance that there can be no conviction. In this I think S. is more correct than in many of his oracular assertions. The President was not present during the greater part of this conversation, which, however, was continued after he came in, canvassing many of the Senators. Some of them, through friends, had made known their doubts and perplexities; the friends of some were confident that this or that Senator was personally kindly and senatorially rightly disposed, and would oppose the outrage, *if* certain appointments were made. The President said he was tired of these things and wished they were over.

Some conversation took place between McCulloch, Browning, and myself in regard to sending in immediately the new carpet-bag constitutions of Arkansas and South Carolina. They urged that it should be done immediately. I asked what of the actual, existing constitutions of those States, which Congress assumed to annul. Both took alarm, hoped the President would not oppose Congress, oppose the Reconstruction law, etc. I expressed the hope that he would do his duty faithfully.

The President had come in from the library during the discussion and seated himself at the desk, my back being towards him. He sent in a brief message which he had prepared for Congress, merely informing that body he transmitted such papers as he had received. This avoided difficulty, for it expressed no opinion. Under the circumstances this, perhaps, is the best he can do, and is not liable to attack.

May 6, *Wednesday.* General Rousseau called on me. His visit to Alaska has not impaired his health, and his quick journey from Oregon has given him a rough and hardy appearance. He has been here three or four days and mingled freely with Congressmen and others, and expresses the fullest confidence in the acquittal of the President. Still I get no facts; no names are given.

May 7, *Thursday.* Bingham has closed the final argument of the Managers, and at its close there was a scene in the galleries got up especially for the occasion and a part of this Radical drama. I have not read all of B.'s speech, but, from the examination given it, I do not think it great, and his friends seem disappointed. The subject is postponed until Monday, and the Court has agreed to come to a vote on Tuesday. If the Senators regard their oaths, and act as judicial officers and statesmen, there will be an acquittal; if partisan action controls all the Radical Senators, or most of them, conviction is likely. The movement has been a partisan one from its inception.

Judge Harris, late New York Senator, called on me, and, discussing the great topic, tells me he had a long conversation with a prominent Radical Senator, a religious, conscientious man, who said to him there was nothing against the President which could be called a crime or misdemeanor, but the President was a troublesome man, was an impediment, and he thought the majority would be justified in availing themselves of a technical advantage in getting rid of him. Although Judge Harris called no names, I inferred from his remarks that Frelinghuysen was the Senator who made these discreditable remarks.

May 8, *Friday.* The Retrenchment Committee, of which Senator Edmunds is chairman, held a session at the Department this morning to inquire into the sale of the ironclads Oneota and Catawba, under a resolution of E. B. Washburne, directing inquiry into the "alleged fraudulent sale." I had directed copies of all the papers to be prepared so that there need be no delay. The Committee chose to examine me orally, also Faxon and Lenthall. Not expecting to be called, I had not given the subject any close attention, but was willing the Committee should know every item of the transaction, satisfied there had been no fraud, but that Congress by its injudicious management had hurt this sale and probably prevented others. There was supercilious arrogance and great ignorance displayed by some of the gentlemen of the Committee, as well as the general disposition of this Congress to usurp executive and, indeed, all power. They wished me to stop the sale, to prevent the boats from sailing, etc. Simpletons! I wish we could sell all.

At the Cabinet-meeting Seward read a dispatch requiring the Venezuelan Government to make indemnity for the Hannah Grant, a whaling-schooner, whose voyage had been broken and some of her crew detained. I said that I had doubts whether the subject should be pursued; that the captain and men of the H. G. were perhaps as culpable as the Venezuelan coast-guard. Our men could not speak Spanish nor the guard English, and before they could come to an understanding the H. G. sailed off and left her men. Seward was taken aback; said the Venezuelans would be let off lightly, but some notice must be taken of the difficulty.

Great confidence was expressed by all the Cabinet that the President would be acquitted; and such also seemed his impression, but I could get no fact, — perhaps ought to expect none. It was said Fessenden was in great distress, — had offered to resign, but the Maine delegation would not listen to it. The vote of Henderson of Missouri is relied upon through the influence of Miss Foote,[1] to whom he expects to be married. Sprague is counted upon through Mrs. S. and her father, etc. These are frail staffs to lean upon, yet they are taken in the absence of better. There may be other circumstances, or facts, which are confidential, but they are not communicated, if there are such.

Colonel Halpine (Miles O'Reilley) and Mr. Roosevelt called on me. They are feeling for information, while professing to communicate. I am satisfied they know nothing certain. Halpine and R. also speak most contemptuously of Morgan, who seems to have sunk in every man's estimation.

May 9, Saturday. There is a good deal of deep feeling; yet no boisterous excitement. The impeachers are less con-

[1] Daughter of Judge Elisha Foote, Commissioner of Patents.

fident than they were, yet express full belief in conviction. Their reliance is on the force, discipline, and necessities of party, not on crime or misdemeanor on the part of the President. How far the Radical Senators who have pretensions to statesmanship will debase themselves to party dictation is the only question. If they are really legislators, judges, and statesmen, men of independence and moral courage, the President will be acquitted; not otherwise. More than one half of the Senators are demagogues and blockheads, party tools, who regard not their oaths nor the welfare of the country.

Numbers influence party men, so that inferior intellects often control superior minds. Fessenden and Morton and Trumbull are fearful of consequences if they boldly and considerately do their duty. I have no faith whatever in Morton, though McCulloch has hopes of him, but McCulloch is deceived. His speech at the beginning of the session exhibited a mind whose moral stamina was gone. . . .

The President tells me this afternoon that he has no doubt that Fessenden will vote for acquittal. I did not ask his newest evidence. Riding out this evening, I met McCulloch, who assures me, emphatically, of an acquittal. Says Grimes, Fessenden, Trumbull, and Van Winkle will vote to acquit, and others also. I conclude he has sources of information which are reliable. I get no facts. Of Grimes', Fessenden's, and Trumbull's honest opinions I have no doubt, but there is a terrible pressure upon them. Of Van Winkle I know nothing.

May 11, Monday. Dixon came in yesterday. Has heard the President intends to resign, if it shall be clearly ascertained that he will be convicted. Told him I gave the rumor no credit, and he said he would not, but that the President once made a remark which the rumor had brought strongly to his mind. In an interview with the President on Saturday, he told D. he wished to know with certainty

WILLIAM PITT FESSENDEN

the result on Monday. "Why on Monday," says D. to me, "unless he has an object in view?"

Doolittle called this morning, feeling, as all do, interested, not to say excited, but craving information. I had none to give. Neither he nor Dixon has confidence. They have no facts. Both, like me, believe that several of the leading minds on the Radical side are against conviction, but whether they have the courage and moral firmness to do their duty is a question. Dixon tells me of two conversations he had with Fessenden, who gave him no assurance, but yet talked in a way that left but little doubt on his mind, — said he did not wish to do an act which would disturb him the rest of his life, wanted always to wake in the morning with a clear conscience.

The afternoon and evening have been exciting. The Senatorial Court sat to-day with closed doors, the members expressing and discussing their views on the articles of impeachment. As they made their speeches, respectively, their opinions got outside the doors. Sherman declared himself opposed to the first article, but would vote for the second. In other words the President had the right to remove Stanton, but no right to order another to discharge the duties. Poor Sherman! He thinks the people fools; they know him better than he does them. Grimes boldly denounced all the articles, and the whole proceeding. Of course he received the indignant censure of all Radicals; but Trumbull and Fessenden, who followed later, came in for even more violent denunciation, and more wrathful abuse.

This evening the Radicals are greatly crestfallen, and have hardly a hope, while their opponents can scarcely restrain their elated feelings over the probable defeat of an infamous and dastardly conspiracy. A marvelous change has come over both parties.

McCulloch came in overjoyed, and wished me to go with him to the President's. We found he had all the news, but was calm, though gratified. He showed us the notes he had from time to time received through the P.M. and evening.

Groesbeck soon came in; said the work was accomplished, but there must be no exulting outbreak. Both he and Mc-Culloch declare there is no question of acquittal. Randall soon joined us, and is even more sanguine. Says the vote will stand at least 22 to 32, likely better than that. I would rather see the votes, though I have no cause to question his accuracy, except he is not an accurate man.

The Senate is in session this evening; and will be, probably, most of the night. A motion was made to reconsider the vote ordering the vote to be taken to-morrow, but failed. Still I am apprehensive. The Radicals have a majority and are alarmed, for there are some who refuse to be disciplined into doing a wrong act.

May 12, *Tuesday.* The Radicals, fearful of the result of the vote which they had ordered should this day be taken on impeachment, have postponed the question until next Saturday. The excuse for this is the illness of Howard,[1] one of their members, who is said to be delirious, — the brain fever, — some say delirium tremens. I suppose he is really ill, though many think not. Had it been one of the Senators friendly to the President, there would have been no four days' postponement, — nor even with Howard's sickness, had they [not] been limited to a two-thirds vote. When Attorney-General Stanbery was taken ill, the leading Radicals would not consent to delay a day, although he was the principal counsel of the President.

The postponement did not greatly surprise me. It required only a majority vote, and very likely a still further postponement will take place, if the Senatorial conspirators have not sufficient force to convict. There is little honor, justice, or truth with the impeaching judges. If by any trick or subterfuge they can succeed, the Radicals will resort to it, however unprincipled. The President was,

---

[1] Jacob M. Howard of Michigan.

I think, more disturbed by the postponement than I have ever seen him, but he soon rallied.

Great consternation prevails among the Radical impeachers, who have never permitted themselves to doubt for a moment the conviction of the President, whether guilty or not. It was a foregone conclusion, a party decree; any one who disobeyed was to be denounced. Such men as the late Assistant Secretary of the Treasury, Chandler, are almost frantic. I have long assured McCulloch that Chandler was playing a double game and deceiving him; but McC. was incredulous, and retained him long in office. . . .

Doctor Horwitz tells me Chandler called on him some days since, and said he had made calls on all the members of the Cabinet, which he designed as farewell visits, for he would feel unpleasant to call on them after the President's conviction. I recollect that he called with his wife some ten days since, and other members of the Cabinet also inform me that they remember a similar visitation, but they had no thought of the purpose of his visit. It is an evidence of the confidence of Radicalism.

May 13, *Wednesday*. There is great rage among the conspirators and leading Radicals. The *Tribune, Chronicle*, and other organs, howl over their defeat, and are very abusive of four Senators whom they denounce as recreants, apostates, Judases, etc., etc. Their greatest violence is against Grimes, a man of strong feelings and acute sensibilities, who was this afternoon struck with paralysis. I trust it may not prove fatal or even serious, but he has for some weeks undergone great mental excitement in consequence of the estrangement of old associates, and malignant assaults from his political friends, for a firm, honest, and conscientious discharge of his duty. This abuse has been trying to his system. While he has a right appreciation of these attacks, he is nevertheless sensitive, and feels it to be a wicked and ungrateful return for many years of faithful party and public service.

3

The flippant remarks of a class of superficial writers, who have little knowledge of the government or the proper working of our political system, is disgraceful, and it is lamentable that so many should be influenced and misled by them. Veteran legislators and statesmen who have grown old in the public service, and who have given thought and mind, and time and labor, to great questions are libeled and defamed by the slanders.

May 14, Thursday. One of the tricks of the whippers-in to influence the doubtful Senators is to send abroad for letters and telegrams favoring and craving impeachment in order to sustain the party; to get Members of the House to call on the Senators and urge them to vote to convict, right or wrong, and in every possible way, by extra means, to extort a decision adverse to the President. This monstrous prostitution of the conspirators is acquiesced in by the Radicals, who seem to think it proper, so utterly are they demoralized; and men making pretensions to character participate in the abuse. Butler, Stevens, and men like them, taking advantage of prejudices and as yet unforgiving hate growing out of the War, do not attempt to cover up intended villainy. One of the schemes now on foot is to admit the bogus Senators, elected under the bogus constitutions which the carpet-baggers, aided by negroes under military dictation, have imposed on the Southern States. Strengthened in numbers by these interlopers, they hope to carry conviction. How long can a government stand which is in the hands of such profligate and unprincipled wretches?

Grimes is no better. I fear the worst. Still I hope he may recover and that soon. But he is of a family subject, I am told, to sudden death, and has himself been apprehensive that such might be his fate. It was this, I am informed, which led him to decline a reëlection. Howard is reported better. Conflicting rumors and opinions prevail in regard to the final result of impeachment. I apprehend but little is known, and nothing with certainty. The doubtful men do not avow themselves, which, I think, is favorable to the President, and the impeachers display distrust and weakness. Still their efforts are unceasing and almost superhuman. But some of the more considerate journals, such as the *New York Evening Post, Chicago Tribune,* etc., rebuke the violent. The thinking and reflecting portion of the country, even Republicans, show symptoms of revolt against the conspiracy.

May 15, *Friday.* Only pressing and necessary public business is being done in these days by the Government. Suggestions or recommendations by the Departments are received with distrust by the Radical Congress, and useful and necessary measures are opposed and often rejected without consideration, so that it is better to be quiescent than active. The Radical leaders are revolutionary, and many of their associates of better mind and temper have become tainted, corrupted, and distempered. They have called the President so many vile names, applied to him such vile epithets, that they persuade themselves he must be in fault, yet they designate nothing, except that he does not lend himself and the Government to their party schemes and usurpations. They denounce him as a traitor because he adheres to the Constitution, holds firmly to his own belief, and refuses to surrender his own judgment to their dictation.

The Managers of the impeachment on the part of the House have summoned witnesses before them to testify in regard to the views and opinions of the Senators and the President. This wholly illegal and unauthorized inquisition, even by this presuming and usurping House, shows the spirit which prevails, and how personal rights are disregarded. In a very short time these men, if not checked, would break up the foundations of the government and of the whole social system. Strange that such men should get the ascendancy over their associates, but it is by party organization and discipline, through secret caucuses, and the tyranny imposed by the majority rule, sharpened by the angry remnants of the Rebellion which still linger and compel the timid, passive, and obedient to violate law, Constitution, equity, justice, morality, right, and any and all the fundamental principles of government. Abject subserviency!

A few matters of current interest were disposed of in Cabinet. Some conversation on the topic which comes up in every meeting of two or more, viz., impeachment. The same general confidence was expressed by Seward, McCulloch, and Randall of acquittal whenever a vote shall be taken, but there is doubt whether another postponement will not take place to-morrow. It is a question whether the sick men will be then in attendance. Doctor H., his physician, tells me that Grimes will ride up, though at some risk, if the vote is to be taken.

I do not yet get from my associates, who express themselves so confidently, any positive assurance of seven Senators from the Republicans. We can count up pretty surely five, perhaps six, but where and who is the seventh or eighth? Is Anthony, or Sprague, certain for acquittal? Pretty certain, at least on most of the articles. How stands Frelinghuysen? How Van Winkle, and Willey? How is Ross, and how are Corbett and Cole? Not one is vouched for when pinned down, though there seems a general impression that Van Winkle and Fowler may be depended upon.[1]

To me the result looks exceedingly doubtful, although I have an inward faith that Providence will not permit so great a wrong or outrage as conviction to be committed. There is some good sense, some self-respect, some integrity

[1] In the final vote Henry B. Anthony and William Sprague of Rhode Island, Frederick T. Frelinghuysen of New Jersey, Waitman T. Willey of West Virginia, Henry W. Corbett of Oregon, and Cornelius Cole of California went for conviction, but Peter G. Van Winkle of West Virginia, Edmund G. Ross of Kansas, and Joseph S. Fowler of Tennessee for acquittal.

and patriotism remaining among a few of the Radicals even, as we see by the course pursued by Grimes and others. These Senators are being vilified and denounced with unsparing malignity by leading Radical presses and politicians, who assume to dictate to them what the party demands should be their vote or judgment in this case. For a conscientious discharge of their official duty and a regard for their oaths, the ablest Senators of long experience are assailed with bitterness as apostates and renegades by the Secretary of the Senate, Forney, through his two papers, and by others.

May 16, *Saturday.* The day has been one of excitement. Such was the outside pressure and such the confidence of the Radical majority, after many secret meetings and much caucus discipline, that the Senate was brought to vote on impeachment. There has been constant caucusing daily and twice a day by these triers — these judges — since Tuesday. Letters and telegrams have been pouring in, especially to the doubtful, and so-called recreant, Senators, all prompted from here. Schenck, chairman of Ways and Means in the House and also of the Congressional Radical Committee, has sent off telegrams, — it is reported a hundred, — calling for instructions from Loyal Leagues to influence the Senatorial judges. Governor Burnside, the weak and feeble general whose silly and incompetent orders at Fredericksburg caused the slaughter of 50,000 men, responded to Schenck, whose telegram was published in Rhode Island and another, *verbatim*, in West Virginia. They show beyond doubt that public opinion is manufactured here in Washington by the conspirators.

Two caucuses of Radical Senators were held yesterday at Senator Pomeroy's, called by Theodore Tilton, a whipper-in on impeachment, — the first at noon, the other in the evening. At this last, the members became satisfied under the sanguine representations of Tilton they would succeed on the eleventh article, provided that would be put first.

Judge Harris of Albany, who called on me this morning on business, said he met Van Horn, Representative from New York, who informed him the vote on impeachment would be taken to-day. They could not afford to delay longer. The necessities of the country and the call of the Party required immediate action.

At twelve-thirty I went to the President's. McCulloch was there, and a messenger with a telegram entered as I did. The telegram stated a vote on the eleventh article had been taken, and the President was acquitted. Soon after, Edgar came in with the particulars on that vote, which had been made the test, and on which the Radicals considered themselves strongest. It was the sheet anchor of Stevens.

The Senate was full, so far as the usurpers have permitted, and the vote was 35 to 19. Seven Republicans voted with the Democrats. Ross, who had been less strongly relied upon than some others, voted for acquittal, while Willey voted guilty. This last was quite a disappointment to the President. He had also hoped for Anthony and Sprague and was not without hopes for Corbett and Cole.

Willey, after being badgered and disciplined to decide against his judgment at a late hour last night, agreed to vote for the eleventh article, which was one reason for reversing the order and making it the first. Ross, it is said, had promised he would go for impeachment, basing his action on the first article, which was the basis for the movement. This, however, he did not communicate, but what he said relieved him from farther importunity, and the great effort was made upon Willey. Bishop Simpson, the high-priest of the Methodists and a sectarian politician of great shrewdness and ability, had brought his clerical and church influence to bear upon W. through Harlan, the Methodist elder and organ in the Senate. While Willey's vote disappointed the Democrats, the vote of Ross disappointed the Radicals.

When the result was known, Williams of Oregon, a third-rate lawyer who got into the Senate from that remote State, moved a postponement of farther proceedings until the 26th inst. The Chief Justice declared this not in order, but his decision was overruled by the majority, on an appeal taken on motion of Conness, a man of about the capacity, and as weak and corrupt, as Williams. Rules, orders, regulations are wholly discarded and disregarded by the Radical revolutionists. Their getting together in caucus, on a judicial question, is a specimen of Radical policy, character, integrity, and sense of duty.

May 18, *Monday.* The wrath of the conspirators and their creatures the Radicals continues with little abatement, but it has, so far as Senators are concerned, turned most vindictively on Ross, who is their latest disappointment. There is, however, a determination on the part of the leaders to formally expel the recreants from their party, and to do this at their Chicago Convention. But for the great folly here, I should hardly believe such folly there. In excited times like these, it is to be remembered that the violent, the impulsive, the inconsiderate, the positive element prevails over the passive and the considerate. Whether there will be cool and reflective men in their convention of sufficient influence to check the madness of party is a question.

As regards the seven Senators themselves, I have doubts. They are intelligent, and, I think, conscientious, but it remains to be seen whether they will have the firmness and moral courage to maintain their position independently through the fiery conflict in the near future. Whatever may be the doings at Chicago, these Senators are marked and spotted men so far as the Radicals are concerned. Yet I am inclined to think that some of them flatter themselves they have not lost caste, — that they will regain their party standing by being more radical than their party. A shallow delusion, which other men, their equals, have fallen into before them.

Senator Trumbull has made haste to report the bogus

constitution of Arkansas with all its enormities, in order
to demonstrate his Radical fidelity. Doctor Horwitz tells
me that in an interview at Grimes' room with Trumbull,
Grimes expressed some concern or made some inquiry in
regard to this movement, when T. said it was for effect,
that the President would let it slide, with a protest, perhaps, and they [who are] now called the apostates would
get the inside track on Reconstruction, and thus prove
themselves the most skillful managers. I asked Doctor
H. if they deceived themselves by believing the President
could in any way assent to such a scheme. He says Trumbull
seemed to so consider it. These men do not know the President. There are rumors, asserted with great positiveness
and apparent sincerity, that when impeachment is disposed of, there is to be a renovation or a reorganization of
the Cabinet. It is too late to be productive of any good if
attempted, and there is no probability that it will be attempted. Whether the rumor is set afloat by the Radicals
to take off the sharp edge of their disappointment, or by
zealous friends of the President to conciliate the Radicals
and help over the trial next week, the 26th, I know not,
nor is it of any consequence.

I called this evening on Senator Grimes, and felt sad to
see him so afflicted, yet gratified to find him so cheerful
and his mind so clear and vigorous. It is a great public
calamity that he should have been stricken down at this
time, when his services are so much wanted. A number
came in while we were there, — too many I thought, —
among them Fessenden, whom I was glad to meet. There
is great friendship between him and Grimes. Both of them
smart under the attacks which are made upon them, and
each tells me he is in daily receipt of atrocious letters.
These they wisely cast aside and destroy without reading
more than what is sufficient to know their contents. They
have, however, many cheering and encouraging letters.
Fessenden says he reads no newspapers. Pike,[1] who came

---

[1] Frederick A. Pike, a Representative from Maine.

in later, had some talk in defense of impeachment. Said
he took a different view from Grimes and others. He was
for removing the President without regard to the charge,
and for mere political party reasons.

Grimes took from his table a piece of paper and read
aloud the oath he had taken as one of the court, said it was
not the first time such appeals had been made to him, and
asked Pike how he would dispose of that oath. This was
a stumper, but Pike undertook to say that he could get
along with that. I said that such getting along showed the
demoralization which was going on, and which actually
pervaded Congress; that if he and his party could succeed
in removing the President for mere party considerations,
regardless of oaths and the Constitution, one of two results must follow, the overthrow of his party, or the government; that the government could not survive such
shocks ten years, probably not five.

Grimes concurred with me. Pike attempted to whistle
away the remarks, but I saw they affected him.

May 19, *Tuesday.* The Senate adjourned over to Thursday, and will then do nothing until their friends get
through at Chicago and return, in other words not till the
26th inst., when impeachment will be again taken up, for
I do not believe the reckless men, the real conspirators,
intend to give up the question, though the sensible men of
their party wish it. Threats and vengeance are abundant
against the seven "recreants," and thunders are threatened from Chicago, but better counsels will be likely to
prevail, — not better feeling, for there is intense and, for
the present at least, unforgiving hate by the conspirators
towards them.

Our friends in the Cabinet pronounce impeachment
dead. I prefer to see the vote. One man would have
turned the scale on Saturday. How he will vote on the
26th remains to be seen. It is a thread on which the result
hangs.

Ross is abused most. He is to be investigated by the House, or his acts are, and the Senate will submit to the indignity. I have no idea that there has been any corruption, as is insinuated and asserted. It is claimed he was pledged, that he has broken his promise, etc. Who tampered with him? Who got his pledge? Who received his promise in advance to give judgment? The enemies of the President who are going to investigate Ross' conduct. The Managers are sitting as a committee to investigate the Senators under authority of the House, and Butler, vile and unscrupulous, is calling men before him and compelling them to disclose their private affairs. Last night he spent several hours at Jay Cooke's bank, overhauling private accounts. These outrages are tamely submitted to, and are justified and upheld by Radical *legislators, patriots, and statesmen.* Heaven save the mark!

May 20, *Wednesday.* Senator Henderson went before one of the House committees and submitted to impertinent interrogatories, but refused to go before Butler and the impeachment Managers. Private individuals do not get off so easily. There is a perfect inquisition by Butler and the chief conspirators, where individual rights are stricken down, and the outrage is sanctioned and enforced by this Radical Congress. The mass of telegrams sent by the public in confidence has been seized by these inquisitors. Men are required to tell how they expended their money, what were their pecuniary transactions, and also explain their correspondence. Nothing is private, nothing sacred.

May 21, *Thursday.* The Chicago Convention is the sensation of the day. As Grant is to be nominated President, the scuffle is over the Vice-Presidency. Wade, Colfax, Wilson, Fenton, and Hamlin are the candidates, with little disposition on the part of either to give way to the other. There is not much to be said in favor of either. Wade has become demoralized, and is not the plain, single-minded, honest, unambitious man he was a few years since. His employment as one of the Committee on the Conduct of the War, his association with Stanton, who was indifferent and regardless of individual rights, and with Chandler, coarse, vulgar, . . . have blunted the better feelings, affected the habits, and tainted the principles of bluff old Ben Wade.

The others are very common men, with no decent pretensions to the second position in the Government, though either for civil service is superior to Grant. The office of Vice-President is without responsibility, patronage, or any duty worthy of honorable aspiration. The Connecticut delegation are reported as bartering the vote of that State to Fenton, if New York will make Hawley president of the Convention. Judd and Logan of Illinois assert that Grant urged impeachment. This has been said of him by others, and accords with what I have understood. He is a man of low instincts, not of a nice sense of honor nor of proper self-respect, is wanting in truthfulness and sincerity, and is grossly, shamefully ignorant of the Constitution and of the structure of the government. Yet he is the designated candidate, if not the choice, of the Radicals for the office of Chief Magistrate. A feeling of gratitude for military services, without one thought of his capacity, intelligence, or experience in civil affairs, has enlisted popular favor for him, and the conspirators have availed themselves of it, though the knowing ones are aware of his unfitness for administrative duties. They expect to use him; he intends to use them. They can intrigue, but he is, with low instincts, a man of cunning and is destitute of affection out of the family circle. . . . The War brought him again into the Army, and E. B. Washburne, his Representative in Congress, made it his study and business to indorse, extol, and advance Grant. . . . Circumstances favored, and he was promoted to be General, — Major-General, Lieutenant-General were not sufficient. There was an attempt to make him Commander-in-Chief over the President, to which Grant was nothing loath, and finally, uniting with the Radicals, he entered into the conspiracy to impeach the President and was slyly active in that intrigue.

I have little doubt that the Radicals intend to make him President the next four years by fraud and force if necessary. Their moral sense is blunted, and politically they are unprincipled. They have Congress, which opens and declares the vote; they have the General of the Army, who is their candidate; and if they can by any means secure the President before the vote is counted next February, they will not hesitate to override the popular verdict, should it be against them. The bogus Senators and Representatives, from the States which have bogus constitutions, will, in the mean time, be admitted to seats, and how is the country to rid itself of the imposition? Bold, honest, firm, and resolute minds are wanted for the work, — some one master-spirit, with tact, courage, and energy, capable and willing to take the lead in rescuing the government from the usurpers. Who is he?

There are some rumors of change of Cabinet and change of policy on the part of the Administration. I do not give them credit, and yet there are some singular and ominous movements which give colorable indication that the rumors are not wholly groundless. I should sooner believe a change might be made in the Cabinet than there would be a change of policy on Reconstruction, were the President to act out his own convictions. But at this day nothing honorable to himself or beneficent to the country is to be obtained by these rumored changes, and I therefore cannot believe they will be made. To give in to the Radical doctrine of destroying the States and inflicting on them new constitutions, repugnant in some respects to the people on whom they are imposed, would be an abasement and abandonment of all principle.

I shall not be surprised, however, if some of his friends advise these measures, and are preparing for them. It is said that Evarts is to take Seward's place. He would be

the man whom Seward would select for a successor, and
the announcement may be a feeler. Some of the Republican Senators who voted against impeachment are opposed
to Seward; they brought in Schofield. It is said Seward
some days or weeks since tendered his resignation. Not
unlikely. He scents trouble and danger in the distance.
No man of sagacity or reflection can be unmindful of it.
The scheme of depriving the ten Southern States of their
rightful governments and imposing sham substitutes will
not be permanent, and if not quietly disposed of by an
overwhelming vote in the Northern States next fall, may,
if the Southern States are not too exhausted, be followed in
the winter and spring by violence and bloodshed. In the
latter event, Seward would be less unpleasantly situated
in Auburn, or abroad, than in Washington. Perhaps the
same could be said of and for each and all of us who are
striving to do our duty.

May 22, *Friday.* Seward brought forward Japan difficulties, — the detention of the Stonewall by Commander
Brown under our flag until the civil war in Japan is ended,
the payment of a draft on the Barings for some $25,000
to pay expenses of the vessel, etc. I made some queries
in relation to the management of our affairs in Japan for
the last seven years, and as to the regularity and legitim-
acy of present proceedings. In his dispatch to our Minister, Van Valkenburg, written in answer to a telegram, via
San Francisco, giving a brief and not very clear statement of affairs, Seward wrote that his proceedings, and
his draft were "approved." I preferred "acquiesced,"
"assented to," or some different word, because until we
knew the facts we could not well approve, and might, when
the whole circumstances were known, actually disapprove;
but, confiding in our representative, we could with propriety, on such information as we had, acquiesce in what
he had done. Seward at no time likes criticism, and is a
correct, though verbose, writer; and he is sensitive on Japan

matters, and to some of his acts I have heretofore taken exceptions. McCulloch saw he was annoyed and thought to relieve him by saying he did not see much difference in the words, and if he preferred "approved" would retain it. I merely remarked that it carried a responsibility with it which might be unpleasant in certain contingencies, from which the Administration might wish itself relieved. I asked about the money which the Japanese had paid the Western Powers, and in which we had participated, I thought unfortunately, for the Japanese were willing to give us commercial advantage over others.

In the scuffle at Chicago, little man Colfax beat his competitors and on the fifth ballot was put on the ticket with Grant. There was some manufactured enthusiasm in the convention, but very little earnest feeling; none for country, but calculations for party. Grant's name is not magnetic, while Colfax has a feeble and superficial hold on sound and enduring public opinion. The candidates were serenaded this evening, but the attendance was slight. Colfax is near my house and I could at my window hear his speech.

The impeachment Managers are prosecuting their inquisitorial inquiries in the basement of the Capitol, and the public are submitting to the outrage with a tameness that is surprising. Outrages are so frequent and enormous, however, that the people look with indifference and even composure on new villainies. Reckless and lawless men like Stevens and Butler, clothed with authority, are ready to abuse it and trample down the Constitution, and law, and individual rights. Their party associates do not object, but lend themselves to the proceeding, provided the outrages and abuses are directed toward their political opponents. These things cannot be long continued, but may be submitted to until the grievance becomes intolerable. Strange how a few bad men in position, sustained by party, can damage society, pervert government, and inflict disorder and evil upon a country!

May 25, Monday. There is deep feeling but no noisy excitement on the subject of impeachment. There is caucusing and canvassing among the Radical Senators for conviction, but it is not allowable for any two men to converse on the subject of acquittal. Butler, violent, cunning, unscrupulous, devilish, has control of the Managers and of the House and is carrying on an extraordinary game of inquisitorial prosecution and persecution. In view of the action of the Court to-morrow, he made a partial report to-day of broken testimony from several witnesses that the inquisitors had before them in secret. It made, as intended, something of a sensation, and may, as intended, lead to a further postponement. This seems the present object; but there are some Radicals, in the Court and out of it, who wish this matter brought to a conclusion, and they may, united with the anti-impeachers, be able to bring on a decision, when the facts and truth, now withheld, may to some extent appear. It is, however, hardly probable, for the party discipline is strong and severely hostile to truth.

The impression among all parties is that there will be an acquittal; but, with the evident determination to convict for the good of the party, I by no means consider acquittal certain. Intrigues pervade the whole atmosphere. I hear of no one but the seven "recreants" who can be relied upon, and it is not certain that Ross will vote for acquittal on every article. He is not expected, I believe, to go for acquittal on the first, which relates to Stanton's removal, and it is claimed he is committed for the second and eighth. Should he fail on these two, the probabilities are strong for conviction. There is some talk of Anthony, Corbett, and Willey, or at least one of them, on these, but I doubt if there is any foundation. Sherman and Howe, it is supposed, will vote against the first article, and if this is strongly defeated it may affect the final result on all.

May 26, Tuesday. The Radical Senators held a caucus

this morning and resolved to postpone further voting on impeachment for four weeks. But all their number did not attend, and no one of the seven "recreants" was invited. The result was that the extreme Radicals could not carry all their friends with them, and after several votes the conclusion was to come to a decision. But here again the indecency and partisanship of the Senatorial impeachers appeared. Williams of Oregon moved to take the vote on the second article instead of the first, and the motion was, of course, carried. Ross had, on matters of postponement, voted with his party through the morning, but when the test came on the second article, and excitement was high, the attention of Senators, spectators, and all concentrated on him, and he in the hush and stillness that prevailed said, "*Not guilty.*" A sense of relief to some and of wrath to others was perceptible.

It was Cabinet day, and a telegram brought us word promptly of every motion made, and every vote that was taken. We had considered matters pretty secure, when word reached us that Ross was voting with the Radicals. This was for a few minutes a damper, but the next telegram announced the vote on the second article to be the same as it was on the eleventh, an acquittal. This was followed by a like vote on the third article, and this by an abandonment of the case, and an adjournment of the Court, *sine die.*

The Cabinet were all present with the President when the various votes were announced. His countenance lightened up and showed a pleasant and satisfied smile, but the same calm, quiet composure remained. He had never believed otherwise than in acquittal.

Butler's report yesterday is printed. It is artful and malicious. Only such testimony or parts of testimony as he and his Radical associates choose to disclose is brought out. There is no Member not of Radical politics or views on the Committee, and the Managers can therefore distort, pervert, and falsify to any extent, and Butler and most of the Managers are not nice in their means.

By seizing the telegraphic dispatches, these unscrupulous men have obtained a clue to the transactions of every person who trusted to that means of communication on any subject in those days, and, finding many things to them inexplicable, they have formed their own conclusions, often erroneous and mere fallacies. All the dispatches which are private and have to them a suspicious appearance and they cannot understand or explain, they charge to impeachment. The lobby men, claim-agents, gold-gamblers, and the whiskey ring who gather about Congress, like buzzards around carrion, use the telegraph extensively, and the Managers have, I doubt not, thrust their noses into the nests of these unclean birds. Not unlikely there were large bets and stock-gambling on the result of the trial, and this flock, like others, entered into speculation and wagers, and had their feelings and purses enlisted. Some of them may have tried to seduce moneyed fools to make them advances for improper purposes, and some may have used impeachment as a blind to cover other operations. But neither the President nor I believe any one of the seven Senators who refused to go with their party for conviction gave or received one cent for their vote. No intelligent, honest, candid man who regarded his oath would have voted otherwise than these seven Senators. Those Senators who voted for conviction are either partisan knaves, or weak, timid blockheads, the tools of knaves. There is not a man among them who is not conscious that he is guilty of wrong in the vote he has given.

That Thurlow Weed should have been sought by the gamblers and tricksters would be expected; but he was too cunning and sagacious to have his name mixed up in the proceeding. I do not think him too honest, provided the matter was feasible and necessary for his purpose. But the Managers give only a part of his testimony, and

3

Butler is as great a rogue as Weed and more criminal. I therefore, without any confidence in either, think full justice may not be done W. in this instance.

Stung and angry over their failure in the court of impeachment, the Managers and Radicals returned to the House filled with venom, which they expended on the witness, Woolley,[1] whom they have under arrest, and after partisan ruling by the Speaker and spiteful voting by the majority he was destined to confinement.

May 27, Wednesday. The Chicago nominations create no enthusiasm. Neither Grant nor Colfax has the ability or power to magnetize the people. Grant has lost moral strength by his untruthfulness, and Colfax is very weak and superficial. Stanton has cleared out of the War Department mad, and "relinquished" all to Assistant Adjutant-General Townsend. Last August he defied the President and refused, for the public good, to resign when requested, and five months since he crawled back into the Department and has held on to the place under Senatorial sanction without discharging its duties, or advising or communicating with the President or any member of the Administration. He was told to "stick," and the public business has in consequence been obstructed, the Government and country been subjected to great inconvenience and loss, and lo! the result. He goes out without respect, except on the part of ignorant and knavish partisans. His administration of the War Department has been wastefully extravagant and a great affliction to the country.

Stanton has executive ability, energy, and bluster. He is imperious to inferiors and abject to superiors. Wanting in sincerity, given to duplicity, and with a taste for intrigue, he has been deep in the conspiracy and one of the

---

[1] Charles W. Woolley of Cincinnati, a lawyer engaged in Washington on whiskey cases, who had been arrested as a recusant witness, having refused to testify before a committee of the House. He was suspected of bribery or attempted bribery in connection with the impeachment trial.

chief instigators of the outrageous proceedings of Congress, a secret opponent of the President's from the commencement of his administration. A host of puffers and toadies have ministered to his vanity by giving him undue praise, and Seward made himself ridiculous by lauding him as "Stanton the Divine," the "Carnot of the War." His administration of the War Department cost the country unnecessarily untold millions of money and the loss of thousands of lives. There was some efficiency, but it was not always well directed.

May 28, *Thursday.* There are strange but almost positive rumors of resignations by Randall, Seward, and others. I am incredulous, not prepared to believe them. The nomination of General Schofield to be Secretary of War in place of *Stanton removed*, which the President sent in sometime since, does not get through the Senate. The extremists do not like to say, by their votes, "Stanton removed"; he was, when Schofield was nominated, holding the place with their sanction. He has since "relinquished" the office. I asked the President if he thought Schofield reliable. He said it depended on the turn things might take. If we were likely to be successful, he would be with us; if the Radicals succeeded, he would be with them. In other words, Schofield is for Schofield. I regret that the President was compelled to select and appoint such a man, nor do I know under what influences the appointment was made. Schofield will likely be under the influence of Grant and the Radicals, and as one of the military governors has done things that cannot be justified.

May 29, *Friday.* Some talk but little done in Cabinet. No Secretary of War yet. General Thomas attends Cabinet-meetings, and is in the way, — doing no good, perhaps not much harm. Is sometimes a little obfuscated and garrulously intrusive, and prevents free, social interchange of views, for he talks too much abroad. McCulloch says

Fogg and Chandler of New Hampshire are in a quarrel. I told him I was glad of it and was sorry it had not opened sooner; that there was a New Hampshire clique that was very mischievous, and which he had never rightly appreciated. Of this clique his Assistant Chandler was one of the worst. McCulloch was a little nettled, for I have for two years warned him of these fellows. He said there were some troublesome men in Connecticut. I replied a good many; that I had nothing to say in their justification.

Some discussion of candidates for the Court of Claims took place. Browning and McCulloch pressed Otto, Assistant Secretary of the Interior. I spoke well of Otto, but remarked that ex-Senator Foster was a candidate and was well qualified for that position. While this had to be admitted, they objected that New England had already its representative on the bench of the Court of Claims. This I did not controvert, but thought if section or locality was to govern, we should select from the South, and for myself I preferred, if the right man could be found, he should be appointed from that quarter.

Seward did not attend until all the members but myself had left. My business was soon concluded, and I withdrew without waiting for him to open his portfolio, — for I was satisfied he wished a Mephistopheles interview. There has been money raised in New York, I have no doubt, to assist the President in defraying his expenses in the impeachment trial, and Seward has been the channel of communicating, etc.

I was struck with the observation of a Seminole chief at a late conference (1868), when told that for wampum paper was substituted, on which was written the promises we mutually pledge ourselves to perform. "I," said the Seminole, "would trust the inviolable faith of wampum sooner than the written promises of your Constitution. Wampum has the faith and devotion of the Indian, while your written Constitution is a mere matter of calculation

and bargain, no longer regarded than your interest and
conscience dictate."

He was opposed to equality of representation on the
part of the tribes. He wanted tribal distinction. Would
consent to federation, but not to consolidation. The Chero-
kees, Creeks, and Choctaws numbered 45,000, while the
Seminoles, Chickasaws, Sacs and Foxes, and the smaller
tribes had scarcely half the number. What security had
the smaller tribes against absorption and destruction by
their greater brethren, if numbers were to control? It would
make the great tribes greater; it would extinguish the
smaller. He loved his people and would preserve them.

LX

Whites and Blacks in the Washington Election — Death of ex-President
Buchanan — His Character — Oregon goes Democratic — Stanbery,
renominated as Attorney-General, is rejected by the Senate — The
Senate compliments Stanton — The Powers of the Comptrollers and
Auditors in the Treasury Department — Chase talked of for the Presidency — Burlingame and the Chinese Ambassadors — City Election
in Washington — Chase's Candidacy for the Democratic Nomination to
the Presidency — Hopelessness of President Johnson's Desire for the
Nomination — Admiral Porter and the Controversy between the Line
and Staff Officers of the Navy — The *Intelligencer* attacks McCulloch —
Congressional Inquiry into the Sale of the Ironclads Oneota and Catawba — The House accepts the Arkansas Constitution over the President's Veto — The Attack on McCulloch instigated by Seward —
Evarts nominated Attorney-General — Intimations of Another Impeachment Movement.

June 1, *Monday.* The election in Washington, D. C.,
took place to-day. There has been considerable excitement, tending to conflict between the whites and blacks.
Although this is but the beginning, the separation has
taken place. Those who did not vote with their own color
were exceptions. A very few, generally of the more modest
and well-behaved, blacks voted with the whites, but they
were very few in number. Those whites who consorted
with the blacks were to a great extent office-hunting
demagogues.

Ex-President Buchanan died this afternoon at Lancaster. He belonged to a past generation of statesmen and
was himself of no mean ability. Without warm attach-
ments himself, he failed to strongly attach others, yet he
was courtly, dignified, and studiously correct in his deportment and social intercourse. He was not a man of impulse but of calculation, and relied on intellect to manage
and shape his actions rather than on rightful instincts or
established principles. What in his estimation was best
for Mr. Buchanan he adopted and pursued, regardless of

others or of his country, — not that he would do wrong
or intentionally injure the country when no benefit was
to inure to himself.

June 2, Tuesday. The anti-Radicals made yesterday a
pretty successful contest in this city and carried a majority
of the wards. It is uncertain who is elected mayor, but
doubtless Bowen, the Radical, will be *declared* elected.
This is perhaps best, for otherwise this Radical Congress
would pass some outrageous law striking down popular
rights still farther, and install ignorance and the blacks in
power.

The election in Oregon has gone Democratic by a decided majority, electing a Democratic Representative to
Congress in place of the present Radical, and decisive
majorities in both branches of the legislature. This is the
first response to Chicago nominations, — the first Representative to the next Congress.

General Schofield, Secretary of War, was at the Cabinet-meeting. Little of interest was discussed.

June 3, Wednesday. The Senate, in its spite, has rejected the nomination of Mr. Stanbery as Attorney-General. There is in this rejection a factious and partisan
exhibition by Senators which all good men must regret to
witness. I know not the vote, but am unwilling to believe
that some of the better class of Radical Senators could have
been guilty of so unworthy an act. Yet after the result of
the impeachment and the proceedings which took place at
the trial I can believe almost anything of that body. It
will not surprise me greatly if Trumbull opposed the confirmation, and perhaps others who voted to acquit the
President, but I hope not. Some of them, and I think Trumbull in particular, are extremely desirous to reinstate
themselves in their party, and therefore in matters of
party go with the extremists. It is a mistake, as they will
learn.

The President sent for me this evening. The House of Representatives has appointed a committee to attend the funeral of Mr. Buchanan to-morrow at Wheatland, and he raised the question whether some of the members of the Administration should not also pay respect to the departed statesman. The suggestion did not strike me with favor, and I expect I showed my feelings in my looks. I asked him if he proposed going. He said that was one of the questions. He had thought that Mr. Seward and myself might do well, perhaps, to consider the subject. [He said] that Mr. Kennedy had spoken to him respecting it and gone to my house and also to Mr. Seward's, but that we were both out, taking our evening rides. I remarked that if Mr. K. called again I would be able to give him an answer.

He has not, at this time, past 10 P.M., called, so I trust the subject has been dropped. I should, under the circumstances, have been compelled to decline and to advise him also to decline. There has been nothing personal or political in the course of Mr. Buchanan which requires extraordinary services from either of us on this occasion. All proper honors to a Chief Magistrate, living or dead, should be rendered, and these have been ordered. There have been Presidents whose obsequies I would have gone farther than Lancaster to have attended, but there is, on my part, no heartfelt grief nor reverence for James Buchanan which calls for this effort; his feeble and erring Administration was calamitous to the country.

June 4, Thursday. The House manifested little feeling and intended slight and disparagement in regard to Mr. Buchanan, but finally appointed a committee to attend his funeral at 2 P.M. this day; but the House refused to adjourn over, as is done for every worthless fellow of their own body who dies here or far away. The Senate adjourned, but, I believe, appointed no committee. The deceased had no strong hold on the affections of his countrymen of any party, and manifestations of sorrow, like his politics, are artificial.

The Senate passed a complimentary resolution to Stanton. It was an unusual proceeding, and done in the spirit of factious partyism. His administration of the War Department was energetic, but not always well directed. By nature he was impulsive, wayward, cruel, unjust, and in his administration was often wasteful and extravagant. To his chiefs, one and all, he was faithless. His intrigues against Buchanan and Johnson are known, but those against Lincoln were less palpable. Had Lincoln's life been spared, some of his duplicity would have been developed. Though long associated with him, I have had no very profound respect for him as the "War Minister." He has considerable legal ability, but when he has a purpose to accomplish very little rectitude of mind. With a different Secretary of War, the War would have terminated sooner, and, I think, with a great saving of life and treasure. For the present he escapes censure because he has identified himself with the extreme men of the dominant party. A vote of thanks would have been given him by those men, had his atrocities been ten times greater. Fessenden took occasion to show that he was in principle and feeling as Radical as any.

At this time the "Reconstruction" acts are under consideration, — all in violation of the Constitution. Congress is trampling on State and personal rights and usurping power in all these proceedings. Trumbull justifies and excuses himself for voting for and supporting these malevolent and wicked enactments on the ground that, being unconstitutional, they are good for nothing, — no law. Others of the little statesmen, who are great factionists, arrogate to themselves authority to make and unmake States, to confer power upon them and to deprive them of inherent and constitutional rights, as if States were mere corporations, subject to the whims and caprices of Congress.

June 5, Friday. At the Cabinet-meeting to-day McCulloch submitted some papers relating to a claim of a road
in Kentucky which had been allowed $170,000 toll for
army transportation by the War Department. This sum
they had received under protest and claimed much more,
and the Kentucky delegation had waited on him, the Secretary of the Treasury, and requested that the claim should
be referred to the Attorney-General.

I asked what business he had with the subject under any
circumstances, the matter belonging to and having been
adjusted by the War Department, — whether he and the
Attorney-General were to revise the other Departments
and overrule their decisions.

McCulloch said he preferred to send it back to the War
Department for it to refer the matter to the Attorney-
General, if it thought proper, and would so inform the
Kentucky delegation. Browning said it was not a legal
question, but an administrative one which belonged to the
War Department alone. After some discussion the papers
went to the Secretary of War.

Subsequently General Schofield presented an act passed
in February last, conferring very extraordinary powers on
the Comptroller and Auditors. The law, he said, would
cause embarrassment in the War Department, for whom,
it seems, the law is to operate. McCulloch undertook to
go into some explanation, which showed a lamentable
want of correct information of his own duties and of the
rights of other Departments of the Government. He assumes that an Auditor or Comptroller can set aside the
decisions of any Department, if they think proper, or can
alter these decisions; in other words, administer the
government or supervise those who do administer it. The
truth is, the First Comptroller, who is probably an honest
man, is manifestly ignorant of the structure of the government, and consequently and measurably of his own position and duties. He does not learn them and will not, because the Secretary of the Treasury is afraid of him and is

to a great extent in certain important particulars governed by him. This man Taylor, First Comptroller, was for some time Treasurer of the State of Ohio, where his word and ruling on financial matters was supreme. There were no checks on his action, no departments, as in the Federal Government, exercising executive powers, and, having the control of the finances as well as the custody of the Treasury, he was a little autocrat. He has the same conception of his duties here, but they are very unlike.

"Why," says McCulloch, "you would make the Comptroller and Auditor clerks." I told him they were clerks, and I did not intend myself to be a clerk to them. I remarked that his labors had been so absorbing that he had not looked into the making of his Department, but had submitted to his subordinates, and I advised him to inform himself on a subject so essential to the Government; told him that from the beginning of his administration of the Department he had failed, I thought, in not thoroughly examining this question and keeping his subordinates in their places, instead of taking their assumptions; requested him to read Crittenden's opinion when Attorney-General, etc.

June 6, *Saturday.* An apparently strong demonstration is being made for Chase for President, particularly in New York. It is not sincere, nor is it a move in the right direction, and the strength which the movement has acquired is itself evidence of political demoralization among Democrats. It is New York party management and means Seymour. Not unlikely Chase has modified his creed since the Radicals have adopted another and different commander, but he was one of the originators of Radicalism, and the promoter of its vagaries, heresies, and wrongs. Whatever may be the popular sentiment, the New York leaders won't have Chase.

June 8, *Monday.* Made a return call on Mr. Burlingame,

who, with the Chinese ambassadors, visited me a few days
since at my house. He thinks we might learn some things
useful of the Chinese, as well as they of us, in matters social
and civil. Their practice of extinguishing annually all in-
debtedness he thinks would be well and have a good effect
if adopted here. A man who does not extinguish his debts
at the close of the year, so as to commence the new year
with a clean record, loses caste and drops to a lower grade.
Their civil war of thirteen years, in which over ten millions
lost their lives and which was desolating in its effects,
closed up without any national debt.

June 9, Tuesday. The arbitrary and outrageous conduct of Butler and the impeachment Managers begins to
tell upon a portion of the Radicals. They cannot justify
the imprisonment of Woolley, who seems, however, to be
a profligate fellow, and was by his own confession on a de-
bauch when a large portion of the $20,000 for which he fails
to account disappeared. He and his associates were probably conniving in intrigues and briberies with Members
of Congress, and, not unlikely, they may have attempted
to swindle and dupe some persons into advances under
the pretense of influencing Senators. . . . It is a corrupt
Congress, and the most corrupt put on the loftiest pretensions.

The President dined the Chinese, members of the Cabinet, some of the principal foreign ministers, and a few
friends of note. Neither Grant nor Sumner was present,
though I am confident Grant was invited. The President
is studiously regardful of official courtesies.

June 10, Wednesday. At the late city election the Radicals claim to have elected the mayor, but their opponents,
the Democrats and conservatives, carried five wards,
which gives them a majority against the mayor. This
result has disconcerted the Radicals in Congress, who have
been modifying and changing the charter of the city.

Nearly every black man in the city voted for Bowen, the
Radical candidate, while probably four fifths of the whites
voted for Given, the Democratic candidate. Since the
election there have been strange doings to get the possession of the city government, and Congress is very much
disposed to interfere and give the government into the
hands of the Radicals. They are educating themselves in
fraud and villainy, and their leaders intend by such means
to disregard and set aside the Presidential election, should
they not be successful at the polls.

There are some strange indications in regard to the
selection of a Democratic candidate for President. In New
York a busy and noisy demonstration is made for Chief
Justice Chase, who, with Sumner, is really the father of
Radicalism, not of Republicanism. Reconstruction and negro suffrage in the States have been pet measures of Chase,
yet the opponents of these measures in New York profess
a wish to make him their candidate. The *New York Herald*
is really casting aside its principles, or the principles of the
Democratic Party, and teaches acquiescence in the usurpations and outrages which have imposed negro suffrage and
bogus constitutions on the Southern States. All this is
designed to pave the way ostensibly for Chase, but there
is a deeper intrigue behind, perhaps the nomination of
Seymour, — New York partyism.

June 11, *Thursday.* The States are preparing for the
July nominating convention in New York. Connecticut,
New Jersey, and Maryland have just chosen their delegates
and left them free to act. Many of the States have improperly tied the hands of their delegates. Such a course
is in conflict with the very object and purpose of a convention.

Woolley is finally released. Congress has disgraced itself in permitting Butler to imprison this man; but Congress itself is at this time a body without character or
ability or any value.

June 12, Friday. Seward has gone to Auburn. Hunter [1] appeared for him in Cabinet-meeting, without anything to present.

I am getting embarrassed by the course of the Academic Board at Annapolis. Some of their decisions are reprehensible. The Examining Board, which attended recently, have permitted themselves to be made instruments to read me a lecture on certain subjects.

Unfortunately we have no man in Congress who is at all conversant with naval affairs, and all legislation and all Congressional action is in a wrong direction. Men having selfish schemes and purposes adapt themselves to party ends, and find ready supporters, regardless of the service.

June 13, Saturday. Was last night at a review at the marine barracks. Had a call to-day from Governor English. He apologizes in regard to his message. Says Ingersoll and Osborn desired to tone down my strong points and make it more local and less national, etc., etc. Although possessed of pretty good common sense, I perceive he has a touch of the fever which gets among aspiring politicians, and is timid and weak in consequence.

June 15, Monday. The papers publish the proceedings of a Chase meeting in Philadelphia.[2] It is represented that Doolittle, Dixon, Jeffries,[3] and others were of the meeting, but none of them were present. Doolittle has been to New York and says the talk for Chase is strong, yet he cannot suppose the leading men can be earnest. Blair says Belmont and the bankers are the instigators, — that it is a money scheme.

I look upon it as an intrigue for Seymour, who months ago announced himself not a candidate. Since then we have been told he was friendly to Pendleton, and latterly that

---

[1] William Hunter, Second Assistant Secretary of State.

[2] On June 10. It was a private conference.

[3] General N. L. Jeffries, Register of the Treasury.

he thinks well of Chase, but all this means Seymour, who is subtle, artful, and not always sincere, and has a ring of special admirers, or cronies, who think much of management. The aspect of things when the Convention meets may be such that Seymour will absolutely decline, but if so, it will be because the prospect is hopelessly adverse. He means to be, and his friends mean that he shall be, nominated, and their side moves are false and deceptive.

His brother-in-law is a Senator and resides in the same town with him, which operates against his Senatorial aspirations. Still, if the Presidency is not attainable or is doubtful, and his friends can make the Senatorship certain, he may acquiesce in that arrangement.

I called with Doolittle on the President this evening, and we had half an hour's talk on Presidential matters. I expressed freely my views in regard to Chase and Seymour, to which they both assented. Doolittle concurred most fully. The President was more cautious and reserved; said it was strange and curious to witness popular movements. During the last two years and more a great political contest has been going on for the Government and the Union, involving their existence, but neither Seymour nor Chase had done anything to sustain those who were battling for the country. They were antagonistic: Seymour, a Democrat, had given no support to the Administration; Chase had thrown his influence with the Radicals, yet there were Democrats who were seriously advocating his claims. Probably Seymour was not.

The tenor of his remarks leaves little doubt on my mind that the President's aspirations have been, or are, in that direction. It has always been so with his predecessors. But, if indulged, it is an idle dream on his part. I do not think he cares so much about the office as an approval of his acts. The retention of Seward in his Cabinet has alienated the Democrats, particularly those of New York, from him. He could not expect to gain their confidence and support when his chief minister is their lifelong opponent.

In keeping Seward and refusing for two years to commit himself to the Democrats, or to give them countenance, he wilted down his influence, weakened his position and his Administration. For a year he has bestowed some favors on Democrats, but Seward was still with him. It is impossible that he should be nominated at New York.

June 16, *Tuesday.* This is the thirty-third anniversary of my marriage. Not much done in Cabinet. McCulloch had a letter about the ironclads at New Orleans which have been sold, and which demagogues and speculators have represented as striving to escape surreptitiously. Wanted the President to issue an order on the subject, for fear the Collector could not detain them. I told him there was no necessity for calling on the President; he could apply to the War and Navy Departments, or the Secretary of State could institute action for their detention if there is any violation of neutrality.

June 17. Am told of intrigues and combinations and cliquism among certain naval men who should be in better business. Vice-Admiral Porter is restless by nature; has his favorites, and uses and presses any and all who will yield into his schemes. He has some good professional qualities, but little administrative talent. Raymond Rodgers has abilities and culture, but not individuality or independence, and makes himself a voluntary dependent. Porter uses him, and he likes to be used.

Junior officers at the Academy are drawn into the schemes of Porter, who has been injured by too rapid promotion, and desires to control the Navy. Members of Congress are imposed upon, and Porter, who is fond of politics without understanding them, and thinks himself shrewd, has covertly, as he supposed, allied himself with the Radicals. There has been a gathering here of some of these spirits, and the Naval Committee has given them a hearing. The principal topic was, I understand, the controversy between line and staff officers. There has been folly and unwise management on both sides in that matter, but this sly intrigue is sowing the seeds of mischief which the authors themselves will repent.

June 18, *Thursday.* The *Intelligencer* is making strange and unjustifiable attacks on Secretary McCulloch. There is something mercenary and vicious in this. While McC. has made mistakes and been imposed upon by Radical intriguers in his appointments, his integrity and intentions are correct, and as a financier he has had no equal since Guthrie. In politics and political training he was unfortunate, but his instincts were right, and experience has contributed to correct, in a measure, the errors resulting from early association. He told me some days since that he had been threatened by Coyle of the *Intelligencer*, a mischievous fellow who makes himself too intimate with the President, with an assault, because he would not prostitute himself to do wrong for Coyle's benefit. This he had resisted, and Coyle's extravagance — for he lives in princely style — was undoubtedly giving him (C.) trouble which the Treasury could not stand.

June 19, *Friday.* Statements, which seem authentic, are made in regard to the political opinions and views of Chief Justice Chase which indicate quite a change. These statements come from those who claim to have had interviews and free intercourse with him. I am glad to see these improved opinions; hope they are true, and that he will vigorously maintain them. But I cannot believe he will obtain the Democratic nomination, however sincere and thorough his conversion. Yet he is very much talked of, and very earnestly pressed, in some quarters where I should not have expected it. I should be sorry to see him nominated, and yet more sorry to see Pendleton, who is prominent, but whom the New York managers no more intend than Chase. Neither is the man for this emergency,

3

provided he could be elected, but either would be likely to put the election in jeopardy, and thus elevate a worse man. The intrigues for Seymour will be apt to elect Grant.

In looking over some bills which were on the President's table for his signature, I took up an act relieving Butler of Tennessee from liabilities and disabilities for having participated in the Rebellion, restoring to him his civil rights, and modifying the ironclad oath so as to permit him to take his seat in the House. I asked what that act was but a pardon, and whether the President ought, by signing it, to sanction the legislative interference with his prerogative. The President, while expressing no opinion, indicated by his manner and words that he was pleased by my suggestions and inquiry. No one of the members, however, squarely came up to the mark. Browning said the act was undoubtedly a pardon, and the President alone had the constitutional pardoning power. All but myself seemed to think it was not best for the President to interpose and assert the rights of the Executive. I cited a case which I knew of in General Jackson, who declared Congress should never intrude on the executive prerogative while he was President. Randall said General Jackson had a power in Congress which enabled him to do this. I replied he had the power because he firmly maintained the rights of the Executive and would not permit them to be trespassed upon, and I had no doubt that if the same course had been pursued by this Administration we should have had strength in Congress. Here the subject dropped; it was getting serious.

The President, who is accused of obstinacy, has often been too yielding, has tried to conciliate, and the greater his effort the more intrusive and the greater the resistance. A usurping and domineering Congress has absorbed the rightful constitutional power of the President in many respects, and crippled his authority in others. Some have advised and encouraged this yielding to wrong; I have never been guilty of it.

WILLIAM FAXON

June 20, *Saturday.* The Reconstruction [= Retrenchment?] Committee to which was referred a scandalous
resolution of E. B. Washburne, relative to an alleged
fraudulent sale of the Oneota and Catawba, two ironclad
vessels which have passed into the hands of the Peruvian
Government, made report yesterday, about as scandalous
as Washburne's resolution. The Assistant Secretary is
directly charged with fraud, and "perhaps" the Secretary
of the Navy. No honest, fair-minded man, with fair intentions, would make this base insinuation, or charge fraud
on Faxon.[1] By misrepresentation and one-sided and dis-
colored testimony, the committee may cast an imputation
on F., but it is without foundation.

Congress ordered, or authorized, the ironclad vessels
of a particular class or classes to be sold, at not less than
the affixed value to be made by five naval officers, after
public advertising. The Board, consisting of Winslow and
others, examined the vessels, affixed a price, the vessels
were advertised, six or seven bids were made for the Oneota
and Catawba. Every bidder failed; some were bogus.
Eventually Swift & Co., the original builders, bought them
at their affixed value. There were six other vessels of the
same class and model, — five of which cost the Government
more than these two, — for which mere nominal prices
were offered, not one tenth their value.

Swift & Co. and their associates have sold these vessels
to the Peruvians — had undoubtedly contracted for them
or for two of that class previously — at a much higher
price than they gave. Of this, however, the Department
knew nothing. No one supposed that any man or firm
would invest half a million in an ironclad, as a matter of
private speculation. But, because the parties purchasing
received a large advance from Peru, the Retrenchment
Committee insinuate fraud.

The Government got the price at which these vessels

[1] William Faxon, formerly Chief Clerk of the Department, had been
made Assistant Secretary on Captain Fox's going to Russia, in 1866.

were valued by a board of its own ordering, a board whose integrity and capacity no one questions; any person or persons might have had them at that, or a higher price. There are six more of this class of vessels, the same model, equally good, which any one can have, but nobody wants at the same price. Yet this Retrenchment Committee insinuate wrong. This is debased partisanship. It so happens that Faxon and the parties are all Republicans, or there would have been stronger assertions in all probability. The wretched committee of partisans were distressed because they could find no vulnerable point to assail me, and, while unjustly assailing Faxon, they say "perhaps the Secretary" had an understanding, — "willing to wound but yet afraid to strike." These dirty, scandalizing *patriots*, who devote their time to scandal and party electioneering instead of legitimate legislation, do not hesitate to insinuate falsehoods or traduce character.

The President put a veto on the Arkansas bogus constitution, and the House, unable to controvert his position, hastened to accept it by a two-thirds vote. One cannot but be ashamed at the debased and subservient partisanship which could not exhibit a single independent mind in behalf of the Federal Constitution and of the great principles on which our political system is founded, among the Radical majority.

June 22, Monday. Mr. Merritt came to see me yesterday. Was in a good deal of distress in consequence of the attempts to belie and misrepresent me for his transaction. Knowing, as he did, my entire ignorance of the whole transaction attending his purchase and sale, — that I was not even aware of his connection with Swift & Co., or that the vessels were for Peru, — ignorant himself, as I verily believe, of any wrong, he seems shocked at the malignity and defamatory exhibition of his political party friends. I assured him that the slanders and insulting assaults would not seriously disturb me, although I claimed no exemption from sensitive feelings under such calumnies.

Letters were received to-day from the European, North and South Atlantic, and North Pacific Squadrons. All in pretty good condition and doing well.

The midshipmen had a merry week at West Point. Miss Loyal, who was there, writes Mrs. Welles that she was mortified to hear Mrs. General Grant speak with confidence of her occupying the White House next season. But she is an ambitious and outspoken woman; her husband has more cunning and more reticence.

Vice-Admiral Porter exhibits a good deal of duplicity. He and the Board reported strongly against a young orphan boy who has no relatives. I ordered him to join the practice ships. Porter, who had resisted this, writes to B——'s friend Mrs. Ann Stephens, that it was his act, etc., etc. His double-dealing in De Camp's case I do not forget, and there are repeated instances of his insincerity and untruthfulness.

June 23, Tuesday. Seward was at Cabinet-meeting. He returned Sunday morning from Auburn. Has been absent about a fortnight. The attacks of the *Intelligencer* on McCulloch commenced while S. was absent. He generally contrives to get away when one of his explosions is to take place. McCulloch is friendly to Chase and wants him nominated and elected. Seward does not, and would be willing to see any active friend of Chase's stricken down. I am inclined to think that McCulloch is more earnest for Chase than he would care to have known, — more than he, perhaps, is aware of. But Seward and Weed are implacable in their hostility to the Chief Justice, and McC.'s adroitness in his behalf is more than counteracted by the two old stagers. But I question if McCulloch knows, or even suspects, the source of the intrigue against him. The President, I apprehend, has an idea prompted by the same set that it would benefit him were McCulloch to leave the Cabinet; but in this he is mistaken. That Mc-Culloch has erred, greatly erred, in appointing to and retaining in office a herd of violent, vindictive, and offensive Radicals there is no doubt. I have repeatedly cautioned him on this head; but I don't think Seward has done so, and McCulloch has always believed, and still does perhaps, that Thurlow Weed was his special friend. He has also believed that Seward was friendly, and has had no suspicion that his support of Chase could cause any alienation.

Governor Buckingham of Connecticut has been quite sick in Illinois. Under the impression that he might die, the Radicals made haste to legislate so as to secure the office [1] to a partisan. A large portion of the legislation of this, and also the last, Congress, was mere party scheming, while great public interests have been neglected. In the case of Governor Buckingham, he is likely to save them trouble by recovering from his illness. The papers report that he is much better, and about going to Chicago, where he can be better served.

June 24, Wednesday. The President has nominated Mr. Evarts to be Attorney-General. It is doubtful whether he will be confirmed, and yet there is no reason why he should not be. I am surprised that the President should nominate him, and surprised that he should accept the office. But the finger of Seward is in this. As a lawyer Mr. E. is at the head of the bar; as a politician he is the opposite of the President. He can, however, accommodate himself pretty readily to any party and any set of principles, — views them much as he does his clients. The Senate might confirm him without question, for he has avowed himself a Radical and opposed to the President's policy, although he was one of his counsel in the impeachment case.

Mr. Pruyn tells me that Seymour or Chase will be nom-

---

[1] William A. Buckingham, the War Governor of Connecticut, had been elected Senator to succeed Dixon. He took his seat March 4, 1869.

inated at New York. "But," said I, "Seymour has peremptorily and repeatedly signified his refusal." "Well,"
said he, "that is so, but if the Convention should nominate
him, I have no doubt he would yield." Pruyn is of Albany,
one of the leading Democratic minds of New York, and he
speaks, I have no doubt, the purpose and intention of the
leaders of that party in that State, which does not mean
Chase. I am sorry there is not more sincerity, frankness,
and straightforward conduct among New York party
leaders. A good and righteous man, such as we now have,
should not be injured by such duplicity.

June 25, *Thursday.* The President has nominated Collector Smythe of New York Minister to Austria, — an
appointment that should not have been made, and I cannot
suppose will be confirmed. In this, as well as Evarts'
nomination, I see the finger of Weed and Seward. Perry
Fuller, an improper selection for such a place, is nominated
Commissioner of Internal Revenue. These nominations
and some other movements leave little doubt on my mind
that the President has hopes of a renomination, and there
are those around him who encourage the delusion. I look
upon it as beyond the bounds of probability, almost of
possibility. He desires to be victor over the conspirators,
more than the office.

June 26, *Friday.* Seward opened his budget to-day with
statements in regard to three or four unimportant consuls.
Grave matters for the Cabinet, while important appointments are slipped through in a different manner! But the
President himself is not without fault in this respect. Some
strange and singular appointments have been made from
time to time without consulting any one, — certainly none
of his Cabinet.

Intimations of another movement for impeachment by
Thad Stevens are thrown out, — it is said, however, not with
any expectation that the House will adopt the charges, but

that Stevens may make a speech, and that the charges may be suspended over the President. I doubt if the malignant and vicious old man will make this demonstration, but he likes notoriety and power, and his threat exhibits both to his satisfaction.

LXI

A Proclamation of General Amnesty read in Cabinet — Jefferson Davis the
only Person excepted — The President draws up another making no
Exception — The New York Convention nominates Horatio Seymour
and Francis P. Blair — An Unfortunate Nomination — The Result
brought about by the Tammany Managers — Disappointment of the
President — Seward Close-mouthed on the Nominations — Conver-
sation with the President in regard to Seward, Stanton, and McCulloch
— Doolittle invited to become an Independent Candidate — The Pre-
sident prepares a Message recommending Certain Changes in the Con-
stitution — Cabinet Discussion of it — A Talk with Montgomery Blair
— The Blairs and the President — Evarts takes his Seat in the Cabinet
— The Two New Cabinet Members, Schofield and Evarts — John A.
Griswold claiming Credit for the Monitor to the Exclusion of the Navy
Department — Congress, instead of adjourning, takes a Recess till
September 21 — Seward reads in Cabinet a Proclamation relating to
the Fourteenth Amendment — General Banks and the Navy Yard
Appointments — Conditions in Georgia.

July 1. Much confusion prevails among Democrats relative to a candidate for President. Delegates to the Convention which meets at New York on the 4th, and many
who are not delegates, have passed through Washington;
others are now here. The aspect of things does not please
me. There has been mismanagement and weakness in New
York, and little vigor or right intention anywhere. A personal demonstration, and extremely partisan too, has been
made for Pendleton, who will probably have the largest vote
of any candidate at the commencement, but who will not
be allowed to be nominated. He may, in the excess of
party feeling, demonstration, and excitement, be nominated, though it seems hardly possible for sensible men to
make such a blunder. Chase, who is conspicuous as an
opponent of the Democrats, as a negro suffragist, and, until
recently, as a Reconstructionist, is strongly pressed. The
New-Yorkers appear to have surrendered all principle in
a feeble, sprawling anxiety to triumph, and will thereby

endanger success. Possibly they have overmanaged in regard to Pendleton, who has been fostered as an auxiliary, merely, to New York.

The President, I perceive, has strong hopes of a nomination. But what he might have made a certainty is, by himself and his course, placed beyond the confines of possibility. He has said nothing to me direct, and I am glad of it, for it would be a subject of extreme embarrassment to me.

Hancock seems a fair man. I know not his mental strength, but have a favorable opinion of it. In many respects he would make a good candidate; he has a good military record, and the military feeling is prevailing at this time. His indorsement of Stanton two or three years ago in New York is to his discredit. I have no doubt it was procured by Stanton himself through Jere Black, — a political manœuvre in which H. was used. Hendricks would unite as many as any one, perhaps, and is a politician as good, perhaps, as any suggested of the anti-War Democrats. He and Hancock have appeared to me most likely to strike the Convention favorably, provided it is composed of sagacious, fair-minded men, unshackled by personal favoritism, and if the majority can swing clear of the great tidal wave of New York which moves for party and not for country.

Doolittle is a fair and good man, whom I should name, if by so doing he would be made President. But he is young and less prominent than others, and the party Democrats are making too much haste to get power for such a man.

.   .   .   .

The President has read to us a form of proclamation prepared by Seward for general amnesty. As usual, the paper is a little verbose and less direct than I like. Exception was made of such persons as are under indictment. The President, I saw, was not pleased with that part of the document; asked how many there were under indictment, why prolong this unhappy controversy by such a clause. Seward thought that was as restricted as we could make

it. There were but two men, — Davis and Surratt. I
asked if exceptions were to be made, and there were but
two, why not name them. I thought, however, Surratt
was arraigned for a criminal, personal matter, rather than
treason. The President said that was so, and there is
really but one man, — Davis.

After the others left, Browning and myself remained
and went over the papers again. I suggested that the preamble did not bring out as distinctly as I wished the fact
that since the proclamation of May, 1865, — his first proclamation for amnesty, — there had been no armed or
organized resistance to the Federal authorities. Browning
agreed with me, and the President took the idea. He said
he should revise the document and wished us to reflect
upon it and make suggestions. He particularly desired we
should consider the subject of an unqualified amnesty to
all, without any exception.

July 2, Thursday. The New York Convention absorbs
more attention than Congress, which, in fact, is little
else than a party convention. I give little heed to the many
strange rumors that prevail; but, looking on, I am constrained to believe there is not much candid, enlightened
intelligence as yet displayed. The New-Yorkers have over-
refined. Have held up, restrained, and not concentrated
sentiment. In the anticipation that there would not be
unity they have designedly left matters loose, and they
continue so. If they supposed they should thereby
eventually control the result and have their own man,
they may have failed. Chase or Pendleton may have become too strong to be controlled. Our New York friends
purposely scattered, and may not be able to rule, the elements.

The President to-day laid before Browning and myself
his proposed proclamation. It is essentially different from
Seward's paper, and is without "exception." Browning
thought this a mistake, said they would try again to im-

peach, etc. The President wished to know if they would frame an article based on his amnesty. I saw he was decided, and remarked he must, for himself, judge of the expediency. There was this fact: if Jeff Davis were tried and not convicted, we should have a strange and unsatisfactory result. Could he be convicted by any jury where he can be legally tried?

July 6, Monday. Went to Hampton Roads, the Capes, and Norfolk on the evening of the 3d and returned this morning. A pleasant respite on the 4th and Sunday. Fox, Faxon, Commodore Jenkins, etc., etc., were of the party. Commodore Kilty, Rodgers,[1] and others were glad to see us at the Norfolk Yard, and came with us to Fortress Monroe on the evening of the 4th to witness the military display of fireworks. A great crowd were assembled in and about the fort. General Barry, who is now in command, and his friends received us most hospitably and kindly.

July 7, Tuesday. While at the President's, two telegrams were received from the Convention in New York, stating the result of the ballots to nominate candidate for President. Pendleton leads, as was expected, and the President was next, which was not expected. Most of his votes must have been from the South. The vote of New York was given for Sanford E. Church. This, I told those present, was a blind and meant Seymour, that the New-Yorkers intended Seymour should be the candidate, and Seymour also intended it, provided he became satisfied he would secure the nomination; but, unless certain, he would persist in declining. New York, I said, had been playing an insincere game; had, though the headquarters and management of the party was in New York, designated no one; had not tried to concentrate, but had endeavored to scatter, and, for effect, have several names

[1] Captain C. R. P. Rodgers.

presented. Puny efforts for local candidates like English of Connecticut, Parker of New Jersey, Packer of Pennsylvania, as well as Church of New York, were encouraged, but all this frittering away strength meant Seymour. New York will control the Convention. McCulloch and Browning thought that the Pendleton men would control, — that they probably would not get two thirds for him, but that they could say who should or should not be the man. "If they move in a body," said I, "but that they will not do. When they break from Pendleton, they will scatter, and ultimately be gathered for Seymour."

Seward during the conversation said nothing, and he made a point to leave early. The President was evidently gratified with the vote he received, and the cheers when it was announced.

July 8, Wednesday. The platform of the Convention is not so good as I expected. The Pendleton policy controls, but it is pretty certain he will not get the nomination. If the New-Yorkers cannot carry Seymour they will likely go for Chase, though he gets no nomination or support at present. At the close of the day's session the run was for Hancock and Hendricks. The fear that Hancock might succeed prompted an adjournment, and there will be intrigue to-night, — perhaps a union on Chase, though I can hardly believe it. Seymour, if nominated, will be defeated. Hancock, if the candidate, will be elected. Some speculations are thrown out for English, but it is mere flummery, though the Connecticut delegates do not understand it. They have done better than New Jersey, which still holds out for Parker. The President's vote is falling off. There has never been any intention to nominate him, except by a few earnest friends in Tennessee and perhaps a few in some of the Southern States. Seward is a stumbling-block for him.

July 9, Thursday. Horatio Seymour and F. P. Blair, Jr.,

were nominated President and Vice-President at New York. Ohio dropped Pendleton and went unanimously for Seymour. This was followed by other States successively, ending in a unanimous vote. "A spontaneous movement," say Seymour's friends, "Unexpected," "A general recognition of the first statesman in the country," etc., with much similar nonsense. The threatened demonstration for Chase appears to have alarmed the Pendletonians, who dislike him. All worked as New York intended. The friends of Pendleton were unwilling, I judge, that Chase, Hendricks, or any Western man should be selected, lest it might interfere with P.'s future prospects. We shall know more in a day or two.

I do not consider the nomination a fortunate one for success or for results. Seymour has intellect, but not courage. His partyism predominates over patriotism. His nomination has been effected by duplicity, deceit, cunning management, and sharp scheming. He is a favorite leader of the Marcy school of Democrats in New York, if not of the Van Buren and Silas Wright school. A general feeling of disappointment will prevail on the first reception of the nomination, discouraging to Union men, but this will be likely to give way in the exciting election contest to the great questions involved. The Radicals will take courage for a moment from the mistakes of the Democrats.

I was at the President's when the telegram announcing Seymour's nomination was received. The President was calm and exhibited very little emotion, but I could see he was disturbed and disappointed. He evidently had considerable expectation.

The nomination of Blair with Seymour gives a ticket which is not homogeneous. Blair is bold, resolute, and determined; has sagacity as well as will. His recent letter enunciates his policy and the underlying principles of the present contest. Seymour, more timid and calculating, does not take the ground openly; but the Radicals will force the Democrats to accept or reject the doctrines. In nominating Blair after the publication of his letter, the Democrats are committed to his views, if there be anything in partyism. Throughout the whole proceedings preliminary to and attending this convention to its close, there has been, on the part of the New York politicians, a selfishness that has narrowed their vision and a want of sagacity and enlarged and comprehensive views that is surprising. The end has not yet been reached. They have put in jeopardy an election which they might have made certain.

When President Johnson refused to adopt the plans and schemes of the Radicals to exclude the Southern States from Congress and to impose upon them constitutions, laws, and governments by Federal authority, he caused a rupture of the Republican Party which, had he been cordially seconded by the Democrats, would have insured the defeat of the Radicals, for the better portion of the Republicans concurred with him and the Democrats. His course was so correct on the subject of Reconstruction, the rights of the States, and kindred measures that the Democrats were generally disposed to sustain him and identify themselves with his Administration, but the managing Tammany men of New York, apprehensive that this might affect the organization and discipline of Tammany, while they encouraged and supported the President's policy, were careful not to identify themselves with and indorse the President himself, to whom they and the country were so much indebted. Confident that the sentiment of the country was against the Radical usurpations, and glad to avail themselves of that sentiment, they feared that the President, who boldly fought those intrigues, a man whom they did not elect, might become popular; they were distant, cold, reserved towards him.

Most of the Democratic managers had been opposed to the War and War measures, had opposed the election and reëlection of Lincoln and Johnson, had sympathized with the Secessionists, and, in their national convention, declared the War a failure. Their unpatriotic and disunion course had kept them in minority for years, from which they now, by the folly and extreme measures of the Radicals, who had become disunionists not by secession but by exclusion, expected to be relieved, and they were impatient to be in power.

But while a large majority of the people were opposed to the vicious, usurping, and centralizing schemes of the Radicals, they were not ready to place a Copperhead or anti-War Democrat at the head of the Republic. The great mistake of the New York Democratic managers was in supposing that the Radical measures were so atrocious that the people would accept and vote for almost any man, even those who were on the opposite extreme. The memories of the War were not, however, forgotten; there was dislike and distrust of the men who opposed it, and there was still a strong military feeling prevailing. Neither of these elements could give a cordial support to Seymour or any one like him.

But the New-Yorkers had neither the tolerance, tact, nor judgment to wait events, give resentment time to cool, and permit a War Democrat to be chosen. They would not allow Hancock or even Hendricks to be nominated. They feared Johnson might be. There was an excuse for the New-Yorkers' not supporting Johnson, because he had retained Seward, whom they abominated, and to whom they could not be reconciled. But why oppose and exclude Hancock, a much more popular man with the military than Grant, a man of more intelligence, and greater capacity, and who, if nominated, would be elected? The reason was that the Tammany politicians were determined to have Seymour, who was neither a military man, nor a friend to the War for the Union.

What, therefore, might have been a certainty, the New York managers have made an uncertainty. They have professed to have no candidate, — were willing to unite on whoever was nominated, — but have intrigued throughout to prevent any man from being nominated but Seymour. As capable politicians, New York being the great State and New York City the headquarters of the party, to have designated and united on one or two men who would have been acceptable to the country would have brought success. Instead of this they professed indifference, encouraged Chase, fostered Pendleton, mentioned Hendricks, and, having the matter in their own hands, voted for Sanford E. Church, whom they intended should not be nominated, and who had not been mentioned.

Had the Tammany managers who make party a trade been sufficiently disinterested and patriotic to have stood back and let a War Democrat opposed to Radical usurpations be nominated, Seymour might, four years hence, be brought forward with success, for he has intellect, but it is given more to party than to country. If he fails now, he fails forever, and I fear our Federal Union will fail also and consolidation obtain an enduring ascendancy.

July 10, *Friday.* The President was, I thought, more affected to-day than yesterday, but was quite reticent on the nominations. McCulloch and Browning expressed, and evidently felt, great dissatisfaction, — said Seymour was, next to Pendleton, the worst selection which could have been made. I said it was not, save in financial matters, preferable to Pendleton; that P., though a demagogue, had played no double game, or cheated and bamboozled his friends, but Seymour and the New York managers had.

McCulloch lamented the failure of Chase, who, he says would have certainly succeeded had not Seymour been taken up, but it was foreordained that Chase should not, and Seymour should be, nominated. I told him I had no regrets for Chase, though I greatly preferred him to Seymour. Browning united with McCulloch in the belief that Chase would have got more popular votes than any other man.

There is a strange desire to make these matters personal. Leading politicians are almost invariably in fault in that

3

respect. They fancy the people are led away by a prominent orator or politician, regardless of principles. A great
mistake. They will abandon a favorite who is in error.
But when a favorite agrees with them in principles, there
is a feeling of enthusiasm around that is irresistible. Seymour can arouse no such enthusiasm, because, though in
feeling and conviction he may now be with the people,
he is timid and insincere. "There is a tide in the affairs
of men," but just at this time the tide, I fear, is not with
Seymour, though he has got the nomination.

Seward was very close-mouthed, and got away as soon
as he could. I shall not be surprised if he goes for Grant.
Yet his friend and crony Thurlow Weed has left the country, as I have sometimes thought to avoid taking part in
this campaign, when Seward cannot perhaps go with him.
They were both accused of favoring Seymour, covertly,
against Wadsworth for Governor in 1862.

July 11, *Saturday.* Senator Doolittle called this morning to breakfast, having just arrived from New York.
He is sore, and dissatisfied with New York trickery and
management. We went together to the President, with
whom I had an appointment at ten. They both manifested feelings almost of resentment. I felt as much disgust
towards the proceedings and towards Seymour's nomination as either of them, but said: "Here is Grant, ignorant,
untruthful, and unreliable, as we all know, and behind
him is the important question of State rights as against
central despotism. Much as we may dislike Seymour and
the disingenuousness of our New York friends, our course
is plain. Seymour, though a heartless politician, timid,
selfish, and the devotee of party discipline and party
management, will be compelled to go with his friends,
whom he has the sagacity to know to be right. Grant we
know to be wholly incompetent." To this both assented.
The President spoke with some bitterness, I thought, of
Blair's letter, as overturning things, etc. I inquired if

JAMES R. DOOLITTLE

they were not to be overturned, — whether these fraudulent governments imposed on the States by a usurping Congress were to be sanctioned and legalized, or whether the legitimate governments were to be permitted in time to regain their place. The President went into the library without a word. Doolittle conversed with me.

On other occasions, when I have brought forward these points, the President has been disinclined to discuss them. They have never been matters of Cabinet discussion, — that is, the future of these Reconstruction questions. I have no doubt that Seward is for submission, acquiescence, although he has never said so in words, but that is the bent of his mind; and he easily influences the President.

After Doolittle left and we had finished business, the President seemed inclined to talk. Said Seymour had not lifted a finger to sustain us through our three years' struggle, that those of us who had maintained the government and its true principles were wholly ignored, that the Democratic Party had for twelve years acted as if demented, and seemed determined to continue in error.

I assented to the fact of their erroneous and factious course, and to their present mistakes; but remarked, in justice to the mass of the New York Democrats and those of some other States, that they could not and would not give their confidence to Mr. Seward and were unwilling to identify themselves with an administration where he was a ruling spirit. Neither he nor Seymour could win the confidence of party opponents. The nominations being over, we might look at this subject truthfully and philosophically.

The President was a little annoyed, I observed, that he had introduced the matter, and that Doolittle, before he left, had said the great error was in retaining Stanton, when over two years ago we knew he was intriguing against us.

The President did not controvert my remark, but, as if by way of defense, said there had been more complaint against McCulloch and the Treasury than against all others. He did not mean to say there was cause for it, or that it was justifiable, but he mentioned the fact and the difficulties he had to encounter. I replied that McCulloch was himself a capable financier and an honest man, but he had committed a great error in retaining Rollins,[1] Chandler, and other Radicals here, and permitting them to crowd in swarms of Radicals all over the country. I believed him, however, a true friend of [the President] personally, and of the Administration.

I again remarked that I spoke freely, as he had introduced the subject; that, the issues and the tickets of the two great parties being made up and before the country, it could not be supposed I had any motive to influence those questions, and I supposed that the two men (Seward and McCulloch) would continue with him to the close. Without expressing either assent or dissent in words, he left the impression that such was the case.

July 14, *Tuesday.* The Democrats and conservatives do not yet get reconciled to the New York nominations. It was undoubtedly a mistake, but they must support it as preferable to Grant in his ignorance and Radicalism in its wickedness. It will not do to sacrifice the country from mere prejudice against, or partiality for, men. I judge from what I hear that Chase and his friends felt a degree of confidence that he would be the nominee. He had, I have no doubt, the money interest in his favor.

When I went to Cabinet to-day, only Seward was in the council room. He said, jocosely, that he understood I was for the New York nominations and he opposed to them. Said the papers so stated. I observed that I had not seen the statement, but I had no hesitation in saying I was opposed to Grant and the Radicals, and, consequently, I had, under the circumstances no alternative but to go for

[1] E. A. Rollins, Commissioner of Internal Revenue and, like Chandler, a New Hampshire man.

Seymour. I tried to draw from him some expression but without success. Others came in, and he turned the conversation.

The President submitted the Edmunds law excluding the electoral vote of certain States. Seward declared himself very explicitly opposed to this, and so did every member present. Browning wanted a short message of not more than ten lines. The President said he was willing any of us should prepare a veto. No one volunteered. From Seward's remarks I supposed he would do it, if requested, and he so said before we left, and though his reasons and mine would not be in all respects alike, I could not compete with him. The President would, in any event, make Seward's the groundwork of his message, if S. prepared one.

July 17, *Friday.* The weather has been so intensely warm that I have tried to keep cool, and, in those dark evenings without a light, have been disinclined to write, although I feel guilty in not noting occurrences as they take place. Some are of interest and may be adverted to hereafter. There is, apparently, unappeasable discontent with the New York nominations. Perhaps I hear more of the complaints than others. Senator Doolittle a day or two since stated he had a letter from a number of persons in Pennsylvania, expressing dissatisfaction with the candidates — they could not vote for Seymour — and inviting Doolittle to be a candidate. He wished to consult me as to his answer. I said there was but one course and that was to decline. I was more and more satisfied the nomination of Seymour was not judicious, but there is now no alternative but to support and try to elect the ticket. That would save the government, reconcile sections, and give us peace. He said he concurred with me, and had a letter partly prepared which he intended to have brought with him.

The President read a veto which he had prepared on the Edmunds Bill excluding certain States from casting electoral votes, or, if cast, to prevent them from being counted.

The veto is very well done and, I think, is the President's own work.

He afterwards laid before us a message suggesting sundry alterations of the Constitution. I was uncomfortable while it was being read, for I could perceive it was a favored bantling which he had prepared with some care.

Seward, at once, and on its conclusion, met the subject frankly and candidly. Said he made no objection to the document as an exhibit of the President's own personal views, but he did object to its giving-out as an Administration or Cabinet paper. He could readily assent to some of the propositions, to others he could not, and, as a general thing, did not admire changes of the fundamental law. He did not wish the Presidential term lengthened, nor did he wish there should be a prohibition to reëlect.

McCulloch said as a general thing he was against constitutional changes, but thought it well for the President to present his views. He rather liked extending the term. Browning had never given the subject much thought, but was favorably impressed with the suggestions that were made.

Schofield and Randall said very little. I concurred generally in the remarks of Seward, but excepted, which he did not, to the encroachments proposed to be made on the federation features of our system. I was not for taking away from the States the single sovereign vote in case there was no election on the first trial. It was not, I think, the expectation, when the Constitution was framed, that the electors would be chosen by the people, but that they would be appointed by the legislatures of the States respectively. That feature had proved a failure, however. The legislatures had surrendered the choice of electors to the people, and I should prefer that the people should vote direct for the candidates than through the making of an electoral ticket. If there was no election and the choice went back to the people, I should, in that event, wish each State to give one vote and but one vote, whether the State was great or small, thus avoiding aggregation or consolidation in the election and preserving the distinctive character and equality of the States. So, as regards the Senators, I preferred they should be chosen by the legislatures instead of being elected by the people, as the President now suggested. The Senators were representatives of the States in their sovereign capacity. Members of the House were the direct representatives of the people. I would sacredly preserve the federation features of our system and did not care to popularize the Senators. And I long since had come to the conclusion that changes in the Constitution should be made with great care and caution.

Perhaps I was not as full and emphatic on all these points as I wished to be, for I was subject to constant interruption. The President wished, evidently, no dissent to his suggestions. He has, I think, prepared this document under an impression that it will strike the popular pulse and possibly make him a candidate.

Mistaken man, if such are his thoughts! This is no time to bring forward and encourage constitutional changes. There are other great and impending questions which supersede theories and speculations like these, — questions affecting the character and stability of the government that must be met and disposed of. The President is, no doubt, sincere in his propositions, but he evidently has not thoroughly examined and considered the subject in all its bearings. He has not reflected on the compromises which were made by the States when surrendering power and framing the Constitution, nor has he that deference and regard for the States and their dedicated rights, which are essential to union, that I should have expected. His propositions, without his intending it, are tending to a great consolidated central government instead of a federal union.

Some one — Randall, I believe — asked which of the parties would adopt these recommendations, or if he expected Seymour would adopt them. I did not fully catch the inquiry, but the President, with some vim, said we did not go to them, they must come to us. He did not know that they supported our measures, and it would be well to understand how they stood on matters of principle, before troubling ourselves about supporting their ticket. This seemed very like Seward, and I think comes from him. He looked much pleased when the remark was made. I am apprehensive that in his disappointment the President will permit himself to be persuaded to take a course which may give him much after regret.

Montgomery Blair came to see me last evening, and reports matters at the New York nominating convention. He says Seymour was for Chase and so was a majority of the New York delegation. The final move for Seymour by the Ohio delegation prevented, he says, the nomination of Frank Blair, who was, he declares, the choice of the Convention. They were tricked out of it, etc. I make all allowance for Mongtomery Blair, for he is a very affectionate and devoted brother, and really thinks Frank the greatest man in the country. Frank has undoubtedly more courage than Seymour and greater sagacity and power than is generally supposed, but I cannot think he has any such hold on the popular mind as Montgomery supposes. A great many eminent men are favorable to him, — some that surprise me; but on the other hand there is a terrible prejudice against him by others. Thurlow Weed and Seward have done much to create this prejudice, and so have Chase and the Treasury agents, but Frank has unfortunately his own infirmities. The elder Blair is a remarkable man and has, in a long and political life, by his talents, power, and influence, incurred enmities; and the whole family, by their bold denunciations, have raised an extensive feeling against them. I have found them honest, positive, egotistical, but remarkably sagacious, early to detect and prompt to expose intrigue and fraud.

The President is under great obligations to the Blairs, but Seward has succeeded in prejudicing him against them, —

much to his own injury, I apprehend. Montgomery Blair does not conceal his defection from the President, who has treated his advice and warnings with but little respect, and in some instances has availed himself of information derived from Blair without giving credit and confidence in return. Blair says he thinks and hopes the President will oppose the Democratic ticket, and finally go for Grant. I do not, and I so told him. The President has been ungenerously treated by leading Democrats, but the people respect him.

July 21, Tuesday. Mr. Evarts appeared in Cabinet council to-day for the first time. He arrived in Washington on Sunday. This appointment makes Seward potent beyond what he has hitherto been with the President, but that fact will not strengthen the Administration. Neither of the political parties like Seward. He is disliked by both, has not public confidence, and there is no affection for him in any quarter. The President does not see this, nor will he; but from this time forward he will probably be too much under the combined influence of his Secretary of State and Attorney-General.

Evarts is, naturally enough, much devoted to Seward, who has patronized, trained, and taught him, though Evarts is possessed of the superior intellect. The pupil is more of a man than his tutor, and it is no disparagement to Seward, who himself is not a common man, to say so. But Evarts, though a remarkably clear-minded man, a stiff, sharp logician, a lawyer of extraordinary ability, is not a sagacious politician, has not got hold of the popular heart, nor can he do so. He is foremost in his profession, but a centralist in policy, with no political convictions. The important movement has brought Schofield, the warrior, and Evarts, the lawyer, into the Cabinet. Both stand deservedly well in their professions, but, I apprehend, neither will prove serviceable administrative officers. Fessenden and Grimes, without personal partiality but from abundant precaution, desired, after the unfortunate selection of Lorenzo Thomas to discharge the duties of the War Department, that a discreet and judicious man should succeed Stanton, which led to the appointment of Schofield; Evarts was brought in by Seward and his friends; the President quietly yielding but not selecting in either case. To Grimes and Fessenden and to Seward also he justly feels under obligations, and has yielded to them in these appointments.

I hope the President will not be induced to favor, in the least, the usurping Radical faction and their unconstitutional Reconstruction schemes. He cannot any more than myself be a personal admirer of Seymour, and, were the approaching election merely personal, neither of us could be interested in the result. Among prominent public men there are few in whom I have not greater confidence than Seymour. He is not a sincere man, and I cannot forget his persistent, wholesale, and disgraceful slanders of New England, his assaults on her population and institutions, so unjust and so unworthy a statesman of his pretensions, so uncalled-for and unmerited. His speech some years since at St. Paul, intended as a bid for the Presidency, had the ingredients of a low-class politician. It was the more inexcusable for the reason of his having intellectual qualities, and also because he is of New England stock. But although he is personally the most objectionable to me of all the proposed Democratic candidates, nevertheless he is the selected opponent of Radicalism. I therefore support him in preference to Grant.

The President will, I am confident, take the same view and do nothing to help Grant, unless persuaded by others, and only two men can do that. They are in position, and Evarts has openly taken ground for Grant months since, but the President, who detests Grant, knowing him to be untruthful and false-hearted, has appointed E.

I have been anxious that the President should hasten his action on bills and send in his vetoes promptly, in order

that Congress might adjourn early, but he seems disinclined to facilitate their departure. Says they have wasted
time, that we are compelled to wait here through the summer, and that they can endure the heat as well as we. Similar remarks were made by Randall and Seward. I think
it a mistake.

July 24, *Friday*. The recklessness and disregard of the
organic law and of the great principles of morality and
right by the Radicals become daily more and more apparent. Their own will, schemes, and intrigues they consider
paramount to the Constitution. Tests and test oaths are
manufactured with facility to exclude by legislative enactments their opponents, and laws and usage are set aside
with equal facility to favor their own partisans.

A very large number of "carpet-baggers" are now admitted into each house of Congress, and the more considerate of the Radicals begin to manifest apprehensions that
these, with the extremists, will control all legislation.
Seward declares that this has been his reliance, and that
therefore he has advised to let them have their own way,
fully satisfied they would not long harmonize. That he has
abstained from opposition, and yielded, and urged the
President to yield, until the Administration is powerless,
and the government has become changed, are palpable
facts. How the government is to right itself and the true
principles of the Constitution be reinstated are matters
beyond his grasp. His advice and influence in this regard
have been neither profound, wise, nor fortunate.

The public do not get reconciled to the nomination of
Seymour and Blair. The indifference, not to say aversion,
is deeper, more extreme, and less easily reconciled than I
anticipated. I trust it may not continue and thus lose the
election. It was without doubt an unfortunate selection,
made under bad leadership, by a body which did not, and
does not, realize the true condition of affairs. The occasion demanded the sacrifice of all personal considerations

for the good of the country, but New York intrigue and
personal spite and disappointment of the Pendletonians
defeated Hendricks and Hancock. The country was sacrificed for personal considerations. I still have hope the
people will rally to save the Constitution, — to rescue and
restore it and to vindicate the cause of free government
and self-government, — but it is not to be denied that our
federal republic system is in danger. The election of Grant
will ratify and confirm the usurpations which have been
made, yet there are some, I fear many, good men who are
not entirely divested of the War feeling, and who, in consequence of their dislike and distrust of Seymour, threaten
to go for Grant or not vote at all.

Little of special interest to-day in Cabinet, and the President was not communicative in relation to appointments,
of which he is making many in which it is supposed we
more or less participate. I am importuned on these matters outside, but, unless requested, I am not disposed to
intermeddle out of my own Department, though one or
two others do.

July 25, Saturday. Received yesterday P.M. a resolution
calling for the contract, payment, facts in relation to construction, etc., of the original Monitor, and replied at some
length to-day. I participated in getting this resolution
passed, in order to give the public the true history of the
case, now gravely misrepresented. John A. Griswold, a
wealthy iron-master and Member of Congress, has been
nominated a candidate for Governor of New York by the
Radicals, and there has been, and is, a persistent attempt
to give him false credit in regard to the Monitor, and this
by systematic and deliberate falsehood and injustice to
the Department. Mr. Griswold is deserving of some credit.
He was one of Ericsson's sureties and assisted in his financial necessities. As such he is deserving of praise, even if
he went into the concern as a business operation, which I
suppose he did. He and his associates, I have understood,

were willing to hazard each $10,000 in the confident expectation it would, as it did, prove a good investment.

After the services of the Monitor at Hampton Roads, Winslow, one of the associates with Griswold, was very importunate and persistent in the claim that he and those associated with him should have the exclusive privilege of building all that class of vessels for the Government. Whilst treating him politely, I assured him his demand could not be complied with; that, if allowable, they could not of themselves furnish all the vessels that were wanted. He said they would sublet, and insisted they were entitled to this privilege as much as if they had procured a patent. The claim was preposterous, and I refused to recognize it, but they were given contracts for several vessels.

General Benjamin F. Butler declared a few days since on the floor of the House, and Mr. Griswold's biographers assert, that he advanced the money for building the Monitor, that he had no remuneration until after the fight with the Merrimac, all of which is false. The work of building the Monitor was paid for as it progressed. Six payments were made between the middle of November and 3d of March, before the vessel was completed and delivered. The last and final payment, save the reservation which by contract was to be retained until after a satisfactory test, was made before she left New York on her trial trip. Yet the Hon. Mr. Griswold, knowing the facts, himself a party, sat quietly in his seat and took to himself this false credit without one word of explanation or any justice to the Navy Department. His biographers have, I am persuaded by his connivance, not only made the same statement as Butler, but have gone farther and tried to ignore the Navy Department, or have slandered and belied it by declaring the Secretary was opposed, or only gave a negative support, to Mr. Griswold and his associates.

Not only this; Chaplain Boynton, the historian of the Navy during the Rebellion, was subsidized — I have no doubt — and induced to give a distorted and unjust statement, in which praise and glory are given to Griswold to which he was not entitled. In this way a fictitious character is manufactured for a party candidate by injustice to others.

July 27, Monday. In conversation with Senator Doolittle yesterday, he informed me that the President intended to nominate Alexander Cummings for Commissioner of Internal Revenue. He wished to know if I was acquainted with Cummings, wished me to see the President, and suggested the name of Judge Bradley of Rhode Island.

I called at the President's an hour or two later and among other matters brought up the subject of the Commissioner of Internal Revenue. Jeffries, who had earnestly sought the place and had the support of McCulloch, was rejected by the Senate on Saturday night by an overwhelming vote. At one time it was thought he would be confirmed, and there are various rumors in regard to him. He is accused of double-dealing, — of making promises to both parties, — there is scandal, etc., etc. I thought the President did not seem grieved greatly at Jeffries' rejection, and he said to me he proposed sending in the name of Cummings. I remarked that Cummings was a very particular friend of Cameron, and expressed a doubt as to his reliability, — particularly where Cameron was interested. There had, I added, also been rumors and charges heretofore against him, but as he has since passed the ordeal of nomination and confirmation to a responsible office, I suppose those charges must have been explained and disproved.

The President said he had heard something of those rumors, but he thought he could depend upon Cummings, even against Cameron.

This morning, when at the Capitol with the President and Cabinet, I found Seward very busy about appoint-

ments, and among others, about Cummings, whom he
indorsed as a capital man for the place, — no better could
be found. Witnessing his movements and hearing his remarks, I remembered old intimacies between Seward and
Cameron. In this connecting link I can see how movements are going on for Grant and the Radicals in quarters
which the President does not suspect. Not that it is certain Cummings will support Grant. He likely will not, but,
in the position of Commissioner, he might, if circumstances
required, have been influenced by Seward and Cameron
to have taken that course, the President not being a candidate.

But few Members of either house called in at the President's room during the two hours we were there. In this
respect, there was a strong contrast with similar occasions
in former years. The Members who voted for impeachment were generally shy and appeared ashamed to show
themselves. There was, I thought, conscious meanness and
abasement in their very looks.

There was little to interest during the closing hours of
the session, — less excitement than usual, and none of the
great absorbing constitutional struggle, such as I have
sometimes seen in other days. Statesmanship was wanting.
The Members talked and acted as if in a village caucus.
Petty intrigues, tricks, and contrivances to help the party
were the great end and aim. Instead of the usual adjournment *sine die* to meet at the regular session in December,
Congress took what they call a recess until the 21st of
September. This was a scheme to cheat the Constitution
and innovate on the executive prerogative, for it is the
President's duty to convene Congress, if public necessity
requires. But it was not pretended there was any public
necessity. The recess was to prolong the session, and watch
and circumscribe the President in the discharge of his
executive duties. There being no cause for assembling,
the Radical Members, before leaving, knowing that an extra
session was unnecessary, signed a paper to the purport

that they would not convene in September unless called
together by E. D. Morgan, Senator, and Schenck, Representative. These two men are chairmen of the Radical
party committees of their respective houses, and on them
was conferred the executive authority of calling an extra
session for party purposes. Such is Radical legislation —
and Radical government.

July 28, Tuesday. Judge Kelley and Stevens of New
Hampshire, two of a committee who had visited the Philadelphia Navy Yard in relation to the purchase of tools by
the Engineering Bureau, called on me to make statements
and exhibit portions of testimony which they had taken.
Stevens made a few brief remarks and left. Ferry, the
other committeeman, did not attend. Their investigation
had of course been *ex parte,* and their showing against
Teller certainly requires explanation. But the committee
had come to no result, — made no specific charges, — had
a rambling talk of matters in which Judge K. manifested
a degree of warm partisanship. After listening to him over
two hours, I requested him to let me have the report when
made, or, if he could present the points, charges, specifica-
tions, in a form so that I could call for an explanation from
Engineer Teller and others, I would demand it.

When I went to the Cabinet-meeting this noon, I found
Seward and General Banks with the President. I seemed to
have interrupted them, not unexpectedly to the President,
who said, "Well, here is the Secretary of the Navy, and
you [General B.] and the Secretary of State can come to
an understanding with him." I inquired the subject-
matter. General Banks said his object was to get me to
conform to the law in navy yard appointments; that I did
not obey the present law, nor the law of last year. I asked
in what particular. He said I appointed master mechanics
from the Navy, — that Navy officers filled the places, and
not civilians who understood the trades. I replied that
he in the House and General Wilson in the Senate had each

of them publicly made that statement, but it was not true; that no officers except sail-makers were master mechanics in any of the yards. He said boatswains were employed as masters. "But," I added, "boatswains are not mechanics, sail-makers are, and the last year's law, enacted for party ends, not the public service, did not embrace master laborers." He insisted that no civilians were masters, but that naval officers were. I defied him to name one. He said he had no details, but he understood there was not a single civilian in place. I told him there were no others except sail-makers and boatswains; that since the War we had, to a considerable extent, dismissed masters in order to save expense and retained only foremen, the gangs being so much reduced. It was a matter of economy.

Driven from this point, he asked if there could not be a change of Naval Constructor at Charlestown. I told him it might be done if there was sufficient reason, but Mr. Hart had commenced work which was unfinished, and it would be hardly fair to take him away and substitute another without cause. With this we parted.

Mr. Seward read a proclamation which he had prepared pursuant to act and directions of Congress in relation to what they call the Fourteenth Constitutional Amendment. I passed some criticism, or rather took some exceptions. Thought he was too compliant, identified himself too much with the proceeding, and did not make his work appear as if the act of Congress. The President fell in with my suggestions, and Mr. Evarts proposed one or two verbal changes to carry out my views. They did not come up to my ideas. Seward, however, was annoyed even with them. Said it was hard business for him at best, and he thought he ought to be satisfied with what he had got to sign. I remarked that was true, and was glad it did not devolve on me to put my name to such a paper; that I would not do it in that form.

July 29, *Wednesday.* General Banks again called, with

3

Mr. Stewart of New York, a member of the Naval Committee. Banks had quoted him yesterday at the President's. Said Stewart told him, when he (B.) introduced the amendment concerning navy yards, that I would pay it no attention. Stewart said it was a mistake, — he had not stated the case so strong. Banks changed his ground somewhat. He had found himself at fault; admitted that the masters were civilians, but under naval officers. I told him that was true. The commandant of the yard, who had general supervision and the administration of the yard, was by law a naval officer. So were the constructor and the chief engineer. He said the commodore who commanded the Charlestown Yard was of no account; that he merely opened and closed the gates, and lit the gas, — nothing else; that he was afraid of Hart, etc., etc. I told him John Rodgers had been esteemed a man of courage, physical and moral. He claimed that the law required me to appoint masters of the several trades. I asked him to show me the law, and he pointed to the provision in the appropriation bill just passed. I denied that the provision established masters, — it merely required that masters should be civilians and not naval officers. I admitted I had not much regard for such legislation. Congress has no authority to say what class of persons shall be appointed, and what class excluded from office. The Executive, not Congress, makes and is responsible for appointments.

"Then," said he, "you do not mean to obey the law." I claimed he had no authority for that remark; that it was my intention to detach both the boatswains and sailmakers; that under the reorganization of the yards we needed no master laborers, nor was a master sail-maker necessary under the reductions.

"Then," said he, "you mean to evade the law by appointing no masters." "That," said I, "is not correct. We have, and probably shall continue to have, some masters of large gangs; but masters are not required for most of the trades; foremen and quarter-men will be sufficient." "That," said he, "is not the law." I asked what was the law. He pointed to the provision already mentioned. "That," said I, "merely requires me *when* masters are appointed to select civilians, not naval officers. Some of the trades have but five, or six, or eight, or ten men. No masters are required in those cases. It would be a useless expense to have masters when not wanted." This he admitted, and wanted to know how many men required a master. I said none were really necessary at this time, but some may be convenient. He still insisted that I was obliged to appoint masters for each of the several trades and wished me to give him a line to the Attorney-General for an opinion. This I declined. Told him I understood the law without making an inquiry in any quarter. He still pressed me for a letter, and I still declined, but told him he could, if he wished, converse with the Attorney-General.

He said he had seen that gentleman already, but he declined to give an opinion without a written request from me, and he (Banks) now asked it of me. The request was almost in the nature of a demand. I, however, continued to refuse, but told him I had no objection to conversing with the Attorney-General when I saw him.

He left in ill temper. Said he should remain in Washington until he accomplished his object.

July 30, *Thursday*. General Banks called again to-day. Said in reply to the usual complimentary inquiry as to his health that he was weary. Wanted to get away, but could not until there was some understanding in regard to navy yard appointments, but he now wished specially to know whether there was to be a change of Naval Constructor. He wanted Hart to be sent to some other yard, and Hanscom ordered to Charlestown. I required some cause for detaching Hart, who is discharging duties faithfully and satisfactorily, without complaint from any one but him, and he did not pretend that Hart was delinquent as a constructor. [I said] that, as regards Hanscom, he had been recently sent to Portsmouth and I did not propose to disturb him. "Then send some other man," said he, "for Hart is a coarse, vulgar fellow, a tyrant, controls the yard, is insolent and incompetent." I questioned the correctness of his analysis; admitted that I thought Hart was sometimes arbitrary and positive, but told him I intended in a few days to visit the Charlestown Yard and would then make personal inquiry.

July 31, *Friday.* Seward and Evarts are absent from Cabinet-meeting. Hunter, who was there for Seward, said the Spanish Minister was very uneasy about the Oneota and Catawba, fearing they would be permitted to leave New Orleans.

Attention was called to a statement from nine Georgians who claim to have been illegally arrested, imprisoned, and cruelly treated. Schofield said the statement was untrue, a pack of lies; that his brother had been sent down there to examine the subject, and he reported that the whole story was untrue.

Browning said he hoped it was untrue, for, as described, it was one of the greatest outrages he had ever heard of, and the credit of the Government, he thought, required it should be clearly and distinctly disproved, if it was really untrue.

I questioned whether it was an entire fabrication. There might be some exaggeration, — probably was, — but that these Georgians had been arrested illegally, carried to a distant prison, were closely confined, etc., could hardly be questioned.

Schofield admitted he had not seen the statement, but there had been so many false reports, and his brother was so convinced of it, that he gave no credit to anything he heard. Besides, the state of society was such there that strong measures were necessary.

The President produced the *Intelligencer*, and the statement was read. It seemed to stagger Schofield, who, however, still quoted his brother and cited the condition of the South. All, however, were emphatic against the extraordinary proceedings, and thought there should be a thorough investigation, — except Randall, who said nothing.

Schofield produced a correspondence between Meade and Grant. Georgia having been reconstructed, Meade finds himself powerless, and wants instructions. Schofield thought the President should delegate authority to Meade to respond with his command to the Governor of Georgia.

I objected and hoped the President would not interfere until the power of the local authorities was exhausted and application was duly and properly made.

LXII

A Tour of Inspection of the Navy Yards — Talk of an Extra Session of
Congress — The Railroads and Congress — Sanford E. Church and
Dean Richmond (the younger) on a Political Mission from New York —
The Power of State Sheriffs to call on Army Officers for Assistance —
Death of Thomas H. Seymour — His Career and the Part played in it by
Mr. Welles — Radical Gains in the Maine Election — The "Alexan-
drine Chain" — Senator Morgan and Representative Schenck issue a
Call for Congress to reassemble — Congress meets and adjourns —
General John A. Dix's Anti-Seymour Letter — His Character and Polit-
ical Views — Marriage of Robert T. Lincoln — The Pacific Railroad.

August 27. I have been absent a few weeks inspecting
the several navy yards and stations. Our yard boat, the
Tallapoosa, having freight to interchange with the different
navy yards, I improved the opportunity of going in her.
Doctor H. and others advised it, and the rest, change,
etc., I was satisfied would be of benefit. Commodore Jenkins, Chief of Bureau of Navigation, Admiral Radford,
and others went with me. I had expected Admiral Smith
to be of the party, but his health was so impaired that he
was compelled to leave earlier. Doctor Horwitz and Mr.
Bridge, of the Medical and of the Provision and Clothing
Bureaus, were expected to join us. Mr. Bridge met us at
Portsmouth and returned with us.

The trip was, throughout, pleasant. Senator Grimes
came on board at Rye Beach, and we made an excursion
on the coast of Maine as far as Mount Desert. The weather
was cool and bracing. Much of the time we wore overcoats. The passage among the islands was delightful. Off
Rockland and its vicinity we fell in with the mackerel-
fishing fleet of some three or four hundred vessels. At
Portsmouth we witnessed the launching of the new sloop
Alaska. The Kenosha was launched at Brooklyn, but an
accident to our boiler detained us from it.

The several navy yards were in good condition. But

little work is being done at any of the yards. There was, however, something to be looked after. I have not visited the yards since 1863, and as I shall soon yield up the administration of the Department, I felt it a duty to give them this last inspection before making my final report.

We returned safe and well on Monday last. Little of striking interest has occurred during our absence. I find on my return some of the members of the Cabinet are absent, and there will be, for a month or more, some absentees. I am anxious to visit Connecticut for a day or two in September, but Mr. Faxon left to-day and will be gone probably for a month.

There is a contrariety of opinion in regard to an extra session of Congress. The decision is not with the legally constituted Executive, who is responsible, but with an irresponsible partisan committee. The impression among the members of the Cabinet is that there will be no extra session. None is necessary. My opinion has been that, as the question is one of party expediency, Congress would probably be convened.

I do not like the aspect of affairs. There are ominous prospects connected with the election. It is evident that the Radicals intend to secure the next President by fraudulent means if others cannot prevail. In fact, all their Reconstruction schemes have had that end in view. The Democrats seem determined not to be defrauded, nor to submit to outrages.

If Congress convenes in extra session, it will be with a design to resort to extreme and illegal measures to overpower a legitimate expression of public opinion. An unchecked partisan body like the present fragmentary Congress, composed in part of usurping carpet-baggers, will, in the heat and fury of an excited national party contest, be a wild, unscrupulous set, restrained by no constitutional barriers, or any principle of legal or moral right. There is no statesmanship or political wisdom in either branch, but there is much that is vicious and wicked.

At the Cabinet-meeting to-day, Seward read a letter from the late Mexican Minister, Romero, stating he would meet Seward at Vera Cruz and escort him to Mexico, etc., etc. Seward is alarmed for the future, and intends to escape from any participation in the approaching election.

He read a letter from a Mr. Sherman of Utica, stating that Roscoe Conkling had recommended him, Sherman, for Collector. Seward indorsed the nomination and wanted Sherman appointed. It would gratify Conkling. I doubted its expediency without farther advice, but Seward was persistent. McCulloch is inclined to make the appointment on Seward's assurance. I have no faith in it.

On the subject of alleged disturbances South, Schofield said they seem altogether exaggerated; that in Virginia there was now less crime than in Massachusetts.

September 1, *Tuesday.* The subject of selling a gunboat to an agent of the Haytian Government was brought forward. In a recent sale of vessels at Portsmouth, the Maratanza was bid off by a person who avers that he bought it for Hayti. I assumed that my duty was ended when the vessel was sold and we had the pay. Whether the State or Treasury Departments would object to granting him or others a clearance were matters not for me to determine. My views were approved in Cabinet, and Seward said no one could object, or would be heard in opposition, to a sale to the Haytian Government; a sale to the rebels would be another thing and might raise a question.

Seward expressed great desire to go to the Rocky Mountains. Urges the President to make the trip with him. I judge there has been previous conversation on the subject. The President gave no definite answer. Said he was embarrassed as to any movement by the proposed session of Congress which Morgan and Schenck might convene. He could go nowhere till that was decided. Seward said if they went to the Rocky Mountains that would be decisive. The Radicals would not come here while he was away. When about breaking up, Seward again asked the President if he should make arrangements for the trip West. The President said he would give no final answer to-day.

The subject of sympathy and aid for the Greek rebels in Crete was mentioned, and some other matters were introduced relating to the Turks. The conduct of Mr. E. J. Morris, our Minister to Constantinople, was discussed. I expressed doubts of the wisdom and judgment of Morris. Seward says he has improved, and has modified and changed his opinions. Seward said every man, woman, and child in the United States were against the Turks. I told him he would please except the Navy and Navy Department. The President said no nation had been more friendly and true to us during our difficulties than the Turks, and instead of interfering against them in their trials, we had better turn our attention to our own affairs and get our own people reconciled. Schofield fully assented to this; thought we had better attend to the affairs of our own household. Seward concurred, but said our consul at Candia was a troublesome man and was in the interest or feeling of the missionaries, who, as usual, were mischievous in the matter. The opinion seemed to be general that the consul had better give way.

The Indian troubles and the plundering schemes of the Pacific and other Western railroads were considered. There has been wild and wicked legislation by Congress. Members are corrupt and dissolute. McCulloch says the ring of railroad men had monopolized that great interest and is controlling Congress.

I mentioned a fact concerning Oakes Ames, Representative from Massachusetts, communicated to me by Paymaster Bridge, who says the half-yearly dividend of Ames, paid a short time ago, was $81,000 on the Sioux City & Omaha road. This was just sixty per cent on his stock. I asked Bridge how he knew the fact. He tells me he got it from his nephew, who is president of the road. McCulloch says he doubts whether Ames ever paid a dollar for his Omaha stock, but that his interest in that road is a trifle compared with his interest in the Pacific. This man, worth millions, takes the position of Representative — seeks and gets it — for the purpose of promoting his private interest.

September 2, Wednesday. I asked the President to-day if he had really any intention of going to the Rocky Mountains. He said he had not. I said that he would, in my opinion, do well to take a respite, if only for ten days; that I would recommend him to visit Tennessee, and, in doing so, go unaccompanied by any of his Cabinet, especially not by Mr. Seward; that Mr. S. was desirous of taking him somewhere, but it would be well for both that he should make one trip alone. The President smiled; said he thought so, too; that he certainly should not go to the Rocky Mountains, never had thought of it for a moment seriously. Congress would probably prevent his going anywhere. Morgan and Schenck, under Radical usurpation, were in this respect the Executive and directed the actions of the Government.

September 3, Thursday. The President invited me to go with him to the German Schützenfest this P.M. Although wholly unprepared and the weather unpromising, I went. It is the first of these festivals I ever attended. We were received with great good will and respect by the managers, escorted to various points, and taken through the grounds when the rain did not prevent. The President tried a shot, and was made a member of the association. We were invited to dine with the managing directors and hospitably entertained throughout. There was much good feeling and fellowship and everything was orderly.

These associations are becoming numerous and popular over the country. They are of German origin, and the associations are composed chiefly of Germans or those of

German descent, but others largely participate. I did not, however, observe any of our Irish brethren on the ground.

September 4, *Friday*. Sanford E. Church of New York called on me and desired, after a little conversation on political matters, that I should go with him to the President, with whom he wished an interview. He is of the Silas Wright school of politics and has, personally, something of the manner of Governor Wright. Our views and opinions corresponded on men and affairs generally.

The President received him kindly, and after a brief conversation appointed to-morrow at 10 A.M. for a meeting. This being Cabinet day, and an hour having been assigned for the reception of the Austrian Minister, he would be occupied with these and other matters.

S[eward] read a multitude of dispatches to Van Valkenburg at Japan and one or two from him. They were not very edifying, although S. seemed to consider them so. His oral efforts to enlighten us were not very successful, although he had some of the strange names of the daimios, etc., by heart.

He also read a long dispatch to Webb at Rio in relation to his course and that of Washburn in demanding as a right that the steamer Wasp might run the blockade. I respectfully differed from some of his positions; told him I was glad Washburn was coming home, although we now had too many of the family on hand, and I wished Webb was returning also. Told him and the Cabinet that I saw no necessity for sending a Minister to Paraguay, where there is not a single American resident, nor had they a Minister here. Seward repeated a remark heretofore made, that the mission disposed of one of the troublesome family of Washburn, who are now all provided for.

McCulloch made some inquiries in relation to payments in coin to the Navy and others. He also asked for information about moneys which, to a considerable amount, had been placed in the hands of Senator Pomeroy several years since for the deportation of negroes. Seward said he remembered all about it, and went into something of a narrative of a black colony sent to Cow Island,[1] most of whom died and the remainder returned in disgust. I told him he had only related the latter part of the movement; that the first was a scheme to send off the negroes to Chiriqui, in which Thompson first and Pomeroy subsequently figured. The subject was new to most, or all, of the others. Seward, in expatiating upon it, magnified his own doings. I do not remember that he took an active, or very active, part for it, but I am confident he took no part against it. In the early stages, when there was a speculating scheme to mine coal by negroes, I had to resist, but good old Mr. Bates was heartily with me, though an advocate for deportation of the negro. Then they were going to mine coal for the Navy, and buy Thompson's grant from Central America, etc., which was finally checked when on the point of consummation by a protest from the Minister, who denied the legality of the Thompson title.[2]

I observed that Seward cared to say little or nothing of those transactions, and was sorry to see that he attempted to belittle Mr. Lincoln, who, he said, knew nothing or next to nothing of public affairs except what related to army movements. In this he does injustice to Mr. Lincoln, who better understood things generally than Mr. Seward. Seward himself was constantly dipping into questions which he did not understand, — would get a slight superficial idea and nothing beyond. Much of this he obtained by hanging on to Mr. Lincoln and pressing him to make inquiries.

Seward's blunders as regards the blockade, his ignorance of admiralty law and of some of the most essential duties of a first minister, were unfortunate for the Administration and the country. Yet his readiness, his suppleness,

[1] Ile à Vache, Hayti. Mr. Charles K. Tuckerman gives an account of this unfortunate venture in the *Magazine of American History* for October, 1886.
[2] See Volume I, pages 123, 150–52.

and his superficial knowledge answered a purpose. I see his object in these derogatory remarks of Mr. Lincoln, which he has made in my presence on one or two occasions that I remember, and how often on other occasions I know not. His purpose is to cast off his blunders and mistakes on the dead President, to whom he meant to impute all the faults of the State Department.

I spoke of releasing the Oneota and Catawba, also the relief of the Glasgow, both of which were to have been attended to some weeks since. He was unprepared and had evidently forgotten them for the time, but said he would be ready in a few days.

September 5, Saturday. Mr. Church informed me this P.M. that he had had a very agreeable and satisfactory interview with the President, and is to see him again to-morrow at 1 P.M., and will call after that at my house with young Mr. Richmond.

September 7, Monday. Mr. Church came to see me yesterday. Spent over an hour with me. Young Dean Richmond was with him. There is a strong desire to bring the Administration into the support of Seymour and Blair. Hitherto but little has been done in this direction. The leading Democrats of New York have not been cordial or really friendly to the President, but, while accepting his principles, they for selfish schemes preferred to be separated from him.

I said to Mr. Church I could make reasonable allowance for this distrust, because the President had continued their old opponent Mr. Seward in his confidence. He at once eagerly and earnestly responded; asked how they could be in harmony with one who had no sympathy or principle with them. Church is, however, very cautious in what he says. He is here on a mission, somewhat diplomatic, and an observer and a witness more than a communicative speaker. He has again called; has seen McCulloch and is confident all will go well. I am not sanguine, nor does he express himself confidently, but has stronger hopes than I can yet command. The New-Yorkers have over-managed, — a mistake of their party leaders for years. They have talked and still talk of and make the financial question prominent, but Reconstruction, as it is called, involving the structure and character of the government, is more important than even that. The New-Yorkers have tried to make this secondary, but that question should strengthen Mr. Johnson, who is at issue with the Radicals on Reconstruction. This was before the nomination, and, having got the financial issue prominent, they continue it. So with Pendleton, who takes anti-Democratic ground. They are talking of the two currencies and in which of them the bonds shall be paid; but they should all go to work and let us have but one currency. There should be no unredeemable paper.

The course and speeches of Pendleton make it clear that he is a disappointed and intriguing man, and that he does not take his disappointment kindly. His speeches, except in ability, are like Webster's when he and Clay were competitors and Clay became the candidate.

September 8, *Tuesday.* Seward had more of the Japanese matters. No one said a word but myself. As usual, I expressed my doubts of the wisdom of combining with the Western Powers, though perhaps we had now become so much committed and involved that there was no ready way of extricating ourselves. In relation to the religious question, I trusted we were not to become propagandists.

Schofield read a general order of General Buchanan, telling the officers under him that they must obey the order of the sheriff when he calls out the *posse comitatus* and they cannot quiet disturbances. I excepted most decidedly to such a doctrine, and so did Randall. Schofield said Attorney-General Evarts had so laid down the law. Seward defended the principle, or rather the order, and said Randall and myself ought to inform ourselves of Evarts' opinion, that the subject had been elaborately discussed when we were absent. I replied that I had opinions of my own on the subject, long since formed, principles in regard to the powers and duties of the Federal and State Governments differing from him and Mr. Evarts. I asked if a military officer of the United States [became] a State officer when the President had, on the application of a State, by its legislature, or by the Governor when the legislature was not in session, issued his proclamation. Seward replied yes. Both he and Schofield cited the Fugitive Slave Law. I said that law was not high authority with me, but in that matter a U. S. Commissioner, if I remembered rightly, was the officer, not the State sheriff. They both said that law and the principle were coming back to torment the inventors. I replied I had no wish to torment any one, — certainly no one for his folly.

In this instance, the order and action under it will be likely to have a good effect, for the very presence of troops will, perhaps, prevent disturbance. Nevertheless, the doctrine of Seward and Evarts is erroneous, and the order wrong.

September 9, Wednesday. Colonel Thomas H. Seymour [1] died last week and was buried on Monday, the 7th, with great parade. He was sixty years old and had great popularity; was genial, affectionate, of pleasant manners and kindly nature. The papers eulogize him highly, and the crowd which attended his funeral attest the estimation or love for him that prevailed. The expectation that distinguished men, and particularly Horatio Seymour, would be present swelled the crowd to some extent.

The eulogies contain some errors of fact, and award him qualities which he never possessed. He is represented as a distinguished lawyer, as having acquired a competence

[1] Governor of Connecticut, 1850–53, then for four years Minister to Russia. He was a Peace Democrat during the War.

in his profession, whereas, though admitted to the bar, it was by courtesy, not that he had legal knowledge or acquirements; he never had a case or managed one, or made a plea in any court, save perhaps that of a justice of the peace. As to earning a competence, he never earned five dollars in any court. He is spoken of as a distinguished and successful editor. He undertook to edit a paper under very favorable circumstances, and utterly failed, and was dismissed by his publishers and friends in a few months.

His military zeal and efforts are highly lauded, and not without some desert. Instead of seeking service in the Mexican War, as stated, I procured his commission for him, unsolicited by himself, and he accepted it with some reluctance. I knew he was poor and desponding, and that he had a fondness for military parade and show. He was educated at Captain Partridge's Military School, and we encouraged him to drill, for a compensation, several military volunteer companies, — as much to help him as the companies. When the New England regiment was raised for the Mexican War, I, then being in Washington, and the only man from our State of any position or influence, saw Governor Marcy, then Secretary of War, and insisted that one of the field offices of that regiment should be given to Connecticut. He admitted the propriety of the demand, but he had committed himself in some degree to a gentleman in Maine, and no candidate had come forward or been presented from Connecticut. He asked if I was prepared to name a man. It was before the days of telegraphs, and communication by mail was slow. The regiment was being made up. I gave him the name of T. H. Seymour on my own responsibility and wrote A. E. Burr and General J. T. Pratt that they must compel him to accept. It was a responsibility by no means pleasant to me, for, had he never returned, his death would have been charged upon me.

Seymour did not, at the time, thank me, or make any acknowledgment, and I had no word or line from him until

after his arrival at Vera Cruz. Some years later, in 1852
I believe, he, in a public speech in Hartford, when he had
been praised for his military services, declared his indebt-
edness to me for his military position. The *Hartford Times*
published, on the day of it, a notice of this acknowledgment.

In 1833 I was nominated for Congress. Seymour was
then editor of the *Jeffersonian* and had expected his father
would be nominated Secretary of the State, for which he
had been many years an unsuccessful candidate. But it
was thought best by the nominating convention to have
an entire new ticket. N. A. Phelps[1] was the active man in
effecting this change. Seymour, in his anger because his
father was not nominated, immediately and violently opposed my election, and in connection with others, the chief
of whom was N. A. Phelps, defeated the ticket.

When all was over, Seymour became aware of his error,
— saw that he had been made a dupe by Phelps, and that
he had done me injustice. This he ever after tried to retrieve and stood firmly by me in subsequent party and
personal conflicts. In 1835 I procured him to be appointed
judge of probate. I had a controlling voice in the legislature, of which I was a member, and the legislature then
elected those judges. I was the same year elected Comptroller over Elisha Phelps, the uncle of N. A. Phelps. The
candidate for judge of probate was Isaac Perkins. Both
he and E. Phelps had two years previously been incumbents
of the two offices; both had been in the combination against
me in 1833 and instigated and misled Seymour.

I was glad of an opportunity to punish them and to heap
coals of fire on Seymour's head, and succeeded. He felt
and appreciated my kindness, and though we have since
differed widely, I am not aware that he ever did aught
against me personally. I have seen little of him, though
always friendly, for the last fifteen years. When he re-

[1] Noah Amherst Phelps, who was himself Secretary of the State of
Connecticut in 1843–44.

turned from Russia we were widely estranged in politics, and I do not remember to have met him since my residence in Washington.

Amiable and kind-hearted, generous without means, indolent by nature, a lawyer who never had a case, retiring but proud, with an imaginative mind, a refined taste, sincere in his convictions and tenacious to obstinacy in his opinions, he retained friends and acquired official distinction.

Probably no man in Connecticut was more opposed to the War or more earnestly sympathized with the Secessionists than T. H. Seymour, yet he did not mean to be unpatriotic or opposed to the Union.

September 10, *Thursday.* Binckley, Solicitor of Internal Revenue,[1] has been to New York to ferret out frauds, of which there are untold amounts which seem to go unpunished and undetected. There must be great remissness somewhere. Whether B. is the right man to unearth these villainies and bring the rascals to justice is another question. He and Courtney, District Attorney, have had a disagreement, and the whole world is down on Binckley. I think he may have been indiscreet, but believe him honest and zealous.

September 11, *Friday.* A thin Cabinet-meeting. Only McCulloch, Schofield, and myself present. A delegation from Tennessee was there on the subject of getting troops into the State.

The report of Binckley was read. It seems he went on to New York by direction of the President, who had received advices from certain parties that villainies could be uncovered, provided a reliable person was sent there. B. thinks he has discovered great frauds and that the District Attorney is implicated. This seems hardly credible. I should be sorry if such be the fact. There are circumstances against

[1] John M. Binckley, formerly Assistant Attorney-General.

Courtney, who claims to have been slighted in the military proceedings. Binckley says it was because he was mixed up in the frauds. The fact that he has done so little is adverse to Courtney. The efforts, for two years, to ridicule and disparage B., with his not always well regulated zeal, have got the current of prejudice against him, which is of course improved by all the rogues and cheats who are defrauding the revenue. They are with C. in this matter and shout loud against B.

The differences between the two led B. to telegraph the Secretary of the Treasury for instructions. McCulloch, without knowing the differences, replied that the law gave these matters to the District Attorney, but failed to request that B. should be associated with him on behalf of the Treasury.

Courtney telegraphed Ashton, Assistant Attorney-General, who utterly ignored B. The result is that B. left New York, and came highly incensed to Washington and made report. The commission at his suggestion postponed the case for a week against the wishes of C. and of the Whiskey Ring. McCulloch feels unpleasant, and the President directs that C. be ordered to Washington, and if he will not faithfully prosecute, he intends another shall.

September 14, *Monday.* Intelligence received of a terrible earthquake extending along the western coast of South America from Cape San Francisco, destroying cities, many thousand lives, and hundreds of millions of property. Two U. S. naval vessels, the Wateree and the Fredonia, were wrecked, and every soul on board the latter but two was lost. Three of the officers were on shore and escaped. There are no remains of the wreck. The Wateree was thrown one third of a mile on shore and must be removed. Received dispatches from Rear-Admiral Turner on the subject and also from other officers.[1]

[1] This was the earthquake of August 13, 1868. The Wateree and the Fredonia were at Arica, Chili.

September 15, *Tuesday*. The election in Maine took place yesterday. The Radicals elect their tickets by increased majorities. Both parties put forth all their efforts, and the vote is the largest, probably, ever given in the State. The relative increase is about the same of the two parties. The result confirms my impression that Seymour's nomination is unfortunate and likely to prove disastrous. There was too much dexterity on the part of the managers in securing the nomination, to inspire confidence and make the election certain. It is not a selection to draw recruits, when recruits are essential to success, and yet such has been the policy in making a ticket at this time. There is no enthusiasm for Seymour on the part of those who vote for him; tens of thousands do it reluctantly, but it is the only alternative to defeat Radicalism. The Democrats in their party zeal and inconsiderate haste have thrown away, I fear, a glorious opportunity, and postponed their triumph for at least four years.

In 1864, when Stanton and Halleck were filled with terror and apprehension, they procured an appropriation of three hundred thousand dollars to place obstructions in the Potomac. Stanton was in constant terror, thought I was negligent, knew not how soon a Rebel steamer would come up the river and carry him and others off. As he got from Congress almost anything he wished, he found no difficulty in procuring this grant. He then appointed Colonel Alexander, an engineer, . . . to invent or devise some plan of obstruction. He proposed a chain, and had one prepared four hundred feet long with twenty-three anchors, and a large number of floats. This crude and worthless contrivance now lies just below Alexandria, at Fort Foote. General Humphreys has written a letter to the Secretary of War inviting coöperation of the Navy to test the Alexandrine Chain; says that enough of the appropriation is, he thinks, unexpended to defray naval expenditures. General Schofield forwards the paper to me with his approval and invitation.

I brought the subject up in Cabinet-meeting. Stated my objection to review and prosecute this matter now that the War was over and four years have elapsed, even if the scheme commended itself, but I thought it worthless, and to go on with it, a waste. Schofield thought we should prepare for war, and not be taken at disadvantage as was the case in 1861, and as this device had been commenced, it had better be completed. I advised that we should stop where we were, save our money to pay our debts, and wait for better days, trusting to our ironclads and torpedoes rather than to Alexander's contrivance. His traps could remain where they were till our needs were less pressing. He admitted the times were not propitious and finally admitted that the subject had perhaps better be postponed.

September 16, *Wednesday.* Some months since, Mr. Seward said Kilpatrick, Minister to Chili, had applied for leave to come home for three months. I remarked that he wanted to be here to electioneer in the coming election. Seward replied not, that he vouched for that, would guarantee he would not. We were both earnest. I told him I should remember his guaranty. I see by the papers Kilpatrick arrived on Monday and made an electioneering speech last evening in New York.

Senator Morgan and Representative Schenck, both chairmen of Radical Congressional Committees, have issued a call for Congress to convene — meet in extra session — and do nothing. These gentlemen were designated by the Radicals in Congress as an authority to assemble Congress on the 21st inst., if they judged proper, or, in plain words, if the interest of the Radical Party in their opinion required it. The Committee say, virtually, in their call, that the public interest does not require it, for they advise an immediate adjournment, after the members shall have assembled, without transacting any business. This is a specimen of Radical statesmanship and Radical regard for the Constitution. That instrument devolves

on the President the duty of calling extra sessions when
the public exigencies require it. This is a device to defeat
that provision and executive authority altogether, and
to have an extra session if the party desires it.

September 17, *Thursday*. The returns from Maine give
a very decided victory to the Radicals. The Democrats
have, it is true, greatly increased their vote, but so have
the Radicals also. All their Members of Congress are
elected. The Democrats failed to get one, and in the legislature they have a less number than last year. This does
not surprise me so much as it grieves me. I am not so
familiar with the public pulse as formerly, but in my view
the prospect of success for the Democratic ticket in November is very remote. Great stress is laid on the central belt of States, from the Delaware to the Mississippi.
I confess to very little confidence in either of them. I
hope, however, I am mistaken.

September 18, *Friday*. Seward read a long document
to-day on the transfer of the Oneota and Catawba, in
which he is careful to embody the report of a partisan
Congressional Committee, calumniating the Navy Department and misrepresenting the facts in relation to the
sale of these vessels. It was wholly erroneous, as I told
him, but nevertheless characteristic. He concludes with
permission for the owners to have a clearance, provided
they will give a bond that the vesssls shall *never* be used
against a government with which the United States are
at peace. This I suggested was absurd.

Mr. Evarts was at the Cabinet to-day. I have not seen
him since July. He was here, however, a week or more in
August when I was absent. All were present but Browning. The subject of the adjourned and party-called extra
session of Congress was discussed and some of the embarrassments likely to result therefrom. These the Radicals have not thought of. Should there be a quorum

present and an immediate adjournment, it may be necessary for the President to call an extra session at once.

The Pacific Railroad swindle was again on the tapis. Villainy and plunder are the great purpose of some of the Radical legislators. Members of Congress are very corrupt.

September 19, *Saturday.* I am apprehensive that the Democrats and conservatives are not managing in all respects wisely. They began wrong in selecting their candidate. He will, however, get the strict Democratic Party vote, but he will not draw one single recruit from the other side, and the War Democrats are indifferent or have very little zeal. Many calm, considerate, conservative men will vote for Seymour, but with no earnest enthusiasm, while many who would cheerfully and earnestly have supported a War Democrat, or a Republican of Democratic antecedents, will not vote for him. Most of this class will, I fear, vote on the other side.

In caucuses and conventions, the noisy, violent, unthinking enthusiasts — the positive men — usually carry the day over the really wise, moderate, and sagacious. The New York Convention was composed of materials that would not tolerate a fair man like Hancock, or Doolittle, or even Hendricks. Pendleton, cunningly led on by Tammany for a diversion, not a nomination, was the strongest in the convention, but the weakest of all before the country.

One of the serious errors in Maine was that of calling Pendleton there to open the campaign. He made not a single convert, cooled good men by his false financial theories, and his going into that field at the beginning of the contest roused the whole Radical element, and all their energies were expended to make their victory decisive and complete.

September 21, *Monday.* Governor Swann came over

to-day from Annapolis at the instigation of Vice-Admiral
Porter to get a change of orders for two more officers. By
regulation, one third of the officers go out annually. On
Porter's personal application, and assignment of reasons
which might perhaps suffice to make their cases exceptional, two officers, Phythian and Matthews, will remain.
He now urges that Luce and Sicard may also have their
orders changed.

It is wrong in Porter to give me this embarrassment.
Not to grant his farther application will be assumed by him
offensive in all probability; to grant it will be violating a
sound rule which should be rigidly adhered to. The officers
themselves are in league with Porter in this matter. A
clique has been growing up at Annapolis under his auspices
which should be broken up. Besides, the best interest of the
Academy and the service require triennial changes.

Governor Swann, sent here by Porter, went first to the
President on this subject and was referred to me. He was
very persistent and has a good deal of address and management. Made the application a personal favor to himself, as well as to Porter, and of great moment to the
Academy. But I must do my duty.

Montgomery Blair, who now devotes his time to electioneering almost exclusively, and who has honesty and
good sense, assures me that the Democrats will carry Indiana and Ohio at the October election, and he is also very
confident of Pennsylvania. I hope he may not be mistaken,
yet I candidly confess I have no confidence of such a result
in either State. That should be the case, but the people
yield passively to party discipline and to a surprising
extent seem indifferent to the welfare of the government,
and, stranger still, they submit with almost abject subserviency to onerous taxation. What but the madness and
blunders of party could have produced such a result as the
late election in Maine? May we not expect like obtuseness
in the Middle States? There is no love for Grant; there is
positive dislike of Seymour.

There was a session of Congress pursuant to the summons of the chairmen of two Radical Party Committees, who stated in their call that nothing must be done, and that, therefore, the Members must convene and do it. I have seen but brief report, but the programme seems to have been carried out. What a burlesque on government! The two or three Democratic Representatives who were present appear to have been bewildered or stupefied, and before recovering themselves a motion to adjourn was made and carried without a test vote or roll call to show that a quorum was or was not present.

September 22, Tuesday. Judge Mason of Annapolis, one of the most sensible and best minds in Maryland, called on me and stated some facts in relation to the intrigues of Vice-Admiral Porter and his partisan conduct. Among other things he mentioned that when General Grant went to Annapolis, a few days after he was nominated at Chicago, Porter fired salutes and made great demonstrations. For two days there was polishing and great exultation. Until about the time of the impeachment movement, Porter had been an open friend, and frank but not partisan supporter of the Administration. But when impeachment was decided upon, Porter became suddenly an intense partisan, scandalizing and abusing the President. About that time impeachment was considered certain, and the arrangement, as understood, was that Wade, if President, should make Porter Secretary of the Navy. Then, if Grant was elected, Porter was to be continued. Before Grant was nominated, he had never been received with salutes at Annapolis, though he frequently visited the Academy.

All but Browning were present at the Cabinet-meeting. The Attorney-General mentioned the difficulties in relation to the appointment of District Attorney for the eastern district of Pennsylvania. Judge Cadwalader refuses to swear in or recognize O'Neal. Mr. Evarts says no other man can officiate.

McCulloch says he has been called upon by the Retrenchment Committee in relation to the appointment of supervisors. Told them Rollins named none but intense Radical partisans, while he wanted business men of integrity.

I inquired if he asked by what authority Congress passed a law giving the appointments virtually to one of his subordinates, — whether it was competent for Congress to say that the Assistant Secretary of State should nominate to the President for appointment ministers and consuls. He said he did not question them on those points, they are so reckless of the Constitution and its restraints and requirements. Evarts said that was one of the points in this question, whenever it comes up. I wish McCulloch had a little more nerve and push in those matters.

September 23, *Wednesday.* General John A. Dix, Minister to France, has written a rancorous and disreputable letter against Seymour and favoring the Radicals. While I might not differ with him essentially as to the qualities of Seymour, I cannot commend the sense or principles of Dix, as disclosed by this ebullition of spleen and disappointment. There were some who spoke of Dix as a candidate for President. He evidently thought more of it than others did, and yet not to secure a vote, or be named even, in the Convention had given him great vexation. This letter is represented as private, but no one is so simple as to believe the statement. Every line is intended for publication. But the letter destroys confidence in the sincerity of General Dix's political professions. As a Democratic State-Rights man he could not, if honest, wish success to the Radical Party, which wholly and entirely discards every principle of the Democracy and strikes down the rights of States, yet he commits himself unequivocally to the Radical candidate.

I long since distrusted General Dix's disinterestedness and sincerity. He has been an inveterate place-seeker. Silas Wright had regard for him, but he knew not Dix, who was obsequious and deferential to Wright. There were circumstances which occurred while Dix was in the Senate which caused me to hesitate and question his reliability. But he, like myself, was then a thorough party man and had the indorsement of Wright. The people would not elect Dix. He strove hard to be Governor of New York. He tried under Pierce to go to France, and if his own statements are to be relied on, — and I believe they are, — was cheated and deceived.

During the Rebellion he was a major-general, without ever entering the field, and while at Fortress Monroe, he cuddled and favored intercourse with the Rebels, not, I think, for his own personal pecuniary benefit, but under the influence of Ludlow, his aide, and an unscrupulous intimate. I do not think Dix pecuniarily dishonest, though he has appeared to me to be somewhat avaricious. But he fears and conforms to the opinions of men in power. His estimate of Seymour's character is pretty correct, but he was not called upon by any consideration for the display of petty spite and malignity which shows out in this letter, and which was intended to assist that party or combination of men who have been his political opponents and are now pursuing a policy inconsistent with all those cherished principles which he and I have supported in the past. I have always considered him intensely selfish.

In reading this uncalled-for and discreditable letter, — discreditable from the position and former course of the writer, — I am painfully impressed with the fact of the injudicious and unwise nomination of Seymour.

September 24, *Thursday.* The papers yesterday and to-day are filled with reports of a discussion and altercation in the Cabinet on the occasion of Seward's avowing his intention to support Grant and Colfax. McCulloch and myself are represented as declaring ourselves for Seymour, etc., etc. There is no word of truth in the statement from beginning to end. The names of neither Grant nor Seymour were mentioned, nor was there any allusion to parties. I have little doubt that Seward originated the report. It is one of those little manœuvres which I dislike.

September 25, Friday. Robert T. Lincoln, son of the late President, was married last evening to Mary Harlan, daughter of Senator Harlan of Iowa. There were but few present. Bishop Simpson of the Methodist Church officiated. Young Lincoln has made my house his home when in Washington during the days of courtship. He and Edgar are intimate. Regard for his father made him always a welcome guest, and I also highly esteem and respect Robert himself and have done so from our first acquaintance in 1861, when he was here with his father at the inauguration. His deportment and character, then and always, impressed me favorably.

The Pacific Railroad was the chief topic to-day in the Cabinet, and changes in the direction, and a board of engineers as commissioners, were ordered. A few men, Members of Congress and others, are sadly plundering the country, I apprehend.

I do not admire the policy which Seward is pursuing in regard to our foreign relations, but it is useless to attempt to change it, or obtrude my opinions. He is allowed to run his course, but certainly he has strange notions, and, it appears, little idea of the effect of his proceedings.

LXIII

Dahlgren's Management of the Ordnance Bureau — The Political Outlook — Getting the Election Returns — Proposal to withdraw Seymour and substitute another Democratic Candidate for the Presidency — The Democratic Mistake and how it came about — The Governor of Arkansas asks for Arms — Troops to be sent to Memphis — Seward's Table of Treaties — Dinner of the New York Bar to Attorney-General Evarts — Grant's Spite against Members of the Cabinet — Minister Washburn in Paraguay — Minister Reverdy Johnson submits a Protocol on the Alabama Claims — Discussion of the Subject.

October 3, Saturday. The country is absorbed with politics and parties. More of the latter than the former. Speakers are overrunning the country with their hateful harangues and excitable trash. I read but few of the speeches. Those of the Radicals are manufactured, so far as I have seen them, of the same material. Hatred of the Rebels, revenge, the evils of reconciliation, the dangers to be apprehended if the whites of the South are not kept under, the certainty that they will, if permitted to enjoy their legitimate constitutional rights, control the government, — the Radicals will be deprived of power, — this is the stuff of which every Radical oration is made, interlarded sometimes with anecdotes. No allusion to the really great questions before the country, — the rights of man, the rights of the States, the grants and limitations of the Constitution.

Had the Democrats made a judicious nomination they would have enlisted the good sense and patriotism of the people and had an easy victory. As it is, they have given the Radicals every advantage and, of course, are likely to suffer a terrible defeat. At all events, things appear so to me. Yet cool and sagacious men, who are abroad among the people and have better opportunities than I can have, express the fullest confidence in a Democratic triumph.

Such ought to be the result. I hope they are right and my apprehensions groundless.

Since Seymour was nominated, the Radicals have succeeded in getting up some feeling for Grant. There was none before, for he is not a man to evoke enthusiasm or win respect. The Democrats have yet much to learn. Adversity has not softened, chastened, and corrected their arrogance and thirst for power, and they have endangered and probably sacrificed a good cause by not being more generous and forbearing. They have not learned to humble themselves in order to be exalted. Why they should, so many of them, have been willing to accept Chase, as to almost lose control, can be accounted for only in one way. The money interest was for him in New York, and principles gave way in that quarter to wealth. The Tammany leaders proposed to have no candidate in that State, — no choice, — and were taken at their word.

Blair tells me that Samuel Tilden wanted to be the candidate of the Democrats for President. It is hardly credible, and yet in that way, better than any other, can his conduct and that of the New York Democratic politicians be accounted for. He and they had professedly no candidate, — could name none, — were, while holding the reins, as meek in their professions as Uriah Heep, waiting for others to move, and similar silly pretensions were made when the country was in agony.

Evarts is absent, attending courts in New York, while great legal questions are pending and the opinion of the Attorney-General is required. We must wait his return and be held accountable for the delay.

Charles L. Woodbury, Peter Harvey, and others of Boston and its vicinity send me a long list of names of persons whom they wish to have appointed to places in the Boston Navy Yard. No disposition is made of the incumbents who are faithfully discharging their duties, — at least no complaint is made and these gentlemen prefer no charges against the men they, or I, would dismiss. They would have me incur the odium and they have no responsibility. If appointed, the men would thank them, not me; the men removed would blame me, not them. Both will be against me if I do my duty, which I will endeavor to discharge faithfully.

Kilpatrick is making a fool of himself, running all over the country making partisan speeches, to the great annoyance of Seward, who guaranteed he should take no part in the political contests. Yesterday he read a letter from K. that was as supercilious as egotistical, flippantly snapping his finger at the Secretary of State and defying him. I thought Seward desired that some of us should press a revocation of his leave of absence, but I was not disposed to gratify him after I had cautioned him of K.'s proper orders before leave was given.

Dahlgren is trying to manage the Ordnance Bureau without responsibility. In his selfish nature he would evade all responsibility whatever. He wants, however, undue credit. In everything he does he has Dahlgren and Dahlgren's interest in view. He is not a favorite with the officers of the Navy, who think, and not without reason, that he has been favored. He covets more favor, however, and that accounts for his anxiety to please all and to offend none. The public money flows freely where he is, — not that he would appropriate it to himself; he is too proud to be dishonest in that way, though he loves money exceedingly. But after great kindness to him in many ways, he would not hesitate to skulk from responsibility which honestly belongs to him and throw it upon me.

Horatio Ames has a large claim for guns which have been rejected, and has besieged the Department for years in regard to them, — first belying and misrepresenting it, hounding Members of Congress and others for two years to get a contract, and at length getting an order from Mr. Lincoln; second, the guns not passing inspection, he has for three years been importuning for pay. Five years have been given to the lobby, — two to get an order, three to get

pay. I have no doubt he has expended a large amount of
money in making the guns, and he doubtless thought he was
doing good service to the country and himself. Under
these circumstances, he has an equitable claim, perhaps,
on the Government. But Congress is the branch of government which can grant relief. I have so told him for two
years, and he finally went to that body. In the mean
time a change has taken place in the Ordnance Bureau.
Dahlgren has been placed at the head, and Ames appeals
to him to reopen the case. Oakes Ames, his brother, is very
rich and a Member of Congress, with a large circle of influential Members in his interest. Dahlgren brings all of
Ames' papers to me. I have stated to him, and he knows,
that the case has been passed upon, — decided, — and
unless he is satisfied or thinks his predecessor's decision is
wrong, or that there is testimony not previously submitted,
it should not be reopened. But he equivocates, and I at
length indorsed on one of the documents, returning it, that
the Department had disposed of it unless he recommended
opening it or there was new evidence. He takes advantage
of this and "recommends" a board to examine all the
papers, etc., etc. I replied that I could not in that way
relieve him of his legitimate duties, etc., etc.

October 10, *Saturday*. Dahlgren sends me another letter,
changing his position, — wants six guns examined and
tested, etc., etc. Was compelled to write him a pretty
pointed letter. I am not disposed to be used, or made an
instrument, to relieve him of responsibility or to gratify
his resentments. He is hostile to Wise, whom he succeeds
in the Bureau, — not without reason, perhaps, for Wise
has secretly reflected on Dahlgren's services. There is no
love lost between them. But I am not to be made a partisan of either.

It has been clearly Dahlgren's wish to have a board
criticize and review Wise's acts in order to detect some
error or mistake. This would humble Wise without Dahl-

gren's implicating himself, though it would be his work. But while I have no exalted opinion of Wise, I shall not intentionally be an instrument in the hands of any man to treat him unfairly.

Mr. Solicitor Bolles has been making pert decisions in regard to punishments under court-martial law; says they may sentence to death for any offense. Sent the case to the Attorney-General, who gives an opinion sustaining the Solicitor; but Evarts evidently did not prepare the opinion nor examine the case. He cites the opinion of Attorney-Generals Black and Bates to sustain him, both of whom gave opinions before the law of 1862 was enacted.

Secretary Browning attended Cabinet-meeting last Tuesday for the first time in several weeks. The Pacific Railroad matters were brought forward by him on Tuesday and yesterday. It is, I apprehend, a giant swindle.

There is much gossip in relation to a projected marriage between Secretary Seward and a Miss Risley. He is in his sixty-eighth year and she in her twenty-eighth. I give the rumor no credit. Yet his conduct is calculated to make gossip. For the last six weeks he has passed my house daily to visit her, is taking her out to ride, etc., etc. Says he is an old friend of the family.[1]

Had last Friday a frost, and for two or three days quite cool weather. Mrs. Welles and Edgar left on Thursday for a week's visit to Irvington.

Received results of court of inquiry relative to the loss of Wateree and Fredonia by the great earthquake at Arica. The conduct of the two commanders, Gillis [2] in leaving, and Doty [3] in remaining absent from, his ship, is reprehensible. No motives of courtesy or of humanity should have caused either to neglect the men and vessel intrusted to him. It was neither humane nor right to be absent at such a time from the post of duty.

[1] Mr. Seward afterwards adopted Miss Olive Risley as his daughter, and she and her sister accompanied him on his journey round the world in 1870 and 1871.

[2] Commander James H. Gillis. [3] T. W. Doty.

3

A letter from General Schofield to General Grant, congratulating him on his nomination and hoping for his election, is published. It was written last May and confirms my impression that Grant was consulted by Fessenden and Grimes and participated in making S. a Cabinet officer. Schofield, like Grant, is shrewd and in the civil service acts with a view to his own interest in all he does. This is the fact as regards both. They each have astuteness, a certain kind of ability. Schofield is much the best-informed of the two, but Grant has more obstinacy and self-will. It was natural enough for Schofield to ally himself to his superior in command. Most of the army officers would be apt to do it. There is not, however, much enthusiasm for Grant. He has not many warm personal friends. Sherman is quite devoted to him, — sincerely, I think, — others because he is the lucky man, in place, and the Democratic nomination renders Grant's election almost certain.

Both parties continue to speak with confidence of success, and have generally persuaded themselves into the belief that their opponents will be defeated. As for the candidates on the ticket, I have little love or regard for either. Blair is the most of a man on either ticket. . . . Seymour, though temperate, is insincere and weakly and selfishly ambitious; was opposed to the Government and sentiment of the country, was at heart with the Rebels. His nomination has given the Rebels a grand opportunity to ring and prolong the War changes, and will be likely to insure Democratic defeat, when victory was, by a fair, discreet, and judicious course, within their reach. It was not a time to nominate a Copperhead. Concession should have been made. Colfax is a small man of narrow views and limited capacity, superficial and light.

The election next Tuesday will probably be decisive of the Presidential election, provided all the States go for either party. If the Radicals succeed in this they will be apt to carry their point in November. I am inclined to think they will take all three, although the Democrats express strong faith in a triumph in all; but they are over-sanguine and too grasping. They might with Hancock have succeeded. I will not discourage any with my unbelief; but, really, I may to myself confess I have had no heart in this campaign since the nominations were made. This Saturday night, alone by myself, I make this jotting, not to prophesy, but to write down frankly my opinions. The elections will, I think, be adverse to the Democrats next Tuesday, and also in November. If so, a sad fate, I fear, awaits our country. Sectional hate will be established.

October 12, *Monday.* Admiral Dahlgren called this morning. Says he thought I desired him to take up and take action in Ames case. I asked him how he could suppose so when I had expressly told him I should not again take up the case if there were no new facts, or unless he should recommend it in consequence of some mistake, and even then I should take time to consider it. The truth is he wanted to rap Wise with other men's knuckles.

There is great excitement in Philadelphia in regard to the election and a threatened conflict of authority between the sheriff and mayor. The judges have been behaving scandalously. I shall not be surprised if there is riot and bloodshed.

Each party continues to express undoubted confidence, and as nothing can be gained by round assertion to-day which the result to-morrow will contradict, the sincerity of their opinion is not to be doubted. But while the Democrats have the best cause, they have sacrificed an opportunity, — mismanaged, — and they have not, I fear, just now, in consequence of mismanagement and too grasping a course, the largest numbers. The Democratic leaders have very skillfully knocked out their own brains, or my impressions are wrong.

October 13, *Tuesday.* Attorney-General Evarts was not

at the Cabinet. He has too much private professional business to do justice to his office. I wished much to see him on some matters.

John P. Hale, Seward's Minister to Spain, has acknowledged the new government. I asked if Hale was authorized to do this; Seward said he was. The Cabinet was not advised or consulted. We had some talk about Hale, when I expressed my opinion of him freely, — his unfitness for the place, and that he had little moral principle. Seward assented; said Hale had threatened him.

Edwards Pierrepont, one of Stanton's jockey lawyers, writes A. T. Stewart, inclosing, or tendering, $20,000 to assist in the election of General Grant, and Stewart duly acknowledges it. Such a donation is, of course, not disinterested or for an honest purpose. Pierrepont has been paid enormous fees by Stanton and Seward. He is a cunning and adroit lawyer, but not a true and trusty man. The Democrats of New York let themselves down when they made him one of the Sachems of Tammany. They are getting justly paid.

Pollard [1] applies for permission to have access to the Rebel archives in writing the life of Jeff Davis, whom he does not like. Schofield was disposed to deny him, and Seward also. I advised that he might, in company with a clerk, take or have taken copies under the supervision and with consent of the Secretary of War. Schofield said he was a prejudiced enemy of Jeff Davis and of the Union cause. I did not deny that, but was willing the Rebels should tell their own story. Thought Doctor Lieber an enthusiast and as much prejudiced as Pollard.

Went this evening to the White House to get early election returns, as usual, on the eve of the election in the three great central States. [2] Found McCulloch there. Only a single dispatch, and that of not much account, from

[1] Edward A. Pollard, author of *Life of Jefferson Davis, with the Secret History of the Southern Confederacy*, and other books on the War.
[2] Pennsylvania, Ohio, and Indiana.

Philadelphia, had been received. McCulloch was quite confident and hopeful. The President cheerful, but gave no opinion. He had asked me after Cabinet-meeting how things were going. I told him I would come over this evening and see.

Remained about an hour, but no dispatches came. Unlike former years. The coming men are the recipients of the news, — Seymour and Grant. I did not say this, but thought it, with something of sadness that human nature should show such qualities. About half-past nine Randall came in with a budget of confused returns, and some very good rumors. After a little time the President's Private Secretary came with returns less favorable but quite as much confused. McCulloch's whole look and tone changed and he soon left.

October 14, *Wednesday.* The election news is far from full and far from cheering. In Philadelphia the Democrats have been successful, and generally, in all the States, should judge they had given a larger vote than ever before. The probabilities are that Hendricks [1] has succeeded in Indiana, though it is not yet certain. General Dunn [2] tells me the counting of the votes is a slow process and cannot be completed in many places until this evening. It is admitted the Democrats have made gains of Representatives to Congress in all three States. It could hardly be otherwise, for the Radicals have almost all in the present Congress.

The President says this P.M. that he had no definite news, — nothing more than is in the papers. No one sends to him. Heretofore he has always had friendly telegrams giving results. He says Randall called just before I did and was feeling very blue, and when he left said he would tele-

[1] Thomas A. Hendricks, the Democratic candidate for Governor of Indiana. He was defeated by the Republican Governor, Conrad Baker, by a very small majority.

[2] General William McKee Dunn of Indiana, afterwards Judge-Advocate-General.

graph Tilden to get Seymour out of the way. It was pretty evident, the President said, that the present ticket could have little hope.

Although guarded in his remarks, I could perceive the President was not greatly displeased with the turn things were taking, and I think begins to have hopes that attention may yet be turned to himself. But his intimacy with and support of Seward forecloses, if nothing else would, any such movement. On that rock he split. It was Seward who contributed to the retention of Stanton; it was Seward who counseled him to submit and yield to Radical usurpation; and it was Seward who broke down his Administration; it was Seward who drove from him the people. The President is bold and firm when he has come to a decision, but is not always prompt in reaching it. The people would have stood by him against the usurping Congress, had he squarely met them at first and asserted the rights of the Executive and the Constitution.

October 15, *Thursday.* Colonel Johnson, formerly one of the editors or writers of the *Union*, called and had a long conversation. He was the friend and editor of Buchanan. Tells me some incidents in relation to the Kansas matters. He is now pretty intimate with President Johnson, as are now many of that class. In the main [Colonel] Johnson's influence is not bad on abstract political questions, for he has studied the Constitution and understands the situation of the government; is sounder and abler on these subjects than some men of higher reputation and distinction, but has been too long a lobbyist to have rigid ideas in pecuniary transactions. His object was, I think, to sound me on the subject of withdrawing Seymour and Blair and substituting other names. I gave him no light, — no encouragement or discouragement. In fact, as things are, I can say little about it. Seymour is doomed to defeat, and at this late day a rally for another can hardly be made, if attempted.

I did not conceal from [Colonel] Johnson my views, — my regret that Seymour was a candidate, that I had never yet seen a man who approved it, that he had been a weight and drag on a good cause. The country required at this time a different candidate to conciliate and reunite differences. He spoke of the popularity of the President and of the zeal which some felt for Chase, especially the banking interest. I avoided saying much as regarded the former, but, whatever might be the banking views, expressed surprise that Democrats should urge Chase. Why not take Sumner or Wade, whose position on living political questions — Reconstruction, negro suffrage, etc. — was much the same as his. There has been a good deal of talk through the day of throwing aside the ticket and taking Chase. The *New York World* and the *Intelligencer* favor it. Wall Street prompts the former, and the President does not dissuade the latter. But this talk is idle. It may not be difficult, since the late elections, to persuade Seymour to withdraw, but the substitution of Chase will not now make the ticket stronger. The talk about the President means nothing. There is no intention to make him the candidate, though there is a strong feeling in his favor among the masses who do not control organization. His name is used by a set as a bank-note for Chase and nothing else. I am sorry he listens to it.

October 16, *Friday*. It is pretty generally conceded that the Radicals have a majority — not large — in the three great central States. This may be considered decisive of the Presidential contest in November. We have not gained so many Members of Congress as I expected, and on the whole I am prepared for a signal Democratic defeat. I have had little hope that the Radicals would be defeated since Seymour was nominated, and am therefore not so much disappointed as others.

The Democratic managers have thought more of party than of country and are reaping their reward. In June there was every probability that the Radicals would be defeated. The country was against them, and there was no feeling or enthusiasm for Grant, who, whatever may be his military talents, has no civil capacity on political questions. There should have been great care to avoid making a War issue, unless a War candidate like Hancock was selected, for therein is Grant's strength. Without a military opponent Grant is formidable. The only hope of the Radicals was in an appeal to the prejudices on bygone questions of war, and the hatred which still lingers and is stimulated by them. With unaccountable stupidity, the Democrats took precisely the course which the Radicals wished them to. They stifled the military and patriotic sentiment for Hancock, and brought forward a Peace Democrat, a man whom the soldiers throughout the land disliked, whose sympathies were notoriously with the Secessionists, and who said and did some foolish things which the Radicals would, of course, seize, exaggerate, and amplify.

Pendleton, an equally pronounced Peace Democrat, was an early and persistent candidate for the office and thought to avoid the great absorbing and real issue — that of preserving the Constitution and the integrity of the Union — by bringing forward a weak and superficial financial scheme which captivated speculators and ignorant persons and men of a low moral standard. He did not maintain the true Democratic doctrine on the currency and money issue, but based his movements on two currencies, — one of paper and one of specie. True Democrats are hard-money men, and can favor no paper which is not convertible into money — coin — at the will of the holder. Paper is not money, but a promise to pay money. A broken promise by the Government is a breach of faith and disturber of confidence.

Seymour, possessed of no nerve, of no courage, a partisan politician of culture and talent, occupying a prominent position in New York, a whilom candidate of his party, seemed to hesitate, shrank from the contest, played fast and loose, but finally, under the influence of Wall Street, assented to and apparently became an advocate for the nomination of Chase, the antagonist of the Democratic party and Democratic principles on the great issues of Reconstruction and strict construction now before the country. Chase was, and still is, the champion of negro equality and favors the Radical laws of Reconstruction. He was, with his committee, the author of the legal-tender system and the father of national treasury banks. In no sense could he honestly be the candidate of the Democrats. Yet Seymour professedly, as did Belmont and company, earnestly favored his nomination.

Pendleton, however, opposed him and opposed Hendricks because, were they elected, it might interfere with his aspirations in the future. No conservative War Democrat would they permit to be the candidate, and when it became obvious to the Pendleton delegates in the New York Convention, and to the wild and turbulent crowd of outsiders who had been sent on from Cincinnati to control the convention, that Pendleton could not be nominated, they selected and nominated Seymour for the clearly manifest purpose of excluding any conservative Democrat, like Hancock, Doolittle, or even Hendricks.

It never entered the minds of these men that it was important to have a candidate who would draw and not repel recruits. They believed the Radical measures were so atrocious that they could elect whoever was nominated, and therefore, having the organization, passed by all War Democrats and nominated a Secession sympathizer. Thousands and tens of thousands who would have gone in for a fair, Union, conservative War Democrat would not, and will not, identify themselves with Seymour, whose course during the War for the Union was as offensive as that of the Radicals now.

A great opportunity has been thrown away, to the irreparable injury of the country. It does not seem possible that Seymour can be elected. The movement for Chase appears to be earnest; but the first step for his supporters is to get Seymour to decline. There are rumors that he has put his resignation in the hands of the National Democratic Committee. If this be so, which I doubt, the President and his friends will be promptly thrust aside and Chase pressed with energy. I am not in the secret of these operations, but hear much of them. If Seymour has resigned or should resign, Hancock or Doolittle should be substituted. Were either of these men at once earnestly and most decisively pressed, possibly something might be accomplished, but a change of front at this late day would be a pretty certain precursor of defeat. I have little faith in anything good being effected.

It would gratify me to see the national nominating convention system overthrown, as it would be were a candidate spontaneously taken up and elected.

I asked Randall, who was uneasy during the whole Cabinet session, what was being done. He said nothing decisive; that the Blairs would rather have Frank on the ticket and be defeated than have any other man elected. This is Seward all over, and I noticed that Seward seemed in excellent spirits.

He does not like Seymour or any Democrat, unless some one like Randall, an active, superficial, and super-serviceable schemer whom he can use. As Schofield had to remain after Cabinet session, Randall went round and said to the President he would come up this evening. I think Randall would, if he had the opportunity, go for the President. I asked who would be named, if Seymour declined. He said Chase, or the President. I asked him what was to be gained by electing Chase, or making him the standard-bearer. It staggered him. "Nothing," said he, "but I want to beat Grant." So do I.

October 17, *Saturday.* Under the circumstances the Democrats and conservatives have done well in the late elections. They have been cheated and wronged to some extent, I have no doubt. I am disappointed that the Democrats did not elect more Representatives. Had Hancock been on the ticket instead of Seymour, we should have carried Pennsylvania and Indiana and, I think, Ohio. As it is, I am satisfied the popular majority for the Radicals is not great in either State.

I think Seymour will not decline. The scheme did not take so easily as the Chase men anticipated, and the whole affair will blow over.

October 19, *Monday.* The Democratic committees and Seymour hold out against any change of ticket. There is some attempt to denounce Belmont, but it is feeble. There are conflicting rumors as regards Chase. I have no doubt he would willingly have lent his name, but since the scheme has failed he quite likely disapproves the attempt. The President, I am constrained to believe, has not been entirely indifferent in this matter. Second-rate men have been willing to please him by flattering assurances that the people wanted him and demanded the change in the ticket. He listened with pleasure to their assurances, if he did not encourage them.

October 20, *Tuesday.* Seward, Randall, and Evarts were absent from the Cabinet session. I know not if there is any political significance in this. Hunter says Seward has gone up the Hudson to see about some real estate of his son's. The papers say he is to meet Peter Cooper and others about the canal across the Isthmus. Randall professes to be engaged on some arrangement for the overland mail. Evarts has some important law-suits in New York. They are all of the same kidney.

Hunter submitted a telegram in cipher from Reverdy Johnson,[1] asking if the Alabama claims should be submitted to the arbitrament of the King of Prussia. McCulloch

[1] Appointed by President Johnson to succeed Charles Francis Adams as Minister to England.

would not trust him because of his family relations with
the Queen. I asked what was meant by the Alabama
claims, — whether it embraced all similar claims and the
other incidental questions. The President thought we
should have the whole proposition in all its parts before
us before deciding.

Pacific Railroad again occupied much attention. Congressional fraud and corruption are, I am satisfied, in this
immense swindle.

There were extensive frauds in the late election, — perhaps on both sides. The Radicals are steeped in them,
and, not yet content, there are villainous plans to cheat
Representatives clearly and fairly elected by the Democrats
out of their seats. Dawes and company will be ready to
help the fraud, as they have lent themselves to great
rascalities in the present Congress. They are destroying
public confidence in popular government.

October 23, Friday. At the Cabinet-meeting General
Schofield read a letter from the Governor of Arkansas,
expressing great apprehension of trouble from the people,
who are armed, and requesting that he might have United
States arms that are in the arsenal to put in the hands of
the militia. The militia are understood to be Radical partisans. General Schofield was very earnest in this matter;
said the opponents to the Governor were Rebels who retained their arms when Kirby Smith surrendered; that
they are organized, and unless something was done, the
loyal men would be overpowered and killed by the Ku-
Klux. After hearing him for some time and a few commonplace expressions of concern from others, I asked if the
Governor of Arkansas was afraid of the people of Arkansas,
— if General S. advised the arming of the Governor's
partisans against their opponents, the people of that State.
In other words, is popular government a failure in Arkansas?
General S. said that he and the military gentlemen generally had believed there was but one way to establish the

Reconstruction of the States South, and that was by martial law. I asked how long martial law should be continued. He said until those governments were able to sustain themselves. "Do you mean by that," I inquired, "until the black and the ignorant element controls the intelligent white population?" The General said he was not a politician nor intending to discuss the subject politically; he was speaking practically, how these governments were to be maintained. "And you come to the conclusion that force is requisite," said I. "There is," said he, "no other way to keep down the Rebels."

"Then," said McCulloch, "if I understand you, General S., the Reconstruction laws are a failure. The people in those States are incapable of self-government."

Browning said it was plain there must be a standing army to carry out the Radical policy, and it would have to be kept up through all time. All agreed that it was not best to let the Governor have the arms for his party.

Seward proposed sending United States troops to Arkansas. This Schofield thought would perhaps answer if we had the troops, but we had not got them. He urged that General Smith, commanding, might be authorized to issue arms if he thought it necessary.

After a long and earnest but not satisfactory discussion, the compromise of Seward was adopted by Schofield, who proposed to order the Twelfth Regiment, stationed here in Washington, to proceed to Memphis, and by the time they reached that point, it could be determined what disposition should be made of them.

I objected to any giving-out of arms, or moving military troops on the eve of an excited election. Claimed that from the showing there was no insurrection, nothing but the unreasonable apprehensions of a party leader who feared the people he professed to govern. He, with one of the bogus Senators, had undertaken a speculation in arms which had been destroyed, and he was in consequence very angry. We ought to keep clear of this party contest.

I could perceive that Schofield was dissatisfied with my
views, that Seward plumed himself on having suggested
a course that was to be adopted. The President did not
concur with Schofield nor fully with Seward, who, however,
had his way.

Our whole governmental system is being overturned by
the military and the Radicals. One after another of the
scalawag and carpet-bag governors is calling for arms and
troops to help him in the elections, and this Administration yields against its honest convictions on the suggestions of a trimmer. Of course the people of Arkansas are
to be borne down under the impression that the Federal
Government is against them. God knows when all this is
to end!

The President asked Browning, Randall, and myself to
stay after the Cabinet adjourned, and submitted a paper,
carefully and elaborately prepared, on government expenditures. It was a faithful exposition and, sent out at
the proper time, would have a good influence. I could
perceive that the President flattered himself it would be
effective and perhaps redound to his credit, perhaps bring
him forward as a candidate. He still has dreams, idle
dreams, that he may be elected. The people may be
with him, but party discipline and party management and
intrigue are all-powerful.

October 27, Tuesday. Horatio Seymour has gone West,
making speeches. He talks very well, but his speeches are
likely to be unavailing. Nevertheless the spirit of the
people who are opposed to Radicalism seems unbroken.
Defeat in the great States has not disheartened or wholly
discouraged them. A few men, anxious for office, have
fallen away, but not one honest man has wavered, so far
as I have heard, yet many will not vote for S.

General Schofield read a telegram from Colonel Campbell of his staff, who had been to Arkansas, stating that
it was not expedient to listen to or be governed by the

representations of the Governor. The tone of Schofield is much moderated.

There is disturbance in Louisiana, and the reconstructed Governor finds himself incompetent to discharge the duties of the executive. Radicalism is there an uneducated, unregulated, and disorganized faction. The negroes are wholly incapable of discharging police duties, and the Governor calls on General Rousseau to help him.

Seward exhibits a table of the number of treaties which have been negotiated, under each administration, and promises the President that he shall have brought forward more than any of his predecessors. I do not think so highly of the doings in this respect as others. There is more or less complication and entanglement in these treaties. Few and simple regulations are best; but Seward, not the most intelligent and discreet diplomatist, will continue by help of Weed and his colleagues to make a good flourish and be extolled for his marvelous labors.

October 30, *Friday.* Seward and Evarts are again absent. Likely both have gone home to vote. That is said and published. Evarts would be glad of such an excuse to be absent and attend to his immense private business. He has been at but one Cabinet-meeting for five weeks; important opinions are consequently postponed and action delayed.

November 17, *Tuesday.* Exhausted and fatigued with office labor during the day and with preparing my Annual Report and receiving company evenings, I have been unable to make note in this book for some time.

But events of interest have transpired, and I regret that I did not from day to day make at least a brief memorandum. There was excitement over the election, but acquiescence in the declared result. In New York and Philadelphia there was a great outcry of fraud by the Radicals, who as a party, now as in other days and under other names, were given to frauds. They denounce the vote of intelligent whites of foreign birth, while they illegally and by fraud polled hundreds of thousands of ignorant negro votes.

The defeat of Seymour did not surprise me. There has been mismanagement and weakness on the part of the Democratic leaders, if nothing worse. The Democratic capitalists in New York were, under New York management, committed for Chase, but with no sincerity on the part of the leaders, and when he was thrown out, the capitalists were indifferent or willing Grant should be elected. Pendleton and his friends have acted like disappointed partisans, very stupidly for themselves, very badly for the country, and as if they were afraid something might happen to hereafter defeat him.

In nominating Seymour the War issue was unavoidably raised and the Democrats have been busy in trying to make people believe Seymour to have been a good War man. They did not convince the voters nor believe their own assertions. Of course, amid shuffling issues and insincerity, all has been uphill work. There was no zeal for Grant until Seymour was nominated, — then men would have been busy had Hancock been his opponent. The Democrats have not only thrown away a great opportunity and injured their party, but done the country irreparable wrong.

Grant has returned to Washington after loitering away several months in Galena and the region roundabout since he was nominated. Colfax has been back here also. He and Wade have again adjourned Congress, — a mockery upon the Constitution and honest government.

A dinner is given by the New York Bar to Attorney-General Evarts this evening, to which all the Cabinet men were invited. I omitted writing the committee until Saturday evening. McCulloch and Randall did not write until yesterday. The others wrote a week ago, declining. The papers state that Grant, who is in New York, declines to attend if Secretaries McCulloch and Welles and Postmaster-General Randall are to be present. This announcement, publicly made, is from his factotum Adam Badeau, but by Grant's authority.

When Seward came into the council room this noon he spoke, before being seated, of his not attending the Attorney-General's dinner because if he went he should have kept away another man. I remarked that writing an equivocal letter answered every purpose and propitiated offended dignity that disliked truth. Seward gave me a singular look and satisfied me he felt the remark.

He said he went to New York last Thursday; that a very good friend who is usually at the depot told him that General Grant was occupying the Presidential car. He, S., said, "Very well, if he wants to see me, he can come here." Soon after his friend came to him with General Grant's compliments, inviting him into his car. "Another tribute," said I, "to the equivocal manner of answering a plain and simple question."

He proceeded to state the incidents, etc., of the journey. I judge that his presence was not particularly acceptable to Grant and that the intercourse was formal. This, however, did not greatly disturb Seward, who ostensibly went to New York to attend the funeral of Mrs. Blatchford and was glad of the opportunity to get into Grant's company.

He says he never has exchanged a word with Grant since the interview at the President's last February. This, I find, is the fact as regards all who were then present. In trying a refined and subtle game the General was exposed, and, in an issue between himself and the President, those of us who were present were called upon to state the facts, and General Grant, it seems, in the exercise of his new social and official position, undertakes to proscribe those who cannot sacrifice the truth for him.

The subject does not trouble me otherwise than, as a citizen, I regret the degradation of the highest office in the country. McCulloch said that had he been aware of any such revengeful feeling on the part of Grant, he would

3

certainly have gone to New York to have shut him off from
the dinner. I said I would not have gone across the room
to have either prevented or aided him in the matter. The
General of our armies and the President-elect might make
this exhibition of malignant spite against truth without
disturbing me in the least.

Mr. Seward had a large budget of letters and newspaper
slips relative to affairs in Paraguay and our late Minister
Washburn, who has been extremely troublesome ever since
he has been there or in that neighborhood. For some years
he has been the persistent friend of Lopez, and the Secretary of State aided him in his absurd claims of insisting on
having a national vessel to run the blockade of the allies,
in order to carry him back and forth.

I have remonstrated against maintaining a mission in
the interior of South America, among a half-savage people,
where there are no citizens of the United States, no commerce, no intercourse of any kind, where no other government sends a minister, and where we should have none.

Washburn sometime since resigned, and General Mc-
Mahon was appointed his successor. Mr. Seward said he
had but a single dispatch from Washburn, but the papers
are filled with his letters, — some of them very discreditable, — and his conduct appears to be reprehensible
throughout. Seward said he had a letter from Webb at
Rio, very well written, but Seward was careful not to read
it. He had prepared a singular letter to me, however,
which he did read, in which he proposed that the whole
affair shall be communicated to Admiral Davis, who is to
proceed with an adequate force to Paraguay and demand
redress.

I asked where McMahon, the representative of the
Government, was, that he was not intrusted with this duty;
why this responsibility was put on Davis, a naval officer.
I was willing he should be directed to consult, coöperate
with, and aid General McMahon, but the Admiral had no
"adequate force" to send up the river and make the de-

mand, even were it proper. Seward said he had great
confidence in Davis as a discreet man who would act pru-
dently, etc., etc. In all this I see Mephistopheles, and do
not mean to be bamboozled by him. The President and
Randall expressed great regard for McMahon.

November 18, *Wednesday.* In a brief interview with the
President I told him I thought it the proper duty of the
Minister we had sent to Paraguay to investigate and make
demands, if demands were to be made; that he might, and
perhaps should, consult with Admiral Davis, but I thought
it improper to impose the Minister's duties on the Admiral
and make him responsible. The President concurred and
wished me to advise with Seward. I remarked that we
differed; that I had for several years thought we needed no
minister at Paraguay, where we had no citizens, no commerce, etc.

I received late this P.M. from Secretary Seward the
letter which he read yesterday to the President and Cabinet relative to intrusting Admiral Davis to proceed with
an "adequate force" to Paraguay, demand redress, etc. I
drafted a rough letter but had not time to copy or complete.

November 19, *Thursday.* Sent my instructions to Admiral Davis, taking care to copy that part of Seward's
letter which advised the President that the Admiral should
proceed with an adequate force, etc., wishing he had such
force. I also wrote Seward that I thought it proper General
McMahon should be associated with the Admiral and
share the responsibility.

Every one seems disgusted with Grant's conditional
acceptance of an invitation to the Evarts dinner. None
of his friends attempt to defend him. The little man is
exhibiting his true traits. Very malignant, revengeful,
because exposed in his equivocation and falsehood. An
enemy of truth and of those who assert it, provided he is
thereby discomfited.

November 20, *Friday*. Told Evarts I was glad I had not kept him or any invited guest from his dinner. He says there was a great strife among the Radicals whether Grant should be allowed to attend; that some extreme Radicals got up a counter-dinner uptown to draw Grant off; that the conditional acceptance was intended to relieve Grant if any of us attended, a cunning device that failed. As none of us attended, there was no escape but for him to give his presence to the Evarts banquet.

Seward said he had received my letter in the Paraguay matter and would attend to my suggestions. Would instruct McMahon and request him to consult with Admiral Davis. Thought it very proper, etc. I asked him to send me a copy of his instructions. Said he would. Gave him again my opinion of Washburn and of his mission.

November 24, *Tuesday*. Seward came to Cabinet council this morning with a queer expression on his countenance. We two were the first arrivals. On exchanging salutations, he said he was sick, quite sick. I asked his malady. He said he had got the damnedest strange thing from Reverdy Johnson for a protocol. Others came in to whom he made similar communication. He submitted the document to the President and Cabinet with a lugubrious look which cannot be described. Intended to be sad and grieved, but with a lurking laugh. The Alabama claims are to be submitted to arbitration; four commissioners, two by each party; if not unanimous, some sovereign to be selected by the two governments as umpire, etc. The whole thing, he said, was wrong, contrary to instructions, must be sent back. The members were surprised and made inquiries into the points of difference. He did not make himself clear, but said he would prepare and submit a dispatch at the next Cabinet-meeting. I was more interested with the distressed looks of McCulloch and Browning than with the muddy exposition. They had evidently expected the Alabama claims were about adjusted. I re-

marked that I had not expected the English Government
would ever consent to a reference of those claims to a commission, that I had now little expectation the claims would
be paid, that the commission was closely locked up. Seward said he would have better terms. I asked if all claims
of either party since 1853 were submitted, including prizes
and captured property. Seward did not give me a direct
answer, and some incidental question from McCulloch
furnished him an opportunity to drop it.

When we left, McCulloch and myself came down together. He expressed his regret that there should be delay in this matter, for the country would be disappointed.
I told him I expected no settlement of those claims during
this administration, — certainly not in our favor.

November 25, Wednesday. Admiral Farragut and wife
arrived late last night and are stopping at our house.
They are both well and enjoy these excursions and their
friends. He is guileless, simple-hearted, and as sincere as
he is brave. Mrs. F. is devoted to him, proud of him, and
very social.

Received a note this morning early from the President,
who wished me to call on him. Found he was anxious about
the treaty. Wished my views. Said he desired to accept
and send in the treaty without fail, and he knew not why
this was not in good shape. I said that I thought Mr.
Seward had no disposition to hasten decision, that I had
never supposed him much in earnest in this matter, and
that as things are with us, he probably wished to prolong
the negotiation. The English had never admitted they
were responsible, and were so confident they would not be
held responsible that they sometime ago had consented
to arbitrament, but Mr. Seward had requested they
should also submit their governmental action. This they
had refused, and I had expected they always would; but
they had surrendered the point, though in a way that hedged
them in against any advantage to us. I told him I was not

sanguine we should get anything, whoever might be the negotiator. The President requested me to read the three articles aloud, and we commented on each. I remarked it was difficult to come to a conclusion, for Mr. Seward carefully abstained from presenting his points, and we knew enough of the English to be aware they did not intend to be overreached. I asked if Seward had been with him on this subject and frankly stated the case. He said he had, and would be in again with a rough draft, and have his dispatch fully prepared by Friday. "Then," said I, "we shall have the case in full. Let us wait."

November 26, Thursday. Spent the day at home socially with Admiral and Mrs. Farragut. The President and Mrs. Patterson dined with us, in company with the Admiral and Mrs. F. and Admiral and Mrs. Radford.

November 27, Friday. Mr. Seward read his letter of instructions to Reverdy Johnson. They were not approved by the President nor any one of the Cabinet. I had expected he would have the support of Mr. Evarts and thought probably he had consulted that gentleman, but from the discussion I infer neither was the fact.

I again inquired how much was covered, — whether claims for captures, destruction of property, prizes, etc., were to be permitted; if so a commission was not desirable. Mr. Evarts thought so too, and said our Alabama claims amounted to only about eight millions, while the English would probably demand a hundred millions from us. I thought the latter not improbable if naval prizes were included, but should be surprised if our claims were not largest. McCulloch asked Seward whether, if he could not get better terms, he would accept the protocol presented, but Seward avoided an explicit answer; was confident it would not reach that ultimatum; the English would give in.

The President thought it would be best to postpone a final decision on Seward's dispatch until Tuesday. This disturbed Seward, who said he wished to send off a cable dispatch this afternoon, and he should receive an answer in a week which he doubted not would be favorable.

Before the meeting closed, the President requested me to go with him into the library, when he asked me what had best be done. Said he wished the subject disposed of during his Administration or that the Senate should be responsible for the delay. I again expressed my doubts whether Mr. Seward was anxious for an immediate disposition; asked what we were to gain by this treaty, — what were the advantages. Told him I had no idea that Mr. Seward or Mr. Reverdy Johnson would overreach the English negotiators. As the subject is in the hands of Seward, he would be dissatisfied if overruled by others and his views set aside, and that, if prepared to conform to him, it would be as well to let him have an opportunity to try Reverdy Johnson farther. This seemed to relieve him, as I supposed it would. On our return to the council room he told Seward to send his telegram and get his answer if he could in a week.

November 28, *Saturday*. When at the President's to-day, relative to some Marine appointments, he reverted to the discussion yesterday. I asked him if he really understood Seward's object; why he did not press the matter of the Alabama claims upon the British Government himself, and compel it to admit the *rightfulness* of the claim; why refer the *principle* to a commission. The English never, in my opinion, would have submitted to arbitration the attack on Copenhagen. Our claim should not be classed with theirs.

November 30, *Monday*. The Attorney-General has given an opinion on the eight-hour law, and the payments under it, which is a specimen of attorneyship unsurpassed. If he is wiser after investigating the subject, he has imparted none of his wisdom to others.

LXIV

Report on the Pacific Railroad — The *New York Evening Post* on Vanderbilt and the Merrimac — The Alabama Claims — Congress assembles — Senator Trumbull makes an Unreasonable Request — The President's Annual Message and its Reception in Congress — Proposal to annex San Domingo — Attorney-General Evarts and the Law relating to Courts Martial — Grant's Probable Course as President — Discussion of the Finances of the Country — Fox's Conversation with Admiral Porter — Formal Acquisition of League Island for the New Navy Yard — Bowles of the *Springfield Republican* arrested at the Suit of Fisk — Relations of Grant with President Johnson and Members of the Cabinet — Cabinet Discussion of the Currency Question — The End of an Eventful Year.

December 1, Tuesday. Most of the session of the Cabinet was consumed with reading a long report of the committee to examine and report on the Pacific Railroad. They report the road well built in the main, but that it will require six and a half millions to put it in proper order so far as built, — Muddy Creek.[1]

December 2, Wednesday. Read final proof of my eighth and last Annual Report as Secretary of the Navy. It has been an irksome task. The composition of a report is more laborious than five times that quantity of ordinary writings, — so much detail, examination, comparison, etc., etc., with such a multitude of documents and statistics. But the work is done. Have had great assistance from Faxon.

The newspapers are in quite a ferment over the case of Dick Meade,[2] who is in the lunatic asylum. Great sympathy is expressed for him, none for his family. They, more than he, have suffered from his malady. I have for

[1] In the southwestern corner of Wyoming.
[2] Richard W. Meade, U.S.N., retired in 1867 as commodore, brother of General Meade.

some time been aware he had an unbalanced and erratic
mind. It is painful that his suffering wife and children
should be dragged before the public and misrepresented.

December 3, Thursday. Had a letter from G. V. Fox inclosing a slip cut from the *New York Evening Post*, giving
credit to Stanton and Vanderbilt and ignoring the Navy
Department in relation to the Merrimac when she came
out of Norfolk. The falsehoods are so palpable that it
would seem no one could be deceived by them. Nevertheless false impressions are made on the public mind. It
is represented that Stanton's scouts had brought him word
that the M. was coming down; that he sent for Vanderbilt,
who came on, went to Hampton Roads, asked the naval
commander if the M. was coming, etc., etc.

Stanton was not informed by any scouts, but I was; and
expected the Monitor would be on hand. Fox went to
Hampton Roads to meet her. Stanton was the most
frightened man that I ever saw. He telegraphed to Northern Governors and the Mayors of the principal cities his
alarm, imparted his fears to Mr. Lincoln and all who saw
and listened to him, created a panic, was vexed at my coolness. But all this was on the day *after* the Merrimac had
come down and sunk the Cumberland and Congress. He
had not sent for Vanderbilt, nor had he done anything
before, for he knew nothing, expected nothing. It was an
uncomfortable day for me, but I had no panic, and when
I heard, as I did by telegraph (which was in operation
from Fortress Monroe on that dark Sunday for the first
time), that the Monitor was there, I felt relieved and was
at comparative ease, while Stanton was flying about,
really very much scared, and mad because I was not.

He did telegraph, that night, I think, or the following
day, to Vanderbilt, for he had no faith in the Navy officers
nor me, nor any one else, but he knew Vanderbilt had big
steamers. Vanderbilt came here and was closeted with
Stanton in regard to naval and military defenses and the

security of Washington. They called on Mr. Lincoln, as he informed me. The bluster and management of Stanton made the panic seriously ridiculous. The steamer Vanderbilt and Vanderbilt himself went to Hampton Roads; the steamer remained there two months or more, out of abundant precaution, and so did the Baltic, and two or three other large and expensive steamers, but Mr. Vanderbilt's military services were earlier dispensed with. Stanton's scare cost the country more than half a million dollars. All his work and expenditure were *after* the Monitor had its fight, and had driven the Merrimac up Elizabeth River. But the lies and falsehoods sent out like this article in the *Post* make up history in these days.

December 4, Friday. Seward expressed great confidence to-day in the success of Reverdy Johnson with his plan. I asked what the plan was. "Does it," said I, "embrace claims of Englishmen for cotton and other property captured or destroyed during the War?" He replied emphatically, "No, it does not." "And, of course, this shuts off any claim for prizes condemned in our courts," said I. "Shuts off all," said he; "they do not come within the treaty."

I was in this matter explicit, and have given, I believe, the words which each of us used. He went on with some other remarks,—that nothing which could come within our admiralty or local jurisdiction was to be considered, and that they suffered like other belligerents when within enemy's limits. I hope his representations and understandings are all correct. It is a relief.

The Pacific Railroad folks are here in force. Do not like any checking-up on their subsidies. Browning submitted a statement from Mr. Williams, showing that the managers have received seventeen millions more than they have expended. Still they are distressed for more money. Mr. Evarts thinks they might be accommodated by the Government. Talks like an attorney for them.

December 5, *Saturday.* The combination of newspaper correspondents centred here in Washington is an unscrupulous and corrupt combination. There may be and there are a few exceptions. For some days past these fellows have been busy with schemes to beg, bluff, steal, bribe, cheat, and in any way get copies of public documents which are to accompany the President's Message. They almost lied McCulloch out of his senses. Schofield caved in without a struggle and surrendered. Says General Grant advised it, who unfortunately knows no better. I would have nothing to say or do with them in a matter so improper and disrespectful to the President, who by the Constitution communicates information to Congress. Of course extra pains have been taken to get hold of my Report. In to-day's *Tribune* there is published what is called a synopsis. It is, undoubtedly, made up from one sheet and no more, stolen from the printer's. This probably was procured by a bribe to some poor printer, who perjured himself, broke his faith, and if found out, would forfeit his place. Such is the morality of the *New York Tribune* and of newspaper correspondents.

The President informed me this P.M. that his Message was not fully completed. He is, he says, bothered with the Treasury statement of the public debt. The point which bothered him does not seem obscure to me, but I could not satisfy him.

December 7, *Monday.* Congress assembled. Both houses pretty full. The President informed them he would transmit his Message on Wednesday. I took to the President my Report and documents in duplicate for transmission. Randall was there with copies of his Report just completed, but had not the appendix. I was glad the President delayed his Message until Wednesday and so told him. Randall says the Members are very uneasy and intend to do but little.

December 8, Tuesday.   Senator Trumbull called this morning. We had about ten minutes' pleasant conversation, when he said he called principally in regard to an extension of leave to Midshipman Webster. He had written me yesterday and received a reply that it could not be granted. I explained the case. Twelve midshipmen came home on the Franklin. Immediately after the vessel arrived I directed that the midshipmen should have leave, and as the vessel did not go out of commission and was to be in port two months or over, six midshipmen should have one month's leave, and then they should relieve the other six, who should have like leave. Of course I could not give an extension of two weeks to one and deny it to the other eleven, unless there were special reasons which would make it an exceptional case. Mr. T. said there were no special reasons, but he had inquired and understood that I had sometimes extended leave. I told him not one of them had such extension. He said he did not mean these midshipmen, but extension was sometimes granted to officers. I said that was true in isolated and exceptional cases when the extension could be granted without injury or marked favoritism, and there was reasonable ground for gratifying it. "Why, then," inquired he, "cannot I have an extension for this boy?" "Because," I replied, "there are twelve on the same footing, and all must be treated alike; a leave to one would be unjust to eleven others, would cause discontent and work harm. The young men must have even-handed justice and be treated alike, and if so treated they would be satisfied, but special favor to any one would have a bad moral influence and impair the authority of the Department."

He manifested at once great ill-temper. Said he asked no favors of this Administration; he had, however, humiliated himself to request that a midshipman should have two weeks' leave of absence, as his vessel would not sail for a month or more, and it was refused. He would not have humiliated himself to ask it but for the fact

that the boy's mother had attended Mrs. T. in her last
sickness.

I said that was considerate and kind on his part towards
the lad, but surely he would not on that account wish me
to break in on the rule and government of the service
under the circumstances.

He grew more excited, said he did not want to break
regulations; he asked a favor for only one person; perhaps
the Department would want a favor one of these days.
He asked no odds. It was in his power to embarrass or
annoy the Navy Department as much as the Department
could annoy him. I told him he could hardly mean all that
he intimated; that we were not here to annoy but to assist
each other, and he ought not to exhibit the feeling he had;
that I, perhaps, had not been fortunate enough to make
the case fairly understood, and I would call Commodore
Jenkins, Chief of Bureau of Navigation, who would state
the facts and my course and principle of action.

I sent for Commodore J., who has immediate charge of
midshipmen, to whom Mr. T. presented the case a little
strong, and was informed almost in my words of the circumstances, and told in his (J.'s) opinion no one of the
boys ought to have an extension; that others were making
similar applications and were denied. Trumbull still continued unreasonable, and I saw expected to carry his point
by covert intimations and boisterous dissatisfaction. I
therefore with some emphasis assured him that I must do
my duty without favor, and if he did not, or would not,
see the impropriety of giving to one of twelve six weeks
and restrict the other eleven to four, I could not help it.
I must do right, and maintain regulations, without partiality or prejudice. He lowered his tone, but went off in
a dudgeon.

The President read, or rather Colonel Moore, his Secretary, read his Message to the Cabinet this P.M. It was in
print and I concluded had been seen by no one of the heads
of the Departments. The document will be distasteful to

the Radicals and some portions of it not acceptable to the Democrats. His views on Reconstruction are sound. On the subject of finance he is not successful, but inexcusably weak and erroneous. This scheme to remodel the Constitution is neither nice nor wise, striking down, as it does, some important features of the federal system. The language and tone of the document are good, but the determined stand which he continues to maintain on matters when he differs from Congress will be assailed.

Each head of a Department furnishes a synopsis of his Report which the President usually embodies or furnishes with sometimes a complimentary expression of his own. This has been the case with both Presidents Lincoln and Johnson on every occasion of an Annual Message. Seward has taken more than usual space this time. But little was said by any one when the reading was concluded. I think there was on the matter of finance and the Constitutional Amendments a feeling of disappointment and regret with all. When that portion which relates to the Navy was read, the President, referring to the exception taken to the reduction of interest from six to three per cent on the naval pension fund, said, "Congress has set the example, declared what the interest ought to be on the public debt." McCulloch said three per cent would pay the Navy pensions. I remarked it was bad faith and unjustifiable.

Mr. Browning, after a little time, got up and came round to the President, congratulating him on the ability of the Message; said he heartily approved every word of the first part of the paper, but that he did not indorse the propositions to amend the Constitution. No other member gave expression to his opinion. We could hardly do it uninvited, and the President asked no criticism, could make no change, for the document is in print, and is to be presented to Congress to-morrow. I would not say to the President that I approved all the first part of the Message, though there is much that I do approve and commend. But I am opposed to repudiation in any form, or any tendency to bad faith towards public creditors or others. I unite with Browning in disapproving the proposed Constitutional Amendments.

The President is not a financier, does not consider his project a breach of faith, but a suggestion or plan to dispose of the debt. It is the plan essentially of Butler and others. But the President will be violently attacked on that part of his Message, which is assailable, because in that way his opponents can vent their spite for the wholesome lecture administered on Reconstruction.

December 9, Wednesday. As I anticipated, Congress ventilated its rage against the President. His Message, in its soundest portions, annoyed them. They felt his rebuke and knew they deserved it. Conness, who is innately vulgar; Cameron, who is an unconscionable party trickster; and Howe, cunning and shrewd but not profound or wise, had their sensibilities aroused. The President had no business to insult Congress by communicating his opinions. It was indecorous to the Senate, and they would not permit it to be read. So they adjourned in a huff.

The House permitted the Message to be read, and then denounced it as infamous, abominable, wicked. Schenck, the leader, was against printing, and others of about the same calibre ranted. They attacked most violently that part which suggests payment of the bonds not in conformity with the original understanding. It is the most weak and indefensible.

December 10, Thursday. The Senators have recovered their senses, and quietly submitted to the reading of the Message, after an exhibition of folly and weakness that would discredit a party caucus. All seemed ashamed. The House, however, prints only the legal number of the Message and documents, — no extras.

These displays of puerile anger by the legislative body are ridiculous. Men assuming to be statesmen, who are

Senators if not legislators, are led away by such fellows as Conness and Cameron. They must all hang together. It is really pitiful. Their inconsiderate spite will have the effect of insuring for the Message a pretty general reading.

December 11, Friday. There was little done by the Cabinet. Seward read a proposition to the effect that San Domingo wished to come under the protection of the United States. In the present condition of the country there can be little done. Radical partyism must have its insane, shallow run. The real interests of the country are neglected, and it would be unwise to attempt to consider the subject now, if ever. Neither San Domingo nor Africa, if annexed or admitted, would strengthen the Union.

Mr. Attorney-General Evarts has been engaged through the week in endeavoring to demonstrate the constitutionality of legal tenders, — that paper which is irredeemable in money, the equivalent of coin. When McCulloch expressed a wish that the Court would decide that only gold and silver were legal currency, — that irredeemable paper is not money, — Evarts said we had just got rid of civil disturbances, but we should be thrown into something worse if we did not sanction the right of the Government to issue paper money.

He evidently thinks that he and the Court can patch up a system better than the Constitution. A rigid adherence to the fundamental law would be temporarily an inconvenience and hardship, and therefore the wise lawyers must contrive to get round it. This man, like Seward and that class of politicians, has no political convictions, no fixed political principles. It is unfortunate for the country that there is such a preponderance of lawyers in our public councils. Their technical training and extensive, absorbing practice unfit them to be statesmen. They are ready to take either side of a case for a fee, and will labor as earnestly for the side which they know to be wrong as for the right. Their influence is often bad. They will, for party ends, warp and pervert the plainest provisions of the Constitution.

I have had for several weeks a perplexing case. A captain's clerk betrayed his principal, — treacherously exposed his correspondence to the King and authorities at Honolulu. The Solicitor charged him with unofficial-like conduct, of which he was convicted and sentenced to ten years' confinement at hard labor in the penitentiary. No man can be sent to the penitentiary by a naval court martial, except for a capital [sic] offense under the statute. No one ever has been. Of course it became necessary to set the sentence aside. The Solicitor had his professional pride touched, claimed the court had the right to sentence to the penitentiary, and requested that the opinion of the Attorney-General might be obtained. Although the case was clear, I acceded to his request. The opinion of the Attorney-General was asked; considerable time elapsed before the opinion was received, when, to my astonishment, it sustained the sentence. I called his attention to certain inconsistencies and fundamental points with which he was in conflict. He seemed embarrassed, said he would examine the subject thoroughly. I requested he should do it himself, for I told him the opinion which he gave me came from the Solicitor of the Navy Department through Assistant Attorney-General Ashton. He admitted Ashton prepared the opinion. I told him I had heard it before Ashton ever saw it.

I then added that the law was prepared under my own eye in the Navy Department; it was intended that none but for capital offenses should be sent to the penitentiary. After meditating for weeks, and pondering over the statutes, he writes me he is confirmed in his opinion, it is strengthened by my adverse suggestions, etc. All of which means that Ashton, Bolles, and himself have studied to make a plain case obscure or to pervert it.

To-day I put before him the military and naval laws, passed contemporaneously, one on the 16th, the other on

3

the 17th, of July, '62. He seemed, and was indeed, surprised. Said he was aware of no such law; that it was explicit; that his attention had never been called to it. Said I could dispose of the case by disapproving the sentence; that I had better do it. Now it is no plainer to me, nor to any fair-minded man, under the military law than under the naval law. The military were in the habit of sending soldiers to the penitentiary. The Navy never did. Congress, to put an end to the military practice, prohibited the sending any person to the penitentiary except for capital offenses, by any court martial. The law officers of the Government, it seems, knew not of the law, and put their heads together to make law, and to defeat the statutes. To do this they had no regard for personal rights, — were ready to make me instrumental in throwing a poor fellow into the penitentiary against law and usage. As a class, lawyers do not respect personal rights, are not statesmen or good administrative officers.

December 12, Saturday. The President is disappointed with the manner in which his Message is received. He did not expect Congress or the Radicals to be pleased with his reiteration of his views on the question of Reconstruction, but he had an idea that his financial suggestions would take with some of the Radicals. Not one, however, has yet stepped forward to defend him, and his friends strive to apologize and explain away his singular views.

Colonel Moore asked me my opinion of the Message. I told him it was, like all the President's documents, calm, deliberate, statesmanlike, but his friends would not unite on his financial propositions, nor his proposed Constitutional Amendments. The clamor of the stupid and ill-mannered dunderheads in Congress, and newspaper correspondents and partisans out of it, who denounced the Message as infamous, and denied his right to lecture Congress, or in plain words give an opinion against their party schemes, was absurd.

There are many, and some very whimsical, rumors and speculations concerning Grant's policy and Cabinet. As regards policy and measures, he has none. He can no more foreshadow, or anticipate, or design a course of political action than he can make a speech to a popular audience, or a plea of abatement, or a sermon on total depravity. Yet he has shrewdness and a certain amount of common sense, with avarice, selfishness, and ambition. Of the structure of the government, and a proper administration of its affairs, he is singularly and wonderfully ignorant.

For personal rights he has as little regard as for the Constitution, — cares nothing for either. He has sustained all the wicked and vicious legislation, so violative of the Constitution, of the rights of the States, and of individual rights, which disgraced the last and present Congress, and has really no idea that the Constitution is any more restraint upon him as President than as General. He may be taught better by his friends, may learn the civil duties of Chief Magistrate, may apprehend and comprehend the powers and limitations of the fundamental law; but he does not now understand them so well as the generality of his countrymen and is stupidly indifferent to them. Nevertheless, he is not destitute of judgment which, with a low order of common sense, enables him to get along by riding on the opinions of others and making them his own. Because he does not know the fundamental law or the statutes, it must not be supposed that he disregards them, unless they are troublesome.

. . . Horse-flesh has more charms for him than brains or intellect. He likes Bonner for his fast horses, not for his sharp transactions and business qualities. The race-course has more attractions for him than the Senate or the council room. He loves money, admires wealth, is fond of power and ready to use it remorselessly. . . . He does not intend to labor like a drudge in office, does not propose to study public affairs, has no taste for books or intellectual employment. If I mistake not, he designs to let his Cabinet perform each his own work, like department military commanders. He will approve or disapprove, listen when convenient, but leave investigation and almost entirely the decision to them. Appointment of his friends to office is the extent of his ideas of administrative duties. . . .

December 14. Had a little talk with Senator Hendricks this morning on naval matters and political affairs. He is sensible and judicious, one of the best and most useful Members of Congress.

Commodore Meade has been turned loose from the lunatic hospital by Judge Sutherland of New York. The press has been used to set him at liberty, and the court yielded. Meade is certainly crazy at times and ought long since to have been cared for. When arrested, he had five or six loaded pistols, and threatened the lives of several of his own family and others; among the latter, I understand was myself. He is, with all his bluster, a great coward, and therefore will scarcely harm any one, yet, should he kill, no punishment can be inflicted, for it would be proved that he is a lunatic.

The Radicals are not inclined to do much business this session. There is a disagreement among themselves, a want of confidence in each other, and they fear a split on almost any important measure that may be considered.

December 15, *Tuesday*. Seward says that within six weeks — probably less — after the 4th of March he intends to be in the City of Mexico; that he will not remain one day in office after the expiration of Mr. Johnson's term. He has, probably, an understanding with Romero, late Mexican Minister.

.   .   .   .

December 16, *Wednesday*. Admiral Dahlgren is too timid and selfish for his position. He will not, if he can help it, give an opinion on any subject involving the slightest responsibility, for fear he shall in some way compromise himself, yet he is covetous of all honors. He wishes the navy yard here. I should be willing to put him almost anywhere, were I to remain. As it is, will make no change. Rear-Admiral Bailey called last evening. He also wants the navy yard; has been intriguing for it through McCulloch, who is a family connection. Not being successful, now asks me to introduce him to the President. I understand his object. Told him there were others desirous of the place who never yet had a navy yard. But he is regardless of the rights of others when they conflict with his objects and wishes. He has been much favored and has little gratitude.

December 17, *Thursday*.

.   .   .   .

December 18, *Friday*. Browning read parts of reports on different railroads. The Government and people have been terribly swindled and plundered by schemers. Congress has been lavish in subsidies, grants, corporations to favorites, and all sorts of favors for party ends. These are some of the means by which the prerogatives and rights of the Executive have been crippled and the character of the government changed.

Seward read part of a memorandum concerning troubles in Corea and the project of a treaty with that country, which cannot at this time be effected. I said we were better without a treaty than with one; that the case of the General Sherman, which had been destroyed in the Ping-Yang River, called for no action by the Government. This whole subject has been investigated by the naval authorities on that station and reported upon. The object of Seward is, I perceive, the future. He avails himself of naval information to place on record a statement of the facts, as if the results of reports to him and of his investigation.

December 19, *Saturday*. There has been some discussion on the finances in Congress, and also in the newspapers. Almost the whole that I see is crude absurdity. Morton of Indiana has submitted propositions, and made a speech which exhibits some ingenuity and talent, but, if sincere, they evince little financial knowledge or ability. There are some clever things, of course.

I do not, I confess, read much of the shallow, silly trash that appears in the debates. There is not, so far as I can perceive, a single financial mind in Congress. Most of the editors are perfect blockheads on the subject. The more ignorant give us the most words.

Senator Doolittle is beginning to bestow attention on financial matters. He made some inquiries of me this evening. I told him I had given the subject very little thought for years. It has been painful for me to do so, from the time Chase commenced issuing irredeemable paper and making it a legal tender for debt. Where the crude, unwise, and stupid management of party schemers and speculators is to lead the country, God only knows. We have no fixed standard of value. Everything is uncertain. There is a redundant currency, all of irredeemable paper, and though Radical leaders may at any time increase it and make what is bad worse, there is no coin in circulation. In this, as in almost everything else, the country is drifting, and the government and all sound principles are likely to be wrecked. Morton is said to be fishing for the Treasury, but it would be a source of regret to see him appointed Secretary, yet I know not who Grant can select. There is talk of E. B. Washburne, who has no capacity for the place. He can — and so could any thick-headed numbskull — oppose appropriations without judgment or discrimination, but this affectation of economy from a notoriously mean man is no qualification for a financier.

The whole pack of Radicals are, as I expected they would be, fierce in their denunciations of the President for his suggestions, yet many of their leaders have made quite as exceptional propositions.

The President did not intend repudiation, although his financial scheme renders him liable to be so represented. I was sorry he made it. His scheme is virtually a plan to extinguish the public debt by paying the interest for sixteen years and a fraction. But the creditors are entitled to the principal.

If our financiers will bring around specie payments the debt can be reduced; loans at reduced rates could be negotiated to advantage. But there is no proposition yet made to effect the first, and until that is done we cannot expect to accomplish the other.

So long as the Government discredits its own paper, there will be no resumption of specie payments. The first step to be taken is to stop the issuing of any more fractional currency. Call it in ; burn it up. The vacuum will be supplied by specie, which will come when invited, treated respectfully and according to its worth. Let the second step be a prohibition against all paper money below five dollars. This might be gradual. Coin would take its place. Specie will come when demanded. Supply and demand in this, as in other matters, will regulate themselves.

These steps cannot be taken without an effort. Values are to be established and prices brought to a proper standard. They are now inflated. We are not to get a return to specie payments without some embarrassment. But the movement can be made, and carried much sooner and easier than is supposed. Senator Morton's plan of hoarding specie until 1871 is ridiculously absurd. Instead of hoarding in the vaults of the Treasury and the banks, let it go into the pockets of the people when demanded for ordinary business transactions. Then there will be a basis for resumption. The gold and silver would be retained in the country, for here the demand would be greatest, until there was a supply.

To discredit its own paper, compel it to be received as money and in payment of debt, and sell the specie which it collects is bad government. While the practice is pursued we cannot expect resumption. Our wise Congressmen think they can order resumption by law without any strain or pressure on the public, but they are careful to fix a distant day, and before it arrives they know and intend it shall be further postponed and abandoned. If they would forbear persecution, hate, and oppression of the South, let war cease when none but themselves make war, give us real peace instead of constant strife, develop the resources of the country, they will contribute to the restoration of confidence and a stable currency.

December 21, *Monday*. Fox, who was at my house last evening, says he had a long conversation with Admiral Porter yesterday. He says Porter is a seriously sick man; that, in regard to a place in the Cabinet, he has never had an intimation or word from Grant. It is his wish to have a board of admiralty on which he may have a place. Probably he is fishing for both positions, and will be satisfied, for a time at least, with either. Fox says he asked P. if he understood the object of Edmunds' proposition to exclude Army and Navy officers from civil positions. P. said it was aimed at Schofield. F. told him it was more direct at him (P.). It is as much at Grant as either. Porter tells Fox that C. F. Adams will be Secretary of State. This may be so, but P. knows nothing about it. Sumner is much disturbed with this rumor. The truth is Grant himself does not know; he has little knowledge of men, of public affairs, or of his approaching duties.

Reverdy Johnson is doing neither himself nor the country credit in England. By last accounts he was corresponding and dining with Laird. There is, in much of his conduct, and especially in this, a degree of servility that is disgusting. Laird ten years ago was professedly an intensified abolitionist, — could not use sugar or anything else that was the product of slave labor. But when the slaveholders attempted to break up the Union to serve slavery, Laird hastened to help them. To injure the Union he was reconciled to slavery, and to fill his pockets was ready to serve slave-owners.

December 22, Tuesday. The Mayor of Philadelphia, Morton McMichael, with a committee of the Council, made a formal call to present a title-deed of League Island. Some complimentary remarks were made by the Mayor, and a general conversation took place. There was an obvious desire on the part of the committee that the proceeding should be more formal than I cared for. It was an opportunity for reviewing and reciprocating compliments, for we had each earnestly and persistently labored to consummate the transfer and acceptance of this location for naval purposes. But while the Mayor was pleased to bestow upon me high commendation for my action, and I was willing to award to the Philadelphians proper acknowledgments for their munificent donation, I cared not to spend time or words on the subject. The place is eligible for naval purposes beyond any other locality that I know of, and in advising its acceptance I have been actuated only by a sense of duty, and yet for years I have been denounced and have received the most ungenerous abuse for faithfully discharging an honest duty. Professor Bache of the Coast Survey first called my attention to League Island. Congress, on my recommendation, voted to accept it, provided a board of officers deemed the situation available, but Senator Foster inserted a proviso that New London should be examined by the committee which the Secretary of the Navy might appoint. I selected a board of such officers as were available without prejudice or partiality, for the duty was plain and required no mental effort. But a majority of them were naval officers who felt disposed to oblige me, and, knowing I was from Connecticut and partial to New London, they made choice of that place, which was destitute of some of the required advantages that were sought, in preference to Philadelphia, which possessed them. They were, moreover, old-time men, with old notions that a naval station should be near the sea. The result has been a long and angry effort on the part of a few speculators in New London to substitute that place for League Island, or the Philadelphia Yard. I was slandered and defamed because, a citizen of Connecticut, I would not give in to their schemes, and in consequence of their opposition the acceptance of League Island was postponed for years.

Subsidies to Pacific Railroad were discussed in the Cabinet. Evarts was in their favor; Browning yields. The President, while doubting, has been seen, and the result is this monstrous concern controls all. I thrust in a doubt or two, but they were of no avail.

December 23, Wednesday. Sam Bowles, editor of the *Springfield Republican,* was arrested and confined a night in Ludlow Street Jail, New York, at the suit of Fisk,[1] one of the Wall Street adventurers, who is largely concerned in the Erie Railroad. The arrest and confinement was a sorry exhibition of petty spite on the part of Fisk that will injure him more than B. in the end, though the latter had been severe and cutting in his remarks. His paper is, however, more correct and more enlarged in its general scope and management than almost any of the party to which it belongs. A great outcry has been made by the whole press over his ill-treatment, which was scandalous enough, but most of those who are so indignant had no mercy or compassion for the hundreds who were seized and thrown into prison by Stanton and Baker,[2] or later by the satraps of the South.

December 24. A general clearing-out has taken place in anticipation of Merry Christmas. But few Members of Congress remain in the city, and many in the Departments have left.

A dispatch from Rear-Admiral Davis of the South

[1] James Fisk, Jr., better known as Jim Fisk.
[2] General Lafayette C. Baker, Chief of the Secret Service.

Atlantic Squadron gives but little additional information concerning Paraguay, but from what he says I infer he has no great apprehensions as regards Bliss and Masterman.[1] The papers announce the arrival of Webb and Washburn at New York, and we shall soon have fulminations and declarations from these worthies.

Seward has gone to Auburn with the British and French Ministers to spend Christmas. All his movements in these days are for political party effect. But his lifelong and devoted friend is reported a confirmed invalid, and he therefore cannot count on the assistance of Weed, which has been for him always potent and effective.

December 28, *Monday.* The papers announce that General Grant leaves Washington with his wife to spend the New Year's Day in Philadelphia; that he does this to avoid calling on the President on that day according to custom. He has never called on the President, nor exchanged a word with him since the deception which he practiced in the Stanton matter and his detection and exposure. I apprehend he has neither called on nor spoken to any of those who witnessed that occurrence; he has not with me. The President-elect proposes to fight truth; is mad that he was exposed. The correspondence between the President and General Grant ought never to have taken place. Certainly the President should not have permitted himself to be drawn into such an altercation, but having done it, we who were witnesses could not do otherwise than state the truth. I should not say that Grant had not spoken with any of the witnesses; Seward, who equivocated after having explicitly and unequivocally confirmed the President's statement, has debased and belittled himself to get in communication with Grant. The papers in Seward's interest speak of his being continued as

[1] Porter C. Bliss and George F. Masterman, United States citizens connected with the Legation at Asuncion, arrested and confined on the charge of being Brazilian spies.

Secretary of State under Grant. I do not believe it, or that any influence can be brought to make G. sincerely consider it. He never liked Seward and must despise his twistings and hesitancy to affirm what he had asserted and knew to be true. Seward and Weed may have flattered themselves with the idea that Grant could be persuaded to continue him.

Grant is malignant and revengeful, is wanting in generosity and magnanimity, for President Johnson showed him great favors and consideration. But for Seward, I question whether the two would have had their disagreement; Seward's temporizing policy and advice brought about misunderstanding, though unintentionally.

It has been surprising to me that Seward, whose views are so unlike President Johnson's, should nevertheless have been so potent and influential in many essential matters. Seward procured the retention of Stanton for more than a year after the President had determined to dismiss him, and he succeeded in bringing Evarts into the Cabinet, and thereby strengthened his position. The two combined are powerful, and, when acting together, they usually carry their points. Yet neither of these men has earnest convictions, — honest, fixed political opinions. They believe in expedients and believe they can best frame expedients. They trust to their own cunning rather than to right principle to effect a purpose. Both have ability. E. has the best legal mind and knowledge, yet he follows Seward, who has official standing and experience, — is a precedent and authority for E.

Stanbery called on me last Thursday. He is looking very well and expressed himself hopeful, though unable to see how the country is to be extricated from the evils and mismanagement in which we are involved.

December 29, *Tuesday.* Quite a discussion took place on the subject of the currency at the Cabinet-meeting. The President insisted, positively and with sincerity, that specie payment might be resumed to-morrow without difficulty or derangement, although believing that gold and silver, like other commodity, is regulated by demand and supply, provided there were no paper substitute. I could not assent to the feasibility of an immediate resumption without causing some embarrassment. It might be less, perhaps, than was generally believed, but whenever we did return to a specie standard there would be suffering and hardship. Fasting is essential to the restoration of health after a plethora. McCulloch came in while we were discussing the subject, and he and the President soon became engaged, the President laying down certain propositions which I did not perhaps fully comprehend, to the effect, if I understood him, that if twenty-five per cent of the greenbacks were redeemed at once, their place would be immediately supplied by gold. McCulloch controverted this, said the customs barely yielded sufficient coin to pay accruing interest and the requisitions of the State and Navy Departments. To resume at once, therefore, he declared an impossibility. The greenbacks and paper must be gradually retired, and had not Congress improperly interfered and prevented the withdrawal of the greenbacks, we should at this time have been near the point of resumption. The President insisted resumption could just as well take place now as if the withdrawal had gone on. Schofield protested it would be most unjust to the whole debtor class to resume without previous notice. I asked if injustice had not been already done the whole creditor class by cheapening the currency, by which they received really but seventy cents on the dollar. This view completely stumped Schofield, who evidently had thought and talked on only one side of the question.

This subject is one of absorbing interest, and its rightful solution is of the utmost importance. It must necessarily be attended with some hardships, but less, I apprehend, than is generally believed. The great body of the supporters of Grant are not hard-money men. They

belong mostly to the old Whig Party, and, while full of
expedients, have no sound or fixed principles on currency,
finance, or any other subject. If Grant has any views in
regard to currency or finance, they are not avowed or declared. I doubt if he has any, and should feel quite as well
satisfied to know that he had none as that he had, for he
may, provided he is well advised, fall into a correct train,
if not already committed to some one or more of the many
wild and vague theories that are pressed. If he has any
opinions on these subjects, my apprehensions are that his
notions are crude, and that from ignorant obstinacy he
will be likely to aggravate existing evils.

The country needs at this time a firm, intelligent, and
able Executive, and he should be sustained in wholesome
efforts by a decisive Congressional majority. A wise policy persistently adhered to is wanted. Our Members of Congress are so weak and uninformed themselves—such demagogues — that they will give way on the least pressure
of hard times, and fluctuate and surrender to any demand
for a change of policy, to obtain relief. If the Executive
and Congress yield to the cry of more paper money, give
up and sell the gold, and try a new path, it will be a vicious
one and there will be no hope. The standard, or measure
of value, must be maintained to insure stability and confidence.

December 30, *Wednesday*. There was, last (Tuesday)
evening, an interesting party of two or three hundred
young folks at the Presidential Mansion, called thither to
meet the grandchildren of the President in a social dance.
It was the President's birthday, he being sixty years old
this day. The gathering was irrespective of parties, and
all were joyous and festive. General Grant, the President-
elect, would not permit his children to attend this party
of innocent youths, manifesting therein his rancorous and
bitter personal and party animosity. Not much that is
good can be expected for the country from such a character.

December 31, *Thursday.* The closing hours of the year are stormy, with the prospect of an unpleasant day to-morrow. The year has been eventful, and there is much that is painful in the recollection. I speak of political and public affairs. There has been much to impair confidence in the intelligence and integrity of the mass of the people to govern themselves. Under the influence of passion and led on by bad men, they hastily plunge into war. Our Constitution, or frame of government, is wise and beneficent, if adhered to and respected. But it is notorious and incontrovertible that the Radical Congress, in the excess of party, have trampled the organic law under foot when party ends were to be subserved, have disregarded the fundamental law without hesitation or scruple, assaulted and broken down the distinctive departments of the government, and violated the reserved and indisputable rights of the States. In all this reckless wickedness they have been under party discipline, sustained by the people, and a majority of the next Congress is elected to support their vicious revolutionary proceedings. An amiable, forbearing, and honest President, striving to uphold the government, has been impeached in party hate, and barely escaped conviction. Representatives and Senators readily forswore themselves, became persecutors of the Chief Magistrate, conspired against him, and committed perjury in obedience to the dictates of party leaders who found him an obstruction to their revolutionary schemes. The President made errors, but they are venial, and he had done nothing to draw down upon him these assaults, except that he at first yielded too much to Radical demands, — hesitated and lost.

LXV

The President's New Year's Reception — Grant's Failure to call on the
President — The President decides not to attend Grant's Inauguration
— The Naval Surgeons seeking to be made Commodores — Death of
General Rousseau — The Tenure-of-Office Repeal Bill passes the House
— Seward concludes his Fifty-sixth Treaty — Evarts favors abandon-
ing Confiscation Proceedings — Senatorial Elections — The Alabama
Claims Treaty discussed in Cabinet — Fenton defeats Morgan for the
Republican Senatorial Nomination — Seward's Subserviency to Grant
— Senator Grimes introduces a Bill to reorganize the Navy.

January 1, 1869, *Friday*. A disagreeable, rainy day.
The ground covered with snow, save where the heavy
rain has melted and washed it away.

At a little before eleven went to the President's with
Mrs. Welles, my sons, and nieces. Found the house already filled with a miscellaneous crowd. The President
and family had not yet made their appearance. Secretary
Seward and Marshal Gooding had, as usual, got everything confused and without order or system. The President had said on Tuesday that the Cabinet should be there
a quarter before eleven, previous to the admission of any
others. Seward, fond of notoriety, of precedence and show,
secretly and without authority or consent invited the
foreign legations there in advance of us, thus, with a crowd
to look on, throwing everything into confusion. As soon
as the President returned to the Blue Room, Seward,
who had placed himself at the door to take precedence,
called aloud for Baron Gerolt, the Senior Minister. The
Baron, who better than Seward knew the proprieties of
the day, was not ready, and Seward continued to call aloud,
like a crier, for his appearance. His object was to lead in
his crowd of some fifty ministers and attendants in advance
of his Cabinet associates. I, with some others, passed him
still calling for the Baron. The room was already pretty

full, and in a few minutes was a jam of Cabinet Ministers, judges, foreign representatives, and a multitude who had smuggled themselves in under Seward's disarrangement.

After exchanging compliments with the President and his family and other officials and friends, we left and, from meridian until past 4 P.M., received calls. It is a tedious, wearisome time to remain so long standing, interchanging civilities, and yet is submitted to with pleasure, I believe, by most persons. Except as a matter of duty, I should prefer to be excused. But few ladies called, the weather was so inclement. Men of all parties and stations in life came, were courteous, and seemed gratified. It is our last official New Year's reception, and I so spoke of it freely.

January 2, Saturday. The weather is still unpleasant. Made a short business call on the President. He says General B. F. Butler called on him yesterday; Butler also called on me and I believe most of the Cabinet. It was impudent and vulgar to intrude himself on the President, the man whom he had vilified, slandered, and abused, for the President could not, if so disposed, treat him as he deserved. Butler undertakes to discriminate between the man and the President; says he has no controversy or difference with Andrew Johnson, and the Senate, wiser than himself, have acquitted the President of official misconduct with which Butler and his co-conspirators deliberately and maliciously charged him. The President, while conversing freely on Butler's call, was careful to express no opinion as to its propriety or otherwise. He says the visit was entirely unexpected, and was prompted as much by the absence of Grant as a desire to be courteous to him.

In running away to Philadelphia at this time in order to avoid the interchange of civilities customary among officials at this season, in restraining his children from the juvenile gathering on Tuesday evening, and in shunning and shrinking from the President, his family, and others, Grant

3

was only bringing out in bolder relief his infirmities and vulgar characteristics. His own letters and correspondence developed his want of sincerity and truth, though he affected to be offended that he had even been doubted in those qualities. If he had any cause to be offended with either the President or the gentlemen of the Cabinet, it was because they had not remained silent and suppressed the truth when he had equivocated and falsified what had taken place. It is the consciousness of unsuccessful guilt and detected error, as much, perhaps, as weak and unhappy traits of character, which excites his animosity. He is deficient in some of the nobler qualities of mind. . . . Ten years ago he was a porter . . . in a leather store; but for the War he would be there still.

We concurred as to his attributes and weakness. I suggested that with his narrow mind and intense malignity he might not consent to a public inauguration in our presence. The President said he had given that subject a thought or two, and it might be well for us all to go to the Capitol together and leave it together. I asked why we should be present at all. If the President-elect was so disrespectful and wanting in courtesy as not to comply with common customary civilities and call, as was his duty, on the Chief Magistrate whom he was to succeed, I did not feel disposed, and hoped he did not, to be a part of the train on the 4th of March. General Jackson declined to call on Mr. J. Q. Adams when he came to Washington in 1829, and Mr. Adams and his Cabinet very properly declined to attend the inauguration. The President said he was not aware of that fact. It was a precedent for us which he was glad to learn.

January 4, *Monday.* Mr. Hubbell[1] and Judge B——of Ohio called on me with an application from young B——, formerly a lieutenant in the Navy, backed by a number of prominent citizens of that State, asking to be reinstated

[1] Probably James R. Hubbell, Member of Congress from Ohio, 1865–67.

in the Navy. He had been dismissed nearly three years since for drunkenness and worthlessness, or rather had been retired. On a previous occasion he had been court-martialed, convicted, and sentenced to be placed at the foot of the list of lieutenants. Senator Sherman had called earlier in his behalf. The Judge appears to be a sensible man, is represented as standing high, and I was assured that the ex-lieutenant had reformed, that the whole Ohio delegation, of all parties, stood ready to sign papers in his behalf, that the President had been seen and was willing to nominate him, and all that was necessary to complete the business was for me to come into the arrangement.

It is painful to have these cases presented. There was, however, but one course for me to pursue, and I therefore informed the father and Hubbell that I could not support their views, — that there were no vacancies of lieutenant-commanders, etc. They asked if there were not in lieutenants, and, learning there was, he was willing to go to the foot of that grade. This I told them was derogatory and would be so considered by every right-minded officer.

After a pretty free conversation, they withdrew, but returned in half an hour with an indorsement on the application by the President, to the effect that he recommended the case favorably, and, if consistent with usage, would, if I sent over the name, forward the nomination to the Senate. I informed the gentlemen that this was embarrassing, but I could not make out a nomination without an explicit order; that I would see the President on the subject to-morrow, but I would frankly inform them I would not recommend it.

They were very earnest, again said the whole Ohio delegation would unite with them. I asked if the delegation, with perhaps one or two exceptions, knew any more of the young man than I did. Told them where there was no responsibility it was easy to give names. The delegation were friendly to the father and willing to oblige him without regard to the welfare of the service. That duty devolved on me, and, with feelings as kind and friendly as theirs, perhaps, there was on my part a duty to the service which I could not disregard, and I could not advise the appointment.

January 5, Tuesday.

. . . .

I had some talk with the President, as I promised, on B——'s case. He said he knew nothing of it, but had turned the parties over to me to dispose of.

We had some conversation respecting Grant and others. The President said he had turned over in his mind the subject of attending the inauguration since our talk the other day, and he thought we owed it to ourselves to take the ground that we could not, with proper self-respect, witness the inauguration of a man whom we knew to be untruthful, faithless, and false, — a dissembler, a deliberate deceiver, — who, in order to extricate himself from the difficulties in which he was involved by his equivocation and intrigues, had attempted to impugn the veracity of all of us. Whatever may be said by him, and whatever prejudices and misconceptions he may, for the time being, spread abroad, we, said the President, *know* him to be a liar, guilty of duplicity, false to his duty and his trust. Knowing these things, shall we debase ourselves by going near him, and thus assist in giving him a false character?

In connection with this he brought forward the published correspondence in relation to Reconstruction. Grant had sent in what appeared to be the whole correspondence, but last Saturday the President said he had obtained a letter written by Grant to Sheridan on the 4th of June, 1867, but which Grant had suppressed, in which he told Sheridan to do as he pleased in Louisiana and Texas without regard to the letter of the Attorney-General. That letter, the President said, relieved Sheridan of much of the odium of his action, justified him in his remark at St. Louis that he acted on the suggestions of Grant, and, had

he carried out Grant's wishes, he should have gone much
further than he did. This letter of the 24th of June Grant
had withheld to conceal his treachery and guilt; this
suppression itself was equivalent to a falsehood.

January 6, Wednesday. Mr. Hubbell called on me again
to-day with a communication headed by Senator Wade and
signed by all the Ohio delegation in behalf of B——, whom
they wished to be reinstated. This is all done without
knowing him. These men would, in sympathy, lend their
names to demoralize the whole service. I shall be glad when
relieved from such miserable legislative influences.

January 7, Thursday. The naval surgeons have for a
long period been laboring to be made commodores and to
have naval rank. It was known that, while I would give
the whole staff personal recognition, I have not favored the
schemes of the staff to take rank and title with the line.
I therefore have not been consulted in their late movements by either line or staff. As there was much controversy, I was glad to be excused by all of them. The line
officers have, many of them, exhibited a want of manly
frankness in the matter. They had not the moral courage to resist what they knew to be wrong. Admiral Farragut himself, in kindness of heart, has given them an
approving letter that conveyed more than he really intended, which was read on the floor of the House. Vice-
Admiral Porter, who is opposed to extending recognition
or even justice to the staff, I am told, gave them a favorable letter, but refused to have it made public. O the duplicity and moral cowardice of some of our heroes! He was
here yesterday, and I doubt not his object. It was not to
back up his letter, but the reverse.

The doctors were in high glee this morning and confident of success in the House, but after a short debate the
scheme was killed by a vote of two to one, and the whole
was laid on the table. The end is not yet.

January 8, Friday. A full Cabinet. Among matters presented, Seward had a long document in regard to St. Thomas which he proposed to send to the Senate. He said it was a statement of the facts. The President did not require it to be read. This I regretted, for there will be likely to be some misunderstanding. I think that in the present condition of affairs we want the money more than St. Thomas, and the purchase has been inconsiderately pushed by Seward, certainly for no present public necessity or purpose.

We received to-day intelligence of the death of General Rousseau at New Orleans. The Radicals, who forget all merit and all service in any man, however patriotic and deserving, and who have made war on R. and threatened to annihilate his office in order to get rid of him, because he was opposed to their wild notions, will now, perhaps, cease their opposition to him. He was brave and patriotic. In the early days of the War, had great and deserved influence in Kentucky, and rendered valuable service there and in the field. He was of the Presidential party in 1866 when we "swung round the circle," and the contrast between his presence and that of Grant—his lofty person and cheerful, joyous countenance beside the diminutive form and stolid face of Grant — was marked. The crowds, when the two were seen together, were disposed to give homage to Rousseau rather than to Grant, which sometimes mortified and annoyed the latter.

January 9, Saturday. The President to-day spoke of comparing our Reconstruction plans, which were printed on slips and were before the Cabinet in 1865, in April, — Stanton's programme, first ordered by President Lincoln, with my amendments. I had informed the President I still retained my copy.

In the afternoon, an hour or two later than this conversation, Garrett Davis[1] and myself, among other matters,

[1] Senator from Kentucky.

fell into conversation on the subject of the Reconstruction acts, — the version given by Stanton, etc., — when Davis, to whom I had related certain circumstances, expressed a strong desire that I would give the facts publicity. I doubted its expediency at this time, but he finally proposed with the President's consent to introduce a resolution calling for information in relation to the early Reconstruction proceedings.

January 11, *Monday.* Had another long interview with Hubbell and B—— relative to the reappointment of the latter to the Navy. They dwelt chiefly on the fact that they had got in their behalf all the Ohio delegation, of all parties. I told them I cared no more about the Ohio delegation than any other equal number of respectable gentlemen, unless they personally knew B—— and his case. They did not claim that more than two knew him, but Hubbell said B.'s father was a reputable man of great influence and it would benefit the President and his friends hereafter. Told him such considerations should have no influence.

Colvocoressis[1] also called. His case is hard, I think, but there is no remedy. Wanted to examine the record.

Congress, or the House, by a vote of 119 to 47 repealed the Civil-Tenure Bill to-day. This is a comment on Radical legislation, — the honesty, consistency, and regard for the Constitution of the Radical majority. To embarrass President Johnson and break down the Executive while being honestly administered by a man to whom they were opposed was the moving cause of their partisan, superficial legislation in that enactment. I shall be glad to see Congress return to its duty and the government reëstablished on right principles, but alas! I fear the latter can never again be restored.

January 12, *Tuesday.* Butler, who yesterday carried the

---

[1] George Musalas Colvocoressis, U.S.N., retired as captain in 1867.

repeal of the Tenure-of-Office Bill through the House, made his long-promised speech to-day in favor of paper money and against specie. In plain words a preference of false promises over truth. Irredeemable paper is a lie: gold is truth. He is a controlling spirit in this Congress and with the Radical party. He is strong-willed when clothed with power; energetic, cunning, unscrupulous, and consequently dangerous; potent for good sometimes, for evil often. There is very little true wisdom or good sense in the House on matters of currency or finance.

Seward had three or four treaties to send up to the Senate. He said, with a self-complacent air of triumph, that they completed the fifty-sixth which he had concluded, — about as many as had been made during the whole previous existence of the government. I could not resist remarking, "Entangling alliances! Our predecessors deemed it wise and prudent to have no more than were absolutely necessary." The remark vexed him.

Evarts brought forward the subject of confiscation, which certain robbers, Radical disunionists, are pressing. He thought the subject had been pursued far enough. Seward wished he would make out a schedule of the amount which would probably accrue to the Government. Schofield thought this would be prudent in view of assaults that might come from those who stood ready to attack such a movement. I said there had been enough of persecution, — let us now have peace. I wished the whole confiscating proceedings to cease, — to be abandoned. Browning and Randall concurred. So did McCulloch, but thought it well to guard against attacks. Schofield said if the whole matter of confiscation had been dropped two years ago all would have been well, and much irritation and animosity prevented, but as things were now situated, it would be best to let Congress take action on the subject, and decide what should be done. Evarts asked if that view had not gone far enough. Why was Congress to absorb and take to itself the executive branch of the government entirely?

Were we doing our duty in yielding everything? This
was a rebuke from the right quarter to a vicious policy.
I could not forbear giving my voice in approval. Seward
seemed puzzled. He abandoned his wish for a schedule.
Said it was a mere suggestion. The final unanimous conclusion was that the Attorney-General should abandon
his policy, and end the suits which had been commenced,
so far as it could be done in good faith. This stand by
Evarts has surprised and delighted me.

January 13, *Wednesday.* A great struggle is going on in
some of the States for Senator, — Maine, New York,
Pennsylvania, Indiana, Missouri, Wisconsin, and Minne-
sota. The Radicals have majorities in the legislatures of
all the States, but are divided among themselves, — not
on any principle, but desire for office. In Maine, Hamlin
and Morrill are contestants. The *Springfield Republican*
styles the former a dirty-shirt demagogue. Morrill, a man
of usually honest interests and intentions, debased himself,
— first in the matter of unseating Stockton, and afterwards in the impeachment villainy. In the Radical nominating caucus, Hamlin got 75 votes, Morrill 74, and there
was one blank. H., having one half the votes, claimed the
nomination; Morrill's friends resisted. Good men will be
glad to have both defeated. Fessenden, who for years has
been all-powerful in Maine and whose potential view would
have decided for either in past years, is said not to have
a friend in the legislature whom he can influence, and the
suspicion that he favors Morrill hurts that gentleman with
the Radicals.

In New York and Pennsylvania money enters largely into
the election, and the longest purse, if freely used, will probably win in the former. Cameron and the railroad interest
have already secured the nomination of John Scott, the attorney for the great central road, a man unknown beyond
the limits of his State. The railroad controls Pennsylvania, and Cameron has had the adroitness to secure it.

Here in Washington, as elsewhere, money, special privileges, luxury, and kindred vices bear sway, and in the current events of the times we have reëxhibited the decadence of the Republic of Rome and the degeneracy of her people. The press is terribly in fault, — is weak and wicked, often corrupt and ignorant. Flippant and ready writers who read novels and magazines, but who are destitute of reflection or profound thought, who have never studied the science of government, and who are deplorably ignorant of the structure of our own, are the editors and stipend correspondents who lead, or mislead, the people.

January 14, Thursday. General Butler's financial speech does not meet the approval of his own party so far as I can perceive. In making the speech he must have had an object, but not a good one. No one but a knave or a fool would take the position he does, and Butler is not a fool. There is, however, very little good sound sense on financial matters in Congress. Indeed, want of statesmanship, want of ability, want of enlightened legislation are daily more perceptible.

January 15, Friday. Seward and myself were a little in advance of others at the Cabinet-meeting. He told me he had got three treaties signed with Great Britain, and the press was not aware of the fact. One is relative to San Juan, one relates to naturalization or expatriation, one relates to the Alabama Claims and all claims on either side. I asked if the English were to present claims for loss of property by their people during our Civil War. He said yes. I said such a treaty, including prize captures and cotton, is in every point of view adverse to us. The balance of account will be against us; but why should we consent to submit to arbitrament at all the destruction of British property sent to assist the Rebels, or which was destroyed within Rebel lines? He said we could not have a treaty unless it included all claims on both sides. But why

permit, or admit, that such property captured on Rebel
vessels or in Rebel territory can be recognized as a claim,
— a matter of controversy? He asked if we did not claim
for the Alabama captures. I answered yes, but that was
a very different question. They had improperly interfered
against our Government, with which they had treaties and
were at peace, without cause, to our injury. We had done
no such wrong towards them. While, therefore, we had a
just and equitable claim, they had none. If they have consented to arbitrament on the question of British municipal law in permitting the Alabama to be built, fitted
out, and manned in England, they have done it to get an
advantage of us in the matter of sovereignty and other
particulars also.

When Seward a short time after stated in full Cabinet
he had made this arrangement, McCulloch said the English
would make a balance against us. He doubted, however,
if these matters would be adjusted in our day, — they
would pass down to another generation. Seward was annoyed, but said nothing. He looked at me as if he thought
McCulloch and I had had consultation on the subject,
which we had not, although we both took the same view.
Browning expressed himself gratified that the Alabama
claims were specifically mentioned, — a remark which
soothed Seward. No other member of Cabinet gave any
opinion; but the President said that, right or wrong, we
would try it. He and Seward have evidently had previous
consultations, and it may be that I have not right impressions of the terms and conditions.

Before we broke up, the President said to me he was so
importuned and pressed in B——'s case that he wished I
would send over a nomination and he would let the Senate
dispose of the matter. I told him it would be a singular
proceeding, and without precedent; besides the Senate had
the subject before it, the Naval Committee had sent to me
for the facts. He said he understood it had not got to the
Senate, and B——'s friends were very importunate. When

leaving, I inquired if I should send in B——'s name for a lieutenancy, or for his position among his former associates who were lieutenant-commanders. He said for lieutenant. Browning, who stood by, remarked that it was against law and usage. It is unpleasant and bad in every point of view that the President should be persuaded into such a proceeding. I ordered the nomination made out and sent when I reached the Department, and wrote a letter to the President that it was by special direction, but Faxon advised against sending it.

January 16, *Saturday.* Wrote a letter to Grimes and Naval Committee and sent documents and charts concerning Midway Islands in the Pacific Ocean.[1]

Stanton has written letters to Michigan for Chandler, and to New York for Morgan, to aid their elections. I can hardly suppose he can influence a vote in either State, — certainly not in New York. Chandler has been nominated, and will, of course, be elected. The Radicals at Albany hold their caucus to-night. The contest is narrowed down to Morgan and Fenton, with a general impression that M. will succeed. He has the most money, though F. is aided by M. O. Roberts, A. T. Stewart, and other capitalists.

January 18, *Monday.* Seward gave a party (dinner) on Saturday to which Grant was invited, and which he accepted. Thus ends the assumption that he would cut all those who convicted him of falsehood, and Seward has crawled abjectly to the man who for two months has not spoken to him. It is a pitiful exhibition of each. Grant

---

[1] Two small islands belonging to the Hawaiian group, but some fourteen hundred miles to the west-northwest of Honolulu. Secretary Welles in his Annual Report of July 1, 1868, had recommended the acquisition of the islands by the United States on account of a good harbor inclosed between them. They had recently been surveyed by order of the Department, and the harbor was named Welles Harbor. The Midway Islands now belong to the United States, having been acquired with the Hawaiian Islands in 1898. They are a station of the Philippine cable.

was convicted of an untruth; Seward was identified by letter, word, and thought with all who witnessed the interview, but equivocated, shuffled, and was false to his colleagues when put to the test. Grant, who professes to be, and doubtless is, offended because his veracity is impeached, shows his real regard for truth by associating and taking to himself this equivocal and faithless shuffler. Fudge on such pretenders!

At the caucus of the Radical members of the New York Legislature at Albany on Saturday evening, Fenton beat Morgan by ten majority, to the surprise of every one. This is the fruit of Morgan's intrigues and labors since he commenced his deceit two or three years since. I am not surprised at this inglorious termination, though disappointed at the result of Saturday night's caucus. Yet, reviewing the subject, now it is over, it is not marvelous.

The papers state that Morgan, who was waiting the result in a private house in Albany near by, on learning the fact that he was beaten, proceeded with all haste to the Delavan House and extended his congratulations to his successful opponent Fenton. This insincere exhibition of magnanimity is despicable. It is well to extinguish animosity, not to retain resentments, to honor the success of an honorable competitor, but there is none of this in this case. Morgan has said to me in past years that Fenton was treacherous, a liar, an intriguer, in whom no confidence could be placed. What sincerity was there in his congratulations to such a man, — one of whom he had such opinions? Fenton is what Morgan said of him. He is cunning, false, selfish, is no statesman, but a shrewd politician of a bad school, a trimmer, industrious and pressing.

Morgan is a preferable man, or was, but he has become sadly debased. No man ever had a better opportunity to obtain a high and honorable name, to have pursued a more quiet and useful career, to have in these days rendered a greater service, but he has labored to forfeit all, and has succeeded. He knew what was right, but did what was wrong, and he has got his reward. I am sorry that Fenton is elected, as he is, virtually, but am not sorry that Morgan is defeated.

Morgan's course on the Reconstruction measures, beginning with the Civil-Rights Bill, was unpatriotic, unwise, mistakenly selfish, partisan, and against his convictions of right. He knew better, for we then consulted. But his most disgraceful and reprehensible conduct was in the matter of impeachment. When I remember how wickedly he voted to admit improper testimony against the President, who had always treated him kindly and who had committed no public impeachable offense, and how he servilely, stolidly, and doggedly voted against admitting truth to be given in evidence which exculpated the President from false charges, I cannot regret that Morgan is defeated. No one who participated in the infamous conspiracy to impeach President Johnson ought ever to be trusted.

January 19, *Tuesday.* Mr. Seward read his letter to the Committee on Foreign Affairs of the Senate relative to the proposed consolidation of several missions in South America into one, opposing the movement. I inquired whether it would not be advisable to abolish the Paraguay Mission, or embody it with some other. That country or people has no minister or representative here; we have no residents there, except persons attached to the legation, nor have we any commercial intercourse with Paraguay. Seward thought it important, in order to prevent Brazil from becoming too formidable, that we should continue the mission, though we had no special interest there. I excepted to any such ulterior purpose or supervisorship, which tended to entangle and embroil us and already caused difficulty. No one made any remarks on either side of the question, for the reason, I presume, that they had given it but little attention and knew little or nothing on the subject. The matter was dropped.

A very sharp and ill-tempered letter from Bancroft to General Dix was read. Napoleon was annoyed by some remark said to have been made at a dinner in Berlin, when B. said that, in the event of a war between France and the North-German States, the United States would favor the Germans, for they had not forgotten the course of France towards us during the Rebellion. The French Minister complained to Dix, who thought B. had been misunderstood, or that, if not, the remarks were his personal opinions. But he communicated the complaint to Bancroft, and also wrote Secretary Seward. B. took fire and wrote a sharp letter to Dix, so personally offensive that the latter will scarcely have further intercourse with him.

McCulloch feels sore and disquieted with Seward for his sneaking subserviency to Grant. The latter had avoided all interviews with him, as well as with the President and the rest of us who had witnessed the last interview between the President and the General, until Seward humbled himself in order to get on speaking terms with the man whom he had declared, as he was, guilty of falsehood. Through the instrumentality of Evarts, Blatchford, Grinnell,[1] and others, Seward succeeded in procuring a recognition, and a consent, on the part of Grant, to dine with him. McCulloch considered it not only degrading in Seward, but discourteous and a breach of faith towards his colleagues, and wrong and insulting to the President in whose Cabinet he sat. I agreed with him fully.

Randall, who joined us, was full of disparaging remarks of Grant, whom he met at Seward's after dinner on Saturday, but who was churlish, reserved, and with whom he exchanged not a word. R. tried to palliate Seward's course; said S. told him he had always kept on speaking terms with Grant. This is not true, and I am not to be deceived by the pretense.

[1] Moses H. Grinnell, "merchant prince" of New York.

January 20, *Wednesday.* The President's first season's reception last evening was one of the pleasantest of these gatherings I have ever been at, and was generally attended by the officials of the Army, Navy, and Civil Service. Grant was not there, not was any one of his staff. Only a few of the opposition Members came. Some sense of shame restrains them.

January 21, *Thursday.* Attorney-General Evarts gave last evening a reception. It was extremely crowded. A multitude of Members of Congress were there who were not at the President's the preceding evening. I was present for a short time, but it was so uncomfortably close and crowded that I left early.

January 22, *Friday.* Our reception last evening was very pleasant, and the guests professed and seemed to be highly pleased. We have never permitted party differences to influence us in the invitations which we send out, but some of the carpet-baggers and scalawags we did not ask. Van Wyck, a New York Representative, was not invited, because, whatever his position, he is a base and untruthful man with whom I want no association, yet the fellow had the impudence to intrude himself. General Grant, having through his aide, Badeau, given public notice through the press that he would not attend a dinner given to Mr. Evarts in New York if I and certain others who witnessed his equivocation and humiliation when [he was] questioned by the President and he attempted to justify and apologize for his treachery, duplicity, and falsehood [were present], I would not permit myself to invite him, although he is President-elect, and although I am always disposed to treat with attention honorable and truthful public men in official stations, whatever may be their opinions. I should, as a matter of duty, extend to him the courtesies and civilities due to the President-elect, whatever might be my own opinions and convictions of him as a man and officer, but he has rendered it impossible. Conscious guilt and abased feeling have influenced him, and self-respect governs me. We are strangers henceforth.

Seward handed me to-day a memorandum in relation to the ironclad steamer Stonewall, sold to the Japanese for $400,000, of which they paid $300,000 at the time of transfer, and the State Department undertook to pay [sic] the remaining $100,000 through Van Valkenburg, the Minister. But a civil war prevailed in Japan when the vessel reached that country, and our Minister, sanctioned by the Secretary of State, forbade her delivery, and assumed to pay the expense of her detention. Seward now wished me to divert over $50,000 from the back pay which is due, to defray the expense which he and Van V. have incurred.

I told him I had no authority to make such diversion; that it was due and should be paid; the non-delivery of the steamer was not a naval act; we were in no way responsible for it, etc., etc. He wished me to take the memorandum and consider it. It is a specimen of a certain kind of management and maladministration of which I cannot be the willing victim. I doubt if the money will ever be paid to the Navy or covered into the Treasury.

January 23, Saturday. Had letters to-day from Rear-Admiral Davis of the South Atlantic Squadron relative to the difficulties with Paraguay, which he appears to have adjusted, and Bliss and Masterman, who were reported to have been tortured and murdered, have been delivered safe and sound on the deck of the Wasp. There has been a vast amount of empty indignation and ignorance exhibited by the press and the public men in this matter, and our Ministers, Webb and Washburn, have demonstrated unfitness for their position in regard to it, now as well as previously.

Called with my brother on the President this evening and had an hour's conversation on various matters. He

3

has sound and correct views, is honest and patriotic, but has not the tact, skill, and talent to wield the administrative power of the government to advantage in times like these, with a factious majority in Congress against him. The opposition, managed by wicked and unscrupulous conspirators, aided by fanatics, has grown up on sectional hate and become powerful, while the Administration, devoted to reconciliation and peace, has fallen away and become feeble.

January 26, Tuesday. I sent yesterday a letter to Seward returning a dispatch from Mr. Harvey, Minister to Lisbon. In the dispatch the Minister denounces naval officers for making purchases of Messrs. Abecassis, whom he vilifies as Jews, adventurers, tavern-keepers, etc. The monopoly of trade has been long previously enjoyed by certain American officials, who gave the trade to favored parties and received therefor a high commission. The brothers Abecassis made sales at less rates than those furnished by the officials, and hence their offense. It was first said the Abecassis could not sell coal at the rates charged without cheating or unless it was a stock owned by Rebels. Now, since we had so supplied ourselves from Abecassis, it is said that coal can be bought cheaper. The Minister has, patriotically or for some cause, taken upon himself the supervision of the naval officers, and is violent against the Jew interlopers who have disturbed old arrangements.

Admiral Farragut, Fleet Paymaster Bradford, Commodore Smith, and others speak highly of Abecassis; so do the Portuguese Minister and others.

I have little confidence in Harvey, who was a mercenary correspondent here prior to, and at the commencement of, the Rebellion, a tool of Seward's who gave notice to the Rebels of the expedition to Sumter, and had his reward in the mission to Lisbon. His animosity and personal feeling betray themselves in his letter, and show unusual interest in contracts for a Minister.

The President gave his first State dinner for the season. There were present the Cabinet Ministers and their families, with those Senators who voted against impeachment. Fessenden and Grimes were not present. The former attends no parties, and Grimes is not well. Nevertheless, it is probable other reasons may have influenced them. Although these two men voted against impeachment, they are both strong Radicals and unwilling to be identified in any manner with the President. It may injure them with their party. They seem not aware that they are already marked and for the time doomed men, or that the Radical organization, while it continues, will not recognize them or admit them to fellowship. These two Senators usually act in concert. Whether they would have declined a State dinner by the President-elect is a problem. Mr. Trumbull, who attended, left the table early, — long before the dinner was over. He had time to see who were his associate guests, and who were absent. After leaving the President's, Mrs. W., her sister, and M. C. went with me to the weekly reception of Sir Edward Thornton; his parties are pleasant and not overcrowded. Most of the foreign ministers were there with their families, Chief Justice Chase, etc.

January 27, Wednesday. Senator Grimes yesterday introduced a bill to reorganize the Navy. He did not consult me in regard to it, nor show me the bill before introducing it, as usage and courtesy would seem to require, especially if the bill comes from the Naval Committee. There are many things in this bill which I approve, and I am, on the whole, glad I was not consulted and have none of the responsibilities, and consequently ought to receive the blame of no one. Still I shall be censured by many who will feel aggrieved if the bill becomes a law, because they will very naturally conclude that, coming from the Naval Committee, I was consulted, — probably think I advised and prepared the bill. I had, when we were together at Portsmouth last summer, one or two conversations with

Grimes, and some of my views are, I perceive, embodied in the act he has introduced. But I had no explanation of it then, and some of his propositions I do not indorse.

January 28, Thursday. The correspondence in relation to Paraguay is published, or so much of it as Mr. Seward deemed proper. Some of Webb's rant is omitted. A few weeks since, our impetuous, heedless, almost senseless press was boisterous for war and fight. The Navy was declared to be too slow and indifferent because it did not bombard their cities and take possession of their harbors, nine hundred miles in the interior of South America.

January 29, Friday. Had last night our last public reception. It was largely attended by a pleasant company, irrespective of parties. The company, male and female, was select; civil, naval, and military officers with their families, and Members of Congress were present.

McCulloch wants us to send a naval vessel to Alaska to protect the seals from extermination. Our appropriations are so reduced by Congress that we have no supernumerary force to aid the revenue department in that quarter.

Seward said to-day that the Senate had confirmed a treaty with Mexico for adjusting claims with that country, which was the same, in words, with the Alabama Treaty. I asked if it involved the same principles, — whether we had a similar difficulty with Mexico as with England. S. did not thank me, I saw by his looks, for the inquiry. He said we had unrequited claims upon Mexico, which were left to commissions. But there were no national wrongs and a grievous injury inflicted or winked at by that Government, said I, no controversies involving questions of public law analogous to that we had against England. He said all disputed points involved questions of public law. I perceived he did not wish points raised, but he invited them. He says there is an authorized agent here from San

Domingo who wishes that country to be annexed to the United States, on whatever terms we please. One of the Japanese princes wishes to sell out his territory to any one who will buy it.

January 30, *Saturday.* Sent a letter to Senator Grimes in relation to defects in the appropriation bill. My intention has been not to urge corrections after the full and explicit statements in my reports and other documents, especially as the Committee on Appropriations have not, in their partisan spite, the courtesy to consult me. But Faxon thinks we had best keep ourselves right on the record, and there is regard for the service and my successor, whoever he may be, that ought not to suffer from the faults and follies of his hasty friends. It is a misfortune that a man so ignorant, so wanting in civility as well as intelligence as E. B. Washburne should be in the position he occupies.

Stockton has been elected to the Senate, while Morrill of Maine, whose vote unjustly displaced him, is defeated by Hamlin. While I am sorry that Hamlin is elected, I am not sorry that Morrill, for whom I have had special regard, is defeated. He and Morgan have, I am constrained to believe, voted against their convictions in the impeachment conspiracy and usurping measures of the Radicals, and they have each got their reward.

LXVI

Students of Georgetown College visit the President — John P. Hale as
Minister to Spain — General Schofield advocates consolidating the War
and Navy Departments — President Lincoln's Clemency towards the
Defeated South — Did Grant and Sherman act under Instructions from
him in making the Terms of the Surrender? — Senator Morrill of Ver-
mont compliments the Administration of the Navy Department —
Insurrection in Cuba — The Butler and Bingham Factions among the
Radicals — General Dix resigns as Minister to France — Hawley urged
for Grant's Cabinet — The Panama Canal Treaty — Grant's Nepotism
— Simeon Johnson and Coombs's Claim — Johnson's Ignorance of the
Duties of the Departments — Grant's Cabinet still in Doubt — The
Question of governing Alaska — The Course to be followed by President
Johnson and his Cabinet on Inauguration Day.

February 1, *Monday.* The students at the Roman Catholic college in Georgetown visited the President this morning with their instructors. By arrangement of Father
McGuire on Saturday, the Secretary of War and myself
were to be present. The President notified us a little before
eleven, and I went over, but the Secretary of War did not
come.

The young men appeared very well, and their speakers,
in a few brief remarks, well expressed, addressed the President, who replied at great length. Had his speech been but
one third the length, he would have acquitted himself with
credit. He dwelt on the Constitution, the importance of
limiting men in office, and of observing with scrupulous
fidelity the fundamental law. General Grant, President-
elect, I am told, declined to receive the young men.

February 2, *Tuesday.* The papers publish a letter of
John P. Hale, Minister to Spain, complaining of the Secretary of Legation, Perry, and attacking Seward, who, he
represents, is concerned in improper speculation with P.
He probably does S. injustice, but I could not forbear tell-

ing Seward that he deserved all the good things Hale might
say of him. Seward said he was unfortunate in some of his
appointments, — alluding to Hale and Nicolay,[1] Consul
at Paris, whom the President inclines to displace. I, without alluding to Nicolay, told him Hale was unfit for the
position of Minister, was undeserving of it; that during
the whole War, most of which time he was chairman of
the Naval Committee of the Senate, he had, as Seward well
knew, thwarted and opposed the Navy Department and
tried to cripple and embarrass my efforts; that this was so
palpable and so offensive that the Senate, without any request or motion from me, felt compelled to displace him;
that his State refused to reëlect him, although the legislature was overwhelmingly of the same party. In the face of
all this, he (S.) had appointed Hale to a first-class mission
abroad. I did not regret that he was manifesting his true
character towards the Secretary of State. Seward did not
deny, but admitted, that Hale was his selection. When the
appointment was made, he put it on Mr. Lincoln, but I
never doubted who was the author of that appointment.

February 3, *Wednesday.* The marriage of General Comstock to Bettie Blair, which had been on the tapis for some
time, took place to-day. Comstock is on the staff of General Grant; Bettie is the daughter of Montgomery, and
niece of General Frank Blair, Democratic candidate for
Vice-President. This brings the Blairs into court influence. Grant attended the wedding at church, and by some
blunder got into the same seat as Mrs. Patterson, the
President's daughter, and her husband Senator Patterson.
Mrs. Grant was at Commodore Lee's party, the uncle of
the bride. We met, but without recognition.

Boyer of Pennsylvania, who is on the Military Committee, tells me that General Schofield, Secretary of War,
was before the committee to-day and advised the consolidation of the War and Navy Departments under one head.

[1] John G. Nicolay, Lincoln's Private Secretary.

This is a natural sequence of late measures, — a repetition of history long since told. A simple government is a military department with one head; a republic is clumsy and troublesome. The Radical Congress, by usurpation, has undertaken to destroy the executive, one of the three constitutional departments of the government, by depriving the President of his rightful powers and to confer them by legislative enactment on the General of the armies. A Radical general was made Secretary of War. It is not strange that he should come to the conclusion that power should be consolidated, and that it should be vested in the military head, instead of the Constitutional Executive. My only surprise in this is that Schofield, who is shrewd and not frank when he is likely to be affected, should have expressed himself so far on the subject. I apprehend he did not expect it would get abroad, but was a supposed quiet effort to plant the seeds of central, despotic military feeling. They are undoubtedly his convictions, and to those who have little faith in public intelligence and virtue, who believe in a government of form and not of opinion, who dislike the turbulence of elections, and who prefer the calm, quiet regularity of despotism, the views of Schofield will be acceptable. Much can be said on that side of the question, but men have not the courage to express their convictions if they are supposed to conflict with the directors of popular sentiment. It appears to me that, were I a centralist, I would openly avow it. I have no hesitation in saying I am opposed to the whole modern scheme of Congressional aggression, and that I have less faith in the exercise of general executive power by the legislative body than by one responsible head.

February 4, Thursday. A telegram brings tidings of the death of my brother-in-law, John Mulholland Hale, who died this morning of typhoid pneumonia at Reading, Pennsylvania. His death is a great loss to his family and friends, and to them his loss is irreparable. He was endowed with great business capacity, and his life and principles were exemplary. Mrs. Welles, Mrs. Morgan, and Edgar left this evening for Reading to attend his obsequies and pay the last earthly duties to the departed.

There was to have been this evening a large but select party at our house, which the death of Mr. Hale prevented. Forty-one and a half years ago, in the month of July, 1827, I alighted from the stage-coach in Lewistown, and among a crowd of men and boys I selected a black-eyed lad with a large black mole on his cheek, as my cousin John. He was a sturdy boy of twelve. After twoscore of years eventful to both of us, he has closed life's journey, and I must soon follow.

February 5, Friday. Seward read the last of the tart and not very creditable correspondence between Bancroft and Dix. I have some time since ceased to be an admirer of these men, and this correspondence fails to restore my former high opinion of either. The weakness of a driveler and the impertinence of a pedagogue are the characteristics.

Montgomery Blair tells me of an article which appeared some four or five weeks ago in Wilkes' paper,[1] which he says was prompted by Grant. It relates to the terms of capitulation at Appomattox Court-House, and of Johnston to Sherman, which the article avers were presented by Mr. Lincoln to the two generals at Bermuda Hundred, when he was there in March, 1865.

Blair called my attention to this article in Wilkes' paper in consequence of some remarks of mine, stating the substance of an interview which I had with Mr. Lincoln, soon after his return from Richmond and only a day or two before his death, in relation to the authority he had given to General Weitzel to call together the legislature of Virginia in order that they might repeal their secession ordinance and enactments. I may have in my notes mentioned this matter. Lest I have not, — for I find many most

[1] George Wilkes's *Spirit of the Times.*

important events are omitted, while some of little consequence are mentioned, — I now state it.

The proclamation, or order, of General Weitzel for reassembling the legislature of Virginia in the early part of April was received with great indignation, and was denounced by Stanton, Speed, and others. Although it was authorized by the President, he was, on his return to Washington, greatly annoyed by their opposition, and he either sent for me or in a business interview brought up the subject, and asked my view of it. In reply, I questioned the policy of his movement. He said his object and intentions were to bring about harmony and reconciliation at the earliest moment, and he should not stickle about forms; that it seemed to him best to meet the Rebels as men and countrymen who were to be trusted; the legislature was composed of leading men from the several counties, who must have a local influence, and he believed if they were to come together and undo their own work, it would hasten amicable feelings and better satisfy them and ourselves also. I suggested that they might not when assembled counsel submission but combine to resist. Besides, in recognizing them as a legislature, was he not giving them character and power never yet conceded them? There was, moreover, a skeleton organization under Pierpont, which we had tried to vitalize and maintain. How could we recognize another?

The President said he had no fears of any further attempts at resistance, — they were too thoroughly whipped and exhausted, — but there might be something in the other suggestion that we were countenancing the Rebel organization. He did not think much of it, however, but public prejudice must be considered, and the manner in which the movement had been received by Stanton and others had caused him to hesitate and he had wanted my views, — complimenting me for calm consideration when others were impulsive.

I related this interview to Blair, and remarked that I

had long ago come to the conclusion that Sherman in his
terms to Johnston had acted under instructions received
from President Lincoln at City Point, and that the clemency of President Lincoln was probably the cause of the
mild conditions extended by Grant to Lee and for which
Grant takes credit. Blair tells me that the article in Wilkes
takes the same view.

February 6, *Saturday.* The schemes for centralization
are becoming stronger and increased in number in Congress. Suffrage is to be wrested from the States and made
national. Corporations are being multiplied and by the
legislative branch of the government special privileges are
granted to all the favored who ask. The government is
being perverted, and its character destroyed. There is a
strange conglomerate in the Senate, where arrogance,
assumption, corruption, littleness — everything but statesmanship and wisdom — are to be found. Lawyers of some
smartness, like Edmunds of Vermont, and Howe of Wisconsin, but who have not calm, fair, deliberate minds, —
necessary qualifications as legislators and statesmen, —
profligate fellows, like Nye and Pomeroy and Stewart; and
expediency men, like Morrill of Maine, Ferry, Cattell, and
Sherman; cunning, unscrupulous managers like Butler
and Cameron, prevail. It is useless to enumerate further.

February 8, *Monday.* Senator Morrill of Vermont in a
conversation to-day complimented my administration of
the Navy Department in terms that were as unexpected
as agreeable. The economy as well as efficiency was commended, and the country, he said, would in time do me
justice, notwithstanding the abuse that had been so abund-
antly and persistently inflicted for years.

February 9, *Tuesday.* Seward read a long dispatch to
the Vice-Consul at Havana, who is clearly with the revolutionists in Cuba and wants our whole squadron there to

give them encouragement and perhaps aid. The accounts which we receive from Cuba are very contradictory. Under the censorship which the Governor-General has established, and the extraordinary efforts to suppress intelligence in regard to the rebels, with whom there is but little outside communication, we cannot expect much reliable information.

February 10, *Wednesday.* Congress to-day counted and declared the Presidential votes. There was nothing novel or interesting in the proceeding, save that certain States were excluded. The truth is, Grant is elected by illegal votes and fraudulent and unconstitutional practices. He would not have had a vote south of Washington but for the usurping and inexcusable acts of Congress.

The folly of the Democrats North in nominating Seymour insured Grant's election and gave encouragement to the outrageous legislation to help them.

Further schemes to tinker the Constitution are before Congress, and the Senate sat the whole night of Monday to force through the measure then before it, giving suffrage to negroes and fools by the Central Government in total disregard of the rights of the States, and of the fundamental principles of our system. How far these schemes are to be pressed, and whether they can be averted in season to save our system of government, is yet to be seen.

February 11, *Thursday.* It seems there were some not very creditable proceedings in Congress yesterday when the two houses were in joint session, followed up by the House after the joint convention was dissolved. The subject has been continued and discussed to-day, though with less heat and rancor. Still there has been sufficient to show the antagonisms in the Radical Party which must break out before Grant shall have been long in office. The hate between Butler and Bingham is intense. Both are unscrupulous and unprincipled; both are cunning and adroit.

Butler has most talent, most will, most daring and persistency; Bingham is more subtle and deceptive, has more suavity, is more snaky and timid with less audacity. Most of the members are with Bingham at present. He has also Stanton and Grant — who are afraid of Butler — to support him. The difficulties yesterday grew out of the Radical intrigue and villainy to exclude the vote of Georgia, and treat her as out of the Union. These revolutionary and wicked proceedings are having their effect in more ways than one on their authors. I do not see how Grant, if he has the comprehension, which is doubtful, can reconcile these differences, and before his Administration will be half served out, serious calamities are likely to befall the country.

February 12, *Friday*. Seward sends me a letter from Harvey at Lisbon, showing a disposition to be impertinently offensive and intrusive in the matter of purchases for the European Squadron. I directed Admiral Radford and the officers of the squadron to exercise their own judgment in obtaining supplies, regardless of Mr. Harvey.

General Dix notifies of his resignation of his place as Minister to France, to take place in about two weeks. It will be well if others will imitate his example. We have a very feeble set of representatives abroad. Not unlikely Dix expects or hopes for a Cabinet appointment. He is an old political soldier.

February 13, *Saturday*. The Congressional Committee officially waited on General Grant and informed him of his election. In reply he made the commonplace response which any ordinary person would make for a smaller office, of doing his duty, collecting the revenue, and practicing economy. This will, of course, be taken up and paraded as wonderful and most satisfactory by toadies of party, but when General Grant comes to act, he will, like others, do and fail to do. He will not be likely to enslave himself like

President Johnson, who has crowded the White House
with clerks, and has rooms filled with records and files, but,
while laboring on details and little matters of a clerical
nature, and which belong more appropriately to the Departments, the weightier and more important concerns
must suffer. Grant will generalize, if he does anything,
and therein will do better than President Johnson, but
most likely will turn over his duties to others, for he is
inexcusably ignorant of the structure and workings of the
Government.

Marshall Jewell, the Radical candidate for Governor in
Connecticut, has been here for a few days in behalf of
General Hawley. The effort is to put Hawley in Grant's
Cabinet. Jewell got an interview with Grant through
General Terry. In this interview Jewell took occasion to
speak of the favorable influence on the Radical cause
which would follow the selection of a Cabinet officer from
Connecticut. He wished to insure his own election, and he
wished to carry the First Congressional District. Grant
said he perceived Dixon was to be a candidate in that district, and hoped he would be defeated; said he had read
the resolutions of the Radical State Convention and liked
them.

The Radicals are not satisfied with Grant. The Democrats, in their folly, are trying to persuade themselves that
he is as much their man as he is of those who elected him.
Butler's demonstration on Wednesday was not successful.
The Democrats could, perhaps, have made it so. The result is hard and distrustful feelings among the Radicals,
but Butler is audacious and Bingham will yield.

February 15, Monday. Caleb Cushing has returned with
a successful treaty, it is said, for a ship canal across the
Isthmus. We shall have particulars, I suppose, by to-
morrow. There have been, and probably still are, some
extensive private speculations in this movement, and
some political and personal intrigues connected with it.

Seward expects great glorification and perpetual fame from it, — smoke, not substance.

February 16, *Tuesday.* The President sent the nomination of one of the Dents [1] to the Senate for the Chilian Mission in place of Kilpatrick, one of Seward's and Weed's pets, who has been here for six months lecturing and speechmaking through the country. The appointment of K. to that mission ought never to have been made. I so said in the day and time of it, but the President yielded to Seward and has been sorry ever since. I know not who prompted the nomination of Dent, but it is injudicious. It is rumored that Butler instigated it. Not unlikely, but the President should not lend himself and office to selfish schemes of Butler nor any one else. Grant has been active in getting all of his relatives as well as those of his wife in place. His father is postmaster, his son a cadet, and how many brothers, brothers-in-law, etc., etc., in office I know not. Why the President should volunteer to send one of the tribe to Chili I am not advised. I regret such movements. No good can come of such temporizing. I would neither court Grant nor embarrass him, and some petty suggestions in relation to appointments have found no favor with me.

The Senate refuse to confirm necessary appointments. Two pension agencies, one at St. Louis and one at Brooklyn, are vacant, and great trouble and difficulty will ensue if there is no agent to make those payments which come due in March. But the Senate is recklessly partisan, and regardless of the necessities of pensioners when party ends are to be served.

February 18, *Thursday.* Simeon Johnson, who is one of the board to revise the laws, appointed in place of Caleb Cushing, has been once or twice to see me in relation to a

---

[1] Judge Louis Dent, one of Grant's brothers-in-law. He was not confirmed by the Senate, and Judson Kilpatrick continued in the office.

claim of Coombs for the steamer Louisville. Early in the War, Coombs, by some contrivance, got a permit from President Lincoln to go within the Rebel lines to trade. The Rebels seized the steamer, sent her on one or more trips to New Orleans. In the mean time, our Navy having captured that place and the river squadron coming down from the North, she could not be used, and the Rebels took her into Red River and laid her up. Then the force under Porter a year later captured her, had her appraised under the law, and took her into service. The case was sent to the Southern District in Illinois for adjudication, and was, I think, first condemned as good prize, which was the fact. By some legerdemain she was subsequently condemned as captured or confiscated property, and the captors were awarded salvage, receiving about $12,000; the appraisal of the vessel was about $68,000. At a later period the court, without notifying the Department or the captors, reopened the case, had a new appraisal by parties in Springfield without their ever seeing the steamer, and had her valued at $150,000. For three years, Coombs, himself first and since by numerous agents, including Guthrie when Senator, Montgomery Blair, Eames, and various parties less worthy, male and female, has prosecuted this claim. Doubtless mention has been made in previous data of this diary of the proceedings. Johnson, who now comes, is a special friend and supporter of the President, and for that reason has the job. He was an editor of the *Union* under Buchanan and is an old claim agent. The call to-day was the second or third he has made on me with a request that I would send the case to the Fourth Auditor or Second Comptroller, or both, for adjudication or decision. I asked him what he meant by such a request. He said his object was to get a final disposition of the case; that he had had one or two interviews with the Second Comptroller, who thought it a clear case, and was ready to take it up and act whenever the Navy Department would submit it to him. If Johnson is sincere, it was an extraordinary application.

I expressed my astonishment at this gross ignorance of this intelligent man on most subjects on mere routine duty, and his manifest want of knowledge of the powers and duties of the Departments and of the organization and principles of the government. He was abashed and embarrassed by my remarks, but at first made a stand and cited the course of the War Department and Third Auditor as his justification. I asked him if his ideas of administration placed the Executive and the Departments under the control and direction of the accounting officers of the Treasury, — if he supposed that cases arising under the Departments and which it was the duty of the Secretaries to decide were subject to appeal and finally to be adjudged and disposed of by an auditor or comptroller or any other subordinate. He said no, but the duties of a head of Department were executive, not judicial. I said they were administrative, ministerial, executive, and if we erred, the remedy was with the courts, or Congress, not with the accounting officers of the Treasury.

The strange, inexcusable ignorance which prevails among intelligent men in regard to the working and organization of the government is amazing. I do not believe it to be ignorance on Johnson's part, whatever may be his protestations. Johnson says Attorney-General Evarts is no better informed than he is; probably not, and McCulloch, I know, submits to the ignorant assumption of the First Comptroller, who claims a supervision over the Departments.

February 19, *Friday.* Seward says he intends to leave Washington on the 8th of March and go to Auburn. The President appears to think that the Cabinet should all go out at noon on the 4th of March. This is my wish, and I believe that of most of the members of the Cabinet, and yet there is an apparent impropriety, if not a positive wrong, in abandoning our posts until there has been a reasonable time for our successors to qualify and take upon themselves

3

the duties. There is some embarrassment in the case, resulting from Grant's conduct towards those of us who witnessed the interview between him and President Johnson a year since, when his insincerity, deceit, double-dealing, duplicity, and want of truth were apparent, when, in plain words, he was detected in a deliberate falsehood. He affects to be in a miff because we stated the truth in regard to that interview, and has had intercourse with none of us, except Seward, who has demeaned himself and played an equivocal part to conciliate the little high official.

For one I want not his favor and shun not his wrath. I do not wish to come under his orders, nor would I be derelict of duty or propriety because he is vulgar. It would be unpleasant to remain one day in office under his administration; it may be wrong, however, to leave until a successor appear.

No intimation is yet made as to any one of the next Cabinet. There is nothing remarkable in this, though many think it strange. I doubt if Grant has fully determined in his own mind. It is not usual with him to make up his mind definitely until the last moment. He is commonly considered, or has the name of being, a judge of men, or that he knows those whom he can use. Rawlins, Sherman, Sheridan, and others, all men of ability, he favors and encourages because they defer to him, have really made him what he is, and do not permit themselves to obstruct him or be in his way. George Thomas, Rosecrans, Hancock, and others are not favorites, though tolerated, and the latter he feels to be in his power. Mixed with jealousies and aspirations, he has constant suspicion and inveterate enmities. He is fond of power, never refuses or declines it, loves wealth, accepts and encourages gifts, is sly, shrewd, cunning, secretive, ambitious, and selfish, with some executive, but little administrative, ability; knows how to appropriate and avail himself of the talent and labor of others. At present he is cajoling the Democrats by letting them hope he may favor them and not the extreme Radicals.

The Radicals distrust him and have apprehensions that he may go over to the Democrats. By these manœuvres he strengthens his position; he weakens the Democrats and brings the Radicals into subjection.

McCulloch brought up, as he has once or twice previously, the question of governing Alaska. No government has yet been established there by Congress, — the Members are busy in efforts to confer power and privileges on the negroes. Some conversation took place. I suggested that there need be no difficulty, — General Sickles, or one of the Reconstruction military governors, might be sent there, who embodied in himself all governmental authority, legislative, executive, or judicial. This touched Schofield slightly, who again sneered at jury trials, asked if they had not better be established in Alaska, contrasted the ready military method of administering justice in the Southern States, with the slow, unending process of jury trial, when a verdict was matter of chance.

February 20, *Saturday.* The President spoke to me several days since in relation to the "Copper Bill" which had been presented to him for approval. I expressed very fully my disapproval of it and of the system of corporations and special privileges which Congress is establishing. He said he coincided with me, and I find the bill will be vetoed.

Mr. Grimes, Chairman, has addressed me a letter from the Naval Committee concerning the transfer of a government vessel for a school ship, to a charitable association in New York. Sent him a pretty full reply to-day. Took occasion to express my repugnance to such donations, or uses, of public property, while I am earnestly friendly to having and training young seamen. Regretted that Congress at its last session had discouraged the apprentice system.

Am importuned, as my exit is near, by retired officers for promotion. The old commodores are, many of them, exceedingly anxious to obtain the advanced grade. I am not surprised at it, although I cannot assist them. Congress has embarrassed the Department and excited these movements by heedless legislation. I am also sadly troubled on the other hand by the President, who kindly yields to the appeals made to him and would, I verily believe, promote all, and pardon all.

Had some talk with the President in relation to inauguration day. Something was said a few days ago about his going to the Capitol and remaining to the close of the session to sign bills, etc. I advised him to do no such thing, but to remain at the White House and discharge his duties there. Unlike preceding inaugurals, the next Congress would assemble on the 4th, — there would be no interruption of business. He should, therefore, put himself to no special inconvenience, and was not requested to do so.

February 22. I inquired how he was to dispose of himself, if at the Capitol at 12 meridian on the 4th prox. Would he go on the platform with the man who had deceived him, been false to his trust, and who had insulted him (the President) because he had detected and exposed his falsehoods? Would he leave the Capitol and go down the steps in view of the throng of partisan spectators, who would be there assembled to witness the triumph of this ignorant, vulgar man? Would he think of leaving the Capitol by any other door than the one by which he entered? To me it was plain he could not go near the Capitol on that day and preserve conscious self-respect.

He assured me he would not; that he would close up his Administration in the room where we were. I do not think he can be persuaded to a different course, though Seward and others, fond of show and parade, will urge him to form part of the pageant.

February 23, *Tuesday*. I asked Seward, whom I found in the council room alone this noon, when he proposed to leave the Cabinet and Washington. He said his resignation would take effect at noon on the 4th of March, and that he should leave Washington that day. This would be personally agreeable to me, but I queried as to the propriety of abandoning our posts before our successors appeared, and were qualified. Later in the day, and in the evening at General Schofield's, where we all dined, the subject was renewed. McCulloch and Browning were very decidedly in favor of continuing at their posts until their successor appeared. Browning said he wished to be very civil and courteous, and proposed, if his successor was a man with whom he could associate on any terms, to go in his carriage and invite him to the Department, introduce him to the clerical force, and initiate him as to his duties. I said, while I would omit no proper courtesy, I was not prepared to make, unasked, any such unseemly concession; that it would, in my view, be demeaning myself, and while I would receive my successor affably and kindly, I would not run after him. Mr. Evarts inclined to the opinion that we should wait and induct our successors. Seward and Randall were very emphatic that they would not remain one moment after the termination of President Johnson's term, — that if the third of March expired legally at meridian on the 4th, they then would leave.

After this discussion, my impression is that, under the circumstances and with a man like Grant, we had best all go out with our chief. The Government and the country need suffer no detriment from our resignation and retirement with the President. All is under the control of the President, who can, by dispensing with forms and parade, take the oath at twelve and at once appoint his Cabinet. He can return proffered civility with churlish discourtesy, and would be likely to do it. I perceived there are movements for a session at 3 P.M., and I also noted, in our discussion to-day, Schofield remarked that the President-elect could, under the prescribed laws, be as well prepared and make his appointment of cabinet officers on the day of inauguration as at any time. The subject has obviously been under consideration.

February 24, Wednesday.

. . . .

Attorney-General Evarts called in behalf of a friend, Chaplain F——, who wanted waiting-orders pay instead of furlough pay. Read to him the laws and told him I had no doubt he was receiving the legal pay. He said the Comptroller and Auditor thought differently, but did not like to pay extra without the sanction of the Department, and were expecting I would get an opinion or write them. I remarked that, being satisfied, I cared not to pursue the subject; that I saw no cause to change the practice, or usage, or law; that if the accounting officers were clearly satisfied I was wrong, they perhaps might, in the days when the Treasury was being plundered, feel justified in giving extra pay to this man, who was already a pensioner without having rendered service.

This matter has been some time in embryo. Claim agents, and loose notions, and practices at the Treasury will likely accomplish the swindle. I so remarked to E., who took it very calmly; said F—— was poor; the amount would not be great on the Treasury. I said it was right or it was wrong; his was not the only case pending, and his had no merit. He had rendered but small service, for which he has been amply paid, and was now a pensioner on the Government, doing nothing. Had he been wholly retired with one year's full pay, his case would have been finally disposed of.

February 25, Thursday.

. . . .

February 26, Friday. An hour or two was spent in Cabinet over the Pacific Railroad. The two companies, one from the East (the Pacific), one from the West (the Central), are approaching each other in the vicinity of Salt Lake, and each is claiming subsidy over the same line. There are statements not wholly reliable, I apprehend, by each. In anticipation of these difficulties, and, if possible, to avoid them, the subject was considered last fall, and as there was then a dispute whether the road should cross Bear Bay or go around it, maps and reports were submitted, and it was decided the route should go round. It is now said that not only the route but the line of the road was decided. This was not my understanding.

In conversing as to the course to be pursued on the termination of the Administration, it was understood that all would resign and leave with the President except Schofield, who said he had been invited and should remain for a brief period. Seward says he has had the files looked up, and finds the practice has not been uniform, that in some instances, and generally, the members of the Cabinet have tendered their resignation to the outgoing President, but some have remained and tendered them to the newly inaugurated. This last, I apprehend, has been in those cases where there has been a mere change of President, but not a change of policy or of party.

A good deal of speculation, some of it absurd, is going forward in regard to the new Cabinet. Not more, perhaps, than in preceding cases. A. K. McClure, an active Republican politician of Pennsylvania and a great friend of Governor Curtin, having learned the fact that Grant had said he should select one member of the Cabinet from that State, hurried on here and had an interview, in which by report Grant appears to better advantage than the Pennsylvania politician.

LXVII

Discussion of the Inauguration Ceremonies — The President's Last Reception — Good-byes at the Department — How President Johnson and his Cabinet spent the Last Moments of the Administration — The Inaugural Ceremonies and Procession — Grant's Cabinet — A. T. Stewart illegally nominated Secretary of the Treasury — Sumner's Wrath at Grant's Course in regard to his Cabinet — Stewart, after offering to trustee his Business, finally declines the Secretaryship — Pressure for Boutwell as Secretary of the Treasury — Mr. Faxon and Mr. E. T. Welles leave the Navy Department — Hamilton Fish succeeds Washburne as Secretary of State and the Latter is appointed Minister to France — General Rawlins made Secretary of War — Admiral Porter, in charge of the Navy Department, appoints Chief Engineer King in Isherwood's Place — Porter's Management of the Department — Debate on the Repeal of the Tenure-of-Office Act — Grant's Scheme of reorganizing the Navy — Moses H. Grinnell made Collector at New York — Porter's Intrusion in the Navy Department — The Story of his Appointment as Vice-Admiral — Butler expresses Contempt for Grant — Ex-President Johnson in Tennessee — Montgomery Blair on Colonel Moore and other Associates of Johnson in Washington — Butler outgeneraled and the Tenure-of-Office Repeal Bill compromised.

March 1, *Monday.* A special Cabinet-meeting was held in regard to the controversy between the Union Pacific and the Central Railroad. An hour was spent, before taking up the subject, on matters relating to inauguration. General Grant, who eight years ago was employed to tend and sweep his brother's leather store in Galena, as a porter and sub-clerk, has given the Committee on Ceremonies, on the 4th of March, to understand he would not ride in the same carriage with the President nor speak to him. The Committee have, of course, been embarrassed how to proceed, and have finally a programme studiously arranged, which is for the President and President-elect to proceed in separate carriages. The President will pass through Pennsylvania Avenue, on the right, the President-elect, on the left, etc., etc. Seward and Evarts opened the subject of the procession and our attendance, and had evidently had some understanding with each other and with the Committee in regard to it. Seward said he did not know but they had intended to shut us off entirely, but since they have been polite enough to provide us a place, he believed he would remain over another day to perform his part. Evarts thought it best we should go in the procession, and he made inquiry about carriages. The President brought out a letter he had from the marshal, inquiring about carriages informally.

I expressed a hope the President would perform no part in the parade, and advised he should remain at the Mansion until meridian, ready to discharge any and all duties. At that time his functions would cease, and ours would cease with his.

A remark or two was made by Browning and McCulloch, each indicating a disposition to go in the procession. Seward offered Browning a seat in his carriage. The President said nothing. I stood alone. Randall expressed no opinion. Seward and Evarts became zealous. Seward was garrulous; told over several egotistical and stale stories, claimed the President and his suite had the post of honor, being on the right; appealed to usage, etc.

I asked when, ever before, there had been such a programme, — two processions, one on each side of the street. What did it indicate but division, and what would be the effect but to irritate and promote hostility? I disclaimed any neglect or want of courtesy, but, on the other hand, I would submit to none. There was a decency and proper self-respect to be observed.

March 2, *Tuesday*. There are many strangers here to attend the inauguration, and a number called from curiosity to see the heads of Departments. This makes a constant interruption, when time is wanted to clear up affairs.

At the Cabinet much time was consumed as to the course to be pursued on the 4th. Seward and Evarts were determined that the President and Cabinet should go to the Capitol and take part in the proceedings. I combated this course, but no one sustained me except Randall, who, near the close, expressed a hope that the President would do nothing derogatory to himself and his position. McCulloch, who has an itching to go, but feels its impropriety, said but little, yet what he did say evinced his feelings. Addressing himself to me, he said he thought it decidedly best that we should go to the Capitol and take part in the ceremonies. It would look small and be considered small if we did not. I remarked that on a somewhat similar occasion, J. Q. Adams and Henry Clay had declined to attend the inauguration of General Jackson, and were not considered small men, nor was their refusal to attend considered a small affair. Those men were less exemplars [*sic*] to me than others who were unwilling to follow their example.

Mr. Evarts had the matter much at heart, and he and Seward proceeded to dispose of it as a matter of course and as if nothing further was to be said. They assumed for granted that things must be as they wished and directed. The President hesitated, yielded in a measure apparently, and it was assumed that the question was decided. The President, however, did not wholly surrender, but said we would meet at nine on Thursday morning at the council room, and then determine. Evarts said we must bring our carriages, and with an understanding that we would go in a body to the Capitol. I claimed that was going further than the President had proposed or than I was willing to go. "We will meet here," said I, "on Thursday." "But," said Evarts and Schofield, "the Committee and managers should know in advance." "By all means," said Evarts, and he sat down and wrote a notice, which he read out to Schofield and then to the President, and the latter did not controvert it. So we are likely to form part of the pageant, — be a tail to the Grant kite. I have my doubts if I participate in that pageant.

It was concluded that we would consider the 3d as terminating at meridian on the 4th, if Congress did not order otherwise.

General Dix's resignation as Minister to France is received, and the indications are that he may go to the State Department.

March 3, Wednesday. There was an immense gathering last evening at the Presidential reception. These "jams," as they are rightly called, are becoming severely oppressive, and if Grant has the courage to effect a reformation he will deserve the thanks of the country. To permit the Executive Mansion and all its approaches to be crowded by the whole population who may choose to push themselves forward without order or system, is preposterous. Hundreds of friends and officials who desired to pay their respects, and whom the President and his family wished to see at this last reception, were driven away, unable to obtain entrance. The evil should be corrected. Some of the crowd came in with their overcoats, hats, and bonnets, and for mere idle curiosity. Not a few were the wild, fanatical partisans who have busied themselves in slandering, defaming, and misrepresenting the President. They, male and female, thronged the Mansion and its parlors, to the exclusion of social friends and political associates of the retiring President.

Went with the Chiefs of Bureaus and officers to the Executive Mansion to introduce each and give all an opportunity to bid the Chief Magistrate farewell. Rear-Admiral Joe Smith, the senior officer, who eight years ago, as now, walked by my side, then addressed President Lincoln with a few remarks, saying there were evidences of approaching convulsion, that "we (Navy officers) will perform our duty, and expect you to do yours." I now introduced the officer to President Johnson with the remark that these are the men who, in war and peace, have stood fast by the Government and the Union. He received them cordially, took each by the hand and bade them farewell.

On returning to the Department, the Chiefs of Bureaus, the clerks, messengers, and employees came successively to take their leave, and express their regard and kind wishes for me and my future welfare. It was something beside mere formality. Some, more sensitive perhaps than others, or possessed of deeper feelings, were unable to give utterance to their thoughts; others with tears expressed their regrets and spoke of lasting obligations. I, not less than they, was moved. Ties of friendship formed and many of them continued through eight active and eventful years cannot be easily and lightly severed or forgotten.

It was past four when, probably for the last time and forever, I left the room and the building where I had labored earnestly and zealously, taken upon myself and carried forward great responsibilities, endured no small degree of abuse, much of it unmerited and undeserved; where also I have had many pleasant and happy hours in the enjoyment of the fruits of my works and of those associated with me.

March 4, Thursday. I went at nine this morning to the Executive Mansion, agreeably to appointment at the last Cabinet-meeting. There was quite a crowd on the portico and walks as I drove up and entered. Schofield was already in the council room, having preceded my arrival a few moments. The President was busy examining and signing bills. As I shook hands with him, he said quietly, "I think we will finish our work here without going to the Capitol." I expressed my gratification. Yesterday I had said to him that Congress had not been so courteous and kind and civil to him as to place him under obligations to dance attendance upon them. They, and General Grant also, had thought it expedient to have the incoming Congress convene on the 4th of March instead of the first Monday of December, in order that the legislative department of the government might be a check on the executive. If any legislation was omitted, the new Congress could remedy it.

The President now said he thought it but right that the Congress should forward the bills to him here. This I knew would be a disappointment to my colleagues, and I had no doubt that a strong effort would be made to bring around a different result. Randall, who came next after me, was very well satisfied. Schofield discreetly said nothing, but I could perceive he was not pleased with the new phase of affairs. McCulloch was disappointed and disturbed. Browning said not a word. Evarts, who did not come in until about ten, was determined to change the programme; said the understanding was that we should go to the Capitol, that we were expected there. When the President occasionally left the room, McCulloch twice told E. that the President would not go to the Capitol unless he put in strong for him to do so. Evarts would not take off his overcoat. Seward came in last, smoking his cigar. Asked if all were ready; meant to have come sooner; seemed to suppose we were waiting for him. The President continued busy at his desk, while Seward, Evarts, and others talked. At length Seward, who sat on the opposite side of the room from the President, asked aloud if we would not be late, — "Ought we not to start immediately?" The President said he was inclined to think we would finish up our work here by ourselves.

There was discomfiture, of course, and it was easy to perceive they thought me the author of their disappointment. McCulloch came to me about twelve, and said, "Well, you have carried your point." I disclaimed this, otherwise than in frankly giving my opinion whenever the subject was broached, but [said] that I had, at no time, introduced the topic.

In this whole matter, I have felt that the President, after the offensive, silly, arrogant, and insolent declarations of Grant to the committees and others that he would not speak to his official superior and predecessor, nor ride, nor associate with him, could not compose a part in the pageant to glorify Grant without a feeling of abasement. These airs are put on by Grant to relieve himself from conscious degradation which he must have felt for his treachery to the President and the odium of falsehood which he knows others heard, saw, and witnessed. But his insulting impudence to the President and others who witnessed that humiliating spectacle will never eradicate the knowledge of the duplicity and falsehood of which he was guilty, — as well as of the ingratitude to the man who had trusted him.

A few minutes past twelve the President said we would part. As he was to leave, it was proposed that we should wait his departure. He then shook hands with each of us, and we with each other and, descending to the portico, where our respective carriages were waiting, the President entered his, mine followed, and we drove away.

At my house were the President's daughter, Mrs. Patterson, and her children, who had come over in the morning. They propose to remain with us a few days before going to Tennessee.

The proceedings at the Capitol are represented to have been without order or system, and the immense crowd swayed and pushed aside the dignitaries. I am more than ever gratified that we did not attend. General Grant rode up in a dogcart with Rawlins. There was a long procession, mostly of negroes, — at least two thirds, I should judge. But few of them had muskets. Congress had passed a resolution authorizing and requesting that four thousand muskets should be placed in the hands of these vagabonds, and quite a crowd came from Baltimore and the country around, expecting each to obtain a musket. But President Johnson refused to approve the bill, which was to place over eighty thousand dollars' worth of arms in the hands of Bowen, the demagogue mayor, to distribute. Of course great dissatisfaction is expressed by the colored crowd towards President Johnson for his meanness in withholding the guns.

March 5, Friday. The city was full of strangers this morning. It was difficult for them to get off in the crowded trains last night and this morning, and there is an immense throng of party expectants, waiting the Cabinet nominations. These nominations were sent in about 2 P.M., and produced a rapid dispersion. The excitement had been great for some days and had reached fever heat, but there was a cold shower-bath on the announcement of the names.

It is obviously a Grant Cabinet. The members belong to the Radical-Republican Party, but neither one, unless it be Creswell, would have been selected by that party. They are not the men the Radicals wanted, but they are such men as Grant wants. Washburne is coarse, comparatively illiterate, a demagogue without statesmanship or enlarged views, with none of the accomplishments or attributes that should belong to a Secretary of State. Jefferson is the first; Washburne is the last. Hamilton, a man of talents and genius, was the first Secretary of the Treasury. He had financial skill and ability to develop the resources of the nation. Stewart, the last Secretary of the Treasury, has made a princely fortune in the trade of silks, calicoes, laces, and stockings. So of the others. From first to last there is not an experienced politician or statesman among them. Most of them are party men. All are Grant men. Creswell was a Secessionist in 1861, and, like Logan, raised a company to resist the Unionists. There is now not a more bitter and intolerant Radical in the country, but his Radicalism is obsequious and subservient to Grant.

It is the plan of Grant to cheat both parties, and he is measurably successful. The Democrats rejoice because none of the Radical leaders have been selected. Sumner,

Wade, Schenck, Curtin, Griswold, Boutwell, and all of that class are ignored. None of the men in whom the Radicals had confidence are chosen. Their minds did not concentrate on the jewels which have been dug up. Grant was the man to unearth and bring forth the brilliant lights which are to govern and illuminate the country, if he acted intelligently and deliberately. He has been reticent; kept his secret well. The great men of the country were hid under a Radical bushel until he brought them forth.

The Radicals are astounded, thunderstruck, mad, but, after taking breath, try to reconcile themselves and be composed that things are no worse, — that Grant has not, besides kicking them one side, selected Democrats. In this is consolation. They therefore try to praise the Cabinet and like it. The Administration is to be Grant's, based on Radical usurpations. Both parties are to be bamboozled, and if he really has any policy, —which I doubt, — it is that the animosity of each is to be played off against the other.

The inaugural address, a mess of trite, flat, newspaper partyism, in a day and time when noble utterances ought to be expected, is praised and extolled by the Radicals. His support of the public credit of a specie standard, — of the payment of the debt, — if such be honestly and squarely his purpose, is well. His idea of digging the precious metals,—his strong-box figure, — to discharge the debt, indicates his narrow, barren thoughts, while some arrogant expressions weaken and do not strengthen it. Still, it is lauded as a remarkable state paper.

It is not to be expected, however, that partisan editors, correspondents, and place-hunters would have — certainly they would not express — opinions against the inaugural address, or the new Cabinet. They are here and everywhere to express approval, although the address is indifferent and the Cabinet distasteful.

As regards the Cabinet, no statesman and patriot with right intentions would have selected it, or any other of untried men for such positions. If General Grant thinks he can take up five or six men, personal adherents, sycophants like Washburne, money-givers like Stewart and Borie, to discharge the highest and most responsible positions, and believes that such persons can successfully administer the government, he is himself unfit for the place of Chief Magistrate. But if General Grant has aspirations above and beyond the Constitution, he might well put in his Cabinet men without knowledge of, or experience in, public affairs, men who themselves mean well and have no unhallowed ambition, but who are ignorant of the structure and workings of our peculiar system. I impute no wrong motives to these men, with the exception of Creswell and Washburne. But, with the limited ideas which most of them possess, they can be easily led into error by a cunning and ambitious man of ability and at the head of the government.

Grant has both avarice and ambition. Two of the men have been liberal in their donations, and he appreciates their gifts. Washburne is servile and obsequious. Of Hoar I know little, and nothing to his personal disparagement. He belongs to the school of centralists, and is, I doubt not, committed to what are called the "Reconstruction" measures, by which States and people, in violation of the Constitution, are despoiled of their rights. Cox is patriotic, but with less ability, perhaps, than Hoar.

March 6, Saturday. There is disturbance and trouble in the Radical camp. Mr. Stewart is not ready to give up his extensive business for the office of Secretary of the Treasury. Grant did not know that it was illegal for an extensive importer to be Secretary of the Treasury. A sagacious and honest-minded man would have seen the incompatibility of such a conjunction, even were there no legal objections. Had Grant been less secretive, he would have been wiser. His friends, had he consulted them, would have advised him properly. Stewart, of course,

3

knew no better. The Senate confirmed Stewart unanimously, supposing, probably, that it was arranged that he should give up his business to take the place. This was the general supposition. But to-day Grant sends in a special message addressed to the Senate only, asking Congress to permit the newly appointed Secretary of the Treasury to be exempted from the law; that the most conspicuous case of the propriety and necessity of the law in the whole United States shall be relieved from the disabilities which the law imposes; that Mr. Stewart, the largest importer, shall have a privilege which the law was enacted to prevent and which is denied every other importer. This message is a more conclusive evidence of unfitness than the ignorance of appointing. The first was from a want of knowledge; the second from a want of honest principle. It is said, however, he had Congressional advices in the last movement, and Patterson of New Hampshire and Sherman, two partisan Senators, showed an obsequious want of moral principle in their movements to relieve Grant from his dilemma.

It is not strange that unscrupulous party papers should advise and urge an abandonment of the laws and regulations which were enacted as safeguards to the country and which have existed from the foundation of the government, to please the King, and there are Senators no better.

Admiral Farragut tells me that Grant told him that he gave the office of Secretary of State to Washburne as a compliment, — not that he is to continue in the place. Here is another evidence of the traits of character of our new Chief Magistrate. High places of the Government he considers his perquisites and he bestows them on personal favorites as a matter of compliment, without regard to fitness or the true interest of the country.

March 8, *Monday.* Uneasiness, discontent, doubt prevail in regard to the Administration. The Cabinet is weak. Whether the President is also weak will soon be more generally known. He is not gaining confidence and strength in the public estimation, but, though ignorant of the structure of the government and of governmental duties, he is not destitute of cunning and is intrenching himself in position by the bestowment of governmental favors. The Cabinet is his, and will be devoted to his use and purpose, whatever that purpose may be, or they will be compelled to give way to others.

Stewart proposes, in order to retain the office of Secretary of the Treasury, to put his immense business in the hands of trustees, and to dedicate all the profits to poor soldiers and their families. This extraordinary bid for the place leaves no doubt of his great anxiety to obtain and hold it. It can hardly be supposed he will be able to purchase this high office under the affectation of benevolence. Mr. S. has never heretofore been renowned for his charities. I have suggested that instead of putting his business in commission it might be better to put the Treasury in commission, and let the trustees manage the finances instead of Stewart's affairs.

Faxon informs me he was summoned to the White House by the President, where he found Washburne, the other Assistant Secretaries, army officers, and a miscellaneous crowd. Grant was sitting in one corner of the fireplace, smoking his cigar. Washburne was at the table, writing orders apparently, and every few moments rising and running from one room to another. There was trouble and anxiety about some pardons which had been granted by President Johnson, which Grant desired to revoke. He ordered the Assistant Secretaries to send out no commissions, and to do only necessary routine work; said his regular Cabinet days would be Tuesdays and Fridays, and directed the Assistants to attend until the Secretaries entered upon their duties. Faxon informed him that no commission would go out which had not the President's signature. This seems not to have been known by him or his Secretary of State, Washburne.

No action was taken to-day in Congress on the Act of 1789, or Grant's message asking exemption for Stewart. Faxon tells me that Sumner does not, when with friends, conceal his wrath and indignation at Grant's course; says that he (Sumner), the father of the Senate, chairman of the Committee on Foreign Relations, was offered nothing, was not even consulted in regard to the Cabinet, appointments abroad, or the policy which the Administration should pursue.

March 9, Tuesday. The *Intelligencer* of this morning contained a very extraordinary leader, first under its head, double-leaded, laudatory of Stewart and Grant, because the former offers to give his income, some two millions a year, to the poor of New York, provided he can thereby be permitted to hold the office of Secretary of the Treasury and manage the finances. Every one on reading the article pronounced the paper purchased. I have no doubt of it, or of its readiness to be purchased for any purpose. When the previous course of the paper is considered, there can be no question that it has been influenced by a consideration. Newspapers, as well as the poor for whom it affects great interest, are soothed by money. It is plain that Stewart wants position. Wealth does not introduce him into the first circles. He thinks official distinction will elevate him. The censorious insist that he will make more money than he gives, if made Secretary of the Treasury.

March 10, Wednesday. The papers published Stewart's deed of trust, and also his letter declining the office of Secretary of the Treasury. It was found, after inquiry and consultation, that the arrangements would not work, and that the rich man could not openly buy the place. To Grant and Mrs. Grant the misgo is a great disappointment. Stewart's silks and laces, scandal says, were potent in the appointment, and in other ways he had also given largely to Grant. Who shall be substituted is now the question. The friends of John A. Griswold are pressing him, but the gossiping rumor alleges he did not contribute so largely as others in proportion to his means, and therefore cannot succeed. He is, however, a better man and better qualified than Stewart. Boutwell is pushed most earnestly, but it seems, though the Radicals urge him, he has not been a free giver and consequently does not suit Grant. Boutwell was tendered the Interior Department, but Grant would not give him the Treasury. Still the demands and clamors of the Radicals are so loud and persistent, he may feel it necessary to yield. He has, moreover, been taken down and tamed by his blunders for Stewart. We shall see how matters operate. It is said he will not give way and the Radical pressure for Boutwell will only make him more determined against that gentleman. It is also claimed that Hoar is from Massachusetts, and there cannot be two Cabinet officers from the same State. Grant has laid this down as a fixed fact, a cardinal principle, from which he will not swerve. But, it is said, this can be arranged by getting through a bill enlarging the number of judges, and putting Hoar on the bench.

All of this trafficking and shuffling seems to be considered right and well enough by the Radical leaders. There is no thought or even a conception that the public are entitled to consideration, — that they are to have a voice or wish worth a moment's attention, or that the public interest and welfare are to be consulted. Places for Grant to give and for Radicals to receive are their ideas of administration.

Vice-Admiral Porter was telegraphed by Grant to come to Washington and take charge of the Navy Department yesterday, and he at once came over from Annapolis by a special train. Borie, the Secretary, who is here, waited his coming, and the two went to the Department arm in arm; Porter told Faxon and others that he had come to "run the Department," that Borie would n't do much, that Borie yielded to him. Faxon commenced to inform B. of the general routine, but Porter stopped him, and said Faxon could inform him (P.) and he would communicate to B., and B. submitted meekly.

The War Department is put in the keeping of the General and the Navy Department is under the control of the Vice-Admiral. All things are tending to centralization and military supremacy.

Faxon and E. T. Welles took leave of the Department to-day. Their resignations were tendered on the 8th and accepted when a successor could relieve them. Faxon took the noon train to-day for Connecticut. He has been associated with me the last eight years, and our intercourse has been always pleasant. I have found him ever faithful and useful, and cannot but feel regret at our parting. He tells me that Schofield is not pleased with the recent order placing the General over the War Department, and has asked to be speedily relieved. The ex-President, Johnson, goes to Baltimore to-morrow to attend a banquet tendered him by the city authorities, and has urged me to go with him, but I declined; wish he had also, and hope he will attend no others.

March 11. Grant has finally surrendered and nominated Boutwell for the Treasury. He would not at the beginning give him the place, but has been humbled and subdued in a measure by the exposure of his ignorance in the first instance; by his readiness to cheat the law in the second; third, by his inability to procure a repeal of the enactment and being finally compelled to withdraw his grossly improper proposition. The Radicals have been very clamorous and violent for distinctive recognition as a power, which Grant has tried to evade, but he at last yields. He yields in another respect from his repeated declarations and immovable principles that he would not have two members of his Cabinet from one State. But it is reported that this difficulty will soon be corrected. The Supreme Court is to

DAVID D. PORTER

be enlarged, and Hoar is to be got rid of by being transferred to the bench. Bargains, intrigues, and arrangements are the order of the day; the country's welfare is of little consideration. There is an inaccuracy and readiness in these vicious proceedings which is startling. But the "party of moral ideas" seem to consider the whole thing proper.

Hamilton Fish of New York is appointed Secretary of State. Washburne held the office four days. He could not fill it. Grant told Farragut that he gave Washburne the place as a compliment. That was in character. Grant considers the government offices his, not the country's. They are bestowed on favorites for their personal service and devotion to him, not for qualification of the recipient nor for the public welfare. Fish is a New-Yorker of medium talents, a man of wealth, of some experience and fair accomplishments, a moderate Republican, an old Whig, not an extreme man, will be rightly disposed, and be likely to do tolerably well, if things move rightly, but without energy or force to correct Presidential errors or to resent wrongs. He is a great improvement on the coarse, uncultured Washburne. This "fellow," as I once heard Mr. Lincoln call Washburne, is appointed Minister to France. He may represent correctly the man who appoints him, but is no credit to the country.

General Rawlins succeeds Schofield as Secretary of War. Of the three persons who figured not very largely eight years ago in the village of Galena, but who are now in the most prominent places in the Republic, I have always considered Rawlins as possessing the superior, though not great, mind. His health is not good, but I think his influence will be in the right direction, beneficial for Grant and the Administration.

Porter has begun his career by an onslaught on Isherwood, who is superseded by Chief Engineer King. Isherwood has his peculiarities, but is mentally superior to any one of the chief engineers with whom I have come in contact. He has not great business talents, but is devoted to

his profession. His engines, which have been assailed and
denounced by rivals and opponents, have rendered good
service and given better satisfaction than any others. He,
as well as the Engineer Corps generally, and all the staff
have erred in their clamor for rank. Isherwood has not
the *suaviter in modo* in his intercourse with others whom he
believes wrong, he is no double-dealer, but speaks his mind,
roughly and offensively at times. He holds a ready pen.
There were rumors of his connection with the Martin boiler
and Lowell's condenser that were never fully cleared up,
and which his opponents have used with some effect
against him. King, who succeeds him, is his antagonist; is
smooth and never uses harsh language. Those who differ
with him charge him with plausibility, insincerity, and
not very great ability. He was at my house this evening,
and says he knew nothing of and had no intimation of his
selection until he saw it in the paper. . . .

I hear of some new and strange orders issued, or about to
be issued, by the Navy Department. Likely there is some
foundation and some exaggeration. Porter will, from his
nature, strive to do something *different* from what has been
done, more likely to be evil than good; will issue some
counter orders, adopt a contrary policy, effect something
novel without much regard to its good or bad qualities.
I have so detailed officers as to avoid cliques, and clannish
aggregations, and therein have dissatisfied Porter, who is
given to favorites and has dislikes and prejudices without
cause. In breaking up cliques, incipiently forming, and
dispensing with those who were indulging in those personal factions, I know I have performed a benefit to the
parties themselves, as well as to the service. But Porter
is resentful because he had not his own way.

March 12, *Friday.* Commodore Glisson called on me this
evening. Is here in relation to League Island and the Ironsides, but says there is such confusion and bewilderment
at the Navy Department that he can accomplish nothing.

It is time to make arrangements for letting the unoccupied lands. Had offers of ten thousand dollars for them for pasturing, to which the lands have been put for the last three years. But they prohibit him from pasturing them; say it is not proper that lands which are to be used for a navy yard, though not occupied, should be pastured. Glisson told them the crops would not be gathered as hay. They did not want it should be. He said to let the grass and weeds grow and perish on the ground would breed disease. But his views were disregarded. Porter, he says, is the man who answered him and gave the orders.

Commodore Melancthon Smith called later in the evening. He says Porter is trying to flourish and make a noise in order to be noticed in the papers. Has appointed a large number of boards to examine ships, engines, etc. Overlooks the Bureaus, which can furnish all the information, but he wants officers to move about and report. Has Goldsborough chairman of one board; has detached Stringham from a court martial and ordered him on another board; and has other boards in embryo. Tells Commodore Smith and other Chiefs, if they want anything, to apply to *him*, not to the Secretary.

The officers of the Navy and Army were presented to-day to the President. He said there were so many Navy officers that he supposed Congress would be for reducing the Navy. There were about sixty of them, and over two hundred of the Army officers, but the Navy men say the President made no remarks to the Navy [*sic*] branch of the service indicating reduction.

March 13, *Saturday*. John P. Hale, the worthless and worse than worthless Minister to Spain, is continued, and Perry, the efficient Secretary of Legation, is dismissed, provided the Senate consents.

The papers contain ten or more general naval orders, most of them frivolous and captious, manifesting great zeal to differ with, or cast reflection on, the late Administration

of the Department. It is not difficult to trace them to
Vice-Admiral Porter, who received many favors from that
administration, to which he was always superciliously obsequious until about the period of the Presidential election.
Among the orders revoked is one suspending and repri-
manding Sawyer, a second assistant engineer who denounced President Johnson as a traitor that ought to
be impeached. Grant indorses the revocation, because
Guyon, the principal witness, spoke disrespectfully of
Congress. Neither the Vice-Admiral nor the President
discriminates between denunciation of a superior, which is
destructive of discipline, and denunciations of a legislature
or other body. Both are improper, but one is criminal
and mutinous, insubordinate, and a high military offense.
Had Sawyer said that Admiral Bailey, his immediate commander and commandant of the yard, was a traitor and
deserved to be court-martialed, he would have been tried
and punished, or had one of the Army subordinates said
the same of Grant, he would have been tried and punished;
but, according to this order, he might berate and assail
the superior of Bailey and Grant, the Commander-in-
Chief of Army and Navy, with impunity.

Had charges been preferred against Guyon for disrespectful language towards Congress, he might or might
not have been court-martialed, although it would not, in
that case, have been a military offense, and he might not
have been found guilty, as Sawyer was, of insubordinate
and disrespectful language towards his superior. Party
feeling has moved the President and his Vice-Admiral in
the wrong direction.

Two general orders are issued in the name of the Secretary of the Navy, revoking the sentence of a court martial
in the case of Collins and Bache, the former commander
and the latter navigating officer of the Sacramento, which
was wrecked in the Bay of Bengal, — a loss to the Government of six or eight hundred thousand dollars. Collins was
playing chess, and Bache smoking, forward, when she

stranded. But the revocation says nothing appeared against the latter. He belongs to a distinguished family and is the nephew of Vice-Admiral Porter; why should not his sentence, and suspension, which has expired, be revoked?

March 17, *Wednesday.* This is St. Patrick's Day, and the Irish do not forget it. An interesting debate is going on in the Senate on the repeal of the civil-tenure law. Trumbull, who was an active partisan for its enactment, and who has forgotten or surrendered most of his old Democratic, strict-construction principles, is unwilling to repeal an unconstitutional act which gives undue power to the Senate; but several of the Radical Senators are disposed to retrace their steps, admit the law was personal, passed to cripple the constitutional authority of the late President, etc. The confession is more candid and more creditable than the persistent wrong of Trumbull and others, who, having by party usurpation and fraud got unauthorized power, are unwilling to relinquish it. Edmunds of Vermont, more of a lawyer than legislator or statesman, takes ground with Trumbull. Carpenter, the new Senator from Wisconsin, made his début in a speech claiming that the power of removal is with the Senate, but is willing to suspend the power. He is another lawyer who is regardless of the fundamental law and not a statesman or wise legislator. On the whole, the Radicals do not appear to advantage in this discussion, and the wickedness and injustice by which a usurping majority embarrassed and thwarted the late administration is apparent.

A smart debate took place between Butler and Schenck, neither very scrupulous men. Schenck has, perhaps, more influence in the House, but Butler knows the most.

The papers say that Attorney-General Hoar has given an opinion that Grant has no authority to revoke the pardons granted by President Johnson, which he had attempted. I know nothing of the merits of any of these cases, and should not be surprised if they were not deserving of pardon, but that Grant should interpose and try, by straining and violating the law, to defeat an act of clemency on the part of his predecessor, displays malevolence as well as ignorance, and is characteristic.

I this evening parted with ex-President Johnson and his family, who leave in the morning for Tennessee. No better persons have occupied the Executive Mansion, and I part from them, socially and personally, with sincere regret. Of the President, politically and officially, I need not here speak further than to say he has been faithful to the Constitution, although his administrative capabilities and management may not equal some of his predecessors. Of measures he was a good judge, but not always of men.

March 18, *Thursday.* The Senate is still debating the Tenure-of-Office Law. There is great reluctance to yield power on the part of mankind generally, especially if improperly obtained, and the Radical majority of the Senate is no exception. Although the most stupid of them must be aware that the power and energy of the Executive are crippled, and that the public business, and especially the collection of the revenue, is thereby greatly impaired, still they cling to power. Office is really the great impelling motive of the Radicals, the alpha and omega of their acts. No regard for the Constitution or principle governs them.

March 19, *Friday.* Honest John Lenthall, Chief Naval Constructor, called on me last evening. He feels unhappy over the condition of affairs at the Navy Department. Thinks Mr. Borie well disposed, but that he is feeble, timid, and inefficient. Porter, on the other hand, is officious, presuming, and meddlesome. Borie is dwarfed and overborne by the self-assuming and arrogant Vice-Admiral. L. says P. displays a great amount of ignorance and puerility in his orders and assumptions; talks of economy but spends recklessly. Bridge (Paymaster) came in later in the evening. Listened attentively; hates Porter, but is afraid to say so. I was amused at his timidity, and also disgusted with it.

Grant sends in no nominations; holds up to compel the Senators to surrender their usurped power. Tells applicants that he wishes the law repealed and holds himself under no obligation to remove incumbents whilst it remains. He does not send in a message to Congress, boldly and explicitly stating these things, but does it, as he aided in the passage of the law, in whispers and behind-the-door conversations.

March 22, *Monday.* The city is filled with a hungry crowd, wanting offices which they can't get. Grant uses them to compel the Senate to repeal the Tenure-of-Office Bill. But the Senators are reluctant to give up power; dislike to back down; are also mad. While Grant has now the right of this question, it is to his discredit that he was guilty of exerting himself to impose and continue that villainy as an embarrassment to the Administration of President Johnson. The Radical Senators are getting much divided among themselves; have never had much confidence in each other, but still adhere together for power and plunder.

March 23, *Tuesday.* There is some satisfaction in looking on the movements, and feeling that one has no responsibility for what is done or omitted. The strife here is great and the disappointments will be many. Some remedy should be devised for the great evil of office-seeking and the greater evil of Congressional intermeddling with appointments. The best men in the community for places of trust and responsibility are not those who rush here to get them. But where is the remedy? Congress itself is made up of vagabond adventurers to a great extent, fellows who sell their votes for money, and who intrigue for the worthless on receiving a consideration. There is but little moral or political principle in Congress. The few who are not vicious and debased are destitute of independence, and yield to the discipline and tyranny of party.

.   .   .   .

The supporters of the Tenure-of-Office Bill, finding that they were in a minority of the Senate but in a majority of the party, resorted to the device which they have practiced extensively for the last three years of calling a caucus, to which they endeavored to transfer legislation, and then by party machinery enable the actual minority to decide the fate of the bill. Edmunds and Conkling, two fierce partisans, projected this scheme. The former is a mere lawyer legislator, with no conception of his duties, although an attorney of some sharpness and ability. Conkling has more legislative capacity, but is an egotistical coxcomb, with less political honesty than Edmunds, who would, at any time, sacrifice the right to benefit his party. The friends of repeal were not insensible to the trick which was sought to be practiced, would not be caught, and declared in caucus they would not be bound by its proceedings. This is a good indication. Party machinery and party tyranny may yet be broken. Morton and Conkling are reputed to have had a sharp passage in caucus.

March 24, *Wednesday*. The bill to reorganize the Navy, which Grimes introduced into the Senate a few days since and hurried through that body without discussion, has been checked up by the Representatives. There was an intention of running it through the House without reference to a committee or any examination, but this did not succeed, and a reference took place. In the committee there was soon a conviction that so important a bill, and one involving such radical changes and such marked discriminations, should be well matured. Porter and Borie went twice to the Capitol and presented themselves before the Naval Committee to urge immediate action, and Isherwood tells me they had a letter from Grant expressing a

wish that there might be no delay in its passage, which
they read to some of the members of the committee. It
was the absorbing subject with the head, or heads, of the
Navy Department, but the House Naval Committee came
unanimously to the conclusion, after patiently listening
to Porter, hearing Grimes, and understanding the wishes
of Grant, that it was best to move slowly, and they therefore deferred the further consideration of the bill until next
December. This is a sockdologer to Porter, who had made
his arrangements, based on this bill. Without it he is
literally an intruder in the Department. The bill, among
other provisions, establishes a Board of Survey to consist
of three admirals, of which it is well understood Porter
was to be the President. This would have placed him in
the Department as superior or superintendent.

It is obvious that the scheme of bringing Porter here to
take charge of the Navy Department and the new Secretary
also has been long since planned, and is a part of Grant's
military policy. When Porter, last autumn, in the midst
of the election campaign, volunteered his testimony to
the effect that Grant was a total abstinence man, it was
a bid which was well understood, and which no man of
position, unless a Porter, would make. Those who know
Porter well are aware he can certify to almost anything.

It was easy for Grant to place the War Department
under the military, but the Navy Department is differently organized and some management was necessary.
The selection of a man like Borie, without knowledge of,
or experience in, public affairs, was made on personal
grounds, with reference to the end to be accomplished.
Weak, as regards the duties, but willing to oblige Grant,
he became an instrument. Porter was summoned here
by Grant, before Borie was permitted to enter the Navy
Department, and B. was at once put in Porter's keeping.
Porter came duly prepared, his pockets filled with general
orders which he had been weeks preparing, — some of
them on the most trivial subjects, others mere repetitions

or verbal alterations of existing orders. The Book of Regulations — the uniform regulations, which would require a tailor some days to prepare — was at once established, a winter's work was at once introduced, and in all this poor Borie was a passive tool. He is now a mere clerk to Vice-Admiral Porter, not the Secretary of the Navy. This is Grant's work and purpose. The government is to be conducted on a military plan and system. Law, usage, and civil service are set aside.

The Judiciary Committee in the Senate reported a bill on the Tenure-of-Office Law which is a perfect cheat and swindle. Grant is said to have been consulted by the committee and a compromise was effected. The lawyers duped and cowed him. The poor devil has neither the sagacity and obstinacy for which he has credit, if he assents to this compromise, where the Executive surrenders everything and gets nothing.

I shall not be surprised, however, if Trumbull has induced and seduced Grant. In heart and sentiment Trumbull has become a perfect Senatorial oligarch, and aims to concentrate all power in the Senate. His original Democratic principles — State-Rights and strict construction — he has almost totally abandoned, and seems to suppose the powers of the government are lodged with the Senate; at all events, he wishes the Senate whilst he is a member to exercise them.

March 25, *Thursday.* There was a rumor prevalent to-day that ex-President Johnson died last night from a sudden attack of paralysis. It was founded on the fact that he had a severe attack of disease of the kidneys, and that his physician, Doctor Norris, had been sent for. The President and his family arrived home at Greenville safely on Saturday, where they were received with greetings cordial and sincere from their old neighbors and friends after their long absence.

Moses H. Grinnell has been nominated Collector of

the Port of New York. I am not surprised at it. He is proud, a man trained in the corrupt and corruptible school of New York politics, an old admirer of Daniel Webster. At one period he was one of the merchant princes; he still has a commercial standing and occupies a prominent social position, which will make him careful about prostituting himself or his office. His restraints will be due as much to his commercial standing as to his moral instincts and he will have a studied desire to guard his reputation. Like Hamilton Fish he was formerly devoted to Seward, and like Fish he has become estranged in a measure from his former leader. Both keep up the formalities of friendly intercourse, but there is no heart-feeling on their part, or Seward's.

Commodore Jenkins tells me that Vice-Admiral Porter devotes his time apparently to criticism, — complains of, and picks flaws in, my administration. He has got his boards organized — by appointment of Borie, who is a mere puppet — to examine the hulls and engines that are building, or that were commenced during the War and have since been completed or suspended. Jenkins says he went into the Secretary's room, where Porter had the ledger and books, and Stribling, who is to be president of one of these boards, was examining them with Porter. Stribling manifested any other emotion than that of pride in his work, and, subsequently, in an apologetic way, made inquiries of Jenkins about the employment of workmen, the form of intercourse at the navy yards, the assumption of the Bureaus and their subordinates, and the want of proper deference to commandants of the yards. Jenkins advised him to examine the method of proceedings at the yards, — to make proper inquiries for himself before coming to a conclusion, — and he would find he was on a false scent, and that he had been imposed upon. Stribling seemed mortified, expressed the greatest respect for me, but supposed that old usage had been sacrificed, that commandants had not their rights, and that a worse practice

3

had been introduced. Jenkins said such was not the fact so far as his Bureau was concerned, nor did he believe such practice existed with any other; certain he was that I was vigilant and that, had any deviation been brought to my notice, it would have been properly corrected.

This is a specimen of the low schemes and intrigues that are being practiced. I have done too much for Porter, who is incapable of gratitude, and is eaten up with selfish ambition. The creation of the office of Admiral, which became necessary in order to have naval rank corresponding with that of the military commander of the armies, necessitated the promotion of some one to the office of Vice-Admiral, made vacant by the appointment of Farragut to the highest grade. There was no Rear-Admiral entitled to such promotion. Goldsborough, who was senior, had not a single qualification but size, belly, and lungs. Davis was literary and a scholar without a strong naval fighting record. Dahlgren was cold, and so calculatingly selfish that he feared to do anything lest he might injure his past reputation, which was on the "gun line," — not in their use but the manufacture or make of them. Porter, who had a mixture of good and bad qualities, was preferable, I thought, to either of them, but yet without just claims for the distinction. He had acquitted himself very well at Fort Fisher by persevering in his efforts to carry into effect the wishes and views of the Navy Department. I had placed him in command of the squadron after Farragut declined, because he had energy, ambition, and I knew he would feel that his future success would depend on accomplishing the work prescribed. When it was over, although there were many things which I disapproved, I could not, when the vacancy occurred, do otherwise than give him the place over the heads of others, and after the War was ended, I placed him in the eligible position of Superintendent of the Naval Academy. He had, I thought, some excellent qualities for the position at that particular time, and for two years he discharged the duties well. The third year his restless nature began to develop itself. Change, novelty, new schemes were introduced. He first wanted the European Squadron when it was given to Farragut. Later the party intrigues and Presidential movements enlisted him. He had fostered a factious clique at Annapolis, and began to use the officers for himself and purposes. I did not accord to him full sway, for I perceived his error. Among others he had Walker, a nephew of Senator Grimes, in the academic staff. I regretted the necessity of ordering Walker to the Academy, for I knew the use that would be made of him.

Secret movements soon commenced against the Department, and Grimes began to change his views. Walker came to Washington every few days, and Grimes became distant, changed his views, had new schemes such as he once disapproved. His broken health subjected him more entirely to the malign influence that was brought to bear upon him. Walker was the unconscious dupe and tool of Porter, and Grimes, in his feeble health, was subject to that influence.

When Farragut returned, and the time had arrived for Porter to have the European Squadron, as he had requested, he asked to be excused; said his health was so impaired he could not discharge the duties; the routine at the Academy was pleasant and beneficial to an invalid who could not perform other duties. All of which I understood and was in no sense deceived. Though still obsequious to me, he was paying his court in another quarter. Grant was likely to be elected President and he had volunteered to testify to Grant's total abstinence, which by his published standard deserves reward. He had been accustomed to say to me that Grant was nothing unless associated with Sherman, whom of the two Porter admired most; that together they made a great general. Latterly nothing is said of Sherman. Gradually his calls on me have fallen off. His visits to Washington have been frequent during the fall and winter, but I have seen him only two or three times.

Grimes introduced a bill for a Board of Survey,—a scheme of Porter to get position in Washington. Until Walker became the messenger of Porter, Grimes steadily opposed this Board. The refusal of the Naval Committee in the House to consider Grimes' bill until next December disconcerts Porter, who is at present a mere intruder in the Navy Department without any legal status.

March 26, Friday. The House by a majority of over twenty refuses concurrence with the Senate in its modification of the Tenure-of-Office Act, and insists on unconditional repeal. Grant is quoted as having surrendered to the lawyer intriguers, but the House, more sensible, more sagacious, and more firm, holds out. Still Bingham, Schenck, and the scheming ultra-Radicals are in concert with the Senate intriguers, and, having made a dupe of Grant, . . . they will labor to have the Senate recognized as a part of the executive power, clothed with authority to check and control the President for party purposes. Trumbull and Edmunds, two Radical lawyers, are active in this scheme.

Borie has sent a letter to the Naval Committee for the repeal of the eight-hour law. Though right in this, it was not wise or politic at this time. The demagogues in Congress enacted the law regardless of the public interest, and dare not repeal it, whatever may be their convictions.

March 27, Saturday. The President has rescinded that part of his order which placed the War Department under the General of the armies. It was a part of a scheme for a military government that Grant has had in view, which neither Congress nor the country was yet prepared to sanction. The Navy Department was in like manner to have been organized, and may be yet. Porter is ready to take on himself any authority which others will permit, with law or without law.

Doolittle tells me he has had a talk with General Butler,

who says the House will to the end insist on repeal of the Civil-Tenure Bill. He, B., has seen Grant and tried to have a conversation with him and make him comprehend the features of this amendment. "But," said Butler, "he is stupidly dull and ignorant and no more comprehends his duty or his power under the Constitution than that dog," pointing to a small dog near them. Butler's expression of ineffable contempt, Doolittle says, cannot be described, when he alluded to Grant.

I am also told by Doolittle that Stewart, when he found he could not be Secretary of the Treasury, requested as a special favor that Ethan Allen might be appointed District Attorney in New York. But Grant regretted to inform Stewart that he had promised that place to a Mr. Ford, the brother of one of Grant's cronies. This promise he had made last summer. Ford is an obscure lawyer, without standing or position. Poor Stewart is mortified and chagrined that he has made himself an ass and expended his money for nothing.

Sprague, though not an orator, has been telling the Senators some truths. At first they were disposed to treat his attacks on, or exposure of, the lawyers with levity, and Nye . . . attacked him with severity, but though this amused the galleries for the moment, Sprague's remarks remain.

March 29, *Monday.* Ex-President Johnson has recovered from the painful attack which prostrated him, and is announced to speak at Greenville, Nashville, a... Memphis. He has been an effective speaker in Tennessee in former years, and may succeed again, but ten years have changed the character of the people, and the people themselves, nor is it likely that he remains unchanged. I shall not be surprised, therefore, if he is not as successful as in former years, and, under the sweeping proscription by which Brownlow and his faction have aimed to disfranchise all who are opposed to them, the ex-President may

find it more difficult than he apprehends to serve the
State.

March 30, *Tuesday*. Montgomery Blair came to see
me. His brother Frank has sued the authorities in St.
Louis, who refused his vote unless he would take the ironclad oath of Missouri, which required him to swear that
he had not opposed the administration of the general
government nor the government of the State of Missouri,
whereas he had opposed and defeated the Rebel governor
and Rebel organization of that State in 1861, and with
General Lyon extricated the State from Rebel control. His
vote being rejected, he brought suit, which was last week
argued before the Supreme Court. Montgomery B. thinks
the case was well presented, and they will gain their case.
He is, however, a sanguine man, and never doubts that
his brother Frank is always right. I think he is in this instance, and is oftener right and has much greater sagacity
than his opponents believe.

Montgomery Blair regretted that President Johnson
should have gone to Coyle's after leaving the Executive
Mansion. The habits, practices, and character of C. should
have prevented it. He says he found it difficult to get to
the President, but he asked Rives, one of his aides, what
he intended doing and where going when he left the White
House, and R. told him where he was to go. As he did so,
R. shrugged his shoulders. B. expressed his regret, and R.
also. He said to Blair — what he declared he had said to
no one else — that Coyle and too many like him had surrounded the President during his whole term. Blair says
they flattered and deceived him, . . . and Blair thinks the
President could not have been entirely ignorant of facts
that were so notorious. But Blair is censorious. He said,
however, he imputed nothing corrupt or venal to President Johnson. The difficulty was he tolerated scoundrels
around him, and permitted them to do what he would
scorn to do himself. I remarked that I had inquired of him

heretofore concerning Moore, who is a Washingtonian.
Blair said that was some time ago and he had given no
attention to the subject then, but since, and recently,
damaging information had come to him, and that he now
knew personally that Moore had played a false part and
deceived Johnson. I had no reason, I said, to suppose he
was unfaithful to the President, except the fact that
Stanton had placed him there and that he had previously been in Stanton's employ. I never heard an expression from him against Stanton, even when Stanton's
treachery was detected and exposed, and on one or two
occasions some facts appear to have reached Stanton
which I could account for in no other way than through
Moore. In everything, aside from Stanton, it always appeared to me he was true to the President and serviceable
to him — and I could not say [*sic*].

March 31, *Wednesday.* The Tenure-of-Office Bill went
to a committee of conference, on which was Trumbull,
Edmunds, and Grimes for the Senate, Butler, Washburn
of Wisconsin, and Bingham for the House. The opponents
of repeal had the advantage, except that Butler was relied
upon as equal to all opponents. But he was flattered by
the association, cajoled, and failed his friends. Like other
too cunning men, and men under the shade, he was too
compliant and shrewd. He gained his points as regards
ultimate removal, but yielded a principle. His sly, tricky
management was outwitted and his fierce energy mollified.
Butler vanquished himself. He has congratulated himself that, if the public denounced him as a knave, no one
asserted he was a fool, but this self-laudation is his no
longer. He has been befooled, flattered, and made an ass
of.

I hear that the compromise passed both houses. Very
likely, and each congratulated itself that it has beaten the
other. Butler has been outgeneraled, has lost reputation
for shrewdness.

LXVIII

The Compromise on the Tenure-of-Office Bill passes Both Houses — Porter as "Lord of the Admiralty" — Connecticut goes Radical in the State Election — Possibility of War with Spain — Congress adjourns after placing the Matter of Reconstruction in the President's Hands — Morton's Amendment requiring the Adoption of the Fifteenth Amendment to the Constitution before a State is given Representation — Corruption not confined to one Party — A General Sweep of Official Incumbents — Diplomatic Appointments — Motley goes to England, Washburne to France — The Senate rejects the Alabama Treaty after a Speech against it by Sumner — Regrets at leaving Washington — A Courtesy from Vice-Admiral Porter — Reflections on relinquishing Office — The Return to Hartford — Call on Admiral Farragut in New York — The Admiral suffering from Official Neglect — Changes in Hartford in Eight Years — Getting settled — Grant's Unfitness for the Presidency — Secretary Borie a Nonentity — Admiral Porter's Order to Change the Names of Men-of-War — The Alabama Question and the British Public.

April 1, Thursday. Secretary Borie has rescinded one of his illegal general orders, issued by direction of Porter. Some one has informed the [indecipherable] that it was not only without authority of law but in violation of law. It is not the only general order liable to the same charge. But Porter never paid much regard to law or regulations at a time when either conflicted with his convenience, and, as for Borie, he seems to know nothing either of his duties or of law, nor cares to know.

The compromise on the Tenure-of-Office Bill has passed both houses. All the Democrats and some of the most sensible and reputable Republicans voted against it. On looking at the subject more deliberately to-day, my last evening's impressions are confirmed. The only question is, Was Butler a treacherous knave or a silly, egotistical dupe? He has betrayed those who trusted him through either design or ignorance, and he is not a fool, though in this instance foolish. But Grimes and Washburne are equally implicated, though Butler was considered the leader. They each trusted the other, doubtless, and thought to patch up and heal a disagreement in the party.

Commodore Jenkins has resigned his position as Chief of the Bureau of Navigation and is assigned to duty as Secretary of the Lighthouse Board. Rear-Admiral Harwood, who was secretary of that board, has been detached and is to be placed as one of the Retiring Board, which is hereafter to hold permanent session in Washington. It is easy to perceive that one object in this movement is to control the action of the retiring, or "ex," board in certain cases. Favorites will be treated lightly; those who are under the displeasure of the "Lord of the Admiralty," as Porter is now called, will be likely to fare hard. A factious clique aims to govern the Navy.

Jenkins is one of the most faithful, industrious, laborious, and best-informed officers in the service; better fitted for the position he occupied than any man of his grade. There were prejudices against him, deeply and cunningly introduced and magnified by the man who has compelled his resignation.

April 2, Friday. President Grant sent in quite a batch of nominations to-day. From this I infer that he acquiesces in the passage of the mongrel, bungling, exceptional piece of legislation on the Tenure-of-Office Bill which was rushed through the two houses. There was some expectation of a veto among his best friends, but it is not in him, and his Cabinet advisers have hardly the stamina for such a step. Besides, the matter is in such a shape that the whole thing is embarrassing.

Butler and the extreme Radicals were defeated yesterday on the Mississippi question by a union of the more considerate Radicals with the Democrats. It was a very handsome rebuke to the despotic demagogue.

An order has gone out from the Navy Department reducing the wages of workmen one fifth below outsiders in consequence of the eight-hour law. The order is correct in principle, but will be fiercely resisted in Congress by the demagogues who passed it.

Borie has sent a letter to the Naval Committee urging the establishment of a Board of Survey; says he shall be compelled to reduce the staff if it is not done, etc. The handiwork of Porter is perceptible in all this, and the threat may accomplish the work. It is disgraceful that there should be such an intrigue in the Navy Department. Borie would not himself have attempted it, but Porter would not hesitate to instigate and pass it. Under menace, the staff officers may yield, though I should be sorry to see it.

April 3, Saturday. An opinion has been obtained from Attorney-General Hoar reversing the opinion given by Attorney-General Bates on which the action of the Department was founded in March, 1863, with the approbation of President Lincoln, increasing the relative rank of staff officers. I have always doubted whether the regulations could be maintained, if dissented to or opposed and brought to a legal test, and therefore advised the staff to have the regulations confirmed by Congress and then legalized. But they were not satisfied with the rank given them and therefore would not move, — not unlikely would have opposed legislation, had it been attempted. But the regulations have been in force six years, have been recognized by the Executive and Congress, have become a usage, are equitable and right in themselves, provided there is to be assimilated rank, and no person avows himself opposed to them. But the staff do not favor a Board of Survey, and without such a board, Vice-Admiral Porter has no legal status in the Department. The Naval Committee have decided they would not consider the subject of such a board until December, and this opinion has been extorted from the Attorney-General, when overwhelmed with more pressing and important business, in order to gratify the grasping aspirations of the Vice-Admiral. Having got Attorney-General Hoar's opinion, reversing that of Attorney-General Bates, Mr. Borie signs an order which had been prepared for him, reducing the rank of the staff. Not unlikely this Congress will be wheedled and dragooned into Porter's schemes of a Board of Survey, by coercing the staff into an assent to that measure, provided they can secure the rank which was given them by me.

April 5, Monday. Great excitement in Congress and New York on the subject of the Pacific Railroad. I have looked upon the transactions connected with that road as in some particulars outrageously fraudulent. Durant, the manager, has the reputation of being a knave, and there are Members of Congress involved in the swindle. Fisk, an adventurer and operator in New York, had a fight with the concern, and, the board refusing to produce their books, the court has authorized the safe to be broken open, which has been finally done, after a day's labor, with sledge-hammers, crowbars, etc., etc.

April 6, Tuesday. Grant yesterday signed the new Tenure-of-Office Bill. He has been defeated and over-reached in this matter. This is not surprising. Thus far he does not promise a very wise or successful administration. The folly of making a Chief Magistrate of a man who is totally ignorant of civil affairs and destitute of statesmanship will perhaps be demonstrated to the satisfaction of all by the present Executive.

Returns from the Connecticut election, which took place yesterday, indicate the success of the Radical ticket. Party, not principle, has controlled. How soon the people will come out from Radical delusion and take care of themselves and their rights, God only knows. The people of Connecticut are as capable as those of any State to govern themselves and take care of their liberties, yet, in the madness and delusion of party, they vote away the foundation principles of free government. They are blind, stupidly and inexcusably blind, to their own best interests, when they strip their State of its sovereignty and transfer it to the Central Government.

There has been less interest, apparently, in the election than usual, though great questions were involved, and there was some not very judicious management. The nomination of Dixon in the First Congressional District as the Democratic candidate was a mistake. He was the candidate of a party which, for a quarter of a century, had opposed him and he it. Although he has placed himself squarely on the Democratic platform, and of late has pursued a course which Democrats approve, still old antagonisms were not forgotten, and with them there was distrust, disgust, and lack of zeal. Dixon flattered himself, and many Democrats deceived themselves, with the belief that he would secure votes from his old party friends and associates, — a not uncommon mistake. Personal influence, under such circumstances, is of little account. It is doubtful whether he got ten such, while he lost hundreds which a different candidate would have secured.

April 7, Wednesday. I hear of quite a number of vessels being ordered to be fitted for immediate service. Other vessels are ordered to join the North Atlantic Squadron. Their movements indicate trouble in the Antilles, and especially in Cuba. It may be proper that the squadron may be reinforced since the disturbances in that island have assumed such magnitude, but great prudence and circumspection, as well as vigilance, are necessary. From the large force which is being fitted out, and the characteristics of Porter, who evidently has entire control of the Navy Department, is reckless of expenditure and ambitious to make a display, and from certain manifestations which I have heretofore observed in Grant, I am somewhat apprehensive that we may become involved in difficulties with Spain. In that case the whole of the maritime countries of southern Europe will sympathize with her. General Banks, who is chairman of the Committee on Foreign Relations in the House, is not a suitable man for the position at any time, and especially not now. He is voluble and shallow, aspiring and pretentious.

A war with so weak a government as Spain in the present unfortunate condition of our exhausted country would be lamentable. The Administration is in feeble and incompetent hands, — men who are partisans or nothings; the Union is disrupted by exclusion; States are plundered of their property and rights, and are governed by force; an immense debt and unreliable measures make the prospect sad. But the people have brought these things upon themselves. They have not yet aroused to their true condition. In devotion to party they have to a great extent forgotten, or been inattentive to, their obligations to the country.

While the Administration is sending a large number of armed ships into Cuban waters, and we have rumors of illegal expeditions fitting out in our country to aid the insurgents there, and our countrymen are sympathizing with them, no proclamation enjoining neutrality is issued by the President.

April 8, Thursday, and 9, Friday. Chief Engineer King called upon me this evening. Says he has had some difficulty with Vice-Admiral Porter. The late order reducing the rank of the staff he thought unjust, and he addressed a letter to Secretary Borie on the subject. This Porter did not like, — he tolerates no differences. I had been told by others of this disagreement, which was represented to be much sharper than K. mentions, and I am also told that P. said he was much disappointed in K. and cared not how soon he resigned.

Commodore Lenthall[1] also called. He laments the change that has been made; thinks the men at the head of the

---

[1] Naval Constructor John Lenthall, as Chief of the Bureau of Construction and Repair, had the rank of Commodore.

government scarcely know what Porter and Borie are about. Orders upon orders are received of a most singular character. Commodore Selfridge, chairman of one of the boards, sent to the different navy yards to examine the vessels, has made reports recommending changes in the vessels which exhibit his own incapacity, and at the same time his desire to please those who sent him on this examination. As a constructor, L. says he finds it necessary that he should take lessons of Selfridge to unlearn the lessons, teachings, and experience of a lifetime. Porter was anxious that L. should adopt Selfridge's recommendations, but L. said he could not adopt and make them his; if, however, explicit orders were given him, he should execute these orders. P. asked if he would not adopt some. L. said he could not. "Well, then," said P., "let them go." L. says, however, he has complied with a request of P. that more sail should be placed upon vessels of the Algoma class.

Each of these bureau officers is, I see, exceedingly dissatisfied, and my sympathies are with them and the staff, who are each subjected to improper treatment, and I freely, too freely perhaps, to them and others expressed my opinions and feelings.

April 10, *Saturday.* Congress adjourned to-day at noon, as agreed by resolution. Sumner, Butler, and some of the extreme Radicals were opposed and would be glad to have a continuous session. They desire to govern.

The President sent a message to Congress on the subject of Reconstruction. Congress passed a resolution, or law, putting the subject in his hands. Morton[1] put on an amendment that the States should not be admitted, or represented, until they adopted the Fifteenth Amendment to the Constitution, which is now pending. As if Congress could override the Constitution, dictate terms to a State, and prescribe conditions on which it should have representation! But this is all in character with the disunion

[1] Senator Oliver P. Morton of Indiana.

proceedings of the Radicals. An amendment of the Constitution, thus forced by a usurping Congress upon the country, is a nullity, and should be so treated whenever the government is rescued from Radical hands.

The Senate is to continue in session to act upon appointments and treaties. But little good can be expected from that body with such a President and Senate as we now have. Office and power are the great end and aim of each. In vain do we look to them for relief and statesmanship. Overwhelmed in debt, no financial scheme is matured; none has been broached, even, which has received or is entitled to decent respect. The Union wrenched asunder by the Radicals, who professed regard for its maintenance, States denied their inherent, reserved, and guaranteed rights, the Constitution and its obligations disregarded and trampled down by those who were elected to carry out its provisions and swore to support them, the country is indeed in a lamentable condition. The tyranny of party is vastly stronger than any ties of patriotism or the obligations of an oath.

Some of the Radical Senators revolted at this new and villainous proposition of Morton and voted against it, but the carpet-baggers came opportunely to his support. A reaction must take place against these atrocious measures, which are a mockery of free government and enlightened public opinion.

April 12, *Monday.* The Senate convened to-day at noon, and the President sent in quite a list of nominations, —many of them renominations, I suppose, that were not acted upon at the regular session which expired on Saturday. Ashley, the impeacher, was confirmed as Governor of Montana, after a long and severe struggle in the Senate, by one majority. The nomination and confirmation of this corrupt wretch after the exposure of his profligacy and baseness in the appointment of Case to be Surveyor-General of Colorado, which he procured from President

Lincoln, and the wrong that he exacted in return, — a share in the profits and plunder which the position gave, etc., etc., — is further evidence of the total debasement of the Radical Party. Some Republican Senators, it seems, opposed him, but, Grant having selected him, the appointment was confirmed. Had one or two more votes been wanting, they would have been forthcoming.

.   .   .   .

The country is becoming, though very slowly, aware of the corruptions and abuses which are being practiced, but does not yet assume resolution to correct them. The people, carried away by party, try to justify or excuse their palpable enormities by declaring that degeneracy is general, and their opponents are as wicked and venal as their friends. I am sorry to be compelled to believe that corruption is not confined to one party. It is the disgrace and wickedness of the times, imputable in part to the evils of war in the first instance and not checked, but encouraged, by the Radicals, who have made corruption common, and from which some of their opponents have not had the firmness and virtue to abstain.

April 15, Thursday. The Administration appears to be making an unusual change or general sweep of all official incumbents, irrespective of party. Friends and supporters, men who are faithful and efficient, many of whom have been for years, some of them a quarter of a century, in public employment, are summarily ejected from office. One cannot but feel sympathy for these suffering individuals, who are unfitted for other employment after having spent a large portion of their lives in the faithful discharge of their duties, from which they have been unexpectedly and without premonition dismissed. But the country is a sufferer as well as the dismissed officials. No new appointee can make good the place of many of these faithful servants in the Departments, who have the traditions of the service and a familiarity with the law, usages, and routines, which are only acquired by experience. There are many worthless fellows in bureaus and at clerical desks who should be displaced, but such are quite as likely to be retained as any in these party, ill-considered, and imprudent changes.

The foreign appointments which are being made of ministers and consuls are, in many instances, discreditable. Scarcely one can be called a first-class selection. Mr. Motley, who has the first mission, that of London, is a literary man, a book-maker, a man of some reputation in that respect, but he has not the proper talent and ability for so important a mission as that of England, at so interesting a period as this. While at Vienna he displayed no diplomatic ability, nor had he, perhaps, an opportunity. He goes, therefore, to the first and most important mission abroad without experience, or any manifestation of diplomatic capacity, and is undoubtedly indebted to the "McCracken letter," and his petulant, querulous, insolent response, and to the controversy and notoriety which followed, for his present appointment. He is selected to spite Seward, — these are the lofty considerations which influence this Administration.

Washburne, the vulgar and mean, represents the Administration, not his country, to France. Then there is a Jones, whom no one knows but Grant and Washburne, . . . is nominated to Belgium. His only recommendation is that he has been an active party electioneerer for Washburne, the contemptible. Pile,[1] an ignorant, prejudiced partisan, formerly a frontier Methodist ranter, is nominated to Brazil. So of others. Small men with limited comprehension and limited capacity, but who are Radical Grant men, are hastily pressed forward by scores. Of their adaptability Grant himself is not competent to judge, nor could a man more familiar with the necessary requirements for these positions have informed himself in so brief a period.

[1] William A. Pile. He was rejected by the Senate, but afterwards was made Governor of New Mexico.

3

The consular appointments are most of them deplorable. The selections made by Seward, I thought, were many of them objectionable, but these now made are worse.

Sickles and his friends aver that he was promised the Spanish Mission by Grant himself, yet the promise was broken and the place was given to Sanford,[1] to the great disgust, as well as disappointment, of Sickles. It does not surprise me that Grant broke his promise, — not that he is an habitual liar, but he can prevaricate and violate the truth when his necessities are great with as much readiness as any man I ever knew. Nor ought I, perhaps, to be surprised, when I see what is going on, that he should have promised a man of the character and reputation of Sickles, so high, and honorable, and responsible a place as the mission to Spain.

Kingly, son-in-law of J. P. Hale, was nominated Secretary of the Spanish Legation in place of Perry, between whom and Hale there has been a controversy.[2] Hale requested his friend Washburne to oust Perry, and Grant ousted him, but has since revoked his action. Hale is charged with having prostituted his office as Minister to smuggling. The subject is undergoing investigation by the Spanish Government. Hale is a canting hypocrite, corrupt and base. He opposed me, and the Navy and Navy Department, throughout the War and as long as he remained in the Senate, because I would not allow him to job the Department. Villainy and baseness ultimately gets its reward.

April 16, *Friday.* Sumner has made an able speech in the Senate on the Alabama Treaty, which received but one vote, that of McCreery of Kentucky. Thus end the labors of Seward and Reverdy Johnson on that important sub-

---

[1] Henry S. Sanford, the Minister to Belgium. He was rejected by the Senate, and General Sickles received the appointment.

[2] If this nomination ever actually reached the Senate, it failed of confirmation. John Hay was eventually appointed to the position.

ject. I never thought that this was the time, or that they rightly appreciated the question, or that they were the proper men to adjust or to attempt the settlement of it. Better would it have been had they not made the attempt.

President Johnson had wrought himself into a desire to arrange a treaty to close that controversy, and identified himself with his Secretary and Minister in the matter. The treaty was such, when first submitted, that I am incredulous as to the sincerity of Seward, and at no time have I believed the Senate would sanction it, — though Sumner would deprecate difficulty with England. This emphatic rejection is not peaceful, yet I do not in the least apprehend hostilities.

I did not admire Mr. Seward's treatment of the subject of those depredations and the part taken by England during the War nor since. He exhibited, I thought, but feeble statesmanship and little knowledge of international law, and, although his present admirers and others award him great diplomatic skill and ability in his management of affairs with both England and France, I think he displayed very little. Sumner, then and now, showed more knowledge and talent and a more correct appreciation of the matter than Mr. Seward. There is more manly vigor and true statesmanship in this speech than in all of Seward's diplomacy with England. Sumner is better informed and better grounded on our foreign relations than on the true principles of our government.

April 17, *Saturday.* The Senate did not adjourn to-day, as many anticipated it would. It is now understood they will adjourn on Tuesday. There seems a strong disposition with some extreme Radicals to get away. Treaties and nominations are before them unacted upon; the Administration is beginning to be understood and is gaining neither strength nor respect.

Grant drove past my house in a dogcart this P.M. His wife and two children were with him. I was sitting at the window, and Mrs. Grant turned to me and made a low bow. I mention the fact because, though we have two or three times met, it is the first sign of recognition since the day her husband left the Cabinet.

McCulloch called on me last evening, and regretted that I leave Washington. Thinks I would be better satisfied here than in Hartford, for eight years' separation from old friends at the latter place have weakened and severed most of the ties which once endeared the place, while here I have formed new friendly associations, and am generally known and properly regarded. There is much truth in these remarks, and I feel that I have an ordeal and trial to pass through for a few weeks to come which I would be glad to avoid. Blair was here this evening and expressed himself even warmer and more feelingly on the subject of our approaching separation. I confess to the reluctance with which I part from the people and society of Washington, where I have experienced unremitting kindness, and especially from the circle of intimate personal and political friends and associates with whom, through storm and sunshine, through trials and vicissitudes, in war and peace, under two administrations, I have had many pleasant and happy, as well as some sad and trying, hours. But it is best that the brief span of life that remains to me should be passed in the land of my nativity.

I have employed the week in preparation for my departure, gathering up, with my wife and sons, our household effects and making ready to leave.

Vice-Admiral Porter, who has charge and control of the Navy and Navy Department, has, with great courtesy, placed the Tallapoosa, dispatch boat, at my service, to convey my effects to Hartford, when on her way to Boston, which will save me much trouble and the necessity of transshipment. This act of the Vice-Admiral is, on his part, a recognition of friendly official benefits conferred, and for which he cannot otherwise than feel grateful. How far his liberality may be justified and approved, is a question which I shall not scan, but the tender he has made I have been glad to accept.

Not a feeling, or one single moment, of regret has crossed my mind on relinquishing office; in leaving the cares, responsibilities, and labors which I have borne and tried faithfully to execute, I feel satisfying relief. I miss, it is true, the daily routine which has become habitual, but the relief from many perplexities more than counterbalances it. My duties were honestly and fearlessly discharged. These facts are known by all who have any knowledge on the subject. They have passed into history. I look back upon the past eight years of my Washington official life with satisfaction and a feeling that I have served my country usefully and well. My ambition has been gratified, and with it a consciousness that the labors I have performed, the anxieties I have experienced, the achievements I have been instrumental in originating and bringing to glorious results, and the great events connected with them will soon pass in a degree from remembrance or be only slightly recollected. Transient are the deeds of men, and often sadly perverted and misunderstood.

May 2, Sunday. Hartford, Allyn House. Two weeks have passed since I have opened this book. The days have been occupied in breaking up our establishment in Washington, closing our affairs, preparing to return, and in returning to Connecticut. Friends called to express regret, many to urge and advise us to remain. Generally, I believe these friendly manifestations were sincere; and I confess to occasional misgivings in leaving W., where I have had many enjoyments, not unmixed with cares and anxieties, it is true. The climate is to me more genial than that of New England, — the springs and autumns in genial mildness surpass ours, — and the society, in many respects is more agreeable and social. But regard for our children, the counsel of my wife, and many circumstances admonished me to again return to the State of my birth, the friends

of early years, and to pass my few remaining days in the
land of my ancestors. Here I expect to, and shall in all
probability, end my earthly pilgrimage, here close the
record of my life, and here lie down beside my children
who have gone before me.

We left Washington on the morning of Tuesday, the
27th of April. Edgar remained to close up our affairs. Most
of our effects were sent on board the Tallapoosa, which
had been tendered me to transport my effects to Hartford;
the remainder were sold on the day we left, at auction.
Mrs. Welles and our sons were faithful and industrious in
packing and preparing to leave.

We have had a pleasant home in Washington. The house
we occupied became our position, and in every respect
matters were made to correspond. The depreciation of
the currency and the great advance in prices have consumed the salary paid me, and in a pecuniary point of
view, I am probably poorer to-day than if I had not been
in office. My business affairs have been neglected, so that
I have made no gains. All my time has been faithfully
given to the public service.

We had a pleasant time from Washington to New York,
and stopped with Mr. Morgan on Washington Square
until the afternoon of the 28th. I called on Admiral Farragut, whom I found quite ill but slightly recovering.
The impression at first was that I had better not see him,
but he soon sent for me, and the interview, I think, bene-
fited him. His ailment is mostly nervous, the result, in a
great measure, of official neglect and the condition of things
at Washington. He feels acutely the slight that is shown
him, and the orders and movements which were calculated
to, and I am constrained to believe were intended to, annoy
him. He and myself have been subjected to similar slights
by Porter, whom we both have favored.

I would not permit the Admiral to dwell on these matters which so keenly and sorely affected him, but told him
we must for the time being patiently bear with any injus-

tice; that, in considering the subject, I philosophized, and
he better than myself could do so; that I had said to one
or two friends who sought to cheer and comfort me that,
in reviewing the past eight years, I was conscious I had
done well, that I should be gratified if those who succeeded
me would do better, satisfied if they did as well, and if they
failed, the failure would be theirs, the credit would be mine.
In a much stronger degree could he take this view. He
need not fear that his countrymen and posterity would
fail to do him justice. My remarks soothed, comforted,
and consoled him.

We left New York at 3 P.M. and reached Hartford at
seven, stopping at the Allyn House. Nearly four years
have passed since I have been here, more than eight since
I left and took up my residence in Washington. In that
period I have only three times come back to Connecticut
for two or three days on each occasion. Changes in that
time have taken place. Hartford itself has greatly altered, — I might say improved, for it has been beautified
and adorned by many magnificent buildings, and the population has increased. These I see and appreciate; but I
feel, more sensibly than these, other changes which come
home to my heart. A new and different people seem to
move in the streets. Few, comparatively, are known to me.
A new generation which knows not Joseph is here. Of those
that remain scarcely one responds to my warm greeting
with equal warmth. Some that were most intimate are
gone, to find homes elsewhere, or have left the scenes we
loved, forever. In looking around in the few days I have
been here, I learn that hearts which I valued have passed
away. They are cold in the grave; others colder are out
of it.

May 3, *Monday.* The papers announce my return and
that with my friends I am at the Allyn House. No cordial
welcome or word of approval appears. I came quietly,
without previous announcement and without show or

ostentation; the moving busy throng have left me alone. I wished no herald to announce my return nor any parade to give it éclat. I should have been glad to have seen and taken by the hand some of the friends of other years, but only A. E. Burr and J. G. Bolles have yet called and welcomed me. I have met many in the street who greeted me kindly, expressed themselves glad to see me, and I doubt not were so; but it was commonplace gladness, for neither they nor their friends have called to see me or mine. This seems a cold return for eight years' devoted service as unsparing and faithful as man ever gave to his country. But, while I cannot be insensible or indifferent to it, I do not impute the slight entirely to estrangement or indifference. The temperament and habit of the people have much to do with it. Nevertheless, it is unpleasant. I come almost as a stranger after years of absence, and wish to rent or purchase a home, but among all my old friends not one extends any friendly aid or assistance, though some of them know my wants.

Property is extremely high in price, and no purchase can be made except at a sacrifice. A little friendly advice and assistance from old friends who are residents and who know values would be acceptable, but I do not get it.

May 9, *Sunday.* The past week has been a busy one. With my sons I have roamed the city looking at houses, but find none for sale which are in all respects satisfactory. Prices are ruinously high to purchase, and yet I do not wish to rent, become familiar, and be again compelled to move. Age is telling upon me.

After considerable cogitation and search we have pretty much concluded to purchase the house . . . on Charter Oak Place. It is a more expensive place than I can well afford, and in several respects not to my mind, but nevertheless is perhaps the best which is immediately obtainable.

I was the more easily persuaded into this large investment in real estate in consequence of the unsettled and uncertain condition of the currency, owing to vicious legislation and bad management of the finances. There is wildness in Congress; we are without stability or system; all is afloat concerning values.

During the week old friends have called and welcomed me back, and I am not aware that any were turned away from me. The prompt cordiality of Washington is not a characteristic of Hartford, and my quiet, unannounced return had doubtless some influence in restraining advances. My old friend Calvin Day was absent from the city when I arrived, and did not get home until midnight on Saturday. As soon as he knew I was here, on Monday morning, he called. H. A. Perkins, Mrs. Colt, Beach, Seymour, etc., etc., called. Mark Howard is absent. Governor Hawley saw me at breakfast on Wednesday last and immediately came and greeted me. He declared he knew nothing of my being in the city until he saw me, although it was a week after my arrival had been announced in his paper.

The government steamer Tallapoosa, which had my effects on board, drew so much water that the pilot feared to cross the bar at Saybrook, and they therefore were landed at New London on Saturday, the 1st, and brought by steamer thence to Hartford on the 3d. This misfortune to me was the occasion of special exultation by party scavengers. The *New York Tribune* had two or three malicious articles on the subject. The *Courant* of this city imitated the *Tribune* in an article by its local contributor, which, however, Governor Hawley, the editor, promptly corrected the following day. The love of scandal and malice is great with many, and the *New York Tribune* is not excelled in this regard. It has little followers.

The General Assembly convened on Wednesday, and the Governor, Jewell, was inaugurated. The day was pleasant and the crowd in attendance great. In days long gone by

I enjoyed and participated in these ceremonies. It is many days since the mere ceremony and forms have given me interest, and to-day, when I see that by mere party force a majority gathered to debase the State and surrender the high attribute of sovereignty to central power, I not only have no interest in, but a positive disinclination to witness, the pageant.

The Governor (Jewell) is a pleasant business man, of light calibre, with no fitness or proper aptitude for the place. He has been pecuniarily successful, and wealth alone, without other qualifications, has given him the office. His intentions are probably well; but of the laws, institutions, wants, and necessities of the State and people he knows but little. His message was written chiefly by others, and its most important declaration of principles was from my teachings, and views, against corporations and special privileges.

May 16, *Sunday.* A letter from McRitchie on the Tallapoosa, received last Sunday evening, informed us that our furniture and things were at New London. Edgar and John went there and returned with them on the steamer Sunshine on Monday. We placed them in our recently purchased house on Tuesday. . . .

May 30, *Sunday.* Two days of incessant employment and care, with family unsettled, effects, books, papers, etc., in confusion, with no servants, or with discontented ones, Mrs. W. disabled and confined to her room from injury by a fall, have made me, unused as I am to these matters, exceedingly uncomfortable. Two hundred and twenty-four boxes were received from Washington, four loads from Glastonbury, besides a considerable amount of furniture which had been left eight years ago with friends in Hartford, have been brought to the house to arrange. To assist in this, with other cares, has left me neither time nor inclination to write.

We came into possession of the house on the 19th inst.,
Wednesday. Our three sons at once commenced vigorously
and earnestly to put the household in order, and have devoted themselves faithfully to that object since.

Edgar left on Thursday for Saratoga via New York, to
be present at the wedding of one of his classmates. Tom
went yesterday to Granville with a fishing party. I have
not been fifty rods from the house for a week until yesterday, when I had to go to the bank on business. Met Mr.
Hamersley on my way, who invited me to his store, where
we had an hour, on political subjects chiefly. It is somewhere about fifteen years since we have had such and so
long a conversation.

So far as I have met and seen old friends, I have had
every reason to be satisfied. Though not very demonstra-
tive, or forward in calling, they have without exception
been cordial and apparently sincere.

The little that I see and hear of public affairs confirms
me in the opinion which I formed in daily personal interviews of the unfitness of Grant. He has no proper ideas of
government, makes his Administration personal, does not
comprehend nor care for great principles. Measures are
to him of minor importance, and his views of government
consist in displacing and appointing men to office, regardless of their qualifications and of the public interest. Grant
has no sympathies, very little patriotism, but intense selfishness. His career previous to the Rebellion was not such
as would be likely to elevate and ennoble his character,
and his rapid and great advancement has intoxicated and
intensified a naturally sordid mind. In his Cabinet appointments he has not been fortunate. One of his limited
capacity and mental power should be aided by competent
advisers.

The Navy Department is strangely administered, but
is much as Grant would have it. Borie seems to be a
nonentity, and Porter a light-headed factotum, spoiled by
favors too freely granted. To make a change from the acts

and policy of the last Administration, to do things differently and pursue a different course, though worse, seems to be the great end and purpose of those who now control the Navy Department. It is necessary to say *those*, for, though done in the name of Borie, these things emanate from Porter, and he desires to have it so understood. Many of the changes are frivolous and puerile; some may be well enough; some are not creditable but objectionable. The last order is to change the names of some of the men-of-war and give them tame, flat, and insipid English names instead of American or Indian. To ape, imitate, and copy the English is the object and pitiful course of too many Americans, and the present managers of the Navy Department are of the number. To extinguish the native names as well as to exterminate the native race has been the narrow purpose of the bigots and fools of our country from the first. In making these changes vessels in actual commission are not exempted, and vessels which have been unfortunate or lost at sea have their names revived.

It is obvious that Porter had intrigued and had an understanding with Grant (who does not know the man who uses him) long before the change of administration, and that through the winter he was preparing to take charge of the Department. Borie is evidently a convenient tool, who was substituted, as the nominal head, after the Senatorial intimation that military and naval men should not be placed in charge of the civil administration of the Departments.

June 6, Sunday. Another toilsome, troubled week has passed. Difficulty in obtaining good and willing servants is annoying and vexatious. To serve is no part of the intention of a large portion of the hired help or assistants, — or only to serve according to their own pleasure, and on their own terms. The great object is to render the least possible service and to obtain the highest amount of wages attainable, with those who perform domestic labor. This, especially the shirking part, is particularly the case with the Irish, — more so than with American or other nationalities, — and the difficulties are on the increase. . . . There has been a class of demagogue politicians who have contributed largely to this state of things by which our domestic affairs are disturbed without benefit to the employers and the employed. The teachings and influence of the *New York Tribune* have been pernicious. General Banks and a class of demagogues in Congress have enacted what is called the "eight-hour law"; that is, workmen shall be paid wages for ten hours, though laboring but eight, when in the employ of the Government.

The Alabama question has stirred up the British public since the rejection of the treaty and the publication of Sumner's speech. There is no doubt the English Government and people feel and are fully conscious of the great wrong they have done us, and the attitude of affairs is to them anything but agreeable. They are more apprehensive of war than they are willing to confess, and hostilities may be nearer than our own people suppose.

[Here ends the diary that my father had kept for seven years. He continued his habit of writing until the end of his life, but his later writings were chiefly in the form of contributions to periodicals upon subjects connected with the War and Reconstruction. — EDGAR T. WELLES.]

THE END

INDEX

PREPARED BY

DAVID M. MATTESON

ABANDONED plantations, Cabinet discussion on control by Treasury agents, 2, 148–150; bureau for, suggested, 150.

Abecassis, Isaac, Portuguese merchant, naval trade with, 3, 514.

Abell, Edmund, removed by Sheridan, 3, 142.

Adams, C. F., Zerman letter, 1, 300; as Minister, 301; protest against Laird rams, 406; ignorant of British intention to seize rams, 437; resigns, 3, 256; suggested as Presidential candidate, 295; and State portfolio, 488.

Adams, H. A., at Pensacola (1861), and Porter, 1, 28–31; and Preble, 163.

Adams, J. Q., diary, 1, xxiii.

Adirondack, wrecked, 1, 109.

Admiral, Farragut's commission, 2, 562, 563. *See also* Rear-admirals, Vice-admiral.

Admiralty, Board of. *See* Board.

Advertisement, official, 2, 490.

Advisory Board, action on subordinate active appointments, 1, 77.

Agassiz, Louis, at Seward's, 1, 506.

Aiken, William, and Reconstruction, 2, 397.

Alabama, rejects Fourteenth Amendment, 2, 636.

Alabama (*290*), at Nassau, 1, 109; depredations and pursuit, 165, 175, 179, 191, 207, 216, 224, 304, 316, 327; and Federal letters of marque, 253; Welles and pursuit,

497; at Cherbourg, 2, 62; sunk, 65, 67, 138; rejoicing over sinking, 67, 70. *See also* Semmes.

Alabama claims, Cabinet discussion of points (1867), 3, 241; question of arbitration by King of Prussia, 459; Cabinet and Johnson's protocol, 468–471, 474; Johnson's treaty, 506, 507, 516, 579; Sumner's speech, 578, 579; Senate rejects treaty, 578; English and rejection, 589.

Alaska, purchase, 3, 66, 68, 75, 83, 84; commissioner, 129, 141, 169; protection of seals, 516; government, 531.

Alaska, launched, 3, 422.

Albany Regency, career, 3, 224–227.

Alden, James, at Norfolk Navy Yard, 1, 43–45; and Bureau of Navigation, 2, 357, 362.

Aldie, engagement, 1, 336, 338.

Alexander, B. S., obstruction of the Potomac, 3, 436.

Allen, ——, Editor of the *Intelligencer*, and Connecticut election (1866), 2, 456, 460.

Allen, C. M., and Georgia peace commissioner, 2, 125.

Allen, Ethan, and district-attorneyship, 3, 565.

Allyn, J. P., and Arizona offices, 1, 409.

Almaden mines, Halleck's interest, 1, 397.

Alta Vela affair, 3, 305, 316–318, 322, 344.

Altoona Conference, 1, 153, 156.

Amendments, Johnson's suggestions, 3, 406, 407. *See also* amendments by number.

Ames, Horatio, claim for guns, 3, 447–449, 451.

Ames, Oakes, graft in Pacific railroads, 3, 425.

Amnesty, Welles favors punishment of leaders, 2, 43; Cabinet discussion (1865), 294, 306; Johnson on pardons (1865), 358; reciprocal, 3, 94; question of general (1867),183,193, 197–199; Seddon's application, 230; Congressional acts of individual, 386; proclamation of general (1868), 394–396.

Anderson, Robert. *See* Sumter.

Anderson, Fort, capture, 2, 245.

Andrew, J. A., on conduct of the War, 1, 162; and coast defense of Massachusetts, 288; and pursuit of *Tacony*, 375; and Weld, 405; on Seward and Johnson, 2, 529.

Andrews, R. F., removal, 2, 155.

Ann Hamilton, trade permit, 1, 537, 543, 544.

Annexations, Seward's project for French West Indies, 2, 393; attempted, of Danish West Indies, 466, 473, 3, 40, 95–98, 124, 125, 502; attempted, of Bay of Samaná, 2, 631, 643, 3, 7, 40; Alaska, 66, 68, 75, 83, 84; question of Culebra Island, 94; basis of Seward's policy, 106, 125; Seward's desire for Panama, 107; desired by San Domingo, 480, 517; suggested, of Midway Islands, 508.

Anthon, W. H., on conviction of Scofield, 2, 201.

Anthony, H. B., impeachment vote, 3, 356, 358, 367.

Antietam campaign, McClellan commands at Washington, 1, 104, 109, 113; Confederates invade Maryland, 110, 111; McClellan in field, 114–117, 122, 124; Burnside declines command, 124; delays, 124, 129; South Mountain, 130; battle, 139, 140; Harper's Ferry, 140; Confederates escape, 140, 142, 145, 146, 156; Halleck's indecision, 153; inaction after, 176; fifth anniversary of battle celebrated, 201–203.

Appomattox campaign, Sailor's Creek, 2, 276; surrender, 278.

Arago, captures *Emma*, 1, 445.

Arbitrary arrests, Vallandigham case, 1, 306, 321, 344, 347; suppression of Chicago *Times*, 321; forged proclamation incident, 2, 36, 38, 67; Arguellis incident, 36, 45; decision against, in Treasury case, 206, 207; Milligan decision, 242, 245, 471, 474, 476. *See also Habeas corpus*.

Archibald, E. M., and *Peterhoff* mails, 1, 266.

Arguellis, ——, arrest as slavetrader, 2, 36, 45.

Argyle, Duke of, on Wilkes in West Indies, 1, 299.

Ariel, captured, 1, 207.

Arizona, officers for, 1, 409.

Arkansas, delegation to Washington (1867), 3, 6; Reconstruction constitution, 347; veto of constitution overruled, 388; disturbances, 460–463.

Arkansas, passes Union fleet, 1, 72; destroyed, 78.

Arkansas Post, captured, 1, 224.

Army, grand review, 2, 310. *See also* Draft, Indians, Negro soldiers, Stanton, and campaigns and officers by name.

Army and Navy Gazette, official connection, 1, 343.

Army of the Potomac, McClellan's popularity, 1, 105, 111, 113, 115, 116, 129; attitude of officers (1862), 118; demoralized after Fredericksburg, 226; responsibility for commanders, 440. *See also* campaigns and commanders by name.

Arnold, I. N., and naval cases, **2**, 262.

Arrests. *See* Arbitrary.

Ashley, J. M., impeachment resolution, **3**, 8; character, 12; Conover allegations, 143 *n*., 144; Governor of Montana, 575; corrupt practices, 575.

Ashton, J. H., and case of Brown, Navy Agent, **2**, 345; and internal revenue frauds, 435.

Aspinwall, W. H., and Sumter expedition, **1**, 38; and emancipation, 163; steamer *Ariel* captured, 207.

Atkinson, Edward, and war-time cotton trade, **2**, 66.

Atlanta. See Fingal.

Atlanta campaign, Resaca, **2**, 33; capture of Atlanta, 135; bearing on Presidential campaign, 140.

Atlantic cable, naval vessels and laying (1866), **2**, 503, 504.

Attorney-General, question of appointment (1864), **2**, 183, 187, 192. *See also* Bates, Evarts, Speed, Stanbery.

Augur, C. C., visit to Fort Foote, **1**, 474.

Augusta, pursues *Alabama*, **1**, 179.

Aulick, J. H., and promotion (1862), **1**, 75; and Ordnance Bureau, 386.

Aulick, Richmond, excursion, **2**, 65.

Austria, and Mexico, **2**, 479, 485.

Averill, W. W., reported success (1864), **2**, 100.

Azuni, D. A., on use of neutral waters by belligerents, **1**, 464.

Babcock, J. F., and Connecticut appointments, **1**, 81, **2**, 597; and Johnson's policy, 424; in Connecticut campaigns (1866), 457, 460; (1868), **3**, 264, 329; and Senatorial election (1866), **2**, 506, 508; on Weed and Grant (1868), **3**, 249.

Bache, A. D., and navy yard at League Island, **1**, 185; and Welles, **2**, 117.

Bache, G. M., and loss of *Sacramento*, **3**, 554.

Bacon, J. G.(?), brings dispatches from Charleston fleet, **1**, 234.

Badeau, Adam, Grant's factotum, **3**, 465.

Bailey, Theodorus, and captured mails, **1**, 270, 272; on Matamoras trade, 283, 289; and *Mont Blanc* incident, 302, 305, 417, 419, 422, 425–427; and Portsmouth Navy Yard, **2**, 148; wants command of Washington Yard, **3**, 485.

Bailor, ——, pretended peace commissioner from Georgia, **2**, 125.

Baird, Absalom, and New Orleans riot, **2**, 572, 573.

Baker, L. C., and graft disclosures, **1**, 518, 522, 525; case against, for false arrest, **2**, 206.

Baldwin, C. H., cruise in *Vanderbilt*, **1**, 224.

Baldwin, J. D., and Reconstruction, **2**, 441, 442.

Baltic, Weed's scheme for government purchase, **1**, 155.

Baltimore, Butler's rule, **2**, 269; election disturbances (1866), 620.

Bancroft, George, oration on Lincoln, **2**, 431; Dix incident, **3**, 511, 521.

Bankhead, J. P., on loss of *Monitor*, **1**, 215.

Banks, N. P., Blair on, **1**, 126; force fitted out, 192; supersedes Butler, 209; as officer, 210; Sabine Pass, 441, 443; and cotton trade, 511; Red River expedition, **2**, 18, 19, 26, 86, 178; character, 18, 26; nominated to Congress, 381; and Radicals, 381; and Navy Department, 381, **3**, 325; and French Exhibition, **2**, 469; and Mexico, 649; and first Reconstruction Bill, **3**, 40; and removal of Hartt, 139; and navy yard appointments, 416–420.

Banks, Chase and circulation, **1**, 530. *See also* National banks.

Barlow, S. L. M. (?), and McClellan, **1**, 117, **2**, 28.

Barnard, J. G., at Fort Foote, **1**, 474.

Barney, Hiram, on McClellan, **1**, 116, 117; G. W. Blunt on, 405; and graft disclosures, 514.

Barney, Mrs. Joshua, and dismissal of son, **2**, 605.

Barney, S. C., dismissal, **2**, 605.

Barnum, W. H., election contested, **3**, 129.

Barron, Samuel, and Seward's interference with Sumter expedition, **1**, 17–19, 36; character, loyalty doubted, 19, 20; joins Confederacy, 36.

Barry, W. F., visit to Fort Foote, **1**, 474.

Bartlett, ——, and Welles, **1**, 184, **2**, 259; and Bennett, 258.

Bates, Edward, and Carrington, **1**, 56, 57; and movement to remove McClellan, 100; and Cabinet-meetings, 138, 320; and dismissal of Preble, 141; and appointment of midshipmen, 146, 147; on colonizing of negroes, 152, 153; and emancipation, 158; and Halleck, 180, 397; and Senate committee on Seward, 195, 196; and admission of West Virginia, 205, 206; on captured mails, 290, 301; on draft and *habeas corpus*, 397, 432; Chase on, 413; and Admiral Milne, 468; and renomination of Lincoln, 500; and Fort Pillow massacre, **2**, 24; and Chase's resignation, 63; and cotton trade, 66; on the Cabinet (1864), 93; on judicial control over prizes, 106; on abandoned plantations, 149; character, 162; and Taney's funeral, 176; resigns, 181, 183.

Beauregard, P. G. T., and demonstration on Washington (1863), **1**, 359, 377.

Beecher, H. W., and slanders of Johnson, **2**, 454.

Belknap, A. A., question of restoration, **3**, 205, 206.

Bell, C. H., Sabine Pass, **1**, 441; and command of Gulf Squadron, **2**, 116; to command West India Squadron, 299; report on Formosa, **3**, 182.

Belligerency, Welles on blockade and recognition, **1**, 86, 174, 414, 440, **2**, 159, 160, 246, 254; withdrawn from Confederacy, 319. *See also* Blockade.

Benham, H. W., and James Island, **1**, 160.

Benjamin, J. P., and Jaquess, **2**, 109.

Bennett, J. G., peace with Weed, **1**, 78; and French mission, **2**, 258. *See also* New York *Herald*.

Benton, T. H., and Marcy's report on Frémont, **2**, 42.

Bermuda, prize, controversy over government purchase, **1**, 170, 304.

Berrett, J. G., and Belknap, **3**, 205.

Bertinatti, Madame, claim, **2**, 522, 526.

Betts, S. R., *Peterhoff* mails case, **1**, 310.

Bigelow, John, on attitude of France (1864), **2**, 39; Chargé, 205; and Mexico, 332, 336, 622; and Slidell (1866), 585; in Washington (1867), **3**, 75; and Seward, 75; on impeachment, 292, 293.

Bigelow, Mrs. John, visits Blairs, **2**, 328.

Binckley, J. M., Conover case, **3**, 165; and Sickles's actions, 182; and Holt, 172; fraud investigations, 434, 435.

Bingham, J. A., and Civil Rights Bill, **2**, 476, 479; and Conover allegations, **3**, 168; and Grant-Johnson controversy, 274; as impeachment manager, 332, 345, 347; and Butler, 524; and repeal of Tenure-of-Office Act, 564, 567.

Birge, H. W., and Welles, **2**, 313.

Black, J. S., and Stanton (1861), **1**, 60; and veto of Reconstruction Bill, **3**, 51; and Goldsborough's claim, 99; attitude (1867), 99; influence over Johnson, 205; impeachment counsel and Alta Vela,

304, 305, 307, 308, 316–319, 322, 323, 344.

Blaine, J. G., attack on Navy Department, 2, 241, 250.

Blair, Bettie, marriage, 3, 519.

Blair, F. P., Sr., and relief of Sumter, 1, 13, 2, 248; and Senate committee on Seward, 1, 203; abandons home during Lee's invasion, 350, 354; on Stanton, 355, 356; and Presidential campaign (1864), 509; and Admiral (Captain) Lee's advancement, 533, 2, 243, 504–507, 512, 513, 569, 578; and prosecution of contractors, 1, 541; and Early's raid, 2, 70; Richmond mission, 219, 221; political sagacity, 364; and calling of Union Convention, 528; and Johnson, 3, 168; character, 408.

Blair, F. P., Jr., on Vicksburg campaign, 1, 405; character, 405; antagonism to Chase, 510, 533, 2, 20; defends Navy Department, 1, 531; returns to army, 2, 20; forged requisitions, 20; nomination as collector rejected, 501; and Austrian mission, 3, 70, 71; and War portfolio, 165, 166, 231, 232; Vice-Presidential candidacy, 397, 398, 408; suit against Missouri on oath, 566. *See also* Elections (*1868*).

Blair, Montgomery, and relief of Sumter, 1, 13, 2, 248, 304; antagonism to Stanton and Seward, 1, 56, 59, 203, 329, 340, 345, 355, 356, 398, 2, 84, 91, 102, 112, 369–371, 374, 378, 523, 528, 3, 72, 166, 195; and McClellan, 1, 95, 104, 2, 28, 322; on Pope, 1, 104, 126; and colonizing of negroes, Chiriqui grant, 123, 150, 151; on War Department under Cameron and Stanton, 125–128; on commanding generals, 126; and emancipation, 146, 159, 210; on killing of Gen. Nelson, 179; and admission of West Virginia, 191, 205, 206; and Senate committee on Seward, 195–

197, 203; influence on Lincoln, 205; character, 205, 2, 20, 370, 413; and McClernand, 1, 217; and Chase, 231, 2, 45; on Seward's difficulties over captured mails, 1, 274; and a fugitive-slave case (1863), 313; and Cabinet-meetings, 320, 2, 17, 86; and Vallandigham case, 1, 344; and Lee's invasion (1863), 352; and Stephens's attempted mission, 360, 361; and promotion of D. D. Porter, 369; foresees end of War (1863), 376; excursions, 394, 2, 31, 65; on dismissal of army officers, 1, 406; Reconstruction theory, 413, 467; on *habeas corpus* and draft, 432; and Speakership (1863), 481; and renomination of Lincoln, 500; and cotton trade permits, 511, 2, 57, 66, 139; reception, 1, 521; campaign contribution (1864), 534; on Fort Pillow massacre, 2, 24; and date of Republican Convention (1864), 28; and Hamlin, 47; and Chase's resignation, 62, 63; and Early's raid, 70; house burned, 76, 80; and Radicals, resignation, 77, 80, 156–158, 174; Bates on, 93; and Greeley's peace negotiations, 94; on Grant as general, 94, 3, 121, 122; and politics in Brooklyn Navy Yard (1864), 136, 137; and collectorship at New York, 137; and Admiral (Captain) Lee, 146, 161, 172, 513; on Weed's antagonism to Welles, 155; and Chief-Justiceship, 181, 182; Senatorial aspirations and removal of Hoffman, 195, 243; Richmond mission, 221; on Bennett and French mission, 258; and New York papers (1865), 322; and Mexico, 329, 333; and Johnson, 343, 414, 437, 3, 120, 409; and Maryland patronage (1865), 2, 343; addresses Democrats (1865), 382; at Grant's reception (1866), 478; expects second rebellion, 484, 552, 555, 556; and Union Convention, 531, 574; in campaign of 1866, 613; and Austrian mission for brother, 3, 71; on Grant's probable candidacy (1867), 121; and Field for State portfolio, 184; and Grant (1867), 184, 185; and rumor of Cabinet reorganization (1867), 203, 204; on Democratic Convention (1868), 408; in the campaign, 440; and Coombs's claim, 528; on Johnson's associates, 566.

Blair, Mrs. Montgomery, character, 2, 329.

Blake, G. S., as officer, 2, 353.

Blatchford, Samuel (or R. M.), and Federal office at New York (1864), 2, 62.

Bliss, George, Jr., and trial of contractors, 1, 540, 2, 19, 57.

Bliss, P. C., arrest as spy, 3, 491, 513.

Blockade, Seward's interference and apprehensions, 1, 74, 79, 82, 154, 155; trade permits through, especially at Norfolk, 165, 172–175, 183, 217, 227, 527, 536, 537, 543, 544, 548, 2, 56–57; reported raising at Charleston, 1, 232, 234; question of raising at Galveston, 233; and Matamoras trade, 283, 334, 388, 443, 2, 4; *Mont Blanc* incident, capture in neutral waters, 1, 302, 305, 416–427; French tobacco at Richmond, 338–340, 2, 9, 12; instructions to officers, especially as to neutral territory, 451, 454–456, 458–465, 535, 2, 34; character of blockading vessels, 1, 496; movement to open certain ports, 510, 511, 514; detention of crew of captured runners, 517; raising at Brownsville, 529; ineffectual at Wilmington, 2, 127. *See also* Belligerency, Prizes.

Blow, H. T., and Johnson's tour, 2, 589.

Blunt, G. W., on Federal officers at New York (1863), 1, 405; character, 406; and speed test of naval

vessels, 512; excursion, 2, 31; on Navy at Fort Fisher, 228; and Henderson case, 306; and appointment as Naval Officer, 532.

Board of Admiralty (Survey), movements for, 2, 233, 236, 240, 241, 3, 247, 570.

Board of Survey. *See* Board of Admiralty.

Bogy, L. V., and Johnson, 3, 203, 204.

Bolles, J. A., superstition, 2, 339; and Brown case, 345; and Semmes case, 410, 423, 424, 471; on court-martial punishments, 449, 481.

Bolles, J. G., and Radicals, 2, 586; removed, 612.

Bond, H. L., and Maryland election (1866), 2, 621.

Booth, J. Wilkes, question of publishing diary, 3, 95.

Border States, and abolition, 1, 402, 403.

Borie, A. E., as Secretary of Navy, 3, 549, 556, 568, 587, 588; and reorganization of Navy, 558; desires Board of Survey, 570.

Boston, criticism of Welles from, 1, 404, 405; Johnson's visit, 3, 109, 114, 116, 119, 123.

Bounties, effect of army, on naval enlistments, 1, 546; in Marine Corps, 2, 174; bill (1866), 564.

Boutwell, G. S., violence, 2, 634; and Reconstruction Bill, 3, 47; and impeachment and arrest of Johnson, 235, 300; character, 239; and Treasury portfolio, 549, 550.

Bowen, S. J., candidacy for mayor, 3, 375, 380.

Bowie, G. W., and Johnson, 3, 288.

Bowles, Samuel, and Jim Fisk, 3, 490. *See also* Springfield *Republican*.

Boynton, C. B., naval history, 2, 360, 366, 3, 413.

Boynton, T. J., and *Mont Blanc* incident, 1, 419.

Bradford, A. W., and Altoona Conference, 1, 156; house burned, 2, 73; at Antietam anniversary, 3, 201.

Bradford, Mrs. A. W., pass to South, 1, 156.

Bradley, Judge, of Rhode Island, and Internal Revenue Commissioner, 3, 414.

Bradley, J. H., Surratt case, 3, 167.

Brady, J. T., and Fenian trials, 3, 283.

Brandegee, Augustus, Chairman of Naval Committee, 1, 484; and Welles, 509, 2, 250; and navy yard at New London, 446.

Brazil, and capture of *Florida*, 2, 184–186, 197, 275.

Breese, Samuel, as officer, 1, 76.

Bridge, Horatio, on Hamlin, 2, 345; inspection tour, 3, 422; and Porter, 556.

Briggs,——, and Trowbridge-Lamar plot, 1, 492.

Bright, John, on attitude of England, 1, 305.

Brinkerhoff, Jacob, and Wilmot Proviso, 2, 386.

Brooklyn Navy Yard, offensive partisanship at, 1, 178; and election of 1864, 2, 97, 98, 108, 122–124, 136, 137, 142–145, 175; ousting of Radicals, 616; Belknap's defalcation, 3, 205. *See also* Navy yards.

Brooks, James, political character, 1, 524, 2, 22; and investigation of Treasury, 22; and McClellan's letter of acceptance, 140; and Butler (1865), 230.

Brown, George, on conditions in South (1863), 1, 316; and delivery of *Stonewall* to Japan, 3, 365.

Brown, Harvey, removed, 1, 406.

Brown, J. P., trouble with Morris, 3, 25.

Brown, S. P., and corrupt contracts, 1, 540; question of reappointment, 2, 342, 344–346.

Browning, O. H., and Union Convention, 2, 533, 538, 574, 581; and

Johnson's tour, 587; and Mexico, 624; and Fourteenth Amendment, 628; and welcome to Congress (1866), 632; and asylum for the Pope, 639, 640; on negro suffrage in the District, 3, 5; on Prussian Convention, 9; and first Reconstruction Bill, 10, 12; and negro suffrage for Territories, 19; on relinquishing of *Dunderberg*, 28; on seizure of *R. R. Cuyler*, 39; and Stanton's report on enforcement of Civil Rights Bill, 45; and Indian affairs, 69, 74, 254; and Danish West Indies, 98; and removal of Sheridan, 150; and Conover allegations, 143, 144; and successor to Stanton, 231; on conduct of military governors, 243; and removal of Stanton, 284; and impeachment, 297, 298, 345; on Johnson's talkativeness, 311; and Democratic nominations (1868), 401; and disturbances in South, 461; on Johnson's message (1868), 478; and holding over under Grant, 533; and inauguration, 537.

Brownlow, W. G., and Fourteenth Amendment, 2, 557; character, 3, 205; Nashville disturbances, 211.

Brownsville, Texas, raising of blockade, 1, 529.

Bruce, Sir F. W. A., and *Stonewall*, 2, 306; and Fenians, 454, 486; death, 3, 203.

Bruzual, Blas (or M. E.), and purchase of a vessel for Venezuela, 1, 474–476.

Bryant, W. C., and charges against Henderson, 2, 60, 61, 78, 228; as editor, 61; and Administration (1864), 104.

Bryson, Andrew, and Fenians, 2, 518–520.

Buchanan, Franklin, and Secessionists, 1, 19.

Buchanan, James, and secession of South Carolina, 2, 256; and Sumter (Dec., 1860), 273; death, 3,

374; character, 374; Government and funeral, 376.

Buckingham, W. A., reëlections, **1**, 262, **2**, 5; and draft, **1**, 406; Senatorship and illness, **2**, 505, **3**, 390.

Budd, William, and Washington chair, **1**, 77; as officer, **2**, 111.

Buel, ——, of Bermuda, and Georgia's peace commissioner, **2**, 125, 126.

Buell, D. C., Perryville, **1**, 165.

Bull Run, second campaign, Cedar Hill, **1**, 78; Pope awaits McClellan, 89; fleet in Potomac, 91, 93; battle, McClellan's conduct, 93, 97, 98, 104, 107, 117, 122, 221, 225, 226; retreat, 98, 100, 104; alarm in Washington, 99, 105, 106, 109; Pope's report, 109, 110, 114; Lincoln on, 116, 126; army demoralized, 117; Porter court martial, 220, 225, 229.

Bullitt, Cuthbert, Union man, **1**, 81.

Burlingame, Anson, on admirable Chinese customs, **3**, 379.

Burnett, D. G., elected to Senate, **2**, 642.

Burnside, A. E., and Navy, **1**, 91; declines command in Antietam campaign, 124; Blair on, 126; commands Army of Potomac, 182; Fredericksburg, 191–193; expected forward movement (Jan.), 226; army demoralized, 226; resigns command, 229; Vallandigham case, 306; suppression of Chicago *Times*, 321; arrival for Wilderness campaign, **2**, 17; and impeachment, **3**, 357.

Burr, A. E., on Welles and Senatorship, **2**, 501; and Connecticut politics, **3**, 264, 328.

Bushnell, C. S., and *Monitor*, **1**, 214.

Butler, B. F., rule at New Orleans, **1**, 209; prospective command in Mississippi movement, 210; as officer, 373, **2**, 223; and trade permits, **1**, 536, 544, 548, **2**, 56, 57; preparation for Virginia campaign, 15, 19, 24; in the campaign, 35; and martial law at Norfolk, 81;

character, 81, 365, 469, **3**, 504, 523; and exchange of naval prisoners, **2**, 168, 169, 171; Wilmington expedition, 209, 210, 213–217, 222; and Grant, 214, 217, 222, 223, 226, **3**, 56; dismissed, **2**, 223; in Washington, and political radicals (1865), 224, 226, 230; rule in Baltimore, 269; and Reconstruction (1865), 348, 349; (1867), **3**, 81, 82; and trial of Davis, **2**, 365, 367; intrigue in *Grey Jacket* case, 469, 492, 493; elected to Congress, 619; and Conover allegations, **3**, 143 *n.*; as impeachment manager, 321, 326, 333, 336; pressure on doubtful Senators, 354, 362; investigation of vote, 366–368; calls on Johnson and Cabinet, 497; currency speech, 503, 506; and Bingham, 524; and repeal of Tenure-of-Office Act, 564, 567, 568; on Grant's ignorance, 564.

Butterfield, A. G., and *Mont Blanc* incident, **1**, 419, 427.

Byington, ——, sends news of Gettysburg, **1**, 357.

Cabinet, Lincoln's, formation, **1**, xx, 81, 230, 325, **2**, 388–392; Seward and proposal of regular meetings (1861), **1**, 6–8, 136–138; Seward's attitude, 104, 124, 400; character of meetings, lack of consultations, 131, 134–136, 274, 320, 348, 351, 391, 401, 429, 526, 546, **2**, 16, 17, 58, 59, 62, 84, 86, 91, 98, 166, 203; and financial matters (1862), **1**, 168; assistants at meetings, 319, **3**, 318; and renomination of Lincoln, **1**, 500; rumors of reorganization (1864), **2**, 102; Fessenden and Seward-Stanton clique, 120; rumors as to, for second administration, 194, 195, 247, 250, 251; Johnson retains Lincoln's, 289; improved meetings under Johnson, 318; relations with Johnson, 481–483, 487, 522–525, 543, 606, 611;

changes in Johnson's, 553, 554, 558, 563; direct communication by Secretaries to Congress, 3, 131; rumors of reorganization of Johnson's (1867), 183, 203, 204; (1868), 364, 371; rumors as to Grant's, 488, 530, 535; Johnson's, and holding over under Grant, 529, 530, 532, 535; Welles on Grant's, 543–549. *See also* members of the Cabinet by name.

Cadwalader, John, Pasco case, 2, 400, 401; and O'Neal, 3, 441.

Calhoun, J. C., and South Carolina aristocracy, 2, 312.

Calhoun, captured, 1, 350.

Calvert, C. B., and Navy Department, 1, 187; and appointment of midshipmen, 234, 236.

Cameron, Simon, delay in taking portfolio, 1, 3; and Seward's interference with Sumter expedition, 25; resigns, 57, 58; and appointment of Stanton, 59; Blair on, as Secretary of War, 126–128; defeated for Senate (1863), 223; on Seward's meddling, 242; patronage and political views (1865), 2, 349; selection to the Cabinet, 389; Senatorial election (1867), 3, 16, 20; character, 16, 20, 479, 523; and removal of Stanton, 285; and impeachment, 301, 333; and Senatorial election (1869), 505.

Campbell, A. F. (?), and politics in Brooklyn Navy Yard, 2, 122.

Campbell, J. A., negotiations with Seward (1861), 1, 26; Hampton Roads Conference, 2, 235, 238; seeks parole, 330; character, 330.

Campbell, Col. J. A., on Arkansas disturbances, 3, 462.

Campbell, Lewis, Mexican mission, 2, 501, 621, 649; instructions, 623, 625, 628.

Canada, Confederate operations, 2, 151–153; Fenian raid (1866), 450, 451, 453, 454, 484, 486, 518–521, 523, 524.

Canby, E. R. S., and cotton trade, 2, 159; Mobile, 165; as military governor, 3, 187, 245.

Capture, legal, of private property used by Confederate Government, 2, 486. *See also* Blockade, Prizes.

Carleton, J. H., report on Mexico, 2, 367.

Carpenter, F. B., Emancipation Proclamation picture, 1, 527, 549.

Carpenter, M. H., and repeal of Tenure-of-Office Act, 3, 555.

Carrington, E. C., candidacy for district attorney, 1, 56.

Carter, J. M., and navy yard for New London, 1, 222.

Carter, S. P., return to Navy, 2, 366; report on Borneo, 3, 182.

Cartter, D. K., and assassination of Lincoln, 2, 286; and dismissal of son, 359; and Stanton, 3, 157, 160; and arrest of Thomas, 286, 294.

Cartter, W. H., dismissal, 2, 359.

Case, F. M., as Surveyor-General of Colorado, 3, 575.

Case, Newton, and A. H. Stephens, 2, 332.

Casey, Joseph, and speculation, 2, 314.

Caswell, Alexis, at Seward's, 1, 506.

Catawba, sale, 3, 348, 387–389, 420, 429, 438.

Cattell, A. G., and removal of Stanton, 3, 285; character, 523.

Cave, Sir Stephen, in Washington, 3, 135.

Cavnach, ——, and Trowbridge-Lamar plot, 1, 492.

Cedar Hill, battle, 1, 78.

Ceres, prize, mails, 1, 491, 492.

Chambers, J. S., question of removal, 1, 218, 219.

Chambersburg, Pa., Stuart's raid, 1, 169.

Chancellorsville, beginning of campaign, 1, 287; rumors, 290, 291; anxiety at Washington, 291–293; Stoneman's raid, 292–295; news

of defeat, 293; reception of news,
294; Sedgwick, 295; death of Jackson, 297; losses, 302; Hooker's
irreverence and drinking, 336, 348.

Chandler, L. H., and trial of Davis,
2, 614.

Chandler, W. E., naval fraud cases,
2, 200, 218, 262; Pasco case, 400,
401; and Butler, 492, 493; and
impeachment, 3, 353; and Fogg,
372.

Chandler, Zachariah, Committee on
Conduct of the War, 2, 198; and
Butler (1865), 224; character,
633, 3, 52; attack on McCulloch,
52; and Fessenden, 138; and impeachment, 301, 332, 339; reëlection (1869), 508.

Charleston, preparation for naval
attack on, 1, 153, 216, 217, 263,
264; reported raising of blockade,
232, 234; Du Pont's delay, 236,
237, 247, 249, 259; Administration's plan of attack, 237; rumors
and anxiety as to attack, 262–265;
repulse, 265, 267–269, 273; Du
Pont's failure to report, 273, 274,
276; failure of his operations and
subsequent controversy, 276, 277,
288, 295, 302, 307, 476–478, 2, 7,
11, 14, 30, 133; question of renew-
ing attack, 1, 273, 309, 313, 324,
338; Du Pont to be relieved, question of successor, 311–318, 325,
326, 337, 341, 342, 346, 347; progress of renewed (Dahlgren's)
movement, 372, 380, 415, 427,
449, 467, 520; Gillmore's force,
382–385; mutual relations of attacking forces, 467, 474; captured,
2, 242; aspect (1865), 311. See also
Sumter.

Charlestown Navy Yard, appointments and politics, 1, 374, 380,
2, 31, 33, 34, 143, 3, 417, 419, 446.
See also Navy yards.

Chase, Kate, and Sprague, 1, 306.

Chase, S. P., attitude towards Cabinet consultations, 1, 7, 320, 525,
526, 546, 2, 17, 58, 166; and Cameron, 57, 59, 127; and appointment of Stanton, 59, 61; intrigue
for removal of McClellan, 93–95,
100–105, 108, 109, 112, 114,
117, 119–122, 139; relations with
Stanton and Seward, 101, 131,
139, 203–205, 231, 397, 402, 447,
536, 2, 174; and patronage, 1, 78,
138; and Pope, 114, 221; and proposed attacks on Richmond (1862),
130; (1863), 349, 351; and Antietam, 142; and coin for foreign
drafts, 147, 2, 10, 29; on conduct
of War Department (Sept., 1862),
1, 148; and Chiriqui Grant, 151;
and emancipation, 159, 209; on
conduct of the Administration
(1862), 161; war-time trade, permits, and agents, 165, 166, 175,
177, 183, 217, 510, 511, 522, 527,
537, 543–545, 548, 2, 33, 34, 36,
66, 258, 343; as financier, 1, 168,
176, 494, 520, 525, 530, 2, 3, 13,
14, 54, 57–59, 61–63; on killing
of Gen. Nelson, 1, 178; Seward-
Chase resignation episode, 196,
201–205; and admission of West
Virginia, 205, 207; on finances and
party loyalty, 223; and Weed, 230,
231, 3, 163; bank bill, 1, 237; and
extra session of Senate (1863),
238; and letters of marque, 246,
247, 250; and John Gilpin prize
case, 297; on a fugitive-slave case
(1863), 313; and Lee's invasion,
331, 335; and Hooker, 335, 348,
349, 444; Presidential candidacy
(1864), 345, 413, 415, 498, 500,
525, 529, 533, 2, 30; and Stephens's attempted mission (1863),
360, 361; and promotion of D. D.
Porter, 369; and command at New
York (1863), 373; and Whiting,
381; on draft and suspension of
habeas corpus, 397, 432–434; on a
departmental administration, 401;
and Halleck, 402, 447; on slavery
and Reconstruction, 402, 410–414;

and Lincoln, 413, 520, **2**, 44; on
Bates, **1**, 413; and Laird rams,
428, 435; and Ohio election (1863),
469; on Trowbridge-Lamar plot,
492, 494; animosity of Blairs, 510,
533, **2**, 20, 45; and policy of opening certain ports, **1**, 514; and cutting of ship-timber in North Carolina, 522, 527, 528; on Charleston
operations, 520; on raising of
Brownsville blockade, 529; favors
bounties on immigration, 543; and
gold premium (April, 1864), **2**, 12–
15; and conduct of subordinates,
Congressional investigation, 20–22;
on Fort Pillow massacre, 25; and
foreign-owned cotton, 40; and
Presidential visits to headquarters,
55; resignation, 62, 63, 69, 93;
Bates on, 93; failure to pay requisitions, 114; support of Lincoln
(1864), 120, 140, 187; character,
121, 183, 192, 366; and Preston
King, 137; and control of abandoned plantations, 149; and Blair's
resignation, 157, 158 *n.*; appointment to Chief-Justiceship, 181,
183, 187, 192, 196; appointment
and political activity, 196, 202,
251, 253, 304, **3**, 135, 244; apprehended decision on arbitrary arrest, **2**, 242, 245, 246; and Blair's
Senatorial aspirations, 243; and
McCulloch, 245; Seward on, as
Cabinet disturber, 246; and blockade, 246, 254; and radical Reconstruction, 253; decision on captured cotton, 263; and negro suffrage, 304, 343, 369; and trial of
Davis, 366, 368; selection to Cabinet, 391; and Johnson, 619; tardi-
ness in holding court in South,
3, 101; and impeachment trial,
293, 301, 306, 327, 328; Presidential candidacy (1868), 379, 381,
382, 385, 389–391, 393, 397, 404,
455, 457–459.
Chattanooga, movement to reinforce, **1**, 442, 444; Welles on change

in commanders, 447; importance,
473.
Chattanooga, Robert Johnson's pro-
posed voyage in, **2**, 472, 479, 491.
Chenango, explosion, **2**, 14.
Cherokee, controversy over purchase,
1, 516.
Chesapeake, seizure and surrender, **1**,
490, 508, 509, 545.
Chicago, Johnson at, **2**, 593.
Chicago *Times*, suppressed, **1**, 321.
Chicago *Tribune*, and impeachment,
3, 355.
Chickamauga, battle, **1**, 438, 441,
444, 446; rumor of Lee at, 439.
Chili, trouble with Spain expected,
2, 357, 365, 495.
Chimo, report on, **2**, 52.
China, mission to United States
(1868), **3**, 380.
Chiriqui Grant, **1**, 123, 150–153, **3**,
428.
Church, S. E., and Presidential nom-
ination (1868), **3**, 396; solicits
Johnson's support of Seymour,
427, 429.
Churchill, J. C., and impeachment,
3, 238.
Cincinnati *Gazette*, attack on Navy
Department, **2**, 80.
Circassian, cartel vessel, **2**, 169.
Cisco, J. J., Assistant Treasurer, **2**,
62.
Cities, Welles on free suffrage and
corruption, **1**, 523, 524.
Civil Rights Bill, Welles on, **2**, 459,
460; Doolittle's substitute, 463;
veto, 463, 464; passage over veto,
475, 477, 479; Trumbull on, 489;
Stanton's report on enforcement,
3, 42–45. *See also* Fourteenth
Amendment.
Civil service, Cabinet and patronage,
1, 138, 218; navy yards and politics, especially assessments, 178,
327, 374, 380, **2**, 97, 98, 108, 122–
124, 136, 137, 142–145, 175, 376,
377, 380, 382; Senatorial confirmation and "courtesy," **1**, 235;

campaign contributions, 534; general political assessments, **2**, 112; Lincoln and patronage, 195; ironclad oath and Southern appointments, 318, 357, 445, 450, 453, 454; Johnson and appointments, 343, **3**, 64, 83–85, 147, 152, 412, 527; Welles and New England patronage, **2**, 356; patronage and split on Reconstruction, 398, 399, 585–587, 596–599, 602, 616, **3**, 52; Congress and patronage under Johnson, **2**, 426 *n.*, **3**, 557; appointment of ex-army officers, 74; rush of office-seekers (1869), 557; Grant's sweep, 576. *See also* Tenure-of-Office Act.

Civil War, warnings ignored at Washington, **1**, 10; Scott's defensive-frontier policy, 84–86, 125, 172, 242; West-Pointism, 85, 125; enthusiasm (1862), 89; despondency (1862), 119, 129, 176, 209; progress to end of 1862, 211; conditions in the South (1863), 223, 316; lack of enthusiasm (1863), 324; Gettysburg, Vicksburg, and termination, 371, 378, 428; character of Davis and termination, 376–379; popular attitude at end of 1863, 499; strain on Administration of opening days, 549; Welles hopeful of termination, **2**, 158, 177, 200, 208, 218; continued arrogance of Confederates (1865), 229; germ in South Carolina aristocracy, 276, 277, 312; mistaken estimates of opponents, 277; grand review of army, 310; official end, 473, 579–581, 583. *See also* Army, Finances, Foreign, Lincoln, Navy, Peace.

Claims. *See* War claims.

Clandaniels, ——, peculations at Philadelphia Navy Yard, **2**, 200.

Clark, ——, of Auburn, N. Y., and cotton speculation, **2**, 37.

Clark, ——, editor of the Norfolk *Régime*, on Wilmington expedition, **2**, 216.

Clark, Daniel, on J. P. Hale and

Navy Department, **1**, 507; appointment as judge, **2**, 565.

Clarke, Freeman, insubordination, **2**, 453.

Clay, Brutus, and Mrs. White, **2**, 21.

Clay, C. C., implication in assassination plot, **2**, 363.

Clay, C. M., discouraged (1862), **1**, 117.

Clay, Henry, character, **1**, 506, 507.

Cleveland, C. D., and Confederate ironclads, **1**, 436.

Cleveland, E. S., and Connecticut election (1866), **2**, 458, 461.

Cleveland, Johnson at, **2**, 593.

Clifford, J. H. (?), of Massachusetts, and trial of Davis, **2**, 365, 367.

Clyde, captured, **1**, 428.

Cobden, Richard, on Wilkes in West Indies, **1**, 298; on attitude of England, 305.

Cochrane, John, and draft, **1**, 380; nomination (1864), **2**, 41; political character, 43; withdraws, 156.

Cole, Cornelius, impeachment vote, **3**, 356, 358.

Coleman, J. A., and naval chaplaincy, **1**, 162.

Coles County, Ill., riots, **2**, 81.

Colfax, Schuyler, election as Speaker, **1**, 481; character, 481, **3**, 24, 30; and Navy Department and Welles, **1**, 482, 484, **2**, 236, 250; and movement to expel Long, 9; and Chase, 21; and assassination of Lincoln, 287; radical speech (1865), 385, 410; and impeachment resolution (1867), **3**, 12; Vice-Presidential candidacy, 362, 366. *See also* Elections (1868).

Collamer, Jacob, Senate committee on Seward, **1**, 194, 196, 198.

Collins, Napoleon, and *Mont Blanc* incident, **1**, 417, 421, 423; captures *Florida*, **2**, 184; trial, 275; and loss of *Sacramento*, **3**, 120, 554.

Colombia, seizure of *R. R. Cuyler*, **3**, 38–42; tax on foreigners, 106.

Colonization of negroes, schemes for

foreign, **1**, 123, 150–153, 162, **3**, 428; Cox's domestic scheme, **2**, 352.

Colorado, Cabinet on bill admitting, **2**, 502, **3**, 22; veto, 30.

Coltman, ——, Union man of Louisiana, **1**, 81.

Columbia, captured, **2**, 242.

Colvocoressis, G. M., retirement, **3**, 503.

Commerce. *See* Blockade, Trade.

Committee on Conduct of the War, report, **1**, 262; purpose, **2**, 198; summons Butler (1865), 224, 226; character, 226.

Comstock, C. B., Wilmington expedition, **2**, 226; marriage, **3**, 519.

Comstock, J. J. (?), and command of the *Baltic*, **1**, 155.

Confederate cruisers, squadron to intercept, **1**, 109, 111, 122, 123, 134; coast defense against, 125, 288, 347, 364, 366, 375, 380, 435, **2**, 256, 257; and Federal agitation for letters of marque, 246, 248, 250, 253; proposed proclamation against, as pirates (1865), **2**, 298, 300, 308. *See also Alabama, Florida, Shenandoah, Tacony, Tallahassee.*

Confederate ironclads, *Fingal*, **1**, 72, 336, 341, 344; *Arkansas*, 72, 78; Laird rams, construction in England, 245, 247, 250, 262; Seward's protest, 399; Dahlgren fears, 406; Chase urges preparation to seize, 428; private knowledge of British intention to seize, 429, 435–438; newspaper anxiety concerning, 435; detention announced, 443; continued anxiety, 448; building in France, **2**, 35, 65; French, stopped, 254. *See also Stonewall.*

Confiscation, Cabinet discussion (1869), **3**, 504.

Congress, *Thirty-seventh:* character, **1**, 186, 206, 224; Senate committee on Seward, 194–205; attacks on management of War, 224; and appointment of midshipmen, 224, 227, 234, 236; "courtesy" in Senate, 235; closing hours (1863), 244; naval bills, 245; Committee on Conduct of the War, 262. *See also* Hale (J. P.).

Thirty-eighth: question of extra session of the Senate, **1**, 238; organization, naval committees, 481–484, 490, **2**, 193; naval affairs, **1**, 522, 528, 531, **2**, 7, 11, 236–238, 240–242, 250; interference of Members with navy yards, **1**, 482, **2**, 224, 225; censure of Long, 9, 12; investigation of Navy Department, 21, 22; of Fort Pillow massacre, 23; and Mexico, 39; and finances, 57; closing hours (1864), 62, 65; (1865), 251; House resolution against Seward, 202; Thirteenth Amendment, 234; Radicals and Reconstruction, 239, 242.

Thirty-ninth: meeting, **2**, 385, 392; ignores Johnson, 392; impending war with Johnson, 412, 414, 421, 434; naval appropriations, 430, 444; Stockton ousted, 464, 475; Colorado, 502; closing hours (1866), 563–565; (1867), **3**, 58; wasteful grants, **2**, 542; bounty bill, 564; second session, 626; Forney's reception and parade, 627, 630–632; probable action, 627, 632, 633, 635; Republican caucus (Dec., 1866), 633; annoyance of Departments, 634, 637, **3**, 13; leaders in Senate, **2**, 635; treatment of Johnson's adherents, 637; character, 644; Southern trip of Members, 649. *See also* Reconstruction, Tenure-of-Office Act.

Fortieth: sessions, **3**, 17, 19, 61, 73, 74, 128, 415, 423, 426, 437, 438, 441, 464, 475; rejection of nominations, 83–85, 527; investigation of Departments, 122; indecision, 129; thanks to Sheridan, 130; character and revolutionary plans, 130, 133, 244, 267, 314, 321, 324, 506, 520, 523; resolution on Cretan insurrection, 138; naval affairs, 264,

265, 280, 325, 341, 348, 384, 387, 515; closing hours of main session, 415; and Johnson's final message, 479, 482; do-nothing policy, 484; Tenure-of-Office Act, 503. *See also* Impeachment, Reconstruction.

Forty-first: Tenure-of-Office Act, **3**, 555, 556, 558, 560, 564, 567, 568, 571; naval affairs, 558; adjourns, 574.

Conkling, F. A., and appointment of midshipmen, **1**, 227.

Conkling, Roscoe, Senatorial election, **3**, 16, 20; character, 16, 20, 558; and impeachment, 301, 336; patronage, 424; and repeal of Tenure-of-Office Act, 558.

Connecticut, Federal appointments, **1**, 78, 81, 510; home guard, 375; coast defense, 380; and draft, 382; elections (1864), **2**, 5; (1866), 427, 429, 433, 452, 454–462, 465, 468, 469, 474; (1867), **3**, 77, 78; (1868), 264, 267, 328, 329; (1869), 571, 572; rejects negro suffrage, **2**, 373, 375; Welles seeks to influence attitude (1866), 426; Democratic Party in, 427–429; Senatorial elections (1866), 501, 505–510; (1868), **3**, 390; adopts Fourteenth Amendment, **2**, 541; delegates to Union Convention (1866), 567; political attitude (1867), **3**, 63; Welles and Gov. English's messages, 87–89, 382; character of Radicals, 88.

Conness, John, and Navy Department, **2**, 234; and removal of Stanton, **3**, 285; and impeachment, 333; character, 479.

Conover, Sanford, allegations, **3**, 143–146, 149, 152, 157, 161, 165, 168.

Constitution. *See* Federal Constitution.

Construction and Repairs, Bureau of. *See* Lenthall.

Contract frauds. *See* Corruption.

Cony, Samuel, and coast protection, **2**, 256.

Cook, B. C., and politics in navy yards, **2**, 142–145.

Cooley, Samuel, and Welles, **2**, 313.

Coombs, ——, *Louisville* war-claim case, **3**, 528, 529.

Cooper, Edmund, relations with Johnson, **2**, 532, **3**, 221; on Brownlow, 205; on elections (1867), 222.

Cooper, Samuel, forged dispatches, **1**, 175, 176.

Copper bill, veto (1869), **3**, 531.

Copperheads, and Johnson, **2**, 590.

Corbett, H. W., impeachment vote, **3**, 356, 358, 367.

Corcoran, W. W., house taken for hospital, **1**, 99.

Corning, Erastus, Lincoln's letter to, **1**, 323, 329; and De Camp, **3**, 18.

Corruption, in Navy Department contracts, **1**, 511, 512, 514, 522; Stover case, 514, 518, 524; Fox and investigation, Welles's attitude, 537–541; Henderson case, 540–544, 547, **2**, 5, 54, 60, 61, 78, 79, 82, 83, 220, 225, 306; Smith Bros. case, 7, 11, 15, 53, 55, 56, 60, 61, 90, 124, 238, 260–264, 334, 359; Scofield case, 57, 58, 176, 177, 199–201; Philadelphia Navy Yard, 200, 205, 208, 224, 231, 238, 400–402; Stiners case, 279; Hoover case, 418; general (1869), **3**, 576.

Cotton, war-time trade, **1**, 498, 511, **2**, 33, 34, 36, 37, 66, 138–140, 159–163, 167; protection of foreign-owned, 40; captured French, 106, 107; participation of officers in trade, 173; disposal of Savannah, 219, 278; Sherman and foreign-claimed, 229; captured by Navy in Red River campaign, 255, 263; tax, 316.

Couch, D. N., and Gettysburg, **1**, 358.

Counterfeit drafts, **2**, 567.

Court martial, punishments by, **3**, 449, 481.

Court of Claims, candidates, **3**, 372.

Courtney, S. G., and internal revenue frauds, **3**, 434, 435.

Covode, John, and removal of Chambers, **1**, 218; character, 219, **2**, 580; Southern trip, 580.

Cow Island, negro colony, **3**, 428.

Cowan, Edgar, and Reconstruction, **2**, 415; and Freedmen's Bureau Bill, 437; and Johnson's attitude, 482, 483; and Union Convention, 533, 538; loses committee position, 637; character, **3**, 20, 58; and Austrian mission, 59.

Cox, ——, of Georgetown, question of restoring property, **2**, 414.

Cox, J. D., and colonizing of negroes, **2**, 352; and Reconstruction, 440; suggested for War portfolio (1867), **3**, 231, 261; Welles on Cabinet appointment (1869), 545.

Cox, W. S., impeachment trial witness, **3**, 333.

Coyle, John, and Johnson, **3**, 566.

Cragin, A. H., Senatorial election, **2**, 51.

Crater, battle, **2**, 89–92.

Craven, T. T., and *Stonewall*, **2**, 261, 267, 392, 396.

Crawford, M. J., Confederate commissioner, Seward intrigue, **1**, 26.

Creswell, J. A. J., political record, **3**, 543.

Crete, insurrection, **3**, 71, 138, 425.

Crittenden, T. L., Chickamauga, **1**, 444, 446.

Crook, George, in Johnson's tour, **2**, 589.

Crosby, A. C., and Radical patronage, **2**, 585.

Crusader, at Pensacola (1861), **1**, 26, 29.

Cuba, assumption of six-mile maritime jurisdiction, **1**, 170, 367, 399, 467, 468; insurrection, **3**, 523; American Navy and insurrection, 572, 573.

Culebra Island, movement to annex, **3**, 94.

Culpeper, cavalry fight, **1**, 326.

Cumberland, at Norfolk Navy Yard, **1**, 42.

Cummings, Alexander, nomination for Commissioner of Internal Revenue, **3**, 414.

Cuniston, ——, spy, **1**, 313.

Curry, Azariah, master of *Mont Blanc*, **1**, 419.

Curtin, A. G., and Lee's invasion, **1**, 330, 350; and Confederate raid (1864), **2**, 89; and Fourteenth Amendment, 529; Senatorial candidacy, **3**, 16; character, 16.

Curtis, B. R., impeachment counsel, **3**, 294, 298, 299, 302, 308, 330, 331.

Curtis, S. R., asks aid of Navy, **1**, 91.

Cushing, Caleb, and Cabinet office, **2**, 183; and naval contract fraud cases, 225, 227; and *Grey Jacket* case, 493; canal treaty, **3**, 526.

Cushing, W. B., and capture of Fort Anderson, **2**, 245.

Custer, G. A., in Johnson's tour, **2**, 589.

Cutts, J. M. (?), and Blair, **2**, 84.

Dacotah, pursues *Alabama*, **1**, 179.

Dahlgren, J. A., and *Merrimac* scare, **1**, 62, 64, 66; Lincoln's partiality, 158, 163; and Du Pont's campaign against Charleston, 158, 164, 277; and promotion, 163, 239; as officer and bureau chief, 164, 179, 317, 338, 341, **2**, 7, **3**, 447; and succession to Du Pont's command, **1**, 311, 314, 315, 337, 341, 342; refuses subordinate command, 317; and guns for monitors, 342; reports on Charleston operations, 372, 382, 434, 547; and Fox, 401; fears Laird rams, 406; and Gillmore, 434; complaints against, and troubles, 449, 474; Florida expedition, 532; visit to Washington, 534; and death of son, 536, 544, 545, **2**, 7; asks to be relieved, 128; and Farragut, 134; and command of Wilmington expedition, 147; as blockader, 173; sends word of Sherman, 200; gun-casting controversy, 202; and Welles's visit to Charleston, 311, 313; return to Washington (1865), 320; ship visited by Johnson and Cabinet, 331; to command South Pacific Squadron, 604; Tucker episode, **3**, 37, 69, 70; and Ames's claim, 448, 449, 451; wants command of Washington Navy Yard, 484; and vice-admiralship, 562.

Dahlgren, Mrs. J. A., journey to husband's station, **3**, 92, 93.

Dahlgren, Ulric, on Lee's invasion, **1**, 331; captures dispatches, 359; loses leg, 380, 470; raid and death, 536–538, 544, 545.

Dakota, Federal politics (1864), **2**, 153.

Dana, C. A., on fall of Vicksburg, **1**, 371.

Dana, R. H., and law of prize, **1**, 531, 532.

Darling, ——, of New York, and release of Scofield, **2**, 199.

Dart, W. A., and Fenians, **2**, 518, 520.

Davidson, Thomas, political complaints against, **2**, 144.

Davies, Charles, seeks office for nephew, **2**, 558.

Davies, H. E., office-seeker, **2**, 558.

Davis, C. H., Mississippi operations, **1**, 72, 75, 91; and W. D. Porter, 145; transferred, 157; as officer, 158, 351; of board on dismissal of Preble, 191; and *Monitor*, 214; promotion, 239; and letters of marque, 260; visit to Fort Foote, 474; and Du Pont, **2**, 118; and command of Wilmington expedition, 147; and Paraguay, **3**, 466–468, 490, 513; and vice-admiralship, 562.

Davis, Garrett, and Reconstruction, **3**, 502.

Davis, H. W., and Du Pont, **1**, 478, 531, **2**, 8, 30, 117, 118; and chair-

manship of Naval Committee (1863), **1**, 482; attacks on Navy Department, 505, 531, **2**, 227, 236, 237; and movement to expel Long, 9; and campaign of 1864, 30; protest, 95, 96, 98, 122, 239; inflated, 153, 202; and Stanton, 166; attack on Seward, 198, 202; and Butler, 224; as Radical leader, 247; and negro suffrage, 326; death, 409; character, 409, 438; memorial services, 438.

Davis, J. C., Cabinet on killing of Nelson, **1**, 178.

Davis, Jefferson, Stephens's mission to Lincoln, **1**, 358; and demonstration on Washington (1863), 359, 376; Welles's estimate, 376; story of, by escaped slave, 515; and Jaquess, **2**, 84, 109; and Blair's mission, 221; and Hampton Roads Conference, 238; and secession of South Carolina, 255; alleged implication in assassination conspiracy, 299; captured, 306; custody, 308, 309; Cabinet discussions on indictment and trial, 335, 337, 365–368, 608, 614, 616; condition in confinement, 339, 365; not to be paroled, 358; attitude of Sumner and Welles (1865), 397; and general amnesty, 395, 396.

Davis, Mrs. Jefferson, slave's story, **1**, 515; at Savannah (1865), **2**, 314.

Dawes, H. L., and Smith Bros., **2**, 56; and Stanton's plan of Reconstruction, 291; in campaign of 1868, **3**, 460.

Day, B. F., disrespect for Congress, **3**, 312.

Day, Calvin, and Johnson's policy, **2**, 426; and Welles's return to Hartford, **3**, 585.

Dayton, W. L., and French mediation, **1**, 235; on *Florida*, 440; on attitude of France (1864), **2**, 39; death, 205; Welles's association with, 205; and Lincoln's cabinet, 392.

Debts, payment of private, in South, 2, 355; repudiation of Confederate, 579. *See also* Chase, Finances, Paper money.

De Camp, John, question of promotion, 3, 18.

Deity, recognition in Constitution, 2, 190.

Delafield, Richard, and Norfolk Navy Yard, 1, 46.

Delano, B. F., on *Alabama* depredations, 1, 165; as naval constructor, 499; and politics in Brooklyn Navy Yard, 2, 145.

Deming, H. C., political character, 2, 434; candidacy for reëlection, 3, 63.

Democratic Party, intrigue and downfall (1844), 2, 387; in Connecticut, 427–429; and Union Convention (1866), 540, 542, 545; and Johnson, 595, 598, 602, 603, 617, 619, 3, 196, 199, 223, 319, 320, 383, 399, 403, 429. *See also* Elections, Politics.

Denmark, complaints against Wilkes, 1, 322, 325, 451; attempted sale of West Indian islands, 2, 466, 473, 3, 40, 95–98, 124, 125, 502.

Dennison, William, and armored fleet for the Ohio, 1, 90; excursion, 394; in campaign of 1864, 509; and speed test of naval vessels, 512; Postmaster-General, 2, 157, 168; and Chief-Justiceship, 182, 183, 192; and Chase, 183; and Pierpont government, 282; and assassination of Lincoln, 288; and informing of Johnson, 288; at funeral of Lincoln, 293; on Sherman's peace terms, 296, 297; and Hamlin, 345; and negro suffrage, 301; trip to Charleston (1865), 310–315; and Mexico, 333, 479, 485; on trial of Davis, 338; on post-War military arrangements, 352, 355, 356; and political assessments, 380; and Chase's appointment to Cabinet, 391; and Johnson's policy, 399,

419, 425, 537, 543; and Freedmen's Bureau Bill, 434; and party split, 443, 446; on ironclad oath, 445, 450, 453; and Fenian raid, 451; and Civil Rights Bill, 464; and trial of Semmes, 467; and report of Reconstruction Committee, 496, 497; and Atlantic cable, 503; on admitting Colorado, 503; serenade speech, 513; on Fourteenth Amendment, 536, 537; resignation, 551, 553, 555; attitude after resigning, political ambition, 577; on Stanton and Grant, 3, 240.

Dent, Louis, appointment by Johnson, 3, 527.

Desertion, exemplary punishment needed, 1, 232.

De Soto, wrecked, 3, 240.

Dickerson, E. N., assault on Isherwood, 1, 504; test of engine, 2, 346, 356, 361.

Dickinson, D. S., and Vice-Presidential nomination, 2, 45.

Dictator, launched, 1, 495; construction, 2, 35, 201, 207, 340.

Dillon, ——, gunpowder invention, 1, 239, 240.

District commanders. *See* Military governors.

District of Columbia, appointments to court, 1, 245; negro suffrage, 2, 422, 640, 3, 3–8, 15. *See also* Washington.

Dix, J. A., and New York politics (1862), 1, 154, 162; and Norfolk trade, 166, 172–175, 177, 183, 227, 318; and Weed and Seward, 231, 356; operations in Suffolk, 287; and demonstration on Richmond (1863), 349, 351; Lincoln's opinion, 350; to command at New York, 373; and Vice-Presidential nomination (1864), 2, 45; arrest for suspending *World*, 67; nominated to Dutch mission, 566; Naval Office and French mission, 602, 607; Welles's estimate, 607, 3, 442,

443; supports Grant, 442; Bancroft incident, 511, 521; resigns, 525, 539.

Dixon, James, and Connecticut appointments, **1**, 78, 235, 239, 246, 510, **2**, 612, **3**, 78–80, 84, 161; and Welles, **1**, 81, 82, 509, **2**, 307, 501; on Stanton, **1**, 206; Sumner and reëlection (1863), 503; and split in party (1865), **2**, 407; and Johnson's policy, 415, 449, 650; and Freedmen's Bureau Bill, 436; and Civil Rights Bill, 475, 479; and Crosby, 585; loses committee position, 637; and removal of Stanton, **3**, 165; defeated, 264; and impeachment vote, 351; and Chase's candidacy (1868), 382; Congressional candidacy, 526, 572.

Dixon, Mrs. James, and Mrs. Lincoln, **2**, 287.

Dolphin, at Norfolk Navy Yard, **1**, 42.

Dolphin, prize, **1**, 302.

Domestic servants, demagogic influences on, **3**, 588.

Donnell, R. S., and reunion, **1**, 407.

Doolittle, J. R., and appointment of Howard, **1**, 235; on Hooker, 305; and cotton trade, 497; on Presidential prospects (1863), 498; excursions, **2**, 31, 547; and Indian affairs (1865), 362; and Reconstruction, 379, 415, 440; and Freedmen's Bureau Bill, 436, 437; and Civil Rights Bill, 463; on Johnson's irresolution, 480, 481; and Union Convention, 528–530, 533–535, 538, 550, 581, **3**, 251; and Dix's appointment to Holland, **2**, 566; urges removal of Stanton, 581, 582; loses committee position, 637; on attaching Grant to the Administration, 646; relations to Johnson, 647; and suspension of Stanton, **3**, 255; speeches (1868), 264, 267, 281; and Democratic Presidential nomination (1868), 295, 394, 402, 405; and impeach-

ment vote, 351; and Chase's candidacy, 382.

Dorsheimer, Philip, removed, **2**, 598.

Doty, T. W., and wreck of *Fredonia*, **3**, 449.

Douglas, S. A., on Seward and Secessionists, **1**, 32–35.

Douglass, Frederick, and headship of Freedmen's Bureau, **3**, 142.

Downes, John, court martial, **2**, 162.

Draft, riots in New York, **1**, 369, 372, 373; enforcement, 380; Welles's opinion, 382; in Connecticut, 382; Lincoln-Seymour correspondence, 395, 396, 399; and clerical force at Washington, 396; exemption of petty officers of Navy, 407; *habeas corpus* suspension to prevent interference with, 432, 433, 435; and naval enlistments, 498, 541, **2**, 121, 129; consideration of new proclamation (1864), **1**, 541.

Draper, Simeon, appointed collector, **2**, 137; cotton agent, 219; character, 220.

Drayton, Percival, on attack on Charleston, **1**, 295, 307, 312; on fellow officers, **2**, 351, 353; illness, 352; death, 353; as officer, 353; funeral, 354.

Dream, British vessel, outrage on, **1**, 308.

Dred Scott decision, Welles on, **2**, 184.

Dudley, T. H., as consul, **1**, 154, 374; and Laird rams, 262, 436; and *Shenandoah*, **2**, 411.

Duhamel, William, and Conover, **3**, 165.

Dulce y Garay, Domingo, at Washington, **2**, 526.

Dunderberg, construction, **1**, 499, **2**, 340, 341; question of relinquishing, 596, 603, 604, **3**, 27–29, 40, 42, 92, 97.

Dunham, C. A. *See* Conover.

Dunnington, J. W., captured, **1**, 224.

Du Pont, S. F., as officer, character, **1**, 72, 160, 477, **2**, 30, 133–135; and command of expedition against

Charleston, 1, 158; preparation for attack, 216, 217; captures mail, 222; on reported raising of blockade, 234; shrinks responsibility of attacking, 236, 247, 259; tests ironclads before Ft. McAllister, 249; rumors of attack, 262, 263–265; repulse, 265, 267–269, 273; failure to report, 273, 274, 276; report, failure, and subsequent controversy, value of ironclads, 276, 277, 295, 302, 307, 311, 314, 320, 326, 344, 476–478, 2, 7, 11, 30; recall, 1, 288, 311, 312, 318, 320, 322, 326, 337, 346, 347; believed deranged, 307, 312; useless, 309, 311; Lincoln's opinion, 440; and Farragut and Porter, 477, 2, 119; and H. W. Davis, 1, 531; early intrigues and cliques, 2, 117; Port Royal expedition, 118, 3, 217; as blockader, 2, 173; death, 320; relations with Department during the War, 320, 321.

Duval, Dr., excursion, 2, 340.

Eads, J. B., in Washington, 2, 208.

Eames, Charles, and *Peterhoff* mails, 1, 284; and Gurowski, 326; and Welles's annual report (1863), 479; and fraudulent contract cases, 2, 11, 53, 57, 59, 227, 260; and prize cases, 12; and Sumner, 363; and trial of Semmes, 423; apoplexy, 3, 13; death, 67; as official, and Welles, 67; and Coombs's claim, 528.

Early, J. A., Shenandoah raid, 2, 68–70; before Washington, 70–77, 80; pursuit, 85; new raid by, expected, 88, 89; defeated by Sheridan, 151, 153, 158.

Earthquake in South America, 3, 435.

Eastport, Maine, Fenians, 2, 484, 486.

Eaton, A. B. (?), and election returns, 2, 178.

Eaton, W. W., defeated, 2, 5.

Eckert, T. T., and election returns, 2, 178; and assassination of Lincoln, 286.

Edmunds, Judge, solicits campaign contributions (1864), 1, 534.

Edmunds, G. F., and removal of Stanton, 3, 285; and naval affairs, 348; character, 523, 558; and repeal of Tenure-of-Office Act, 555, 558, 567.

Edmunds, J. M., and proposed removal of Lines, 2, 148.

Eggleston, Benjamin, pretended interview with Johnson, 2, 649.

Eight-hour law, Evarts's opinion, 3, 471; movement for repeal, 564; and reduction in wages, 569.

Elections, *1862, 1863:* New York, 1, 153, 154, 162, 171, 177, 219, 2, 27; results to Administration, 1, 183; Connecticut, 262; Ohio and Pennsylvania, 469–471.

1864: McClellan and Presidency (1862), 1, 163; Blair on candidates (1863), 345; Chase's candidacy, 345, 413, 415, 525, 529, 531, 533; prospects of candidature (1863), 498, 500; Lincoln and renomination, 521, 530, 2, 4, 44; meeting of Republican National Committee, 1, 529; campaign contributions and assessments, 534, 2, 112; date of Republican Convention, 4, 28, 30, 142; State, 5, 141, 175; conservative movement in Cabinet, 29; and resignation of Chase, 69; nomination of Frémont and Cochrane, 41–43; gathering of Republican delegates, 44, 45; Republican Vice-Presidential timber, 44, 384; nomination of Lincoln and Johnson, 46; Wade-Davis protest, 95, 96, 98, 122; navy-yard patronage and assessment, 97, 98, 108, 122–124, 136, 137, 142–145, 175; Republican despondency, 102, 103; attitude of New York papers, 103–105; interest in Democratic Convention, 120; Seward as political manager, 120, 131; Chase's support of Lincoln, 120, 140, 187; Frémont's withdrawal expected, 120; and Smith Bros. case, 124; nomination of McClellan, 129, 132; hopes for Lincoln's success, 132, 176; enthusiasm for McClellan, 135; Democratic platform and capture of Atlanta, 135, 140; McClellan's letter, 140; Seward's keynote speech, 140; Forbes on issue, 141; and Sheridan's victories, 153; elements of Democratic Party, 153; Confederates and McClellan, 154; resignation of Blair and retirement of Frémont, 156–158; soldiers' and sailors' votes, 175; returns at Washington, 178; Senatorial tour, 186; Radicals support Lincoln, 187.

1865: Reconstruction issue, **2,** 373; Republican success, 381; Blair and Democrats, 382.

1866: State, **2,** 427, 429, 433, 452, 454–462, 465, 468, 469, 474, 613–615; politics and navy yards, 586, 596–599, 602, 616; Radical victory expected, 608, 613; Fourteenth Amendment as issue, 608–610; effect of Cabinet discord, 611, 613; results, 616–620; Maryland controversy, 620. *See also* Presidential tour, Union Convention.

1867: Connecticut, **3,** 77, 78; expected influence, 222, 232; results, 232.

1868: Grant's candidacy, **3,** 121, 175 *n.,* 180, 189, 244, 277, 363, 364; Johnson's candidacy, 166, 189, 383, 391, 394; Chase's candidacy, 244, 379, 381, 382, 385, 389–391, 393, 397, 404, 455, 457–459; Weed and Grant movement (1867), 249; State, 267, 309, 328, 329, 375, 436, 438, 450–453, 455, 458; meeting of Democratic National Committee, 294; Seymour's candidacy, 295, 382, 383, 390; Democratic timber, 295, 393, 394; Republican Conven-

tion, 362; Republican Vice-Presidential timber, 362, 363; force and fraud for Grant if needed, 364, 423; nomination of Grant and Colfax, 366; Democratic Convention, nomination of Seymour and Blair, 381, 395–399, 408; Democratic nominations invite defeat, 398–402, 436, 439, 440, 443, 446, 450, 455–458, 464; attitude of Johnson and Cabinet after nominations, 401, 402, 404, 408–410, 415, 429, 443, 450; attitude of Conservatives, 404, 405, 411, 462; movement for third candidate, 405; exclusion of vote of certain States, 405; issues, 430, 445; movement to withdraw Seymour, 454, 458, 459; frauds in State, 460; results, 463; frauds in Federal, 463; electoral vote counted, 524; Grant officially informed, 525; Connecticut (1869) as barometer of reaction, 571, 572.

Eliot, T. D., report on Louisiana, **3,** 41.

Ella and Annie, captures *Chesapeake,* **1,** 508.

Ellet, H. W., and control by Navy Department, **1,** 180, 272, 273.

Elliott, H. H., on New York sentiment (1862), **1,** 119.

Ely, J. S., removed, **2,** 597.

Emancipation, Lincoln's first reference, **1,** 70; Cabinet on preliminary proclamation, 142–145, 158–160; Lincoln serenaded, 147; effect of preliminary proclamation, 158; Cabinet on final proclamation, 209, 210; proclamation published, 212; Welles on importance, 212; probable effect in South, 219; and Reconstruction, 403, 415, **2,** 579; Carpenter's picture, **1,** 527, 549; Lincoln and compensated, **2,** 237; Welles on results, 431. *See also* Slavery, Thirteenth Amendment.

Emma, Queen, of Hawaiian Islands, at Washington, **2,** 575, 577, 582,

596, 598; to return home in war vessel, 596, 598, 601, 604.

Emma, prize, sale to Navy, 1, 437, 438, 445, 446.

Emory, W. H., pursuit of Early, 2, 85; on Red River campaign, 86; and removal of Stanton, 3, 283, 288, 289, 299, 338.

Engineer Corps of Navy, movement to reorganize, 3, 252–254, 283, 385. *See also* Isherwood.

Engle, Frederick, and Chiriqui Grant, 1, 151.

English, J. E., gubernatorial candidacy and Reconstruction views (1866), 2, 427, 429, 452, 454–462, 465, 468, 474; elected (1867), 3, 77; messages (1867), 87–89; (1868), 382; political career, 88; reëlection, 267, 329.

Enlistments, *habeas corpus* proceedings (1867), 3, 208–222. *See also* Draft.

Equipment and Recruiting, Bureau of. *See* Foote (A. H.), Smith (A. N.), Smith (Melancthon).

Ericsson, John, *Passaic*, 1, 179; *Monitor*, 214; and guns for monitors, 342; and light-draft monitors, 2, 81, 108, 241, 350.

Erie, Lake, Confederate operations (1864), 2, 151–153.

Etheridge, Emerson, and Lincoln's Cabinet, 2, 390.

Etiquette, official, 2, 251.

Etting, F. M., and Fort Pickens, 1, 30; and Norfolk Navy Yard, 43.

Eutaw, test of speed, 1, 512, 516, 519.

Evarts, W. M., and Chief-Justiceship, 2, 181; and Attorney-Generalship (1864), 183; Henderson case, 220; and trial of Davis, 365, 367; impeachment counsel, 3, 298, 307, 308, 330, 342; character, 307, 409, 492; and State portfolio (1868), 364; Attorney-General, 390, 409; on use of troops as *posse*, 430; absenteeism, 446, 451, 463; Cabinet

and public dinner to, 464–468; and Alabama claims, 470; opinion on eight-hour law, 471; and Pacific Railroad, 474; and legal tender, 480; on court-martial punishments, 481; on confiscation, 504; and Grant and Seward, 511; reception, 512; and holding over under Grant, 533; and inauguration, 537, 538, 541.

Everett, Edward, and Dahlgren, 2, 7; death, 225; Welles on career, 225.

Ewing, Thomas, Sr., and Wilkes case, 2, 203; and Dahlgren, 3, 92; and Cabinet office (1867), 232; (1868), 286.

Fairion, ——, master in Brooklyn Navy Yard, offensive partisanship, 1, 178.

Farragut, D. G., Vicksburg operations, 1, 72, 79, 218, 249, 274, 314; and W. D. Porter, 88, 145; and dismissal of Preble, 190, 191; and loss of Galveston, 230; as officer, 230, 237, 431, 2, 133; and command against Charleston, 1, 311; at New York (1863), 396; visits to Welles, 431, 2, 223, 490, 3, 101, 469; Lincoln on, 1, 440; predicts defeat of Sabine Pass expedition, 441; and Du Pont, 477, 2, 119; Mobile Bay, 100, 105, 124, 133; how selected for New Orleans expedition, 116, 134; and command against Wilmington, 127, 146, 165; desires rest, 145; and cotton trade, 159; visits James River force, 230, 232; and Fox's presumptions, 232, 233; favors an Admiralty Board, 233; of Board of Promotions, 235; Craven court martial, 396; commission as Admiral, 562, 563; in Johnson's tour, 584, 588; European cruise, 3, 104, 123; and line and staff differences, 501; ill and feels slighted (1869), 582.

Farragut, Mrs. D. G., in Johnson's tour, 2, 589.

Fast, national (1863), **1**, 288; (1864), **2**, 93.

Faunce, John, captain of the *Harriet Lane*, **1**, 23.

Faxon, William, Chief Clerk, **1**, 75, 92; illness, 250, **2**, 80, 100; excursions, **1**, 394, **2**, 65, **3**, 396; and Laird's statement, **1**, 401; and Welles's paper on neutral rights, 451; and captured mails, 491; Hale's animosity, 523; and frauds of contractors, 540, **2**, 53; and relief of naval contractors, 207; and Osborn, 219; vacations, 269, **3**, 423; and Fox's official trip abroad, **2**, 509; and sale of ironclads, **3**, 387; as official, 550; resigns, 550.

Federal Constitution, recognition of Deity, **2**, 190; sacredness, **3**, 372; Johnson's suggested amendments, 406, 407. *See also* Reconstruction, and amendments by number.

Felton, S. M., and Lee's invasion, **1**, 332, 343; and Early's raid, **2**, 69.

Fenians, raid (1866), **2**, 450, 451, 453, 454, 484, 486, 518–521, 523, 524; counsel for trials in England, 283.

Fenton, R. E., on partisanship in Brooklyn Navy Yard, **1**, 178; and Johnson's tour, slights Seward, **2**, 592; and Welles (1867), **3**, 201; Vice-Presidential candidacy, 362; Senatorial election, 508, 509.

Ferry, O. S., election to Senate, **2**, 505, 509; character, **3**, 523.

Ferry, T. W., investigation of Philadelphia Navy Yard, **3**, 416.

Fessenden, W. P., and dismissal of Preble, **1**, 162, 163, 188–190, 228; Senate committee on Seward, 196–198; on Welles's administration, 228; and coast defense, 364, 366; wants prize court at Portland, 366, 491; and J. P. Hale, 491; and naval contract frauds, 541; Secretary of the Treasury, **2**, 64, 65; and cotton trade regulations, 66, 138, 162, 240, 258; and Greeley's peace negotiations, 84, 99; adver-

tises a loan, 86; and honoring of naval requisitions, 114, 141; and Seward-Stanton clique, 120, 173, **3**, 173; and collectorship at New York, **2**, 137; on control of abandoned plantations, 150; as financier, 163, 180, 239, 329; criticism of naval officers, 172; and Cabinet consultations, 203; and Draper, 220; and Nasby's book, 238; and successor in Treasury, 244, 245; attitude on Reconstruction, 415; relation to Radicals and to Johnson, 447–449; and Foster, 510; as leader in Senate, 635, **3**, 14; and Bay of Samaná, **2**, 643; and Chandler, **3**, 138; and Chase, 306; impeachment vote, 345, 349–351, 360; and successor to Stanton, 409; loses political power, 505; and party fealty, 515.

Field, D. D., and naval affairs, **1**, 112; and *Evening Post*, **2**, 61; and State portfolio, **3**, 184; and impeachment counsel, 303, 308; Seward on, 303.

Field, M. B., as official, **2**, 62.

Field, S. J., appointment to Supreme Court, **1**, 245; on Johnson, **3**, 64, 65; McCardle case, 320.

Field, T. Y., court martial, **3**, 140.

Fifteenth Amendment, in Senate, **3**, 524; as prerequisite to Reconstruction, 574, 575.

Finances, cost of foreign drafts, **1**, 147; and military success, 520; differences on policy (1864), **2**, 57; Johnson's message on (1868), **3**, 478, 479, 482, 487. *See also* Chase, Fessenden, McCulloch, Paper money, Taxation.

Fingal, Confederate ironclad, **1**, 72; captured, 336, 341, 344.

Fish, Hamilton, and English mission, **3**, 257; Secretary of State, 551; character, 551.

Fisher, G. P., and Stanton, **3**, 160.

Fisher, Fort. *See* Wilmington.

Fisk, James, Jr., and Bowles, **3**, 490.

Five Forks, battle, **2**, 272.

Flagg, A. C., as politician, **3**, 226.

Flambeau, brings news of attack on Charleston, **1**, 266.

Flanders, B. F., control of abandoned plantations, **2**, 148, 149.

Fleming, C. E., promotion, **1**, 77.

Florida, Thayer's scheme to colonize, **1**, 206; Federal defeat in (1864), 531.

Florida, (*Oreto*), discharged at Nassau, **1**, 109; passes blockade at Mobile, 140, 141, 230; question of blockading at Brest, 438, 440; pursuit, **2**, 39; capture in neutral waters, 184–186, 197, 275.

Flusser, C. W., death, **2**, 17.

Fogg, G. G., recall, **2**, 388; on formation of Lincoln's Cabinet, 388–392; political character, 599; Reconstruction views, 600, 601; and Chandler, **3**, 372.

Fontané, P. H. W., on conditions in South, **1**, 316.

Foot, Solomon, and appointment of midshipmen, **1**, 227; resigns from Naval Committee, 227; and *John Gilpin* prize case, 297; and Reconstruction, **2**, 415; death, 465; funeral, 466; Welles's relations, 466.

Foote, A. H., as bureau chief, **1**, 74, 75, 92, 93; on Pope and Halleck, 120; Mississippi River operations, 167; of board on dismissal of Preble, 191; and letters of marque, 256, 260; and command against Charleston, 311, 314, 317, 318, 325, 326, 346, 347; illness, 334–336; Welles's relations, 335, 345, **2**, 135; death, **1**, 345; as officer, **2**, 353.

Foote, Fort, useless, **1**, 474.

Forbes, J. M., on Wilkes in West Indies, **1**, 298; and Lincoln's renomination, **2**, 4; on issues of Presidential campaign (1864), 141; and Smith Bros., 263.

Forbes, P. S., and Dickerson's engine, **2**, 346, 356, 361; contract for *Idaho*, 418, **3**, 29.

Forbes, R. B., and purchase of *Cherokee*, **1**, 516.

Ford, ——, and Indian affairs (1865), **2**, 362.

Ford, ——, and district-attorneyship in New York (1869), **3**, 565.

Ford's Theatre, movement to purchase, **2**, 317; closed by Stanton, 331.

Foreign affairs, character of Grant's appointments, **3**, 577, 578. *See also* Blockade, Neutrality, Seward, and nations by name.

Forged proclamation incident, **2**, 35, 37, 38.

Formosa, attack on natives (1867), **3**, 182.

Forney, J. M., and Welles, **1**, 386; and Hoover case, **2**, 418; on Washington's Birthday speech, 438; and Stevens, 486; and Maryland election (1866), 620; reception for Congress, 627, 630–632; and Johnson, **3**, 6; Senatorial candidacy, 16; and impeachment, 26. *See also* Washington *Chronicle*.

Forrest, Moreau, brings news of attack on Charleston, **1**, 267.

Forrest, N. B., Kentucky raid (1864), **2**, 12; Fort Pillow massacre, 23–25.

Forsyth, John, Confederate commissioner, Seward's intrigue, **1**, 26; on Pope's administration, **3**, 242.

Foster, J. G., captures Goldsborough, **1**, 206; preparation against Charleston, 236, 237, 265; Lincoln's opinion, 350; operations in North Carolina, 381.

Foster, L. S., and Indian affairs (1865), **2**, 362; fails of reëlection, 505, 507, 508; and Johnson, 510; and Italian mission, **3**, 24; end of Senatorship, 58; and Austrian mission, 68, 70; and Court of Claims, 372.

Fourteenth Amendment, Welles on, **2**, 516, 522, 549; amendment and passage, 526, 527; and Union Convention, 529, 534, 539; attitude of Johnson and Cabinet, 532, 533, 535–537, 628, 630, 649; adoption by States, 541, 557; as issue (1866), 608–610, 618; rejection in South, 636; Grant favors, **3**, 8; proclamation of ratification, 417.

Fowler, J. S., impeachment vote, **3**, 356.

Fox, G. V., and relief of Sumter, **1**, 9, 14, 15, 21–23, **2**, 248, 374; and *Monitor*, **1**, 64; at Portsmouth, 87; and J. P. Hale, 150, 485, 488, **2**, 6; and ironclads, **1**, 179, 495; and Lord Lyons, 192; on question of Galveston blockade, 234; and preparations against Charleston, 236, 265, 266; and letters of marque, 261; and failure before Charleston, relations with Du Pont, 276, 302, 311, 344, **2**, 8; and renewal of operations, and Dahlgren, **1**, 390, 313, 317; and *Tacony*, 327, 333; and guns for monitors, 342; excursions, 394, **2**, 31, 65, 340, **3**, 396; and Laird's statement, **1**, 395, 401; weakness for seeming authority, other qualities as official, 401, **2**, 232, 233, 308, 418; inspects *Clyde*, **1**, 428; and Welles's paper on neutral rights, 451; and Welles's annual report (1863), 479; and speed test of naval vessels, 511, 512; H. W. Davis's antagonism, 531; and trade permits, 536; and naval contract frauds, 536, 538–541, 547, **2**, 5, 53, 54, 56, 58; and transfer of soldier seamen to Navy, **1**, 546, 547; and Butler, **2**, 16, 17, 19; and light-draft monitors, 52, 81, 108, 241, 350, 351; on Presidential visits to headquarters, 55; vacation, 100; and D. D. Porter, 129, 235; and Wilmington expedition, 133, 146–148, 150, 209, 214, 215, 230; and Farragut, 134; and exchange of naval prisoners, 168, 169; and Admiral Lee, 172, 173; and politics in navy yards, 175; and relief of naval contractors, 207; and Osborn, 219; attacks on, 241, 247; reply, 248, 251; and Blaine, 250; trip to Havana, 267; and Stimers, 351; and Pendergrast case, 364; and Seward, 384; talks of resigning, 395, 418; official trip to Russia, 506, 509, 512, 514; on impeachment, **3**, 338.

Fractional currency, discussion in Cabinet, **1**, 168.

Frailey, J. M., and Jefferson Davis, **2**, 308.

France, mediation, **1**, 235; tobacco at Richmond, 338–340, **2**, 9, 12; better attitude (1863), **1**, 443, 445, 494, 495; (1864), **2**, 35, 39; ironclads for Confederates, 35, 65, 254; captured cotton claimed by, 106, 107; and Confederate privateering, 159; withdraws right of belligerency, 319; Seward and American possessions, 393; Exhibition, 462, 469; purchase of ironclads, **3**, 92. *See also* Mexico.

Franklin, W. B., Peninsular campaign, **1**, 96; and Second Bull Run, 97, 104, 110.

Frauds. *See* Corruption.

Fredericksburg, battle, **1**, 191–193.

Fredonia, wrecked, **3**, 435, 449.

Freedmen's Bureau, lack of funds, **2**, 413; bill and veto (1866), 431–437; second bill passed over veto, 554; headship (1867), **3**, 142. *See also* Abandoned plantations.

Frelinghuysen, F. T., and impeachment, **3**, 335, 346, 348.

Frémont, J. C., candidacy (1864), **1**, 525; nomination, **2**, 41; 1856 campaign, 41; Benton said to have written his journals and War Department report on (1848), 42; as officer in War, 42; withdrawal of nomination expected, 120; withdraws, 156.

French Exhibition, use of naval vessels to transport exhibits, **2**, 462, 469.

Frontier policy, Scott's, for Civil War, **1**, 84–86, 125, 172, 242.

Fry, J. B., and Stanton, **3**, 279.

Fugitive Slave Law, late case in the District, **1**, 313.

Fuller, Perry, nominated as Commissioner of Internal Revenue, **3**, 391.

Galiani, F. A., on use of neutral waters by belligerents, **1**, 464.

Galveston, captured by Confederates, **1**, 220, 230; question of blockade, 234.

Garcia y Tassara. *See* Tassara.

Garfield, J. A., as Radical, **2**, 247.

Geary, J. W., at Antietam anniversary, **3**, 202.

General, Grant's commission, **2**, 562, 563; attempt to bestow brevet on Sherman and Thomas, **3**, 279, 282, 284. *See also* Lieutenant-general.

General Sherman, destruction, **3**, 485.

Georgia, supposed peace commissioner, **2**, 125, 126; desire for reunion, 158; case of illegal imprisonment (1868), **3**, 420, 421; vote excluded (1868), 525.

Germantown, at Norfolk Navy Yard, **1**, 42.

Gerolt, Baron von, Prussian Minister, **1**, 95.

Gettysburg campaign, first rumors of invasion, **1**, 328, 330; Milroy, 328, 330–333; insecurity and uncertainty at Washington, 329, 338, 342, 343, 350, 351, 353; Curtin's alarm, 330, 350, 358; call for volunteers, 331; passivity of Federal army, 331, 335; invasion denied, 332; fight at Aldie, 336, 338; depression of Administration, 340; Lincoln and Hooker, 344, 348; McClellan rumor, 345; Meade supersedes Hooker, 348; question of counter-movement on Richmond, 349, 351, 359; Meade as commander, 349, 351; Lee in Pennsylvania, 350, 352; policy of merely driving Confederates back, 352, 358, 363, 369; battle, 354, 356–358; Lee's escape, 357, 363, 364, 366, 368–375; proposed demonstration on Washington by Beauregard, 359, 376; and draft riots and Stephens's mission, 369; Sickles on selection of field, 472.

Gillem, A. C., and military governorship, **3**, 245.

Gillett, R. H., interview with Taney, **2**, 184.

Gillis, J. H., wreck of *Wateree*, **3**, 449.

Gillis, J. P., Sumter expedition, **1**, 23.

Gillmore, Q. A., Charleston operations, **1**, 310, 317, 380, 382–385, 449, 475, 547; and Dahlgren, 434, 474; and Wilmington expedition, **2**, 128, 133; and Welles's visit to Beaufort, 313.

Gilmore, J. R., mission to Richmond, **2**, 109.

Gilpin, Charles, and navy-yard frauds, **2**, 205.

Given, J. T., candidacy for mayor, **3**, 381.

Glisson, O. S., and League Island, **3**, 552.

Glover, Samuel, and impeachment counsel, **3**, 307.

Godon, S. W., in Washington, **2**, 317; and Paraguay (1866), 491, 543; and Webb, **3**, 208; on Port Royal, 217.

Godwin, Parke, and Henderson case, **1**, 542, **2**, 60, 104; as editor, 61.

Gold, discoveries (1864) and currency problem, **2**, 179, 180. *See also* Paper money.

Gold bill, enacted, **2**, 54.

Goldsborough, L. M., and Wilkes's command in James River, **1**, 73; fear of *Merrimac*, 142; and Early's raid, **2**, 73; and command of Wilmington expedition, 147; and promotion, 604; and Surratt, **3**, 29; and Cretans, 70; question of retirement, 85, 86, 99, 107–109, 135; and vice-admiralship, 562.

Goldsborough, Mrs. L. M., and retirement of husband, **3**, 107.

Goldsborough, N. C., captured, **1**, 206.

Gooch, D. W., and Charlestown Navy Yard, **1**, 374, 380, **2**, 31, 34; and Smith Bros. case, **1**, 540, **2**, 53, 263; of Committee on Conduct of the War, 198; and Stanton's plan of Reconstruction, 291; and naval patronage, 325; and Boston collectorship, 357; Naval Officer, 381.

Gooding, D. S., excursion, **2**, 330.

Goodman, ——, of Connecticut, candidate for internal revenue office (1862), **1**, 78.

Goodman, ——, on guilt of Smith Bros., **2**, 53.

Goodrich, J. Z., position threatened, **2**, 356.

Goodwin, J. N., Arizona office, **1**, 409.

Governors, Altoona Conference, **1**, 153, 156; character of messages (1863), 219.

Graham, W. A., and Lincoln's Cabinet, **2**, 390.

Grand Gulf, captured, **1**, 295.

Granger, Gordon, Mobile Bay, **2**, 114; and command at Washington (1868), **3**, 317.

Grant, H. A., appointment to collectorship, **2**, 612, 651.

Grant, U. S., Welles's portraiture, **1**, xlvii; Vicksburg, 308, 309, 311, 314, 320, 324, 364, 371; intercepts supplies from Texas, 379; and Navy, 379, **2**, 6; and McClernand, **1**, 387; and drink, 388, **2**, 214; and cotton trade, **1**, 511; at Lincoln's reception, Welles's first impressions, 538, 539; presentation of commission, 539; and Early's raid, **2**, 68, 69; as

commander, 68, 70, 73, 90, 91, 94, 276, **3**, 121, 122; reported disagreement with Stanton (1864), **2**, 79; puts Sheridan in the Valley, 96; and Wilmington expedition, Butler's command, 133, 146, 150, 214–216, 222; and exchange of naval prisoners, 171; and dismissal of Butler, 223; and naval force in James River, 230, 232; goes to Fort Fisher, 230; and resumption of trade, 280, 281; on Stone's River, 283; character, 283 *n.*, **3**, 274, 363, 530, 587; and Sherman's peace terms, **2**, 294, 295, 310; and custody of Davis, 309; and Mexico, 317, 322, 333, 621, 624; and post-War army movements, 352, 355–357, 361, 362; Johnson's attitude (1865), 367; Southern tour (1865), 397, 398; and Fenian raid, 451, 453, 518, 519; and Confederate paroles, 476; reception attended by both elements (1866), 477, 478; and proposal to oust Stanton (1866), 529; commission as General, 562, 563; in Johnson's tour, 584, 588, 591–593; and Union Convention, 582; on Johnson's Copperhead supporters, 591, 592, 595; and Indian affairs, 613, **3**, 98, 100; importance of political attitude (1866), **2**, 646; and negro suffrage for the District, **3**, 5, 15; and Fourteenth Amendment, 8; and Constitution, 15; and revolutionary plans of Radicals, 27; and enforcement of Civil Rights Bill, **3**, 42, 44; changing attitude towards Johnson, 56, 72, 141, 155, 184, 185, 196, 199, 232; and selection of military governors, 62, 63, 65; and Sheridan's letters, 117, 125–127; and Tennessee disturbances, 140, 211; and Maryland election (1866), 140, 141; and removal of Sheridan, 154, 174, 186, 187, 500; Secretary of War *ad interim*, 160, 167–169, 240; and execution of Reconstruction Acts, 169,

182, 183, 185, 187–190, 193, 242, 277, 298; and charges against Holt, 172, 173; secret opposition to the Administration (1867), 175 n.; talk with Welles on Reconstruction Acts, 177–181; Welles and Butler on, as political ignoramus, 180, 181, 565; and Cabinet-meetings, 188, 190; reception to generals, 208; and *habeas corpus* proceedings on enlistments, 212, 213; and Reconstruction elections, 207; and court of inquiry for Sickles, 207, 232; Sherman expected to influence, 221, 232; opposes further pardons (1867), 231; letter on Stanton, 240; Johnson's attempt to have understanding with, 233–235; and question of arresting Johnson, 235, 238; Welles fears "man on horseback," 245, 246, 249, 270, 545, 559, 564; and reinstatement of Stanton, Johnson controversy, 258–262, 266–279, 465, 491, 500; and Radical society, 278; and currency question, 494; proscribes Johnson and Cabinet, Evarts dinner, 464–468, 491, 494, 497, 512; Johnson and Cabinet and inauguration, 498, 500, 532, 536–538, 540–542; Welles forecasts character as President, 483, 525; Cabinet, 488, 530, 535, 543–549; dines with Seward, 508, 511; attends a Blair wedding, 519; political attitude before inauguration, 526, 530; nepotism, 527; Johnson's Cabinet on holding over under, 529, 530, 532, 535; inauguration parade, 542; inaugural, 544; and Johnson's last pardons, 547, 555; and Tenure-of-Office Act, 557, 569, 571; and reorganization of the Navy, 558–560; character of appointments, 575–578. *See also* Elections (*1868*), Virginia campaign.

Grant, Mrs. U. S., confident of husband's election, **3**, 389.

Gray, J. G. C., and *Evening Post*, **2**, 61.

Great Britain, hostile attitude, **1**, 74, 79, 299, **2**, 431; and Confederate cruisers, **1**, 109, 111, 165, 175, 207, 245, 247, 250–252, 255, 262; slave-trade cruising convention, 155, 163, 166, 192, 193; and the *Bermuda*, 170; and captured mails, 180, 266, 269–289, 290, 302–304; and Wilkes in West Indies, 298; better attitude, 299, 305, 445, 495; ministry and Roebuck's motion, 374; and Federal successes, 379, 385; Laird rams, 399, 406, 428, 435–438, 443, 448; *Mont Blanc* incident, capture in neutral waters, 416–427; and sale of prize *Emma* to Navy, 438, 445, 446; Welles on attitude and policy toward, 453; visit of Admiral Milne, 468, 469; *Chesapeake* incident, 490, 508; change in ministry threatened (1864), **2**, 67, 71; and Confederate privateering, 159; question of refusing hospitality to navy of, 319, 320, 327; withdraws right of belligerency, 319. *See also* Alabama claims.

Greece, seeks ironclads, **3**, 207.

Greeley, Horace, on loss of Norfolk Navy Yard, **1**, 50, 51; and Welles, **2**, 12, 260; peace negotiations, 83, 94, 99, 110, 271, 272; attitude toward Lincoln (1864), 87, 104, 130; Lincoln likens him to an old shoe, 112; and Butler, 222–224; appetite for notoriety, 272; and formation of Lincoln's cabinet, 391; on Alaska, **3**, 84; and Stanton, 173. *See also* New York *Tribune*.

Gregory, F. H., and ironclads, **1**, 153; and Charleston expedition, 276, 311, 315; report on *Chimo*, **2**, 52; as officer, 116.

Grey Jacket, prize case, **2**, 469, 492, 493.

Grier, R. C., McCardle case, **3**, 320.

Griffin, Charles, and Second Bull Run, **1**, 110.

Griffin, J. Q. A., Congressional aspirations (1865), **2**, 381.

Griffiths, J. W., and frauds, **1**, 511.

Grimes, J. W., and loss of Norfolk Navy Yard, **1**, 54; Senate committee on Seward, 196, 197, 206; on J. P. Hale, 227, 490; and naval affairs, 485, 488, 490, 519, **2**, 11, **3**, 252, 515, 531, 558, 563, 564; and prosecution of fraudulent contractors, **1**, 540, 541; excursions, **2**, 31, 422; and relief of contractors, 207; attitude towards Radicals and towards Johnson, 379, 447–450; Presidential aspirations, 405; attitude towards South (1866), 444; political character, 447; and tariff, 542; on popular support of Congress, 632; as leader of Senate, 635, **3**, 14; and Bay of Samaná, **2**, 643; and dismissal of Radicals from navy yards, **3**, 13, 18; and Danish West Indies, 97; and impeachment, 338, 342, 346, 350, 351, 360, 361; paralysis, 353, 354, 356; and successor to Stanton, 409; and party fealty, 515; and repeal of Tenure-of-Office Act, 567, 568.

Grinnell, M. H., and Navy Department, **1**, 216, 512–514; and Seward and Grant, **3**, 511; collectorship, 560; character, 561.

Griswold, J. A., defends Navy Department, **1**, 531; excursion, **2**, 31; and Sherman, **3**, 265; and *Monitor*, 412–414; and Treasury portfolio, 549.

Groesbeck, W. S., impeachment counsel, **3**, 302, 308, 330, 352.

Grover, Cuvier, at Savannah, **2**, 313.

Grover, Martin, and Wilmot Proviso, **2**, 386.

Grow, G. A., and Welles, **1**, 482.

Gulf Squadron, command (1861), **1**, 76. *See also* Pickens, West Gulf Squadron.

Gurley, J. A., death, **1**, 408; and Welles, 408.

Gurley, P. D., at death-bed of Lincoln, **2**, 288, 292, 294.

Gurowski, Count Adam, character, **1**, 187, 326, **2**, 100; on Radicals and selection of Lincoln's cabinet, **1**, 325; diary, **2**, 101; and Welles, 101; on Johnson's habits, 438.

Guthrie, James, and restriction of movement of naval officers, **2**, 494; and Coombs's claim, **3**, 528.

Gwathmey, Washington, and Fort Pickens, **1**, 29.

Habeas corpus, writ of, privilege suspended, **1**, 150; suspension to prevent defeat of draft, 432, 433, 435; power to suspend, 433; post-War conditions in South, **2**, 366; proceedings on enlistments (1867), **3**, 208–222. *See also* Arbitrary arrests.

Hahn, Michael, in Washington (1864), **2**, 99.

Hale, Charles, excursion, **2**, 31.

Hale, J. M., death, **3**, 520, 521.

Hale, J. P., Welles's portraiture, **1**, xxx; and loss of Norfolk Navy Yard, 48–54; and appointment of midshipmen, 146, 147, 149; relations with Welles and Navy Department, 187, 206, 224, 227, 308, 384, 386, 505, 507, 509, 522, 523, **2**, 5, 6, 51, 52, 193, 231, 234, 238, 250, 251, 275, **3**, 25; and chairmanship of Naval Committee (1863), **1**, 482, 484, 490; Welles's plain speech with, 485–489; antagonism to Fox, 485, 488, **2**, 6; and bribe, **1**, 489, 522; and naval enlistments, 499; Grimes's opinion, 490; and purchase of *Cherokee*, 516; and Faxon, 523, 529; fails of reelection, **2**, 51; and Farragut, 116; loses chairmanship of Naval Committee, 193; Minister to Spain, 255, 257; question of public ship for, 268; as Minister, 3, 452, 518, 553, 578.

Hale, R. C., death, 1, 354.

Hall, ——, fugitive-slave case in the District (1863), 1, 313.

Hall, J. C., at death-bed of Lincoln, 2, 286.

Halleck, master, and politics in Brooklyn Navy Yard, 2, 123.

Halleck, H. W., Welles's portraiture, 1, xxix; and Navy in James River, 83; and Second Bull Run, 93, 97, 99, 105, 122; Welles's opinion of, as general-in-chief, 107, 119, 134, 179, 180, 192, 209, 216, 218, 320, 324, 329, 364, 373, 376, 379, 383, 392, 442, 444, 471, 472, 2, 92; origin of general command, 1, 108, 119, 221; and McClellan, 116, 120, 122, 124, 179; and Navy, 121, 365, 2, 12; indecision after Antietam, 1, 153; and Norfolk trade, 173; and forged Cooper dispatch, 176; and control over war vessels on Mississippi, 180; and McClernand, 217, 388; and renewal of attack on Charleston, 309, 324, 382, 383, 385; and Vicksburg, 314, 320, 324, 365, 367; Lincoln's reliance on, 320, 329, 364, 371, 526; and Gettysburg campaign, 328, 330, 331, 338, 342, 349–352, 358, 363, 366, 368–370, 373; Blair's plan for McClellan to supersede, 345; and expedition into western Texas, 390–392, 442; and Almaden mines, 397; Chase's final antagonism, 402, 447; and Chickamauga, 438, 442; and commanders of the Army of the Potomac, 440; and Sabine Pass expedition, 441; and Chattanooga, 444, 447; and Meade's autumn campaign, 473; at presentation of Grant's commission, 539; and new draft (1864), 542; and transfer of men to Navy, 547; and Red River campaign, 2, 18, 27; and Early's raid, 69, 70, 72, 76–78, 84; Bates's antagonism, 93; and Mobile, 100,

165; and exchange of naval prisoners, 170; fears at second inauguration, 251; and capture of Richmond, 272; and Sherman, 309; and custody of Davis, 309; and Alaskan commission, 3, 129, 141; obstruction of the Potomac, 436.

Halpine, C. G., and impeachment, 3, 349.

Hamersley, W. J., and Welles, 3, 587.

Hamilton, A. J., cotton-trade permit, 2, 159, 162, 163, 167; as Governor of Texas, 2, 315, 316, 420, 580; character, 315.

Hamlin, Hannibal, and Welles, 1, 82; and coast defense, 364, 366; request for prize court, 366; question of renomination, 2, 44, 46, 47; and reappointment of Brown, 342, 344–346; and Boston collectorship, 356; and formation of Lincoln's cabinet, 389; Vice-Presidential candidacy (1868), 3, 362; Senatorial contest (1869), 505, 517.

Hammond, Henry, appointment, 1, 510.

Hampton Roads Conference, 2, 235, 236, 238.

Hancock, W. S., Gettysburg, 1, 472; Spottsylvania, 2, 29; and Indian troubles, 3, 99; as military governor, 186, 204, 241, 242, 245, 277, 298; and Democratic Presidential nomination (1868), 295, 394, 397, 400, 456; in Washington (1868), 317.

Hannah Grant, seizure by Venezuela, 3, 296, 349.

Hanscom, Isaiah, and navy-yard position, 3, 139.

Hanscom, S. P., and Banks, 2, 178; character, 653; and attack on Navy Department, 3, 325.

Harcourt, Sir W. G. V., on captured mails, 1, 315.

Hardie, W. J., Savannah, 2, 208.

Harlan, James, Secretary of the Interior, 2, 307; on ironclad oath, 318, 445, 450; and closing of Ford's

Theatre, 331; and Mexico, 333, 485; and trial of Davis, 338, 339; on Pope, 357; and political assessments, 380, 381; and Johnson's policy, 395, 419, 425, 481, 524, 537, 543; political aspirations, 405; on Freedmen's Bureau Bill, 434; on Civil Rights Bill, 464; on report of Reconstruction Committee, 497; and Fenian raid, 451; and Colorado Bill, 503; and Atlantic cable, 503; on Fourteenth Amendment, 537; resigns, 563; and impeachment, 3, 358.

Harlan, Mary, marriage, 3, 444.

Harney, W. S., Indian Commission, 3, 254.

Harper's Ferry, capture (1862), 1, 140.

Harriet Lane, Sumter expedition, 1, 16, 22; captured, 220; at Havana (1865), 2, 378.

Harrington, George, and Bankhead, 1, 131.

Harris, Clara W., and Mrs. Lincoln, 2, 287.

Harris, Ira, Senate committee on Seward, 1, 196, 198; and Weed, 2, 154; Reconstruction views, 401; failure of reëlection, 542, 3, 20; and impeachment, 348.

Harris, John, reproved, 1, 89; death, 2, 31; and Marine bounty, 174.

Hartt, Edward, attempt to force removal, 3, 139, 417, 419.

Harvey, J. E., and Confederate commissioners, 1, 32, 2, 248; and naval purchases in Portugal, 3, 514, 525.

Harvey, Peter, and navy-yard appointments, 3, 446.

Harwood, A. A., of Retiring Board, 3, 569.

Hastings, Dr., displaced from marine hospital position, 2, 629.

Hatch, J. P., and Welles's visit to Charleston, 2, 312.

Haupt, Herman, and naval frauds, 1, 511.

Hautefeuille, L. B., on use of neutral waters by belligerents, 1, 464.

Hawaiian Islands, affairs (1868), 3, 322, 329.

Hawley, J. R., question of army promotion, 1, 235, 535; and Dahlgren, 474, 535; and Welles's visit to Wilmington, 2, 314; restored to duty, 369; and negro equality, 369; political views, 433, 3, 87; gubernatorial candidacy and Reconstruction views, 2, 452, 454–462, 465, 468, 469, 474; and Cabinet office, 3, 526; and Welles's return to Hartford, 585.

Hay, John, at Port Royal, 1, 532; on Raymond's annoyance of Lincoln, 2, 175; and election returns, 178.

Hayti, buys gunboat, 3, 424.

Heap, G. H., and Porter, 1, 249; brings news of Red River campaign, 2, 26.

Heaton, David, and trade permits, 1, 527.

Heintzelman, S. P., Blair on, 1, 126; on McClellan's treasonable intentions, 2, 204.

Henderson, G. A., and graft, 1, 518; reappointed, 2, 316.

Henderson, Isaac, and naval frauds, arrest and trial, 1, 518, 540, 542, 2, 54, 59, 60, 78, 79, 83, 104, 185, 220, 225, 306.

Henderson, J. B., resolution on civil service in Navy Department, 2, 633, 3, 13, 21; impeachment vote, 349, 362.

Hendricks, T. A., as Presidential timber, 3, 295, 394, 397; gubernatorial campaign (1868), 453; as Senator, 484.

Hicks, T. H., and Maryland patronage, 2, 195, 196; death, 243.

Hill, Isaac, as politician, 3, 309.

Hillhouse, ——, and Assistant Treasurer at New York, 2, 62.

Hillyer, W. S., and Grant's political position, 2, 646.

Hitchcock, E. A., and exchange of

naval prisoners of war, **2**, 169–171.

Hoar, E. R., Attorney-General, **3**, 545; to go on the bench, 551; opinion on revoking pardons, 555; on relative rank of staff officers, 570.

Hoffman, H. W., question of removal, **2**, 195.

Hogan, John, and Johnson's tour, **2**, 591.

Holden, W. W., as governor, **2**, 580.

Hollister, Gideon, and Cuban Consul-Generalship, **3**, 78–80, 84, 85.

Holman, W. S., assault on Navy Department, **1**, 531.

Holt, Joseph, holds over under Lincoln, **1**, 3; and protection of Washington, 4; to review Scofield case, **2**, 176; and Attorney-Generalship, 183, 187; and relief of Sumter, 274, 374; and implication of Davis, 299; Blair's attack, Welles's opinion (1865), 370, 374, 423, 424; desires a court of inquiry, 601, 604, 616; and Reconstruction, **3**, 118; Conover allegations, 143 *n.*, 144; Welles urges removal, 163, 167; removal considered, 171; affidavits of conspiracy against, 172–174.

Hood, J. B., Nashville, **2**, 200.

Hooker, Joseph, commands Army of the Potomac, **1**, 229; Welles's opinion, 229, 294, 329; and drink, 229, 230, 324, 336, 349; Lincoln visits headquarters, 263, 264, 294; Chancellorsville, 287, 290–295, 302; irreverence, 305, 336; and Lee's invasion, 331, 335, 340, 342; Lincoln's attitude during Gettysburg campaign, 344, 348; relieved, 348, 349; sent West, 444; leaves Sherman's army, **2**, 93.

Hooper, Samuel, and Charlestown Navy Yard, **1**, 374, 380; and Smith Bros., **2**, 224, 263; and collectorship at Boston, 357.

Hoover, Henry, movement to reinstate, **2**, 418.

Horwitz, P. J., excursions, **1**, 394, **2**, 31, 65, 80.

Hovey, ——, of Norwich, Conn., and Cuban Consul-Generalship, **3**, 80.

Hovey, A. P., and Tucker episode, **3**, 37.

Howard, ——, of Brooklyn, and Laird's statement, **1**, 291, 395, 396, 401.

Howard, J. M., Senate committee on Seward, **1**, 196, 198; and bank bill, 237; and Toucey, 355; character, **2**, 633; report on suspension of Stanton, **3**, 255; and impeachment, 301, 333.

Howard, Joseph, forged proclamation, **2**, 37.

Howard, Mark, nomination, **1**, 78, 81; and Welles, 81, 82; nomination suspended, 235, 239, 246.

Howard, O. O., and escape of Lee, **1**, 374; Gettysburg, 472; report on enforcement of Civil Rights Act, **3**, 42; as head of Freedmen's Bureau, 142; and Stanton's intrenchment in office, 323; pious fraud, 323.

Howe, T. O., and Reconstruction, **2**, 415; impeachment vote, **3**, 367; character, 479, 523.

Howell, ——, Matamoras trade permit, **1**, 300 *n.*

Hubbard, C. D., and Johnson-Grant controversy, **3**, 269, 274.

Hubbell, J. R., and reinstatement of a naval officer, **3**, 498, 501, 503.

Hübner, Martin, on use of neutral waters by belligerents, **1**, 464.

Humphrey, James, and politics in Brooklyn Navy Yard, **2**, 122, 142–145.

Hunter, David, and James Island, **1**, 160; and attack on Charleston, 216; in western Virginia (1864), **2**, 61; and burning of Letcher's house, 87; retreat before Early, 87; relieved by Sheridan, 96.

Hunter, R. M. T., Hampton Roads Conference, **2**, 235, 238.

Hunter, William, on raising of Galveston blockade, 1, 233; and *Peterhoff* mails, 286; Secretary of State *ad interim*, 2, 289; and implication of Davis, 300; and Welles, 320; and *Shenandoah*, 411.

Idaho, character of Governor (1867), 3, 186.
Idaho, construction, 2, 418, 3, 29.
Ile à Vache. *See* Cow Island.
Illinois, Senatorial election (1867), 3, 21.
Immigration, proposed bounties, 1, 543.
Impeachment, Welles's diary on, 1, 1; threats (1866), 2, 395, 399, 627, 636; Ashley's resolution, 3, 8; Cabinet discussion of resolution, 12; spirit and outlook of movement, 12, 17, 293, 296, 300, 301, 313, 314, 321, 324, 329, 330, 332, 334, 336, 337, 344, 350; consideration of resolution, 3, 19, 20; attitude of Johnson and Cabinet towards, and arrest or suspension, 21, 27, 50, 57, 60, 62, 151, 200, 235, 237, 238, 291, 313; progress, 26, 61; vacation meetings of Judiciary Committee, 90, 95, 102; character of scrutiny, 102; attitude of House (July, 1867), 131; Conover allegations, 143–146; reports, 238, 239; House votes, 292, 295; counsel for defense, 294, 298, 299, 302, 304–308, 319, 322, 323; Cabinet discussion on consultations, 297; articles, 299; precedents for Stanton's removal, 302, 303, 311, 322; attendance of accused, 302; notice served, 303; Chase's importance and conduct, 306, 327, 328; Johnson divulges defense, 311; preliminaries of trial, 312, 313; public apathy, 315, 319; attitude of Democrats, 319; opening of trial, 319; Johnson's reply, 319; State resolutions on, 320; replication, 321; Butler's opening, 326; consultations of defense, 329–332, 337; Curtis's opening for defense, 330, 331; General Sherman's letters, 330, 331; testimony, 332–336; Wilson's injected speech, 334; acquittal in return for Presidential discretion, 338, 360; arguments, 338, 340–342, 345, 347; and nomination of Schofield, 339, 340; acquittal expected, Welles's skepticism, 341, 342, 345, 347, 349, 351, 356, 361, 367; doubtful Senators, pressure on them, 345–347, 349, 350, 354–356; policy of conviction on general principles, 348, 361; rumors of Johnson's resignation, 350; secret session, opinions of Senators, 351; Johnson and acquittal, 351, 352, 368; vote postponed, Radical consternation and rage, 353, 354; acquittal on eleventh article, 357; further postponement, 359; the seven Senators and party discipline, 359, 361; abuse and threats against them, 360, 362; investigation of vote, 362, 366–370, 380, 381; attempt at further postponement, 368; acquittal on other articles, 368; Johnson's expenses, 372; Stevens and renewal, 391; Johnson and the seven Senators, 515.
Indiana, State elections (1864), 2, 175; (1868), 3, 452, 453.
Indianapolis, Johnson at, 2, 594.
Indianola, Texas, plan to occupy, 1, 391, 443.
Indians, execution of Northwestern, 1, 170, 186; army movements (1865), 2, 355, 357, 360–362; departmental strife for control over, 3, 30, 74, 98–100; agents, 30, 69; report of Commission (1868), 254.
Ingalls, Rufus, and Wilderness, 2, 26.
Ingersoll, E. C., and Navy Department, 2, 430.
Ino, pursues *Alabama*, 1, 179.

Interior, Department of. *See* Browning (O. H.), Harlan (James), Smith (C. B.), Usher (J. P.).

Internal revenue, frauds (1868), **3**, 434.

International law. *See* Belligerency, Blockade, Maritime jurisdiction, Neutrality, Prizes.

Irish, and the army, **1**, 324.

Ironclads, construction for attack on Charleston, **1**, 153, 179; in attack, 217, 249, 265–269, 273, 295, 302, 307, 311, 314; seaworthiness, 225, 226; Welles's satisfaction with, 342, 351, 495, 499; guns, 342; Welles and navy yard for, **2**, 17; light-draft monitors, 52, 81, 86, 108, 241, 349–351; loss of *Tecumseh*, 101; *Dictator* and *Puritan*, 340; *Dunderberg*, 340, 341, **3**, 27–29, 40, 42, 92; sale authorized, **2**, 602; sale, **3**, 92, 206, 341, 384, 420, 429, 438; investigation of sale, 348, 387–389; history of construction of *Monitor*, 412. *See also* Confederate ironclads.

Ironsides, in attack on Charleston, **1**, 265, 273; burned, **2**, 643.

Isaac Smith, captured, **1**, 231.

Isherwood, B. F., at Norfolk Navy Yard, **1**, 43, 44; Dickerson's assault on, 504; as officer, 505, **3**, 552; and speed test of naval vessels, **1**, 511; and light-draft monitors, **2**, 349, 350; engines of *Wampanoag*, **3**, 283.

Island Queen, captured on Lake Erie, **2**, 152.

Isthmus of Panama, Seward desires to annex, **3**, 107; Cushing's canal treaty, 526.

Jackson, Andrew, as general, **1**, 86.

Jackson, M. M., and *Tallahassee*, **2**, 110.

Jackson, T. J., Cedar Hill, **1**, 78; death, 297.

Jacobs, ——, and contract frauds, **1**, 516.

James Island, affairs at, **1**, 160.

Japan, vessels built for, **1**, 225, **2**, 188–192, 561; joint expedition against, indemnity, 189, 210, 560–562, **3**, 135; delegation to purchase ships (1867), 87, 89, 91; *Stonewall*, 97, 99, 365, 513; treatment of native Christians, 230.

Jaquess, J. F., mission to Richmond, **2**, 83, 109.

Jayne, William, and Dakota politics, **2**, 153.

Jeffries, N. L., counsels Johnson to resist (1868), **3**, 288; and Chase's candidacy (1868), 382; internal-revenue nomination rejected, 414.

Jenkins, T. A., as bureau chief, **2**, 357, 362, **3**, 569; and Japanese delegation, 92; excursion, 396; inspection tour, 422; on Porter at Navy Department, 561; transferred, 569.

Jewell, Marshall, and Hawley for Cabinet office, **3**, 526; inauguration, 585; character, 586.

John Gilpin, prize, **1**, 297.

Johnson, ——, and frauds, **1**, 548.

Johnson, Judge, of Ohio, on Wade-Davis protest, **2**, 121.

Johnson, Andrew, Welles's portraiture, **1**, xlvii; Vice-Presidential nomination, **2**, 46, 384; address as Vice-President, 252, 253; informed of Lincoln's death, 288; takes oath, 289; first meeting with Cabinet, 289; temporary office, 289; favors punishment of Southern leaders, 291; at funeral of Lincoln, 292; and proclamation against Confederate "pirates," 298; delegations to, 300; and opening of trade in South, 300; calls on Seward, 304; and negro suffrage, 304, 422, 580; failure to generalize, 305; and Sherman's peace terms, 310 *n.*, **3**, 247; and Texas affairs, **2**, 315, 316; and blockade, 320; appointment of midshipmen, 317, 526; Trumbull's attitude (1865),

322; and Preston King, 323, 380; overrun with visitors, 323; and Radicals (June, 1865), 325; overwork and illness, 327, 329, 342, 347, 348, 352; excursions, 329, 331, 340; use of patronage, character of appointments, 332, 398, 399, 484, 487, 565, 616, **3**, 52, 64, 74, 83, 85, 147, 412, 414; and Smith Bros. case, **2**, 334; and trial of Davis, 335–337, 365, 366, 368; and Hamlin, 342, 344, 345; and Blairs, 343, 511, 513, 514, 578, 569, **3**, 120, 165, 166, 168, 408; plan to relieve of extra burdens, **2**, 354; amnesty policy and pardons, 358, 382, **3**, 193, 197–199, 394–396; first indications of opposition to policy, **2**, 363, 381; Cabinet support of policy (1865), 364; and Chase, 366, 368, 619; and Reconstruction judges, 366; relations with Thomas and Grant (1865), 367; intended visit to Richmond, 375; and political assessments, 376, 379; and Amos Kendall, 376; on sufficiency of executive Reconstruction, 378, 379; Congress ignores on meeting, 392; annual messages (1865), 392; (1866), 628; (1867), **3**, 237, 239; (1868), 475, 477–480, 482; Sumner and Welles on policy and attitude of Cabinet (1865), 393–395, 397, 398, 400, 415, 424–426 *n.*, 430; and refusal to admit Southern Congressmen, 387; Welles warns of intrigue, 396, 398; and rumor of Stanton's intention to resign (1865), 399, 400; and pardon of naval swindlers, 400, 401, 412; Stanton's espionage, 403 *n.*; and case of Captain Meade, 407, **3**, 250, 251; receptions, **2**, 408, **3**, 3, 22, 252, 281, 496, 512, 539; on the Radicals (Jan., 1866), 409, 432; impending war with Congress, 412, 414, 421, 434; and trial of Semmes, 420, 423, 424, 432, 457, 467, 471, 474, 476, 477; Welles

urges to public enunciation of policy, 421; and Holt, 423, **3**, 171; evil influence of Seward and Stanton, **2**, 425 *n.*, 426 *n.*, 523, 527, 528, 532, 540, 544, 556, 566, 627, 630, 652, **3**, 26, 47, 64–66, 72, 73, 83, 90, 100, 116, 118–120, 123, 132– 134, 160, 191, 195, 263, 383, 403, 411, 454, 492; veto of Freedmen's Bureau bills, **2**, 432–435, 437, 554; Washington's Birthday speech, 438–440, 647; and admission of Tennessee Members, 442, 443, 559; and party split, 443, 446, 454, 456, 480; and Grimes and Fessenden (1865), 448, 449; slanders on, 454, 461; and Connecticut election (1866), 454–461, 465, 474; veto of Civil Rights Bill, 461, 463, 464, 475, 477, 479; and sea voyage for son, 472, 479, 491; proclaims end of Civil War, 473; at Grant's reception (1866), 478; and Cabinet (1866), 481–483, 487, 498, 522–525, 527, 537, 543, 555, 556, 606, 611; effects of speechmaking, 488, 647, 648, **3**, 99; and Cabinet opinions on Reconstruction Committee, **2**, 495–498; and Atlantic cable, 504; and Fox's official trip abroad, 509, 512, 514; and Fenians, 518– 520, 523, **3**, 283; and Fourteenth Amendment, **2**, 527, 532, 533, 535; and calling of Union Convention, 528, 531, 534, 535, 538–541; and military interference with Tennessee legislature, 554, 557; reticence, hesitancy, rashness, 558, **3**, 7, 46, 61, 63, 64, 127, 148, 190–192, 200, 221, 289, 290, 293, 315, 338; and bounty bill, **2**, 564; and New Orleans riot, 572–574; Welles on Reconstruction requirements and appointments, 579; and Stanton's opposition to Union Convention, 574, 575; and Queen Emma, 577, 582; and report of Union Convention, 581; and Slidell's desire to return, 585; character of support

(1866), 590, 595, 600, 602, 615, **3,** 62; Democratic pressure on, for offices, **2,** 598; and dismissal of Barney, 605; Gen. Sherman indorses policy, 606; on legality of Congress, 615; and results of election of 1866, 616–619; and Maryland election controversy, 620; and Mexico, 622–624, **3,** 115, 138; consistency of policy, **2,** 629; and Bay of Samaná, 631; Congress aims to destroy executive power, 637; and Doolittle, 647; and Reconstruction Bills, vetoes, 650, **3,** 9, 11, 51, 54, 55, 137; need of Washington organ, **2,** 653; vetoes District suffrage bill, **3,** 3–8; and act convening Congress, 19; Sumner's speech denouncing (1867), 23; diplomatic appointments, 24, 70. 256, 257, 285; and resignation of Motley, 24; vetoes Colorado and Nebraska bills, 30; and Surratt, 31; and North Carolina's proposal of compromise on Reconstruction, 31–33; opposes official pleasure trips, 40; and Stanton's report on enforcement of Civil Rights Act, 42–46, 49; veto of Tenure-of-Office Act, 51, 54, 55; dejection, 56; and Reverdy Johnson, 56, 58, 59; selection of military governors, 60, 62–65; and Tucker episode, 69; Congress as watch over, 73, 74; and injunction against Reconstruction Act, 80; rejection of nominations, 83–85; plan for calm address to people, 99; trip to Raleigh, 100, 101, 104; execution of Reconstruction Acts, 107, 161, 164; and retirement of Goldsborough, 108; trip to Boston, 109, 114, 116, 119, 123; and Stanbery's opinion on Reconstruction Acts, 109, 110, 115; and Sheridan's letter, 125–127, 129; and insurrection in Crete, 138, 425; and Field court martial, 140; pardon of criminals, 140, 547, 555; removal of Sheridan, 142, 149–155, 157,

174, 186, 187; and Conover allegations, 143–146, 149, 152, 157, 161, 168; character of associates, 147, 200, 566; suspension of Stanton, 155, 157–160, 162, 163, 165, 167–169; dissatisfied with Randall, 156, 183; fatal delay in Stanton case, 158; candidacy for renomination, 166, 189, 383, 391, 394, 397, 398, 401, 402, 407; distrusts Seward, 168; and execution of Tenure-of-Office Act, 171, 194; Grant's secret opposition (1867), 175 *n.*; rumors of reorganization of Cabinet (1867), 183, 203, 204; talk with Grant on Reconstruction Acts, 188, 189; disinclined to controvert, 194; and Democrats (1867–68), 196, 199, 223, 229, 399, 403, 429; at Antietam anniversary, 201, 202; and Jeremiah Black, 205; and Reconstruction elections, 207; and disturbances in Tennessee (1867), 211; effort to attach Sherman, 221, 222, 232, 233, 254, 272, 279, 281–283; and successor to Stanton, 231, 286, 287; attempted understanding with Grant, 233–235; message on suspension of Stanton, 240, 242; and Hancock, 241, 242; and reinstatement of Stanton, Grant controversy, 255, 259–262, 266–279, 465, 491, 500; and Welles, 266, 470; social relations with Radicals, 278; removes Stanton, 280, 284, 285, 291; plans for crisis, 282, 288, 291, 316, 317; attempt to advance G. H. Thomas, 284; need of energetic counselors, 287; accused of planning a dictatorship, 291; proneness for newspaper talks, 311; wrong action in Stanton case, 315; and Alta Vela affair, 317, 318, 322; political isolation and neglect, 317, 453; significance of nominations of Schofield and Evarts, 338, 409; and Reconstruction constitutions, 347, 388; rumored change of policy and Cabinet,

(May, 1868), 364, 371; and Buchanan's funeral, 376; and Chinese
ambassadors, 380; and Congressional acts of pardon, 386; veto of
bill excluding vote of unrecon-
structed States, 405; suggests
Constitutional amendments, 406;
attitude towards Presidential nominations, 408, 410, 429, 454; at a
Schützenfest, 426; and internal-
revenue frauds, 434, 435; still
hopeful of a nomination (Oct.),
454, 455, 459, 462; paper on government expenditures, 462; and
Paraguay, 467; and Alabama
claims, 469–471, 507, 579; and
finances, 478, 479, 482, 487, 492;
and Pacific Railroad, 490; Grant
proscribes, 491, 494, 497, 512; children's party, 494; and Grant's inauguration, 498, 500, 532, 536–
538, 540–542; failure of Administration, 514; receives students of
Georgetown College, 518; labors
over details, 526; nominates one
of Mrs. Grant's relatives, 527;
vetoes bill arming negroes for inauguration parade, 542; takes
leave of Cabinet, 542; Baltimore
banquet, 550; Welles's final opinion, 556; illness, reported death,
560; reënters Tennessee politics,
565. *See also* Cabinet, Impeachment, Presidential tour, Reconstruction.

Johnson, Edward, captured, 2, 29.

Johnson, Reverdy, report on Union
Convention, 2, 582; and Reconstruction Bill, 3, 49, 55; and office
for son-in-law, 56, 58; and Johnson-Grant controversy, 260, 261;
Alabama claims negotiations, 459,
468–471, 474, 506, 507; and Laird,
488.

Johnson, Robert, intemperance, proposed sea trip, 2, 468, 472, 479,
491, 604, 605.

Johnson, Simeon, and Black, 3, 317;
and late nomination of Johnson,

(1868), 454, 455; and Coombs's
claim, 527–529.

Johnston, J. E., after fall of Vicksburg, 1, 375, 379; Atlanta campaign, 2, 33; Sherman's peace
terms, 294.

Johnston, W. F., and politics in navy
yards, 2, 602.

Jones, J. G., and Johnson's removals,
2, 598.

Jones, J. R., Minister to Belgium, 3,
577.

Jones, Laura, pass, 2, 207.

Juarez, Madame Benito, in Washington, 3, 91.

Judd, N. B., and Lincoln's cabinet,
2, 390.

Kearny, Philip, letter on McClellan,
1, 174.

Kearsarge, sinks *Alabama*, 2, 65, 67.

Keeler, ——, and contract frauds, 1,
540.

Kelley, W. D., defends Navy Department, 1, 531; and frauds at
navy yard, 2, 224; Welles's estimate, 413; radicalism, 634; Senatorial candidacy, 3, 16; investigation of navy yard, 416.

Kelly, Lieutenant, dismissed, 1, 406.

Kelly, James, postmaster at New
York, 2, 155.

Kendall, Amos, and Johnson, 2, 376.

Kennedy, J. P., and Goldsborough,
3, 86.

Kenosha, launched, 3, 422.

Kentucky, movement to exclude Representatives (1867), 3, 129.

Keokuk, in attack on Charleston, 1,
265.

Kernan, Francis, and resolution to
expel Long, 2, 9.

Kerr, Orpheus C. *See* Newell (R. H.).

Key, J. J., rebuked and dismissed,
1, 146, 156.

Keyes, E. D., demonstration towards
Richmond (1863), 1, 359.

Keystone State, injured, 1, 234.

Kilpatrick, H. J., raid on Richmond,

1, 534; Chilian mission, 3, 24; return to electioneer, 437, 447; attempt to supersede, 527.

King, J. W., report on *Chimo*, 2, 52; heads Engineer Corps, 3, 551; as officer, 551; disagreement with Porter, 573.

King, Preston, and Welles, 1, 82, 523; and Seward's resignation (1862), 194, 202; not to be re-elected, 232, 233; trust in free suffrage, 523; and collectorship at New York, 2, 137; political opinions (1864), 197; at funeral of Lincoln, 293; and Sherman's peace terms, 294; and reconstruction of North Carolina, 305; and Henderson case, 306; excursion, 340; and Johnson, 380; suicide, 385; importance in anti-slavery movement, 385; insanity, 386; as Democrat, 387.

King, Rufus, and the Pope, 2, 638.

Kingly, ——, and Spanish appointment, 3, 578.

Kinney, Mrs., and Mrs. Lincoln, 2, 287.

Kittery Navy Yard, and politics, 2, 143, 586. *See also* Navy yards.

Knower, Benjamin, financial embarrassment, 3, 226.

Koerner, Gustav, at Washington (1864), 2, 138.

Koons, ——, and contract frauds, 1, 540.

Korea, relations with, 3, 485.

Ku-Klux Klan, in Arkansas (1868), 3, 460.

Laird, John, statement on Federal application for ships, 1, 291, 306, 394–396, 401; and slavery and Civil War, 3, 488.

Lamar, C. A. L., supposed plot, 1, 492, 494.

Lamb, ——, appointment as assessor at Norwich, Conn., 2, 597.

Lamon, W. H., trip to Charleston, 1, 9; and Chase, 2, 391.

Lane, G. W., trade through blockade, 2, 56.

Lane, J. H., solicits campaign contributions, 1, 534; wants removal of Lines, 2, 148.

Lansing, C. B., and vessel for Japan, 2, 188, 191, 192, 561.

Lardner, J. L., commands West India Squadron, 1, 309, 318, 319.

Latimer, Captain, and Stover, 1, 515.

La Verte, Madame, in Washington (1866), 2, 427.

Law, John, and Johnson, 3, 62.

Law, R. L., court martial, 1, 505.

Lawyers, bad influence in government councils, 3, 480.

League Island Navy Yard, controversy over establishing, 1, 185, 207, 222, 227, 285, 2, 445; bill to establish, 547, 563; acquired, 3, 489; use of unoccupied land, 553.

Leas, ——, on Matamoras trade, 1, 388.

Leavenworth, J. H., report on Indian war, 3, 98.

Lee, R. E., autumn campaign (1863), 1, 469–473. *See also* campaigns by name.

Lee, S. P., and Norfolk trade through blockade, 1, 166, 172, 173, 177, 318, 527, 536, 2, 56; on operations in Suffolk, 1, 287; and Wilmington blockade, 306, 2, 127; and mission of A. H. Stephens, 1, 358, 360; F. P. Blair's efforts for promotion, 533, 2, 161, 243; and export of French tobacco, 9; and command of Wilmington expedition, 146; transferred, 146, 147, 161; as officer, 161, 504; and M. Blair, 172, 513; and assignment to Mare Island, 504–507, 511–514; further troubles with, 569, 578, 3, 90.

Legal tender. *See* Paper money.

Lenthall, John, as bureau chief, 1, 74, 499; and Fox, 401; and Welles's annual report, 479; and light-draft monitors, 2, 87, 108, 241, 349–351; and relief of contractors, 207; and turrets, 340, 341; and Porter in Navy Department, 3, 556, 573.

Le Roy, W. E., and Morgan's invasion, 1, 379.

Letcher, John, house burned, 2, 76, 87.

Letters of marque, controversy over issuing, 1, 155, 246–262; and attitude of England, 248, 250, 256–259; Welles's letter and views, 252–256, 262; Seward's attempt to involve Navy, 256, 260; Sybert's application for, 260, 261; Confederate, feared (1864), 2, 158.

Lewis, Judge (Ellis?), and removal of Chambers, 1, 218.

Lewis, J. V., as preacher, 2, 393.

Lieber, Francis, and Confederate papers, 2, 335; on trial of Semmes, 407.

Lieutenant-general, Grant's commission, 1, 539. See also General.

Lincoln, Abraham, formation of Cabinet, 1, xx, 81, 230, 2, 388–392; Welles's portraiture, 1, xl–xlii; and relief of Sumter, 5, 9, 13–39; reluctance to offend South, 6, 40; convinced of necessity by Blair, 13; and Seward's interference with expedition, 16–18, 24, 39; and Fort Pickens, 25, 29; and D. D. Porter, 36, 158, 259, 369, 449; and Seward's assumption of leadership, 37; and Norfolk Navy Yard, 41, 54, 84; appointment of Stanton, 57–59; and Merrimac scare, 62, 65, 66; General Order No. 1, on McClellan's "slows," 63, 95–97; on Stanton's "navy," 67; and Welles's administration, 69, 81, 428, 440, 451; Emancipation Proclamation, 70, 130, 145, 209, 210; and Wilkes, 73, 109, 2, 203; Seward's evil influence, 1, 80, 131–139, 204, 274, 284, 287, 526, 2, 36, 38, 86, 112, 130, 155, 160, 166, 176; and Louisiana Union men (1862), 1, 81; and patron-age, 81, 510, 2, 137, 195; and new recruits (1862), 1, 89; Stanton's attitude, 98, 149; and McClellan after Second Bull Run, 104, 112, 113, 122, 124; reliance on Halleck, 108, 120, 134, 179, 180, 320, 329, 364, 371, 526; and bringing east of Pope and Halleck, 108, 113, 120; visit to Scott (1862), 109, 120; on Second Bull Run, 116, 126; and colonizing of negroes, 123, 150–153; estimate of McClellan, 124; and administration by Departments, 134; and Stanton, time spent at War Department, 134, 2, 55, 91, 92, 112, 203; and Cabinet-meetings, 1, 136, 546, 547, 2, 17; and dismissal of Preble, 1, 141, 162, 191, 235; serenaded after Emancipation Proclamation, 147; suspends privilege of habeas corpus, 150; and Altoona Conference, 153, 156; Tod's confidence, 153; rebuke of Key, 146 n., 156; visits to army (1862), 157, 161; (1863), 263, 264, 266, 294; (1864), 2, 55, 58, 90; (1865), 264, 272, 274; and Dahlgren, 1, 158–163, 238, 315, 337, 341; and naval chaplains, 162; and Norfolk trade, 165, 166, 183; and Scott's war policy, 172, 2, 515; and forged Cooper dispatches, 1, 176; orders McClellan to advance (Nov., 1862), 179; and admission of West Virginia, 191, 207; and Seward-Chase resignations, interference of Senate, 194–205; Blair's influence, 205; and Butler, 210; receptions, 212, 490, 501, 2, 15; and McClernand, 1, 217, 220, 387, 388; and removal of Chambers, 218; and negro troops, 218; and gauge of Pacific Railroad, 228; and Hooker (Jan.), 229; and preparations against Charleston, 236, 247, 259, 265; correspondence with Fernando Wood, 237; and extra session of Senate (1863), 238; and a religious meeting, 238; and promotion of military invention, 239; and letters of marque, 250, 256, 259, 261; and failure of Charleston expedition, 268; and captured mails controversy, 270, 274, 275, 277–280, 282, 286, 287, 289, 302, 315; fears war with Europe, 275, 287, 398, 452; and Chancellorsville, 291–294; and *John Gilpin* prize case, 298; and Vicksburg, 308, 364; and fugitive-slave case in the District, 313; and Vallandigham case, 321, 345, 347; reply to Corning, 323, 329; and beginning of Lee's invasion (1863), 328, 331–333, 340; on Orpheus C. Kerr, 333; and Hooker during Gettysburg campaign, 344, 348; and plan for McClellan to supersede Halleck, 345; relieves Hooker, 348, 349; on Dix and Foster, 350; and countermovement on Richmond, 350, 351; and battle of Gettysburg, 354, 356; and attempted mission of A. H. Stephens, 358–363; and escape of Lee, 363, 364, 366, 370, 374; serenaded in honor of victories, 364; and Hamlin's request for a prize court at Portland, 366; and Whiting, 381; and Gillmore's force before Charleston, 382; correspondence with Seymour on draft, 395, 396, 399; and Halleck and Almaden mines, 398; and instructions to naval officers on neutral rights, 398, 399, 409; Stanton on his letter-writing, 399; and Gurley, 408; officers for Arizona, 409; Chase on character, 413; and Reconstruction, 413, 2, 99, 179, 269, 279, 281, 630; and *Mont Blanc* incident, 1, 420, 423; and defeat of draft through *habeas corpus* proceedings, 431–435; secret knowledge of England's intention to seize Laird rams, 437; and Chickamauga, 438, 446; despair over Meade's inaction (Sept., Oct.), 439, 440, 471; and failure of chiefs of Army of the Potomac, 440; on Farragut, 440; on Du Pont, 440; and *Emma* incident, 446; and successor to Rosecrans, 447; and Schofield-Missouri Radicals affair, 448, 471; and Ohio election (1863), 469, 470; has varioloid, 480; and Colfax, 481; and renomination, 498, 500–502, 509, 521, 530, 2, 4, 44, 46; and transfer of soldiers to Navy, 1, 498, 546; popular trust in, 500; stories, 504, 506, 519, 528; on Lowell's article, 504; and sentence of R. L. Law, 505; as judge of character, 506; on Clay, 506, 507; on J. P. Hale and Navy Department, 509; and policy of opening certain ports, 510; and cotton trade, 511, 2, 56, 66, 138, 159, 163, 167; official dinners, 1, 512; and San Domingo, 520; and Chase's candidacy, 520, 525, 529, 531; Welles's estimate, 521, 2, 131; and raising of Brownsville blockade, 1, 529; and Florida expedition (1864), 532; and promotion of Hawley, 535; and Dahlgren's raid, 536; Grant at reception, 538; presents commission to Grant, 539; and new draft (1864), 542; and French tobacco at Richmond, 2, 9; and finances, 11, 59, 65, 180; and fairs, 15; and failure of Red River campaign, 18, 26; restores F. P. Blair to army, 20; pass for wife's sister, 21; and Fort Pillow massacre, 23; and news of Wilderness, 25; and politics in navy yards, 33, 175; appointment of midshipmen, 41, 526; resignation of Chase, 62, 64, 65, 93; and forged proclamation, 67; and Early's raid, 69, 74, 75, 77, 88; and naval contracts fraud cases, 78, 90, 124, 176, 177, 199, 201, 220, 225, 231, 260–262; and private peace missions, 83, 84, 94, 99, 109, 111, 271; and Wade-Davis protest, 95, 96, 98; and Mobile Bay, 100; factional assaults on (1864), 103;

attitude of New York papers, 103–105; on Greeley, 112; and Georgia "peace commissioner," 126; mistakes in counselors, 130; and newsmongers, 131; Welles expects reelection, 132; and H. W. Davis, 153; and Senator Lane, 148; and control of abandoned plantations, 148, 150; and Dakota politics, 153; Weed's hold on New York patronage, 154; and Blair's resignation, 156–158; and admission of Nevada, 163, 164; and land movement against Mobile, 165; and exchange of naval prisoners of war, 168–171; and Marine bounty, 174; and naval votes, 175; and political managers, 171, 175; receives election returns, 178; preparation of message (1864), 179, 190; and Chief-Justiceship, 181–183, 187, 192, 196; and vessel built for Japan, 191; second Cabinet, 194, 195, 247, 250, 251; and disclosure of Wilmington expedition plans, 207; and the expedition, 210, 214; and law as to public records, 211–213, 220; and negroes in Confederate army, 222; on freedom of action after reëlection, 227; and idea of peace negotiations, 232, 269; Hampton Roads Conference, 235, 236, 238; and compensated emancipation, 237; and Nasby, 238; on State rights, 239; and Blair's Senatorial aspirations, 243; selection of Secretary of the Treasury (1865), 243–245, 251; and apprehended decision on arbitrary arrests, 242, 245; and dictation of Radicals, 247; second inauguration, 251, 252; favors easy terms to South, 269; closes Southern ports (1865), 278; proclamation on naval reciprocity, 279; Virginia legislature incident, 279, 296, 3, 522; and resumption of trade with South, 2, 280; on position of Pierpont government, 282; prescient dream,

282; assassination, 283–288; grief of negroes, 290, 293; funeral, 292–294; implication of Davis and others, 299; trial of conspirators, 303–305; and Trumbull, 322; conspirators sent to Tortugas, 334; Bancroft's oration, 431; Surratt case, 630, 3, 29, 31, 166, 167; Booth's diary, 95; Conover allegations, 143–146; Seward's belittlement, 428; believed to have prescribed Appomattox and Sherman's terms, 521, 523. *See also* Cabinet, Elections (1864).

Lincoln, Mrs. Abraham, and public playing of Marine Band, 1, 325; and Mrs. White, 2, 21; and assassination of husband, 287, 290.

Lincoln, G. B., and slanders on Johnson, 2, 454.

Lincoln, R. T., and death of father, 2, 288; marriage, 3, 444.

Lincoln, Tad, and death of father, 2, 290.

Lines, C. L., removal proposed, 2, 147.

Lippitt, A. J., nomination rejected, 3, 85.

Loan, B. F., denounces Johnson, 3, 24.

Locke, D. R. (Petroleum V. Nasby), Lincoln and writings, 2, 238.

Lockport, N. Y., question of postmaster (1866), 2, 607.

Logan, J. A., as Minister to Mexico, 2, 401; and Kentucky Representatives (1867), 3, 129.

Lombard, Captain, and Matamoras trade, 1, 389.

Long, Alexander, movement to expel, 2, 9; censured, 12; and McClellan's letter of acceptance, 140.

Longstreet, James, Chickamauga, 1, 439, 444.

Loomis, ——, Treasury agent at Richmond, claim to Confederate naval material, 2, 336.

Louisiana, Lincoln's policy, 1, 81; policy of opening cotton trade,

511; Congressional report against government (1867), **3**, 41; disturbances, 463. *See also* Sheridan.

Louisville, War claim case, **3**, 528, 529.

Lowell, J. R., article on Lincoln, **1**, 504.

Lowrey, ——, and Henderson case, **2**, 306.

Lowrie, W. H., *habeas corpus* proceedings on draft, **1**, 432.

Luce, S. B., Naval Academy assignment, **3**, 440.

Ludlow, W. H., and Stephens's mission (1863), **1**, 359; and Dix, **2**, 608.

Lyons, Lord, and slave-trade convention, **1**, 193; charges against Wilkes in West Indies, 217; and captured mails, 266, 270, 280, 288, 302; and prizes, 296, 297; and naval violation of neutral rights, 398, 399, 409, 451, 452; and free ships, free goods, 400; influence over Seward, 409; *Mont Blanc* incident, 416, 419, 420, 424; and visit of Admiral Milne, 467, 468; and Mexico, 493; and capture of *Chesapeake*, 508; and detention of crews of blockade-runners, 517; and English-owned cotton, **2**, 40.

McAllister, Fort, ironclads attack, **1**, 249.

McCall, G. A., Peninsular campaign, **1**, 96; Second Bull Run, 99.

McCann, W. P., and New Orleans riot, **2**, 575.

McCardle case, **3**, 314, 320.

McCauley, C. S., at Norfolk Navy Yard, character, **1**, 43–46, 51, 52.

McClellan, G. B., Welles's portraiture, **1**, xxviii; and New Orleans expedition, 60; and Stanton (1861), 57; Welles's estimate as general, 61, 107, 115, 118, 124, 209, 329; Lincoln's estimate, 63, 95–97, 124; Wilkes on, 81, 106; withdrawn from Peninsula, 83, 89, 97; Cabinet intrigue for removal, 83, 93–98, 100–104, 108, 112, 117, 119, 129, 139, 221, 226; Pope awaits, 89; war policy, 92, 107, 117, 145, 156, 242, **2**, 204; and Second Bull Run, **1**, 93, 97, 98, 100, 104, 107, 110, 116, 117, 122, 221; Stanton's review of conduct (Aug., 1862), 95–97; and opening of Potomac (1861), 102, 103; confidence of army in, 105, 111, 113, 115, 116, 129; and Blairs, 126, **2**, 28, 322; Tod's confidence, **1**, 153; Lincoln visits (Oct., 1862), 157, 161; and Emancipation Proclamation, 163; and Stuart's raid on Chambersburg, 169; Kearny's letter on, 174; inaction, 176, 177; ordered to advance, 179; relieved of command, 182; and Porter, 231; disrespect to Scott, 241, 242; Blair's plan for, to supersede Halleck (1863), 345; and Stanton after Seven Days, 355; political letter (1863), 469, 471; Lincoln's deference, 526; and English mission, **3**, 257, 285. *See also* Antietam, Elections (1864).

McClellan, G. W., and Boston collectorship, **2**, 356; and Radical control of patronage, **3**, 156.

McClernand, J. A., and Vicksburg command, **1**, 167, 217, 220, 386, 387; Arkansas Post, 224.

McClure, A. K., and Grant's cabinet, **3**, 535.

McCook, A. McD., Chickamauga, **1**, 444, 446; defends Washington (1864), **2**, 72, 75.

McCracken, G. W., and Motley, **3**, 36, 37.

McCulloch, Hugh, Secretary of the Treasury, **2**, 245, 251; as financier, 253, 299, 576, **3**, 153, 385; and drawing on next year's appropriations, **2**, 264, 266, 268; and Savannah cotton, 278; on resumption of trade with South, 280, 296, 299, 300; and assassination of Lincoln, 287; and informing of Johnson, 289;

first Cabinet-meeting with Johnson, 289; and implication of Davis, 300; on proclamation against Confederate "pirates" (1865), 300; and negro suffrage, 301, 3, 4, 6; and trial of conspirators, 2, 303; and Treasury agents, 316, 343; on ironclad oath in South, 319, 357, 445, 453, 454; alarmed for the Treasury (1865), 328; and closing of Ford's Theatre, 331; and Mexico, 333, 485, 622, 625; and trial of Davis, 335, 338; and right to Confederate naval material, 336, 337; and Indian affairs, 357, 3, 74; assumptions of subordinates, 2, 360, 3, 378, 379, 442, 529; and Johnson's policy (1865), 2, 393, 398; and Freedmen's Bureau Bill, 434; and movement for reconciliation, 446; and Fenians, 451, 519; sensitive on state papers, 453; and Civil Rights Bill, 464; and *Grey Jacket* case, 469; and Butler, 492, 493; on report of Reconstruction Committee, 496, 500; on Colorado Bill, 503; and Atlantic cable, 503; on attitude of Cabinet (1866), 522, 524, 525, 537; and Union Convention, 531, 534, 538, 546, 582; on Fourteenth Amendment, 536; on bounty bill (1866), 564; and Blairs and Admiral Lee, 569; and removal of Dorsheimer, 598; on relinquishing the *Dunderberg*, 603, 604, 3, 28; and Dix as Naval Officer, 2, 607; removes Bolles, 612; and welcome to Congress, 630; and Bay of Samaná, 631; and asylum for the Pope, 639, 640; and first Reconstruction Bill, 3, 10; discouraged, 17, 65, 147; and Stanton's report on enforcement of civil rights, 43; attack on, in Senate, 52; and woolens bill (1867), 58; gives Radicals patronage, 64, 83, 126, 147, 152, 390; and ousting of Stanton, 90, 159, 284; and Danish West Indies, 95, 97, 124; and

Johnson's trip to Raleigh, 101; and execution of Reconstruction Acts, 110, 113; on Sheridan's letter, 126; and Conover allegations, 143–145; and removal of Sheridan, 149, 152; rumors of retirement, 203; question of Seward's influence, 204; and sale of ironclads, 207, 384; and *habeas corpus* proceedings on enlistments, 213; on conduct of military governors, 243; on impeachment counsel, 304, 307; expects an acquittal, 345, 350, 352; Seward and attack on, 385, 389; and Chase's candidacy, 389; and Democratic nominees (1868), 401; and Johnson (1868), 404; and Johnson's suggested amendments, 406; on Pacific railroads, 425; and State elections (1868), 453; and Alabama claims, 459, 468–470, 507; and disturbances in the South, 461; Grant proscribes, 464, 465; and Bailey, 485; and resumption, 492; and confiscation, 504; on Seward's fawning on Grant, 511; and protection of seals, 516; and government for Alaska, 531; and holding over under Grant, 533; and the inauguration, 537, 538, 541.

McDougal, David, and Shimonoseki attack, 2, 560.

McDowell, Irvin, Peninsular campaign, 1, 96; as officer, 373.

Macedonian, practice ship, 1, 324.

McKay, Donald, on Navy Department, 1, 519; and monitors, 2, 86.

McKean, W. W., and command of Gulf Squadron, 2, 116.

McKinstry, J. P., and Robert Johnson, 2, 472, 487, 491.

McMahon, M. T., Minister to Paraguay, 3, 466–468.

McMichael, Morton, and League Island, 3, 489.

Magrath, A. G., and Reconstruction, 2, 397.

Magruder, G. A., and Secessionists, 1, 19.

Mails, controversy over captured foreign official, *Peterhoff* incident, 1, 180, 266, 269–290, 310; judicial or executive question, 266, 278, 279, 281; Seward's illegal concessions, 269, 271, 279, 281, 300; Welles's letter of instructions and views, 270–272, 301–304; Lincoln and order giving up the mails, 274, 275, 280, 282, 284, 287; Earl Russell on, 300; precedent, 303, 310; newspapers on, 306; English view, 315.

Maine, desires coast defense, 1, 364, 2, 256, 257; elections (1864), 141; (1868), 3, 436, 438; Senatorial election (1869), 505, 517.

Mallory, S. R., and Mrs. White, 2, 21; and exchange of naval prisoners, 168, 171; and Fort Sumter, 374; question of paroling, 395.

Mansfield, J. K. F., defensive policy, 1, 84; killed, 140.

Marble, Manton, as editor, 2, 322.

Marcy, W. L., Benton and report on Frémont's explorations, 2, 42; as politician, 3, 225, 226.

Marigold, charges against, 2, 34.

Marine Band, Mrs. Lincoln and public playing, 1, 325, 327; character of selections, 368.

Marine Corps, question of increasing, 2, 6; successor to Col. Harris, 31, 51; unauthorized bounty, 174.

Maritime jurisdiction, Spain's claim to six miles around Cuba, 1, 170, 367, 399, 467, 468.

Marshall, C. H., and Navy Department, 1, 215, 513, 514.

Marshall, D. D. T., retention of position, 2, 323.

Marston, Gilman, on McClellan, 1, 118; character, 118; and coast defense, 375; and Reconstruction, 2, 584.

Martin, Earl, office for, 3, 78.

Marvin, William, and *Mont Blanc* incident, 1, 417, 421.

Maryland, political malcontents, 2, 153, 195, 243; Blairs and patronage, 343; election controversy (1866), 620, 3, 140, 141. *See also* Antietam, Early.

Mason, Judge, of Annapolis, on Porter, 3, 441.

Massachusetts, question of coast defense, 1, 288; Republicans and Johnson (1865), 2, 373, 381.

Masterman, G. F., arrest as spy, 3, 491, 513.

Matamoras, Confederate trade through, 1, 283, 334, 388, 443, 2, 4.

Matchett, D. F., and Conover allegations, 3, 168.

Matthews, E. O., Naval Academy assignment, 3, 440.

Maury, M. F., and Secessionists, 1, 19.

Maximilian. *See* Mexico.

Maynard, Horace, excursion, 2, 330; right to seat in Congress, 387, 388; fears dual government, 484; character, 3, 205.

Meade, G. G., commands Army of the Potomac, 1, 348; as commander, 349, 351, 382, 404, 469, 471–473, 2, 91; Gettysburg campaign, 1, 352, 354, 356–358, 363; escape of Lee, 363, 366, 368–375, 383; meets Cabinet, 404; Lincoln's despair over inaction (Sept.), 439, 440; autumn campaign, 442, 444, 469–473; Lincoln urges to fight (Oct.), 471; and Fenians, 2, 486; and retirement of brother, 3, 250; as military governor, 256; and illegal imprisonment in Georgia, 421.

Meade, R. W., suspension, 2, 401, 407; second trial, 432; retirement, 3, 250; insanity, 472, 484.

Medicine and Surgery, Bureau of. *See* Naval surgeons.

Meigs, M. C., and Seward's interference with Sumter expedition, 1, 17, 23, 25, 38, 172, 2, 374; and *Merrimac* scare, 1, 62, 64; reply to Wilkinson's attack, 224; and Seward's meddling with other departments, 243; and Milroy (1863), 332; and Early's raid, 2, 72; and assassination of Lincoln, 285; and purchase of Danish West Indies, 3, 40.

Meigs, R. J., and suspension of Meade, 2, 401.

Mercedita, rumored loss, 1, 232, 234.

Mercer, Samuel, Sumter expedition, 1, 22; and Du Pont, 2, 118.

Mercier, Henri, attitude (1863), 1, 494.

Merriam, M. H., and politics in Charlestown Navy Yard, 2, 31, 34.

Merrick, R. T., impeachment trial witness, 3, 333.

Merrimac, at Norfolk Navy Yard, efforts to save, 1, 42, 43; scare in Washington, 61–67, 3, 473; Goldsborough's fear, 1, 142.

Merrimac, U. S. S., and pursuit of *Tallahassee*, 2, 111.

Merrimac No. 2, rumors concerning, 1, 72.

Merritt, M. F., and Osborn, 2, 219; and sale of ironclads, 3, 388.

Mervine, William, and rear-admiralship, 1, 76; as officer, 76; command of Gulf Squadron, 313, 2, 116.

Mexico, Empire set up, 1, 385; Seward's blundering policy, 493, 2, 393, 648; House resolution on Monroe Doctrine, 39; Cabinet discussions (1865), 317, 322, 332, 333, 336; war over, feared, 348; Republican reverses, 367; better tone, 401; French to withdraw, 479, 485; Austria and, 485; paper blockade, 579; Sherman sent to, 621, 649; Cabinet on delay in departure of French, Seward's dispatch to Bigelow, 622–626; seizure of Santa Anna, 3, 115, 128; execution of Maximilian, 128; filibustering, 138; claims treaty, 516.

Miami, and *Chesapeake*, 1, 545.

Michigan, rejects negro suffrage, 3, 329; Senatorial election (1869), 3, 508.

Michigan, on Lake Erie, 2, 151.

Midshipmen, troubles over appointment, 1, 82, 146, 147, 149, 188, 224, 227, 234, 236, 319, 393, 2, 41, 163, 317, 526.

Midway Islands, acquisition favored, 3, 508.

Miles, D. S., at Harper's Ferry, death, 1, 140.

Military governors under Reconstruction Acts, powers, 3, 59, 105, 111; expenditures, 92; actions, 142, 146, 170, 176, 182, 185, 241–244, 256, 277, 298; removal of Sheridan, 149–152, 174, 186, 187; removal of Sickles, 187; Grant's order on appointments by, 193. *See also* Reconstruction.

Milligan case, 2, 471, 474, 476.

Milne, Sir Alexander, visit to United States, 1, 467, 468.

Milroy, R. H., at Winchester, 1, 328, 330–332.

Mississippi, executive reconstruction, 2, 315, 316, 366.

Mississippi, loss, 1, 249.

Mississippi River, naval operations, 1, 72, 75, 167; Porter commands squadron, 157, 167; control over war vessels on, 180, 272; policy of opening western bank to trade, 510, 511, 514. *See also* Porter (D. D.), Vicksburg.

Mississippi Squadron. *See* Foote (A. H.), Porter (D. D.).

Missouri, Radicals and Schofield, 1, 448, 471; delegation to Union Convention (1866), 2, 46; ironclad oath, 3, 566.

Missroon, ——, contract frauds, 1, 516.

Mobile, land movement to capture, 2, 165.

Mobile Bay, battle, 2, 100, 101, 105, 114, 124, 133; Stanton claims credit for the army, 115.

Mohawk, at Pensacola, 1, 26.

Monitor, founders, 1, 213, 215; origin, 213–215, 3, 412–414.

Monitors. *See* Ironclads.

Monocacy Bridge, battle, 2, 71, 73.

Monongahela, wrecked, 3, 240.

Mont Blanc, prize case, 1, 302, 305, 394, 416–427.

Montgomery, cruise after *Tacony*, 1, 328.

Montholon, Marquis, and appointment of Logan, 2, 401; large reception, 430.

Moore, W. G., in Johnson's tour, 2, 589; question of loyalty to Johnson, 3, 73, 567.

Morgan, E. D., and Welles for Cabinet, 1, 82; not renominated for Governor, 154, 162; on McClellan and Presidency, 163; Senatorship, 231, 232; alarm for safety of New York, 347; and draft, 380; on Hale, 484; Welles's estimate, 523, 3, 509, 510; and contract frauds, 1, 540, 2, 60, 306; and date of National Convention (1864), 28; and cotton trade, 33, 138; and finances, 62; on Weed's antagonism to Welles, 155; political tour (1864), 186; and Chief-Justiceship, 187; and Treasury portfolio, 240, 243–245; Reconstruction views, 405, 521, 548, 549; Presidential aspirations, 405; and Freedmen's Bureau Bill, 436; and Civil Rights Bill, 475, 477, 479, 547; and Johnson, 487; and Radicals, 633; and impeachment, 3, 332, 334, 346, 349; and Seward, 336; calls special session of Congress, 437; contest for reëlection, 508, 509.

Morgan, G. D., purchases for Navy, 1, 487.

Morgan, J. H., invasion of Ohio, 1, 379.

Morgan, J. S., and Welles, 2, 599, 3, 582.

Morgan, Fort, capture, 2, 124, 133. *See also* Mobile Bay.

Morrill, J. S., and impeachment, 3, 346; on Welles's administration, 523.

Morrill, L. M., and coast defense, 1, 364, 366; and cotton trade, 2, 34, 138; political despondency (1864), 102; political tour, 186; and impeachment, 3, 345, 346; candidacy for reëlection (1869), 505, 517; character, 505, 523.

Morris, Dwight, on draft, 1, 382.

Morris, E. J., trouble with Secretary of Legation, 3, 25; and Cretans, 71, 139, 425.

Morrissey, John, elected to Congress, 2, 619.

Morse, F. H., report on Laird rams, 1, 245.

Morton, O. P., and Johnson's tour, 2, 594; and impeachment, 3, 335, 350; and finances, 486, 487; and Fifteenth Amendment, 574.

Motley, J. L., and Mexico, 2, 485; resignation of Austrian mission, 3, 24, 34–38; Minister to England, 577; as diplomat, 577.

Mulholland, John, cotton purchase, 2, 40.

Murfreesborough, battle, 1, 213, 216, 218; Grant on, 2, 283.

Murray, Robert, and Trowbridge, 1, 493; and arrest of Arguellis, 2, 45.

Myers, Leonard, on admission of Tennessee Representatives, 2, 446.

Nahant, and great storm, 1, 225, 226.

Napoleon III. *See* France, Mexico.

Narragansett Bay, effort for navy yard in, 1, 185.

Nasby, Petroleum V. *See* Locke.

Nashville, battle, 2, 200; disturbance (1867), 3, 211.

Nassau, and blockade-running, 1, 74; and Confederate cruisers, 109.

National bank bill, Cabinet on, 1, 237.

National Intelligencer, on Welles's annual report (1862), 1, 185; in campaign of 1864, 2, 154; and official advertising, 490; character, 653; attack on McCulloch, 3, 385.

National Union Convention. *See* Union Convention.

Naval Academy, success, 1, 324; official visits, 2, 34, 525, 3, 103; Porter as head, 2, 321, 353, 360, 362, 3, 103, 247, 562, 563; condition (1867), 103; Welles and Academic Board, 382, 440. *See also* Midshipmen.

Naval code, question of making, 1, 245.

Naval Committee, chairmanship of House (1863), 1, 482, 484. *See also* Grimes, Hale (J. P.), Rice.

Naval surgeons, effort for naval rank, 3, 501.

Navigation Bureau, Drayton as chief, 2, 353; question of his successor, 357, 362. *See also* Davis (C. H.), Jenkins (T. A.).

Navy, loyalty of officers doubted, 1, 5, 19, 20; hindered by the army, 71; attitude of War Department, 121; enlistment problems, 498, 545–548, 2, 3, 121, 129, 420; question of withholding hospitality from English, 279, 305, 319, 320, 327; bill to reorganize, 3, 515, 558–560; and Cuban insurrection, 572, 573; names of vessels changed, 588. *See also* Admiral, Blockade, Board of Admiralty, Confederate cruisers, Confederate ironclads, Ironclads, Naval Academy, Naval Committee, Navy Department, Navy yards, Neutrality, Prizes, Retirement, Staff, Welles, and campaigns, officers, and squadrons by name.

Navy Department, suggested consolidation with War Department, 3, 519; Porter as actual head, 549, 551–556, 559, 561, 568, 570, 573, 574, 587, 588. *See also* Corruption, Welles, and bureaus by name.

Navy yards, and politics, 1, 327, 2, 376, 377, 380–382; Welles visits, 1, 428, 431; interference of Congressmen, 483; for ironclads, 2, 17; appointment of masters, 379; Welles

and political considerations in appointments, 586, 596–599, 602, 616, 3, 325, 416–420; work curtailed, 247; condition (1868), 422; eight-hour law, 471, 564, 569; Lenthall on Selfridge's report on construction of vessels (1869), 574. *See also* Brooklyn, Charlestown, Corruption, Kittery, League Island, Norfolk, Philadelphia, Washington.

Nebraska, bill for admission vetoed, 3, 22, 30.

Negro soldiers, question of employment, 1, 218; dependence on, 324; Fort Pillow massacre, 2, 23, 24; and exchange of prisoners of war, 168, 170; Lincoln on, for Confederate Army, 222.

Negro suffrage, Cabinet discussion (1865), 2, 301–303; Chase's attitude, 304, 343; Welles on, 324, 373, 3, 137; party demonstration (1865), 2, 324; Sumner on (1865), 330; Stanton's views, 364; advocacy by Radicals, 369; Connecticut rejects, 373, 375; for the District, veto, 422, 640, 3, 3–8, 15; attitude of Congress (1866), 2, 490; and Colorado and Nebraska bills, 502, 3, 22, 23; and executive Reconstruction, 2, 580; for Territories, 3, 19; in action in the District, 102, 374; Michigan rejects, 329; Fifteenth Amendment, 524.

Negroes, foreign colonization, 1, 123, 150–153, 162, 3, 428; problem of war government, 2, 222; grief for Lincoln, 290, 293; colonization in South, 352; Welles and Sumner on condition (1866), 431; story of kidnapping for Cuban market, 570; Welles on appointments, 3, 142; destitution (1867), 245, 246; at Grant's inauguration, 542. *See also* Civil Rights, Emancipation, Freedmen's Bureau, Fugitive, Negro soldiers, Negro suffrage, Slavery.

Nelson, Samuel, negotiations with Seward, 1, 27; controlled by Seward (1867), 3, 320.

Nelson, T. A. R., impeachment counsel, 3, 308, 330.

Nelson, William, Cabinet on killing, 1, 178.

Neutrality, Spanish complaint of violation, 1, 308; instructions to naval officers on respecting, 398, 409, 450–466; violation of free ships, free goods, 400; *Mont Blanc* incident, capture in neutral waters, 416–427; altruistic assertion of rights, 2, 4; *Florida* case, 184–186, 197; sale of war vessels by United States, 3, 92, 206, 387–389, 424, 438. *See also* Belligerency, Blockade.

Nevada, question of proclaiming admission, 2, 163, 164.

New Hampshire, Senatorship (1864), 2, 51; State election (1868), 3, 309; history of politics, 309–311.

New Jersey, Senatorial election (1866), 2, 464, 475.

New London, efforts for a navy yard, 1, 185, 207, 222, 2, 446, 3, 489.

New Orleans, Stanton and expedition, 1, 60; Butler and Banks as rulers, 209; selection of Farragut to command expedition, 2, 116, 134; riot (1866), 567, 569, 570, 572–575, 611.

New York, election (1862), 1, 153, 154, 162, 171, 177, 219, 2, 27; Senatorial elections (1863), 1, 231, 232; (1867), 3, 16, 20; (1869), 508, 509; Democrats and Johnson, 2, 373, 3, 223, 229; political affairs (1866), 2, 607, 608, 610; history of politics, 3, 223–229.

New York City, war sentiment (1862), 1, 119; demand for coast defense, 123, 347, 435; draft riots, 369, 372, 373; evils of free suffrage, 523, 524; Federal appointments, 2, 62, 63, 137, 155, 484, 3, 560; and naval enlistments, 2, 240.

New York *Commercial Advertiser*, and Welles, 2, 260.

New York *Express*, and Welles, 2, 260.

New York *Evening Post*, and Navy Department, 1, 184, 2, 185, 228; on Confederate ironclads, 1, 435; deterioration, 2, 61; and arrest of Henderson, 78, 79, 83, 104; political character (1864), 104; and impeachment, 3, 355.

New York *Herald*, and Navy Department, 1, 184, 2, 259; vicious leadership, 103; and impeachment, 3, 26; and negro suffrage, 381. *See also* Bennett.

New York *Journal of Commerce*, forged proclamation incident, 2, 35, 38, 67; and Welles, 260.

New York *Times*, Seward's control, 1, 123; and Navy Department, 184, 2, 87, 194, 260; on letters of marque, 1, 248; on Confederate ironclads, 435; political character (1864), 2, 104; and party unity, (1866), 533, 542, 544, 545. *See also* Raymond (H. J.).

New York *Tribune*, on *Peterhoff* mails, 1, 306; on Seward and Welles, 366; assault on Navy Department, 2, 87; and failure of impeachment, 3, 353; advance publication of public documents, 475. *See also* Greeley.

New York *World*, and Welles's report (1862), 1, 185; forged proclamation incident, 2, 35, 38, 67; character (1865), 322; and Union Convention, 542; and Johnson, 3, 199, 320, 328.

Newell, R. H. (Orpheus C. Kerr), Lincoln on writings, 1, 333.

Newspapers, misrepresentation in Confederate, 2, 218; advance publication of public documents, 3, 475; degeneracy, 506.

Niagara, cruise to Europe (1864), 2, 38, 39.

Nichols, J. H., visits Welles, 1, 86.

Nicolay, J. G., and playing of Marine

Band, **1**, 368; as consul at Paris, **3**, 519.

Niles, J. M., and Democratic Party in Connecticut, **2**, 429.

Norfolk, trade through blockade, **1**, 165, 172–175, 177, 183, 227, 318; martial law (1864), **2**, 81. *See also* next title.

Norfolk Navy Yard, loss, **1**, 41–54; no troops for, 41, 45, 83; ships at, 42; Welles's efforts to save ships, 42–47; character of commander, 43; criticism of loss considered, 47–54; loss and defection of Union men, 84; controversy over dismissals (1867), **3**, 13, 21. *See also* Navy yards.

Norris, Basil, and Robert Johnson, **2**, 468.

Norris, Hamilton, contract frauds, **1**, 511.

North Atlantic Squadron, question of commander (1864), **2**, 127. *See also* Lee (S. P.), Porter (D. D.), Wilmington.

North Carolina, Federal operations (1861), **1**, 381; desire for reunion, 410; disaster in (1864), **2**, 16, 17; plan of Reconstruction, 301, 305; interference of Sickles (1866), 642; amnesty act, **3**, 9; compromise Reconstruction proposal submitted to the President, 32; proposal published in Richmond, 37.

Noyes, W. C., and Henderson case, **2**, 220.

Nye, J. W., and admission of Nevada, **2**, 163, 164; and Reconstruction, 396; and Connecticut politics (1867), **3**, 63; and Board of Survey, 247; and naval officers, 326; and impeachment, 332; character, 523.

Oath, ironclad, and Southern appointments, **2**, 318, 358, 445, 450; Missouri ironclad, **3**, 566.

Ocean Spray, and Fenian raid, **2**, 486.

O'Conor, Charles, and Henderson case, **2**, 220, 225; and Reconstruction injunction cases, **3**, 86; and Fenian trials, 283; and impeachment trial, 298.

Odell, M. F., and contract frauds, **1**, 540, **2**, 54, 60.

Offices. *See* Civil service.

Ohio, Morgan's invasion, **1**, 379; State elections (1863), 469–471; (1864), **2**, 175; (1867), **3**, 232; (1868), 452, 453, 455.

Ohio River, Welles and armored fleet for, **1**, 90.

Olcott, H. S., and contract frauds, **1**, 525, 536, 539–542, 547, **2**, 5, 11, 15, 54, 114, 263, 265.

Olin, A. B., and Stanton, **3**, 160.

Oliver & Co., and trade permits, **1**, 536.

O'Neill, J. P., and district-attorneyship, **3**, 441.

Oneota, sale, **3**, 348, 387–389, 420, 429, 438.

Onondaga, sale, **3**, 92.

Opdyke, George, and Fernando Wood, **1**, 237; alarm for safety of New York, 347; and *Evening Post*, **2**, 61; suit against Weed, 208.

Opequon Creek, battle, **2**, 151, 153.

Ord, E. O. C., attack on Petersburg lines, **2**, 272; as military governor, **3**, 245, 249.

Ordnance, Dahlgren as head of Bureau, **1**, 164, **3**, 447; for monitors, **1**, 342; Wise and headship, **2**, 7; efficiency of Dahlgren's smoothbores, 67; controversy over casting, 202; Congressional investigation of Bureau, **3**, 122; Ames's claim, 447–449, 451.

Oregon, State election (1868), **3**, 375.

Oreto. *See Florida*.

Orr, J. L., question of amnesty, **2**, 358.

Orth, G. S., and resolution to expel Long, **2**, 9.

Osborn, ——, New York newspaper man, discloses plans of Wilmington expedition, **2**, 205–209, 219.

Otterbourg, Marcus, and Mexican mission, 3, 135.

Otto, W. T., at Cabinet-meeting, 1, 319, 2, 147; and *habeas corpus* proceedings on enlistments, 3, 213; and Court of Claims, 372.

Ould, Robert, and A. H. Stephens's mission (1863), 1, 358; and exchange of naval prisoners, 2, 169.

Owen, E. H., and Connecticut election (1866), 2, 458, 459.

Pacific Railroad, Cabinet discussion of gauge, 1, 228; plundering schemes, 3, 425, 439, 444, 449, 460, 485, 571; report on progress, 472; payment of subsidies, 474, 490, 534.

Page, R. L., surrender of Fort Morgan, 2, 133.

Page, T. J. *See Stonewall*.

Palmerston, Lord, Seward's opinion, 1, 437.

Panama. *See* Isthmus.

Paper money, Welles's antagonism, 1, 147, 148, 167–169, 232, 494, 520, 530, 2, 10, 12–14, 16, 29, 55, 61, 180, 3, 486, 504; and payment of foreign bills, 1, 147, 2, 10, 29; premium on gold (1864), 12, 55, 61, 158, 163; gold premium and forged proclamation, 35; gold bill (1864), 54; Evarts on, 3, 480; Cabinet on plans of resumption (1869), 487, 492, 493; importance of question under Grant, 494. *See also* Finances.

Paraguay, war and American mission, 2, 491, 492, 543, 3, 427, 466–468, 491, 510, 513, 516.

Pardons, Johnson and criminal, 2, 140; Grant and Johnson's final, 3, 547, 555. *See also* Amnesty.

Parke, J. G., attack on Petersburg lines, 2, 272.

Parker, W. A., Grant desires removal, 2, 230, 232.

Parsons, L. E., Sumner denounces, 2, 398.

Parsons, seized by Confederates on Lake Erie, 2, 152.

Pasco, ——, of Philadelphia Navy Yard, pardon, 2, 400–402, 412.

Passaic, construction, 1, 179.

Patterson, D. T., in Johnson's tour, 2, 589; on Brownlow, 3, 205.

Patterson, Mrs. D. T., in Johnson's tour, 2, 589; visits Welles, 3, 542.

Patterson, J. W., and appointment of Stewart, 3, 546.

Patton, W. W., and emancipation, 1, 130.

Paulding, Hiram, at Norfolk Navy Yard, 1, 46; and Breese, 76; and Washington chair, 77; and Mervine, 313, 2, 116; and Trowbridge-Lamar plot, 1, 493; and Stover, 515; and pursuit of *Tallahassee*, 2, 110, 113; and Du Pont, 118; and politics in Brooklyn Navy Yard, 123, 137.

Pawnee, Sumter expedition, 1, 16, 22.

Paymaster's accounts, confusion, 2, 265.

Peace negotiations, Stephens's mission (1863), 1, 358–363, 369; Greeley's, 2, 83, 84, 94, 99, 111, 271; Jaquess and Gilmore's, 109; attitude of Lincoln and Seward, 109, 231, 3, 521; "peace commissioner" from Georgia, 2, 125; Blair's mission, 219, 221; Hampton Roads Conference, 235, 236, 238; controversy over Sherman's terms, 294–297, 309.

Pearson, Frederick, British decoration offered to, 2, 209.

Pearson, G. F., transferred from South Pacific Squadron, 2, 604.

Pease, E. M., Governor of Texas, 2, 316, 3, 146; on conditions in Texas, 2, 568, 3, 105; on attitude of South (1866), 2, 641; character, 3, 147.

Pease, J. J. R., seeks collectorship, 2, 398.

Peirpoint, F. H., his controversy with Gen. Butler, 2, 81; post-War position of his government, 281, 282, 301.

Pemberton, J. C. *See* Vicksburg.

Pendergrast, Austin, suspended, **2**, 364.

Pendergrast, G. J., at Vera Cruz, **1**, 16; at Norfolk Navy Yard, 42, 46.

Pendleton, G. H., Presidential candidacy (1868), **3**, 382, 385, 393, 396, 456; in the campaign, 430, 439.

Peninsular campaign, naval force, **1**, 72, 81, 83, 86, 91, 121; troops withdrawn, 83, 89, 97, 120; Stanton's review, 95–97; Wilkes on McClellan, 106; McClellan accused of treasonable intentions, **2**, 204.

Pennock, A. M., in Washington, **1**, 431.

Pennsylvania, State elections (1863), **1**, 469, 471; (1864), **2**, 175; (1866), 613, 615; (1867), **3**, 232; (1868), 451–453, 455; Confederate raid (1864), **2**, 88, 89; Senatorial elections (1867), **3**, 15, 16, 20; (1869), 505. *See also* Gettysburg.

Pennsylvania Railroad, in politics, **3**, 505.

Pensacola. *See* Pickens.

Perkins, Isaac, and Welles, **3**, 433.

Perry, Amos, resigns, **3**, 24.

Perry, B. F., and Fourteenth Amendment, **2**, 636; Sumner denounces, 398.

Perry, H. J., and J. P. Hale, **3**, 518, 553, 578.

Perryville, battle, **1**, 165.

Peru, trouble with Spain expected, **2**, 357, 365; controversy over Admiral Tucker, 650, **3**, 37, 45, 66, 68–71; purchase of ironclads, 387, 420, 429, 438.

Peterhoff, captured-mails incident, **1**, 266, 269–290, 299–304, 306, 310.

Petersburg, Federal army before, **2**, 54, 55; Crater, 89–92; final attack and capture, 272.

Phelps, James, and Cuban Consul-Generalship, **3**, 80, 85.

Phelps, N. A., and Welles, **3**, 433.

Phelps, S. L., of board on dismissal of Preble, **1**, 191; on Red River campaign and cotton speculation, **2**, 37.

Philadelphia, and Johnson (1867), **3**, 116.

Philadelphia, trade through blockade, **2**, 56.

Philadelphia Navy Yard, frauds, **2**, 200, 205, 208, 224, 231, 238, 400–402; pressure for removal of Radicals (1866), 596, 599, 602; investigation (1868), **3**, 416. *See also* Navy yards.

Phillimore, Sir R. J., on use of neutral waters by belligerents, **1**, 461; on prize crew as witnesses, 465, 466.

Phillips, Wendell, Welles's opinion, **2**, 383.

Phythian, R. L., Naval Academy assignment, **3**, 440.

Pickens, Fort, Seward and relief expedition, **1**, 14, 25, 28–32, 172.

Pickering, Timothy, precedent in removal, **3**, 302, 311.

Pierpont, F. H. *See* Peirpoint.

Pierce, Franklin, as President, **3**, 310.

Pierrepont, Edwards, Henderson case, **2**, 220; campaign contribution (1868), **3**, 452; character, 452.

Pike, F. A., as Chairman of Naval Committee, **3**, 280; and impeachment, 360, 361.

Pile, W. A., nomination as Minister to Brazil, **3**, 577.

Pillow, Fort, Cabinet opinions on massacre, **2**, 23–25.

Pius IX, and asylum in United States, **2**, 638–640, 642.

Plantations. *See* Abandoned plantations.

Platt, O. H., and Connecticut appointments, **1**, 81.

Pleasonton, Alfred, and escape of Lee, **1**, 374.

Plymouth, at Norfolk Navy Yard, **1**, 42.

Pocahontas, Sumter expedition, **1**, 22.

Politics, in Washington before outbreak of the War, 1, 10, 34; indications of new alignment (1866), 2, 370, 372, 407; civil service assessment, 376, 377, 380, 382; history in New York, 3, 223–229; history in New Hampshire, 309–311. See also Civil service, Elections, Union Convention, and parties by name.

Pollard, E. A., and Confederate archives, 3, 452.

Pomeroy, S. C., and Chiriqui scheme, 1, 123, 152, 3, 427; Senate committee on Seward, 1, 196, 198; and Chase's candidacy (1864), 529; slanders Johnson, 2, 454, 461; and Johnson's tour, 593; and impeachment, 3, 357; character, 523.

Pontoosuc, pursuit of Tallahassee, 2, 111, 113.

Poor, J. A., of Maine, and coast defense, 2, 256, 257.

Poor, C. H., promotion, 1, 77.

Pope, John, Cedar Hill, 1, 78; awaits McClellan, 89; battle, 93, 97, 98, 104; retreat, 98, 100, 104; Blair on, 104, 126; a failure, 104; origin of eastern command, 108, 113, 120, 221, 226; report, 109, 110, 114; on McClellan's generals, 110, 112, 220, 226; Lincoln's estimate, 116, 126; Foote on, 120; and execution of Indians, 170; Indian campaign (1865), 2, 357; as military governor, 3, 174, 242, 245, 249; removed, 251.

Pope, Nathaniel, M. Blair on, 1, 126.

Port Hudson, fall, 1, 372, 375.

Port Lavaca. See Indianola.

Port Royal expedition, preparation, 2, 118; battle, 3, 217.

Porter, B. H., killed at Fort Fisher, 2, 226.

Porter, D. D., and Seward's interference with Sumter expedition, 1, 17, 24, 25, 35, 38; character as officer, 19, 87, 88, 274, 2, 215, 3, 384, 389; loyalty doubted, 1, 19, 20; at Pensacola, 28, 31; Lincoln's attitude, 36, 158, 440; commands Mississippi Squadron, 157, 167; and McClernand, 167, 220; and West Point training, 167; sends news of Arkansas Post, 224; announces captures on White River, 227; reports on Vicksburg operations, 238, 249, 259, 295, 311, 364, 367; caricatures, 249; Stanton's opinion, 273; directed to run past Vicksburg, 274, 285; and command against Charleston, 311; promotions, 369, 2, 235, 3, 562; Yazoo expedition, 1, 379; and Chattanooga, 473; on Red River campaign, 2, 18, 26, 178; and cotton speculation, 37, 173, 228; at Washington (1864), 67; on Grant and Sherman as mutual complements, 92; and Farragut, 116, 134; and Du Pont, 119; problem of command for (1864), 129; Wilmington expedition, 146, 148, 150, 172, 209, 210, 213–216, 220, 226, 227; on Mrs. Davis and secession of South Carolina, 255; as head of Naval Academy, 321, 353, 360, 362, 3, 103, 247, 440, 562, 563; and Pendergrast case, 2, 364; and Bay of Samaná, 643, 3, 7; and De Camp, 18; and Board of Survey, 247, 248, 570; and Engineer Corps, 252, 253, 283, 385; and Navy portfolio, 340; sycophancy, 441; desire for civil position, 488; and line and staff differences, 501; as real head of Navy Department, 549, 551–556, 568, 570, 573, 574, 587, 588; and reorganization of the Navy, 558; and Grant in the Presidential campaign, 559, 563; shirks European cruise, 563; courtesy to Welles, 580.

Porter, F. J., and Second Bull Run, 1, 104, 110; court martial, 220, 225, 226, 229; unpopular, 231.

Porter, W. D., not promoted, 1, 77, 88; forged letter, 87; destroys Ar-

kansas, 88; reproved and retired, 145.

Portland, Maine, and prize court, 1, 366, 491.

Portsmouth, N. H., additional defenses, 1, 375. *See also* Kittery.

Posse comitatus, use of troops in South, 3, 430, 431.

Post. *See* Mails.

Postmaster-General. *See* Blair (M.), Dennison, Randall (A. W.).

Potomac River, Welles and opening, 1, 61, 102, 103; flotilla (1862), 91, 93, 109; Fort Foote, 474; obstructions, 3, 436.

Powhatan, and Sumter expedition, 1, 15, 22, 24, 27; at Pensacola, 31.

Preble, G. H., allows *Florida* to pass blockade, 1, 140, 141; to be dismissed, 141; attempt to restore, 162, 163, 188–191, 228, 235.

Prentiss, G. A., on capture of *John Gilpin*, 1, 297.

Presidential receptions, mismanagement, 2, 408, 3, 496, 539.

Presidential tour, plans and dangers, 2, 585, 587; itinerary, 588; party, 588, 3, 502; Johnson's speeches, 2, 589, 590, 593; attitude of officials and Congressmen, 589, 593; 594; Grant's attitude, 591, 592, 595; reception, 592; slight to Seward at Albany, 592, 593; Cleveland, 593; Chicago and St. Louis, 594; Indianapolis, 594; Seward's illness, 594.

Preston, S. W., and Wilmington expedition, 2, 210, 213, 216; killed, 226.

Princess Royal, captured, 1, 231, 234.

Princeton, trade permit, 1, 527, 536, 537, 543, 544, 548.

Prisoners of war, appearance of Confederate (1864), 2, 31; exchange of naval (1864), 168–171.

Privateering. *See* Letters of marque.

Prizes, question of judicial or executive control over, 1, 296, 297, 302, 424–426, 452, 2, 106, 107; *John*

Gilpin case, 1, 297; location of adjudication, 366; detaining crew of neutral, as witnesses, 451, 453, 457, 465; *Grey Jacket* case, 2, 469, 492, 493. *See also* Blockade, Mails, *Mont Blanc*, Neutrality.

Promotion, before retirement, 3, 531.

Protestant Episcopal Church, and Civil War, 2, 382.

Prussia, claims convention, 3, 9.

Pruyn, R. H., and vessels for Japan, 1, 188, 225; and joint attack on Japan, 2, 560; on Seymour's candidacy (1868), 3, 390.

Pryor, Roger, and Holt, 3, 172, 174.

Public records, right to copies, 2, 211–213, 220.

Puritan, construction, 2, 201, 207, 340.

Pyne, Smith, fast-day sermon, 1, 288.

Quarantine, suggestion of national, 2, 480.

Queen of the West, captured, 1, 240.

R. R. Cuyler, Downes court martial, 2, 162; seizure, 3, 38–40, 42.

Raasloff, W. R., and sale of Danish West Indies, 3, 95.

Radford, William, and Confederate ship-timber, 2, 336; in Johnson's tour, 585, 588; and Bay of Samaná, 631; inspection tour, 3, 422.

Railroads. *See* Pacific.

Raleigh, Johnson's trip, 3, 100, 101, 104.

Randall, A. W., and Union Convention, 2, 533–535, 574, 582, 617, 3, 251; Postmaster-General, 2, 563; and Johnson's tour, 587, 588; and Fourteenth Amendment, 609, 628; and Mexico, 622, 623, 625; on welcome to Congress, 632; and asylum for the Pope, 640; and negro suffrage for the District, 3, 5, 6; and Stanton's report on enforcement of civil rights, 43, 45; use of patronage, 52, 64; and impeachment, 57; Welles distrusts, 57, 64, 83, 91, 101, 162; and Danish West Indies, 98, 124; in Johnson's trip to Raleigh, 101; on Stanbery's opinion on the Reconstruction Acts, 111, 114; in Johnson's trip to Boston, 114; and Otterbourg, 135; and Conover allegations, 143–146, 149; and removal of Sheridan, 151; Johnson dissatisfied with, 156, 183; and suspension of Stanton, 163; rumors of retirement, 203; and *habeas corpus* proceedings on enlistments, 213, 221; and question of arrest of Johnson, 238; and nomination of Schofield, 340; expects acquittal, 352; and election of 1868, 453, 458; and Seward, 458; Grant proscribes, 464; on Seward and Grant, 511; and holding over under Grant, 533; and the inauguration, 538, 541.

Randall, S. J., and Field court martial, 3, 140.

Rathbun, George, and Wilmot Proviso, 2, 386.

Rawlins, J. A., reports Vicksburg operations to Lincoln, 1, 386, 387; character, 386, 3, 551; Secretary of War, 551.

Raymond, ——, contract frauds, 1, 537.

Raymond, H. J., political character, as manager, 2, 87, 171, 175, 177; and political control of Brooklyn Navy Yard, 97, 98, 108, 122, 136, 142, 175; and general political assessment, 112; and release of Scofield, 199, 201; and Welles, 201; and French mission, 205; and Reconstruction, 406; and Civil Rights Bill, 479; relations with Johnson, 517, 523, 549, 552, 555, 610, 613, 618, 3, 191, 251; and calling of Union Convention, 2, 530, 534; and Fourteenth Amendment, 541. *See also* New York *Times*.

Read, C. W., career in *Tacony*, 1, 327, 333, 342, 350, 375 *n*.

Reagan, J. H., paroled, 2, 382.

Rear-admirals, appointment on the retired list, 1, 75–77.

Reconstruction, value of Welles's diary, 1, xlii–l; theories, 400, 408, 410, 411, 414, 415, 429, 2, 84, 109, 197, 301, 349, 430, 568, 600, 645, 3, 81; Chase and Welles on slavery and (1863), 1, 402, 403, 410–415, 429, 2, 234; need of a Constitutional amendment, 1, 430; division of Cabinet on (1863), 467; question of amnesty, 2, 43, 294, 301, 358, 3, 9, 183, 193, 197–199, 386, 394–396; Wade-Davis manifesto, 2, 95, 96, 98; Welles on difficulties (1864), 98, 99; Lincoln's proclamation, 99; Lincoln's dilemma, 179; Thirteenth Amendment, 234; attitude of Radicals (1865), 239, 242; Lincoln's last speech, 279; Virginia legislature incident, 279, 280, 296, 3, 522; Stanton's plan (1865), 2, 281, 282, 291, 294, 301; plans and progress of executive, 281, 282, 291, 301, 305, 315, 316, 379, 579, 580; Johnson's first attitude, 291; negro suffrage, 301–304, 324, 330, 343, 364, 369, 373, 375, 422, 490, 502, 640, 3, 3–8, 15, 19, 22, 23, 102, 137, 329, 374, 524; Southern appointments and ironclad oath, 2, 318, 357, 445, 450, 453, 454; unfavorable tone in South (1865), 347, 352; (1866), 641; military departments (1865), 355, 356; beginning of opposition to Johnson's policy, 363, 364, 381; Cabinet and Johnson's policy, Welles and Sumner on (1865), 364, 393–395, 397, 398, 400, 411, 415–417, 419, 424–426 *n*., 430; political issues (1865), 373; sufficiency of executive, 378, 379; exclusion of Southern Representatives, 387, 388, 392, 440–444, 446, 488, 489, 559; Grant's tour of South, 396, 398; Johnson on the Radicals (Jan., 1866), 410; tone of Governors' messages (1866), 410; and party split, 412, 414, 421, 425, 434, 443, 446, 454, 456, 480–483, 485, 522–525, 571; Freedmen's Bureau, 413, 431–437, 554, 3, 142; Welles foretells effect of Congressional, 2, 420, 433; Welles urges Johnson to make a public statement, 421; Joint Committee, 436, 438, 441, 449; political errors of Radicals, 437; Johnson's Washington's Birthday speech, 438–440, 647; Welles on necessity of action (1866), 449, 450; revolutionary plans, 451, 636, 653, 3, 12, 17, 25, 55, 86, 87, 128, 245, 314, 321; and State elections (1866), 2, 452, 454–462, 468, 469, 474; Civil Rights Bill, 459, 460, 463, 464, 475, 477, 479, 489; both sides seek Grant, 477, 478; dual government feared, 484, 552, 555, 557; Cabinet discussion of report of Joint Committee, 494–501; Fourteenth Amendment, 516, 521, 526, 527, 529, 532–537, 539, 541, 549, 557, 558, 608–610, 618, 630, 636, 649, 3, 7, 8, 417; Union Convention, 528–531, 533–535, 538–542, 545–548, 550, 552–554, 567, 571, 573, 574, 576–578, 581, 608, 609, 617, 3, 251; Radical caucus and program (July, 1866), 2, 552, 555; New Orleans riot, 567, 569, 570, 572–575, 611; conditions in the South, 568, 569, 3, 34, 105, 208, 245, 246, 248; government by majority, 2, 576; character of Johnson's requirements and appointments, 579; inconsistency and ignorance of Radicals, 583, 645; character of Johnson's support (1866), 590, 595, 602, 603, 615; and Congressional election, 616–619; Johnson's consistency, 629; probable action of Congress at second session, 635, 636; military interference with States (1866), 642, 644; Administration and first bill, veto, 650, 3, 10–12,

29, 40, 46–49, 51, 54, 55; Johnson and North Carolina's proposal of compromise, 31–33; report against Louisiana government, 41; interpretation of Act, Stanbery's opinion, 59, 60, 94, 96–99, 105, 107, 109–117; selection of military governors, 62–65; injunction case against the Act, 80, 86; Wilson's tour in South, 86, 89; expenditures and appropriations under Act, 93, 119, 131; conduct of military governors, 104, 117, 125–127, 130, 142, 170, 174–176, 182, 185–188, 193, 241–244, 256, 277; bungling action of Congress, 129; explanatory act, 132, 137; Welles's policy of non-execution of Acts, 161, 164, 169; Grant and Welles discuss the Acts, 177–181; Grant and execution of Acts, 182, 183, 185, 187–190, 242, 298; date of elections, 207; signs of reaction, 208; disturbances and requests for troops, 211, 424, 460–463; McCardle case, 314, 320; hampering of Supreme Court, 314, 323; constitutions, 347, 360; rumors of Johnson's change of policy, 360, 364; question of future policy (1868), 403; exclusion of Presidential vote, 405; carpet-bag representation, 411; use of troops as *posse*, 430, 431; confiscation, 504; Georgia excluded, 525.

Red River campaign, Porter's reports, 2, 18, 26; Halleck on, 18; condemnation of Banks, 19; Lincoln on failure, 26; origin, 27; cotton speculation, 37, 86, 173; dam, 37; naval complaints, 178; captured cotton, 255, 263.

Reed, W. B., paper for Union Convention, 2, 574; character, 3, 184.

Republican Party, Welles on Whig element, 2, 122; preservation and Johnson-Congress conflict, 421, 425, 443, 446, 454, 456, 462, 522–525, 528; character in New England (1867), 3, 88; Welles foretells

Liberal movement, 524, 526. *See also* Elections, Politics, Union Convention.

Repudiation of Confederate debt, and Reconstruction, 2, 579.

Requisitions, held up, 2, 58, 59, 69, 106, 114, 264, 266, 268, 274.

Resaca, battle, 2, 33.

Resumption, Cabinet on (1869), 3, 487, 492, 493. *See also* Paper money.

Retirement of naval officers, Welles's attitude, 1, 532; Board, 2, 41; efforts to escape, 3, 85, 86, 107–109, 135, 250, 251; and promotion, 531; control of the Board (1869), 569.

Reynolds, J. F., killed, 1, 354.

Reynolds, J. G., reproved, 1, 89.

Reynolds, William, and Hawaii, 3, 322, 329.

Rhett, Barnwell, character, 2, 312.

Rhind, A. C., report on the attack on Charleston, 1, 267; and ironclads, 268.

Rice, A. H., on test of *Eutaw*, 1, 519; on conduct of J. P. Hale, 2, 6; and investigation of contractors, 7; as Chairman of Navy Committee, 11, 236; excursion, 31; and Smith Bros., 53, 56, 124; on differences in financial policy, 57; and Reconstruction, 498, 499.

Richardson, W. A., of Illinois, election to Senate, 2, 153.

Richmond, proposed attack (Sept., 1862), 1, 130; conditions (Jan., 1863), 223; and Stoneman's raid (1863), 295; Dahlgren raid, 534, 536–538; fall, 2, 272, 275; municipal election (1865), 347, 348.

Ricketts, J. B., and Second Bull Run, 1, 110.

Riddle, A. G., Conover allegations, 3, 143 n., 170.

Ridgeley, A. S., appointed districtattorney, 3, 56, 58, 59.

Riggs, G. W., and Southern sympathy (1864), 1, 521.

Ringgold, Cadwalader, intrigue for vote of thanks, 1, 534.

Risley, Olive, and Seward, 3, 449.

Rives, J. C., *Army and Navy Gazette*, 1, 343; death, 2, 8; Welles's association with, 8.

Rives, Wright, excursion, 2, 340; on Johnson's associates, 3, 566.

Roanoke, at New York, 1, 347, 435.

Robert Anderson, and Matamoras trade, 1, 389.

Roberts, M. O., and Fenton, 3, 508.

Robinson, J. C., wounded, 2, 29.

Rodgers, G. W., death, 1, 415.

Rodgers, John, in James River, 1, 72; weathers storm in *Weehawken*, 226; capture of *Fingal*, 337; official congratulations, 344, 351; and Du Pont, 344, 373; on Butler and first Wilmington expedition, 2, 216; as head of Charlestown Navy Yard, 3, 418.

Rodgers, Raymond, as officer, 2, 353, 3, 384.

Roe, F. A., seizure of Santa Anna, 3, 115, 128, 131.

Roebuck, J. A., motion for recognition, 1, 374.

Rolando, Henry, capture of *William Peel*, 1, 548.

Rollins, E. A., and Radicals, 3, 404, 442.

Romero, Matias, Schenck correspondence, 2, 527, 528.

Roosevelt, R. B., and impeachment, 3, 349.

Root, J. M., and Wilmot Proviso, 2, 386.

Rosecrans, W. S., Murfreesborough, 1, 213, 216, 218, 2, 283; Chickamauga, 1, 438, 441, 444, 446; movement to reinforce, 442; Lincoln loses confidence in, 447.

Roselius, Christian, Union man, 1, 81; on conditions in Louisiana (1867), 3, 208.

Rosen, Count, excursion, 2, 31.

Ross, E. G., impeachment vote, 3, 356, 358, 359, 362, 367, 368.

Ross, Samuel, on draft, 1, 382.

Rousseau, L. H., and Pendergrast, 2, 364; in Johnson's tour, 589, 3, 502; and Alaskan commission, 141, 169; and military governorship, 142; return to Washington, 347; death, 502; as officer, 502.

Rowan, S. C., Sumter expedition, 1, 23; and Norfolk Navy Yard, 43; and Charleston, 276; on need of sailors, 545; and dismissal of Radicals, 3, 13, 21.

Ruger, T. J., and postmastership, 3, 52.

Russell, Earl, hostile attitude, 1, 250; dispatch on English attitude, 298; lessened hostility, 299; on captured mails, 300; and Roebuck's motion, 374.

Russia, visit of fleet, 1, 443, 480, 481, 484; Fox's official visit, 2, 506, 509, 512, 514; sale of Alaska, 3, 66, 68, 75, 83, 84.

Rynders, Isaiah, R. C. Winthrop and, 2, 154.

Sabine, alleged detention, 3, 337.

Sabine Pass expedition, 1, 441, 443.

Sacramento, wrecked, 3, 120, 554.

St. Albans, Confederate raid, 2, 198.

St. Louis, Johnson at, 2, 593.

St. Thomas Island, Wilkes's violation of neutrality, 1, 322, 325, 451; proposed purchase, 2, 466, 473, 3, 40, 95–98, 124, 502.

Sailor's Creek, battle, 2, 276.

Salgar, Eustorjio, and seizure of the R. R. Cuyler, 3, 38.

Samaná, Bay of, proposed purchase, 2, 631, 643, 3, 7, 40.

San Domingo, Seward's embarrassment (1864), 1, 519; proposed sale of Bay of Samaná, 2, 631, 643, 3, 7, 40; protectorate for, 480; desires annexation, 517.

San Jacinto, Alabama escapes from, 1, 191; and pursuit of Tallahassee, 2, 110.

San Juan Island, treaty on (1869), 3, 506.

Sanders, G. N., and Greeley's negotiations, 2, 83; implication in assassination of Lincoln, 299.

Sanford, H. S., desire for passage in Niagara, 2, 38, 39; Venezuelan claim, 3, 297; and Spanish mission, 578.

Santa Anna, A. L. de, seizure (1867), 3, 115, 128, 131, 132.

Saunders, Reed, and captured mails, 1, 222.

Savage, J. L., fraudulent contracts, 1, 537, 2, 54, 78.

Savannah, the Fingal, 1, 72; captured, 2, 208, 209; cotton, 220, 278; Stanton on conditions (1865), 228; aspect (1865), 313.

Sawyer, G. F.(?), suspension revoked, 3, 554.

Schenck, J. F., and retiring board, 2, 41.

Schenck, R. C., Second Bull Run, 1, 98; denies invasion by Lee (1863), 332; and chairmanship of Naval Committee (1863), 482; and naval retiring board, 2, 41; and attack on Navy Department, 236; as Radical, 247; Romero correspondence, 527, 528; and Kentucky Representatives, 3, 129; and retirement of Goldsborough, 135; and doubtful Senators, 357; calls special session, 437; and Johnson's message (1868), 479; and repeal of Tenure-of-Office Act, 564.

Schofield, J. M., and Missouri Radicals, 1, 448, 471; nomination to War Department, 3, 338–340, 371; first Cabinet-meeting, 375; and case of arrests in Georgia, 420; and insurrection in Crete, 425; and use of troops as posse, 430; and test of the Alexandrine chain, 436, 437; supports Grant, 450; and Pollard, 452; and disturbances in the South, 460, 461, 463; advance publication of annual report, 475;

on resumption, 493; and confiscation, 504; advises consolidation of War and Navy Departments, 519; and holding over under Grant, 533, 535; and the inauguration, 541.

Schoolships, Welles on government vessels for private, 3, 531.

Schützenfest, Welles on, 3, 426.

Schurz, Carl, and Chase for Cabinet, 2, 391; Southern trip, 580; political character, 580.

Scofield, C. W., fraudulent contracts, 1, 537, 2, 19; trial, 57, 58, 60; sentence, efforts for release, 176, 177, 199–201.

Scott, John, Senatorial candidacy (1869), 3, 505.

Scott, T. A., as Assistant Secretary of War, 1, 127; and Lee's invasion, 331.

Scott, Winfield, and relief of Sumter, 1, 3–8, 12, 15; protection of Washington, 4; and Fort Pickens, 26, 29; and defense of Norfolk Navy Yard, 41, 44, 45, 52, 83; defensive-frontier policy, 84–86, 242, 2, 515; Lincoln's interview (1862), 1, 109, 120; letter on Secession, 171; McClellan's disrespect, 241, 242; and Lincoln, 526; death, 2, 514; character, 514.

Seals, protection, 3, 516.

Secession, Welles on impossibility, 1, 414, 429; armistice, 2, 374, 378. See also Reconstruction (theories).

Second Bull Run. See Bull Run.

Secor and Swift, bid for ironclads, 3, 92, 387.

Seddon, J. A., application for amnesty, 3, 230, 231.

Sedgwick, C. B., and codification of naval laws, 1, 245; and Laird's statement, 396; and fraudulent contract cases, 512, 518, 524; and prize law, 531.

Sedgwick, John, Chancellorsville campaign, 1, 295; and escape of Lee, 374; killed, 2, 27.

Segar, J. E.(?), trade permit, 2, 257.

Selfridge, T. O., Sr., not promoted, 1, 77.

Selfridge, T. O., Jr., pressure for removal, 2, 597, 599; and habeas corpus proceedings, 3, 208–221; report on vessels under construction (1869), 574.

Semmes, Raphael, question of arrest and trial, 2, 404, 406, 407, 410, 414, 420, 423, 424, 432, 436, 457, 467, 471; released, 476, 477. See also Alabama.

Seven Days' Battle, Stanton and McClellan after, 1, 355. See also Peninsular campaign.

Seward, F. W., and Sumter expedition, 1, 23; and father's resignation (1862), 194; at Cabinet-meetings, 319, 3, 318; and trial of Wilkes, 1, 530; assault on, 2, 283–285, 291, 307; and Bay of Samaná, 643, 3, 7, 40.

Seward, Mrs. F. W., and assault on husband, 2, 284.

Seward, W. H., under Lincoln: Welles's portraiture, 1, xxxii–xxxv; and relief of Sumter, 6, 9, 12–39, 2, 248; assumption of leadership, 1, 7, 12, 14, 36–39, 79, 133, 136, 198, 203, 2, 515, 3, 428; expected to compromise with Secessionists, 1, 11, 172, 355; and Confederate commissioners, 12, 26–28, 32–35; and Fort Pickens, 14, 25; and Harvey, 32; and appointment of Stanton, 56, 58–60, 68, 127, 128; and Merrimac scare, 63; and emancipation, 70, 143, 144, 210; and Wilkes, 73, 109, 134, 298, 299, 304; and the blockade and belligerency, 74, 79, 82, 174, 414, 2, 160; and Norfolk Navy Yard, 1, 84; and movement to remove McClellan, 100, 104, 112, 241; and Pope's report, 110; and Caleb Smith, 119, 193; and New York Times, 123; attitude toward Cabinet consultations, 104, 124, 138, 381, 390, 391, 400, 2,

16, 58, 203; and appointment of
Cameron, 1, 126; private influence
over Lincoln, 131–139, 274, 284,
287, 526, 2, 36, 38, 86, 92, 112, 130,
155, 166, 176; interference with
other Departments, 1, 132, 137,
139, 241–243, 274, 290, 300, 305,
416, 2, 160, 328; and Stanton, 1, 135,
355, 447; and dismissal of Preble,
141; and colonizing of negroes, 152,
153, 3, 428; and New York election (1862), 1, 154, 162, 177, 219;
fears European combination
against the blockade, 154, 155;
and letters of marque, 155, 246–
250, 252, 256, 259–262; and slave-
trade cruising convention, 155,
163, 166, 193, 236; and pass for
Mrs. Bradford, 156; and Confederate cruisers, 165, 438, 440; and
trade through blockade, 166, 177;
and Spain's assumption of six-mile
jurisdiction around Cuba, 170,
399, 467, 468; as diplomatist, inconsiderate yielding to foreign
demands, 170, 171, 181, 217, 269,
273, 398, 409, 445, 446, 451, 502, 2,
36, 164, 3, 444; hoaxed by forged
Confederate dispatches, 1, 175,
176; and captured mails, 180, 222,
266, 269–290, 300, 315; and Gurowski, 188; resignation episode,
Lincoln and the Senate committee, 194–205; and Chase, 203–205,
536; and Welles, 204, 326, 366, 2,
155, 194, 384; and admission of
West Virginia, 1, 205; and Butler at
New Orleans, 210; and vessels for
Japan, 225, 2, 190; Weed's *alter
ego*, 1, 231, 2, 105, 155, 548; desire for Senatorship (1863), 1, 231;
and reported raising of Charleston
blockade, 232; and question of
Galveston blockade, 233; ignorance of international law, 233,
285, 394, 2, 106; and French mediation, 1, 235; and extra session of
the Senate (1863), 238; and Scott,
241, 242; and Matamoras trade

and expedition to Texas, 283, 335,
387, 442; interference with judicial control of prizes, 296, 297, 302,
305, 2, 106, 107; and Wilson, Secretary of Legation at London, 1,
301; Blair's antagonism, 329, 345,
2, 91, 370, 3, 72; and French tobacco at Richmond, 1, 338–340, 2,
9, 12; prevents restoration of Mc-
Clellan (1863), 1, 345; and relieving
of Hooker, 348; and Stephens's attempted mission (1863), 358, 360–
363; and serenade after Vicksburg, 364; and promotion of D. D.
Porter, 369; and Dix, 373; and
Whiting, 381, 2, 85; credulity as to
foreign news, 1, 374; and instruction of naval officers as to neutral
rights, 398, 409, 450, 535, 2, 34;
and Laird rams, 1, 399, 429, 435–
438, 443, 448; excursion, 404; Lyons's influence over, 409; avoids
Reconstruction theorizing, 413,
467; *Mont Blanc* incident, 416–427;
shirks responsibility, 416, 2, 392,
403, 409, 413, 518, 625, 628, 3, 424;
on draft and *habeas corpus* proceedings, 1, 432, 433; on Palmerston, 437; *Emma* incident, 445;
draft of Thanksgiving proclamation, 449; and Admiral Milne, 467,
468; and sale of a naval vessel to
an unrecognized government, 474–
476; and visit of Russian fleet, 481;
and Trowbridge-Lamar plot, 492,
493; and Mexico, 493; and renomination of Lincoln, 500; and Sumner, 503; entertains American
Academy, 506; on Clay, 507;
Chesapeake incident, 508, 545; and
cotton trade, 511, 2, 57, 66, 159–
163, 167; and Grinnell, 1, 513; and
detention of crews of captured
blockade-runners, 517; and San
Domingo (1864), 519; and raising
of Brownsville blockade, 529; and
defeat in Florida, 531; campaign
contribution (1864), 534; and
Grant at Lincoln's reception, 538;

and new draft (1864), 542; on bounty on immigration, 543; *William Peel* case, 548, 2, 4, 12; on the responsibility of opening days of the War, 1, 549; and Banks, 2, 18; and conservative movement (1864), 29; and forged proclamation incident, 35, 38, 67; and attitude of France (1864), 35, 39; extradition of Arguellis for slave-trading, 36, 45; and Sanford, 38, 39; and foreign-owned cotton, 40; and Hamlin, 47; and Chase's resignation (1864), 62, 65; and Early's raid, 74; and E. D. Smith, 83; and arrest of Henderson, 83; and Greeley's peace negotiations, 84, 99, 110; Bates on, 93; outburst in Cabinet, 106, 107; and Du Pont, 117; influence over Fessenden, 120, 173; as campaign manager, 120, 131; and Georgia "peace commissioner," 126; easily imposed upon by intrigants, 126; Auburn keynote speech (1864), 140; and date of Republican Convention, 142; and Blair's resignation, 157, 158 *n.*; political dishonesty, 160; and admission of Nevada, 163, 164; denunciation by Radicals, 174, 198, 274; and naval votes, 175; hopeful of Lincoln's reëlection, 176; and Taney's funeral, 176; and Chief-Justiceship, 182; and capture of the *Florida*, 185, 186, 197; and Lincoln's second Cabinet, 194; constitutional views, 197; House resolution against, 202; on law as to public records, 211–213; and Butler (1865), 224; and idea of peace negotiations, 231; Hampton Roads Conference, 235, 236, 238; favors Morgan for the Treasury, 244; and apprehended decision on arbitrary arrests, 246; on Chase as Cabinet disturber, 246; on Johnson's speech as Vice-President, 252, 253; and Hale's appointment to Spanish mission, 255, 257, 268;

and flag-raising at Sumter, 267; goes to headquarters, 269; and proclamation closing Southern ports (1865), 275; accident, 275; attempted assassination, 283–285, 291, 307; speech on war-time administration, 383, 384; and nomination of Johnson, 384; selection to the Cabinet, 388–392; claim to have shaped the Cabinet, 3, 76.

Under Johnson: views Lincoln's funeral, 2, 293; call by Johnson and Cabinet, 304; and *Stonewall*, 306, 335; resumes work, 307; and opening of ports, 307; and proclamation on Confederate "pirates" (1865), 307; Mexican policy and action, 317, 332, 333, 336, 348, 367, 393, 401, 430, 479, 485, 486, 579, 622–626, 628, 648, 3, 115, 131, 132, 138; and purchase of Ford's Theatre, 2, 317; and withdrawal of belligerency, 319; and refusing hospitality to English navy, 319, 320, 327; and Campbell, 330; and closing of Ford's Theatre, 331; exercise of arbitrary power, 331; and trial of Davis, 335, 337, 339, 365; vacation, 348; plan to relieve Johnson of burdens, 354; and Spanish-Peruvian affairs, 357, 365; and ironclad oath, 358; and Johnson's policy and party preservation, 363, 378, 393, 399, 424, 425 *n.*, 426 *n.*, 437, 516, 523, 525, 527, 528, 530, 533, 538, 540, 544, 545, 556, 566, 591, 595, 610, 3, 47; recalls Fogg, 2, 388; and Johnson's annual message (1865), 392; trip to Cuba and escape from Congress, 392, 403, 406, 409, 413; desire for French West Indies, 393; and rumor of Stanton's intention to resign (1865), 399, 400; blunders, 404; Presidential aspirations, 405; and *Shenandoah*, 411; and Freedmen's Bureau Bill, 434; and French Exhibition, 463, 469; and purchase of Danish West Indies, 466, 473, 3,

40, 95–97, 124, 125, 502; and sea-trip for Robert Johnson, **2**, 472, 491; and Fenians, 484, 486, 518, 520, 521, 524, **3**, 283; troubles with Paraguay, **2**, 491, 492, 543, **3**, 427, 466–468, 510, 516; on report of Reconstruction Committee, **2**, 495, 498; and Atlantic cable, 503; and Fox's official trip, 509, 512; harangues, 510, **3**, 87; and Mme. Bertinatti's claim, **2**, 522, 526; and Schenck-Romero correspondence, 527, 528; and call of Union Convention, 530, 534, 535, 538–541, 547, 548, 553, 609, 617, **3**, 251; and Fourteenth Amendment, **2**, 531, 532, 535, 541, 628, **3**, 417; excursion, **2**, 547; and Japan, 560–562, **3**, 87, 89, 91, 92, 135, 229, 365, 513; and bounty bill (1866), **2**, 564; and sending Dix abroad, 566, 607; dodges Union Convention, 575; and Stanbery, 575; proclamation of peace, 579, 580; and Queen Emma, 582; plans Presidential tour, 584, 587; and return of Slidell, 585; in Johnson's tour, 588, 591; slighted at Albany, 592; and Johnson's speeches, 594; illness on tour, 594, 598; and Senatorship, 607, 611; and arrest of Surratt, 630; proposed purchase of Bay of Samaná, 631, 643, **3**, 7; and welcome of Congress (1866), **2**, 632; on asylum for the Pope, 638, 639, 642; and negro suffrage, **3**, 4; and Arkansas delegation (1867), 6; Prussian negotiations, 9; and first Reconstruction Bill, 10; and impeachment movement (1867), 12, 50, 57; appointment of Kilpatrick, 24; seeks to placate Radicals, 25; and resignation of Motley, 24, 34–38; and relinquishment of the *Dunderberg*, 27; and seizure of the *R. R. Cuyler*, 38, 39, 42; and Stanton's report on enforcement of civil rights, 43, 44; and Tucker episode, 45, 66, 71; and veto of Tenure-of-

Office Bill, 51, 52, 54; on Grant and Butler, 56; evil influence over Johnson, 64–66, 83, 100, 116, 119, 120, 132–134, 160, 191, 195, 263, 383, 403, 409, 411, 454, 492; purchase of Alaska, 66, 75; and Foster for Austrian mission, 68, 70; and expediency, 71; and Indian affairs, 74; egotism, 75; and Connecticut election (1867), 78, 80; and sale of ironclads, 92, 438; desires Culebra Island, 94; before impeachment committee, 95; sycophantic toward Stanton and Grant (1867), 100; in Johnson's trip to Raleigh, 100, 101; annexation fever and Presidential aspirations, 106, 120, 125; and tax on foreigners in Colombia, 106; and Stanbery's opinion on Reconstruction Acts, 110, 111, 114, 116; in Johnson's trip to Boston, 109, 114, 120; and Sheridan's letter, 125; on direct departmental communications to Congress, 131; and Otterbourg, 135; and Cretan insurrection, 138, 425; and suspension of Stanton, 159, 160, 162, 163, 326; and Conover allegations, 161, 170; Johnson distrusts, 168; rumors of retirement, 183, 184, 203, 364, 371; Blair urges dismissal, 195; influence over Mc-Culloch, 204, 389; and *habeas corpus* proceedings on enlistments, 213, 221; as politician, 227, 228; and amnesty for Seddon, 230; Alabama claims negotiations, 241, 468–471, 474, 506, 507, 516, 579; and conditions in the South (1867), 246; and English mission, 256; and Johnson-Grant controversy, 263, 266, 271, 276; arrogance towards Venezuela, 296, 349; and Cabinet consultations, 297; and impeachment trial, 297, 298, 304, 305, 307, 308, 335, 337; official retrospections, 301; on D. D. Field, 303; and Alta Vela, 305, 316, 318, 322; and Chase (1868), 306, 389; on Mc-

Cardle case, 320; and Hawaiian Islands, 322, 329; and removal of Stanton, 335; and Morgan, 336; expects acquittal of the President, 345; attitude towards nominees (1868), 402, 408, 415, 443, 458, 459, 463; and veto of bill excluding electoral vote of South, 405; and Johnson's suggested amendments, 406; and nomination of Cummings, 414; plans trips (1868), 424, 484; and use of army as *posse*, 430; and Kilpatrick's return to electioneer, 437, 447; rumor of intended marriage, 449; influence over Randall, 458; and disturbances in the South, 461, 462; character of treaties, 463, 504; and Grant after election, 465, 508, 511; and dinner to Evarts, 465; and Korea, 485; and portfolio under Grant, 491; officious disarrangements at New Year's reception (1869), 496; and confiscation, 504; and Hale as Minister, 519; and canal treaty, 526; and holding over under Grant, 532, 533, 535; and the inauguration, 537, 538, 541.

Seward, W. H., Jr., wounded, 2, 71.

Seward, Mrs. W. H., death, 2, 319.

Seymour, Horatio, nominated for Governor, 1, 154; spirit of message (1863), 219; Blair on Seward and, 345; speech on Fourth, 363; and draft riots, 372; correspondence with Lincoln, 395, 396, 399; and State portfolio, 3, 203. *See also* Elections (1868).

Seymour, O. S., defeat, 2, 5; character, 5.

Seymour, T. H., campaign for Governor, 1, 262; speech on Fourth, 363; career and character 2, 5, 3, 431–434; and McClellan's letter of acceptance, 2, 140; death, 3, 431.

Sharkey, W. L., and Reconstruction of Mississippi, 2, 315, 316, 366.

Shellabarger, Samuel, report on Louisiana, 3, 41.

Shenandoah, disposal, 2, 411, 417, 427.

Shenandoah Valley, Early's raid (1864), 2, 68, 69, 87; Sheridan in command, 96; Sheridan's campaign, 151, 153, 158.

Sheridan, P. H., in Virginia campaign, 2, 29; command in the Valley, 96; Valley campaign, 151, 153, 158; Five Forks, 272; Sailor's Creek, 276; and Mexico, 333; on New Orleans riot, 569, 570, 572; and Indian depredations in Texas, 613; as military governor, 3, 93, 104, 117, 125–127, 130, 142, 146, 500; removal, 149–157, 174, 186, 187.

Sherman, John, and exclusion of Southern Congressmen, 2, 440, 443; amendment to Reconstruction Bill, 3, 47; and reinstatement of Stanton, 258, 263; and impeachment, 335, 351, 367; character, 523; and appointment of Stewart, 546.

Sherman, R. U. (?), seeks collectorship, 3, 424.

Sherman, Roger, watch, 3, 265.

Sherman, W. T., Vicksburg, 1, 220; and Johnston after Vicksburg, 375, 379; Atlanta campaign, 2, 33, 135, 140; as commander, 92, 242; reaches the sea, 200; at Savannah, 208, 209; and D. D. Porter, 221; plans of Carolina march, 221; and foreign-claimed cotton, 229; controversy over peace terms, 294–297, 309, 3, 247, 521, 523; indorses Johnson's policy, 2, 606; goes to Mexico, 621, 649; called to Washington to influence Grant (1867), 3, 221, 232, 233, 254; mission to the Indians, 254; and Johnson-Grant controversy, 260, 261, 263, 266, 272; presented with Roger Sherman's watch, 265; new department for, Johnson's efforts to attach, 272, 279, 281–283; letters as impeachment evidence, 330,

331; testimony, 332; and War Department after Grant's inauguration, 550, 564.

Ship-timber, cutting in North Carolina, 1, 522, 527, 528.

Shubrick, W. B., reception, 1, 521; and Du Pont, 2, 30, 118; and Farragut, 116.

Shufeldt, R. W., as officer, 1, 434; on attack on Charleston, 466.

Sicard, Montgomery, Naval Academy assignment, 3, 440.

Sickles, D. E., on Gettysburg, 1, 472; interference with North Carolina laws, 2, 642, 644; as military governor, 3, 65, 170, 176, 182, 185, 187; letter on Welles and Reconstruction Act, 119; removed, 187; wants court of inquiry, 207, 232; and Spanish mission, 578.

Sigel, Franz, defeat in the Valley (1864), 2, 68.

Silliman, Benjamin, at Seward's, 1, 506.

Simpson, Edward, Foote's fleet captain, 1, 318.

Simpson, Matthew, and impeachment, 3, 358.

Sisson, H. T., in North Carolina, 1, 350.

Slave-trade, controversy over cruising convention, 1, 155, 163, 166, 192, 193, 236; arrest of Arguellis, 2, 36, 45; story of, to Cuba (1866), 570.

Slavery, Welles's attitude, 1, xix; and Reconstruction, 402, 403, 407, 410. See also Emancipation, Fugitive, Negroes, Slave-trade.

Slidell, John, desires to return, 2, 585.

Slocum, H. W., on New York politics (1866), 2, 606; and Weed, 3, 24.

Smalley, D. A., and Johnson's removals, 2, 598.

Smith, A. N., heads Bureau of Equipment, 1, 343.

Smith, Ashbel, letter on Texas affairs, 2, 332.

Smith, C. B., and movement to remove McClellan, 1, 94, 95, 100, 101; and Seward, 119, 193; on Banks, 126; on Pope, 126; on Cabinet-meetings, 131; and McClellan's delay after Antietam, 146; and colonizing of negroes, 150–152; on fractional currency, 168; threatens to resign, 193; and Seward's resignation, 203; selection to the Cabinet, 2, 390.

Smith, E. D., and Peterhoff mails, 1, 284, 310; and contract frauds, 2, 78, 82, 114.

Smith, E, K., supplies intercepted, 1, 379.

Smith, F. W., collector at Bridgeport, and Connecticut election (1866), 2, 457, 460.

Smith, Franklin W. See Smith Brothers.

Smith, Mrs. Franklin W., and arrest of husband, 2, 61.

Smith, G. C., Montana appointment, 2, 527.

Smith, J. B., death, 1, 142.

Smith, J. C., and Connecticut election (1868), 3, 329.

Smith, James, messenger of Navy Department, 2, 283.

Smith, Joseph, and Merrimac scare, 1, 64; and ironclads, 179; and Monitor, 214; Hale's attacks on, 224, 2, 6; and Preble, 1, 228; and guns for monitors, 342; and Fox, 401; and Charlestown Navy Yard, 2, 31, 34; and contract frauds, 53; and Farragut, 116, 134; and relief of naval contractors, 2, 207; and Grimes, 3, 13, 14; at Lincoln's first, and Johnson's last, reception, 539.

Smith, Kilby, nomination, 3, 85.

Smith, Melancthon, and Lane's trade permit, 2, 56; as exchange agent, 169, 171; and Bureau of Navigation, 357; heads Bureau of Equipment, 597; and habeas corpus proceedings on enlistments, 3, 208, 211.

Smith, Truman, and Reconstruction, 2, 434.

Smith, Watson, report on Warrington, 1, 510.

Smith Brothers, charged with contract frauds, 2, 7; arrest and trial, 53–57, 60, 90, 224; petition in behalf of, 124; Lincoln's concern, 124; efforts for release, 231, 238; sentence reversed, 260–264, 334, 359; Welles on guilt, 266.

Smythe, H. A., collector at New York, 2, 484; and Connecticut Senatorial election, 507, 508; and Johnson, 558, 566; nominated to Austrian mission, 3, 391.

South Atlantic Squadron. *See* Charleston, Dahlgren, Du Pont, Port Royal.

South Carolina, humbled, 2, 242; aristocracy of, and cause of the Civil War, 276, 312; Reconstruction constitution, 3, 347.

South Mountain, battle, 1, 130.

Spain, and Confederacy, 1, 399; appointment of Minister to (1865), 2, 254, 255; trouble with Peru expected, 357, 365; and Chili, 495. *See also* Cuba.

Spaulding, E. G., and Du Pont's intrigue, 2, 7.

Spaulding, R. P., and Johnson's tour, 2, 589; and Navy Department, 3, 265.

Speed, James, Attorney-General, 2, 192, 197; and law as to public records, 212, 220; on government of negroes, 222; and State rights, 239; and apprehended decision on arbitrary arrests, 242, 245; on Chase and politics, 251; on Johnson's speech as Vice-President, 252; on drawing on next year's appropriations, 264; and fall of Richmond, 273; and assassination of Lincoln, 287, 288; and informing of Johnson, 288, 289; first Cabinet-meeting under Johnson, 289; and amnesty, 294, 301; on Sherman's peace terms, 294, 296, 297; and trade regulations (1865), 299; and proclamation against Confederate "pirates," 300, 308; and negro suffrage, 301; and trial of conspirators, 303, 305; on ironclad oath, 318; and trial of Davis, 338, 365, 367, 368, 614; vacation, 348; and Reconstruction judges, 366; on Freedmen's Bureau Bill, 434; and trial of Semmes, 467; as official, 480, 481; and Mexico, 485; and Fenians, 520, 524; and Johnson's policy, 524, 537, 543; resigns, 554, 555.

Spencer, ——, of New York, and release of Scofield, 2, 199.

Sperry, N. D., and Administration (1866), 2, 485; and Senatorial election, 506.

Spinner, F. E., on elected officers, 1, 406.

Spooner, Thomas, and date of National Convention (1864), 2, 30.

Spottsylvania Court-House, battle, death of Sedgwick, 2, 27; news awaited, 28; battle reports, 29; anxiety, 33.

Sprague, Peleg, and prize laws, 1, 531, 532.

Sprague, William, and Kate Chase, 1, 306; impeachment vote, 3, 349, 356, 358; attack on lawyers, 565.

Springfield *Republican*, character, 3, 490.

Staff officers, differences with line, 3, 252, 253, 384; desire of surgeons for naval rank, 501; relative rank, 570, 573.

Stahl, ——, master blacksmith, removed, 2, 597.

Stanbery, Henry, nominated to Supreme Court, 2, 487; Attorney-General, 558, 560; on bounty bill, 564; on New Orleans riot, 572, 573; and Seward, 575; and visit of Queen Emma, 577; and proclamation of peace in Texas, 580; on Tenure-of-Office Act, 583; and Johnson's tour, 587; and trial of Davis, 608, 614, 616; and Indian depredations in Texas, 614; and Mexico, 622; and asylum for the Pope, 639; on negro suffrage for the District, 3, 4, 5; on Reconstruction Bill, 11, 54; and seizure of the *R. R. Cuyler*, 39, 41; and Stanton's report on enforcement of civil rights, 43; interpretation of Reconstruction Acts, 59, 60, 63, 93, 96–99, 105, 109–117; and Tucker episode, 66; and injunction cases against Reconstruction Acts, 81, 86; and purchase of Danish West Indies, 97, 124; on tax on foreigners in Colombia, 106; and Sheridan's letter, 126; and veto of explanatory Reconstruction Act, 137; urges dismissal of Stanton (1867), 173; as Presidential adviser, 209, 287; on *habeas corpus* proceedings on enlistments, 209–222; and successor to Stanton, 231, 286; and message on suspension of Stanton, 240; and Alabama claims, 241; and conduct of military governors, 242, 243; on conditions in the South (1867), 246; and retirement of Capt. Meade, 250, 251; on Tenure-of-Office Act and Lincoln's Cabinet appointments, 290; impeachment counsel, 299, 302, 308, 331, 341; counsel and resignation, 299, 303, 308, 311; and Johnson's talkativeness, 311; rejected for reappointment, 375; hopeful after election (1868), 492.

Stanton, E. M., *under Lincoln:* Welles's portraiture, 1, xxxi; and Seward, 12, 58, 203, 355, 356, 2, 91; attitude towards Administration before joining it, 1, 54, 55, 58; candidacy for district attorney, 56; antagonism of the Blairs, 56, 59, 125–128, 203, 329, 345, 355, 398, 2, 91, 102; appointment to Cabinet, 1, 57–60, 68, 128, 355, 356; and McClellan (1861), 57; personal relations with Welles, 60,

61, 64–67, 127, 128; and Chase, 61, 101, 402, 536; and New Orleans expedition, 61; and Potomac operations, 61, 67, 3, 436; personal character and management of Department, 62, 68, 69, 125, 128, 148, 161, 442, 447, 2, 328, 331, 3, 309, 370, 377; *Merrimac* scare, 1, 62–68, 3, 473; and Lincoln's General Order No. 1, 1, 63; intrigue for removal of McClellan (Aug., 1862), 83, 93, 95–101, 104, 108, 109, 112, 118–122, 129; and Second Bull Run, 93, 105; and Lincoln, 98, 149, 2, 92, 112, 130; and New York *Times*, 1, 123; and Antietam, 142; and Chiriqui Grant, 151; and emancipation, 159; threatens to resign (1862), 160, 161, 202; and Norfolk trade, 165, 175, 178, 183; after Antietam, 176; and Navy Department control of Mississippi gunboats, 180, 272, 273; and Senate committee on Seward, 195, 200–202, 206; and admission of West Virginia, 205, 207, 208; and McClernand, 217, 388; and negro troops, 218; and Pope, 221; and capture of *Queen of the West*, 240; and D. D. Porter, 273, 369; and Chancellorsville, 293, 294; and renewal of Charleston operations, 309, 385; and Cabinet consultations, 319, 320, 546, 2, 16, 17, 58; unpopular with army, 1, 324; visits headquarters (1863), 327; and Lee's invasion (1863), 328, 330, 332, 338, 342, 353; and *Army and Navy Gazette*, 343; and relieving of Hooker, 348, 349; and countermovement on Richmond, 351; and battle of Gettysburg, 354, 356, 358; and McClellan after Seven Days, 355; and Stephens's attempted mission, 358, 360, 361; and fall of Vicksburg, 365, 367, 371; and escape of Lee, 366, 370; and Dix, 373; and expedition to western Texas, 390, 442; and draft exemptions, 397, 407; and Halleck and Almaden mines, 398; and Lincoln's letter-writing, 399; proposes an excursion, 406; Reconstruction theory and plan, 413, 2, 179, 281, 282, 291, 294, 301; and *habeas corpus* proceedings on the draft, 1, 432, 433; and commanders of the Army of the Potomac, 440; and Sabine Pass expedition, 441; and Chattanooga, 444; and Trowbridge-Lamar plot, 492; and transfer of soldiers to Navy, 498, 546, 548; and renomination of Lincoln, 500; and cotton trade, 511, 537, 2, 66, 139; at presentation of Grant's commission, 1, 539; and new draft (1864), 542; and Fort Pillow massacre, 2, 25; and forged proclamation incident, 35, 38; and Presidential visits to headquarters, 55; and Early's raid, 68–70, 72, 74, 77, 78, 84; reported disagreement with Grant, 79; and Whiting, 85; and the Crater, 89; no intention to resign (1864), 102; influence over Fessenden, 120, 173; and Wilmington expedition, 128, 205–207, 209, 214, 215; and control of abandoned plantations, 149, 150; and Confederate operations on Lake Erie, 151–153; and Blair's resignation, 158 n.; and land movement against Mobile, 165; intimacy with Radicals (1864), 166, 173, 247; and exchange of naval prisoners, 168–171; and appointment of Chase as Chief-Justice, 192; uses Committee on Conduct of the War, 198; avoids responsibility, 206; and government of negroes, 222; on Savannah trip, 228; and Blair's Senatorial aspirations, 243; on Johnson's speech as Vice-President 252; and flag-raising at Sumter, 267; and capture of Richmond, 272; on Buchanan and Sumter (Dec., 1860), 273; Virginia legislature incident, 279; and resump-

tion of trade with South, 280, 281, 296; and assault on Seward, 285; and assassination of Lincoln, 285; Seward on services, 384, 399; and contract frauds, 3, 23. *See also* Halleck.

Under Johnson: and informing of Johnson, 2, 288; first Cabinet-meeting under Johnson, 289; attitude toward, and influence over, Johnson (1865), 289, 290, 394, 398, 399, 405; (1866), 424, 437, 523, 538, 541, 556, 557, 627, 652; (1867), 3, 26, 47, 72, 118, 119, 123, 132–134; Reconstruction plan, 2, 291, 294, 301; at funeral of Lincoln, 292–294; Sherman controversy, 294–297, 309, 3, 247; and proclamation against Confederate "pirates," 2, 298, 300, 308; and implication of Davis, 300; and negro suffrage, 301, 303, 364, 3, 4, 22, 23; and trial of conspirators, 2, 303–305, 334; and custody of Davis, 308, 309; on ironclad oath and Southern appointments, 318, 319, 358, 445, 450; closes Ford's Theatre, 331; and favors for state prisoners, 332; and trial of Davis, 335, 338, 365, 614; and Mexico, 348, 485, 621, 622, 624, 625; illness, 352; and post-War movements of Army, 352, 355–357, 360–362; fears and bodyguard, 362; and Radicals (1865), 364; Blair's attack (1865), 370; and political assessment, 380, 382; and parole for Mallory, 395; rumor of intended resignation (1865), 399, 402; espionage over Johnson, 403 n.; Presidential aspirations, 403; and Cox house case, 414; and Freedmen's Bureau Bill, 434, 439; and Fenian raid, 451, 453, 486, 518–520; and Civil Rights Bill, 464; and trial of Semmes, 467; and national quarantine, 480; removal urged, 480, 481, 581–583, 606, 611, 613, 630, 3, 45, 49, 90, 91; and report of the Reconstruction Committee, **2,** 495–501; and Colorado Bill, 503; and Atlantic cable, 503; serenade speech, 513; and Mme. Bertinatti's claim, 522, 526; and Schenck-Romero correspondence, 528; and Thomas and the Tennessee legislature (1866), 554; and Grant's nomination as General, 562; and bounty bill (1866), 564; and New Orleans riot, 569–571, 611; and story of negroes kidnapped to Cuba, 570; and final proclamation of peace, 580, 581; opposes Union Convention, 582; and Johnson's tour, 585, 587, 592; and return of Slidell, 585; and court of inquiry for Holt, 601; and relinquishment of *Dunderberg,* 604, **3,** 28; and Indian depredations in Texas, 613; and Maryland election controversy (1866), 620, **3,** 140, 141; and Fourteenth Amendment, **2,** 628, 630; and arrest of Surratt, 630; and Bay of Samaná, 631; and welcome to Congress, 632; and asylum for the Pope, 640; and Prussian convention, **3,** 9; and reciprocal amnesty, 9; and Reconstruction bills, helps frame them, 11, 17, 49, 94, 96, 110; and control of Indian affairs, 30, 69, 74, 98, 254; and seizure of *R. R. Cuyler,* 38, 39, 42; and Danish West Indies, 40, 98, 124; report on enforcement of civil rights, 42–46; and impeachment movement, (1867), 50; and veto of Tenure-of-Office Bill, 50, 52, 54, 158, 162, 168; and interpretation of Reconstruction Act, on Stanbery's opinion, 59, 64, 105, 111, 114; and appointment of military governors, 64, 65; and Tucker episode, 66, 69; and sessions of Congress, 74; and sale of ironclads, 92; and expenditures of military governors, 93; and Booth's diary, 95; and Sheridan's letter, 117, 118, 125–127; direct communications to Congress, 131,

132; and Tennessee troubles (1867), 140; responsibility for Sheridan's actions, 154; suspension foreshadowed, 155; refuses to resign, 157, 158; action on, considered, 159, 160, 162, 163, 165, 167; suspended, 168, 169; public reception of suspension, 173; question of successor, 231; message on suspension, 240, 242; return to Washington, 246; Senate disapproves of suspension, 255, 258, 259; Grant-Johnson controversy over reinstatement, 259–262, 266–279; question of resignation after repossession, 263, 267; official taboo, 278; Thomas to watch, 279; removal, 280, 284, 289–291; Senate on removal, 285; arrest of Thomas, 294; Ewing nominated to succeed, 286, 287; removal and impeachment of Johnson, 292; *quo warranto* writ, 299; precedent for removal, 302, 311; intrenched in office, nitro-glycerine scare, 297, 309, 323, 338; Schofield to succeed, 338–340, 371, 375; relinquishes office in ignominy, 370; Senate's complimentary resolution, 377; political influence (1869), 508.

Starkweather, H. H., and Connecticut election (1866), **2,** 458; and Senatorial election, 508; and *Sabine,* **3,** 337.

State Department. *See* Seward (W. H.), and foreign nations by name.

State-rights, Cabinet discussion (1865), **2,** 239. *See also* Reconstruction (theories).

Steam Engineering, Bureau of. *See* Engineer Corps, Isherwood, Stimers.

Stedman, G. A., mortal wound and promotion, **2,** 94, 96.

Steedman, J. B., in Johnson's tour, **2,** 589; and War portfolio, **3,** 165.

Stephens, A. H., attempted mission (1863), **1,** 358–363; mission and draft riots, 369; Hampton Road

Conference, **2**, 235, 238; in custody, 308; Stanton's discourtesy, 332; not to be paroled, 358; paroled, 382; at Grant's reception, 478.

Stevens, A. F., investigation of Philadelphia Navy Yard, **3**, 416.

Stevens, Thaddeus, opposition to Seward (1864), **2**, 198; and Butler (1865), 230; and Navy Department, 237; and Johnson (1865), 325; and exclusion of Southern Congressmen, 387, 388, 392, 440, 442; revolutionary designs, 432, 451, 633, **3**, 87, 133; and veto of Freedmen's Bureau Bill, **2**, 436; and Reconstruction Committee, 441; Grimes on, 447; at Grant's reception (1866), 478; and distribution of Forney's *Chronicle*, 486; control of Radicals, 626, **3**, 130; and Bay of Samaná, **2**, 643; and impeachment (1867), **3**, 12; Senatorial candidacy, 16, 21; character, 21, 26; and Reconstruction Bill, 40, 47; as impeachment manager, 301, 340, 354; and renewal of impeachment, 391.

Stewart, A. T., and Fenton, **3**, 508; character, 523; and Treasury portfolio, 543, 545–548, 565.

Stewart, Charles, and rear-admiralship, **1**, 77.

Stewart, W. M., and Civil Rights Bill, **2**, 475.

Stimers, A. C., and preparation against Charleston, **1**, 247; Du Pont's charges against, 307; and light-draft monitors, **2**, 52, 81, 108, 241, 349–351; resigns, 349, 351.

Stimson, ——, storekeeper at Kittery Navy Yard, appointment, **2**, 586.

Stiners, ——, contract frauds, **2**, 279.

Stockton, John, ousted from Senate, **2**, 464, 475; return candidacy, 475; reëlected to Senate, **3**, 517.

Stockton, R. F., and son's return to Senate, **2**, 475.

Stoeckel, Baron, and visit of Russian fleet, **1**, 481; Alaska treaty, **3**, 75.

Stokes, W. B., character, **3**, 205.

Stone, J. M., Congressional aspirations (1865), **2**, 381.

Stone River. *See* Murfreesborough.

Stoneman, George, raid (1863), **1**, 292–295; in Johnson's tour, **2**, 589.

Stonewall, stopped at Corunna, **2**, 254; watched by *Niagara*, 261, 267; in West Indies, 305–307; to be surrendered by Spain, 335; Craven court-martial, 392, 396; sold to Japan, **3**, 97, 99, 365, 513.

Stover, H. D., fraudulent contracts, **1**, 514, 515, **2**, 54; implication of others, **1**, 518, 524; witness in Opdyke-Weed suit, **2**, 208, 211.

Stowell, Lord, on use of neutral waters by belligerents, **1**, 461; on prize crew as witnesses, 465, 466.

Stribling, C. K., and sale of vessel to Venezuela, **1**, 474, 476; lighthouse duty, **2**, 578; and Porter's conduct of Navy Department, **3**, 561.

Stringham, S. H., and relief of Sumter, **1**, 5, 8, 9, 12, 15; ordered to Pensacola, 16; and navy yard at League Island, 185; and Wise, **2**, 7; and Charlestown Navy Yard, 34; and Du Pont, 118.

Stuart, J. E. B., in Lee's invasion (1863), **1**, 350; Chambersburg raid, 169; death, **2**, 33.

Stuart, William, and slave-trade cruising convention, **1**, 155; and the *Bermuda*, 170; and captured mails, 181; and *Emma* incident, 445.

Suffolk County, Virginia, operations (1863), **1**, 285, 287.

Suffrage, Welles distrusts free, in cities, **1**, 523, 524; under Reconstruction Act, **3**, 94, 96–99. *See also* Negro suffrage.

Sumter, Fort, question of relief, **1**, 3–39, **2**, 248, 374; scarcity at, **1**, 4;

Ward's plan, 5–10; Seward's understanding with Secessionists, 12; Seward and Confederate commissioners, 12, 26–28, 32–35; Blair convinces Lincoln on relief, 13; Fox's plan, 14–16, 21–23; Seward's interference with plan, 16–21, 23–26, 31, 35–39; Federal attack (1863), 427, 434; flag-raising (1865), 2, 267; Buchanan's administration and (Dec., 1860), 273.

Supreme Court, Field's appointment, 1, 245; death of Taney, 2, 176; question of successor, Chase's appointment, 181–183, 187, 192, 196; apprehended decision on arbitrary arrests, 242, 245; on captured cotton, 255, 263; Milligan case, 471, 474, 476; Stanbery's nomination, 487; and Reconstruction Act, 3, 80; injunction cases against Reconstruction Act, 86; war of Radicals on, 258, 282, 314, 323; McCardle case, 314, 320.

Surratt, J. H., arrest, 2, 630; sent to America, 3, 29, 31; Johnson's attitude, 31; trial, 166, 167.

"Swamp Angel," and foreign attitude, 1, 445.

Swann, Thomas, and election controversy (1866), 2, 620.

Swatara, brings Surratt, 3, 29, 31.

Swayne, N. H., and armored fleet for the Ohio, 1, 90; and Chief-Justiceship, 2, 182.

Swett, Leonard, and Cameron, 2, 390; and impeachment counsel, 3, 306, 307.

Swift & Co. *See* Secor and Swift.

Sybert, ——, application for letters of marque, 1, 260, 261.

Sykes, George, Blair on, 1, 126; and escape of Lee, 375.

Tacony, depredations and pursuit, 1, 327, 333, 342, 350, 375 n.

Tallahassee, depredations and pursuit, 2, 102, 105, 110, 111, 113, 119.

Taney, R. B., Cabinet and funeral, 2, 176; Welles's opinion, 177, 184; on Welles's administration, 184.

Tariff, Grimes on (1866), 2, 542; woolens bill (1867), 3, 58; veto of copper bill (1869), 531.

Tassara, D. G. Garcia y, and assumption of six-mile maritime jurisdiction, 1, 170, 399; complaint of violated neutrality, 308; reception, 522; and *Stonewall*, 2, 307; dinner to Dulce, 526.

Tatnall, Josiah, plantation, 2, 313.

Taxation, Welles on necessity, 2, 3, 16; cotton, 316. *See also* Finances, Tariff.

Taylor, Bayard, on attitude of Napoleon (1863), 1, 495.

Taylor, Mrs. N. G., buries clothes, 3, 15.

Taylor, R. W., and payments out of next year's appropriations, 2, 264, 266, 268, 274; as official, 3, 378.

Taylor, Richard, and Johnson's policy, 3, 72.

Taylor, Zachary, as general, 1, 86.

Tecumseh, loss, 2, 101.

Telegraph, naval vessels and laying of Atlantic cable (1866), 2, 503, 504.

Tennessee, exclusion of Representatives (1865), 2, 434, 436, 441–444, 446; Gen. Thomas and legislature, 554, 557; ratifies Fourteenth Amendment, 557, 558; Representatives admitted, 559; eastern, during the War, 3, 15; disturbances, troops ordered to (1867), 140, 141, 211.

Tenure-of-Office Act, introduced, 2, 549; Stanbery and Welles on, 583; Cabinet discussion, 3, 49, 50, 158, 162, 163, 171; veto, 51, 52, 54, 55; and suspension of Stanton, 159, 162; execution, 194; effects, 199; and removal of Stanton, 285, 286, 288; Cabinet on status of Lincoln's appointees, 290; and impeachment, 292; consideration of repeal and modification, 503, 555, 556, 558, 560, 564, 567–569, 571; Grant's attitude, 557, 560.

Territories, negro suffrage, **3**, 19.

Terry, A. H., and Dahlgren, **1**, 474; Wilmington expedition, **2**, 222, 226; Indian Commission, **3**, 254.

Texas, proposed occupation of western, and Matamoras trade, **1**, 387–392, 443; executive Reconstruction, **2**, 315, 316, 579, 580; conditions (1866), 568; (1867), **3**, 105; Indian depredations, **2**, 613; change in Governors (1867), **3**, 146.

Thanksgiving, Welles on (1863), **1**, 372; (1865), **2**, 393; (1866), 628; draft of proclamation, **1**, 449; Welles on State celebration, 450.

Thayer, Eli, scheme to colonize Florida, **1**, 206.

Thayer, J. M., and removal of Stanton, **3**, 285; on Johnson's plans for dictatorship, 291; and impeachment, 332.

Thirteenth Amendment, passes House, **2**, 234.

Thomas, B. F., and trial of Smith Bros., **2**, 90.

Thomas, G. H., Chickamauga, **1**, 444; as successor to Rosecrans, 447; Nashville, **2**, 200; Johnson's opinion, 367; Welles's opinion, 382; and Tennessee legislature (1866), 554, 557; and disturbances in Tennessee (1867), **3**, 140, 211; and military governorship, 186; nominated as Brevet General, **3**, 284.

Thomas, Lorenzo, and forged Cooper dispatch, **1**, 176; and removal of Stanton, **3**, 279; Secretary *ad interim*, and Stanton, 284, 289, 290; arrested, 285, 286, 294; and Cabinet-meetings, 303; character, 371.

Thomas, P. F., and interests of Commodore Ringgold, **1**, 534; and Belknap, **3**, 205.

Thompson, A. W., Chiriqui Grant, **1**, 123, 150–153.

Thompson, Jacob, alleged implica-

tion in assassination of Lincoln, **2**, 299.

Thornton, Sir Edward, reception, **3**, 515.

Throckmorton, J. W., and Indian depredations, **2**, 613; removed, **3**, 146.

Thurman, A. G., and impeachment counsel, **3**, 305.

Tilden, S. J., and draft, **1**, 380; as politician, **2**, 602, **3**, 228; and Johnson (1866), **2**, 602, **3**, 223, 229; Presidential bee, 446.

Tilton, Theodore, and Civil Rights Bill, **2**, 478; and impeachment, **3**, 357.

Tobacco, French, at Richmond, **1**, 338–340, **2**, 9, 12; at Fredericksburg (1865), 257.

Tod, David, hopefulness (1862), **1**, 153; spirit of message (1863), 219; character, 404; nominated as Secretary of Treasury, **2**, 62, 63; declines, 64; and Johnson's speeches, 594.

Todd, J. B. S., and Dakota politics, **2**, 153.

Toombs, Robert, letter on Southern conditions (1863), **1**, 428; character, 428.

Torpedo, Confederate vessel, **1**, 358.

Totten, J. G., and relief of Sumter, **1**, 3; and Wilmington, 307.

Toucey, Isaac, and Chiriqui Grant, **1**, 151; treason, 355; and Sumter, **2**, 274, 374.

Townsend, E. D., and Stanton, **3**, 279.

Trade, proclamation closing Southern ports to foreign (1865), **2**, 275, 278; plan of resumption with South (1865), 280, 296, 298–300, 308. *See also* Blockade, Cotton, Treasury agents.

Train, C. R., and trial of Smith Bros., **2**, 90.

Treason, Welles on punishment, **2**, 43.

Treasury Department, Tod's appointment and declination, **2**, 62,

63; Morgan and, 240, 243. *See also* Chase, Fessenden, Finances, McCulloch.

Treasury agents, misconduct, 2, 33, 34; movement to abolish, 316; and Confederate naval material, 336, 337; demoralization, 343. *See also* Cotton.

Trenholm, G. A., paroled, 2, 382.

Trent affair, Seward and Welles and, 1, 299; Wilkes's mistake, 466.

Trowbridge, N. C., supposed plot, 1, 492, 493.

Trumbull, Lyman, Senate committee on Seward, 1, 196, 197; and bank bill, 237; and J. P. Hale, 490; and Dakota politics (1864), 2, 153; and Johnson's policy (1865), 322; and Lincoln, 322; and Radicals, 435; at Grant's reception (1866), 478; and Welles, 488; on Presidential speechmaking, 488; on Southern representation, Johnson's conduct, Civil Rights Bill, 488–490; Tenure-of-Office Bill, 549; and bounty bill, 564; and radicalism, 638; reëlection, 3, 21; impeachment vote, 346, 350; vote and party fidelity, 359, 375; and Reconstruction, 377; and leave for midshipman, 476, 477; at Johnson's state dinner (1869), 515; and repeal of Tenure-of-Office Act, 555, 567; deserts Democratic principles, 560.

Tucker, J. R., and American naval officers, 2, 650, 3, 37, 45, 66, 71.

Turkey, insurrection in Crete, 3, 71, 138, 425; seeks ironclads, 206.

Turner, L. C., and Key, 1, 146.

Turner, Thomas, and Norfolk trade through blockade, 1, 184; and Dahlgren, 314; on monitors, 314; and Philadelphia Navy Yard, 2, 597; report on earthquake, 3, 435.

Turner, W. F., Arizona office, 1, 409.

Twee Gebroeders, case, 1, 462.

Tyler, E. B., reported capture, 2, 71.

Union Convention, calling and probable control, 2, 528–531, 533–535, 538–541, 545, 550, 608, 609, 3, 251; attitude of Democrats, 2, 542, 545; Cabinet letters on, 546–548, 552–554; Connecticut delegates, 567; prospects, 571; Stanton opposes, 573; papers for, 574; gathering, 576; proceedings, 577, 578; report to Johnson, 581; ultimate result, 617.

Union League, and radical Reconstruction, 2, 444.

Union men, Lincoln and Louisiana, 1, 81; and loss of Norfolk Navy Yard, 84; and Scott's defensive-frontier policy, 85, 86; engulfed, 219; Welles's belief in (1864), 2, 139.

Upshur, J. H., brings reports of attack on Charleston, 1, 267.

Upton, F. H., and *Peterhoff* mails, 1, 285, 310; on prize crew as witnesses, 466.

Usher, J. P., and bank bill, 1, 237; and Halleck and Almaden mines, 397; Reconstruction theory, 413; on draft and *habeas corpus* proceedings, 432; and visit of Russian fleet, 481; and renomination of Lincoln, 500; and social affairs, 530; campaign contribution (1864), 534; and new draft (1864), 542; and bounty on immigration, 543; and finances, 2, 11; and Chase, 20; and conservative movement (1864), 29; and cotton trade, 66; and politics in Brooklyn Navy Yard, 137; anxiety about retention of portfolio, 195, 251, 254; and Wilkes's case, 203; and assassination of Lincoln, 287, 288; and informing of Johnson, 288; and negro suffrage, 301.

Vallandigham, C. L., Cabinet on military trial, 1, 306, 321, 344; Lincoln on, 347; defeat, 470, 471; and McClellan's letter of acceptance, 2, 140.

Van Brunt, G. J., and J. P. Hale, **1**, 308, 384.

Van Buren, John, use of Scott's letter on secession, **1**, 171.

Van Buren, Martin, as politician, **3**, 225.

Vanderbilt, Cornelius, and *Merrimac*, **3**, 473.

Vanderbilt, cruise for *Alabama*, **1**, 224, 304, 316; to convey Queen Emma, **2**, 601, 604.

Van Valkenburg, R. B., and Christians in Japan, **3**, 229.

Van Winkle, P. G., impeachment vote, **3**, 350.

Van Wyck, C. H., proscribed by Welles, **3**, 512.

Varuna, inquiry concerning, **1**, 234.

Venezuela, question of sale of naval vessel to, **1**, 474–476; *Hannah Grant* seizure, **3**, 296, 349; Sanford claim, 297.

Verdi, T. S., attends Seward, **2**, 285.

Vice-admiral, grade created, **2**, 204; question of successor to Farragut, **3**, 562.

Vicksburg, lost opportunity to capture (1862), **1**, 71, 218, 314; ram *Arkansas*, 72; McClernand and command against, 217; news of fighting (Jan., 1863), 218, 220; canal operations, 238, 259; Porter's reports, 249; Farragut below (1863), 249, 274; Welles orders Porter to run past, 274, 285; Grand Gulf captured, 295; rumor concerning Grant, 308; defeat of Pemberton, 309; rumor of capture (May), 311; public anxiety, 314, 324; Cabinet discussion, 320; Halleck's attitude, 320, 324; fall, 364, 367; rejoicing, 365; Yazoo expedition, 379; Rawlins's personal report to Lincoln, McClernand and Grant, 387, 388.

Virginia, Lincoln's desire not to offend (1861), **1**, 6, 40; and secession, 39–41; Lincoln and calling of legislature (1865), **2**, 279, **3**, 522; Cabinet discussion on Reconstruction, **2**, 281, 282, 291, 301.

Virginia. See Merrimac.

Virginia campaign (1864), Navy and Butler's preparation, Welles on plan, **2**, 16, 19, 24; Burnside's corps arrives, 17; anticipation, 22, 25; first rumors, Lincoln's anxiety, 25, 26; first official dispatches of Wilderness, 27; death of Wadsworth and Sedgwick, 27; news of Spottsylvania awaited, 28; Sheridan's movements, 29; reports of Spottsylvania, 29; Confederate prisoners at Belle Plain, 31; anxiety at Washington during Spottsylvania, 33; Butler's movements, 35; forged proclamation, 35; confidence and slaughter, 44–46, 53, 92; army before Petersburg, 54, 78; Lincoln at headquarters (1864), 55, 90; (1865), 264; discouragement, 61, 72; and the Valley, 68, 69; Crater, 89–92; naval force, 230, 232; final actions pending, 271; capture of Petersburg and Richmond, 272, 275; Appomattox, 276, 278, **3**, 521, 523; Grant's reason for final movement against Richmond, 122.

Virginia Military Institute, destruction, **2**, 87.

Vogdes, Israel, and Fort Pickens, **1**, 14, 29, 31.

Wade, B. F., Senate committee on Seward, **1**, 196; and Early's raid, **2**, 74; Wade-Davis manifesto (1864), 95, 96, 98, 122, 239; intimacy with Stanton, 166; and Lincoln, 198; Committee on Conduct of the War, 198; and Butler (1865), 224; attack on Welles's administration, 240; on executive usurpation, 325; and Chase's appointment to the Cabinet, 391; and Johnson's appointments, 501; and first Reconstruction Bill, **3**, 46; and Danish West Indies, 97;

hedges, 130, 135; and impeachment, 293; Vice-Presidential candidacy, 362; later character, 362.

Wadsworth, J. S., gubernatorial campaign (1862), 1, 154, 219, 2, 27; on partisanship in Brooklyn Navy Yard, 1, 178; on escape of Lee, 374; killed, 2, 27; character, 27.

Wagner, Fort, assault on, 1, 380.

Wakeman, Abram, G. W. Blunt on, 1, 405; and politics in Brooklyn Navy Yard, 2, 122; appointed Naval Officer, 155.

Walke, Henry, promotion, 1, 77.

Walker, J. G., as Porter's emissary to Grimes, 3, 563.

Walker, W. M., question of reprimand, 2, 403.

Wallace, Lew, Monocacy, 2, 71, 73.

Wampanoag, engines, 3, 283.

War claims, early, 2, 411; British, 480; Mme. Bertinatti's, 522, 526; and Prussian convention, 3, 9; court, 372; Ames's case, 447–449, 451; Coombs's case, 528, 529.

War Department, General of the Army in charge (1869), 3, 550, 564; Rawlins appointed Secretary, 551. *See also* Cameron, Halleck, Schofield, Stanton.

Ward, J. H., and relief of Sumter, 1, 4–10, 2, 248.

Warrington, Fla., effect of blockade, 1, 510.

Washburn, C. A., difficulties of Paraguay mission, 2, 491, 492, 543, 3, 427, 446, 513.

Washburn, C. C., and repeal of the Tenure-of-Office Act, 3, 567, 568.

Washburne, E. B., and Navy Department, 1, 234, 236, 2, 137, 430, 3, 265, 341, 517; and speakership (1863), 1, 481; and Blair's resignation, 2, 157; and Grant-Johnson controversy, 3, 274; and impeachment, 292; toadies to Grant, 341; character, and State portfolio, 345, 543, 545, 546, 551; and finances,

345; Minister to France, 551.

Washington, George, chair, 1, 77.

Washington, measures to protect, 1, 4; political atmosphere before outbreak of War, 10, 34; *Merrimac* scare, 61–67, 3, 473; after Second Bull Run, 1, 99, 104, 105, 106, 109; during Gettysburg campaign, 329, 350, 351; Confederate plan for demonstration on (1863), 359, 376; Early's raid, 2, 71–77, 80; and fall of Richmond, 272; elections under negro suffrage, 3, 102, 374, 375, 380; Radical *ton* (1868), 278.

Washington *Chronicle*, and letters of marque, 1, 248; and official advertising, 2, 490; Radical organ, 653; and failure of impeachment, 3, 353. *See also* Forney.

Washington *Intelligencer*. *See National Intelligencer*.

Washington Navy Yard, graft, 1, 483; contention, 2, 225.

Wateree, wrecked, 3, 435, 449.

Watkins, G. S., and *Peterhoff* mails, 1, 284, 303; and trade permits, 536; and fraudulent contracts, 2, 53, 57.

Watson, P. H., on Welles and McClellan, 1, 98; as official, 127.

Webb, J. W., and Napoleon III, 2, 410; and Paraguay troubles, 3, 208, 513, 516.

Webb, W. A., and exchange of naval prisoners of war, 2, 168.

Webb, W. H., and Navy Department, 1, 499; *Dunderberg*, 2, 341, 596, 603, 604, 3, 27–29, 40, 42, 92, 97.

Webster, Daniel, political character, 1, 507.

Weed, Thurlow, peace with Bennett, 1, 78; and New York *Times*, 123, 435; and Cameron, 127; and New York election (1862), 154, 162, 219; Comstock and *Baltic* intrigue, 155; Welles's antagonism, 204, 230, 2, 155, 171, 175–177, 188, 189, 201; retirement from *Evening*

Journal, **1**, 230; and formation of Lincoln's Cabinet, 230, **2**, 388–391; Seward's *alter ego*, **1**, 231, **2**, 105, 548; Senatorial intrigues (1863), **1**, 231; (1866), **2**, 607; political errand to Washington (1863), **1**, 235, 236; and date of Republican Convention (1864), **2**, 28; and arrest of Henderson, 83; political position (1864), 105; political character, 142, 155, **3**, 227, 228; hold on New York patronage (1864), **2**, 154; and Blair's resignation, 157; and cotton trade, 160; and vessels for Japan, 188, 189, 191, 192, 561, **3**, 89; and release of Scofield, **2**, 200, 201; Opdyke suit, 208, 211; and Morgan for Treasury, 244; and Johnson (1865), 333; and Seward's speech (1865), 383, 384; and party preservation and Union Convention (1866), 527, 534, 535, 538, 539, 545, 548, 609, 610, **3**, 251; and Fourteenth Amendment, **2**, 541; and Dix's appointment to Holland, 566; effort to regain power (1866), 610; and Kilpatrick's appointment, **3**, 24; attack on Chase (1867), **3**, 163; Cabinet intrigue (1867), 203, 204; and Grant movement (1867), 249; and Alta Vela affair, 305, 318; and investigation of impeachment vote, 369; and McCulloch, 389, 390; and Presidential campaign (1868), 402.

Weehawken, weathers great storm, **1**, 225, 226.

Weitzel, Godfrey, and Wilmington expedition, **2**, 210, 213; and Virginia legislature incident, 279, **3**, 522.

Weld, ——, of Boston, criticism of Navy Department, **1**, 405.

Welles, E. T., examines *Clyde*, **1**, 428; in Washington, 494, **2**, 113; at Fortress Monroe, 17, 19; returns to college, 23; trip to Havana, 267; in Johnson's tour, 589; leaves Navy Department, **3**, 550.

Welles, Gideon, *Departmental affairs under Lincoln:* as Secretary of the Navy, **1**, xxi–xxiii, xxxviii–xl; and Fort Pickens, 14, 26, 28–32; Fort Sumter expedition, 15, 21–23; Seward's interference with it, 16–21, 23–25, 37; and Norfolk Navy Yard, 41–54, 83; and *Merrimac* scare, 61–67, **3**, 473; Vicksburg operations, **1**, 72, 274, 285, 364, 367; and reorganization of the Department, 74, 75; appointment of rear-admirals, 75–77; and subordinate active appointments, 77; Seward's interference with the blockade, 79, 82, 132, 138; appointment of midshipmen, 82, 146, 147, 149, 188, 224, 227, 234, 236, 319, 393, **2**, 163; and W. D. Porter, **1**, 87, 88; and armored fleet for the Ohio, 90; and Potomac operations, 102, 103, **3**, 437; pursuit of Confederate cruisers, popular complaints, **1**, 109–111, 122, 123, 134, 179, 207, 216, 316, 327, 333, 342, 375, 438, 440, 497, **2**, 67, 105, 110, 111, 113, 119; popularity of administration, **1**, 128, 206, 228; and dismissal of Preble, 140–142, 163, 188–191, 228, 235; and J. P. Hale, 149, 227, 308, 384, 386, 482–491, 505, 507, 509, 522, 523, 529, **2**, 5, 6, 51, 52, 193, 231, 234, 238, 268, **3**, 25; policy toward European attitude, **1**, 154, 155, 217, 235, 247, 250, 251, 255–259, 263, 299, 374, 379, 385, 399, 443, 445, 453, 495, **2**, 7, 431; and letters of marque, **1**, 155, 246–262; and purchase of *Baltic*, 155; and slave-trade cruising convention, 155, 163, 166, 192, 236; and appointment of chaplains, 162; and trade through the blockade, **1**, 165, 173–175, 177, 183, 217, 227, 318, 498, 527, 536, 537, 543, 544, 548, **2**, 159, 162, 163, 167, 257; and six-mile maritime jurisdiction around Cuba, **1**, 170, 467, 468; and the *Bermuda*, 170; opposition to blockade and belligerency policy, 174, 440, **2**, 159, 160, 246, **3**, 241; and politics in navy yards, **1**, 178, 327, **2**, 31, 34, 97, 98, 108, 122–124, 136, 137, 142–145, 175; and ironclads, **1**, 179, 268, 295, 311, 342, 351, 495, 499, **2**, 101; and captured foreign mails, **1**, 180, 222, 266, 269–286, 300–304, 315; and control over Mississippi gunboats, 180, 272; annual reports (1862), 184; (1863), 472, 479; (1864), **2**, 187, 194, 197; and navy yard at League Island, **1**, 185, 207, 222, 227, 285; and complaints of Congressmen, 187, 206; and the *Monitor*, 213, 214; and criticism and abuse of the Department, 215, 404, 405, 496, 497, 499, 519, 522, 531, **2**, 17, 37, 67, 79, 80, 87, 105, 114, 185, 236–238, 240–242, 250, 259; and vessels for Japan, **1**, 225, **2**, 188, 191; and reported raising of Charleston blockade, **1**, 232, 234; question of Galveston blockade, 233; preparations against Charleston, 236, 247, 249, 263, 264; anxiety about the expedition, 263–265; on Lincoln's irregular encouragement of inventions, 239; ignored as to naval bills (1863), 245; and codification of naval laws, 245; and Du Pont's failure before Charleston, subsequent controversy, 267–269, 273, 276, 277, 288, 309, 311, 322, 344, 476–478, **2**, 7, 11, 14, 30, 117–119, 320, 321; and Matamoras trade and expedition to check it, **1**, 283, 334, 387, 443; and calls for naval coast defense, Navy and duties of Army, 288, 347, 364, 366, 375, 380, 435, **2**, 256, 257; and Laird's statement, **1**, 291, 306, 394–396, 401; on judicial control over prizes, 296, 297, 302, **2**, 106, 107; and *John Gilpin* prize case, 297, 298; and Wilkes in West Indies, 299, 304, 316, 322; and *Trent* affair, 299; and renewed operations against Charleston, suc-

cessor to Du Pont, 309, 312–318, 324, 337, 346, 347, 380, 382–385, 427, 449, 467, 520, 547; and Naval Academy, 324, **2**, 34; and playing of the Marine Band, **1**, 325, 368; and Foote, 335, 345, **2**, 135; and French tobacco at Richmond, **1**, 339, 340, **2**, 9; and *Army and Navy Gazette*, **1**, 344; congratulates Rodgers, 344; on attitude of War Department toward the Navy, 365, 519, 525, **2**, 6, 13, 100, 115, 165; and location of prize courts, **1**, 366, 491; and promotion of D. D. Porter (1863), 369; and instruction of naval officers as to neutral rights, 398, 409, 450–466, 535, **2**, 4; and Laird rams, **1**, 399, 406, 429, 435–438, 443, 448; *Mont Blanc* incident, capture in neutral waters, 416–427; official visits to navy yards, 428, 431; Lincoln on administration, 440, 451; on Sabine Pass expedition, 441, 443; and purchase of the *Emma*, 437, 438, 445, 446; on visit of the Russian fleet, 443, 480, 481, 484; meets Admiral Milne, 467, 468; and sale of naval vessel to an unrecognized government, 474–476; paragraphs for annual message (1863), 480; and Colfax's committee appointments (1863), 482, 484; and fraudulent contracts, trials, and pardons, 483, 511, 512, 514, 518, 522, 524, 537–544, 547, **2**, 5, 7, 11, 53–61, 78, 79, 82, 83, 90, 124, 176, 177, 199–201, 220, 224, 225, 231, 260–262, 266, 306, 334, 359, 400–402, 418, **3**, 23; routine, **1**, 484; and Morgan's purchases, 487; Wilkes's insubordination and trial, 489–491, 505, 515, 528, 530, 531, 544, **2**, 6, 19, 21, 203; and surrender of the *Chesapeake*, **1**, 490, 508, 509, 545; enlistment problems, draft complications, 498, 541, 545–548, **2**, 3, 121, 129, 240; and Webb, **1**, 499; advises policy of opening cer-

tain ports, 510, 511, 514; and speed test of naval vessels, 511, 515; and M. H. Grinnell, 512–514; London *Times* on administration, 516; and purchase of the *Cherokee*, 516; and Congressional inquiries, 522, 528; and cutting ship-timber in South, 522, 527, 528; and raising of Brownsville blockade, 529; and Florida expedition (1864), 532; and new prize law, 532; and retirement of officers, 532; solicitations for promotion, Lee and Ringgold cases, 533, 534, **2**, 147, 161, 243; and increase of Marine Corps, 6; and navy yard for ironclads, 17; and foreign-owned cotton, 40; and Commandant for Marine Corps, 51; on Treasury's failure to pay naval requisitions, 58, 59, 69, 106, 114, 141, 264–266, 268, 274; and light-draft monitors, 81, 108, 241, 349–351; Bates's opinion, 93; on writing congratulatory letters, 106; on ignoring of the Department in naval victories, 115; discovery of Farragut, 116, 134, 135, **3**, 104; selecting new commander for North Atlantic Squadron, **2**, 127–129; and Wilmington expedition, 127, 146–148, 194, 205–217, 219, 226–228; and Confederate operations on Lake Erie, 151–153; and exchange of naval prisoners, 168–171; and Fessenden's criticism of naval officers, 172; and unauthorized Marine bounty, 174; and naval votes (1864), 175; Taney's praise of administration, 184; and capture of *Florida*, 185, 186, 197; and relief of contractors, 202, 207, 227, 418; on his labors, 218; and Board of Admiralty, 233, 240, 241; and *Stonewall*, 254, 261, 267; and closing of Southern ports (1865), 278.
  General affairs under Lincoln: early career, **1**, xvii; as Democrat, xviii; and slavery, xix; appoint-
ment to Cabinet, xx, 81, 204, 230, 325, **2**, 388; character of diary, **1**, xxiv–xxvii; portraiture of contemporaries, xxvii–xxxv, xlvii–l; own portraiture, xxxv–xxxviii; and society, lii; death, liii; and Seward and Confederate commissioners, 32–35; first meets Stanton, 54; personal relations with him, 60, 61, 64, 83, 91, 127, 128, 447; and General Order No. 1, 63; and emancipation 70, 144, 159, 209, 212, 403, 415, **2**, 237, 431; and captured Washington chair, **1**, 77; and Connecticut patronage, 78, 81, 235, 239, 246, 510; relations with Lincoln, 81, 88; and Scott's defensive-frontier policy, 84–86; on West Point training, 85, 125; and movement to remove McClellan, 94, 97, 101–104, 107, 112, 114, 115, 118, 124; and alarm after Second Bull Run, 99; and Pope's report, 110, 114; and colonizing of negroes, 123, 150–153, **3**, 428; and Blair, **1**, 125, 181; and proposed attack on Richmond (Sept., 1862), 130; on paper money, 147, 148, 167–169, 232, 494, 520, 530, **2**, 10–14, 16, 29, 55, 61, 180; and suspension of writ of *habeas corpus*, **1**, 150, 432, 433, 435; on Altoona Conference, 153; on wives of officers in camp, 170; and forged Cooper dispatches, 176; on killing of Gen. Nelson, 179; on final removal of McClellan, 182, 220, 225; on execution of Northwest Indians, 186; on admission of West Virginia, 188, 191, 205, 207, 208; and Senate committee on Seward, 196, 198–201; relations with Seward, 204, 366; and Weed, 204, 230, 235, 236, **2**, 155, 171, 175–177, 188, 189, 201; review of the year (1862), 211, 212; (1863), 499; and Cameron, 223; on gauge of Pacific Railroad, 228; and Hooker, 229, 294, 348; and shooting of deserters, 232; and Hawley, 235, 535; and Chase's

bank bill, 237; and extra session of Senate (1863), 238; exhausted, 245, 249, 395; on Chancellorsville, 291, 293; and condemnation of a spy, 313; on arbitrary arrests, 321, 322; and Gurowski, 326, 2, 101; and Lee's invasion (1863), 1, 328, 330, 331, 342, 343, 350, 352; and counter-movement on Richmond, 349, 352; and Gettysburg, 354, 356-358; and Stephens's attempted mission, 358-363; and escape of Lee, 364, 366, 368-371, 373; on coincidence of riots and Lee's invasion, 369; on mockery of Thanksgiving (1863), 372; on Jefferson Davis and continuation of War, 376-379; and the draft, 382, 397, 407, 432, 435, 541; and Forney, 386; excursions, 393, 394, 2, 31-33, 65; Reconstruction theory and plans, 1, 402, 403, 407-415, 429, 2, 84, 98, 99, 109, 179, 190, 197, 239; meets Meade, 1, 404; on Secession, 414, 429; on Chickamauga, 438, 444; and successor to Rosecrans, 447; on uselessness of Fort Foote, 474; and Gettysburg dedication, 480; and Trowbridge-Lamar plot, 492, 493; Christmas (1863), 494; receptions, 501, 521, 548, 2, 15, 238; and renomination of Lincoln, 1, 509, 529; and internal cotton trade, 511, 2, 33, 34, 36, 66, 139, 220; on free suffrage and municipal evils, 1, 523, 524; attends National Committee, 529; on suppressing news of defeats, 531; and Chase's candidacy, 533; and campaign contributions, 534; first impressions of Grant, 538, 539; at presentation of Grant's commission, 539; opposes bounty on immigration, 543; on fearful responsibility of opening days of the War, 549; on necessity of heavy taxation, 2, 3, 16; and date of Republican Convention, 4, 28; and J. C. Rives, 8; at Capitol, 9, 251; on Fort Pillow massacre,

24; talk with Confederate prisoner, 32; and Frémont in 1856, 41; favors punishment of Confederate leaders, 43; and Hamlin, 44, 46; and Arguellis incident, 45; and Presidential excursions to headquarters, 55; and resignation of Chase, 62; and nomination of Tod, 63; birthday, 64; and forged proclamation incident, 67; and Early's raid, 69-76, 80; and son's enlistment, 82; on indiscriminate destruction, 87; and peace negotiations, 94, 97, 109, 271; and political assessment, 113; and Bache, 117; on Whig element, 122; and Georgia "peace commissioner," 125; and New York collectorship, 137; movement for removal, 142, 155, 247, 250; and proposed removal of Lines, 147; on abandoned plantations, 149; and resignation of Blair, 156-158; and Banks, 177; gets election returns, 178; and appointment of Chief-Justice, 181, 192; and Maryland patronage, 195; on law as to public records, 211-213; on need of further punishment of Confederates (1865), 229; and choice for Treasury, 244, 245; on special passes, 258; and Bennett and French mission, 258; and flag-raising at Sumter, 258; and fall of Richmond, 272, 273; and Savannah cotton, 278; and Virginia legislature incident, 279, 280, 3, 522; and resumption of trade with the South, 2, 280, 281, 296, 298; and reconstruction of Virginia, 281, 282; and Stanton's plan, 291, 301; and assassination of Lincoln, 283-288, 290, 292.

Departmental affairs under Johnson: and proclamation against Confederate "pirates" (1865), 2, 298, 300; and *Stonewall*, 306; Dixon on administration, 307; and custody of Davis, 308, 309; appointment of midshipmen, 317, 526;

Department's claim to all Confederate naval material, 336, 337; in new quarters, 339; and *Dunderberg*, 340, 341, **3**, 27, 28, 42, 97; and assaults on the Department, 341; and Dickerson's engine, 346, 356, 361; selection of head for Navigation Bureau, 357, 362; and Pendergrast case, 364; and political assessment in navy yards, 376, 377, 380–382; annual reports (1865), 385; (1866), 628; (1868), **3**, 472, 475; and Craven court martial, **2**, 393, 396; and trial of Semmes, 404, 406, 407, 410, 420, 423, 424, 432, 436, 467, 471, 474, 476, 477; and *Shenandoah*, 411, 417; naval estimates and appropriations (1866), 430, 444; (1868), **3**, 264, 265, 280, 325; (1869), 517; and League Island Navy Yard, **2**, 445, **3**, 489; and Fenian raids, **2**, 451, 484, 486, 518–521, 524; and French Exhibition exhibits, 462; and seatrip for Robert Johnson, 468, 472, 479, 491; Butler and *Grey Jacket* case, 469, 492; Farragut visits, 490, **3**, 101, 469, 470; Paraguay troubles, **2**, 491, 492, 543, **3**, 427, 466–468, 491, 510, 513, 516; and order restricting naval officers' movements, **2**, 494; and laying of Atlantic cable, 503; trouble with S. P. Lee, 504–507, 511–514, 569, 578, **3**, 90; and Fox's official trip abroad, **2**, 506, 509, 512, 514; and Naval Academy, 525, **3**, 103, 382, 440; and promotions, **2**, 559, 560, 562, 563, 571; and bounty bill (1866), 564; and dismissal of Barney, 605; Congressional inquiries and investigations, 633, **3**, 13, 21, 122, 337; and Grimes, 14; and retirement of Goldsborough, 85, 86, 107–109, 135; and sale of ships to Japan (1867), 91; and sale of ironclads, 92, 207, 348, 384, 387–389; and travel of officers' wives on naval vessels, 92, 93; and

seizure of Santa Anna, 115; on direct Departmental communications to Congress, 132; and retirement of Com. Schenck, 135; and interference of Congressmen with navy yards, 139; and Field court martial, 140; and Belknap case, 206; and *habeas corpus* proceedings on enlistments, 208–222; and proposed Board of Admiralty, 247, 248; and relievement of Capt. Meade, 250; and differences between line and staff, 253, 283, 384, 501; on officers' right of free speech, 312; navy yard appointments, 325, 416–420, 446; tour of navy yards, 422; and Ames's claim for guns, 448, 451; and Alabama claims, 469–471, 506, 516, 579; and leave for midshipmen, 476, 477; and court-martial punishments, 481; and Congressional requests for reinstatement of officers, 498–501, 503, 507; and Grimes's bill to reorganize the Navy, 515; J. S. Morrill on administration, 523; and Coombs's claim, 528, 529; on use of naval vessels as private school ships, 531; and promotion before retirement, 531; and request for illegal pay, 534; takes leave of subordinates, 540; relations with Porter, 562, 563; and relative rank of staff officers, 570; Porter tenders use of naval vessel to, 580, 585, 586; reviews his official career, 581; no pecuniary gain, 582; philosophizes with Farragut over slights, 582.

General affairs under Johnson: value of diary on Reconstruction, **1**, xlii; Reconstruction theory, 402, 403, 407–415, 429, **2**, 84, 98, 99, 109, 179, 190, 197, 239, 430, 568, 569, 576, 600, 645, **3**, 81; and informing of Johnson, **2**, 288; first Cabinet-meeting under Johnson, 289; and Stanton's plan of Reconstruction, 291, 301; at funeral of

Lincoln, 292–294; and Sherman's peace terms, 295–297; and implication of Davis, 300; and negro suffrage, 301–303, 324, 373, 640, **3**, 4, 6, 8, 19, 137; and trial of conspirators, **2**, 303, 304, 334; trip to Charleston and Savannah, 310–315; and Gov. Hamilton, 315, 316; on ironclad oath and Southern appointments, 319, 358, 445, 454; on withdrawal of right of belligerency, 319, 320; birthday, 327; and the Blairs, 328, 343, 364, 370, 513, **3**, 165, 166, 231, 232; excursions, **2**, 329, 340, 547, **3**, 343, 396; and closing of Ford's Theatre, **2**, 331; and Mexico, 333, 348, 479, 485, 623, 624; and trial of Davis, 335, 338, 339, 365; and Hamlin, 342, 344–346; and patronage, 356, 363, 398, 484, 487, 532, 612, 651, **3**, 79, 80, 84, 85, 161; and Hawley, **2**, 369; vacation, 372; and Democrats (1865), 383; and Seward, 384, **3**, 195; and annexation of French West Indies, **2**, 393; and Johnson's policy (1865), 393–395, 397, 416, 419; on exclusion of Southern Congressmen, 396, 442, 446, 488, 489, 559; warns Johnson of intrigue, 396, 398; urges removal of Radicals, 398, 399, 585–587, 596–599, 602, 616, **3**, 147; and Seward's trip to Cuba (1865), **2**, 403, 406; and split in Union Party, 407, 421, 425, 481, 522–525; receptions, 409, **3**, 252, 266, 277, 497, 512; and Freedmen's Bureau Bill, **2**, 413, 431–433, 437; urges on Johnson public statement of position (Jan., 1866), 421; society sought by Confederate sympathizers (1866), 421; and Connecticut elections (1866), 426, 455–462; (1867), **3**, 77, 81; and Democratic Party in Connecticut, **2**, 428, 429; apprehends effects of Congressional Reconstruction, 433; and movement for reconciliation, 446; and Civil Rights

Bill, 459, 460, 463, 464, 488, 489; and Senator Foot, 466; and purchase of Danish West Indies, 466, 467, 473, **3**, 95, 97, 98, 124, 125; and national quarantine, **2**, 480; and report of Reconstruction Committee, 497, 499; attitude towards Senatorship, 501, 508; and Colorado Bill, 502; on serenade addresses, 512; and Gen. Dulce, 526; and Schenck-Romero correspondence, 528; and Union Convention, 528–531, 533–535, 538–541, 546, 552, 553, 574, 582, 583; and Fourteenth Amendment, 536, 537, 549, 608, 628, **3**, 7, 8, 417; and relations with Japan, **2**, 561, 562, **3**, 135, 230, 430; and appointment of Judge Clark, **2**, 565; on New Orleans riot, 569, 572, 573; urges removal of Stanton, 582, 630, 652, **3**, 45, 49, 91, 155; and Tenure-of-Office Bill, **2**, 583, **3**, 49, 51, 52, 54, 171, 194; and plan for Presidential tour, **2**, 584, 587; and return of Slidell, 585; in the tour, 589; on Presidential speechmaking, **2**, 593, 647, 648; and J. S. Morgan, 599, **3**, 582; and court of inquiry for Holt, **2**, 601, 604; on results of the election (1866), 616–620, 632; and welcome to Congress, 630; and arrest of Surratt, 630; and acquirement of Bay of Samaná, 631, 643, **3**, 7, 40; on asylum for the Pope, **2**, 639; and Sickles's interference with North Carolina laws (1866), 642, 644; on need of an Administration organ, 653; and the Prussian convention, **3**, 9; and first Reconstruction Bill, 11, 48, 49; and impeachment movement (1867), 12, 21, 50, 57, 60; and proposal of compromise on Reconstruction, 31–33, 37; and seizure of the *R. R. Cuyler*, 38, 39; and Stanton's report on enforcement of civil rights, 43, 45; at Capitol, 58, 59; interpretation of Reconstruction Act, on Stanbery's opinion, 59, 60, 63, 96–98, 105, 110–115; and Indian affairs, 69; and Gov. English's messages, 87–89, 382; and purchase of Culebra Island, 94; on Booth's diary, 95; not called before impeachment committee (1867), 102; and tax on foreigners in Colombia, 106; and Johnson's trip to Boston, 109; Sickles's letter on, and expenditures under Reconstruction Act, 119; and Sheridan's letter, 126, 127; on Teutonic and Latin races, 136–137; and Alaskan affairs, 141, 531; and removal of Sheridan, 142, 150, 151, 153, 154, 156, 175; and appointment of negroes, 142; and Conover allegations, 143–146; and Gov. Pease, 146, 147; and suspension of Stanton, 157, 163, 167; urges non-execution of Reconstruction Acts, 161, 164, 169; and Holt affidavits, 172; talk with Grant on Reconstruction Acts, 177–181; and general amnesty, 183, 193, 197, 198, 395; at Antietam anniversary, 201; and Fenton (1867), 201; fears Cabinet intrigue by Weed, 203, 204; and pardon for Seddon, 230, 231; urges Johnson to have an understanding with Grant, 233, 234; illness, 237, 313: and question of arrest of Johnson, 238; and message on suspension of Stanton, 240, 242; and conduct of military governors, 243; fears military absolutism, 245, 246, 249, 270, 271, 545, 550, 559, 564; and conditions in the South, 246; and filling of the English mission (1867), 256; and Grant-Johnson controversy, 262, 266, 271–273; and removal of Stanton, 284; and Ewing for the War Department, 286; and preparation for the crisis (1868), 288; and preparation for impeachment trial, 294, 297; on candidates for the Democratic nomination, 295; opposes Stanbery's resignation, 304, 308; on impeachment counsel, 304–307, 331, 332; and impeachment outlook, 313, 324, 329, 330, 332, 334, 336, 344; and Alta Vela affair, 316, 322; subpœnaed, 326; suggestions for the defense, 331, 337; testimony, 333; and nomination of Schofield, 340; and Reconstruction constitutions, 347; and Buchanan's funeral, 376; supports Seymour, 402, 404, 405, 410; and Johnson's Constitutional amendments, 406, 407; on use of troops as *posse*, 431; and career of T. H. Seymour, 432–434; and Pollard, 452; and disturbances in the South, 460–462; Grant proscribes and is proscribed by, 464, 465, 512; on Johnson's message (1868), 478, 479, 482; on resumption, 486–488, 493, 494, 504; review of 1868, 495; and confiscation, 504; suggests acquisition of Midway Islands, 508; and holding over under Grant, 529, 530, 532, 533, 537, 538, 541; and the inauguration, 537, 538, 541; at Johnson's last reception, 539; Mrs. Patterson visits, 542; reluctance to leave Washington, 580; return to Hartford, 583; quality of welcome, 584, 585, 587; purchases a house, 584; getting settled, 586–588.

Welles, Mrs. Gideon, and Mrs. Lincoln, 2, 290; in Johnson's tour, 589.
Welles, Hubert, death, 1, 181.
Welles, J. A., in Washington, 2, 113; in Johnson's tour, 589.
Welles, R. G., suicide, 2, 651, 652.
Welles, Samuel, injury and death, 2, 550, 551.
Welles, T. G., and Ulric Dahlgren's body, 1, 544, 545; desire for service, 2, 24; in army, 71, 80, 82, 90, 271.
Wells, J. M., removal by Sheridan, 3, 104.

Welsh, John, and Philadelphia Navy Yard removals, **2**, 597.

Wentworth, M. F., removed, **2**, 586.

West Gulf Squadron. *See* Farragut.

West India Squadron, organized, **1**, 109–111, 122, 123, 134; Wilkes's work, 217; and Confederate cruisers, 255; England and Wilkes, 298; Bell to command, 299; Lardner commands, 309, 319; inadequate force, 363.

West Indies, Seward and French islands, **2**, 393; attempted purchase of Danish, 466, 473, **3**, 40, 95–98, 124, 125, 502; Culebra Island, 94.

West Point, Welles on training, **1**, 85, 125.

West Virginia, question of admitting, **1**, 188, 191, 205, 206, 208.

Whelan, William, attends Foote, **1**, 336.

Whigs, Welles on, **2**, 122.

Whipple, H. B., sermon, **2**, 5.

Whiskey Ring, operations (1868), **3**, 435.

White, Mrs. ——, Mrs. Lincoln's half-sister, pass, **2**, 21.

White, Dr., attends Seward, **2**, 285.

White House, fire, **3**, 22.

White River, captures on, **1**, 227.

Whitin, L. F., and Welles, **2**, 208.

Whiting, William, character and importance, **1**, 381, 544, **2**, 85, 184; and Reconstruction, **1**, 400, 408, **2**, 84; and Seward, **1**, 544; on Early's raid, **2**, 77; and Smith Bros. case, 125; and Attorney-Generalship, 183, 187; and negro suffrage, 437.

Whittlesey, Elisha, and payments out of next year's appropriations, **2**, 268.

Wiard, Norman, and monitors, **2**, 88.

Wilderness campaign, anxiety at Washington, **2**, 25; impression of success, 26; first official dispatches, 27.

Wilkes, Charles, command on James River, **1**, 72, 73, 81, 83, 86, 91; as officer, 73, 87, 110, **2**, 351; on Potomac River, **1**, 93, 109; on McClellan, 106; command of West India Squadron, neutral complaints, 109–111, 134, 217, 298, 309, 322, 325, 451; diverts *Vanderbilt* from pursuit of *Alabama*, 225, 304, 316; recall, 299, 304, 316, 318, 322; inadequate force, 363; *Trent* affair, 466; insubordination and trial, 489–491, 505, 515, 528, 543, **2**, 6, 19, 21, 203; equivocates as to his age, **1**, 505.

Wilkes, Mrs. Charles, and recall of husband, **1**, 323.

Wilkes, George, article in his paper on Lincoln and Sherman's peace terms, **3**, 521.

Wilkinson, M. S., Meigs's reply to, **1**, 224.

Willey, W. T., impeachment vote, **3**, 356, 358, 367.

William I of Prussia, and arbitration of Alabama claims, **3**, 459.

William Peel, capture, **1**, 548, **2**, 4, 12.

Williams, G. H., and reinstatement of Stanton, **3**, 258; and impeachment, 358, 368.

Williams, Thomas, and Johnson's policy, **2**, 412; character, 633, **3**, 239.

Wilmington, expedition against, put off (1863), **1**, 216; character of blockade, 306, **2**, 127; plans to capture (1863), **1**, 307; joint expedition considered (1864), **2**, 127, 133, 146, 148, 150; responsibility for delay, 194; plans disclosed, 205–209, 219; news of expedition awaited, 209; powder vessel, 209, 210, 222, 226; failure of first expedition, 213–217; organization of second expedition, 215, 220–222; naval force locked up by, 221; success of second expedition, 226–228.

Wilmot Proviso, Preston King's services, **2**, 386.

Wilson, Charles, as Secretary of Legation, 1, 301.

Wilson, Henry, fears army conspiracy, 1, 118; and coast defense, 364; and investigation of contractors, 2, 7; and arrest of Smith Bros., 56; Reconstruction views (1865), 405; and split of party, 421; and Grimes, 3, 14; in South, 86, 89; and naval appropriations (1868), 325; Vice-Presidential candidacy, 362.

Wilson J. F., as impeachment manager, 3, 334.

Wilson, Nathaniel, and prosecution of contractors, 1, 540 n., 543, 544, 547, 2, 5, 15, 19, 53, 55–58, 78, 82.

Winans, Ross, Butler's plan to hang, 2, 270.

Winchester, capture (1863), 1, 328, 330, 331.

Wing, ——, Tribune correspondent, brings news of Wilderness, 2, 25.

Winooski, and Fenian raid, 2, 484, 486.

Winslow, J. A., Alabama fight, 2, 65, 67; in Washington, 202; and New Orleans riot, 575, 578.

Winthrop, R. C., in campaign of 1864, 2, 153; political character and mistakes, 153.

Wise, H. A., and headship of Ordnance Bureau, 1, 337, 343, 386, 2, 7; excursion, 31; and gun-casting controversy, 202; and Congressional investigation, 3, 122; and Dahlgren, 448.

Wood, Benjamin, R. C. Winthrop and, 2, 154; and Holt, 3, 172, 174.

Wood, Fernando, Lincoln correspondence, 1, 237; and corrupt government, 523; and McClellan's letter of acceptance, 2, 140; R. C. Winthrop and, 153.

Woodbridge, F. E., and impeachment, 3, 295.

Woodbridge, Wylly, in Washington (1865), 2, 269.

Woodbury, C. L., and navy yard appointments, 3, 446.

Woodward, G. W., candidacy (1863), 1, 469, 471.

Wool, J. E., alarm for safety of New York, 1, 347; and draft riots, 373, 405; to be relieved, 373.

Woolley, C. W., imprisonment, 3, 370, 380, 381.

Worden, John, secret journey to Pensacola, 1, 30; first prisoner of war, 31; and Wise, 2, 7; and Bureau of Navigation, 357.

Wright, ——, and his abandoned plantation, 2, 148.

Wright, H. G., at Norfolk Navy Yard, 1, 46; defends Washington, (1864), 2, 72, 75; attack on Petersburg lines, 272.

Wright, Silas, and Preston King, 2, 387; as politician, 3, 226.

Wright, William, and Civil Rights Bill, 2, 475.

Wylie, Andrew, decision in Baker case, 2, 206, 207; and Stanton (1867), 3, 160.

Wynkoop, E. W., report on Indian war, 3, 98.

Wyoming, ordered to East Indies, 2, 267.

Wytheville, Va., raid (1863), 1, 382.

Yankees and South-Carolinians, 2, 277.

Yards and Docks, Bureau of. See Navy yards, Smith (Joseph).

Yeaman, G. H., and negotiations for Danish West Indies, 3, 95.

Young, Samuel, as politician, 3, 225, 226.

Zeilin, Jacob, to command Marine Corps, 2, 51.

Zerman, ——, C. F. Adams's letter to, 1, 300.

The Riverside Press

CAMBRIDGE . MASSACHUSETTS

U . S . A

Date Due
